GERMAN SHORT STORIES:
Dual Language German-English Interlinear & Parallel Text

GERMAN BOOKS AND AUDIO BY L2 PRESS

GERMAN SHORT STORIES: Dual Language German-English, Interlinear & Parallel Text

GERMAN GRAMMAR BY EXAMPLE: Dual Language German-English, Interlinear & Parallel Text

1000 GERMAN SENTENCES: Dual Language German-English, Interlinear & Parallel Text

This series of three books provides over 5000 sentences of interlinear + parallel text plus audio for maximum comprehension of every word and sentence.

GERMAN SHORT STORIES:
Dual Language German-English Interlinear & Parallel Text

Copyright © 2020 by Aron Levin

All Rights Reserved. No part of this book, or associated audio files, may be reproduced, stored in a retrieval system, or transmitted, in any form or by any means, electronic, mechanical, photocopying, recording, internet usage, or otherwise, without the prior written permission from the publisher.

ISBN 978-1-952161-03-2

www.L2Press.com

First Edition

Contents

- i | Introduction
- iv | Alphabet and Pronunciation

PART I
STORIES IN INTERLINEAR AND PARALLEL TEXT

- **1** | Story 1 — Garden Variety
- **13** | Story 2 — A Good Sport
- **23** | Story 3 — Truth Will Out
- **35** | Story 4 — Child's Play
- **47** | Story 5 — Selling Out
- **57** | Story 6 — Don't Stop and Smell the Roses
- **69** | Story 7 — Fool's Gold
- **79** | Story 8 — Dumbbells Everywhere
- **97** | Story 9 — In Good Repair
- **115** | Story 10 — All Inclusive
- **135** | Story 11 — Murder Mystery in L.A.
- **155** | Story 12 — Mommy and Me
- **187** | Story 13 — Evolution

PART II
STORIES IN GERMAN ONLY

319 | **Story 1**
Garden Variety

323 | **Story 2**
A Good Sport

327 | **Story 3**
Truth Will Out

331 | **Story 4**
Child's Play

335 | **Story 5**
Selling Out

339 | **Story 6**
Don't Stop and Smell the Roses

343 | **Story 7**
Fool's Gold

347 | **Story 8**
Dumbbells Everywhere

353 | **Story 9**
In Good Repair

359 | **Story 10**
All Inclusive

365 | **Story 11**
Murder Mystery in L.A.

371 | **Story 12**
Mommy and Me

379 | **Story 13**
Evolution

Introduction

DEAR LANGUAGE LEARNER: This is a dual language book of German and English stories presented in a combined *interlinear + parallel text* format. The combination of parallel text with interlinear is the best of both worlds — the word-by-word translations and pronunciation guide of the interlinear and the broad translations of the parallel text. This single volume streamlines the process of reading in a foreign language by giving you everything needed to read, pronounce, and understand.

Reading is highly beneficial to acquiring a foreign language. Exposure to new words and phrases in the context of a larger story is productive and interesting, but reading in a foreign language can be slow and frustrating. The typical process of reading in a foreign language involves continuously stopping to look up the meaning of words and phrases, which is a slow process that interferes with comprehending the story. Even if all the words in a sentence are familiar, sometimes the meaning of the sentence remains elusive because it contains unfamiliar grammar concepts or idioms. Furthermore, pronunciation is not always obvious. Interlinear text combined with parallel text solves these problems in a compact and convenient way.

The page layout is consistent and logical, with parallel text located next to the corresponding interlinear text. Parallel text occupies the outer section of each page while interlinear text occupies the inner section. The translation style of the interlinear is essentially literal, whereas the parallel text is a free translation. Linguistically speaking, this is an interlinear gloss containing three lines of interlinear text: (1) the first line is the German source text; (2) the second line is the phonetic notation using the International Phonetic Alphabet (IPA), which improves speaking and provides a better overall understanding of the word; and (3) the third line is the English translation of the German word(s) directly above. The interlinear translations give more context-specific information than a dictionary possibly could.

This book is intended for those who want to learn Standard High German as spoken in Germany. The language style is conversational and not overly formal or particularly different from the register that you would encounter in the everyday life of an educated person, yet the grammar is proper.

Intensive and Extensive Reading

Language learners use two methods to read stories – intensive reading and extensive reading. **Intensive reading** is a way of reading a small amount of text in a detailed manner with the goal of understanding as much as possible while extracting new vocabulary and grammar. **Extensive reading** is reading quickly, for pleasure, without looking up anything, for as long as you want, with the goal of gaining massive exposure to the language. Intensive reading is typically utilized in the early stages of language learning, while extensive reading is utilized in the later stages of language learning.

This book allows language learners at any stage to easily perform both intensive and extensive reading. The practice of intensive reading involves looking up the meaning and pronunciation of every unfamiliar word and phrase in a reading session. Even with the help of a dictionary, the meaning can remain elusive, particularly if the word is conjugated, if there are multiple words with the same spelling, or if the word has multiple meanings in English. Professionally edited translations and IPA eliminate such problems and allow for reading intensively in an efficient and less frustrating manner. Similarly, this book assists learners with extensive reading by providing a large amount of engaging text in story form. Even though extensive reading does not involve stopping to look up words, the compact and convenient nature of the interlinear + parallel text allows for quick clarifications that won't distract from your extensive reading flow.

Introduction

Active Listening

Written text with a corresponding audio file is a powerful combination of language learning tools. This book has an associated German audio file (available for purchase at L2Press.com) that was recorded by a professional voice actor. By hearing the language spoken, you can appreciate and imitate the prosody, melody, and intonation of the language. Combined, the audio and IPA will instill confidence, consistency, and clarity in how the language is spoken.

Prioritize active listening, which requires all of your attention and concentration, over passive listening, which requires little effort and yields minimal results. Productive active listening exercises include:

- *Shadowing*: listen to audio while repeating it nearly simultaneously, directly following the sound like a shadow. Ideally do this both with and without looking at a written version of the audio. Try to speak, as best as you can, like the native speaker, focusing on vowel sounds, vowel length, new consonant sounds, stress, and intonation.

- *Repeating*: listen to audio and then pause to repeat. Like shadowing, ideally do this both with and without looking at a written version of the audio, and try to mimic the native speaker as closely as possible. This technique, along with shadowing, is useful for developing a good accent.

- *Listening-Reading*: listen to German audio while reading English text. Following along in English while listening to German audio helps you understand what is being said. Can also combine this technique with shadowing (Listen to German, shadow in German, read English). This technique is great for developing your ability to understand spoken German.

- *Transcribing*: listen to an audio file while pausing frequently to write down exactly what you heard. Correct your transcription against the original text. This technique is good for *focused* listening comprehension.

- *Summarizing*: listen to a short piece of audio and summarize what you heard. Summarize in either written or spoken form. Ideally, summarize in front of a tutor/teacher for immediate feedback. This technique is good for *global* listening comprehension.

How To Use This Book

Mastering the meaning, pronunciation, and usage of every word, phrase, and sentence in this book will unavoidably yield a high level of German proficiency because there is so much material - roughly 3600 sentences. Considering that books containing 1000 or fewer sentences claim learners can reach CEFR level B2 by mastering their material, imagine the results of mastering 3600 sentences. That said, it is unrealistic for a single work to give you full proficiency in a foreign language, but mastering everything in this book through consistent effort will get you farther than almost anything else. This begs the question: How does one master all of the material in this book? Here are tips to get you started:

1. *Extensive and Intensive reading*. As described above, both extensive and intensive reading are made much easier with this book, and they are the main techniques that you will use when reading. If you want to improve your speaking abilities, then read aloud. If you aren't sure of the correct pronunciation, then

look at the line below for immediate feedback and correction. And if you don't know the meaning of the word, look at the third line for immediate feedback and correction of the meaning. If you don't understand the meaning of a phrase or sentence, then look at the parallel text. This constant cycle of instant feedback and correction is a key attribute of deliberate practice and will accelerate your learning like never before.

2. *Active listening.* Use techniques such as Shadowing, Repeating, Listening-Reading, Transcribing, and Summarizing, as described above.

3. *Spaced repetition with chunks.* Spaced repetition software (SRS) is an electronic flashcard system with a built-in algorithm that shows you the cards at optimal times for memorizing. If you are having trouble remembering certain words, phrases, and sentences after reading them many times, and you like to review flashcards, then put them into an SRS, such as Anki or Memrise, and review daily. "Chunks" are groups of two or more words that you should learn as a single unit. Chunks give you vocabulary, context, and grammar all in a short phrase. As an example, take the simple sentence "Last night I ate dinner with my family." Instead of breaking up the sentence into eight individual words and learning them all separately, it would be far more productive to learn it in three chunks - "last night", "I ate dinner", and "with my family". Now you know three chunks of words that work together and can be applied in new situations. "I was at my friend's house *last night*", "*I ate dinner* already", "I'm visiting New York *with my family*". Intuiting the grammar through context is more enjoyable and useful than laboring through tedious grammar exercises.

4. *Converse with a speaking partner.* In parallel to mastering the content of this book using the above techniques, find a native speaker and converse with them on a consistent basis, preferably at least one hour per week. The ideal practice partner is patient and will not simply correct your errors but will prompt you to self-correct. If you desire to speak fluently, there is no substitute for conversation practice.

5. *Part 1 vs Part 2.* This book is divided into two Parts. Part 1 contains the German stories formatted with interlinear and parallel translations. Part 2 contains the same stories but purely in German with no translations. Part 2 has been provided so that you can test your learning progress and accustom yourself to reading in German without any help from translations. Continuously cycle between the two Parts of the book to build further confidence in your new language skills.

Special notes about the German

1. Arrows are used in the third line of the interlinear to indicate separable verbs, passive voice, and several *Perfekt* verb tenses. See the *German Grammar By Example* book for more on these topics.

2. Exclamation marks (!) are used in the third line of the interlinear to translate words that are used as "emphasis particles". See the *German Grammar By Example* book for a more comprehensive description with examples.

Alphabet and Pronunciation

The German Alphabet and Pronunciation

Letter[1]	IPA[2]	Similar sound in English[3]
A, a	/ɑː/	f<u>a</u>ther
B, b	/beː/	<u>b</u>oy / to<u>p</u> (at end of word)
C, c	/tseː/	ha<u>ts</u> / <u>c</u>at
D, d	/deː/	<u>d</u>og / ha<u>t</u> (at end of word)
E, e	/eː/	f<u>a</u>te / g<u>e</u>t
F, f	/ɛf/	<u>f</u>ind
G, g	/geː/	<u>g</u>et
H, h	/hɑː/	<u>h</u>elp
I, i	/iː/	j<u>ea</u>ns / s<u>i</u>t
J, j	/jot/	<u>y</u>ear
K, k	/kɑː/	<u>k</u>ite
L, l	/ɛl/	<u>l</u>ip
M, m	/ɛm/	<u>m</u>other
N, n	/ɛn/	<u>n</u>ever
O, o	/oː/	h<u>o</u>pe / h<u>o</u>t
P, p	/peː/	<u>p</u>et
Q, q	/kuː/	always "qu" which makes /kv/ sound
R, r	/ɛʀ/	guttural R / open *a* at end of word
S, s	/ɛs/	<u>s</u>and / <u>z</u>oo
T, t	/teː/	<u>t</u>oe
U, u	/uː/	sp<u>oo</u>n / p<u>u</u>t
V, v	/faʊ/	<u>f</u>ind
W, w	/veː/	<u>v</u>ibe
X, x	/ɪks/	ki<u>ck</u>s
Y, y	/ʏpsɪlon/	like U with pursed lips
Z, z	/tsɛt/	ha<u>ts</u>
Ä, ä	/ɛː/	b<u>e</u>d
Ö, ö	/øː/	b<u>ir</u>d (New Zealand pronunciation)
Ü, ü	/yː/	like U with pursed lips
ß	/ɛs tsɛt/	<u>s</u>and

(1) The first column lists the German letters in alphabetical order, including the three umlauts and Eszett.
(2) The second column shows the phonemic notation for each German letter as described by the International Phonetic Alphabet (IPA).
(3) The third and final column lists English words with comparable consonant and vowel sounds. The relevant sound is underlined.

Part I

STORIES IN INTERLINEAR AND PARALLEL TEXT

STORY 1

Garden Variety

Einen Garten zu haben ist nicht der richtige Weg, Geld zu sparen. Man glaubt, dass all das selbst angebaute Gemüse Lebensmittelkosten verringern werde. Aber man vergisst die Kosten, die bei der Bewirtschaftung eines eigenen Gartens anfallen. Man sollte daher Gemüse nur wegen der psychologischen Vorteile anbauen.

Having a garden is not a good way to save money. You think that all the home-grown vegetables will lower your grocery costs. But you forget about the costs associated with cultivating your own garden. So you should raise vegetables only for the psychological benefits.

Kaum zu glauben, wie sehr meine Frau ihren Garten liebt. Gemüse wachsen zu sehen, gibt ihr ein unglaubliches Gefühl von Zufriedenheit. Ich empfinde dagegen etwas anderes. Nämlich Schmerz!

I can't believe how much my wife loves her garden. She gets an incredible sense of satisfaction seeing the vegetables grow. In contrast, I get a different sense. It's called pain!

Einen Garten einzuzäunen macht keinen Spaß. Es kostet ungefähr 250 Euro an Material, einen 5 mal 6 Meter großen Garten mit einem 2,5 Meter hohen Zaun einzuzäunen. Es

Putting a fence around the garden is not fun. It costs about 250 Euro in materials for a 2.5 meter high fence to surround a 5 by 6 meter garden. It's got to be 2.5 meters high to discourage the deer from turning the garden into a salad bar.

Story 1

	braucht	einen	2,5	Meter	hohen	Zaun,	um	die Rehe davon
	bʁaʊxt	ˈaɪnən	tsvaɪaɪnˈhalp	ˈmeːtɐ	ˈhoːən	tsaʊn	ʊm	diː ˈʁeːə daˈfɔn
	it needs	a	2.5	meters	high	fence	in order to	the deer from it

Even then, they can get in via other methods. Sometimes they hang around near the gate, hiding behind the shrubs. They slip in unnoticed when you go to weed. One deer tried to parachute in last summer. Luckily the wind shifted and he wound up putting a hole through the neighbor's roof.

abzuhalten, den Garten in ein Salatbuffet zu verwandeln.
ˈaptsuˌhaltən deːn ˈɡaʁtn̩ ɪn aɪn zaˈlaːtˌbʏˈfeː tsuː fɛɐ̯ˈvandl̩n
to deter the garden into a salad bar to to turn into

Und trotzdem können sie auf andere Art und Weise
ʊnt ˈtʁɔtsdeːm ˈkœnən ziː aʊf ˈandəʁə aʁt ʊnt ˈvaɪzə
and anyhow they can they by other method

hineingelangen. Durch die Sträucher verdeckt, halten sie sich
hɪˈnaɪŋəˌlaŋən dʊʁç diː ˈʃtʁɔʏçɐ fɛɐ̯ˈdɛkt ˈhaltən ziː zɪç
to get inside by the shrubbery hidden they stay→ they themselves

manchmal ganz in der Nähe der Gartentüre auf. Unbemerkt
ˈmançmaːl ɡants ɪn deːɐ̯ ˈnɛːə deːɐ̯ ˈɡaʁtntyːʁə aʊf ˈʊnbəˌmɛʁkt
sometimes entirely near the garden gates ← unnoticed

schlüpfen sie hinein, wenn man zum Unkrautjäten geht. Letzten
ˈʃlʏpfən ziː hiːˈnaɪn vɛn man tsʊm ˈʊnkʁaʊtˌjɛːtn̩ ɡeːt ˈlɛtstən
they slip in→ they ← when one weeding he goes last

Sommer versuchte ein Reh, mit einem Fallschirm im Garten zu
ˈzɔmɐ fɛɐ̯ˈzuːxtə aɪn ʁeː mɪt ˈaɪnəm ˈfalʃɪʁm ɪm ˈɡaʁtn̩ tsuː
summer it tried a deer with a parachute in the garden to

landen. Glücklicherweise drehte der Wind und es blieb mit
ˈlandn̩ ˈɡlʏklɪçɐˌvaɪzə ˈdʁeːtə deːɐ̯ vɪnt ʊnt ɛs bliːp mɪt
to land luckily it turned the wind and it it got stuck→ with

seinem Huf im Dach meines Nachbarn hängen.
ˈzaɪnəm huːf ɪm dax ˈmaɪnəs ˈnaxbaːʁn ˈhɛŋən
its hoof in the roof of my neighbor ←

Tilling the soil is not a small matter. First, you have to go to the local rental place and find a tiller that fits in your car. Unless you have a four by four truck, you wind up with a small tiller.

Es ist keine leichte Angelegenheit, den Boden zu bestellen. Zuerst
ɛs ɪst ˈkaɪnə ˈlaɪçtə ˈanɡəˌleːɡn̩haɪt deːn ˈboːdn̩ tsuː bəˈʃtɛlən tsuˈeːɐ̯st
it it is no easy matter the soil to to till first

muss man zum örtlichen Geräteverleih gehen und eine Fräse
mʊs man tsʊm ˈœʁtlɪçən ɡəˈʁɛːtəfɛɐ̯ˌlaɪ ˈɡeːən ʊnt ˈaɪnə ˈfʁɛːzə
one has to one to the local equipment rental to go and a rotavator

finden, die in sein Fahrzeug passt. Wenn man nicht gerade einen
ˈfɪndən diː ɪn zaɪn ˈfaːɐ̯tsɔɪk past vɛn man nɪçt ɡəˈʁaːdə ˈaɪnən
to find that in one's vehicle it fits if one not ! a

Lastwagen mit Vierradantrieb hat, bleibt einem nur eine kleine
ˈlastˌvaːɡən mɪt ˈfiːɐ̯ˌʁaːtʔantʁiːp hat blaɪpt ˈaɪnəm nuːɐ̯ ˈaɪnə ˈklaɪnə
truck with four wheel drive one has one is left with only a small

Fräse.
ˈfʁɛːzə
rotavator

The little ones weigh about a kilo and just skip along the top of the soil. This means you have to push the blades of the tiller into the hard ground as they

Die Kleinen wiegen ungefähr ein Kilo und schlittern auf
diː ˈklaɪnən ˈviːɡn̩ ˈʊnɡəfɛːɐ̯ aɪn ˈkiːlo ʊnt ˈʃlɪtɐn aʊf
the small ones they weigh about one kilo and they skid on

Garden Variety

der	Erdoberfläche	nur	so	dahin.	Das	bedeutet,	man	muss	are spinning.
deːɐ	ˈeːɐtˌoːbɐˌflɛçə	nuːɐ	zoː	daˈhɪn	das	bəˈdɔɪtət	man	mʊs	
the	soil surface	just	around		this	it means	one	one has to	

die	rotierenden	Messer	der	Fräse	in	den	harten	Boden
diː	ʁoˈtiːʁəndn	ˈmɛsɐ	deːɐ	ˈfʁɛːzə	ɪn	deːn	ˈhaʁtn	ˈboːdən
the	rotating	blades	of the	rotavator	into	the	hard	ground

hineindrücken.
hɪˈnaɪndʁʏkn
to push

Bodenfräsen	für	zwei	Stunden.	Versuchen Sie das mal, wenn	Ihre	Try rototilling for two hours when your usual exercise is only lifting a wine glass and zipping through TV channels.
ˈboːdnˌfʁɛːzn	fyːɐ	tsvaɪ	ˈʃtʊndən	fɛɐˈzuːxn ziː das maːl	vɛn ˈiːʁə	
rotavating	for	two	hours	try this	if your	

sonst	üblichen	Leibesübungen	nur	darin bestehen,	ein	Weinglas
zɔnst	ˈyːplɪçən	ˈlaɪbəsˌyːbʊŋən	nuːɐ	daˈʁɪn bəˈʃteːən	aɪn	ˈvaɪnˌglaːs
otherwise	usual	exercise	only	it consists of	a	wine glass

zu	heben	oder	sich	durch	Fersehprogramme	zu	zappen.
tsuː	ˈheːbən	ˈoːdɐ	zɪç	dʊʁç	ˈfɛʁnzeːpʁoˌgʁamə	tsuː	ˈtsapən
to	to lift	or	→	through	TV channels	to	← to zap

Dann	muss	man	seiner	Frau	helfen,	die	Löcher	für	die	Samen	zu	Then you have to help the wife dig holes for the seeds. OK, they are small holes. But digging is not fun unless you find buried treasure.
dan	mʊs	man	ˈzaɪnɐ	fʁaʊ	ˈhɛlfən	diː	ˈlœçɐ	fyːɐ	diː	ˈzaːmən	tsuː	
then	one has to	one	one's	wife	to help	the	holes	for	the	seeds	to	

buddeln.	Zugegeben,	es	sind	kleine	Löcher.	Aber	Buddeln	macht
ˈbʊdəln	tsuːgəˈgeːbn	ɛs	zɪnt	ˈklaɪnə	ˈlœçɐ	ˈaːbɐ	ˈbʊdəln	maxt
to dig	admittedly	they are		small	holes	but	digging	it makes

keinen	Spaß,	es	sei	denn,	man	findet	einen	vergrabenen	Schatz.
ˈkaɪnən	ʃpas	ɛs	zaɪ	dɛn	man	ˈfɪndət	ˈaɪnən	fɛɐˈgʁaːbənən	ʃaːts
not a	fun	unless			one	he finds	a	buried	treasure

Nach	einigen	Wochen,	wenn	es	nicht	zu	viel	und	nicht	zu	wenig	After a few weeks, if it doesn't rain too much, but it rains enough, and the rabbits don't sneak through the fence, you then get to pull weeds and harvest a little produce.
naːx	ˈaɪnɪgən	ˈvɔxən	vɛn	ɛs	nɪçt	tsuː	fiːl	ʊnt	nɪçt	tsuː	ˈveːnɪç	
after	a few	weeks	if	it	not	too much		and	not	too	little	

geregnet	hat	und	die	Hasen	nicht	durch	den	Zaun	geschlüpft	sind,
gəˈʁeːgnət	hat	ʊnt	diː	ˈhaːzən	nɪçt	dʊʁç	deːn	tsaʊn	gəˈʃlʏpft	zɪnt
it rained		and	the	rabbits	not	through	the	fence	they slipped	

darf	man	dann	Unkraut	zupfen	und	ein	bisschen	Gemüse	ernten.
daʁf	man	dan	ˈʊnkʁaʊt	ˈtsʊpfən	ʊnt	aɪn	ˈbɪsçən	gəˈmyːzə	ˈɛʁntən
one may	one	then	weeds	to pull out	and	a	little	produce	to harvest

Ich	versuche	immer,	zu	verreisen,	wenn	das	Unkraut	aus	dem	I always try to be out of town when the weeds burst out of the ground, but sometimes I can't take the time off and get roped into the weeding.
ɪç	fɛɐˈzuːxə	ˈɪmɐ	tsuː	fɛɐˈʁaɪzn	vɛn	das	ˈʊnkʁaʊt	aʊs	deːm	
I	I try	always	to	to be out of town	when	the	weed	out of	the	

Boden	schießt,	aber	manchmal	kann	ich	mir	nicht	freinehmen
ˈboːdən	ʃiːst	ˈaːbɐ	ˈmançmaːl	kan	ɪç	miːɐ	nɪçt	ˈfʁaɪˌneːmən
ground	it shoots	but	sometimes	I can	I	myself	not	to take time off

und	dann	lasse	ich	mich	zum	Jäten	breitschlagen.
ʊnt	dan	ˈlasə	ɪç	mɪç	tsʊm	ˈjɛːtən	ˈbʁaɪtʃlaːgn
and	then	I let	I	myself	to the	weeding	to get roped into

Story 1

Then I get to spend several sessions at the chiropractor's office while he makes a few adjustments so I can stand normally again.

Dann	verbringe	ich	einige	Sitzungen	beim	Chiropraktiker,	der
dan	fɛɐ̯ˈbʁɪŋə	ɪç	ˈaɪnɪgə	ˈzɪtsʊŋən	baɪm	çiʁoˈpʁaktikɐ	deːɐ̯
then	I spend	I	several	sessions	at the	chiropractor	who

dann	meinen	Rücken	wieder	so	hinbiegt,	dass	ich	normal
dan	ˈmaɪnən	ˈʁʏkən	ˈviːdɐ	zoː	ˈhɪnbiːkt	das	ɪç	nɔʁˈmaːl
then	my	back	again	so	he bends straight	that	I	normal

stehen	kann.
ˈʃteːən	kan
to stand	I can

Harvesting also requires a lot of stooped labor. Just pick one bag of beans and it's back to the chiropractor, who just bought a small yacht from the fees I've paid him during the gardening season.

Die	Erntearbeit	erfordert	viele	Tätigkeiten	in	gebückter	Haltung.
diː	ˈɛʁntəˌaʁbaɪt	ɛɐ̯ˈfɔʁdɐt	ˈfiːlə	ˈtɛːtɪçˌkaɪtən	ɪn	ɡəˈbʏktɐ	ˈhaltʊŋ
the	harvesting	it requires	a lot	activity	in	bent over	posture

Heben	Sie	nur	einen	Sack	Bohnen	auf	und	schon	geht	es	wieder
ˈheːbn̩	ziː	nuːɐ̯	ˈaɪnən	zak	ˈboːnən	aʊf	ʊnt	ʃoːn	ɡeːt	ɛs	ˈviːdɐ
pick up→		just	one	bag	beans	←	and	soon	it goes	it	again

zum	Chiropraktiker,	der	sich	gerade	eine	kleine	Jacht	gekauft	hat
tsʊm	çiʁoˈpʁaktikɐ	deːɐ̯	zɪç	ɡəˈʁaːdə	ˈaɪnə	ˈklaɪnə	jaxt	ɡəˈkaʊft	hat
to the	chiropractor	who	himself	just	a	small	yacht	he bought	

von	den	Gebühren,	die	ich	ihm	während	der	Gartensaison
fɔn	deːn	ɡəˈbyːʁən	diː	ɪç	iːm	ˈvɛːʁənt	deːɐ̯	ˈɡaʁtnzɛˌzɔ̃ː
from	the	fees	that	I	to him	during	the	gardening season

gezahlt	habe.
ɡəˈtsaːlt	ˈhaːbə
	I paid

When the kids were younger we had a much bigger garden and always planted too much. We used to grow four zucchini plants each year. What normal family can possibly eat the fruits of four zucchini plants?

Als	die	Kinder	noch	kleiner	waren,	hatten	wir	einen	viel	größeren
als	diː	ˈkɪndɐ	nɔx	ˈklaɪnɐ	ˈvaːʁən	ˈhatn̩	viːɐ̯	ˈaɪnən	fiːl	ˈɡʁøːsəʁən
when	the	kids	still	younger	they were	we had	we	a	much	bigger

Garten	und	pflanzten	immer	viel	zu	viel	an.	Jedes	Jahr	pflanzten
ˈɡaʁtn̩	ʊnt	ˈpflantstən	ˈɪmɐ	fiːl	tsuː	fiːl	an	ˈjeːdəs	jaːɐ̯	ˈpflantstən
garden	and	we planted→	always	much	too	much	←	each	year	we grew

wir	vier	Zucchinipflanzen.	Welche	normale	Familie	kann	denn	die
viːɐ̯	fiːɐ̯	tsʊˈkiːniˌpflantsən	ˈvɛlçə	nɔʁˈmaːlə	faˈmiːljə	kan	dɛn	diː
we	four	zucchini plants	which	normal	family	it can	!	the

Ernte	von	vier	Zucchinipflanzen	essen?
ˈɛʁntə	fɔn	fiːɐ̯	tsʊˈkiːniˌpflantsən	ˈɛsən
harvest	from	four	zucchini plants	to eat

We had so much zucchini that we had to give it away. We loaded the kids into a little red wagon, covered them with zucchini, gave them snorkels so they wouldn't suffocate, and marched down the street.

Wir	hatten	immer	so	viele	Zucchini,	dass	wir	sie	verschenken
viːɐ̯	ˈhatən	ˈɪmɐ	zoː	ˈfiːlə	tsʊˈkiːni	das	viːɐ̯	ziː	fɛɐ̯ˈʃɛŋkən
we	we had	invariably	so	much	zucchini	that	we	them	to give away

mussten.	Wir	luden	die	Kinder	in	einen	kleinen	roten
ˈmʊstən	viːɐ̯	ˈluːdn̩	diː	ˈkɪndɐ	ɪn	ˈaɪnən	ˈklaɪnən	ˈʁoːtən
we had to	we	we loaded	the	kids	in	a	small	red

Leiterwagen,	packten	die	Zucchini	oben	drauf,	gaben	ihnen
ˈlaɪtɐˌvaːɡən	ˈpaktən	diː	tsʊˈkiːni	ˈoːbən	dʁaʊf	ˈɡaːbən	ˈiːnən
wagon	we packed	the	zucchini	on top	on them	we gave	them

Garden Variety

Schnorchel, sodass sie nicht erstickten und marschierten die Straße hinunter.

Alle unsere Nachbarn bekamen Gemüse. Nach etwa ein bis zwei Wochen erkannten die Nachbarn das Quietschen unseres Leiterwagens, als wir unsere Runden machten. Sie zogen die Vorhänge zu und versperrten die Haustüren. Niemand war zu Hause in der gesamten Nachbarschaft.

All of our neighbors got vegetables. After a week or two, the neighbors heard the squeak of the wagon wheels as we made our rounds. They drew their curtains and locked their doors. Nobody was at home in the whole neighborhood.

Was soll mit den übrigen Zucchini geschehen? Wir errichteten einen Zucchini-Verkaufsstand in unserer Einfahrt. Selbst unsere Tochter, die jedem alles verkaufen kann, war nicht in der Lage, unsere Ware zu verkaufen.

What to do with the extra zucchini? We set up a zucchini stand in our driveway. Our daughter, who can sell anything to anyone, was not able to sell our produce.

Meine Frau entdeckte schließlich Rezepte für Zucchinisuppe, Zucchinikekse, Zucchinipopcorn, usw.

So the wife uncovered recipes for zucchini soup, zucchini cookies, zucchini popcorn, etc.

Nachts schlich ich in unseren Garten hinaus und gab den Zucchinipflanzen heimlich Tabletten zur Empfängnisverhütung.

At night, I would sneak out to our garden and secretly feed birth control pills to the zucchini plants, anything to stop them from producing.

Story 1

Ich	versuchte	einfach	alles,	damit	die	Vermehrung	ein Ende
ɪç	fɛɐ̯ˈzuːxtə	ˈaɪnfax	ˈaləs	daˈmɪt	diː	fɛɐ̯ˈmeːʁʊŋ	aɪn ˈɛndə
I	I tried	simply	everything	so that	the	propagation	an end

habe.
ˈhaːbə
it has

My wife also grew lots of eggplant. I had never heard of eggplant until I moved from Berlin to the wilds of Eutin. Of course, most people in Eutin didn't know what a Spezi was, so that evened things out a bit.

Meine Frau pflanzte auch viele Auberginen. Ich hatte noch nie
ˈmaɪnə fʁaʊ ˈpflantstə aʊx ˈfiːlə obɛɐ̯ˈʒiːnən ɪç ˈhatə nɔx niː
my wife she grew also many eggplants I → never before

etwas von Auberginen gehört, bis ich von Berlin in die
ˈɛtvas fɔn obɛɐ̯ˈʒiːnən ɡəˈhøːɐ̯t bɪs ɪç fɔn bɛɐ̯ˈliːn ɪn diː
something of eggplants ←I had heard until I from Berlin into the

Eutiner Wildnis gezogen bin. Natürlich haben die meisten Leute in
ɔɪˈtiːnɐ ˈvɪltnɪs ɡəˈtsoːɡən bɪn naˈtyːɐ̯lɪç ˈhaːbn̩ diː ˈmaɪstən ˈlɔɪtə ɪn
Eutin's wilderness I moved of course → the most people in

Eutin nicht gewusst, was eine Spezi ist, damit war ein gewisser
ɔɪˈtiːn nɪçt ɡəˈvʊst vas ˈaɪnə ˈʃpeːtsi ɪst daˈmɪt vaːɐ̯ aɪn ɡəˈvɪsɐ
Eutin not ←they knew what a Spezi it is so that → a certain

Ausgleich gegeben.
ˈaʊsɡlaɪç ɡəˈɡeːbən
balancing ←it gave

Since my wife is from Hamburg, I have no idea where she ever got the idea that eggplants were something that normal people ate. Nobody in Hamburg ate eggplant.

Da meine Frau aus Hamburg stammt, habe ich keine Ahnung,
daː ˈmaɪnə fʁaʊ aʊs ˈhambʊʁk ʃtamt ˈhaːbə ɪç ˈkaɪnə ˈaːnʊŋ
since my wife from Hamburg she comes from I have I not an idea

wo sie jemals den Gedanken aufgriff, dass Auberginen etwas
voː ziː ˈjeːmaːls deːn ɡəˈdaŋkən ˈaʊfˌɡʁɪf das obɛɐ̯ˈʒiːnən ˈɛtvas
where she ever the idea she picked up that eggplants something

wären, was normale Menschen essen würden. Kein Mensch in
ˈvɛːʁən vas nɔʁˈmaːlə ˈmɛnʃən ˈɛsən ˈvʏʁdən kaɪn mɛnʃ ɪn
they were that normal people to eat they would not a person in

Hamburg aß Auberginen.
ˈhambʊʁk aːs obɛɐ̯ˈʒiːnən
Hamburg he ate eggplants

Anyway, I didn't like the idea of growing eggplant or eating anything that contained eggplant. They had a funny color. Who ever heard of purple vegetables? They were too mushy when they were cooked. They gave me cholera, or warts, or something like that.

Ich konnte mich mit der Idee, Auberginen anzupflanzen oder
ɪç ˈkɔntə mɪç mɪt deːɐ̯ iːˈdeː obɛɐ̯ˈʒiːnən ˈantsʊˌpflantsən ˈoːdɐ
I I could myself with the idea eggplants to plant or

auch nur irgendetwas zu essen, das Auberginen enthält, nicht
aʊx nuːɐ̯ ˈɪʁɡəndɛtvas tsuː ˈɛsən das obɛɐ̯ˈʒiːnən ɛntˈhɛlt nɪçt
also only anything to to eat that eggplants it contains not

anfreunden. Sie hatten eine komische Farbe. Wer hat je von
ˈanfʁɔɪndən ziː ˈhatən ˈaɪnə ˈkoːmɪʃə ˈfaʁbə veːɐ̯ hat jeː fɔn
to reconcile with they they had a funny color who → ever of

lilafarbenem Gemüse gehört? Sie waren zu matschig, wenn sie
ˈliːlaˌfaʁbənəm ɡəˈmyːzə ɡəˈhøːɐ̯t ziː ˈvaːʁən tsuː ˈmatʃɪç vɛn ziː
purple-colored vegetables ←he heard they they were too mushy when they

6

Garden Variety

gekocht waren. Sie haben bei mir Cholera, Warzen oder ähnliche
gəˈkɔxt ˈvaːʁən ziː ˈhaːbn baɪ miːɐ ˈkoːleʁa ˈvaʁtsən ˈoːdɐ ˈɛːnlɪçə
cooked they were they → on me cholera warts or similar

Sachen hervorgerufen.
ˈzaxən hɛɐˈfoːɐɡəˌʁuːfn
things ← they induced

Trotz allem bauten wir viele Auberginen an. Jeden Abend
tʁɔts ˈaləm ˈbaʊtən viːɐ ˈfiːlə obɛʁˈʒiːnən an ˈjeːdən ˈaːbənt
in spite of everything we grew→ we many eggplants ← every night

No matter, we grew plenty of eggplant. Every night we played "hide and seek". The wife would hide eggplant somewhere in the dinner, and the kids and I would try to find it and to then drop it on the floor.

spielten wir »Verstecken«. Meine Frau versteckte irgendwo im
ˈʃpiːltən viːɐ fɛɐˈʃtɛkən ˈmaɪnə fʁaʊ fɛɐˈʃtɛktə ˈɪʁɡəntvoː ɪm
we played we hide and seek my wife she hid somewhere in the

Abendessen Auberginen und die Kinder und ich versuchten, sie
ˈaːbntˌɛsn obɛʁˈʒiːnən ʊnt diː ˈkɪndɐ ʊnt ɪç fɛɐˈzuːxtən ziː
dinner eggplants and the kids and I we tried them

zu finden, um sie dann auf den Boden fallen zu lassen.
tsuː ˈfɪndən ʊm ziː dan aʊf deːn ˈboːdən ˈfalən tsuː ˈlasən
to to find in order to them then on the floor to drop to to let

Wir haben uns so oft beschwert, dass meine Frau in einen
viːɐ ˈhaːbn ʊns zoː ɔft bəˈʃveːɐt das ˈmaɪnə fʁaʊ ɪn ˈaɪnən
we → so often ←we complained that my wife in a

Kochstreik getreten ist. Das war nicht gut. Wir überlebten meine
ˈkɔxʃtʁaɪk ɡəˈtʁeːtən ɪst das vaːɐ nɪçt guːt viːɐ yːbɐˈleːptn ˈmaɪnə
she went on a cooking strike that it was not good we we survived my

Kochkunst gerade drei Tage. Dann haben die Kinder das Handtuch
ˈkɔxˌkʊnst ɡəˈʁaːdə dʁaɪ ˈtaːɡə dan ˈhaːbn diː ˈkɪndɐ das ˈhantˌtuːx
cooking just three days then → the kids the towel

We complained so much that the wife went on a cooking strike. That was bad. We survived for three days eating my cooking. Then the kids threw in the towel. I held out for another twenty minutes, to show them what I was made of. Then I also gave up. After that, it was eggplants day and night.

geworfen. Ich hielt noch weitere zwanzig Minuten durch,
ɡəˈvɔʁfən ɪç hiːlt nɔx ˈvaɪtəʁə ˈtsvantsɪç mɪˈnuːtən dʊʁç
←they threw I I held on→ another twenty minutes ←

um ihnen zu zeigen, was in mir steckt. Dann habe auch ich
ʊm ˈiːnən tsuː ˈtsaɪɡən vas ɪn miːɐ ʃtɛkt dan ˈhaːbə aʊx ɪç
in order to them to to show what was hidden in me then → also I

aufgegeben. Danach gab es Tag und Nacht Auberginen.
ˈaʊfɡəˌɡeːbən daˈnaːx ɡaːp ɛs taːk ʊnt naːxt obɛʁˈʒiːnən
←I gave up after that there was day and night eggplants

Die Tomaten waren der sogenannte Gnadenstoß in unserem
diː toˈmaːtən ˈvaːʁən deːɐ ˈzoːɡəˌnantə ˈɡnaːdənʃtoːs ɪn ˈʊnzəʁəm
the tomatoes they were the so-called coup de grâce in our

Tomatoes were the coup de grace in our garden. Each year we planted twelve, yes I said twelve, tomato plants.

Garten. Jedes Jahr haben wir zwölf, jawohl, ich sagte zwölf,
ˈɡaʁtn ˈjeːdəs jaːɐ ˈhaːbn viːɐ tsvœlf jaˈvoːl ɪç ˈzaktə tsvœlf
garden each year → we twelve that's right I I said twelve

Tomatenpflanzen angepflanzt.
toˈmaːtnˌpflantsn ˈanɡəˌpflantst
tomato plants ←we planted

7

Story 1

I wanted to cage them. I thought it would limit the output. But the suckers grew right through the bars of the cages.

Ich	wollte	sie	einsperren.	Ich	dachte,	das	würde	den	Ertrag
ɪç	ˈvɔltə	ziː	ˈaɪnˌʃpɛʁən	ɪç	ˈdaxtə	das	ˈvʏʁdə	deːn	ɛɐ̯ˈtʁaːk
I	I wanted	them	to cage	I	I thought	this	it would	the	yield

verringern.	Aber	diese	Schmarotzer	sind	einfach	zwischen	den
fɛɐ̯ˈʁɪŋɐn	ˈaːbɐ	ˈdiːzə	ʃmaˈʁɔtsɐ	zɪnt	ˈaɪnfax	ˈtsvɪʃən	deːn
to reduce	but	these	freeloaders	→	simply	between	the

Stäben	der	Käfige	hindurchgewachsen.
ˈʃtɛbən	deːɐ̯	ˈkɛːfɪɡə	hɪnˈdʊʁçɡəˌvaksən
bars	the	cages	←they grew through

Every year, all the tomatoes ripened within eight minutes of each other, on the third Thursday in August. This has always meant one thing - tomato sauce. I hate making tomato sauce. It takes about three days.

Jedes	Jahr	am	dritten	Donnerstag	im	August	reiften	alle
ˈjeːdəs	jaːɐ̯	am	ˈdʁɪtən	ˈdɔnɐsˌtaːk	ɪm	auˈɡʊst	ˈʁaɪftən	ˈalə
every	year	on the	third	Thursday	in the	August	they ripened	all

Tomaten	nacheinander	im	Abstand	von	acht	Minuten.	Dies
toˈmaːtən	ˈnaːxaɪˌnandɐ	ɪm	ˈapʃtant	fɔn	axt	mɪˈnuːtən	diːs
tomatoes	one after the other	in the	interval	of	eight	minutes	this

bedeutete	immer	nur	das	eine	– Tomatensauce.	Ich	hasse	es,
bəˈdɔɪtətə	ˈɪmɐ	nuːɐ̯	das	ˈaɪnə	toˈmaːtnˌzoːsə	ɪç	ˈhasə	ɛs
it meant	always	only	the	one	tomato sauce	I	I hate	it

Tomatensauce	zu	machen.	Das	dauert	ungefähr	drei	Tage.
toˈmaːtnˌzoːsə	tsu	ˈmaxən	das	ˈdaʊɐt	ˈʊnɡəfɛːɐ̯	dʁaɪ	ˈtaːɡə
tomato sauce	to	to make	that	it takes	about	three	days

First you have to pick about three thousand tomatoes. Then you have to throw them in a pot of boiling water. We usually build a fire under the upstairs Jacuzzi and use that as our pot.

Zuerst	muss	man	ungefähr	dreitausend	Tomaten	pflücken.	Dann
tsuˈeːɐ̯st	mʊs	man	ˈʊnɡəfɛːɐ̯	ˈdʁaɪˌtaʊzənt	toˈmaːtən	ˈpflʏkən	dan
first	one has to	one	about	three thousand	tomatoes	to pick	then

muss	man	sie	in	einen	Topf	mit	kochendem	Wasser	werfen.
mʊs	man	ziː	ɪn	ˈaɪnən	tɔpf	mɪt	ˈkɔxəndəm	ˈvasɐ	ˈvɛʁfən
one has to	one	them	in	a	pot	with	boiling	water	to throw

Normalerweise	machen	wir	ein	Feuer	unter	dem	Jacuzzi	im
nɔʁˈmaːlɐvaɪzə	ˈmaxən	viːɐ̯	aɪn	ˈfɔɪɐ	ˈʊntɐ	deːm	dʒəˈkuːzi	ɪm
usually	we make	we	a	fire	under	the	Jacuzzi	in the

Obergeschoss	und	benutzen	ihn	als	Kochtopf.
ˈoːbɐɡəʃɔs	ʊnt	bəˈnʊtsən	iːn	als	ˈkɔxˌtɔpf
upstairs	and	we use	it	as	cooking pot

The tomatoes scream when you throw them in. It's a terrible thing to hear. Well, come to think of it, the noise actually comes from me. I always throw the tomatoes into the jacuzzi a little too hard and splatter myself with scalding spray. That hurts!

Die	Tomaten	kreischen,	wenn	man	sie	hineinwirft.	Es	hört	sich
diː	toˈmaːtən	ˈkʁaɪʃən	vɛn	man	ziː	hɪˈnaɪnˌvɪʁft	ɛs	høːɐ̯t	zɪç
the	tomatoes	they scream	when	you	them	to throw in	it	it sounds	→

fürchterlich	an.	Naja,	wenn	ich	darüber	nachdenke,	kommt	der
ˈfʏʁçtɐlɪç	an	ˈnaˌja	vɛn	ɪç	daˈʁyːbɐ	ˈnaːxˌdɛŋkə	kɔmt	deːɐ̯
terrible	←	well	if	I	about it	I think	it comes	the

Lärm	eigentlich	von	mir.	Ich	werfe	die	Tomaten	immer	etwas
lɛʁm	ˈaɪɡəntlɪç	fɔn	miːɐ̯	ɪç	ˈvɛʁfə	diː	toˈmaːtən	ˈɪmɐ	ˈɛtvas
noise	actually	from	me	I	I throw	the	tomatoes	always	slightly

zu	heftig	in	den	Jacuzzi	und	bespritze	mich	dabei	selbst	mit	dem
tsu	ˈhɛftɪç	ɪn	deːn	dʒəˈkuːzi	ʊnt	bəˈʃpʁɪtsə	mɪç	daˈbaɪ	zɛlpst	mɪt	deːm
too	hard	in	the	Jacuzzi	and	I splash		thereby	myself	with	the

Garden Variety

kochend	heißen	Wasser.	Das	tut	weh!
ˈkɔxnt	ˈhaɪsən	ˈvasɐ	das	tuːt	veː
scalding	hot	water	that	it hurts	

Nach	ein paar	Minuten	muss	man	die	Tomaten	aus	dem	heißen
naːx	aɪn paːɐ	mɪˈnuːtən	mʊs	man	diː	tɔˈmaːtən	aʊs	deːm	ˈhaɪsən
after	a few	minutes	one has to	one	the	tomatoes	out of	the	hot

Wasser	herausnehmen	und	schälen.	Sie	lassen sich	nicht	gerne
ˈvasɐ	hɛˈʁaʊsˌneːmən	ʊnt	ˈʃɛːlən	ziː	ˈlasn zɪç	nɪçt	ˈɡɛʁnə
water	to take out	and	to peel	they	they let themselves	not	willingly

schälen.	Sie	winden sich	und	rutschen weg	und	versuchen	zu
ˈʃɛːlən	ziː	ˈvɪndən zɪç	ʊnt	ˈʁʊtʃn vɛk	ʊnt	fɛɐˈzuːxən	tsuː
to be peeled	they	they squirm	and	they slide away	and	they try	to

entkommen.
ɛntˈkɔmən
to escape

After a few minutes, you have to take the tomatoes out of the hot water and peel them. They don't like being peeled. They squirm and slide and try to get away.

Man	darf	sie	nicht	aus	seinem	Griff	rutschen	lassen,	sonst
man	daʁf	ziː	nɪçt	aʊs	ˈzaɪnəm	ɡʁɪf	ˈʁʊtʃn	ˈlasən	zɔnst
one	one must	them	not	from	one's	grip	to slip	to let	otherwise

wird	man	mit	dem	»bösen	Blick«	bestraft.	Der	böse	Blick	ist
vɪʁt	man	mɪt	deːm	ˈbøːzn	blɪk	bəˈʃtʁaːft	deːɐ	ˈbøːzə	blɪk	ɪst
→		with	the	evil	glare	← one is punished	the	evil	glare	is

ein	Gesichtsausdruck,	mit	dem	mein	Vater	experimentierte	und
aɪn	ɡəˈzɪçtsaʊsˌdʁʊk	mɪt	deːm	maɪn	ˈfaːtɐ	ɛkspeʁimɛnˈtiːɐtə	ʊnt
a	facial expression	with	which	my	father	he experimented	and

den	meine	Frau	perfektionierte.	Ich	kann	fühlen,	wie	der	böse
deːn	ˈmaɪnə	fʁaʊ	pɛʁfɛktsjoˈniːɐtə	ɪç	kan	ˈfyːlən	viː	deːɐ	ˈbøːzə
that	my	wife	she perfected	I	I can	to feel	as	the	evil

Blick	mich	durchdringt,	wenn	ich	eine	entschlüpfte,	halbnackte
blɪk	mɪç	ˈdʊʁçˌdʁɪŋt	vɛn	ɪç	ˈaɪnə	ɛntˈʃlʏpftə	ˈhalpˌnaktə
glare	me	it penetrates	as	I	an	escaping	half-naked

Tomate	ins	Wohnzimmer	verfolge.
tɔˈmaːtə	ɪns	ˈvoːnˌtsɪmɐ	fɛɐˈfɔlɡə
tomato	in the	living room	to chase

You can't let them slip from your grasp or you get The Glare. The Glare is a look that my father experimented with, and my wife has perfected. I can feel The Glare burn through me as I chase an escaping, half-naked tomato into the dining room.

Wenn	die	Tomaten	alle	geschält	sind	und	zitternd	am	Jacuzzi
vɛn	diː	tɔˈmaːtən	ˈalə	ɡəˈʃɛlt	zɪnt	ʊnt	ˈtsɪtɐnt	am	dʒəˈkuːzi
when	the	tomatoes	all	peeled	they are	and	shivering	by the	Jacuzzi

liegen,	muss	man	die	Samen	herausnehmen.	Ich	kann	die	Qualen,
ˈliːɡən	mʊs	man	diː	ˈzaːmən	hɛˈʁaʊsˌneːmən	ɪç	kan	diː	ˈkvaːlən
they lie	one has to	one	the	seeds	to take out	I	I can	the	agony

die	ich	dabei	fühle,	kaum	beschreiben,	während	ich	eines	nach
diː	ɪç	daˈbaɪ	ˈfyːlə	kaʊm	bəˈʃʁaɪbən	ˈvɛːʁənt	ɪç	ˈaɪnəs	naːx
that	I	in doing so	I feel	hardly	to describe	as	I	one	after

dem	anderen	dieser	armen,	kleinen	Dinger	nehme	und	drücke,
deːm	ˈandəʁən	ˈdiːzɐ	ˈaʁmən	ˈklaɪnən	ˈdɪŋɐ	ˈneːmə	ʊnt	ˈdʁʏkə
the	other	of these	poor	little	things	I take	and	I squeeze

When the tomatoes are all peeled and lie shivering on the side of the jacuzzi, you have to take out the seeds. I can't tell you the anguish I feel as I take one after another of the poor little things and squeeze them until their many little seeds pop out. I can't tell you how many future generations of these tomatoes have been squashed by my calloused fingers.

9

Story 1

	bis ihre vielen kleinen Samen herausgequetscht sind. Ich kann
	bis ˈiːʁə ˈfiːlən ˈklaɪnən ˈzaːmən hɛˈʁaʊsɡəˌkvɛtʃt zɪnt ɪç kan
	until their many little seeds squeezed out they are I I can
	kaum sagen, wie viele künftige Generationen dieser Tomaten von
	kaʊm ˈzaːɡən viː ˈfiːlə ˈkʏnftɪɡə ɡenɛʁaˈtsjoːnən ˈdiːzɐ toˈmaːtən fɔn
	hardly to tell how many future generations of these tomatoes by
	meinen schwieligen Fingern zerquetscht worden sind.
	ˈmaɪnən ˈʃviːlɪɡən ˈfɪŋɐn tsɛɐˈkvɛtʃt ˈvɔʁdən zɪnt
	my calloused fingers they have been squashed

Finally, you puree the tomatoes in a blender and hand them to your wife, the master sauce maker. I do not know what unspeakable acts she commits from that point on.

Schließlich püriert man die Tomaten in einem Mixer und
ˈʃliːslɪç pyˈʁiːʁt man diː toˈmaːtən ɪn ˈaɪnəm ˈmɪksɐ ʊnt
finally one purees one the tomatoes in a blender and
übergibt sie seiner Frau, der Meisterin der Soßenherstellung.
yːbɐˈɡiːpt ziː ˈzaɪnɐ fʁaʊ deːɐ ˈmaɪstəʁɪn deːɐ ˈzoːsənˌhɛɐˌʃtɛlʊŋ
one hands over them to one's wife the master of the sauce production
Ich weiß nicht, zu welchen unbeschreiblichen Handlungen sie von
ɪç vaɪs nɪçt tsuː ˈvɛlçən ʊnbəˈʃʁaɪplɪçn̩ ˈhandlʊŋən ziː fɔn
I I know not to which indescribable acts she from
da an übergeht.
daː an ˈyːbɐˌɡeːt
there on she proceeds to

I usually run from the kitchen after the puree part. But I do know that the result is very tasty, so I don't lose too much sleep. Unfortunately, three days work with thousands of tomatoes results in about a half a cup of sauce, so the rewards are fleeting.

Nach dem Püree-Teil flüchte ich normalerweise aus der Küche.
naːx deːm pyˈʁeːˌtaɪl ˈflʏçtə ɪç nɔɐˈmaːlɐvaɪzə aʊs deːɐ ˈkʏçə
after the puree part I flee I usually out of the kitchen
Da ich jedoch weiß, dass das Ergebnis sehr gut schmeckt,
daː ɪç jeˈdɔx vaɪs das das ɛɐˈɡeːpnɪs zeːɐ ɡuːt ʃmɛkt
as I however I know that the result very good it tastes
zerbreche ich mir darüber nicht allzu sehr den Kopf. Leider
tsɛɐˈbʁɛçə ɪç miːɐ daˈʁyːbɐ nɪçt ˈaltsuː zeːɐ deːn kɔpf ˈlaɪdɐ
I agonize→ about it not too much ← unfortunately
beträgt die Ausbeute aus tausenden Tomaten nach drei Tagen
bəˈtʁɛːkt diː ˈaʊsˌbɔɪtə aʊs ˈtaʊzndən toˈmaːtən naːx dʁaɪ ˈtaːɡn̩
it amounts to the yield out of thousands tomatoes after three days of
Arbeit ungefähr eine halbe Tasse Soße. Die Frucht dieser Arbeit
ˈaʁbaɪt ˈʊŋɡəfɛːɐ ˈaɪnə ˈhalbə ˈtasə ˈzoːsə diː fʁʊxt ˈdiːzɐ ˈaʁbaɪt
work about a half cup sauce the fruit of this work
ist also recht kurzlebig.
ɪst ˈalzo ʁɛçt ˈkʊʁtsˌleːbɪç
it is thus quite short-lived

As I write this, I am remembering the smell of tomato sauce coming from the kitchen. It was a wonderful smell.

Während ich dies schreibe, erinnere ich mich an den Geruch der
ˈvɛːʁənt ɪç diːs ˈʃʁaɪbə ɛɐˈɪnəʁə ɪç mɪç an deːn ɡəˈʁuːx deːɐ
as I this I write I remember→ I ← on the smell of the
Tomatensoße, der aus der Küche kam. Es war ein wundervoller
toˈmaːtn̩ˌzoːsə deːɐ aʊs deːɐ ˈkʏçə kaːm ɛs vaːɐ aɪn ˈvʊndɐˌfɔlɐ
tomato sauce that out of the kitchen it came it it was a wonderful

Garden Variety

Geruch.
gəˈʁuːx
smell

Heutzutage ist unser Garten viel kleiner. Gott sei Dank für diese
ˈhɔɪttsuˌtaːgə ɪst ˈʊnzɐ ˈgaʁtn fiːl ˈklaɪnɐ gɔt zaɪ daŋk fyːɐ ˈdiːzə
these days it is our garden much smaller thank god for these

kleinen, guten Taten.
ˈklaɪnən ˈguːtn ˈtaːtn
little good deeds

      These days, our garden is a lot smaller. Thank God for little favors.

Der Leiterwagen rostet im Keller vor sich hin und die Räder
deːɐ ˈlaɪtɐˌvaːgən ˈʁɔstət ɪm ˈkɛlɐ foːɐ zɪç hɪn ʊnt diː ˈʁɛdɐ
the wagon it rusts away→ in the basement ← and the wheels

quietschen immer noch. Die Kinder sind nicht mehr hier, um
ˈkviːtʃn ˈɪmɐ nɔx diː ˈkɪndɐ zɪnt nɪçt meːɐ hiːɐ ʊm
they squeak still the kids they are no longer here in order to

»Aubergine-Verstecken« zu spielen. Die Nachbarn sind verreist,
obɛʁˈʒiːnə-fɛɐˈʃtɛkn tsuː ˈʃpiːlən diː ˈnaxbaʁn zɪnt fɛɐˈʁaɪst
eggplant hide and seek to to play the neighbors they are gone away

für den Fall, dass wir versuchen, mit ihnen unser Gemüse zu
fyːɐ deːn fal das viːɐ fɛɐˈzuːxən mɪt ˈiːnən ˈʊnzɐ gəˈmyːzə tsuː
just in case that we we try with them our vegetables to

teilen.
ˈtaɪlən
to share

      The wagon is rusting in the basement, the wheels still squeak. The kids no longer are here to play "hide the eggplant". The neighbors are out of town, just in case we try to share our vegetables with them.

Aber die Pflege des Gartens kostet immer noch weitaus mehr,
ˈaːbɐ diː ˈpfleːgə dɛs ˈgaʁtns ˈkɔstət ˈɪmɐ nɔx ˈvaɪtˌaʊs meːɐ
but the maintenance of the garden it costs still much more

als man beim Lebensmitteleinkauf spart.
als man baɪm ˈleːbnsmɪtlˌaɪnkaʊf ʃpaːɐt
than one on the grocery shopping one saves

      But the garden still costs a lot more money to maintain than it saves you on grocery bills.

Im letzten April habe ich den Garten für die Ernte dieses Jahres
ɪm ˈlɛtstən aˈpʁɪl ˈhaːbə ɪç deːn ˈgaʁtn fyːɐ diː ˈɛʁntə ˈdiːzəs ˈjaːʁəs
in the last April → I the garden for the crop this year

umgegraben und laufe immer noch herum wie jemand, der
ˈʊmgəˌgʁaːbən ʊnt ˈlaʊfə ˈɪmɐ nɔx hɛˈʁʊm viː ˈjeːmant deːɐ
←I dug and I walk around→ still ← like someone who

einen 20 Kilo schweren Stein auf seinem Rücken trägt. Ich
ˈaɪnən ˈtsvantsɪç ˈkiːlo ˈʃveːʁən ʃtaɪn aʊf ˈzaɪnəm ˈʁʏkən tʁɛkt ɪç
a 20 kilo heavy stone on his back he carries I

muss wieder zurück zum Chiropraktiker!
mʊs ˈviːdɐ tsuˈʁʏk tsʊm çiʁoˈpʁaktikɐ
I have to again back to the chiropractor

      Last April I did the rototilling for this year's crop and I'm still walking like a man carrying a 20 kilo stone on his back. I've got to go back to the chiropractor!

STORY 2

A Good Sport

»Hört auf, Dreck aufeinander zu werfen!«, brüllte ich. — "Stop throwing mud at each other," I yelled.

»Christian hat mich mit seiner Wasserflasche bespritzt.« — "Christian squirted me with his water bottle."

»Christian, hör auf!« — "Christian, don't do that."

Christian, mein Sohn, sollte eigentlich ein gutes Beispiel für die anderen Jungen sein. — Christian, my son, was supposed to be setting a good example for the other boys.

»Trainer Daniel, ich kann zum Spiel am Samstag nicht kommen«, sagte Peter. »Ich will nicht mehr trainieren.« — "Coach Daniel, I can't come to the game Saturday," said Peter. "I don't want to practice any more."

»Warum nicht?«, fragte ich. — "Why not?" I asked.

»Ich mag Fußball nicht.« — "I don't like soccer."

»Warum bist du dann in die Mannschaft eingetreten?« — "Then why did you join the team?"

»Meine Mutter hat mich dazu gezwungen.« — "My mother made me."

In diesem Moment traf mich ein Dreckklumpen. — Just then I was hit with a chunk of mud.

Story 2

"Stop throwing mud," I yelled. "We have our first game in two days. Everyone sit and listen for a few minutes."

»Hört auf, Dreck zu werfen!«, schrie ich. »In zwei Tagen haben
| hø:ɐt aʊf | dʁɛk | tsu: | ˈvɛʁfən | ʃʁi: | ɪç | ɪn | tsvaɪ | ˈta:ɡən | ˈha:bn̩ |
| stop | mud | to | to throw | I yelled | I | in | two | days | we have |

wir unser erstes Spiel. Jeder setzt sich jetzt und hört für ein paar
| vi:ɐ | ˈʊnzɐ | ˈeːɐstəs | ʃpi:l | ˈjeːdɐ | zɛtst zɪç | jɛtst | ʊnt | høːɐt | fyːɐ | aɪn paːɐ |
| we | our | first | game | everyone sit | now | and | listen→ | for | a few |

Minuten zu.«
| mɪˈnu:tən | tsu: |
| minutes | ← |

My team of nine and ten year old boys finally sat down on the grass. They had been running hard and were sweaty and tired.

Endlich setzte sich meine Mannschaft, die aus neun- und
| ˈɛntlɪç | ˈzɛtstə zɪç | ˈmaɪnə | ˈmanʃaft | di: | aʊs | nɔɪn | ʊnt |
| finally | it sat down | my | team | that | of | nine | and |

zehnjährigen Jungen bestand, ins Gras. Sie waren sehr viel
| ˈtseːnˌjɛːʁɪɡn̩ | ˈjʊŋən | bəˈʃtant | ɪns | ɡʁas | zi: | ˈva:ʁən | ze:ɐ | fi:l |
| ten year old | boys | it consisted | in the | grass | they | → | very | much |

gelaufen und waren verschwitzt und müde.
| ɡəˈlaʊfən | ʊnt | ˈva:ʁən | fɛʁˈʃvɪtst | ʊnt | ˈmy:də |
| ←they had run | and | they were | sweaty | and | tired |

I spoke quickly. Boys don't sit for long. After five minutes of explaining strategy, we were running again.

Ich sprach schnell. Jungs können nicht allzu lange stillsitzen.
| ɪç | ʃpʁa:x | ʃnɛl | jʊŋs | ˈkœnən | nɪçt | ˈaltsu: | ˈlaŋə | ˈʃtɪlˌzɪtsn̩ |
| I | I spoke | quickly | boys | they can | not | too | long | to sit still |

Nachdem wir fünf Minuten lang die Vorgehensweise
| na:xˈdeːm | vi:ɐ | fʏnf | mɪˈnu:tən | laŋ | di: | ˈfoːɐɡeːənsˌvaɪzə |
| after | we | five | minutes | long | the | approach |

besprochen hatten, trainierten wir wieder.
| bəˈʃpʁɔxn̩ ˈhatn̩ | tʁɛˈni:ɐtn̩ | vi:ɐ | ˈvi:dɐ |
| we had discussed | we practiced | we | again |

An hour later practice was over. I had to wait twenty minutes before the last mother showed up to collect her child.

Eine Stunde später war das Training vorbei. Ich musste zwanzig
| ˈaɪnə | ˈʃtʊndə | ˈʃpɛ:tɐ | va:ɐ | das | ˈtʁɛ:nɪŋ | foːɐˈbaɪ | ɪç | ˈmʊstə | ˈtsvantsɪç |
| an | hour | later | it was | the | practice | over | I | I had to | twenty |

Minuten warten, bis die letzte Mutter erschien, um ihr Kind
| mɪˈnu:tən | ˈvaʁtn̩ | bɪs | di: | ˈlɛtstə | ˈmʊtɐ | ɛɐˈʃi:n | ʊm | i:ɐ | kɪnt |
| minutes | to wait | until | the | last | mother | she showed up | in order to | her | kid |

abzuholen.
| ˈaptsuˌho:lən |
| to pick up |

"If you are late next time, I'm selling him," I told her.

»Wenn Sie nächstes Mal spät dran sind, werde ich ihn verkaufen«,
| vɛn | zi: | ˈnɛçstəs | ma:l | ʃpɛ:t dʁan zɪnt | ˈve:ɐdə | ɪç | i:n | fɛɐˈkaʊfn̩ |
| if | you | next | time | you are late | I will | I | him | to sell |

sagte ich ihr.
| ˈzaktə | ɪç | i:ɐ |
| I told | I | her |

A Good Sport

Zu unserem ersten Spiel erschienen elf der insgesamt fünfzehn Spieler unserer Mannschaft.
tsuː ˈʊnzəʁəm ˈeːʁstn ʃpiːl ɛɐ̯ˈʃiːnən ɛlf deːɐ̯ ˈɪnsgəzamt ˈfʏnftsɛn ˈʃpiːlɐ ˈʊnzəʁɐ ˈmanʃaft
to our first game they showed up eleven of the overall fifteen players of our team

Eleven of the fifteen boys on our team showed up for our first game.

»Wo sind sie denn alle?«, fragte meine Frau Ingrid.
voː zɪnt ziː dɛn ˈalə ˈfʁaːktə ˈmaɪnə fʁaʊ ˈɪŋgʁɪt
where they are they ! all she asked my wife Ingrid

"Where is everyone?" my wife Ingrid asked.

»Das ist doch nur eine Ortsliga«, sagte einer der Väter. »Die Eltern und die Kinder nehmen es nicht ernst. Es ist für sie nur eine Samstagsbeschäftigung, wenn sie sonst nichts zu tun haben.«
das ɪst dɔx nuːɐ̯ ˈaɪnə ˈɔʁtsˌliːga ˈzaktə ˈaɪnɐ deːɐ̯ ˈfɛːtɐ diː ˈɛltɐn ʊnt diː ˈkɪndɐ ˈneːmən ɛs nɪçt ɛʁnst ɛs ɪst fyːɐ̯ ziː nuːɐ̯ ˈaɪnə ˈzamstaːksbəˌʃɛftɪgʊŋ vɛn ziː zɔnst nɪçts tsuː tuːn ˈhaːbn̩
this is ! only a local league he said one of the fathers the parents and the kids they take it not seriously it it is for them only a Saturday activity if they otherwise nothing to to do they have

"This is just a town league," one of the fathers said. "The parents and kids don't take it seriously. It's just something for them to do on Saturdays if they have nothing else going on."

»Es ist unfair gegenüber denjenigen, die kommen«, sagte ich.
ɛs ɪst ˈʊnfɛːɐ̯ geːgn̩ˈyːbɐ ˈdeːnjeːnɪgn̩ diː ˈkɔmən ˈzaktə ɪç
it is unfair towards those who they come I said I

"It's unfair to the ones who do show up," I said.

Klaus kam während des Aufwärmens zu mir herüber.
klaʊs kaːm ˈvɛːʁənt dɛs ˈaʊfˌvɛʁmənz tsuː miːɐ̯ heˈʁyːbɐ
Klaus he came over→ during the warm-up to me ←

Klaus came over to me during warm ups.

»Ich will heute nicht spielen.«
ɪç vɪl ˈhɔɪtə nɪçt ˈʃpiːlən
I I want today not to play

"I don't want to play today."

»Warum nicht?«
vaˈʁʊm nɪçt
why not

"Why not?"

»Der große Junge aus der anderen Mannschaft hat mir gesagt, dass er mich umhauen wird.«
deːɐ̯ ˈgʁoːsə ˈjʊŋə aʊs deːɐ̯ ˈandəʁən ˈmanʃaft hat miːɐ̯ gəˈzaːkt das eːɐ̯ mɪç ˈʊmhaʊən vɪʁt
the big boy from the other team hat→ me ←he told that he me to knock down he will

"That big kid on the other team told me he's going to knock me down."

»Hans wird dich beschützen.«
hans vɪʁt dɪç bəˈʃʏtsən
Hans he will you to protect

"Hans will protect you."

Story 2

"No, I won't," yelled Hans.

»Nein, werde ich nicht!«, schrie Hans.
naɪn 'veːɐdə ɪç nɪçt ʃʁiː hans
no I will I not he yelled Hans

"Peter, why are you taking off your cleats?"

»Peter, warum ziehst du deine Stollenschuhe aus?«
'peːtɐ vaˈʁʊm tsiːst duː 'daɪnə ʃtɔlənʃuːə aʊs
Peter why you take off→ you your cleats ←

"I don't want to play."

»Ich will nicht spielen.«
ɪç vɪl nɪçt 'ʃpiːlən
I I want not to play

Just then, Peter's mother came over and twisted his ear. He started putting his cleats back on.

Gerade in diesem Moment kam die Mutter von Peter und nahm
gəˈʁaːdə ɪn ˈdiːzəm moˈmɛnt kaːm diː ˈmʊtɐ fɔn ˈpeːtɐ ʊnt naːm
just in this moment she came the mother of Peter and she took

ihm beim Ohr. Er begann, seine Stollenschuhe wieder anzuziehen.
iːm baɪm oːɐ eːɐ bəˈgan ˈzaɪnə ʃtɔlənʃuːə ˈviːdɐ ˈantsuˌtsiːən
him by the ear he he started his cleats again to put on

The game started a few minutes later. Klaus promptly ran off the field and hid behind a chair. We had to play a man down after that.

Ein paar Minuten später fing das Spiel an. Prompt verließ Klaus
aɪn paːɐ mɪˈnuːtən ˈʃpɛːtɐ fɪŋ das ʃpiːl an pʁɔmpt fɛɐˈliːs klaʊs
a few minutes later it started→ the game ← promptly he left Klaus

den Platz und versteckte sich hinter einem Stuhl. Wir mussten
deːn plats ʊnt fɛɐˈʃtɛktə zɪç ˈhɪntɐ ˈaɪnəm ʃtuːl viːɐ ˈmʊstən
the field and he hid behind a chair we we had to

daraufhin mit einem Mann weniger spielen.
daʁaʊfˈhɪn mɪt ˈaɪnəm man ˈveːnɪgɐ ˈʃpiːlən
after that with a man fewer to play

Our team parents were very quiet. Most of the time they sat on folding chairs and talked with each other. I caught a few of them glancing at the game for a second or two. But most of the time they weren't too interested. They were annoyed at half time when they had to stop gossiping and give their kids a snack.

Die Eltern unserer Spieler waren sehr ruhig. Die meiste Zeit saßen
diː ˈɛltɐn ˈʊnzəʁɐ ˈʃpiːlɐ ˈvaːʁən zeːɐ ˈʁuːɪç diː ˈmaɪstə tsaɪt ˈzaːsən
the parents of our players they were very quiet most of the time they sat

sie auf ihren Klappstühlen und redeten miteinander. Ich bemerkte,
ziː aʊf ˈiːʁən ˈklapʃtyːlən ʊnt ˈʁeːdətən ˈmɪtaɪˌnandɐ ɪç bəˈmɛʁktə
they on their folding chairs and they talked with each other I I noticed

wie einige von ihnen etwa eine oder zwei Sekunden dem Spiel
viː ˈaɪnɪgə fɔn ˈiːnən ˈɛtva ˈaɪnə ˈoːdɐ tsvaɪ zeˈkʊndən deːm ʃpiːl
how a few of them about one or two seconds of the game

zusahen. Aber die meiste Zeit interessierten sie sich nicht zu sehr
ˈtsuːˌzaːən ˈaːbɐ diː ˈmaɪstə tsaɪt ɪntəʁɛˈsiːɐtən ziː zɪç nɪçt tsuː zeːɐ
they watched but most of the time they were interested→ they ← not too very

dafür. Sie ärgerten sich zur Halbzeit, da sie mit dem Plaudern
daˈfyːɐ ziː ˈɛʁgɐtn zɪç tsuːɐ ˈhalptsaɪt daː ziː mɪt deːm ˈplaʊdɐn
in it they they were annoyed at halftime because they with the chatter

aufhören mussten, um ihren Kindern einen Pausensnack zu
ˈaʊfˌhøːʁən ˈmʊstən ʊm ˈiːʁən ˈkɪndɐn ˈaɪnən ˈpaʊznˌsnɛk tsuː
to stop they had to in order to their kids a snack break to

geben.
ˈgeːbən
to give

A Good Sport

»Die Sache hat auch etwas Positives«, sagte Ingrid. »Sie könnten
di: ˈzaxə hat aʊx ˈɛtvas ˈpo:ziti:vəs ˈzaktə ˈɪŋgʁɪt zi: ˈkœntən
the thing it has also something positive she said Ingrid they they could

ja auch wie die Eltern der Spieler der gegnerischen Mannschaft
ja: aʊx vi: di: ˈɛltɐn deːɐ ˈʃpi:lɐ deːɐ ˈge:gnəʁɪʃn ˈmanʃaft
! also like the parents of the players of the opposing team

sein.«
zaɪn
to be

"Look on the bright side," Ingrid said. "They could be like the other team parents."

»Diese Leute sind wirklich laut und nicht nett. Ich habe noch nie
ˈdi:zə ˈlɔɪtə zɪnt ˈvɪʁklɪç laʊt ʊnt nɪçt nɛt ɪç ˈha:bə nɔx ni:
those people they are really loud and not nice I → never

zuvor einen Vater gesehen, der wegen eines Handspiels einen
tsuˈfo:ɐ ˈaɪnən ˈfa:tɐ gəˈze:ən deːɐ ˈve:gən ˈaɪnəs ˈhantʃpi:ls ˈaɪnən
before a father ←I have seen who because of a hand ball a

Stuhl nach seinem eigenen Kind wirft.«
ʃtʊl na:x ˈzaɪnəm ˈaɪgənən kɪnt vɪʁft
chair toward his own kid he threw

"Those people really are loud and not nice. I've never seen a father throw a chair at his own kid for getting a hand ball foul."

»Wir haben beim Freistoß ein Tor erzielt«, erinnerte mich Ingrid.
vi:ɐ ˈha:bn baɪm ˈfʁaɪʃto:s aɪn to:ɐ ɛɐˈtsi:lt ɛɐˈɪnɐtə mɪç ˈɪŋgʁɪt
we → on the free kick a goal ←we scored she reminded me Ingrid

"We did score on the free kick," Ingrid reminded me.

»Wird Christian in dieser Halbzeit wieder Torwart?«, fuhr
vɪʁt ˈkʁɪstjan ɪn ˈdi:zɐ ˈhalptsaɪt ˈvi:dɐ ˈto:ɐˌvaʁt fu:ɐ
he will Christian in this half again goalie she continued→

sie fort.
zi: fɔʁt
she ←

"Is Christian going to play goalie again in this half?" she continued.

»Nein.«
naɪn
no

"No."

»Prima. Ich will nicht wieder dabei zusehen, wie sich seine Beine
ˈpʁi:ma ɪç vɪl nɪçt ˈvi:dɐ daˈbaɪ ˈtsu:ˌze:ən vi: zɪç ˈzaɪnə ˈbaɪnə
great I I want not again at that to watch how → his legs

im Tornetz verfangen.«
ɪm ˈto:ɐˌnɛts fɐˈfaŋən
in the goal net ←they get caught

"Good. I don't want to see him getting his legs all tangled up in the net again."

»Wie hat er das bloß gemacht, ausgerechnet, als die andere
vi: hat eːɐ das blo:s gəˈmaxt ˈaʊsgəˌʁɛçnət als di: ˈandəʁə
how → he that even ←he did right when the other

Mannschaft einen Angriff startete?«
ˈmanʃaft ˈaɪnən ˈanˌgʁɪf ˈʃtaʁtətə
team an attack it was starting

"How did he do that just when the other team had a breakaway?"

Story 2

"I don't know, but it's a good thing that Dieter is so fast," Ingrid said.

»Ich weiß es nicht, aber Gott sei Dank ist Dieter so schnell«,
ɪç vaɪs ɛs nɪçt 'aːbɐ gɔt zaɪ daŋk ɪst 'diːtɐ zoː ʃnɛl
I I know it not but thank god he is Dieter so fast

sagte Ingrid.
'zaktə 'ɪŋgʁɪt
she said Ingrid

"If he hadn't caught up with their forward and kicked the ball out of bounds, Christian would have felt terrible," I said.

»Hätte er nicht den Stürmer eingeholt und den Ball ins Aus
'hɛtə eːɐ nɪçt deːn 'ʃtʏʁmɐ 'aɪngə̯hoːlt ʊnt deːn bal ɪns aʊs
→→ he not the forward ←he would have caught and the ball out

geschossen, hätte Christian traurig ausgesehen«, sagte ich.
gə'ʃɔsn 'hɛtə 'kʁɪstjan 'tʁaʊʁɪç 'aʊsgə̯zeːən 'zaktə ɪç
←he would have kicked → Christian unhappy ←he would have looked I said I

---3---

The big boy on the other team was slow. Some man on the other side of the field started running up and down the sideline yelling at him to run faster.

Der große Junge der anderen Mannschaft war langsam. Irgendein
deːɐ 'gʁoːsə 'jʊŋə deːɐ 'andəʁən 'manʃaft vaːɐ 'laŋzaːm 'ɪʁgnt'aɪn
the big boy of the other team he was slow some

Mann auf der anderen Seite des Fußballfeldes begann, entlang
man aʊf deːɐ 'andəʁən 'zaɪtə dɛs 'fuːsbal fɛldəs bə'gan 'ɛntlaŋ
man on the other side of the soccer field he started alongside

der Seitenlinie auf- und abzulaufen und rief ihm zu, schneller
deːɐ 'zaɪtn̩ˌliːniə aʊf ʊnt 'aptsuˌlaʊfn ʊnt ʁiːf iːm tsuː 'ʃnɛlɐ
the sideline to run up and down and he yelled→ him ← faster

zu laufen.
tsuː 'laʊfən
to to run

"Who is that nut?" I asked.

»Wer ist dieser Spinner?«, fragte ich.
veːɐ ɪst 'diːzɐ 'ʃpɪnɐ 'fʁaːktə ɪç
who is that nutjob I asked I

"That's his father," said Ingrid.

»Das ist sein Vater«, sagte Ingrid.
das ɪst zaɪn 'faːtɐ 'zaktə 'ɪŋgʁɪt
that is his father she said Ingrid

After ten minutes, the kid was so angry that he left the field. He sat down and cried while his father and mother were arguing.

Nach zehn Minuten war der Junge so sauer, dass er das Feld
naːx tseːn mɪ'nuːtən vaːɐ deːɐ 'jʊŋə zoː 'zaʊɐ das eːɐ das fɛlt
after ten minutes he was the boy so angry that he the field

verließ. Er setzte sich hin und weinte, während sich sein Vater
fɛɐ'liːs eːɐ 'zɛtstə zɪç hɪn ʊnt 'vaɪntə 'vɛːʁənt zɪç zaɪn 'faːtɐ
he left he he sat down and he cried while → his father

und seine Mutter stritten.
ʊnt 'zaɪnə 'mʊtɐ 'ʃtʁɪtən
and his mother ←they argued

"Since that big kid is quitting, I can play now," said Klaus.

»Da der Große ja aufgegeben hat, kann ich jetzt spielen«, sagte
daː deːɐ 'gʁoːsə jaː 'aʊfgəˌgeːbn hat kan ɪç jɛtst 'ʃpiːlən 'zaktə
since the big (kid) ! he has quit I can I now to play he said

A Good Sport

Klaus.
klaʊs
Klaus

»Großartig. Geh rein als Innenverteidiger. Wir haben das ganze Spiel ohne einen gespielt.«
ˈgʁoːsˌaːʁtɪç geː ʁaɪn als ˈɪnənfɛɐ̯ˌtaɪdɪgɐ viːɐ̯ ˈhaːbn̩ das ˈgantsə ʃpiːl ˈoːnə ˈaɪnən gəˈʃpiːlt
great go in as center-back we → the whole game without one ← we have played

"Great. Go in at center-back. We've been playing without one all game."

Zwei Minuten später bemerkte ich etwas.
tsvaɪ mɪˈnuːtən ˈʃpɛːtɐ bəˈmɛʁktə ɪç ˈɛtvas
two minutes later I noticed I something

Two minutes later, I noticed something.

»Niemand spielt in seiner Position«, sagte ich. »Die rennen alle einfach dem Ball nach.«
ˈniːmant ʃpiːlt ɪn ˈzaɪnɐ poziˈtsjoːn ˈzaktə ɪç diː ˈʁɛnən ˈalə ˈaɪnfax deːm bal naːx
nobody he is playing in his position I said I they they run after → all just the ball ←

"Nobody is playing their position," I said. "They're all just running after the ball."

»Das kommt in dieser Liga oft vor«, sagte Martins Vater.
das kɔmt ɪn ˈdiːzɐ ˈliːga ɔft foːɐ̯ ˈzaktə ˈmaʁtiːns ˈfaːtɐ
that it happens → in this league often ← he said Martin's father

"That happens a lot in this league," Martin's father said.

»Wie soll ich sie dazu bringen, damit aufzuhören?«
viː zɔl ɪç ziː daˈtsuː ˈbʁɪŋən daˈmɪt ˈaʊftsuˌhøːʁən
how should I I to make them with that to stop

"How do I stop them?"

»Ich weiß nicht. Sie sind doch der Trainer.«
ɪç vaɪs nɪçt ziː zɪnt dɔx deːɐ̯ ˈtʁɛːnɐ
I I know not you you are ! the coach

"I don't know. You're the coach."

»Ingrid, lass Irma von der Leine.«
ˈɪŋgʁɪt las ˈɪʁma fɔn deːɐ̯ ˈlaɪnə
Ingrid let Irma off the leash

"Ingrid, let Irma off the leash."

Irma war unser Hund. Wir hatten sie zum Spiel mitgebracht.
ˈɪʁma vaːɐ̯ ˈʊnzɐ hʊnt viːɐ̯ ˈhatən ziː tsʊm ʃpiːl ˈmɪtgəˌbʁaxt
Irma she was our dog we → her to the game ← we had brought

Irma was our dog. We had brought her to the game.

»Sie wird auf das Feld laufen und hinter dem Ball herrennen«, sagte Ingrid.
ziː vɪʁt aʊf das fɛlt ˈlaʊfən ʊnt ˈhɪntɐ deːm bal ˈheːɐ̯ˌʁɛnən ˈzaktə ˈɪŋgʁɪt
she she will onto the field to run and to chase after the ball she said Ingrid

"She will run onto the field and chase the ball," Ingrid said.

»Genau das soll sie machen. Der Schiedsrichter wird das Spiel«
gəˈnaʊ das zɔl ziː ˈmaxən deːɐ̯ ˈʃiːtsˌʁɪçtɐ vɪʁt das ʃpiːl
exactly that she should she to do the referee he will the game

"That's what I want her to do. The referee will stop the game and I can talk to the team."

Story 2

	unterbrechen	und	ich	kann	mit	der	Mannschaft	reden.«
	ʊntɐˈbʁɛçən	ʊnt	ɪç	kan	mɪt	deːɐ	ˈmanʃaft	ˈʁeːdən
	to halt	and	I	I can	with	the	team	to talk

"That's not fair. I'm not doing it."

»Das ist nicht fair. Das mache ich nicht.«
das ɪst nɪçt fɛːɐ das ˈmaxə ɪç nɪçt
that is not fair that I do I not

"Tell one of the kids to fake an injury," Martin's father suggested.

»Sag einem der Kinder, es soll eine Verletzung vortäuschen«,
zaːk ˈaɪnəm deːɐ ˈkɪndɐ ɛs zɔl ˈaɪnə fɛɐˈlɛtsʊŋ ˈfoːɐtsuˌtɔʏʃn̩
tell one of the kids it it should an injury to feign

schlug Martins Vater vor.
ʃluːk ˈmaʁtiːns ˈfaːtɐ foːɐ
he suggested→ Martin's father ←

"That's not nice either," Ingrid said.

»Das ist auch nicht gerade nett«, sagte Ingrid.
das ɪst aʊx nɪçt gəˈʁaːdə nɛt ˈzaktə ˈɪŋgʁɪt
that it is also not ! nice she said Ingrid

"They do it in the European leagues all the time," I told her. "It's an art form with some of those professional players."

»Das wird in der Europaliga immer so gemacht«, sagte ich ihr.
das vɪʁt ɪn deːɐ ɔɪˈʁoːpaˌliːga ˈɪmɐ zoː gəˈmaxt ˈzaktə ɪç iːɐ
that → in the European league always ←it is done I told I her

»Einige Berufsfußballer machen das wirklich geschickt.«
ˈaɪnɪgə bəˈʁuːfsˌfuːsbalɐ ˈmaxən das ˈvɪʁklɪç gəˈʃɪkt
some professional soccer players they do this really skillfully

"But these are ten year old children. You don't want to teach them things like that at such an early age."

»Aber das hier sind zehn Jahre alte Kinder. So etwas sollte
ˈaːbɐ das hiːɐ zɪnt tseːn ˈjaːʁə ˈaltə ˈkɪndɐ zoː ˈɛtvas ˈzɔltə
but these here they are ten year old children such a thing one should

man ihnen nicht beibringen, in ihren jungen Jahren.«
man ˈiːnən nɪçt ˈbaɪˌbʁɪŋən ɪn ˈiːʁən ˈjʊŋən ˈjaːʁən
one them not to teach sth. in their young years

"Well no, but they want to win."

»Sicher nicht, aber sie wollen doch gewinnen.«
ˈzɪçɐ nɪçt ˈaːbɐ ziː ˈvɔlən dɔx gəˈvɪnən
certainly not but they they want ! to win

"They don't care about winning," Ingrid said. "You care."

»Ihnen ist es egal, ob sie gewinnen«, sagte Ingrid. »Dir bedeutet
ˈiːnən ɪst ɛs eˈgaːl ɔp ziː gəˈvɪnən ˈzaktə ˈɪŋgʁɪt diːɐ bəˈdɔɪtət
they don't care if they they win she said Ingrid to you it means

es etwas.«
ɛs ˈɛtvas
it something

Just then, the opposing team scored.

In diesem Moment erzielte die gegnerische Mannschaft ein Tor.
ɪn ˈdiːzəm moˈmɛnt ɛɐˈtsiːltə diː ˈgeːgnɐɪʃə ˈmanʃaft aɪn toːɐ
in this moment it scored the opposing team a goal

A Good Sport

»War das nicht ein tolles Spiel?«, fragte ich Christian.

"Wasn't that a great game?" I asked Christian.

»Es hat wirklich Spaß gemacht«, antwortete er.

"It was really fun," he replied.

»Schade für den Trainer der anderen Mannschaft«, sagte Ingrid.

"Too bad about the other team's coach," Ingrid said.

»Warum hat der Schiedsrichter ihn kurz vor dem Ende vom Platz geschickt?«, fragte Christian.

"Why did the referee send him off near the end?" Christian asked.

»Der Trainer war nicht davon überzeugt, dass der Schiedsrichter eine gute Arbeit geleistet hat«, sagte ich.

"The coach didn't think the referee was doing a good job," I said.

»Er benutzte viele schlimme Wörter, die man nicht in der Gegenwart anständiger Leute gebrauchen sollte«, fügte Ingrid hinzu.

"He used a lot of bad words that you are not supposed to say in front of nice people," added Ingrid.

»Wir haben nicht gewonnen«, sagte Christian. »Aber wir haben gut gespielt. Ein Unentschieden ist ziemlich gut.«

"We didn't win," said Christian. "But we played well. A draw is pretty good."

»Du hast lustig ausgesehen, als du nach dem Tor auf- und abgesprungen bist«, sagte Christian.

"You looked funny jumping up and down after their goal," Christian said.

Story 2

"Do you remember what I was screaming?"

»Erinnerst du dich noch daran, was ich gerufen habe?«
ɛɐˈɪnɐst duː dɪç nɔx daˈʁan vas ɪç gəˈʁuːfən ˈhaːbə
do you remember still on it what I I shouted

"Stay in your positions, stay in your positions."

»Bleibt auf eurer Position, bleibt auf eurer Position.«
blaɪpt aʊf ˈɔɪʁɐ poːziˈtsjoːn blaɪpt aʊf ˈɔɪʁɐ poːziˈtsjoːn
stay in your position stay in your position

"Right. And you all did that for the rest of the game. So the jumping worked."

»Richtig. Und in der verbleibenden Spielzeit habt ihr das alle beherzigt. Also hat sich das Herumhüpfen gelohnt.«
ˈʁɪçtɪç ʊnt ɪn deːɐ fɛɐˈblaɪbəndən ˈʃpiːltsaɪt haːpt iːɐ das ˈalə bəˈhɛɐtsɪçt ˈalzo hat zɪç das hɛˈʁʊmˌhʏpfn̩ gəˈloːnt
correct and in the remaining playing time → you that all ←you took to heart so → the jumping ←it was worth it

"Did you like my header?"

»Hat dir mein Kopfball gefallen?«
hat diːɐ maɪn ˈkɔpfˌbal gəˈfalən
→ you my head ball ←it has pleased

"It was pretty good. Next time try to use the top of your head. Not your face."

»Er war ziemlich gut. Das nächste Mal solltest du den oberen Teil deines Kopfes verwenden, nicht dein Gesicht.«
eːɐ vaːɐ ˈtsiːmlɪç guːt das ˈnɛçstə maːl ˈzɔltɛst duː deːn ˈoːbəʁən taɪl ˈdaɪnəs ˈkɔpfɛs fɛɐˈvɛndn̩ nɪçt daɪn gəˈzɪçt
it it was pretty good the next time you should you the top part of your head to use not your face

"My nose still hurts."

»Meine Nase tut immer noch weh.«
ˈmaɪnə ˈnaːzə tuːt ˈɪmɐ nɔx veː
my nose it hurts→ still ←

"The ice cream will make you feel better."

»Nach dem Eisessen wird es dir besser gehen.«
naːx deːm ˈaɪsˌɛsən vɪɐt ɛs diːɐ ˈbɛsɐ ˈgeːən
after the ice cream eating it will it you better to go

"When can we go home?"

»Wann können wir nach Hause gehen?«
van ˈkœnən viːɐ naːx ˈhaʊzə ˈgeːən
when we can we home to go

"As soon as the swelling goes down and the bleeding stops," Ingrid said. "I don't want you getting blood on the carpet."

»Sobald die Schwellung zurückgeht und es aufhört, zu bluten«, sagte Ingrid. »Mama will nicht, das Blut auf den Teppich kommt.«
zoˈbalt diː ˈʃvɛlʊŋ tsuˈʁʏkˌgeːt ʊnt ɛs ˈaʊfˌhøːɐt tsuː ˈbluːtən ˈzaktə ˈɪŋgʁɪt ˈmama vɪl nɪçt das bluːt aʊf deːn ˈtɛpɪç kɔmt
as soon as the swelling it goes down and it it stops to to bleed she said Ingrid mommy she wants not that blood on the rug to get on

STORY 3

Truth Will Out

Ich habe Rolf, meinen Nachbarn und Börsenmakler, angerufen, um ihm ein paar Fragen über einen Investmentfonds, den er mir verkauft hat, zu stellen.

I called Rolf, my neighbor and stock broker, and asked him a few questions about a mutual fund he sold me.

»Klaus, ich kann heute nicht mit dir sprechen«, sagte er zu mir.

"Klaus, I can't speak with you today," he said to me.

»Warum nicht«, fragte ich.

"Why not?" I asked.

»Ich nehme Medikamente gegen meine Rückenschmerzen. Sie haben eine sonderbare Nebenwirkung. Sie zwingen mich, die Wahrheit zu sagen.«

"I'm taking drugs for my back pain. It has a strange side effect. It causes me to tell the truth."

»Ist das so schlimm?«, fragte ich.

"Is that bad?" I asked.

»Es ist das Schlimmste, was einem Börsenmakler passieren könnte. Wir erzählen nie die Wahrheit. Ups. Das hätte ich nicht sagen sollen. Siehst du, welche Wirkung diese Tabletten auf

"It's the worst thing that could happen to a stock broker. We never tell the truth. Oops. I shouldn't have said that. See how these pills are affecting me?"

Story 3

mich haben?«
mɪç 'ha:bn
me they have

"I'm your friend and neighbor. You can tell me the truth."

»Ich bin dein Freund und Nachbar. Du kannst mir die Wahrheit
ɪç bɪn daɪn fʁɔɪnt ʊnt 'naxˌba:ɐ du: kanst mi:ɐ di: 'va:ɐhaɪt
I I am your friend and neighbor you you can me the truth
erzählen.«
ɛɐ'tsɛ:lən
to tell

"I'm not talking to anyone until these pills are finished. It's too dangerous. The only reason I answered this call is because I thought you wanted to set up a golf game. All my other calls are going straight to voice mail."

»Ich spreche mit niemandem, bis ich mit diesen Tabletten fertig
ɪç 'ʃpʁɛçə mɪt 'ni:mandəm bɪs ɪç mɪt 'di:zən ta'blɛtn 'fɛɐtɪç
I I talk with nobody until I with these pills finished
bin. Es ist zu gefährlich. Der einzige Grund, weshalb ich diesen
bɪn ɛs ɪst tsu: gə'fɛ:ɐlɪç de:ɐ 'aɪntsɪgə gʁʊnt vɛs'halp ɪç 'di:zən
I am it it is too dangerous the only reason why I this
Anruf angenommen habe, ist, dass ich dachte, du willst dich mit
'anˌʁu:f 'angəˌnɔmən 'ha:bə ɪst das ɪç 'daxtə du: vɪlst dɪç mɪt
call I have answered it is that I I thought you want→ with
mir zu einem Golfspiel verabreden. Alle anderen Anrufe werden
mi:ɐ tsu: 'aɪnəm 'gɔlfʃpi:l fɛɐ'apʁe:dən 'alə 'andəʁən 'anˌʁu:fə 've:ɐdn
me to a golf game ←to arrange all other calls they are
direkt zur Mailbox weitergeleitet.«
dɪ'ʁɛkt tsu:ɐ 'meɪlˌbɔks 'vaɪtɐgəˌlaɪtət
directly to the voice mail forwarded

I hung up the phone and walked into the kitchen.

Ich legte auf und ging in die Küche.
ɪç 'le:ktə 'aʊf ʊnt gɪŋ ɪn di: 'kʏçə
I I hung up and I went in the kitchen

"Rolf won't talk to me," I said to my wife Ingrid.

»Rolf will nicht mit mir reden«, sagte ich zu meiner Frau
ʁɔlf vɪl nɪçt mɪt mi:ɐ 'ʁe:dən 'zaktə ɪç tsu: 'maɪnɐ fʁaʊ
Rolf he wants not with me to talk I said I to my wife
Ingrid.
'ɪŋgʁɪt
Ingrid

"That sounds strange."

»Das klingt aber komisch.«
das klɪŋt 'a:bɐ 'ko:mɪʃ
that it sounds ! strange

"He's taking pills for his back that make him tell the truth all the time," I said. "So he's afraid to talk to his clients."

»Er nimmt Tabletten für seinen Rücken und die zwingen ihn,
e:ɐ nɪmt ta'blɛtn fy:ɐ 'zaɪnən 'ʁʏkən ʊnt di: 'tsvɪŋən i:n
he he takes pills for his back and they they compel him
immer nur die Wahrheit zu sagen«, sagte ich. »Daher hat er
'ɪmɐ nu:ɐ di: 'va:ɐhaɪt tsu: 'za:gən 'zaktə ɪç da'he:ɐ hat e:ɐ
always only the truth to to tell he said I therefore he has he
Angst, mit seinen Kunden zu sprechen.«
aŋst mɪt 'zaɪnən 'kʊndən tsu: 'ʃpʁɛçən
fear with his clients to to speak

Truth Will Out

Ingrid saß am Küchentisch und aß ein Plätzchen. Sie runzelte die Stirn. Ich wusste, dass ihr etwas in den Sinn kam.

Ingrid was sitting at the kitchen table eating a cookie. Her forehead wrinkled. I could tell she was getting an idea.

»Das wäre doch der richtige Zeitpunkt, herauszufinden, ob Rolf uns die richtigen Anlagen verkauft hat«, sagte sie.

"Now would be a great time to find out if Rolf has been selling us the right investments," she said.

Ich dachte eine Minute darüber nach.

I thought about that for a minute.

»Du hast Recht«, sagte ich. »Besuchen wir ihn, wenn er heimkommt. Seine Frau ist auf einer Geschäftsreise und wird ihn nicht beschützen können.«

"You're right," I said. "Let's go visit him when he gets home. His wife is away on a business trip and won't be able to protect him."

»Ich werde eine Babysitterin für die Kinder anrufen, damit wir uns nicht sorgen müssen, dass das Haus abbrennt, während wir Rolf zur Wahrheit zwingen«, sagte Ingrid.

"I'll call a sitter for the kids so we don't have to worry about the house burning down while we're forcing the truth out of Rolf," said Ingrid.

Zwei Stunden später machte Rolf seine Haustür auf. Ingrid und ich traten hinter der großen Hecke neben der Tür hervor. Rolf sprang einen Meter hoch in die Luft. Dann erkannte er uns.

Two hours later, Rolf opened the front door of his house. Ingrid and I stepped out from behind the large hedge next to the door. Rolf jumped a meter into the air. Then he recognized us.

»Klaus, ich habe beinahe einen Herzinfarkt bekommen. Warum

"Klaus, you almost gave me a heart attack. Why are you and Ingrid hiding in the bush?"

Story 3

	versteckst du dich mit Ingrid hinter dem Gebüsch?«
	fɛɐ̯ˈʃtɛkst duː dɪç mɪt ˈɪŋɡʁɪt ˈhɪntɐ deːm ɡəˈbʏʃ
	you hide→ you ← with Ingrid behind the bush

"We want to ask you a few questions about our investments," I said.

»Wir wollen dir ein paar Fragen über unsere Investitionen stellen«,
viːɐ̯ ˈvɔlən diːɐ̯ aɪn paːɐ̯ ˈfʁaːɡən ˈyːbɐ ˈʊnzəʁə ɪnvɛstiˈtsjoːnən ˈʃtɛlən
we we want you a few questions about our investments to ask

sagte ich.
ˈzaktə ɪç
I said I

Ingrid opened the door and escorted Rolf inside.

Ingrid öffnete die Tür und begleitete Rolf hinein.
ˈɪŋɡʁɪt ˈœfnətə diː tyːɐ̯ ʊnt bəˈɡlaɪtətə ʁɔlf hɪˈnaɪn
Ingrid she opened the door and she escorted Rolf inside

"Sit over there, Rolf," ordered Ingrid. She pointed to a sofa in the living room.

»Setze dich da drüben hin, Rolf«, befahl Ingrid. Sie zeigte auf
ˈzɛtsə dɪç daː ˈdʁyːbən hɪn ʁɔlf bəˈfaːl ˈɪŋɡʁɪt ziː ˈtsaɪktə aʊf
sit down→ over there ← Rolf she ordered Ingrid she she pointed at

ein Sofa im Wohnzimmer.
aɪn ˈzoːfa ɪm ˈvoːnˌtsɪmɐ
a sofa in the living room

"Maybe I should lie down," said Rolf. "My back has been aching so much."

»Vielleicht sollte ich mich hinlegen«, sagte Rolf. »Mein Rücken
fiˈlaɪçt ˈzɔltə ɪç mɪç ˈhɪnˌleːɡən ˈzaktə ʁɔlf maɪn ˈʁʏkən
maybe I should lie down he said Rolf my back

schmerzt so sehr.«
ʃmɛʁtst zoː zeːɐ̯
it hurts so much

"Go ahead," said Ingrid.

»Nur zu«, sagte Ingrid.
nuːɐ̯ tsuː ˈzaktə ˈɪŋɡʁɪt
go ahead she said Ingrid

"If only my wife was here," Rolf muttered as he lay down.

»Wenn doch nur meine Frau hier wäre«, murmelte Rolf, als er
vɛn dɔx nuːɐ̯ ˈmaɪnə fʁaʊ hiːɐ̯ ˈvɛːʁə ˈmʊʁməltə ʁɔlf als eːɐ̯
if ! only my wife here she were he muttered Rolf as he

sich hinlegte.
zɪç ˈhɪnˌleːktə
he lay down

"Don't look so worried," I said. "We're your friends."

»Schau nicht so besorgt«, sagte ich. »Wir sind doch deine
ʃaʊ nɪçt zoː bəˈzɔʁkt ˈzaktə ɪç viːɐ̯ zɪnt dɔx ˈdaɪnə
look not so worried I said I we we are ! your

Freunde.«
ˈfʁɔɪndə
friends

"Have you been selling us the right investments?" Ingrid demanded to know.

»Hast du uns die richtigen Geldanlagen verkauft?«, verlangte
hast duː ʊns diː ˈʁɪçtɪɡən ˈɡɛltˌanlaːɡən fɛɐ̯ˈkaʊft fɛɐ̯ˈlaŋtə
→ you us the right financial investments ←you sold she demanded

Truth Will Out

Ingrid zu wissen.
ˈɪŋgʁɪt tsu: ˈvɪsən
Ingrid to to know

»Ich sollte nicht über meine Arbeit sprechen, bis ich meine
ɪç ˈzɔltə nɪçt ˈyːbɐ ˈmaɪnə ˈaʁbaɪt ˈʃpʁɛçən bɪs ɪç ˈmaɪnə
I I should not about my work to talk until I my

Tabletten alle genommen habe«, sagte Rolf.
taˈblɛtn ˈalə gəˈnɔmən ˈhaːbə ˈzaktə ʁɔlf
pills all I took he said Rolf

"I shouldn't talk about work until I finish taking my pills," Rolf said.

Ingrid kniff ihre Augen zusammen, während sie unseren
ˈɪŋgʁɪt knɪf ˈiːʁə ˈaʊgən tsuˈzamən ˈvɛːʁənt ziː ˈʊnzəʁən
Ingrid she squinted→ her eyes ← as she our

Nachbarn anstarrte.
ˈnaxbaːɐn ˈanʃtaʁtə
neighbor she stared at

Ingrid's eyes narrowed as she stared at our neighbor.

»Wenn du nicht mitmachst, erzähle ich allen in der Nachbarschaft
vɛn duː nɪçt ˈmɪtˌmaxst ɛɐˈtsɛːlə ɪç ˈalən ɪn deːɐ ˈnaxbaːɐʃaft
if you not you cooperate I tell I everyone in the neighborhood

von deiner Nasenoperation und deinen Brustmuskelnimplantaten«,
fɔn ˈdaɪnɐ ˈnaːzn̩ʔopəʁaˈtsjoːn ʊnt ˈdaɪnən ˈbʁʊstˌmʊskl̩n̩ʔɪmplanˈtaːtn̩
about your nose surgery and your pectoral implants

sagte Ingrid.
ˈzaktə ˈɪŋgʁɪt
she said Ingrid

"If you don't cooperate, I'll tell everyone in the neighborhood about your nose job and pec implants," Ingrid said.

»Das ist Erpressung«, sagte Rolf.
das ɪst ɛɐˈpʁɛsʊŋ ˈzaktə ʁɔlf
that it is blackmail he said Rolf

"That's blackmail," Rolf said.

»Du hast zwei Möglichkeiten«, sagte ich. »Entweder du redest
duː hast tsvaɪ ˈmøːklɪçkaɪtən ˈzaktə ɪç ˈɛntˌveːdɐ duː ˈʁeːdəst
you you have two possibilities I said I either you you talk

mit uns oder die ganze Nachbarschaft wird dich auslachen.«
mɪt ʊns ˈoːdɐ diː ˈgantsə ˈnaxbaːɐʃaft vɪʁt dɪç ˈaʊsˌlaxən
with us or the whole neighborhood it will you to laugh at

"You have two choices," I said. "Talk to us or have the whole neighborhood laughing at you."

Ich bemerkte einen Ausdruck der Resignation in Rolfs Augen.
ɪç bəˈmɛʁktə ˈaɪnən ˈaʊsˌdʁʊk deːɐ ʁezɪgnaˈtsjoːn ɪn ʁɔlfs ˈaʊgən
I I noticed a look of the resignation in Rolf's eyes

I saw a look of resignation in Rolf's eyes.

»Also gut, ich werde reden. Um eure Frage zu beantworten,
ˈalzo guːt ɪç ˈveːɐdə ˈʁeːdən ʊm ˈɔɪʁə ˈfʁaːgə tsuː bəˈantvɔʁtən
okay then I I will to talk in order to your question to to answer

ich verkaufe die Produkte, die mir die höchsten Provisionen
ɪç fɛɐˈkaʊfə diː pʁoˈdʊktə diː miːɐ diː ˈhøːçstən pʁoviˈzjoːnən
I I sell the products that me the highest commissions

"OK, I'll talk. To answer your question, I sell the products that pay me the biggest commissions. I don't care if they are the right investments for you."

Story 3

	einbringen.	Mir ist es egal,	ob	das	die	richtigen	Geldanlagen	für
	ˈaɪnˌbʁɪŋən	miːɐ ɪst ɛs eˈgaːl	ɔp	das	diː	ˈʁɪçtɪɡən	ˈɡɛltˌanlaːɡən	fyːɐ
	to bring in	I don't care	if	this	the	right	financial investments	for

euch sind.«
ɔɪç zɪnt
you they are

"This is what we get for trusting our neighbors," Ingrid said to me.

»Das haben wir davon, dass wir unseren Nachbarn vertrauen«,
das ˈhaːbn viːɐ daˈfɔn das viːɐ ˈʊnzəʁən ˈnaxbaːɐn fɛɐˈtʁaʊən
this we have we from it that we our neighbors to trust

sagte Ingrid zu mir.
ˈzaktə ˈɪŋɡʁɪt tsuː miːɐ
she said Ingrid to me

"Who told you about my plastic surgeries?" Rolf asked.

»Wer hat euch von meinen Schönheitsoperationen erzählt?«, fragte
veːɐ hat ɔɪç fɔn ˈmaɪnən ˈʃøːnhaɪtsˌopəʁaˈtsjoːn ɛɐˈtsɛːlt ˈfʁaːktə
who → you of my plastic surgeries ←he told he asked

Rolf.
ʁɔlf
Rolf

"That's my secret," said Ingrid. "After what you just told me, consider yourself lucky that your new nose isn't broken."

»Das ist mein Geheimnis«, sagte Ingrid. »Nach dem, was du mir
das ɪst maɪn ɡəˈhaɪmnɪs ˈzaktə ˈɪŋɡʁɪt naːx deːm vas duː miːɐ
that it is my secret she said Ingrid after that what you to me

erzählt hast, kannst du dich glücklich schätzen, dass deine neue
ɛɐˈtsɛːlt hast kanst duː dɪç ˈɡlʏklɪç ˈʃɛtsən das ˈdaɪnə ˈnɔɪə
you told you can you you consider yourself lucky that your new

Nase nicht gebrochen ist.«
ˈnaːzə nɪçt ɡəˈbʁɔxən ɪst
nose not broken it is

Ingrid stood over the couch and stared down into Rolf's eyes. I could see sweat building up on his forehead.

Ingrid beugte sich über das Sofa und starrte in Rolfs Augen. Ich
ˈɪŋɡʁɪt ˈbɔɪktə zɪç ˈyːbɐ das ˈzoːfa ʊnt ˈʃtaʁtə ɪn ʁɔlfs ˈaʊɡən ɪç
Ingrid she bent over the sofa and she stared in Rolf's eyes I

sah wie sich Schweißperlen auf seiner Stirn bildeten.
zaː viː zɪç ˈʃvaɪsˌpɛʁlən aʊf ˈzaɪnɐ ʃtɪʁn ˈbɪldətən
I saw how → beads of sweat on his forehead ←they formed

"What's the best way to invest our money?" Ingrid asked.

»Wie investieren wir am besten unser Geld?«, fragte Ingrid.
viː ɪnvɛsˈtiːʁən viːɐ am ˈbɛstən ˈʊnzɐ ɡɛlt ˈfʁaːktə ˈɪŋɡʁɪt
how we invest we best our money she asked Ingrid

"Buy a bond fund, a fund that specializes in domestic stocks, and another fund that invests in foreign stocks."

»Kauft einen Rentenfonds, einen Fonds der sich auf inländische
ˈkaʊft ˈaɪnən ˈʁɛntn̩ˌfɔ̃ː ˈaɪnən fɔ̃ː deːɐ zɪç aʊf ˈɪnlɛndɪʃə
buy a bond fund a fund that → in domestic

Aktien spezialisiert, und einen anderen Fonds, der in ausländische
ˈaktsjən ʃpetsjaliˈziːɐt ʊnt ˈaɪnən ˈandəʁən fɔ̃ː deːɐ ɪn ˈaʊslɛndɪʃə
stocks ←it specializes and a different fund that in foreign

Aktien investiert.«
ˈaktsjən ɪnvɛsˈtiːɐt
stocks it invests

German	IPA	Gloss	English

»Wie viel Geld sollen wir in jeden Fonds einzahlen?«, fragte ich.
vi: fi:l gɛlt ˈzɔlən vi:ɐ ɪn ˈjeːdən fõ: ˈaɪnˌtsaːlən ˈfʁaːktə ɪç
how much money we should we in each fund to pay into I asked I

"How much money do we put into each fund?" I asked.

»In eurem Alter würde ich dreißig Prozent in Rentenfonds,
ɪn ˈɔɪʁəm ˈaltɐ ˈvʏʁdə ɪç ˈdʁaɪsɪç pʁoˈtsɛnt ɪn ˈʁɛntn̩ˌfõːs
at your age I would I thirty percent in bond funds

fünfzehn Prozent in ausländische Aktienfonds und den Rest in
ˈfʏnftsɛn pʁoˈtsɛnt ɪn ˈaʊslɛndɪʃə ˈaktsjənˌfõːs ʊnt deːn ʁɛst ɪn
fifteen percent in foreign stock funds and the rest in

inländische Aktienfonds investieren.«
ˈɪnlɛndɪʃə ˈaktsjənˌfõːs ɪnvɛsˈtiːʁən
domestic stock funds to invest

"At your age, I would put thirty percent into bonds, fifteen percent into foreign stocks, and the rest into domestic stocks."

Ingrid und ich verdauten diese neuen Informationen einige
ˈɪŋgʁɪt ʊnt ɪç fɛɐˈdaʊtn̩ ˈdiːzə ˈnɔɪən ɪnfɔʁmaˈtsjoːnən ˈaɪnɪgə
Ingrid and I we digested this new information a few

Minuten lang.
mɪˈnuːtən laŋ
minutes long

Ingrid and I digested this new information for a few minutes.

»Ich will wirklich keine Fragen mehr beantworten«, jammerte
ɪç vɪl ˈvɪʁklɪç ˈkaɪnə ˈfʁaːgən meːɐ bəˈantvɔʁtən ˈjamɐtə
I I want really not any questions more to answer he whined

Rolf.
ʁɔlf
Rolf

"I really don't want to answer any more questions," Rolf whined.

»Vielleicht sollte ich deiner Frau von den wöchentlichen Besuchen
fiˈlaɪçt ˈzɔltə ɪç ˈdaɪnɐ fʁaʊ fɔn deːn ˈvœçəntlɪçən bəˈzuːxən
maybe I should I your wife about the weekly visits

im Massagesalon in der Nähe deines Büros erzählen«, erwähnte
ɪm maˈsaːʒəzaˌlõː ɪn deːɐ ˈnɛːə ˈdaɪnəs byːˈʁoːs ɛɐˈtsɛːlən ɛɐˈvɛːntə
in the massage parlor near of your office to tell she mentioned

Ingrid.
ˈɪŋgʁɪt
Ingrid

"Maybe I'll have to tell your wife about your weekly visits to the massage parlor near your office," Ingrid mentioned.

»Bist du mir etwa nachgeschlichen?«, keuchte Rolf.
bɪst du: miːɐ ˈɛtva ˈnaːxgəˌʃlɪçn̩ ˈkɔɪçtə ʁɔlf
→ you me ! ← were you following he gasped Rolf

"Were you following me?" Rolf gasped.

Ingrid setzte ihr gnadenloses Verhör fort.
ˈɪŋgʁɪt ˈzɛtstə iːɐ ˈgnaːdənloːzəs fɛɐˈhøːɐ fɔʁt
Ingrid she continued→ her relentless interrogation ←

Ingrid continued her relentless interrogation.

»Was sind die besten Geldanlagen, die wir kaufen können?«,
vas zɪnt di: ˈbəstən ˈgɛltˌanlaːgən di: viːɐ ˈkaʊfən ˈkœnən
what they are the best financial investments that we to buy we can

"What are the best investments that we can buy?" asked Ingrid.

Story 3

	fragte Ingrid.
	ˈfʁaːktə ˈɪŋɡʁɪt
	she asked Ingrid

"Low cost index funds."	»Preisgünstige Indexfonds.«
	ˈpʁaɪsˌɡynstɪɡə ˈɪndɛksˌfõːs
	low-priced index funds

"This is also what you buy for yourself?" I asked.	»Und die hast du auch selbst gekauft?«, fragte ich.
	ʊnt diː hast duː aʊx zɛlpst ɡəˈkaʊft ˈfʁaːktə ɪç
	and these → you also yourself ← you bought I asked I

"Of course. All stock brokers have index funds in their own investment portfolio."	»Selbstverständlich. Alle Börsenmakler haben Indexfonds in ihrem eigenen Anlagenportfolio.«
	zɛlpstfɛɐ̯ˈʃtɛntlɪç ˈalə ˈbœʁznˌmaːklɐ ˈhaːbn̩ ˈɪndɛksˌfõːs ɪn ˈiːʁəm ˈaɪɡənən ˈanˌlaːɡn̩pɔʁtˈfoliːoː
	of course all stock brokers they have index funds in their own investment portfolio

"How come you never told us that before?" I asked.	»Wieso hast du uns das vorher nie erzählt?«, fragte ich.
	viˈzoː hast duː ʊns das ˈfoːɐ̯heːɐ̯ niː ɛɐ̯ˈtsɛːlt ˈfʁaːktə ɪç
	how come → you us that before never ← you told I asked I

"I don't sell index funds."	»Ich verkaufe keine Indexfonds.«
	ɪç fɛɐ̯ˈkaʊfə ˈkaɪnə ˈɪndɛksˌfõːs
	I I sell not any index funds

Ingrid grabbed a large vase that was sitting on a nearby table.	Ingrid ergriff eine große Vase, die auf einem Tisch in der Nähe stand.
	ˈɪŋɡʁɪt ɛɐ̯ˈɡʁɪf ˈaɪnə ˈɡʁoːsə ˈvaːzə diː aʊf ˈaɪnəm tɪʃ ɪn deːɐ̯ ˈnɛːə ʃtant
	Ingrid she grabbed a large vase that on a table nearby it stood

"Do not even think of breaking that on his head," I told her.	»Denk nicht mal daran, die auf seinem Kopf zu zertrümmern«, sagte ich zu ihr.
	dɛŋk nɪçt maːl daˈʁan diː aʊf ˈzaɪnəm kɔpf tsuː tsɛɐ̯ˈtʁʏmɐn ˈzaktə ɪç tsuː iːɐ̯
	think not even about it that on his head to to break I said I to to her

Rolf looked very nervous while Ingrid held the vase. Finally she set it back onto the table.	Rolf wirkte sehr unruhig, als Ingrid die Vase in der Hand hielt. Schließlich stellte sie sie zurück auf den Tisch.
	ʁɔlf ˈvɪʁktə zeːɐ̯ ˈʊnʁuːɪç als ˈɪŋɡʁɪt diː ˈvaːzə ɪn deːɐ̯ hant hiːlt ˈʃliːslɪç ˈʃtɛltə ziː ziː tsuˈʁʏk aʊf deːn tɪʃ
	Rolf he appeared very nervous as Ingrid the vase in the hand he held finally she put she it back on the table

"Should we switch funds every year?" I asked.	»Sollen wir die Fonds jedes Jahr umschichten?«, fragte ich.
	ˈzɔlən viːɐ̯ diː fõːs ˈjeːdəs jaːɐ̯ ˈʊmʃɪçtən ˈfʁaːktə ɪç
	we should we the funds each year to reallocate I asked I

»Nein, die meisten Leute, die jedes Jahr ihr Geld umschichten, verlieren dabei Geld auf lange Sicht.«

"No, most people who switch funds every year lose money in the long run."

»Und warum schiebst du dann unser Geld alle paar Monate von einem Fonds zum anderen?«, schrie Ingrid.

"Then why do you move our money from fund to fund every few months?" Ingrid shouted.

»Jedes Mal wenn ihr eine Transaktion durchführt, verdiene ich eine Provision. Je öfter ihr Aktien kauft oder verkauft, desto mehr verdiene ich.«

"I make a commission every time you make a transaction. The more trades you make, the more money I earn."

Ingrid wandte sich mir mit finsterer Miene zu: »Dein Freund wird gleich in seiner Unterwäsche an die Stoßstange unseres Wagens gebunden und durch die Stadt geschleift.«

Ingrid scowled at me. "Your friend is about to be tied to the bumper of our car in his underwear and dragged around town."

»Bitte tut mir nicht weh«, sagte Rolf. »Ich versuche doch bloß, genug zu verdienen, um mir dieses schöne Haus hier, ein Ferienhaus in Florida und ein paar schicke Autos leisten zu können.«

"Please don't hurt me," Rolf said. "I'm just trying to make enough money to afford this nice house, a summer place in Florida, and a couple of fancy cars."

Ingrids Gesicht lief nun rot an. Ihre Augen wurden

Ingrid's face got really red. Her eyes became bloodshot. It was scary. Rolf and I gaped at her. She breathed

Story 3

deeply until she got control of herself. Finally, she was able to speak in a normal voice.

blutunterlaufen. Es war erschreckend. Rolf und ich starrten
ˈbluːtʊntɐˌlaʊfn̩ ɛs vaːɐ̯ ɛɐ̯ˈʃʁɛknt ʁɔlf ʊnt ɪç ˈʃtaʁtn̩
bloodshot it it was scary Rolf and I we gaped at →

sie an. Sie holte tief Luft, bis sie sich wieder unter Kontrolle
ziː an ziː ˈhoːltə tiːf lʊft bɪs ziː zɪç ˈviːdɐ ˈʊntɐ kɔnˈtʁɔlə
her ← she she took a deep breath until she herself again under control

hatte. Endlich konnte sie mit einer normalen Stimme sprechen.
ˈhatə ˈɛntlɪç ˈkɔntə ziː mɪt ˈaɪnɐ nɔʁˈmaːlən ˈʃtɪmə ˈʃpʁɛçn̩
she had finally she was able she with a normal voice to speak

"I'm leaving now. Rolf, if I see you again I am going to carve my initials into one of your fake pecs."

»Ich gehe jetzt. Rolf, wenn ich dich wiedersehe, werde ich meine
ɪç ˈgeːə jɛtst ʁɔlf vɛn ɪç dɪç ˈviːdɐˌzeːə ˈveːɐ̯də ɪç ˈmaɪnə
I I go now Rolf if I I see you again I will I my

Initialen in eine deiner unechten Brustmuskeln ritzen.«
iniˈtsjaːlən ɪn ˈaɪnə ˈdaɪnɐ ˈʊnˌɛçtn̩ ˈbʁʊstˌmʊskl̩n ˈʁɪtsn̩
initials into one of your fake pecs to carve

She stomped out of the front door.

Dann stampfte sie durch die Haustür ins Freie.
dan ˈʃtampftə ziː dʊʁç diː ˈhaʊsˌtyːɐ̯ ɪns ˈfʁaɪə
then she stomped she through the front door outside

"You were right," I said to Rolf. "Those pills are really dangerous. Don't leave the house until they are finished."

»Du hattest Recht«, sagte ich zu Rolf. »Diese Tabletten sind
duː ˈhatəst ʁɛçt ˈzaktə ɪç tsuː ʁɔlf ˈdiːzə taˈblɛtn̩ zɪnt
you were right I said I to Rolf those pills they are

wirklich gefährlich. Verlasse besser nicht das Haus, bis sie
ˈvɪʁklɪç ɡəˈfɛːɐ̯lɪç fɛɐ̯ˈlasə ˈbɛsɐ nɪçt das haʊs bɪs ziː
really dangerous leave better not the house until they

alle sind.«
ˈalə zɪnt
they are used up

"How does she know all those things about me?" Rolf asked.

»Woher weiß sie all diese Sachen von mir?«, fragte Rolf.
voˈheːɐ̯ vaɪs ziː al ˈdiːzə ˈzaxən fɔn miːɐ̯ ˈfʁaːktə ʁɔlf
from where she knows she all those things about me he asked Rolf

I could have told Rolf the truth. That Ingrid's sister works for Rolf's plastic surgeon and her brother owns the massage parlor. Since Ingrid talks to her siblings all the time, she knows which neighbors have had their tummies tucked and what type of massages they like to get. But I wanted Rolf to squirm a little bit.

Ich hätte Rolf die Wahrheit sagen können. Dass Ingrids Schwester
ɪç ˈhɛtə ʁɔlf diː ˈvaːɐ̯haɪt ˈzaːɡn̩ ˈkœnən das ˈɪŋɡʁɪts ˈʃvɛstɐ
I → Rolf the truth ← I could have told that Ingrid's sister

für Rolfs Schönheitschirurgen arbeitet und ihr Bruder der Inhaber
fyːɐ̯ ʁɔlfs ˈʃøːnhaɪtsçiˌʁʊʁɡən ˈaʁbaɪtət ʊnt iːɐ̯ ˈbʁuːdɐ deːɐ̯ ˈɪnhaːbɐ
for Rolf's plastic surgeon she works and her brother the owner

des Massagesalons ist. Da Ingrid mit ihren Geschwistern
dɛs maˈsaːʒəˌlɔ̃ːs ɪst daː ˈɪŋɡʁɪt mɪt ˈiːʁən ɡəˈʃvɪstɐn
of the massage parlor he is since Ingrid with her siblings

ständig Kontakt hat, weiß sie, welche Nachbarn eine
ˈʃtɛndɪç kɔnˈtakt hat vaɪs ziː ˈvɛlçə ˈnaxbaːɐ̯n ˈaɪnə
steady contact she has she knows she which neighbors a

Bauchdeckenstraffung machen ließen und welche Massagen sie
ˈbaʊxˌdɛknˌʃtʁafʊŋ ˈmaxn̩ ˈliːsn̩ ʊnt ˈvɛlçə maˈsaːʒn̩ ziː
tummy tuck they got done and which massages they

Truth Will Out

bevorzugen.	Aber	ich	wollte,	dass	Rolf	ein bisschen	leidet.
bəˈfoːɐtsuːgn̩	ˈaːbɐ	ɪç	ˈvɔltə	das	ʁɔlf	aɪn ˈbɪsçən	ˈlaɪdət
they prefer	but	I	I wanted	that	Rolf	a little bit	he suffers

»Sie	arbeitet	für	den	Geheimdienst«,	erzählte	ich	ihm.
ziː	ˈaʁbaɪtət	fyːɐ	deːn	gəˈhaɪmˌdiːnst	ɛɐˈtsɛːltə	ɪç	iːm
she	she works	for	the	secret service	I told	I	him

"She works for a secret government agency," I told him.

Ich	machte	mich	auf	den	Weg	zur	Tür.
ɪç	ˈmaxtə	mɪç	aʊf	deːn	vɛk	tsuːɐ	tyːɐ
I	I set out	on	the	way	to the	door

I made my way to the door.

»Noch etwas«,	sagte	ich.	»Ich	werde	mein	ganzes	Geld	in
nɔx ˈɛtvas	ˈzaktə	ɪç	ɪç	ˈveːɐdə	maɪn	ˈgantsəs	gɛlt	ɪn
something else	I said	I	I	I will	my	whole	money	in

preisgünstige	Indexfonds	umbuchen.	Ich	brauche	dich	nicht mehr
ˈpʁaɪsˌgʏnstɪgə	ˈɪndɛksˌfõːs	ˈʊmˌbuːxən	ɪç	ˈbʁaʊxə	dɪç	nɪçt meːɐ
low-cost	index funds	to transfer	I	I need	you	no longer

als	meinen	Börsenmakler.«
als	ˈmaɪnən	ˈbœɐzn̩ˌmaːklɐ
as	my	stock broker

"One more thing," I said. "I plan to switch all of my money into low cost index funds. I don't need you to be my stock broker anymore."

STORY 4

Child's Play

»Worüber schimpfst du?«, fragt mich Ingrid.
vo:ʁy:bɐ ʃɪmpfst du: fʁa:kt mɪç ˈɪŋɡʁɪt
what about   you curse you she asks me Ingrid

"Why are you cursing?" Ingrid asks me.

»Das Internet funktioniert nicht.«
das ˈɪntɐnɛt fʊŋktsjoˈniːɐt nɪçt
the internet it works not

"The internet isn't working."

»Ist der Computer angeschlossen?«
ɪst deːɐ kɔmˈpjuːtɐ ˈaŋɡəʃlɔsən
it is the computer connected

"Is the computer plugged in?"

»Laptops haben einen Akku. Im Gegensatz zu Toastern müssen
ˈlɛptɔps ˈhaːbn ˈaɪnən ˈaku ɪm ˈɡeːɡənˌzats tsuː ˈtoːstɐn ˈmʏsən
laptops they have a battery in contrast to toasters they have to

sie nicht eingesteckt werden.«
ziː nɪçt ˈaɪŋəʃtɛkt ˈveːɐdn
they not to be plugged in

"Laptops have a battery. Unlike toasters, they don't need to be plugged in."

»Klaus, du brauchst nicht sarkastisch zu sein. Ich versuche
klaʊs duː bʁaʊxst nɪçt zaʁˈkastɪʃ tsuː zaɪn ɪç fɛɐˈzuːxə
Klaus you you need not sarcastic to to be I I try

doch nur zu helfen. Warum rufst du nicht den technischen
dɔx nuːɐ tsuː ˈhɛlfən vaˈʁʊm ʁuːfst duː nɪçt deːn ˈtɛçnɪʃn
! only to to help why you call→ you not the technical

Kundendienst an?«
ˈkʊndənˌdiːnst an
customer service ←

"Klaus, you don't have to be sarcastic. I'm just trying to help. Why don't you call technical support?"

»Vielleicht kann Jörg mir helfen.«
fiːˈlaɪçt kan jœʁk miːɐ ˈhɛlfən
maybe he can Jörg me to help

"Maybe Jörg can help me."

»Das letzte Mal, als Jörg dir mit einem Computerproblem
das ˈlɛtstə maːl als jœʁk diːɐ mɪt ˈaɪnəm kɔmˈpjuːtɐpʁoˌbleːm
the last time when Jörg you with a computer problem

geholfen hat, hat er die Festplatte kaputtgemacht.«
ɡəˈhɔlfən hat hat eːɐ diː ˈfɛstplatə kaˈpʊtɡəˌmaxt
he helped → he the hard drive ←he broke

"The last time Jörg helped you with a computer problem, he broke the hard drive."

»Ach, genau. Ich werde eines der Kinder bitten, das Problem zu
ax ɡəˈnaʊ ɪç ˈveːɐdə ˈaɪnəs deːɐ ˈkɪndɐ ˈbɪtn das pʁoˈbleːm tsuː
oh right I I will one of the kids to ask the problem to

"Oh, right. I'll ask one of the kids to fix it."

35

Story 4

	beheben.«
	bə'he:bn
	to resolve

"I don't want them fooling around with our computer. The last time you asked them to help, we ended up with Disney princesses as the desktop background."

»Ich will nicht, dass sie mit dem Computer herumspielen.
ɪç vɪl nɪçt das ziː mɪt deːm kɔmˈpjuːtɐ hɛˈʁʊmˌʃpiːlən
I I want not that they with the computer they fool around

Das letzte Mal, als du sie um Hilfe gebeten hast, hatten wir
das ˈlɛtstə maːl als duː ziː ʊm ˈhɪlfə gəˈbeːtən hast ˈhatən viːɐ
the last time when you they for help you asked we had we

Disney-Prinzessinnen als Bildschirmhintergrund.«
ˈdɪzniː-pʁɪnˈtsɛsɪnən als ˈbɪltʃɪʁmˈhɪntɐˌgʁʊnt
Disney princesses as desktop background

"I'll call the computer company," I say.

»Ich werde die Computerfirma anrufen«, sage ich.
ɪç ˈveːɐdə diː kɔmˈpjuːɐˌfɪʁma ˈanˌʁuːfən ˈzaːgə ɪç
I I will the computer company to call I say I

I wait on the phone for twenty minutes for the next available technician. He makes me re-do all the steps I have already tried. After a few minutes, we find the problem.

Ich warte zwanzig Minuten lang am Telefon auf den nächsten
ɪç ˈvaʁtə ˈtsvantsɪç mɪˈnuːtən laŋ am teːleˈfoːn aʊf deːn ˈnɛçstən
I I wait twenty minutes long on the telephone for the next

verfügbaren Techniker. Er lässt mich Schritt für Schritt alles
fɛɐˈfyːkˌbaːʁən ˈtɛçnɪkɐ eːɐ lɛst mɪç ʃʁɪt fyːɐ ʃʁɪt ˈaləs
available technician he he gets me to step-by-step everything

wiederholen, was ich vorher schon versucht habe. Nach einigen
viːdɐˈhoːlən vas ɪç ˈfoːɐheːɐ ʃoːn fɛɐˈzuːxt ˈhaːbə naːx ˈaɪnɪgən
to repeat that I previously already I tried after a few

Minuten finden wir das Problem.
mɪˈnuːtən ˈfɪndən viːɐ das pʁoˈbleːm
minutes we find we the problem

"I will email a software download to correct the problem," he tells me.

»Ich werde per E-Mail einen Software-Download schicken, um
ɪç ˈveːɐdə pɛɐ ˈiːmeːl ˈaɪnən ˈzɔftvɛːɐ-ˈdaʊnloʊd ˈʃɪkən ʊm
I I will by email a software download to send in order to

das Problem zu korrigieren«, sagt er mir.
das pʁoˈbleːm tsu kɔʁiˈgiːʁən zakt eːɐ miːɐ
the problem to to correct he says he to me

"That won't help, since I can't get onto the internet."

»Das wird nichts nützen, da ich nicht ins Internet komme.«
das vɪʁt nɪçts ˈnʏtsən daː ɪç nɪçt ɪns ˈɪntɐnɛt ˈkɔmə
that it will not to be of use since I not on the internet I get on

"I forgot about that," he says.

»Das habe ich vergessen«, sagt er.
das ˈhaːbə ɪç fɛɐˈgɛsən zakt eːɐ
that → I ← I forgot he says he

"On second thought, send me the email. I'll open it on my neighbor's computer, copy the software onto a flash drive, and install it on my computer."

»Da fällt mir ein, schicken Sie mir die E-Mail. Ich werde sie auf
daː fɛlt miːɐ aɪn ˈʃɪkən ziː miːɐ diː ˈiːmeːl ɪç ˈveːɐdə ziː aʊf
it occurs to me (oh! I know...) send me the email I I will it on

36

Child's Play

dem Computer meines Nachbarn öffnen und die Software auf einen USB-Stick kopieren, um sie dann auf meinem Computer zu installieren.«

»Ausgezeichnet.« — "Excellent."

Ich laufe zu Jörgs Haus hinüber, um die E-Mail zu öffnen. Vierzig Minuten später ist mein Computer aktualisiert.

"I run over to Jörg's house to get the email. Forty minutes later my computer is updated."

»Schau dir das an«, sage ich zu Ingrid. — "Look at this," I say to Ingrid.

»Funktioniert das Internet immer noch nicht?« — "Is the internet still not working?"

»Es läuft jetzt, aber ich habe gerade eine Meldung von Microsoft erhalten. Sie raten mir, ihr neuestes Software-Upgrade nicht herunterzuladen, weil es mit dem Internet nicht kompatibel ist.«

"It's fine now, but I just received a notice from Microsoft. They tell me not to download their latest software upgrade because it interferes with the internet."

»Genau das hast du vor zwei Tagen gemacht.« — "You did that two days ago."

»Und das ist der Grund, warum das Internet nicht mehr funktioniert.« — "And that's the reason the internet stopped working."

Story 4

"Do you want a glass of wine?"

»Möchtest du ein Glas Wein?«
'møçtɛst du: aɪn glaːs vaɪn
would you like you a glass wine

"I think so."

»Ich denke schon.«
ɪç 'dɛŋkə ʃoːn
I I think !

---- 2 ----

Two days later, Ingrid is pulling her hair out.

Zwei Tage später rauft sich Ingrid die Haare.
tsvaɪ 'taːɡə 'ʃpɛːtɐ raʊft zɪç 'ɪŋɡrɪt diː 'haːrə
two days later she pulls out her hair→ Ingrid ←

"The printer isn't working."

»Der Drucker funktioniert nicht.«
deːɐ 'dʁʊkɐ fʊŋktsjoˈniːɐt nɪçt
the printer it works not

"Did you disconnect the laptop from the printer today?"

»Hast du heute den Laptop vom Drucker getrennt?«
hast duː 'hɔɪtə deːn 'lɛptɔp fɔm 'dʁʊkɐ ɡəˈtʁɛnt
→ you today the laptop from the printer ←you disconnected

"Yes. I was using it in the kitchen."

»Ja. Ich brauchte ihn in der Küche.«
jaː ɪç 'bʁaʊxtə iːn ɪn deːɐ 'kʏçə
yes I I needed it in the kitchen

"Sometimes that screws things up," I say.

»Manchmal entstehen dabei die Schwierigkeiten«, sage ich.
'mançmaːl ɛntˈʃteːən daˈbaɪ diː 'ʃviːʁɪçkaɪtən 'zaːɡə ɪç
sometimes they arise with it the difficulties I say I

"Can you fix it?"

»Kannst du ihn in Ordnung bringen?«
kanst duː iːn ɪn 'ɔʁdnʊŋ 'bʁɪŋən
you can you it to fix

"I've already shown you how to correct that particular problem."

»Ich habe dir schon einmal gezeigt, wie du genau dieses Problem
ɪç 'haːbə diːɐ ʃoːn 'aɪnmaːl ɡəˈtsaɪkt viː duː ɡəˈnaʊ 'diːzəs pʁoˈbleːm
I → you already once ←I showed how you exactly this problem

beheben kannst.«
bəˈheːbn̩ kanst
to resolve you can

"I forget."

»Ich habe es vergessen.«
ɪç 'haːbə ɛs fɛɐˈɡɛsən
I → it ←I forgot

"I'm reading right now," I tell her.

»Ich lese aber gerade«, sage ich ihr.
ɪç 'leːsə 'aːbɐ ɡəˈʁaːdə 'zaːɡə ɪç iːɐ
I I read right now I tell I to her

"Klaus, get over here and fix this printer, or I won't cook dinner tonight."

»Klaus, komm her und repariere den Drucker, sonst koche ich
klaʊs kɔm heːɐ ʊnt ʁepaˈʁiːʁə deːn 'dʁʊkɐ zɔnst 'kɔxə ɪç
Klaus come here and fix the printer otherwise I cook I

heute kein Abendessen.«
ˈhɔɪtə kaɪn ˈaːbnt̩ˌɛsn
today no dinner

Ich behebe das Problem sofort. Ingrid ist eine ausgezeichnete
ɪç bəˈheːbə das pʁoˈbleːm zoˈfɔʁt ˈɪŋɡʁɪt ɪst ˈaɪnə ˈaʊsɡəˌtsaɪçnətə
I I resolve the problem immediately Ingrid she is an excellent

Köchin. Ich will nicht, dass sie streikt.
ˈkœçɪn ɪç vɪl nɪçt das ziː ʃtʁaɪkt
cook I I want not that she she goes on strike

I fix the problem immediately. Ingrid is a great cook. I don't want her going on strike.

»Warum kannst du es dir nie merken, wenn ich dir zeige,
vaˈʁʊm kanst duː ɛs diːɐ niː ˈmɛʁkn vɛn ɪç diːɐ ˈtsaɪɡə
why you can you it → never ←you remember when I to you I show

wie man kleinere Probleme mit dem Computer und Drucker
viː man ˈklaɪnəʁə pʁoˈbleːmə mɪt deːm kɔmˈpjuːtɐ ʊnt ˈdʁʊkɐ
how you small problems with the computer and printer

korrigieren kann?«, frage ich Ingrid während des Abendessens.
kɔʁiˈɡiːʁən kan ˈfʁaːɡə ɪç ˈɪŋɡʁɪt ˈvɛːʁənt dɛs ˈaːbnt̩ˌɛsns
to correct you can I ask I Ingrid during the dinner

"Why can't you remember when I show you how to correct minor problems with the computer and printer?" I ask Ingrid during dinner.

»Das ist deine Aufgabe. Ich will mit der Reparatur von
das ɪst ˈdaɪnə ˈaʊfˌɡaːbə ɪç vɪl mɪt deːɐ ʁepaʁaˈtuːɐ fɔn
that it is your job I I want with the fixing of

Elektrogeräten nichts zu tun haben.«
eˈlɛktʁoɡəˌʁɛːtn nɪçts tsuː tuːn ˈhaːbn
electronic devices nothing to to do with

"That's your job. I don't want anything to do with fixing electronic devices."

»Das ist nicht fair«, sage ich.
das ɪst nɪçt fɛːɐ ˈzaːɡə ɪç
that it is not fair I say I

"That's unfair," I say.

»Das Leben ist hart. Gewöhne dich daran.«
das ˈleːbən ɪst haʁt ɡəˈvøːnə dɪç daˈʁan
the life it is tough accustom yourself to it

"Life is tough. Deal with it."

———3———

»Kannst du Onkel Friedrich zum Telefonbuch auf meinem Handy
kanst duː ˈɔnkəl ˈfʁiːdʁɪç tsʊm teləˈfoːnˌbuːx aʊf ˈmaɪnəm ˈhɛndɪ
you can you uncle Friedrich to the contact list on my cell phone

hinzufügen«, frage ich meinen sechs Jahre alten Sohn.
hɪnˈtsuːˌfyːɡn ˈfʁaːɡə ɪç ˈmaɪnən zɛks ˈjaːʁə ˈaltən zoːn
to add I ask I my six year old son

"Can you add Uncle Friedrich to the contact list on my cell phone?" I ask my six year old son.

»Ich habe dir schon einmal gezeigt, wie man das macht«, sagt
ɪç ˈhaːbə diːɐ ʃoːn ˈaɪnmaːl ɡəˈtsaɪkt viː man das maxt zakt
I → you already once ←I showed how one that he does he says

er zu mir.
eːɐ tsuː miːɐ
he to me

"I showed you how to do this already," he says to me.

Story 4

"Show me again."

»Zeig es mir noch einmal.«
tsaɪk ɛs miːɐ nɔx ˈamaːl
show it to me one more time

"There's an instruction manual on your desk," he says.

»In deinem Schreibtisch ist eine Bedienungsanleitung«, sagt er.
ɪn ˈdaɪnəm ˈʃʁaɪpˌtɪʃ ɪst ˈaɪnə bəˈdiːnʊŋsˌanlaɪtʊŋ zakt eːɐ
on your desk it is an instruction manual he says he

"My foot hurts. I can't walk to my desk."

»Mein Fuß tut weh. Ich kann nicht zum Schreibtisch gehen.«
maɪn fuːs tuːt veː ɪç kan nɪçt tsʊm ˈʃʁaɪpˌtɪʃ ˈɡeːən
my foot it hurts I I can not to the desk to walk

"Are you just saying that?" he asks me.

»Sagst du das nur so?«, fragt er mich.
zaːkst duː das nuːɐ zoː fʁaːkt eːɐ mɪç
you say you that only he asks he me

"Maybe."

»Vielleicht.«
fiːˈlaɪçt
maybe

"If you don't like it when mommy doesn't remember things you show her about the computer, why should I have to keep explaining how to update a contact list?"

»Wenn du es nicht leiden kannst, dass Mama sich nicht an die
vɛn duː ɛs nɪçt ˈlaɪdn kanst das ˈmama zɪç nɪçt an diː
if you it you dislike that mommy → not about the

Sachen erinnert, die du ihr am Computer zeigst, warum sollte
ˈzaxən ɛɐˈɪnɐt diː duː iːɐ am kɔmˈpjuːtɐ tsaɪkst vaˈʁʊm ˈzɔltə
things ←she remembers that you to her on the computer you show why I should

ich dann dauernd erklären müssen, wie man seine Kontaktliste
ɪç dan ˈdaʊɐnt ɛɐˈklɛːʁən ˈmʏsən viː man ˈzaɪnə kɔnˈtaktˌlɪstə
I then constantly to explain to have to how one one's contact list

aktualisiert?«
aktualiˈziːɐt
one updates

Apparently, my son has very good hearing and an excellent memory. I make a mental note to be careful what I say in the future when he is nearby.

Offensichtlich hat mein Sohn ein sehr gutes Gehör und ein
ˈɔfnˌzɪçtlɪç hat maɪn zoːn aɪn zeːɐ ˈɡuːtəs ɡəˈhøːɐ ʊnt aɪn
apparently he has my son a very good hearing and an

ausgezeichnetes Gedächtnis. Ich mache mir eine geistige Notiz
ˈaʊsɡəˌtsaɪçnətəs ɡəˈdɛçtnɪs ɪç ˈmaxə miːɐ ˈaɪnə ˈɡaɪstɪɡə noˈtiːts
excellent memory I I make myself a mental note

darüber, vorsichtig damit zu sein, was ich in Zukunft sage, wenn
daˈʁyːbɐ ˈfoːɐˌzɪçtɪç daˈmɪt tsuː zaɪn vas ɪç ɪn ˈtsuːˌkʊnft ˈzaːɡə vɛn
about it careful with it to to be what I in the future I say when

er in der Nähe ist.
eːɐ ɪn deːɐ ˈnɛːə ɪst
he nearby he is

"Because I'm your father and I always drive you to soccer practice," I tell him.

»Weil ich dein Vater bin und dich immer zum Fußballtraining
vaɪl ɪç daɪn ˈfaːtɐ bɪn ʊnt dɪç ˈɪmɐ tsʊm ˈfuːsbalˌtʁɛːnɪŋ
because I your father I am and you always to the soccer practice

Child's Play

fahre«, sage ich zu ihm.
ˈfaːʁə ˈzaːgə ɪç tsuː iːm
I drive I say I to him

»Das ist das letzte Mal, dass ich das mache. Schau genau hin.«
das ɪst das ˈlɛtstə maːl das ɪç das ˈmaxə ʃaʊ gənaʊ hɪn
this is the last time that I this I do look→ closely ←

"This is the last time I'm doing this. Watch closely."

Er fügt die Telefonnummer meines Bruders zu meiner
eːʁ fyːkt diː teləˈfoːnˌnʊmɐ ˈmaɪnəs ˈbʁuːdɐs tsuː ˈmaɪnɐ
he he adds→ the telephone number of my brother to my

Kontaktliste hinzu. Ich gebe vor, sehr aufmerksam zu
kɔnˈtaktˌlɪstə hɪnˈtsuː ɪç ˈgeːbə foːʁ zeːʁ ˈaʊfˌmɛʁkzaːm tsuː
contact list ← I I pretend very attentively to

sein. In Wahrheit fällt mir dabei nur auf, dass seine
zaɪn ɪn ˈvaːʁhaɪt fɛlt miːʁ daˈbaɪ nuːʁ aʊf das ˈzaɪnə
to be in reality I notice→ in the process only ← that his

Fingernägel geputzt werden müssen. Es ist schlimm genug, ein
ˈfɪŋɐˌnɛːgl gəˈpʊtst ˈveːʁdn ˈmʏsən ɛs ɪst ʃlɪm gəˈnuːk aɪn
fingernails they have to be cleaned it it is bad enough a

Kind, das gerade einmal den Kindergarten abgeschlossen hat,
kɪnt das gəˈʁaːdə ˈaɪnmaːl deːn ˈkɪndɐˌgaʁtn ˈapgəʃlɔsn hat
kid that → the kindergarten ←he was just finishing

bitten zu müssen, mir mit meinem Handy zu helfen. Aber es
ˈbɪtn tsuː ˈmʏsən miːʁ mɪt ˈmaɪnəm ˈhɛndi tsuː ˈhɛlfən ˈaːbɐ ɛs
to have to ask me with my cell phone to to help but it

ist sogar noch schlimmer, dass ich ihn zwei Stunden später bitte,
ɪst zoˈgaːʁ nɔx ˈʃlɪmɐ das ɪç iːn tsvaɪ ˈʃtʊndən ˈʃpɛːtɐ ˈbɪtə
it is even worse that I him two hours later I ask

das Surround-Sound-System zu reparieren.
das səˈʁaʊnd-saʊnt-zʏsˈteːm tsuː ʁɛpaˈʁiːʁən
the surround sound system to to fix

He adds my brother's phone number to my contact list. I pretend to be concentrating very hard. Actually, I am noticing that his fingernails need to be cleaned. It's bad enough that I have to ask a kid who barely graduated kindergarten to help me with my cell phone. But it's even worse when I ask him to fix the surround sound system two hours later.

»Wo liegt das Problem?«, fragt er.
voː liːkt das pʁoˈbleːm fʁaːkt eːʁ
where it lies the problem he asks he

"What's the problem?" he asks.

»Aus den vier zusätzlichen Lautsprechern kommt kein Ton«, sage
aʊs deːn fiːʁ ˈtsuːzɛtslɪçn ˈlaʊtʃpʁɛçɐn kɔmt kaɪn toːn ˈzaːgə
out of the four extra speakers it comes no sound I say

ich.
ɪç
I

"No sound coming out of the four extra speakers," I say.

Er zwängt sich hinter den Fernsehapparat in der Ecke unseres
eːʁ tsvɛŋt zɪç ˈhɪntɐ deːn ˈfɛʁnzeːʔapaˌʁaːt ɪn deːʁ ˈɛkə ˈʊnzəʁəs
he he squeezes himself behind the television set in the corner of our

Wohnzimmers und betrachtet die vierhundert Kabel, die am
ˈvoːnˌtsɪmɐs ʊnt bəˈtʁaxtət diː ˈfiːʁˌhʊndɐt ˈkaːbəl diː am
living room and he studies the four hundred cables that in the

He worms himself behind the television set in the corner of our family room and studies the four hundred wires hooked into the TV, DVD player, and cable box.

Story 4

	Fernseher,	DVD-Player,	und	der	Kabel-TV-Box	angeschlossen	sind.
	ˈfɛʁnˌzeːɐ	dɛfaʊˈdeːˈpleːɐ	ʊnt	deːɐ	ˈkaːbl̩-teːˈfaʊ-bɔks	ˈangəʃlɔsən	zɪnt
	TV	DVD player	and	the	cable box	connected	they are

"Someone pushed this button by accident," he says.

»Jemand	hat	diesen	Knopf	versehentlich	gedrückt«,	sagt	er.
ˈjeːmant	hat	ˈdiːzən	knɔpf	fɛɐˈzeːəntlɪç	gəˈdʁʏkt	zakt	eːɐ
someone	→	this	button	accidentally	←he pushed	he says	he

I peak behind the television and see him sitting in a nest of cords and cables. He is pointing to a small switch on the back of the cable box.

Ich	luge	hinter	den	Fernseher	und	sehe	ihn	in	einem	Nest	aus
ɪç	ˈluːgə	ˈhɪntɐ	deːn	ˈfɛʁnˌzeːɐ	ʊnt	ˈzeːə	iːn	ɪn	ˈaɪnəm	nɛst	aʊs
I	I peak	behind	the	TV	and	I see	him	in	a	nest	of

Schnüren	und	Kabeln	sitzen.	Er	zeigt	auf	einen	kleinen	Schalter
ˈʃnyːʁən	ʊnt	ˈkaːbəln	ˈzɪtsən	eːɐ	tsaɪkt	aʊf	ˈaɪnən	ˈklaɪnən	ˈʃaltɐ
cords	and	cables	sitting	he	he points	at	a	small	switch

auf	der	Rückseite	der	Kabel-TV-Box.
aʊf	deːɐ	ˈʁʏkˌzaɪtə	dɛs	ˈkaːbl̩-teːˈfaʊ-bɔks
on	the	back	of the	cable box

"It's in the 'off' position," he says.

»Er	steht	auf	›Aus‹«,	sagt	er.
eːɐ	ʃteːt	aʊf	aʊs	zakt	eːɐ
it	it is standing	on	off	he says	he

"Well, turn it on then."

»Gut,	dann	schalte	ihn	an.«
guːt	dan	ˈʃaltə	iːn	an
well	then	turn on→	it	←

He pushes the button and the four extra speakers come alive with sound.

Er	drückt	den	Knopf	und	die	vier	zusätzlichen	Lautsprecher
eːɐ	dʁʏkt	deːn	knɔpf	ʊnt	diː	fiːɐ	ˈtsuːˌzɛtslɪçn	ˈlaʊtˌʃpʁɛçɐ
he	he pushes	the	button	and	the	four	extra	speakers

erwachen	lautstark	zum	Leben.
ɛɐˈvaxn	ˈlaʊtʃtaʁk	tsʊm	ˈleːbən
they awaken	loudly	to the	life

"Don't touch that button again," he says.

»Diesen	Knopf	ja	nicht	wieder	anfassen«,	sagt	er.
ˈdiːzən	knɔpf	jaː	nɪçt	ˈviːdɐ	ˈanˌfasn	zakt	eːɐ
this	button	!	not	again	to touch	he says	he

"I didn't touch it."

»Ich	habe	ihn	nicht	angerührt.«
ɪç	ˈhaːbə	iːn	nɪçt	ˈangəˌʁyːɐt
I	→	it	not	←I touched

"If you have any more problems, ask the geek," he tells me.

»Wenn	du	noch	weitere	Probleme	hast,	frag	den	Computerfreak«,
vɛn	duː	nɔx	ˈvaɪtəʁə	pʁoˈbleːmə	hast	fʁaːk	deːn	kɔmˈpjuːtɐˌfʁiːk
if	you	still	further	problems	you have	ask	the	geek

sagt	er	zu	mir.
zakt	eːɐ	tsuː	miːɐ
he says	he	to	me

"Stop calling your sister that name. And why should I ask her?"

»Hör	auf,	deine	Schwester	so	zu	nennen.	Und	überhaupt,
høːɐ	aʊf	ˈdaɪnə	ˈʃvɛstɐ	zoː	tsuː	ˈnɛnən	ʊnt	yːbɐˈhaʊpt
stop		your	sister	in that way	to	to call	and	actually

Child's Play

»warum sollte ich sie fragen?«
why should I ask her?

»Sie weiß mehr als ich. Herr Salzmann von nebenan bezahlt ihr zwanzig Euro pro Woche, damit sie sein Heimkino und seine Alarmanlage am Laufen hält.«

"She knows more than I do. Mr. Salzmann next door pays her twenty Euro a week to keep his home theater and house alarm working right."

4

Etwas später am Abend sage ich zu Ingrid: »Der Fortschritt der Technologie geht uns einfach zu schnell.«

"Technology is moving too fast for us," I tell Ingrid later that night.

»Hast du wieder Probleme damit, den Wecker zu stellen?«, fragt sie mich.

"Are you having problems setting the alarm clock again?" she asks me.

»Ja. Warum haben wir dieses digitale Unding gekauft? Man braucht ja einen Meisterbrief in Elektronik, um es in Gang zu bringen.«

"Yes. Why did we buy this digital thing? You need a master's degree in electronics to make it work."

»Du ärgerst dich nur, dass die Kinder mehr Ahnung haben als du.«

"You're just upset that the kids know more than you do."

»Unsere Tochter hat einen Technologie-Beratungsvertrag mit

"Our daughter has a tech consulting contract with Mr. Salzmann."

43

Story 4

Herrn Salzmann.«
hɛʁn ˈzaltsˌman
Mr. Salzmann

"He doesn't have any kids, so he needs her expertise."

»Er hat keine Kinder, deshalb braucht er ihre Fachkenntnisse.«
eːʁ hat ˈkaɪnə ˈkɪndɐ dɛsˈhalp bʁaʊxt eːʁ ˈiːʁə ˈfaxˌkɛntnɪsə
he he has not any kids therefore he needs he her expertise

I sit in bed shaking my head in amazement.

Ich sitze im Bett und schüttle verwundert meinen Kopf.
ɪç ˈzɪtsə ɪm bɛt ʊnt ˈʃʏtlə fɛʁˈvʊndɐt ˈmaɪnən kɔpf
I I sit in the bed and I shake in amazement my head

"The calculator she uses in her math class can solve equations," I tell Ingrid. "I didn't even know how to spell the word 'equation' when I was ten."

»Der Taschenrechner, den sie im Matheunterricht benutzt, kann
deːʁ ˈtaʃnˌʁɛçnɐ deːn ziː ɪm ˈmatəˌʊntɐʁɪçt bəˈnʊtst kan
the calculator that she in the math class she uses it can

Gleichungen lösen«, sage ich zu Ingrid. »Ich wusste nicht einmal,
ˈglaɪçʊŋən ˈløːzən ˈzaːgə ɪç tsuː ˈɪŋgʁɪt ɪç ˈvʊstə nɪçt ˈaɪnmaːl
equations to solve I say I to Ingrid I I knew not even

wie man das Wort ›Gleichung‹ buchstabiert, als ich zehn war.«
viː man das vɔʁt ˈglaɪçʊŋ buːxʃtaˈbiːʁt als ɪç tseːn vaːʁ
how one the word equation he spells when I ten I was

"Our kids are growing up with advanced technology," Ingrid says. "They aren't afraid to push all the buttons, and they learn a lot more quickly than we do."

»Unsere Kinder wachsen mit hochentwickelter Technologie auf«,
ˈʊnzəʁə ˈkɪndɐ ˈvaksən mɪt ˈhoːxʔɛntˈvɪkltɐ tɛçnoloˈgiː aʊf
our kids they grow up→ with advanced technology ←

sagt Ingrid. »Sie haben keine Angst vor all diesen Tasten und
zakt ˈɪŋgʁɪt ziː ˈhaːbn̩ ˈkaɪnə aŋst foːʁ al ˈdiːzən ˈtastən ʊnt
she says Ingrid they they have no fear of all those buttons and

Knöpfen, und sie lernen viel schneller als wir.«
ˈknœpfn̩ ʊnt ziː ˈlɛʁnən fiːl ˈʃnɛlɐ als viːʁ
knobs and they they learn much faster than us

"I wonder how senior citizens manage," I say.

»Ich frage mich, wie die Senioren damit zurechtkommen«, sage
ɪç ˈfʁaːgə mɪç viː diː zeˈnjoːʁən daˈmɪt tsuˈʁɛçtˌkɔmən ˈzaːgə
I I wonder how the senior citizens with it they manage I say

ich.
ɪç
I

"They call their grandchildren for help, or they just don't bother with sophisticated gadgets."

»Sie rufen ihre Enkelkinder zu Hilfe oder sie halten sich mit
ziː ˈʁuːfn̩ ˈiːʁə ˈɛŋklˌkɪndɐ tsuː ˈhɪlfə ˈoːdɐ ziː ˈhaltn̩ zɪç mɪt
they they call their grandchildren for help or they they waste time→ with

diesen komplizierten Geräten erst gar nicht auf.«
ˈdiːzən kɔmpliˈtsiːʁtn̩ gəˈʁɛːtən eːʁst gaːʁ nɪçt aʊf
these complicated devices just not at all ←

"Like your mother, who refuses to touch a computer and won't buy a cell phone."

»Genau wie deine Mutter, die sich weigert, einen Computer
gəˈnaʊ viː ˈdaɪnə ˈmʊtɐ diː zɪç ˈvaɪgɐt ˈaɪnən kɔmˈpjuːtɐ
just like your mother who she refuses a computer

Child's Play

»anzufassen, und sie wird auch nie ein Handy kaufen.«
ˈantsuˌfasn ʊnt ziː vɪʁt aʊx niː aɪn ˈhɛndɪ ˈkaʊfən
to touch and she she will also never a cell phone to buy

»Genau«, sagt sie.
gəˈnaʊ zakt ziː
exactly she says she

"Exactly," she says.

»Aber was ist, wenn sie eine Autopanne hat und einen
ˈaːbɐ vas ɪst vɛn ziː ˈaɪnə ˈaʊtoˌpanə hat ʊnt ˈaɪnən
but what it is if she a breakdown she has and a

Abschleppwagen rufen muss?«
ˈapʃlɛpˌvaːgn̩ ˈʁuːfən mʊs
tow truck she has to call

"But what if her car breaks down and she needs to call a tow truck?"

»Sie fährt sowieso nicht mehr.«
ziː fɛːɐ̯t zoviˈzoː nɪçt meːɐ̯
she she drives anyway not more

"She doesn't drive any more."

»Stimmt, ich vergaß.«
ʃtɪmt ɪç fɛɐ̯ˈgaːs
that's right I I forgot

"That's right. I forgot."

»Was wirst du machen, wenn die Kinder ausziehen?«, fragt
vas vɪʁst duː ˈmaxən vɛn diː ˈkɪndɐ ˈaʊsˌtsiːən fʁaːkt
what you will you to do when the kids they move out she asks

Ingrid.
ˈɪŋgʁɪt
Ingrid

"What are you going to do when the kids move out of the house?" Ingrid asks.

»Die Hersteller werden bis dahin Geräte produzieren, die so
diː ˈheːɐ̯ʃtɛlɐ ˈveːɐ̯dn̩ bɪs daˈhɪn gəˈʁɛːtə pʁoduˈtsiːʁən diː zoː
the manufacturers they will by then devices to produce that so

einfach sind, das sie sogar ein Erwachsener bedienen kann.
ˈaɪnfax zɪnt das ziː zoˈgaːɐ̯ aɪn ɛɐ̯ˈvaksənɐ bəˈdiːnən kan
simple they are that they even an adult to operate he can

Andernfalls musst du noch ein paar Kinder zur Welt bringen.«
ˈandɐnfals mʊst duː nɔx aɪn paːɐ̯ ˈkɪndɐ tsuːɐ̯ vɛlt ˈbʁɪŋən
otherwise you have to you a few more children to give birth

"By then the manufacturers will be making devices that are so simple, that even a grown up can make them work. Either that, or you will need to give birth to a few more children."

»Ich denke, zwei genügen«, sagt Ingrid.
ɪç ˈdɛŋkə tsvaɪ gəˈnyːgən zakt ˈɪŋgʁɪt
I I think two they suffice she says Ingrid

"I think two is enough," Ingrid says.

45

STORY 5

Selling Out

Es ist Samstagmorgen um halb neun. Viel zu früh, um wach zu sein. Trotzdem bin ich hier mit meiner Ehefrau Ingrid und wir räumen mit Gerümpel beladene Tische von unserer Garage in unsere Einfahrt.

It is eight thirty on Saturday morning. Much too early to be awake. Yet here I am with my wife Ingrid, moving tables of junk from our garage into our driveway.

»Wie haben wir bloß dieses ganze Gerümpel angesammelt?«, fragt sie.

"How did we ever accumulate all this junk?" she asks.

»Es ist ein Teufelskreis. Wir kaufen Dinge, die wir nicht brauchen, weil sie im Angebot sind. Schließlich verstauen wir die Sachen im Schuppen. Nach einigen Jahren ist der Schuppen voll. Wir veranstalten einen privaten Flohmarkt, um alles aus dem Schuppen loszuwerden. Und der Kreislauf beginnt von neuem.«

"It's a vicious cycle. We buy things we don't need because they are on sale. Eventually, we store the things in the shed. After a few years, the shed is full. We have a yard sale to get rid of everything in the shed. And the cycle begins again."

Plötzlich höre ich eine andere Stimme.

Suddenly I hear another voice.

Story 5

"I'll give you two Euro for this lamp."

»Ich gebe Ihnen zwei Euro für diese Lampe.«
ɪç 'geːbə 'iːnən tsvaɪ ˈɔɪʁo fyːɐ 'diːzə 'lampə
I I give you two Euro for this lamp

I turn around. A small woman with gray hair and large eyeglasses is standing next to one of the tables we dragged out of the garage. She is holding up one of the items we are trying to sell.

Ich drehe mich um. Eine kleine Frau mit grauem Haar und großer
ɪç 'dʁeːə mɪç ʊm 'aɪnə 'klaɪnə fʁaʊ mɪt 'gʁaʊəm haːɐ ʊnt 'gʁoːsɐ
I I turn around a small woman with gray hair and large

Brille steht neben einem der Tische, die wir aus der Garage
'bʁɪlə ʃteːt 'neːbən 'aɪnəm deːɐ 'tɪʃə diː viːɐ aʊs deːɐ gaˈʁaːʒə
eyeglasses she stands next to one of the tables that we from the garage

geschleppt haben. Sie hält einen der Gegenstände, die wir
gəˈʃlɛpt 'haːbən ziː hɛlt 'aɪnən deːɐ 'geːgnʃtɛndə diː viːɐ
we dragged out she she holds up→ one of the items that we

verkaufen wollen, hoch.
fɛɐˈkaʊfən 'vɔlən hoːx
to sell we wanted ←

"It's a genuine Tiffany lamp," I say. "The price is twenty Euro."

»Es ist ein echte Tiffany-Lampe«, sage ich. »Der Preis dafür ist
ɛs ɪst aɪn 'ɛçtə 'tɪfəni-'lampə 'zaːgə ɪç deːɐ pʁaɪs daˈfyːɐ ɪst
it it is a genuine Tiffany lamp I say I the price for it it is

zwanzig Euro.«
'tsvantsɪç 'ɔɪʁo
twenty Euro

"You'll never get twenty Euro. Will you take five?"

»Zwanzig Euro werden Sie dafür nie bekommen. Wie wäre es mit
'tsvantsɪç 'ɔɪʁo 'veːɐdn ziː daˈfyːɐ niː bəˈkɔmən viː 'vɛːʁə ɛs mɪt
twenty Euro you will you for that never to get how about

fünf?«
fʏnf
five

"Lady, the sale starts in thirty minutes. Come back then and we can talk."

»Meine Dame, der Verkauf beginnt in dreißig Minuten.
'maɪnə 'daːmə deːɐ fɛɐˈkaʊf bəˈgɪnt ɪn 'dʁaɪsɪç mɪˈnuːtən
my lady the sale it begins in thirty minutes

Kommen Sie dann wieder und wir können darüber reden.«
'kɔmən ziː dan 'viːdɐ ʊnt viːɐ 'kœnən daˈʁyːbɐ 'ʁɛːdən
come then again and we we can about it to speak

"The electrical wire is frayed," she says.

»Das Stromkabel ist ausgefranst«, sagt sie.
das 'ʃtʁoːmˌkaːbl ɪst 'aʊsgəˌfʁanst zakt ziː
the electrical wire it is frayed she says she

She holds up the wire with her left hand and points to a frayed part.

Sie hält das Kabel mit ihrer linken Hand hoch und zeigt auf
ziː hɛlt das 'kaːbl mɪt 'iːɐ 'lɪŋkən hant hoːx ʊnt tsaɪkt aʊf
she she holds up→ the wire with her left hand ← and she points

eine zerfranste Stelle.
'aɪnə tsɛɐˈfʁanstə 'ʃtɛlə
a frayed spot

Selling Out

»Das hat sie mit ihren Zähnen gemacht, während wir diesen Tisch herausgetragen haben«, sagt Ingrid. »Ich habe es gesehen.«

"She did that with her teeth while we were pulling this table out," Ingrid says. "I saw her."

»Die Strafe für Manipulationen an der Ware ist eine Verdoppelung des ausgezeichneten Preises«, sage ich zu der Dame. »Vierzig Euro für die Lampe.«

"The penalty for tampering with the merchandise is double the price marked on the tag," I tell the lady. "Forty Euro for the lamp."

Die Dame stampft, etwas vor sich her brummelnd, davon. Am Ende der Einfahrt tritt sie gegen unseren Laternenpfahl.

The lady stomps away, muttering something to herself. At the end of the driveway, she kicks our lamp post.

Zehn Minuten später kommt eine Gruppe Schnäppchenjäger in verschiedenen Fahrzeugen an. Sie durchstöbern den Klimperkram und die Kleingeräte, die Ingrid und ich auf den Tischen verteilt haben.

Ten minutes later a crowd of bargain hunters arrives in assorted vehicles. They rummage through the knickknacks and small appliances Ingrid and I have arranged on the tables.

Ingrid schlendert zu zwei älteren Herren hinüber, die sich gerade über unsere Sachen bücken. »Ich habe gesehen, wie Sie die Preisschilder vertauscht haben«, sagt sie zu ihnen. Ihre Gesichter laufen rot an und sie gehen beschämt davon.

Ingrid strolls over to two senior gentlemen bending over our goods. "I saw you switching the price tags," she tells them. Their faces turn red, and they walk away embarrassed.

Story 5

I sell a few things after some haggling. More people arrive.

Nach	einigem	Feilschen	verkaufe	ich	ein	paar	Sachen.	Noch	mehr
naːx	ˈaɪnɪɡəm	ˈfaɪlʃn	fɛɐ̯ˈkaʊfə	ɪç	aɪn	paːɐ̯	ˈzaxən	nɔx	meːɐ̯
after	some	haggling	I sell	I	a	few	things		even more

Leute	treffen	ein.
ˈlɔɪtə	ˈtʁɛfən	aɪn
people		they arrive

Ingrid drags a teenage girl with orange spiked hair over to me. The girl has a few tattoos on her arms and black lipstick. Both eyebrows are pierced with multiple rings.

Ingrid	zerrt	eine	Jugendliche	mit	orangefarbener	Stachelfrisur
ˈɪŋɡʁɪt	tsɛɐ̯t	ˈaɪnə	ˈjuːɡəntlɪçə	mɪt	oˈʁɑ̃ːʒəˌfaʁbənɐ	ˈʃtaxl̩fʁɪˌzuːɐ̯
Ingrid	she drags over→	a	teenager	with	orange-colored	spiked hair-do

zu	mir	herüber.	Das	Mädchen	hat	ein	paar	Tätowierungen	an
tsuː	miːɐ̯	heˈʁyːbɐ	das	ˈmɛːtçən	hat	aɪn	paːɐ̯	tɛtoˈviːʁʊŋən	an
to	me	←	the	girl	she has	a	few	tattoos	on

den	Armen	und	trägt	schwarzen	Lippenstift.	Beide	Augenbrauen
deːn	ˈaʁmən	ʊnt	tʁɛːkt	ˈʃvaʁtsən	ˈlɪpn̩ˌʃtɪft	ˈbaɪdə	ˈaʊɡənˌbʁaʊən
the	arm	and	she wears	black	lipstick	both	eyebrows

sind	mehrfach	mit	Ringen	gepierct.
zɪnt	ˈmeːɐ̯fax	mɪt	ˈʁɪŋən	ɡəˈpiːɐ̯st
they are	several times	with	rings	pierced

"She tried to slip this CD into her purse," Ingrid tells me.

»Sie	wollte	diese	CD	in	ihre	Handtasche	stecken«,	berichtet
ziː	ˈvɔltə	ˈdiːzə	tseːˈdeː	ɪn	ˈiːʁə	ˈhantˌtaʃə	ˈʃtɛkən	bəˈʁɪçtət
she	she wanted	this	CD	into	her	purse	to put	she informs

mir	Ingrid.
miːɐ̯	ˈɪŋɡʁɪt
to me	Ingrid

I look at the CD. "Best of The Beach Boys," I say to the girl. "Isn't this a little light for you?"

Ich	schaue	mir	die	CD	an.	»Das	Beste	der	Beach Boys«,	sage
ɪç	ˈʃaʊə	miːɐ̯	diː	tseːˈdeː	an	das	ˈbɛstə	deːɐ̯	biːtʃ bɔɪz	ˈzaːɡə
I	I look at→		the	CD	←	the	best	of the	Beach Boys	I say

ich	zu	dem	Mädchen.	»Ist	die	nicht	etwas	zu	heiter	für	dich?«
ɪç	tsuː	deːm	ˈmɛːtçən	ɪst	diː	nɪçt	ˈɛtvas	tsuː	ˈhaɪtɐ	fyːɐ̯	dɪç
I	to	the	girl	it is	this	not	somewhat	to	cheerful	for	you

"It's for my boyfriend," she whines.

»Die	ist	für	meinen	Freund«,	heult	sie.
diː	ɪst	fyːɐ̯	ˈmaɪnən	fʁɔɪnt	hɔɪlt	ziː
it	it is	for	my	boyfriend	she whines	she

"Is he sixty years old?"

»Ist	er	sechzig	Jahre	alt?«
ɪst	eːɐ̯	ˈzɛçtsɪç	ˈjaːʁə	alt
he is	he	sixty	years	old

"He's twenty. He likes surfing music."

»Er	ist	zwanzig.	Er	steht	auf	Surfmusik.«
eːɐ̯	ɪst	ˈtsvantsɪç	eːɐ̯	ʃteːt	aʊf	ˈzœɐ̯fmuˌziːk
he	is	twenty	he	he likes		surfing music

"Go steal a Rammstein CD from the sale down the street."

»Geh	und	klau	eine	Rammstein-CD	von	einem	Flohmarkt
ɡeː	ʊnt	klaʊ	ˈaɪnə	ˈʁamʃtaɪn-tseːˈdeː	fɔn	ˈaɪnəm	ˈfloːˌmaʁkt
go	and	steal	a	Rammstein CD	from	a	yard sale

Selling Out

weiter unten an der Straße.«
'vaɪtɐ 'ʊntən an deːɐ ʃtʁaːsə
further down on the street

»Lauf nach Hause, Sara, bevor ich deine Mutter anrufe«, sagt Ingrid.
lauf naːx 'hauzə 'zaːʁa bə'foːɐ ɪç 'daɪnə 'mʊtɐ 'anˌʁuːfə zakt 'ɪŋɡʁɪt
run homeword Sara before I your mother I call she says Ingrid

"Run home, Sara, before I call your mother," Ingrid says.

»Kennen wir die?«, frage ich, während wir dem Mädchen nachschauen, wie es die Straße hinunterläuft.
'kɛnən viːɐ diː 'fʁaːɡə ɪç 'vɛːʁənt viːɐ deːm 'mɛːtçən 'naːxʃauən viː ɛs diː ʃtʁaːsə hɪ'nʊntɐˌlɔyft
we know we her I ask I as we the girl we watch how she the street she runs down

"Do we know her?" I ask as we watch the girl run down the street.

»Sie hat immer auf unsere Kinder aufgepasst.«
ziː hat 'ɪmɐ auf 'ʊnzəʁə 'kɪndɐ 'aufɡəˌpast
she → always → our kids ← ← she looked after

"She used to babysit the kids."

»Wie unheimlich.«
viː 'ʊnhaɪmlɪç
how scary

"Scary."

Die nächsten zwanzig Minuten sind Ingrid und ich ganz schön beschäftigt. Unser Ramsch verkauft sich schneller als erwartet.
diː 'nɛçstən 'tsvantsɪç mɪ'nuːtən zɪnt 'ɪŋɡʁɪt ʊnt ɪç ɡants ʃøːn bə'ʃɛftɪçt 'ʊnzɐ ʁamʃ fɛɐ'kauft zɪç 'ʃnɛlɐ als ɛɐ'vaʁtət
the next twenty minutes they are Ingrid and I really busy our junk it sells faster than expected

For the next twenty minutes Ingrid and I are really busy. Our junk is selling faster than expected.

»Der Verkauf läuft so gut. Ich denke, ich werde die Preise für die übrigen Sachen um dreißig Prozent erhöhen«, sagt Ingrid, während sie einen Marker in die Hand nimmt.
deːɐ fɛɐ'kauf lɔyft zoː ɡuːt ɪç 'dɛŋkə ɪç 'veːɐdə diː 'pʁaɪzə fyːɐ diː 'yːbʁɪɡn̩ 'zaxən ʊm 'dʁaɪsɪç pʁo'tsɛnt ɛɐ'høːən zakt 'ɪŋɡʁɪt 'vɛːʁənt ziː 'aɪnən 'maːɐkɐ ɪn diː hant nɪmt
the sale it goes so well I I think I will the prices for the remaining things by thirty percent to increase she says Ingrid as she a marker in the hand she takes

"This sale is going so well. I think I will increase the prices for the remaining items by thirty percent," Ingrid says as she grabs a marker.

»Lieber nicht«, sage ich zu ihr. »Die Leute befinden sich in einem Kaufrausch. Du könntest einen Aufstand verursachen, wenn du
'liːbɐ nɪçt 'zaːɡə ɪç tsuː iːɐ diː 'lɔytə bə'fɪndən zɪç ɪn 'aɪnəm 'kaufˌʁauʃ duː 'kœntəst 'aɪnən 'aufʃtant fɛɐ'uːɐˌzaxən vɛn duː
rather not I say I to her the people they are situated in a spending frenzy you you could a riot to provoke if you

"Better not," I tell her. "These people are in a spending frenzy. You could start a riot if you try to milk more money out of them."

51

Story 5

	versuchst, mehr Geld aus ihnen herauszuquetschen.«	
	fɐɐˈzuːxst meːɐ ɡɛlt aʊs ˈiːnən hɛˈʁaʊstsuˌkvɛtʃn̩	
	you try more money out of them to squeeze out	
A well dressed gentleman approaches me.	Ein gut gekleideter Herr kommt auf mich zu. aɪn ɡuːt ɡəˈklaɪdətɐ hɛʁ kɔmt aʊf mɪç tsuː a well dressed gentleman he approaches→ to me ←	
"I want to purchase the expanding table," he says with a slight accent.	»Ich möchte den ausziehbaren Tisch kaufen«, sagt er mit einem ɪç ˈmœçtə deːn ˈaʊsˌtsiːbaːʁən tɪʃ ˈkaʊfən zakt eːɐ mɪt ˈaɪnəm I I would like the expanding table to buy he says he with a leichten Akzent. ˈlaɪçtən akˈtsɛnt slight accent	
"That will be thirty-two Euro."	»Das macht zweiunddreißig Euro.« das maxt tsvaɪʊntˈdʁaɪsɪç ˈɔɪʁo that it comes to thirty-two Euro	
"Will you put a 'Sold' sign on the table and hold it for me until I return later in the day?"	»Könnten Sie ein ›Verkauft‹-Schild auf den Tisch stellen und ihn ˈkœntən ziː aɪn fɐɐˈkaʊft-ʃɪlt aʊf deːn tɪʃ ˈʃtɛlən ʊnt iːn could you a sold sign on the table to put and it für mich reservieren, bis ich heute etwas später zurückkehre?« fyːɐ mɪç ʁezɛʁˈviːʁən bɪs ɪç ˈhɔɪtə ˈɛtvas ˈʃpɛːtɐ tsuˈʁʏkˌkeːʁə for me to reserve until I today somewhat later I return	
"Sure, if you pay me thirty-two Euro."	»Klar, wenn Sie mir zweiunddreißig Euro bezahlen.« klaːɐ vɛn ziː miːɐ tsvaɪʊntˈdʁaɪsɪç ˈɔɪʁo bəˈtsaːlən sure if you to me thirty-two Euro you pay	
"I'll give you a down payment of five Euro."	»Ich gebe Ihnen eine Anzahlung über fünf Euro.« ɪç ˈgeːbə ˈiːnən ˈaɪnə ˈanˌtsaːlʊŋ ˈyːbɐ fʏnf ˈɔɪʁo I I give you a down payment of five Euro	
"No. Pay me the full sum now if you want me to hold the table for you."	»Nein. Sie zahlen mir jetzt den vollen Betrag, wenn ich den Tisch naɪn ziː ˈtsaːlən miːɐ jɛtst deːn ˈfɔlən bəˈtʁaːk vɛn ɪç deːn tɪʃ no pay to me now the full sum if I the table für Sie reservieren soll.« fyːɐ ziː ʁezɛʁˈviːʁən zɔl for you to reserve I should	
"But I have to go home to get more money."	»Aber ich muss doch nach Hause gehen, um mehr Geld zu ˈaːbɐ ɪç mʊs dɔx naːx ˈhaʊzə ˈgeːən ʊm meːɐ gɛlt tsuː but I I have to ! home to go in order to more money to holen.« ˈhoːlən to get	
"Are you trying to tell me that you came to a yard sale with less than thirty-two Euro?"	»Wollen Sie mir weismachen, dass Sie mit weniger als ˈvɔlən ziː miːɐ ˈvaɪsˌmaxn̩ das ziː mɪt ˈveːnɪgɐ als you want to make me believe that you with less than	

Selling Out

zweiunddreißig Euro auf einen Flohmarkt gekommen sind?«
tsvaɪʊntˈdʁaɪsɪç ˈɔɪʁo aʊf ˈaɪnən ˈfloːˌmaʁkt ɡəˈkɔmən zɪnt
thirty-two Euro on a yard sale you came

»Ich habe nicht gedacht, dass ich irgendetwas Teures kaufen
ɪç ˈhaːbə nɪçt ɡəˈdaxt das ɪç ˈɪʁɡntˌɛtvas ˈtɔɪʁəs ˈkaʊfən
I → not ←I thought that I anything expensive to buy

"I didn't think I would buy anything expensive."

würde.«
ˈvʏʁdə
I would

»Ich kenne diesen Trick«, sage ich. »Ich reserviere Ihnen den
ɪç ˈkɛnə ˈdiːzən tʁɪk ˈzaːɡə ɪç ɪç ʁezɛʁˈviːʁə ˈiːnən deːn
I I know this trick I say I I reserve for you the

Tisch bis zum Ende des Tages. Sie kommen dann zurück und
tɪʃ bɪs tsʊm ˈɛndə dɛs ˈtaːɡəs ziː ˈkɔmən dan tsuˈʁʏk ʊnt
table until to the end of the day you you come then back and

"I know this trick," I say. "I hold the table for you until the end of the day. You return and refuse to pay the price we agreed on. You figure you can steal it from me for ten Euro, since there are no more customers. That's an old scam. Go away."

wollen den vereinbarten Preis nicht bezahlen. Sie rechnen damit,
ˈvɔlən deːn fɛɐ̯ˈaɪnbaːʁtən pʁaɪs nɪçt bəˈtsaːlən ziː ˈʁɛçnən daˈmɪt
you want the agreed-upon price not to pay you you figure

ihn für zehn Euro stehlen zu können, weil dann eh schon alle
iːn fyːɐ̯ tseːn ˈɔɪʁo ˈʃteːlən tsuː ˈkœnən vaɪl dan eː ʃoːn ˈalə
it for ten Euro to steal to to be able to since then ! already all

Kunden weg sind. Das ist eine alte Masche. Verschwinden Sie.«
ˈkʊndən vɛk zɪnt das ɪst ˈaɪnə ˈaltə ˈmaʃə fɛɐ̯ˈʃvɪndən ziː
customers gone they are that is an old scam go away

»Sie sind kein netter Mensch. Zu Ihrem nächsten Flohmarkt
ziː zɪnt kaɪn ˈnɛtɐ mɛnʃ tsuː ˈiːʁəm ˈnɛçstən ˈfloːˌmaʁkt
you you are not a nice person to your next yard sale

"You are not a nice person. I'm not coming to your next yard sale."

komme ich nicht.«
ˈkɔmə ɪç nɪçt
I come I not

»Ich werde Sie von unserer Mailingliste streichen«, sage ich
ɪç ˈveːɐ̯də ziː fɔn ˈʊnzəʁɐ ˈmeɪlɪŋˌlɪstə ˈʃtʁaɪçən ˈzaːɡə ɪç
I I will you from our mailing list to delete I say I

"I'll take you off our mailing list," I say sarcastically.

sarkastisch.
zaʁˈkastɪʃ
sarcastically

Der Mann geht weg und tritt gegen unseren Laternenpfahl.
deːɐ̯ man ɡeːt vɛk ʊnt tʁɪt ˈɡeːɡən ˈʊnzəʁən laˈtɛʁnənˌpfaːl
the man he walks away and he kicks against our lamp post

Ich mache eine Bekanntgabe.
ɪç ˈmaxə ˈaɪnə bəˈkantˌɡaːbə
I I make an announcement

The man walks away and kicks our lamp post. I make an announcement.

»Wenn noch einer gegen meinen Laternenpfahl tritt, werde ich
vɛn nɔx ˈaɪnɐ ˈɡeːɡən ˈmaɪnən laˈtɛʁnənˌpfaːl tʁɪt ˈveːɐ̯də ɪç
if another against my lamp post he kicks I will I

"If one more person kicks my lamp post, I will lock them in the trunk of my car for a week."

53

Story 5

	ihn	eine	Woche	lang	im	Kofferraum	meines	Autos	einsperren.«
	iːn	ˈaɪnə	ˈvɔxə	laŋ	ɪm	ˈkɔfɐˌʁaʊm	ˈmaɪnəs	ˈaʊtos	ˈaɪnˌʃpɛʁən
	him	a	week	long	in the	trunk	of my	car	to lock up

Nobody pays any attention to me.
Kein Mensch beachtet mich.
kaɪn mɛnʃ bəˈaxtət mɪç
not a person he pays attention to me

"Can I return this toaster if I don't like it?" one lady asks Ingrid.
Eine Dame fragt Ingrid: »Kann ich diesen Toaster zurückbringen,
ˈaɪnə ˈdaːmə fʁaːkt ˈɪŋɡʁɪt kan ɪç ˈdiːzən ˈtoːstɐ tsuˈʁʏkˌbʁɪŋən
a lady she asks Ingrid I can I this toaster to bring back

wenn er mir nicht gefällt?«
vɛn eːɐ miːɐ nɪçt ɡəˈfɛlt
if it to me not it pleases

"It's a toaster," Ingrid says. "Decide now if you like it."
»Es ist ein Toaster«, sagt Ingrid. »Entscheiden Sie jetzt, ob er
ɛs ɪst aɪn ˈtoːstɐ zakt ˈɪŋɡʁɪt ɛntˈʃaɪdən ziː jɛtst ɔp eːɐ
it it is a toaster she says Ingrid decide now if it

Ihnen gefällt.«
ˈiːnən ɡəˈfɛlt
you like

"It may not fit on my counter."
»Vielleicht passt er nicht auf meine Küchentheke.«
fiːˈlaɪçt past eːɐ nɪçt aʊf ˈmaɪnə ˈkʏçnˌteːkə
maybe it fits it not on my (food prep) counter

"All sales are final. No returns."
»Jeder Verkauf ist endgültig, es gibt keine Rücknahmen.«
ˈjeːdɐ fɛɐˈkaʊf ɪst ˈɛntɡʏltɪç ɛs ɡiːpt ˈkaɪnə ˈʁʏkˌnaːmən
every sale it is final there are not any returns

"I'll pay you fifty cents for it."
»Ich gebe Ihnen fünfzig Cent dafür.«
ɪç ˈɡeːbə ˈiːnən ˈfʏnftsɪç sɛnt daˈfyːɐ
I I give you fifty cent for it

"I'd rather smash it with a hammer and throw it in the garbage than sell it for fifty cents," Ingrid says. "The price is five Euro."
»Eher zertrümmere ich ihn mit einem Hammer und werfe ihn
ˈeːɐ tsɛɐˈtʁʏmərə ɪç iːn mɪt ˈaɪnəm ˈhamɐ ʊnt ˈvɛʁfə iːn
rather I smash I it with a hammer and I throw it

in den Abfall, als dass ich ihn für fünfzig Cent hergebe«, sagt
ɪn deːn ˈapˌfal als das ɪç iːn fyːɐ ˈfʏnftsɪç tsɛnt ˈheːɐˌɡeːbə zakt
in the garbage than that I it for fifty cent I give away he says

Ingrid. »Der Preis beträgt fünf Euro.«
ˈɪŋɡʁɪt deːɐ pʁaɪs bəˈtʁɛːkt fʏnf ˈɔɪʁo
Ingrid the price it is five Euro

"How about four?"
»Wie wäre es mit vier?«
viː ˈvɛːʁə ɛs mɪt fiːɐ
how about four

"Sold. Cash only. No checks, please."
»Verkauft. Nur Bargeld. Keine Schecks, bitte.«
fɛɐˈkaʊft nuːɐ ˈbaːɐˌɡɛlt ˈkaɪnə ʃɛks ˈbɪtə
sold only cash not any checks please

Selling Out

Die Dame bezahlt mit einer Tasche voller Kleingeld. Sie geht mit ihrem Toaster davon. »Du bist eine sehr gute Verkäuferin«, sage ich zu Ingrid.

The lady pays with a bag full of change. She walks away with her toaster. "You are a great saleslady," I say to Ingrid.

Sie strahlt vor Freude.

She beams with pleasure.

Gegen Ende des Tages sind nur noch ein paar Sachen übrig. Ingrid und ich sind hundemüde. Mit Kunden feilschen und sich mit Ladendieben anlegen ist harte Arbeit. Wir sind nahe am Zusammenbruch. Die Organisierung eines Flohmarktes könnte sogar den Buddha zum Mörder werden lassen.

Toward the end of the day, just a few items are left. Ingrid and I are bone tired. Haggling with customers and wrestling with shoplifters is tough work. We are close to the breaking point. Running a yard sale could drive the Buddha to commit murder.

Ein Kunde ist noch da.

One customer remains.

»Ich gebe Ihnen drei Euro für diesen Bilderrahmen«, sagt er zu mir.

"I will pay three Euro for this picture frame," he tells me.

»Der Preis beträgt zwölf Euro. Da Sie der letzte Kunde sind, können Sie ihn für sechs haben.«

"The price is twelve Euro. Since you are the last customer, I will let you have it for six."

»Ich habe nur drei Euro.«

"I only have three Euro."

Story 5

I think for a second. I'm ready for a nice bottle of wine. Maybe I should just sell the frame for three Euro and get rid of this guy.

Ich	überlege	eine	Sekunde	lang.	Ich	sehne	mich	nach	einer	guten
ıç	yːbɐˈleːɡə	ˈaɪnə	zeːˈkʊndə	laŋ	ıç	ˈzeːnə	mıç	naːx	ˈaɪnɐ	ˈɡuːtn
I	I think about	a	second	long	I	I crave			a	good

Flasche	Wein.	Vielleicht	sollte	ich	einfach	den	Rahmen	für	drei
ˈflaʃə	vaɪn	fiːˈlaɪçt	ˈzɔltə	ıç	ˈaɪnfax	deːn	ˈʁaːmən	fyːɐ	dʁaɪ
bottle	wine	maybe	I should	I	just	the	frame	for	three

Euro	verkaufen	und	ich	wäre	diesen	Kerl	los.
ˈɔɪʁo	fɛɐˈkaʊfən	ʊnt	ıç	ˈvɛːʁə	ˈdiːzən	kɛʁl	loːs
Euro	to sell	and	I	I would be rid of →	this	guy	←

"OK, three Euro," Ingrid says. She must have been reading my mind.

»Einverstanden,	drei	Euro«,	sagt	Ingrid.	Sie	muss	meine
ˈaɪnfɛɐʃtandn	dʁaɪ	ˈɔɪʁo	zakt	ˈɪŋɡʁɪt	ziː	mʊs	ˈmaɪnə
okay	three	Euro	she says	Ingrid	she	she must	my

Gedanken	gelesen	haben.
ɡəˈdaŋkən	ɡəˈleːzən	ˈhaːbən
thoughts	to read	to have

"Is it acceptable to pay with pennies?" he asks.

»Sind	Sie	einverstanden,	wenn	ich	mit	Centstücken	bezahle«,	fragt
zɪnt	ziː	ˈaɪnfɛɐʃtandn	vɛn	ıç	mɪt	ˈsɛntʃtʏkn	bəˈtsaːlə	fʁaːkt
are you		okay	if	I	with	cents	I pay	he asks

er.
eːɐ
he

I uncork the wine as Ingrid chases the man down the street with a shovel.

Ich	entkorke	den	Wein,	während	Ingrid	den	Mann	mit	einer
ıç	ɛntˈkɔʁkə	deːn	vaɪn	ˈvɛːʁənt	ˈɪŋɡʁɪt	deːn	man	mɪt	ˈaɪnɐ
I	I uncork	the	wine	as	Ingrid	the	man	with	a

Schaufel	die	Straße	hinunterjagt.
ˈʃaʊfl	diː	ˈʃtʁaːsə	hɪˈnʊntɐjaːkt
shovel	the	street	she chases down

STORY 6

Don't Stop and Smell the Roses

»Ich habe noch drei getötet«, rief ich Ingrid zu.
ɪç 'ha:bə nɔx dʁaɪ gə'tø:tət ʁi:f ɪç 'ɪŋgʁɪt tsu:
I → another three ←I killed I yelled at→ I Ingrid ←

"I killed three more," I yelled to Ingrid.

»Kämpfe weiter und wir kommen hier eventuell lebend hinaus«,
'kɛmpfə 'vaɪtɐ ʊnt vi:ɐ 'kɔmən hi:ɐ eventu'ɛl 'le:bənt hɪ'naʊs
keep fighting and we we come out→ here possibly alive ←

kreischte sie zurück.
'kʁaɪʃtə zi: tsu'ʁʏk
she shrieked she back

"Keep fighting and we might get out of this alive," she shrieked back.

Ich wandte mich für den Bruchteil einer Sekunde lang von
ɪç 'vantə mɪç fy:ɐ de:n 'bʁʊx,taɪl 'aɪnɐ ze'kʊndə laŋ fɔn
I I turned away→ for the fraction of a second long from

meinen Angreifern ab und bemerkte, dass Ingrid vom Feind auf
'maɪnən 'an,gʁaɪfɐn ap ʊnt bə'mɛʁktə das 'ɪŋgʁɪt fɔm faɪnt aʊf
my attackers ← and I noticed that Ingrid by the enemy on

allen Seiten umzingelt war. Ich verlor keinen Gedanken über meine
'alən 'zaɪtən 'ʊm,tsɪŋəlt va:ɐ ɪç fɛɐ'lo:ɐ 'kaɪnən gə'daŋkən 'y:bɐ 'maɪnə
all sides she was surrounded I I was unconcerned about my

eigene Sicherheit und eilte ihr zu Hilfe.
'aɪgənə 'zɪçɐhaɪt ʊnt 'aɪltə i:ɐ tsu: 'hɪlfə
own safety and I rushed to her aid

I turned my head from my attackers for a split second and saw that Ingrid was surrounded by the enemy on all sides. With no thought for my own safety I rushed to her aide.

»Kommt doch her, ihr Blutsauger«, schrie ich unsere Gegner
kɔmt dɔx he:ɐ i:ɐ 'blu:t,zaʊgɐ ʃʁi: ɪç 'ʊnzəʁə 'ge:gnɐ
come here→ ! ← you bloodsuckers I screamed at→ I our foes

an.
an
←

"Bring it on, suckers," I screamed at our foes.

Rücken an Rücken standen wir und boxten und hauten auf
'ʁʏkən an 'ʁʏkən 'ʃtandən vi:ɐ ʊnt 'bɔkstən ʊnt 'haʊtn aʊf
back-to-back we stood we and we punched and we smacked→ at

unsere Gegner ein, während sie ihre Angriffe fortsetzten.
'ʊnzəʁə 'ge:gnɐ aɪn 'vɛːʁənt zi: 'i:ʁə 'an,gʁɪfə 'fɔʁt,zɛtstn̩
our adversaries ← as they their attack they continued

Nach ein paar Minuten waren wir erschöpft. Unsere Feinde
na:x aɪn pa:ɐ mɪ'nu:tən 'va:ʁən vi:ɐ ɛɐ'ʃœpft 'ʊnzəʁə 'faɪndə
after a few minutes we were we exhausted our enemies

We stood back to back, punching and smacking our adversaries as they continued their attack. After a few minutes, we were exhausted. Our enemies just kept attacking.

57

Story 6

	griffen ständig weiter an.
	ˈgʁɪfən ˈʃtɛndɪç ˈvaɪtɐ an
	they kept on attacking→ steadily ←

"Klaus, we have no choice," Ingrid gasped. "We have to use the toxic chemicals."

»Klaus, wir haben keine Wahl«, keuchte Ingrid. »Wir müssen die
klaʊs viːɐ ˈhaːbən ˈkaɪnə vaːl ˈkɔɪçtə ˈɪŋgʁɪt viːɐ ˈmʏsən diː
Klaus we we have not a choice she gasped Ingrid we we have to the

Giftstoffe einsetzen.«
ˈgɪftˌʃtɔfə ˈaɪnzɛtsən
poisons to use

"There is very little left."

»Es ist sehr wenig davon übrig.«
ɛs ɪst zeːɐ ˈveːnɪç daˈfɔn ˈyːbʁɪç
it it is very little of it remaining

"It's the only chance we have." The desperation in her voice made me turn to look at my lovely wife. Her eyes brimmed with tears. Her hair was disheveled.

»Das ist die einzige Chance, die wir haben.« Die Verzweiflung
das ɪst diː ˈaɪntsɪgə ˈʃãːsə diː viːɐ ˈhaːbən diː fɛɐˈtsvaɪflʊŋ
this it is the only chance that we we have the desperation

in ihrer Stimme brachte mich dazu, mich umzudrehen, um einen
ɪn ˈiːɐ ˈʃtɪmə ˈbʁaxtə mɪç daˈtsuː mɪç ˈʊmtsuˌdʁeːən ʊm ˈaɪnən
in her voice it made me to turn myself around to a

Blick auf meine schöne Frau zu werfen. Ihre Augen waren mit
blɪk aʊf ˈmaɪnə ˈʃøːnə fʁaʊ tsuː ˈvɛʁfn̩ ˈiːʁə ˈaʊgən ˈvaːʁən mɪt
look at my beautiful wife to to throw her eyes → with

Tränen gefüllt. Ihr Haar war zerzaust.
ˈtʁɛːnən gəˈfʏlt iːɐ haːɐ vaːɐ tsɛɐˈtsaʊst
tears ←they filled her hair it was disheveled

I pulled the can of mosquito repellent from the pocket of my shorts. I sprayed some on Ingrid's bare arms and legs. Then I sprayed the rest on myself. I threw the can at the swarm of deadly little killers that was hovering in front of us.

Ich zog die Mückenspraydose aus der Tasche meiner Shorts. Ich
ɪç tsoːk diː ˈmʏknˌʃpʁeːˈdoːzə aʊs deːɐ ˈtaʃə ˈmaɪnɐ ʃɔːɐts ɪç
I I pulled the mosquito repellent can from the pocket of my shorts I

besprühte damit Ingrids nackte Arme und Beine. Den Rest sprühte
bəˈʃpʁyːtə daˈmɪt ˈɪŋgʁɪts ˈnaktə ˈaʁmə ʊnt ˈbaɪnə deːn ʁɛst ˈʃpʁyːtə
I sprayed with it Ingrid's bare arms and legs the rest I sprayed

ich auf mich selbst. Die Dose warf ich in den Schwarm der
ɪç aʊf mɪç zɛlpst diː ˈdoːzə vaʁf ɪç ɪn deːn ʃvaʁm deːɐ
I on myself the can I threw I into the swarm of the

tödlichen kleinen Mörder, die unmittelbar vor uns schwebten.
ˈtøːtlɪçən ˈklaɪnən ˈmœʁdɐ diː ʊnˈmɪtlbaːɐ foːɐ ʊns ˈʃveːptən
deadly little killers that directly in front of us they floated

The mosquitoes pulled back to reform their lines. They knew better than to land on skin that had just been coated with spray. I could see the mosquito officers rally their troops for another onslaught.

Die Mücken zogen sich zurück, um ihre Angriffsreihen neu zu
diː ˈmʏkən ˈtsoːgən zɪç tsuˈʁʏk ʊm ˈiːʁə ˈaŋgʁɪfsˌʁaɪən nɔɪ tsuː
the mosquitoes they move back to their attack lines new to

formieren. Sie waren klug genug, nicht auf der Haut zu landen,
fɔʁˈmiːʁən ziː ˈvaːʁən kluːk gəˈnuːk nɪçt aʊf deːɐ haʊt tsuː ˈlandən
to reform they they were clever enough not on the skin to to land

die gerade mit Insektenschutzmittel eingesprüht wurde. Ich konnte
diː gəˈʁaːdə mɪt ɪnˈzɛktnˌʃʊtsˌmɪtl ˈaɪngəʃpʁyːt ˈvʊʁdə ɪç ˈkɔntə
that just with insect repellent it had been sprayed I I could

58

beobachten,	wie	die	Mücken-Kommandanten	ihre	Truppen	für
bəˈoːbaxtən	viː	diː	ˈmʏkn-kɔmanˈdantn	ˈiːʁə	ˈtʁʊpən	fyːɐ
to observe	how	the	mosquito-commanders	their	troops	for

einen	neuen	Angriff	versammelten.
ˈaɪnən	ˈnɔɪən	ˈaŋɡʁɪf	fɛɐˈzamltn
a	new	attack	they mustered

»Die	Schutzwirkung	hält	nur	ein paar	Minuten	an«,	sagte	Ingrid.
diː	ˈʃʊtsˌvɪʁkʊŋ	hɛlt	nuːɐ	aɪn paːɐ	mɪˈnuːtən	an	ˈzaktə	ˈɪŋɡʁɪt
the	protection	it lasts→	only	a few	minutes	←	she said	Ingrid

"The protection only lasts for a few minutes," Ingrid said. "Run to the car as fast as you can."

»Lauf	zum	Auto	so	schnell	du	kannst.«
laʊf	tsʊm	ˈaʊto	zoː	ʃnɛl	duː	kanst
run	to the	car	as	fast	you	you can

Wir	waren	zwei	Kilometer	vom	Parkplatz	entfernt,	tief	im
viːɐ	ˈvaːʁən	tsvaɪ	kɪloːˈmeːtɐ	fɔm	ˈpaʁkˌplats	ɛntˈfɛʁnt	tiːf	ɪm
we	we were	two	kilometer	from the	parking lot	away	deep	in the

We were two kilometers from the parking lot. Deep in a swamp in the Yucatan Peninsula. We saw a small wooden sign with an arrow. The word 'Salida' was painted on it.

Sumpfgebiet	der	Halbinsel	Yucatan.	Wir	sahen	ein	kleines
ˈzʊmpfɡəˌbiːt	deːɐ	ˈhalpˌɪnzl	jʊkataːn	viːɐ	ˈzaːən	aɪn	ˈklaɪnəs
swamp	of the	peninsula	Yucatan	we	we saw	a	small

Holzschild	mit	einem	Pfeil.	Das	Wort	›Salida‹	war	darauf
ˈhɔltsˌʃɪlt	mɪt	ˈaɪnəm	pfaɪl	das	vɔʁt	saˈliða	vaːɐ	daˈʁaʊf
wooden sign	with	an	arrow	the	word	salida	→	on it

gemalt.
ɡəˈmaːlt
← it was painted

»Folge	mir«,	rief	ich.	Über	das	Gesumme	von	Millionen
ˈfɔlɡə	miːɐ	ʁiːf	ɪç	ˈyːbɐ	das	ɡəˈzʊmə	fɔn	mɪlˈjoːnən
follow	me	I shouted	I	over→	the	buzzing	of	millions of

"Follow me," I shouted. It was hard to make myself heard over the buzzing of millions of mosquito wings. I ran in the direction the arrow pointed. Ingrid was close behind.

Mückenflügeln	hinweg	konnte	ich	mir	nur	mühsam	Gehör
ˈmʏknˌflyːɡln	hɪnˈvɛk	ˈkɔntə	ɪç	miːɐ	nuːɐ	ˈmyːzaːm	ɡəˈhøːɐ
mosquito wings	←	I could	I	for me	only	with difficulty	hearing

verschaffen.	Ich	lief	in	die	Richtung,	die	der	Pfeil	anzeigte.	Ingrid
fɛɐˈʃafn	ɪç	liːf	ɪn	diː	ˈʁɪçtʊŋ	diː	deːɐ	pfaɪl	ˈanˌtsaɪktə	ˈɪŋɡʁɪt
to gain	I	I ran	in	the	direction	that	the	arrow	it indicated	Ingrid

war	dicht	hinter	mir.
vaːɐ	dɪçt	ˈhɪntɐ	miːɐ
she was	close	behind	me

»Bedeutet	›Salida‹,	dass	das	der	Weg	zum	Parkplatz	ist?«,	keuchte
bəˈdɔɪtət	saˈliða	das	das	deːɐ	vɛk	tsʊm	ˈpaʁkˌplats	ɪst	ˈkɔɪçtə
it means	salida	that	this	the	way	to the	parking lot	it is	she panted

"Does 'Salida' mean this is the way to the parking lot?" she panted.

sie.
ziː
she

»Es	könnte	bedeuten,	dass	wir	zu	einem	großen	Salat
ɛs	ˈkœntə	bəˈdɔɪtən	das	viːɐ	tsuː	ˈaɪnəm	ˈɡʁoːsən	zaˈlaːt
it	it could	to mean	that	we	to	a	large	salad

"It might mean we are headed toward a large salad." I answered. "My Spanish is not very good."

Don't Stop and Smell the Roses

Story 6

	geführt werden«,	antwortete	ich.	»Mein Spanisch ist nicht sehr
	gəˈfyːɐt ˈveːɐdn	ˈantvɔɐtətə	ɪç	maɪn ˈʃpaːnɪʃ ɪst nɪçt zeːɐ
	we are being led	I answered	I	my Spanish it is not very

gut.«
guːt
good

At the beginning of our hike, I had stepped on a tree root and twisted my ankle. My foot throbbed with pain. This did not stop me from running with all of my speed to escape.

Zu Beginn unserer Wanderung war ich auf eine Baumwurzel
tsuː bəˈgɪn ˈʊnzɐɐ ˈvandəʁʊŋ vaːɐ ɪç aʊf ˈaɪnə ˈbaʊmˌvʊɐtsl̩
at the beginning of our hike → I on a tree root

getreten und hatte mir den Knöchel verdreht. Mein Fuß pochte
gəˈtʁeːtən ʊnt ˈhatə miːɐ deːn ˈknœçəl fɛɐˈdʁeːt maɪn fuːs ˈpɔçtə
←I had stepped and → my ankle ←I had twisted my foot it throbbed

vor Schmerz. Aber das konnte mich nicht davon abhalten, so
foːɐ ʃmɛɐts ˈaːbɐ das ˈkɔntə mɪç nɪçt daˈfɔn ˈapˌhaltən zoː
with pain but this it could me not from it to prevent so

schnell zu laufen, wie ich konnte, um zu entkommen.
ʃnɛl tsuː ˈlaʊfən viː ɪç ˈkɔntə ʊm tsuː ɛntˈkɔmən
fast to to run as I I could in order to to escape

Sweat mixed with suntan lotion ran down my forehead and into my eyes, which started to burn. The forest became blurry.

Schweiß vermischt mit Sonnenmilch lief mir von der Stirn in
ʃvaɪs fɛɐˈmɪʃt mɪt ˈzɔnənˌmɪlx liːf miːɐ fɔn deːɐ ʃtɪɐn ɪn
sweat mixed with suntan lotion it ran from my forehead into

die Augen, die zu brennen begannen. Ich fing an, den Urwald
diː ˈaʊgən diː tsuː ˈbʁɛnən bəˈganən ɪç fɪŋ an deːn ˈuːɐˌvalt
the eyes which to to burn they began I I began the jungle

nur noch verschwommen zu sehen.
nuːɐ nɔx fɛɐˈʃvɔmən tsuː ˈzeːən
only blurry to to see

"I can't see," I said to Ingrid in a voiced that contained a large dose of panic. "You go first."

»Ich kann nichts sehen«, sagte ich zu Ingrid mit einer Stimme
ɪç kan nɪçts ˈzeːən ˈzaktə ɪç tsuː ˈɪŋɡʁɪt mɪt ˈaɪnɐ ˈʃtɪmə
I I can nothing to see I said I to Ingrid with a voice

voller Panik. »Du gehst voran.«
ˈfɔlɐ ˈpaːnɪk duː ɡeːst foˈʁan
full of panic you you go ahead

We passed a man sitting on a chair and selling lemonade from a multi-colored wagon.

Wir kamen an einem Mann vorbei, der auf einem Stuhl saß und
viːɐ ˈkaːmən an ˈaɪnəm man foːɐˈbaɪ deːɐ aʊf ˈaɪnəm ʃtuːl zaːs ʊnt
we we passed by → a man ← who on a chair he sat and

Limonade aus einem bunten Wagen verkaufte.
limoˈnaːdə aʊs ˈaɪnəm ˈbʊntn̩ ˈvaːgən fɛɐˈkaʊftə
lemonade from a colorful wagon he sold

"Run," I said to him. "They are right behind us."

»Laufen Sie«, sagte ich zu ihm. »Sie sind direkt hinter uns.«
ˈlaʊfn̩ ziː ˈzaktə ɪç tsuː iːm ziː zɪnt diˈʁɛkt ˈhɪntɐ ʊns
run I said I to him they they are directly behind us

"Would you like to purchase a Coke?" asked the man.

»Möchten Sie eine Cola kaufen?«, fragte der Mann.
ˈmœçtən ziː ˈaɪnə ˈkoːla ˈkaʊfən ˈfʁaːktə deːɐ man
would you a cola to buy he asked the man

Don't Stop and Smell the Roses

Ich hatte keine Zeit für einen Verrückten, der sich nicht um seine eigene Sicherheit kümmerte. Wir ließen ihn zurück und liefen weiter.

I had no time for a crazy man who was not concerned for his own safety. We left him and kept running.

Eine Gruppe von sieben Schulkindern und zwei Lehrern ging an uns vorbei. Während sie sich glücklich miteinander unterhielten, liefen sie in ihr sicheres Verderben.

A group of seven school children and two adult teachers passed us. They chatted happily to each other as they walked toward certain doom.

Ingrid blieb einen Moment stehen und ergriff den Arm eines Lehrers. »Gehen Sie zurück. Kein Mensch kann im Sumpf überleben.«

Ingrid stopped for a second and grabbed the arm of one of the teachers. "Go back. No human can survive in the swamp."

Er musterte uns mit einem ruhigen Gesichtsausdruck. Vermutlich war er es gewohnt, verschwitzten Touristen mit irrem Gesichtsausdruck zu begegnen, bei denen sich abertausende Mückenstiche im Gesicht und auf den Armen und Beinen abzeichneten.

He looked at us with a calm expression. I guess he was used to encountering sweaty tourists with wild expressions on their faces and thousands of mosquito bites erupting on their faces, arms, and legs.

»Lass sie doch«, sagte ich zu Ingrid. »Vielleicht werden unsere

"Leave them," I said to Ingrid. "Maybe our pursuers will devour them. It will give us a few extra seconds to get back to our rental car."

Story 6

	Verfolger	sie	verschlingen.	Dadurch	gewinnen	wir	ein paar
	fɛɐ'fɔlgɐ	ziː	fɛɐ'ʃlɪŋən	da'dʊʁç	gə'vɪnən	viːɐ	aɪn paːɐ
	pursuers	them	to devour	thus	we gain	we	a few

	zusätzliche	Sekunden,	um	zu	unserem	Mietauto	zu	gelangen.«
	tsuː'zɛtslɪçə	ze'kʊndən	ʊm	tsuː	'ʊnzəʁəm	'miːt͜aʊto	tsuː	gə'laŋən
	additional	seconds	in order to	to	our	rental car	to	to reach

"But they are just children," Ingrid cried.

»Aber es sind doch Kinder«, weinte Ingrid.
'aːbɐ ɛs zɪnt dɔx 'kɪndɐ 'vaɪntə 'ɪŋgʁɪt
but they are ! children she cried Ingrid

"It's them or us," I said, as I pulled her away from the school group.

»Entweder die oder wir«, sagte ich, während ich sie von den
ɛnt'veːdɐ diː 'oːdɐ viːɐ 'zaktə ɪç 'vɛːʁənt ɪç ziː fɔn deːn
either them or us I said I as I her from the

Schulkindern wegzog.
'ʃuːlˌkɪndɐn 'vɛkˌtsoːk
school children I pulled away

The rocky dirt trail became paved as we rounded a bend.

Nach einer Kurve wurde der steinige Feldweg zur Asphaltstraße.
naːx 'aɪnɐ 'kʊʁvə 'vʊʁdə deːɐ 'ʃtaɪnɪgə 'fɛltˌveːk tsuːɐ as'faltʃtʁaːsə
after a bend it became the rocky dirt trail to the asphalt street

"There's a building ahead," Ingrid howled.

»Da vorne ist ein Gebäude«, schrie Ingrid.
daː 'fɔʁnə ɪst aɪn gə'bɔʏdə ʃʁiː 'ɪŋgʁɪt
ahead it is a building she howled Ingrid

We ran another twenty meters, opened a screen door, and tumbled into a large room. Seven people were in the room. They looked up as I slammed the door shut behind us.

Wir rannten noch weitere zwanzig Meter, öffneten eine
viːɐ 'ʁantən nɔx 'vaɪtəʁə 'tsvantsɪç 'meːtɐ 'œfnətən 'aɪnə
we we ran another twenty meter we opened a

Fliegengittertür und taumelten in einen großen Raum. Sieben
'fliːgn̩ˌgɪtɐˌtyːɐ ʊnt 'taʊməltən ɪn 'aɪnən 'gʁoːsən ʁaʊm 'ziːbən
screen door and we tumbled into a large room seven

Leute befanden sich in diesem Raum. Sie blickten auf, als ich die
'lɔʏtə bə'fandən zɪç ɪn 'diːzəm ʁaʊm ziː 'blɪktən aʊf als ɪç diː
people they were located in this room they they looked up as I the

Tür hinter uns zuschlug.
tyːɐ 'hɪntɐ ʊns 'tsuːʃluːk
door behind us I slammed shut

"Call the police and an ambulance," I said, breathing heavily. "We need medical and psychiatric help."

»Rufen Sie die Polizei und einen Krankenwagen«, sagte ich
'ʁuːfn̩ ziː diː pɔliːˈtsaɪ ʊnt 'aɪnən 'kʁaŋkn̩ˌvaːgn̩ 'zaːktə ɪç
call the police and an ambulance I said I

schwer atmend. »Wir brauchen medizinische und psychiatrische
ʃveːɐ 'aːtmənt viːɐ 'bʁaʊxən mediˈtsiːnɪʃə ʊnt psyˈçjaːtʁɪʃə
panting we we need medical and psychiatric

Hilfe.«
'hɪlfə
help

Don't Stop and Smell the Roses

Ein	älterer	Mann	schlenderte	zu	uns	herüber.
aɪn	ˈɛltəʁɐ	man	ˈʃlɛndɐtə	tsuː	ʊns	heˈʁyːbɐ
a	elderly	man	he ambled	to	us	over

An elderly man ambled over to us.

»Sie	haben	Schwierigkeiten	mit	dem	Ungeziefer«,	sagte	er	in
ziː	ˈhaːbn	ˈʃviːʁɪçkaɪtən	mɪt	deːm	ˈʊŋɡəˌtsiːfɐ	ˈzaktə	eːɐ	ɪn
you	you have	troubles	with	the	bugs	he said	he	in

perfektem	Englisch.
pɛɐˈfɛktəm	ˈɛŋlɪʃ
perfect	English

"You are having troubles with the bugs," he said in perfect English.

»Jawohl«,	keuchte	ich.	»Wir	wurden	angegriffen,	als	wir	den
jaˈvoːl	ˈkɔɪçtə	ɪç	viːɐ	ˈvʊʁdn	ˈaŋɡəˌɡʁɪfən	als	viːɐ	deːn
yes	I gasped	I	we	we were attacked		since	we	the

Kakteen-	und	Farnkrautbereich	verließen.«
kakˈteːən	ʊnt	ˈfaʁnˌkʁaʊtbəˌʁaɪç	fɛɐˈliːsən
cactus-	and	fern-area	we left

"Yes," I gasped. "We have been under attack since we left the cactus and fern areas."

»Haben	Sie	kein	Mückenspray	mitgenommen?«,	fragte	er.
ˈhaːbn	ziː	kaɪn	ˈmʏknˌspʁeː	ˈmɪtɡəˌnɔmən	ˈfʁaːktə	eːɐ
→	you	not any	mosquito spray	← you took with	he asked	he

"Did you not bring mosquito repellent?" he asked.

»Wir	haben	ein	bisschen	mitgenommen.	Es	sollte	angeblich
viːɐ	ˈhaːbən	aɪn	ˈbɪsçən	ˈmɪtɡəˌnɔmən	ɛs	ˈzɔltə	ˈanˌɡeːplɪç
we	→	a little		← we took with	it	it should	supposedly

sechs	Stunden	wirken,	aber	es	schreckte	unseren	Feind	nur
zɛks	ˈʃtʊndən	ˈvɪʁkən	ˈaːbɐ	ɛs	ˈʃʁɛktə	ˈʊnzəʁən	faɪnt	nuːɐ
six	hours	to be effective	but	it	it deterred →	our	enemy	only

ein paar	Minuten	lang	ab«,	sagte	ich.	»Sie	können	sicher	sein,
aɪn paːɐ	mɪˈnuːtən	laŋ	ap	ˈzaktə	ɪç	ziː	ˈkœnən	ˈzɪçɐ	zaɪn
a few	minutes	long	←	I said	I	you	you can	sure	to be

dass	ich	dem	Hersteller	einen	fiesen	Brief	schreiben	und	eine
das	ɪç	deːm	ˈheːɐˌʃtɛlɐ	ˈaɪnən	ˈfiːzn	bʁiːf	ˈʃʁaɪbən	ʊnt	ˈaɪnə
that	I	the	manufacturer	a	nasty	letter	to write	and	a

komplette	Geldrückerstattung	verlangen werde.	Wir	besprühten
kɔmˈplɛtə	ˈɡɛltˌʁʏkɐˌʃtatʊŋ	fɛɐˈlaŋən ˈveːɐdə	viːɐ	bəˈʃpʁyːtən
complete	refund	I will demand	we	we sprayed

uns	immer wieder,	bis	die	Dose	leer	war.	Dann	rannten	wir
ʊns	ˈɪmɐ ˈviːdɐ	bɪs	diː	ˈdoːzə	leːɐ	vaːɐ	dan	ˈʁantən	viːɐ
ourselves	again and again	until	the	can	empty	it was	then	we sprinted	we

zum	Parkplatz.	Wir	schafften	es	hierher,	bevor	der	Schwarm	uns
tsʊm	ˈpaʁkˌplats	viːɐ	ˈʃaftən	ɛs	ˈhiːɐˈheːɐ	bəˈfoːɐ	deːɐ	ʃvaʁm	ʊns
to the	parking lot	we	we managed	it	here	before	the	swarm	us

wieder	eingeholt hat.«
ˈviːdɐ	ˈaɪnɡəˌhoːlt hat
again	it caught up

"We brought some. It was supposed to last for six hours but it only deterred our enemy for a few minutes," I said. "You can be sure I'm going to write a nasty letter to the manufacturer and demand a full refund. We kept re-spraying, until the can was empty. Then we made a run for the parking lot. We managed to get here before the horde caught up with us again."

»Da	draußen	sind	Kinder«,	schluchzte	Ingrid.	»Jemand	muss	sie
daː	ˈdʁaʊsən	zɪnt	ˈkɪndɐ	ˈʃlʊxtstə	ˈɪŋɡʁɪt	ˈjeːmant	mʊs	ziː
out there		they are	children	he sniveled	Ingrid	someone	he must	them

"There are children out there," Ingrid sniveled. "Someone needs to save them."

Story 6

retten.«
to save

"It will be alright," the man explained. "We are used to the pests."

»Es wird schon gut ausgehen«, erklärte der Mann. »Wir sind an
it it will to turn out all right he explained the man we are to

diese Plagegeister gewöhnt.«
these pests accustomed

"Where are we?" I asked.

»Wo sind wir?«, fragte ich.
where we are we I asked I

"At the information center. We have a small library where you can read about the swamps and the different types of flora in our Gardens. The parking lot is a few meters from here. Would you like to drink something?"

»Im Informationszentrum. Wir haben eine kleine Bücherei, wo
at the information center we we have a small library where

Sie sich über die Sümpfe und die verschiedenen Arten der Flora
you → about the swamps and the different types of the flora

in unseren Gärten informieren können. Der Parkplatz ist nur
in our gardens ← to read up on to be able the parking lot it is only

ein paar Meter von hier. Möchten Sie vielleicht etwas trinken?«
a few meter from here would you like perhaps something to drink

"Do you have any tequila?"

»Haben Sie irgendeinen Tequila?«
do you have any tequila

He laughed. "You tourists are so funny. We have juice, water, tea, and coffee."

Er lachte. »Ihr Touristen seid vielleicht lustig. Wir haben Saft,
he he laughed you tourists you are ! funny we we have juice

Wasser, Tee und Kaffee.«
water tea and coffee

Ingrid and I sat down on stools, sipped bottled water and tried to compose ourselves. We leafed through the pages of a book that explained all about the different types of plants that were contained in the Botanical Garden. My eyes still burned and my ankle was starting to swell.

Ingrid und ich ließen uns auf den Hockern nieder, nippten
Ingrid and I we settled→ ourselves on the stools ← we sipped

an Wasserflaschen und versuchten, uns zusammenzureißen. Wir
on water bottles and we tried to pull ourselves together we

blätterten in einem Buch, das die verschiedenen Pflanzenarten
we leafed through in a book that the different types of plants

im Botanischen Garten erläuterte. Meine Augen brannten
in the botanical garden it explained my eyes they burned

64

Don't Stop and Smell the Roses

immer noch und mein Knöchel begann, anzuschwellen.
ˈɪmɐ nɔx ʊnt maɪn ˈknøːçəl bəˈgan ˈantsuˌʃvɛlən
still and my ankle it started to swell

»Wie konnten wir dieses Gebäude übersehen, als wir anfangs
viː ˈkɔntən viːɐ ˈdiːzəs gəˈbɔʏdə yːbɐˈzeːən als viːɐ ˈanfaŋs
how they could we this building to overlook when we initially

hier ankamen«, fragte Ingrid.
hiːɐ ˈanˌkamən ˈfʁaːktə ˈɪŋgʁɪt
here we arrived she asked Ingrid

"How did we miss this building when we first got here?" Ingrid asked.

»Es gibt keine Beschilderung«, sagte ich. »Ich parkte das Auto
ɛs giːpt ˈkaɪnə bəˈʃɪldəʁʊŋ ˈzaktə ɪç ɪç ˈpaʁktə das ˈaʊto
there is not any signage I said I I parked the car

am falschen Ende des Parkplatzes.«
am ˈfalʃən ˈɛndə dɛs ˈpaʁkˌplatsəs
on the wrong end of the parking lot

"There are no signs," I said. "I parked the car at the wrong end of the parking lot."

»Wir hätten die Leute im Ferienort fragen sollen, ob sie eine
viːɐ ˈhɛtən diː ˈlɔɪtə ɪm ˈfeːʁjənˌɔʁt ˈfʁaːgən ˈzɔlən ɔp ziː ˈaɪnə
we → the people at the resort ←we should have asked if they a

Karte dieser Gegend haben«, sagte Ingrid.
ˈkaʁtə ˈdiːzɐ ˈgeːgnt ˈhaːbən ˈzaktə ˈɪŋgʁɪt
map of this area they have she said Ingrid

"We should have asked the people at the resort if they had a map of this area," Ingrid said.

»Kannst du zurückfahren?«, fragte ich sie.
kanst duː tsuˈʁʏkˌfaːʁən ˈfʁaːktə ɪç ziː
can you you to drive back I asked I her

"Can you drive back?" I asked her.

»Ich weiß nicht, wie man mit Gangschaltung fährt«, sagte sie.
ɪç vaɪs nɪçt viː man mɪt ˈgaŋʃaltʊŋ fɛːɐt ˈzaktə ziː
I I know not how one with stick shift one drives she said she

"I don't know how to use a stick shift," she said.

»Aber mein Fuß tut weh«, jammerte ich.
ˈaːbɐ maɪn fuːs tuːt veː ˈjamɐtə ɪç
but my foot it hurts I whined I

"But my foot hurts," I whined.

»Du kannst später ein Fußbad im Whirlpool nehmen.«
duː kanst ˈʃpɛːtɐ aɪn ˈfuːsˌbaːt ɪm ˈvøːɐlˌpuːl ˈneːmən
you you can later a footbath in the hot tub to take

"You can soak it in the hot tub later."

Nach einer Weile waren wir bereit, einen Fluchtversuch zu
naːx ˈaɪnɐ ˈvaɪlə ˈvaːʁən viːɐ bəˈʁaɪt ˈaɪnən ˈflʊxtfɛɐˌzuːx tsuː
after a while we were we ready an escape attempt to

unserem Mietwagen zu machen.
ˈʊnzɐʁəm ˈmiːtˌvaːgən tsuː ˈmaxn
our rental car to to make

After a while we were ready to make a break for our rental car.

»Ich gehe nicht über den ganzen Parkplatz«, sagte Ingrid. »Die
ɪç ˈgeːə nɪçt ˈyːbɐ deːn ˈgantsən ˈpaʁkˌplats ˈzaktə ˈɪŋgʁɪt diː
I I go not across the whole parking lot she said Ingrid the

"I'm not going across the whole parking lot," Ingrid said. "The mosquitoes have probably set some kind of trap for us."

Story 6

	Mücken	haben	uns	wahrscheinlich	irgendeine	Falle	gestellt.«
	ˈmʏkən	ˈhaːbən	ʊns	vaːɐ̯ˈʃaɪnlɪç	ˈɪɐ̯gntaɪnə	ˈfalə	gəˈʃtɛlt
	mosquitoes	→	us	probably	some	trap	← they set

I argued with her, but it was useless. Once Ingrid decides something, she will not change her mind.

Ich	stritt	mit	ihr	darüber,	aber	es	war	umsonst.	Wenn	Ingrid
ɪç	ʃtʁɪt	mɪt	iːɐ̯	daˈʁyːbɐ	ˈaːbɐ	ɛs	vaːɐ̯	ʊmˈzɔnst	vɛn	ˈɪŋgʁɪt
I	I argued	with	her	about it	but	it	it was	in vain	when	Ingrid

sich	einmal	entschieden hat,	wird	sie	ihre	Meinung	nicht	ändern.
zɪç	ˈaɪnmaːl	ɛntˈʃiːdən hat	vɪɐ̯t	ziː	ˈiːʁə	ˈmaɪnʊŋ	nɪçt	ˈɛndɐn
→	once	← she decided	she will	she	her	mind	not	to change

I hopped to our car as fast as I could, watching over my shoulder for our enemies. Luckily, they were busy elsewhere. Probably stripping the carcass of another tourist that they had hunted down in the swamp. I drove the car to the entrance of the information center and Ingrid jumped in.

So	schnell	ich	konnte	sprang	ich	in	unser	Auto	und	hielt	über
zoː	ʃnɛl	ɪç	ˈkɔntə	ʃpʁaŋ	ɪç	ɪn	ˈʊnzɐ	ˈaʊto	ʊnt	hiːlt	ˈyːbɐ
so	fast	I	I could	I jumped	I	into	our	car	and	I kept	over

meine	Schulter	Ausschau	nach	unseren	Feinden.	Glücklicherweise
ˈmaɪnə	ˈʃʊltɐ	ˈaʊsʃaʊ	naːx	ˈʊnzəʁən	ˈfaɪndən	ˈglʏklɪçɐˈvaɪzə
my	shoulder	lookout	for	our	enemies	luckily

waren	sie	anderweitig	beschäftigt.	Wahrscheinlich	zerlegten
ˈvaːʁən	ziː	ˈandɐˌvaɪtɪç	bəˈʃɛftɪçt	vaːɐ̯ˈʃaɪnlɪç	tsɛɐ̯ˈleːktn
they were	they	elsewhere	busy	probably	they stripped

sie	gerade	die	Leiche	eines	anderen	Touristen,	den	sie	im
ziː	gəˈʁaːdə	diː	ˈlaɪçə	ˈaɪnəs	ˈandəʁən	tuˈʁɪstn	deːn	ziː	ɪm
they	right now	the	corpse	one of	other	tourist	who	they	in the

Sumpf	erlegt hatten.	Ich	fuhr	das	Auto	zum	Eingang	des
zʊmpf	ɛɐ̯ˈleːkt ˈhatn	ɪç	fyːɐ̯	das	ˈaʊto	tsʊm	ˈaɪnˌgaŋ	dɛs
swamp	they had hunted down	I	I drove	the	car	to the	entrance	of the

Informationszentrums	und	Ingrid	sprang rein.
ɪnfɔʁmaˈtsjoːnˌtsɛntʁʊms	ʊnt	ˈɪŋgʁɪt	ʃpʁaŋ ʁaɪn
information center	and	Ingrid	she jumped in

As we sped back to our hotel, Ingrid tried to count the number of bites on her body. She stopped at two hundred and punched me in the arm.

Als	wir	zu	unserem	Hotel	zurückrasten,	versuchte	Ingrid,	die
als	viːɐ̯	tsuː	ˈʊnzəʁəm	hoːˈtɛl	tsuˈʁʏkˌʁastən	fɛɐ̯ˈzuːxtə	ˈɪŋgʁɪt	diː
as	we	to	our	hotel	we rushed back	we tried	Ingrid	the

Anzahl	der	Stiche	auf	ihrem	Körper	zu	zählen.	Bei	zweihundert
ˈantsaːl	deːɐ̯	ˈʃtɪçə	aʊf	ˈiːʁəm	ˈkœɐ̯pɐ	tsuː	ˈtsɛːlən	baɪ	ˈtsvaɪˌhʊndɐt
number of	the	bites	on	her	body	to	to count	at	two hundred

hörte	sie	auf	und	schlug	mir	auf	den	Arm.
ˈhøːɐ̯tə	ziː	aʊf	ʊnt	ʃluːk	miːɐ̯	aʊf	deːn	aʁm
she stopped →	she	←	and	she punched	me	on	the	arm

"Ow," I said. "What was that for?"

»Aua«,	sagte	ich.	»Wofür	war	das	denn?«
ˈaua	ˈzaktə	ɪç	voˈfyːɐ̯	vaːɐ̯	das	dɛn
ow	I said	I	for what	it was	that	!

"For taking me to this stupid Botanical Garden," she said.

»Dafür,	dass	du	mich	in	diesen	bescheuerten	Botanischen	Garten
daˈfyːɐ̯	das	duː	mɪç	ɪn	ˈdiːzən	bəˈʃɔɪɐtən	boˈtaːnɪʃən	ˈgaʁtn
for it	that	you	me	in	this	stupid	botanical	garden

geschleppt hast«,	sagte	sie.
gəˈʃlɛpt hast	ˈzaktə	ziː
you have dragged	she said	she

Don't Stop and Smell the Roses

»Du   hast   mich   gezwungen,   hierherzukommen«,   sagte   ich.   »Ich
du: hast   mɪç   gəˈtsvʊŋən   ˈhiːɐ̯ˌhɛɐ̯ˈtsuːkɔmən   ˈzaktə   ɪç   ɪç
you   →   me   ←you forced   to come here   I said   I   I

wollte   am   Pool   sitzen   und   Limonade   trinken.«
ˈvɔltə   am   puːl   ˈzɪtsən   ʊnt   limoˈnaːdə   ˈtʁɪŋkn̩
I wanted   at the   pool   to sit   and   lemonade   to drink

"You forced me to come here," I said. "I wanted to sit around the pool and drink lemonade."

»Das   hätten   wir   tun   sollen.   Das   ist   deine   Schuld.«
das   ˈhɛtən   viːɐ̯   tuːn   ˈzɔlən   das   ɪst   ˈdaɪnə   ʃʊlt
that   we had   we   to do   should   that   it is   your   fault

"That's what we should have done. It's your fault."

STORY 7

Fool's Gold

»Pass auf den Lastwagen auf!«, schrie meine Frau Ingrid.
pas aʊf deːn ˈlastˌvaːgən aʊf ʃʁiː ˈmaɪnə fʁaʊ ˈɪŋgʁɪt
watch out→ to the truck ← she yelled my wife Ingrid

"Watch out for that truck!" my wife Ingrid yelled.

»Ich sehe ihn. Willst du fahren?«
ɪç ˈzeːə iːn vɪlst duː ˈfaːʁən
I I see it you want you to drive

"I see it. Would you like to drive?"

»Nein, Klaus, es macht mich nervös, in Manhattan zu fahren.«
naɪn klaʊs ɛs maxt mɪç nɛʁˈvøːs ɪn mɛnˈhɛtn tsuː ˈfaːʁən
no Klaus it it makes me nervous in Manhattan to to drive

"No, Klaus, driving in Manhattan makes me nervous."

»Gut, dann hör auf, Lärm zu machen. Du lenkst mich ab«, sagte ich, während ich einem Taxi auf der Tenth Avenue den Weg abschnitt.
guːt dan høːɐ aʊf lɛʁm tsuː ˈmaxən duː lɛŋkst mɪç ap ˈzaktə ɪç ˈvɛːʁənt ɪç ˈaɪnəm ˈtaksi aʊf deːɐ tɛnθ ˈævɪnjuː deːn vɛk ˈapʃnɪt
well then stop noise to to make you you distract→ me ← I said I as I a taxi on the tenth avenue I cut off

"Well stop making noise. You're distracting me," I said as I cut off a taxi cab on Tenth Avenue.

»Der Taxifahrer hat eine obszöne Geste gemacht«, sagte Ingrid.
deːɐ ˈtaksiˌfaːʁɐ hat ˈaɪnə ɔpsˈtsøːnə ˈgeːstə gəˈmaxt ˈzaktə ˈɪŋgʁɪt
the taxi driver → an obscene gesture ←he made she said Ingrid

"That taxi driver made an obscene gesture at us," Ingrid said. "What a rude man."

»So ein unverschämter Mensch.«
zoː aɪn ˈʊnfɐʃɛːmtɐ mɛnʃ
such a rude man

»Er winkte nur zur Begrüßung.«
eːɐ ˈvɪŋktə nuːɐ tsuːɐ bəˈgʁyːsʊŋ
he he waved only as a greeting

"He was just waving hello."

»Warum hupen denn alle? An jeder Ecke stehen Schilder, die besagen, dass das eine Dreihundertfünfzig-Dollar-Geldstrafe bedeutet.«
vaˈʁʊm ˈhuːpən dɛn ˈalə an ˈjeːdɐ ˈɛkə ˈʃteːən ˈʃɪldɐ diː bəˈzaːgən das das ˈaɪnə dʁaɪˈhʊndɐtˈfʏnftsɪç-ˈdɔlaʁ-ˈgɛlt ʃtʁaːfə bəˈdɔɪtət
why they honk ! everyone on every corner they stand signs that they indicate that this a $350 fine it means

"Why does everyone honk their horns? They have signs on every corner saying it's a three hundred fifty dollar fine."

Story 7

"The cops don't give tickets to the local drivers. Since we don't have New York license plates, we would get a ticket. I guarantee that if I hit the horn one time, a horde of police officers would descend on us and write as many tickets as we could carry."

»Die Polizisten geben den einheimischen Fahrern keine Strafzettel. Da wir keine New Yorker Kennzeichen haben, bekämen wir einen Strafzettel. Ich garantiere dir, wenn ich einmal hupen würde, würde sich eine Horde von Polizisten auf uns stürzen und so viele Strafzettel schreiben, wie wir nur tragen könnten.«

"How come none of the drivers stay in their lane?" Ingrid asked.

»Wieso bleibt kein Autofahrer in seiner Spur«, fragte Ingrid.

"They are too busy avoiding potholes, double parked cars, and those crazy bicycle riders to pay attention to the striped lines on the street."

»Sie sind zu beschäftigt damit, auf die gestrichelten Linien auf der Straße zu achten, weil sie Schlaglöchern, in zweiter Reihe geparkten Autos und diesen verrückten Fahrradfahrern ausweichen müssen.«

"You just went through a red light."

»Du bist gerade über Rot gefahren.«

"So did the three cars behind us. If I had stopped, they would have rammed us."

»So wie die drei Autos hinter uns. Wenn ich gehalten hätte, wären wir gerammt worden.«

"I'm so glad we're driving an old car. It's got so many dents that any additional ones will be an improvement."

»Ich bin so froh, dass wir ein altes Auto fahren. Es hat so viele Dellen, dass jede weitere eine Verschönerung bedeuten würde.«

Fool's Gold

»Genau. Die Leute mit schicken, neuen Autos sind im Nachteil. Sie können es sich nicht leisten, aggressiv zu sein«, sagte ich.

"Yeah. The people with fancy new cars are at a disadvantage. They can't afford to be aggressive," I said.

»Warum hältst du an?«

"Why are you stopping?"

»Ich will einen Hotdog.«

"I want a hot dog."

»Musst du das Auto nicht parken?«

"Shouldn't you park the car?"

»Alle Parkplätze sind besetzt. Man kann rechts neben dem Imbisswagen in zweiter Reihe parken.«

"All the parking spaces are taken. It's okay to double park right here next to this food truck."

»Aber da warten schon zwei Busse und drei Lastwagen hinter uns und hupen. Werden die nicht sauer sein?«

"But there are two buses and three trucks backed up behind us honking their horns. Won't they be angry?"

»Wir sind hier in Manhattan. Sie müssen mit ein paar Verzögerungen rechnen«, sagte ich.

"This is Manhattan. They have to expect a few delays," I said.

Ich öffnete mein Fenster. Der Geruch des Hotdogwagens breitete sich im Auto aus.

I opened my window. The smell from the hot dog food truck filled the car.

»Einen Hotdog mit Sauerkraut und Ketchup«, schrie ich auf.

"A hot dog with sauerkraut and ketchup," I yelled in English above the sound of jackhammers.

Story 7

	Englisch	über	den	Lärm	der	Presslufthämmer	hinweg.
	ˈɛŋlɪʃ	ˈyːbɐ	deːn	lɛʁm	deːɐ	ˈpʁɛsluftˌhɛmɐ	hɪnˈvɛk
	English	over	the	sound	of the	jackhammers	above

"Do you think the food is safe to eat?" asked Ingrid.

»Denkst du, das Essen ist unbedenklich?«, fragte Ingrid.
ˈdɛŋkst duː das ˈɛsən ɪst ˈʊnbəˌdɛŋklɪç ˈfʁaːktə ˈɪŋʁɪt
you think you the food it is safe she asked Ingrid

"Sure. This is a construction site. Only the best hot dog vendors are allowed to sell their food here. Do you want anything?"

»Sicher. Das ist eine Baustelle. Nur den besten Hotdogverkäufern
ˈzɪçɐ das ɪst ˈaɪnə ˈbaʊʃtɛlə nuːɐ deːn ˈbəstən ˈhɔtdɔkfɛɐˌkɔɪfɐn
sure this it is a construction site only the best hot dog vendor

ist es erlaubt, ihr Essen hier zu verkaufen. Willst du etwas
ɪst ɛs ɛɐˈlaʊpt iːɐ ˈɛsən hiːɐ tsuː fɛɐˈkaʊfən vɪlst duː ˈɛtvas
it is it allowed their food here to to sell you want you something

haben?«
ˈhaːbn̩
to have

"I think I'll wait until later."

»Ich denke, ich warte bis später.«
ɪç ˈdɛŋkə ɪç ˈvaʁtə bɪs ˈʃpɛːtɐ
I I think I I wait until later

"You're missing out on a real treat," I said as I took my food from the friendly vendor and paid him four dollars.

»Du lässt dir hier einen wirklichen Leckerbissen entgehen«,
duː lɛst diːɐ hiːɐ ˈaɪnən ˈvɪʁklɪçən ˈlɛkɐˌbɪsən ɛntˈgeːən
you → here a real delicacy ←you are missing out

sagte ich, während ich mein Essen von dem freundlichen Verkäufer
ˈzaktə ɪç ˈvɛːʁənt ɪç maɪn ˈɛsən fɔn deːm ˈfʁɔɪntlɪçən fɛɐˈkɔʏfɐ
I said I as I my food from the friendly vendor

entgegennahm und ihm vier Dollar gab.
ɛntˈgeːgn̩ˌnaːm ʊnt iːm fiːɐ ˈdɔlaʁ gaːp
I accepted and him four dollar I gave

"The driver of the bus behind us got out of the bus and is walking toward you," Ingrid said fearfully.

»Der Busfahrer hinter uns steigt gerade aus und geht
deːɐ ˈbʊsˌfaːʁɐ ˈhɪntɐ ʊns ʃtaɪkt gəˈʁaːdə aʊs ʊnt geːt
the bus driver behind us he got out→ just ← and he approaches→

geradewegs auf dich zu«, sagte Ingrid ängstlich.
gəˈʁaːdəˌveːks aʊf dɪç tsuː ˈzaktə ˈɪŋʁɪt ˈɛŋstlɪç
straight to you ← she said Ingrid fearfully

"He probably wants a hot dog too," I said.

»Er will wahrscheinlich auch einen Hotdog haben«, sagte ich.
eːɐ vɪl vaːɐˈʃaɪnlɪç aʊx ˈaɪnən ˈhɔtdɔk ˈhaːbn̩ ˈzaktə ɪç
he he wants probably also a hot dog to have I said I

I hit the gas and pulled away just as the bus driver got to my window.

Genau in dem Moment, als der Busfahrer mein Fenster erreichte,
gəˈnaʊ ɪn deːm moˈmɛnt als deːɐ ˈbʊsˌfaːʁɐ maɪn ˈfɛnstɐ ɛɐˈʁaɪçtə
just then as the bus driver my window he reached

trat ich auf das Gaspedal und fuhr weg.
tʁaːt ɪç aʊf das ˈgaːspeˌdaːl ʊnt fuːɐ vɛk
I stepped I on the gas pedal and I drove off

Fool's Gold

»Er droht dir mit seiner Faust«, sagte Ingrid. "He's shaking his fist at you," Ingrid said.

»Hör doch auf, durch das Rückfenster zu schauen«, sagte ich. »Du wirst dir noch einen steifen Hals holen.« "Quit looking through the rear window," I said. "You'll get a stiff neck."

Ich aß meinen Hotdog, während ich mit nur einer Hand am Steuer die Tenth Avenue hinauffuhr. Ingrid stieß ein paar kleine Angstschreie aus. Ich weiß nicht, warum. Der Verkehr war heute ziemlich überschaubar. Ich bog unvermittelt nach links in die Neunundvierzigste Straße ein. I ate my hot dog as I drove up Tenth Avenue with one hand on the wheel. Ingrid let out a few mild shrieks of fear. I don't know why. Traffic was pretty manageable today. I took a sharp left turn onto Forty-Ninth street.

»Schau, wie die Leute uns aus dem Weg springen«, sagte Ingrid. "Look at those people jump out of our way," Ingrid said.

»Diese Nonnen sind ganz schön schnell. Sogar die Alte mit dem Spazierstock kann sich ganz schön schnell bewegen.« "Those nuns are pretty quick. Even the old one with the cane can move pretty fast."

Ich fuhr in ein Parkhaus. Es sah aus, als wäre es schon vor zehn Jahren außer Betrieb genommen worden, aber es hatte die besten Preise in New York City. Wir zahlten bei dem freundlichen russischen Parkwächter und gingen in östliche Richtung. I pulled into a parking garage. It looked like it had ceased operating ten years ago, but it had the best prices in New York City. We paid the friendly Russian attendant and walked east.

73

Story 7

"Do you think that this neighborhood is safe?" Ingrid asked.

»Denkst du, dass wir in dieser Nachbarschaft sicher sind?«, fragte Ingrid.
dɛŋkst duː das viːɐ ɪn ˈdiːzɐ ˈnaxbaːɐ̯ʃaft ˈzɪçɐ zɪnt ˈfʁaːktə ˈɪŋɡʁɪt
you think you that we in this neighborhood safe we are she asked Ingrid

"Don't worry. The criminals in this area only work at night," I said.

»Mach dir keine Sorgen. Die Gauner in dieser Gegend arbeiten nur nachts«, sagte ich.
max diːɐ ˈkaɪ̯nə ˈzɔʁɡən diː ˈɡaʊ̯nɐ ɪn ˈdiːzɐ ˈɡeːɡənt ˈaʁbaɪ̯tən nuːɐ ˈnaxts ˈzaktə ɪç
don't worry the criminals in this area they work only at night I said I

"Are you being sarcastic?" Ingrid asked.

»Hast du das sarkastisch gemeint?«, fragte Ingrid.
hast duː das zaʁˈkastɪʃ ɡəˈmaɪ̯nt ˈfʁaːktə ˈɪŋɡʁɪt
→ you that sarcastically ←you meant she asked Ingrid

"Yes."

»Ja.«
jaː
yes

Ten minutes later we were in the Diamond District. Forty-seventh street, between Fifth Avenue and Sixth Avenue. I stopped and leaned against a parked van.

Zehn Minuten später waren wir im Diamond District.
tseːn mɪˈnuːtən ˈʃpɛːtɐ ˈvaːʁən viːɐ ɪm ˈdaɪ̯əmənd ˈdɪstʁɪkt
ten minutes later we were we in the diamond district

Siebenundvierzigste Straße, zwischen der Fifth und Sixth Avenue.
ˈziːbn̩ʊntˌfɪʁtsɪçstə ˈʃtʁaːsə ˈtsvɪʃən deːɐ fɪfθ ʊnt sɪksθ ˈævɪnjuː
forty-seventh street between the fifth and sixth avenue

Ich hielt an und lehnte mich an einen geparkten Lieferwagen.
ɪç hiːlt an ʊnt ˈleːntə mɪç an ˈaɪ̯nən ɡəˈpaʁktən ˈliːfɐˌvaːɡn̩
I I stopped and I leaned on a parked van

"Give me some time to catch my breath," I said to Ingrid.

»Warte einen Moment, damit ich Luft holen kann«, sagte ich zu Ingrid.
ˈvaʁtə ˈaɪ̯nən moˈmɛnt daˈmɪt ɪç lʊft ˈhoːlən kan ˈzaktə ɪç tsuː ˈɪŋɡʁɪt
wait a moment so that I to draw breath I can I said I to Ingrid

"You really are out of shape," Ingrid said.

»Du bist wirklich nicht in Form«, sagte Ingrid.
duː bɪst ˈvɪʁklɪç nɪçt ɪn fɔʁm ˈzaktə ˈɪŋɡʁɪt
you you are really not in shape she said Ingrid

"How come we had to run all the way from Eighth Avenue to here?" I asked.

»Wieso mussten wir den ganzen Weg von der Eighth Avenue bis hierher rennen«, fragte ich.
viˈzoː ˈmʊstən viːɐ deːn ˈɡantsən veːk fɔn deːɐ eɪtθ ˈævɪnjuː bɪs ˈhiːɐ̯ˈheːɐ ˈʁɛnən ˈfʁaːktə ɪç
how come we had to we the whole way from the eighth avenue to here to run I asked I

Fool's Gold

»Ich dachte, dass uns jemand verfolgt.«

"I thought someone was following us."

»Ich wurde beinahe von einer Limousine angefahren, als wir über den Broadway sprinteten. Wir sollten eigentlich auf das grüne Licht warten.« Es dauerte eine Weile, bis ich meine Sätze hervorbrachte, da ich noch damit zu kämpfen hatte, Luft in meine Lungen zu bekommen.

"I almost got hit by a limousine when we sprinted across Broadway. We're supposed to wait for the green light." It took a while to get the words out, since I was still struggling to get air into my lungs.

»Hör mit dem Jammern auf«, sagte Ingrid. »Wir haben es bis hierher geschafft, ohne die Goldketten zu verlieren. Lass uns hinaufgehen und sehen, wie viel sie wert sind.«

"Stop complaining," Ingrid said. "We made it here without losing the gold necklaces. Let's go up and see how much they are worth."

Nach ein paar weiteren Minuten konnte ich wieder normal atmen. In der Mitte des Blocks betraten wir ein Gebäude mit zehn Stockwerken und fuhren mit dem Aufzug zum sechsten Stock. Zimmer 604 hatte ein Schild an der Tür mit dem Namen des Geschäfts in Gold eingraviert. Ein Türöffner ließ uns in ein kleines Empfangszimmer. Eine junge Dame saß an einem

After a few more minutes I was able to breathe normally. We walked into a ten story building in the middle of the block and took the elevator to the sixth floor. Room 604 had a plaque on the door with the name of the business engraved in gold. We were buzzed into a little reception room. A young lady sat at a desk behind a bullet proof panel.

Story 7

Schreibtisch hinter einer kugelsicheren Scheibe.
ˈʃʁaɪpˌtɪʃ ˈhɪntɐ ˈaɪnɐ ˈkuːglˌzɪçɐʁən ˈʃaɪbə
desk behind a bulletproof pane (of glass)

"We would like to sell some gold necklaces," Ingrid said to the lady.

»Wir möchten ein paar goldene Halsketten verkaufen,« sagte
viːɐ ˈmϭçtn aɪn paːɐ ˈɡɔldənə ˈhalsˌkətən fɛɐˈkaʊfən ˈzaktə
we we would like some golden necklaces to sell she said

Ingrid zu der Dame.
ˈɪŋɡʁɪt tsuː deːɐ ˈdaːmə
Ingrid to the lady

"Step into booth number one. Lock the door behind you, and I'll send someone."

»Gehen Sie in die Kabine Nummer eins. Schließen Sie die Tür
ˈɡeːən ziː ɪn diː kaˈbiːnə ˈnʊmɐ aɪns ˈʃliːsən ziː diː tyːɐ
go into the booth number one lock the door

hinter sich und ich werde jemanden schicken.«
ˈhɪntɐ zɪç ʊnt ɪç ˈveːɐdə ˈjeːmandən ˈʃɪkən
behind yourselves and I I will someone to send

There were three numbered doors on a wall to the left of the receptionist. We walked through door number one. There was another bullet proof panel in front of us. Within three minutes a short, thin, young man with a small mustache appeared behind the panel.

An einer Wand links von der Empfangsdame befanden sich drei
an ˈaɪnɐ vant lɪŋks fɔn deːɐ ɛmˈpfaŋsˌdaːmə bəˈfandən zɪç dʁaɪ
on a wall left of the receptionist they were arranged three

nummerierte Türen. Wir gingen in die Tür mit der Nummer
nʊmɐˈʁiːɐtə ˈtyːʁən viːɐ ˈɡɪŋən ɪn diː tyːɐ mɪt deːɐ ˈnʊmɐ
numbered doors we we walked in the door with the number

eins. Vor uns befand sich noch eine kugelsichere Scheibe.
aɪns foːɐ ʊns bəˈfant zɪç nɔx ˈaɪnə ˈkuːglˌzɪçɐʁə ˈʃaɪbə
one in front of us it was situated another bulletproof pane

Innerhalb von drei Minuten erschien hinter der Scheibe ein kleiner,
ˈɪnɐhalp fɔn dʁaɪ mɪˈnuːtən ɛɐˈʃiːn ˈhɪntɐ deːɐ ˈʃaɪbə aɪn ˈklaɪnɐ
in the space of three minutes he appeared behind the pane a small

schlanker, junger Mann mit einem kleinen Schnurrbart.
ˈʃlaŋkɐ ˈjʊŋɐ man mɪt ˈaɪnəm ˈklaɪnən ˈʃnʊʁˌbaːɐt
thin young man with a small mustache

"Hi," he said. "You have gold for me?"

»Hallo«, sagte er. »Sie haben Gold für mich?«
haˈlɔ ˈzaktə eːɐ ziː ˈhaːbn̩ ɡɔlt fyːɐ mɪç
hello he said he you you have gold for me

"You have an interesting accent," I said as Ingrid fished a plastic bag out of her pocketbook. "Where are you from?"

»Sie haben aber einen interessanten Akzent«, sagte ich, während
ziː ˈhaːbn̩ ˈaːbɐ ˈaɪnən ɪntəʁɛˈsantn̩ akˈtsɛnt ˈzaktə ɪç ˈvɛːʁənt
you you have ! an interesting accent I said I as

Ingrid eine Plastiktüte aus ihrer Handtasche herausfischte.
ˈɪŋɡʁɪt ˈaɪnə ˈplastɪkˌtyːtə aʊs ˈiːʁɐ ˈhantˌtaʃə hɛˈʁaʊsˌfɪʃtə
Ingrid a plastic bag out of her pocketbook she fished out

»Wo kommen Sie her?«
voː ˈkɔmən ziː heːɐ
where are you from

"Lithuania," he answered.

»Litauen«, antwortete er.
ˈlitaʊən ˈantˌvɔʁtətə eːɐ
Lithuania he answered he

Fool's Gold

»Ist das in der Nähe von Chicago?«, fragte ich.

"Is that near Chicago?" I asked.

»Nein«, lachte er.

"No," he laughed.

Ingrid holte ihre Tüte voller Goldketten hervor und schob sie durch einen Schlitz in der Glastrennwand, auf eine Ablage. Zwanzig Minuten später gingen wir mit vierhundert Dollar in bar hinaus.

Ingrid produced her bag full of gold chains and pushed it through a slot in the barrier onto a countertop. Twenty minutes later, we walked out with four hundred dollars in cash.

»Sie gaben uns fünfzig Prozent mehr als die Juwelierläden in Brooklyn uns zahlen wollten«, sagte Ingrid. »Damit gönnen wir uns ein nettes Abendessen.«

"They paid us fifty percent more than the jewelry stores in New Jersey were willing to pay," Ingrid said. "Let's treat ourselves to a nice dinner."

»Wir sollten Hamburger essen gehen«, sagte ich. »Sonst geben wir am Ende unseren zusätzlichen Gewinn für unnötiges, teures Essen und Wein aus.«

"We should go eat hamburgers," I said. "Otherwise, we'll wind up spending our extra profits on fancy food and wine that we don't need."

»Ich habe eine Reservierung zum Abendessen gemacht, bevor wir das Hotel verlassen haben«, sagte Ingrid. »Es ist ein französisches Restaurant, nur zwei Kreuzungen von hier entfernt.«

"I made a dinner reservation before we left the hotel," Ingrid said. "It's a French place just two blocks from here."

77

Story 7

I thought for a minute.

Ich überlegte eine Minute.
ɪç   yːbɐˈleːktə   ˈaɪnə   mɪˈnuːtə
I   I thought   a   minute

"This whole adventure was all part of a clever plan to eat dinner at a fancy restaurant in Manhattan, wasn't it?" I said to Ingrid.

»Dieses ganze Abenteuer war Teil eines raffinierten Plans, um
ˈdiːzəs   ˈgantsə   ˈaːbəntɔʁɐ   vaːʁ   taɪl   ˈaɪnəs   ʁafiˈniːɐtn   plaːns   ʊm
this   whole   adventure   it was part   of a   clever   plan   in order to

in einem schicken Restaurant in Manhattan zu Abend zu essen,
ɪn   ˈaɪnəm   ˈʃɪkən   ʁɛstoˈʁãː   ɪn   mɛnˈhɛtn   tsuː   ˈaːbənt tsuː ˈɛsən
in   a   fancy   restaurant in   Manhattan to   to eat dinner

oder?«, sagte ich zu Ingrid.
ˈoːdɐ   ˈzaktə   ɪç   tsuː   ˈɪŋɡʁɪt
"was it not" I said I   to   Ingrid

"What if it was?"

»Was ist, wenn es so war?«
vas   ɪst   vɛn   ɛs   zoː   vaːʁ
what it is if   it   so   it was

"We can go there as long as you don't make me run," I said.

»Wir können dorthin gehen, solange du mich nicht zum Laufen
viːʁ   ˈkœnən   ˈdɔʁthɪn   ˈgeːən   zoˈlaŋə   duː   mɪç   nɪçt   tsʊm   ˈlaʊfən
we   we can   there   to go   as long as you   me   not   to the running

zwingst«, sagte ich.
tsvɪŋst   ˈzaktə   ɪç
you force I said   I

STORY 8

Dumbbells Everywhere

»Nimm etwas ab, Klaus.«
lose weight → some ← Klaus

»Das ist alles?«, fragte ich. »Hundertfünfzehn Euro für eine komplette Untersuchung und alles, was du mir zu sagen hast, ist, dass ich abnehmen muss? Für so viel Geld hättest du mindestens vier weitere Beschwerden finden können. Ich möchte eine zweite Meinung einholen.«

»Okay«, sagte mein lieber Freund Dr. Michael Werner, »deine Nase sieht auch komisch aus.«

»Bist du freitagabends im Krankenhaus als Bühnenkomiker tätig?«, fragte ich.

»Hör zu«, sagte er, »wir kennen uns seit der Hochschulzeit. Du kannst mir vertrauen. Ich sage dir, du musst anfangen, jeden

"Lose some weight, Klaus."

"That's it?" I asked. "One hundred fifteen Euro for a complete physical and all you tell me is that I need to lose weight? For that kind of money, you should have found at least four other problems. I want a second opinion."

"Okay," my good friend Dr. Michael Werner said, "your nose looks funny, too."

"Do you do stand-up comedy at the hospital on Friday nights?" I asked.

"Listen," he said, "we've known each other since college. You can trust me. I'm telling you that you have to start exercising every day."

Story 8

"I'm working fifty hours a week right now," I said. "I've got three small kids who I try to spend time with. And Ingrid, my lovely wife, wants me to talk with her every once in a while. I don't have any time to exercise."

»Ich arbeite bereits fünfzig Stunden pro Woche«, sagte ich. »Ich habe drei kleine Kinder, mit denen ich versuche, Zeit zu verbringen. Und Ingrid, meine liebenswerte Frau, möchte sich mit mir auch hin und wieder unterhalten. Ich habe keine Zeit zum Sporttreiben.«

"What do you do after work?"

»Was machst du nach der Arbeit?«

"I hope you don't intend to bill me for this conversation," I said. "I've heard about how doctors charge patients just for talking with them."

»Ich hoffe, du hast nicht vor, mir diese Unterhaltung in Rechnung zu stellen«, sagte ich. »Ich habe gehört, dass Ärzte ihren Patienten einfache Gespräche berechnen.«

"Do you want me to give you a couple of injections that you don't need?" he asked.

»Willst du, dass ich dir ein paar Spritzen gebe, die du nicht brauchst?«, fragte er.

Unfair. He knew I was afraid of needles.

Das ist ungerecht. Er wusste, dass ich vor Nadeln Angst hatte.

"Okay, I'll talk," I said as I waved the imaginary needles away. "After work we eat dinner. We play with the kids, put them to bed, and then watch a few hours of television."

»Einverstanden, ich werde es dir sagen«, erwiderte ich, während ich die imaginären Nadeln zur Seite schob. »Nach der Arbeit

Dumbbells Everywhere

essen wir zu Abend. Wir spielen mit den Kindern, bringen sie ins Bett und schauen dann ein paar Stunden fern.«

»Da hast du schon die Antwort. Anstatt fernzusehen, kannst du eine Stunde lang Sport treiben.«

"There's the answer. Instead of watching television, you can exercise for an hour."

»So spät am Abend?«, fragte ich.

"That late at night?" I asked.

»Es ist nicht ideal, aber es ist besser, als sich in ein Marshmallow zu verwandeln.«

"It's not perfect, but it's better than turning into a marshmallow."

»Ich habe gerade einen Großbildfernseher mit Surroundtonanlage gekauft.«

"I just bought a big screen television with surround sound."

»Nimm deine Lieblingssendungen auf, während du Sport treibst, und schaue sie dir am Wochenende an«, sagte er.

"Record your favorite shows while you are exercising and watch them on weekends," he said.

»Es ist nicht dasselbe, am Wochenende«, beschwerte ich mich.

"It's not the same on the weekend," I complained.

Dr. Werner betrachtete mich mit stechendem Blick.

Dr. Werner gave me a piercing look.

»Hör auf, Ausreden zu suchen, und versuche, wenigstens etwas

"Quit making excuses and figure out a way to get some exercise instead of watching television."

Story 8

Sport zu treiben, anstatt fernzusehen.«

He took out a prescription pad and started writing. "This is the title of a great exercise book. There are three or four simple routines that you can use to vary your workout. Buy this book and start sweating."

Er griff zu einem Rezeptblock und begann zu schreiben. »Das ist der Titel eines ausgezeichneten Trainingsbuches. Es gibt drei oder vier einfache Routineübungen, mit welchen du dein Training variieren kannst. Kauf dieses Buch und fang an zu schwitzen.«

"I don't like to sweat," I told him. "When I sweat, it makes me feel icky."

»Ich mag es nicht, wenn ich schwitze«, sagte ich zu ihm. »Wenn ich schwitze, fühle ich mich klebrig.«

"I don't want to hear anymore excuses," he said.

»Ich will keine Ausreden mehr hören«, sagte er.

"My underwear sticks to my skin," I continued. "Funny smells come out of my armpits."

»Meine Unterwäsche klebt an meiner Haut«, fuhr ich fort. »Komische Gerüche kommen aus meinen Achselhöhlen.«

"Shower after you exercise. Ingrid will appreciate that," he said.

»Dusche nach dem Training. Ingrid wird das begrüßen«, sagte er.

"Who wants to shower more than once a week? Nobody! It's a waste of good water."

»Wer will denn schon öfter als einmal pro Woche duschen? Niemand! Das ist Trinkwasserverschwendung.«

Dumbbells Everywhere

»Jetzt hast du mich aber wirklich verärgert«, sagte er. »Dafür mache ich nächste Woche am Samstag einen Hausbesuch um ein Uhr.«

"Now you've gotten me really annoyed," he said. "Just for that, I'm making a house call next week on Saturday at one o'clock."

»Wird der von der Versicherung übernommen?«

"Is it covered by insurance?"

»Nein, ich bringe den Arztkoffer mit und messe deinen Blutdruck. Da du diesen schönen neuen Fernseher hast, werde ich auch zum Fußballspiel dableiben. Und obendrein werde ich beim Zuschauen in deinem Lieblingsfernsehsessel sitzen.«

"No. I'm bringing my doctor's bag and checking your blood pressure. I'm staying for the soccer game, too, since you have that nice new television. Finally, I'm sitting in your favorite recliner while I watch."

»In dem mit dem eingebauten Becherhalter in der Armlehne für die Bierdose?«

"The one with the cup holder built into the armrest for your beer can?"

»Genau dem. Stell sicher, dass du jede Menge Bier und Knabberzeug da hast«, sagte er.

"That one. Make sure you have plenty of beer and snacks," he said.

»Was ist, wenn mein Blutdruck nicht niedriger ist?«

"And what if my blood pressure isn't lower?"

»Dann werde ich jeden Samstag kommen, bis ich eine wesentliche Verbesserung sehe. Vielleicht werde ich meine Familie mitbringen.

"I'll come back every Saturday until I see a big improvement. Maybe I'll bring my family. The snacks will cost you a fortune."

83

Story 8

	Das	Knabberzeug	wird	dich	ein	Vermögen	kosten.«
	das	ˈknabɐˌtsɔɪk	vɪʁt	dɪç	aɪn	fɛɐˈmøːɡən	ˈkɔstən
	the	snack food	it will	you	a	fortune	to cost

———————————— 2 ————————————

"Why is all the living room furniture in the garage except for the television and the two reclining chairs?" Ingrid asked me later that evening.

»Warum	sind	alle	Wohnzimmermöbel	außer	dem	Fernseher	und
vaˈʁʊm	zɪnt	ˈalə	ˈvoːnˌtsɪmɐˌmøːbəl	ˈaʊsɐ	deːm	ˈfɛʁnˌzeːɐ	ʊnt
why	they are	all	living room furniture	besides	the	TV	and

den	zwei	Lehnstühlen	in	der	Garage?«,	fragte	mich	Ingrid	später
deːn	tsvaɪ	ˈleːnˌʃtyːlən	ɪn	deːɐ	ɡaˈʁaːʒə	ˈfʁaːktə	mɪç	ˈɪŋɡʁɪt	ˈʃpeːtɐ
the	two	armchairs	in	the	garage	she asked	me	Ingrid	later

an	jenem	Abend.
an	ˈjeːnəm	ˈaːbənt
in	that	evening

"I need space to exercise."

»Ich	brauche	Platz	zum	Trainieren.«
ɪç	ˈbʁaʊxə	plats	tsʊm	tʁɛˈniːʁən
I	I need	space	for the	training

"Can't you exercise outside?"

»Kannst	du	nicht	draußen	trainieren?«
kanst	duː	nɪçt	ˈdʁaʊsən	tʁɛˈniːʁən
can you	you	not	outside	to exercise

"I'll be exercising after we put the kids to bed. It's too dark outside by then."

»Ich	werde	trainieren,	nachdem	wir	die	Kinder	ins	Bett
ɪç	ˈveːɐdə	tʁɛˈniːʁən	naːxˈdeːm	viːɐ	diː	ˈkɪndɐ	ɪns	bɛt
I	I will	to exercise	after	we	the	kids	in the	bed

gebracht	haben.	Um	diese	Zeit	ist	es	draußen	zu	dunkel.«
ɡəˈbʁaxt	ˈhaːbən	ʊm	ˈdiːzə	tsaɪt	ɪst	ɛs	ˈdʁaʊsən	tsuː	ˈdʊŋkəl
we brought		at	this	time	it is	it	outside	too	dark

"Go to a gym."

»Geh	ins	Fitnessstudio.«
ɡeː	ɪns	ˈfɪtnɛsˌʃtuːdjo
go	into the	gym

"I want to exercise at home, where I can watch the TV shows that I like."

»Ich	will	zu	Hause	trainieren,	wo	ich	die	Fernsehsendungen
ɪç	vɪl	tsuː	ˈhaʊzə	tʁɛˈniːʁən	voː	ɪç	diː	ˈfɛʁnzeːˌzɛndʊŋən
I	I want	at home		to exercise	where	I	the	TV shows

anschauen	kann,	die	mir	gefallen.«
ˈanˌʃaʊən	kan	diː	miːɐ	ɡəˈfalən
to watch	I can	that	I like	

"This doesn't sound good," she said.

»Das	hört	sich	nicht	gut	an«,	sagte	sie.
das	høːɐt	zɪç	nɪçt	ɡuːt	an	ˈzaktə	ziː
this	it sounds →		not	good	←	she said	she

"Michael said he would come over every Saturday, watch sports, and eat all our food until I get in shape again."

»Michael	sagte,	er	würde	jeden	Samstag	kommen	und
ˈmɪçaːeːl	ˈzaktə	eːɐ	ˈvʏʁdə	ˈjeːdən	ˈzamstaːk	ˈkɔmən	ʊnt
Michael	he said	he	he would	every	Saturday	to come	and

Sportsendungen	schauen.	Er	würde	uns	alles	wegessen,	bis
ˈʃpɔʁtˌzɛndʊŋən	ˈʃaʊən	eːɐ	ˈvʏʁdə	ʊns	ˈaləs	ˈvɛkˌɛsn	bɪs
sports programs	to watch	he	he would	from us	everything	to eat up	until

Dumbbells Everywhere

ich wieder in Form bin.«
ɪç 'viːdɐ ɪn fɔʁm bɪn
I again in shape I am

»Lieber er als deine Eltern«, sagte sie.
'liːbɐ eːɐ als 'daɪnə 'ɛltɐn 'zaktə ziː
preferable him than your parents she said she

"Better him than your parents," she said.

»Fange nicht an, an meinen Eltern herumzunörgeln«, sagte ich.
'faŋə nɪçt an an 'maɪnən 'ɛltɐn hɛ'ʁʊmˌtsuːˌnœʁgln 'zaktə ɪç
start→ not ← on my parents to pick on I said I

»Konzentrieren wir uns auf das Trainieren.«
kɔntsɛn'tʁiːʁən viːɐ ʊns aʊf das tʁɛ'niːʁən
let's focus on the training

"Don't start picking on my parents," I said. "Let's focus on exercising."

»Du konzentrierst dich auf das Trainieren. Ich mache das nicht«,
duː kɔntsɛn'tʁiːɐst dɪç aʊf das tʁɛ'niːʁən ɪç 'maxə das nɪçt
you you focus on the exercise I I do that not

sagte sie.
'zaktə ziː
she said she

"You focus on exercising. I'm not going to do it," she said.

»Warum nicht?«, fragte ich.
va'ʁʊm nɪçt 'fʁaːktə ɪç
why not I asked I

"Why not?" I asked.

»Ich trainiere im Fitnessstudio fünfmal pro Woche während
ɪç tʁɛ'niːʁə ɪm 'fɪtnɛsˌʃtuːdjo 'fʏnfmaːl pʁo 'vɔxə 'vɛːʁənt
I I exercise at the gym five times per week during

meiner Mittagspause.«
'maɪnɐ 'mɪtaːksˌpaʊzə
my lunch break

"I exercise at a gym five days a week during my lunch break."

»Wir könnten eine Menge Geld sparen, wenn du zu Hause
viːɐ 'kœntən 'aɪnə 'mɛŋə gɛlt 'ʃpaːʁən vɛn duː tsuː 'haʊzə
we we could a great deal money to save if you at home

trainieren würdest.«
tʁɛ'niːʁən 'vʏʁdəst
to exercise you would

"We could save lots of money if you exercised at home."

»Nein, danke. Ich trainiere gerne während der Mittagszeit.
naɪn 'daŋkə ɪç tʁɛ'niːʁə 'gɛʁnə 'vɛːʁənt deːɐ 'mɪtaːksˌtsaɪt
no thank you I I like to exercise during the lunchtime

Anschließend esse ich etwas Gesundes zu Mittag - Obst und
'anʃliːsənt 'ɛsə ɪç 'ɛtvas gə'zʊndəs tsuː 'mɪtaːk oːpst ʊnt
afterwards I eat lunch→ I something healthy ← fruits and

Joghurt. Du solltest versuchen, gesünder zu essen.«
'joːgʊʁt duː 'zɔltəst fɛɐ'zuːxən gə'zʏndɐ tsuː 'ɛsən
yogurt you you should to try healthier to to eat

"No thank you. I like exercising at noon. Afterwards I eat a healthy lunch - fruit and yogurt. You should try eating healthier food."

Story 8

"I become irritable if I don't eat at least two hamburgers and fries every day," I said.

»Ich werde gereizt, wenn ich nicht jeden Tag mindestens zwei Hamburger und Pommes esse«, sagte ich.

Ingrid picked up the book that was sitting on the recliner and started leafing through the pages.

Ingrid hob das Buch auf, das am Lehnstuhl lag, und fing an, durch die Seiten zu blättern.

"Michael recommended that exercise book. I'll do the aerobic part of the workouts in this open space between the recliner and the television while we watch our shows each night."

»Michael hat dieses Trainingsbuch empfohlen. Den Aerobic-Teil des Fitnesstrainings werde ich zwischen dem Lehnsessel und dem Fernseher machen, wo genügend Platz ist, während wir abends unsere Sendungen ansehen.«

"The routine on page twenty five wants you to walk fast while you swing dumbbells," she said. "How are you going to do that in here?"

»Bei der Übung auf Seite zwanzig sollst du schnell gehen und dabei Hanteln schwingen«, sagte sie. »Wie willst du das hier drinnen machen?«

"There's enough room to walk back and forth a few steps at a time."

»Da ist genügend Platz, um jeweils ein paar Schritte vor und zurück zu laufen.«

"What if you hit one of the kids in the head while you're doing this? The dumbbell would probably kill them."

»Was passiert, wenn du eins der Kinder am Kopf triffst, wenn du das machst? Die Hantel würde sie wahrscheinlich umbringen.«

Dumbbells Everywhere

»Die Kinder werden schon im Bett sein.«
diː 'kɪndɐ 'veːɐdn ʃoːn ɪm bɛt zaɪn
the kids they will already in the bed to be

"The kids will already be in bed."

Sie warf nochmal einen Blick auf die Übungen.
ziː vaʁf 'nɔxmaːl 'aɪnən blɪk aʊf diː 'yːbʊŋən
she she threw again a glance at the exercises

She took another glance at the exercises.

»Hampelmannsprünge«, sagte sie. »Du sollst zwanzig
'hamplmanʃpʁʏŋə 'zaktə ziː duː zɔlst 'tsvantsɪç
jumping jacks she said she you you are supposed to twenty

Minuten lang Hampelmannsprünge machen.«
mɪ'nuːtən laŋ 'hamplmanʃpʁʏŋə 'maxən
minutes long jumping jacks to do

"Jumping jacks," she said. "They want you to do twenty minutes of jumping jacks."

»Was soll daran falsch sein?«
vas zɔl da'ʁan falʃ zaɪn
what it should with that wrong to be

"What's wrong with that?"

»Es macht Krach. Das ganze Haus wird wackeln. Ich werde nicht
ɛs maxt kʁax das 'gantsə haʊs vɪʁt 'vakəln ɪç 'veːɐdə nɪçt
it it makes noise the whole house it will to shake I I will not

in der Lage sein, den Fernseher zu hören.«
ɪn deːɐ 'laːgə zaɪn deːn 'fɛʁnˌzeːɐ tsuː 'høːʁən
to be able the TV to to hear

"It's noisy. The whole house will shake. I won't be able to hear the television."

»Das Zimmer ist ja mit Teppich ausgelegt. Das wird den Lärm
das 'tsɪmɐ ɪst jaː mɪt 'tɛpɪç 'aʊsgəˌleːkt das vɪʁt deːn lɛʁm
the room it is ! with rug it is laid out that it will the sound

dämpfen. Und ich werde ganz leicht springen, wie ein Ninja.«
'dɛmpfən ʊnt ɪç 'veːɐdə gants laɪçt 'ʃpʁɪŋən viː aɪn 'nɪnja
to muffle and I I will quite lightly to jump like a ninja

"There's a rug in the room. That will muffle the sound. And I'll jump really lightly, like a ninja."

Ingrid schüttelte den Kopf.
'ɪŋgʁɪt 'ʃʏtəltə deːn kɔpf
Ingrid she shook the head

Ingrid shook her head.

»Ich werde in unserem Schlafzimmer fernsehen, während du
ɪç 'veːɐdə ɪn 'ʊnzɐəm 'ʃlaːfˌtsɪmɐ 'fɛʁnˌzeːən 'veːʁənt duː
I I will in our bedroom to watch TV while you

trainierst«, beschloss sie. »Das ist einfacher für uns beide.«
tʁɛ'niːɐst bə'ʃlɔs ziː das ɪst 'aɪnfaxɐ fyːɐ ʊns 'baɪdə
you exercise she decided she that is easier for us both

"I'll watch television in our bedroom while you're exercising," she decided. "It will be easier on both of us."

»Was ist mit unserer wertvollen gemeinsamen Zeit?«
vas ɪst mɪt 'ʊnzɐɐ 'veːɐtˌfɔlən gə'maɪnzaːmən tsaɪt
what about our precious shared time

"What about our quality time together?"

»Wir verbringen gemeinsam Zeit, wenn wir mit den Kindern
viːɐ fɛɐ'bʁɪŋən gə'maɪnzaːm tsaɪt vɛn viːɐ mɪt deːn 'kɪndɐn
we we spend shared time when we with the kids

"We have our quality time when we play with the kids. Watching television is relaxing time. I'll relax better in the bedroom."

Story 8

spielen. Fernsehen ist Entspannungszeit. Ich werde mich im
Schlafzimmer besser entspannen können.«

"Then I'll put one of the recliner chairs in the garage. That will give me more room," I said.

»Dann werde ich einen der Lehnsessel in die Garage bringen. Dadurch werde ich mehr Platz gewinnen«, sagte ich.

---- 3 ----

Doctor Michael showed up the next Saturday with a bottle of wine and a bag of pretzels. Ingrid ushered him into our living room. All the furniture was back in place. Ernst and Karl, two other college friends, were already sitting on the couch drinking beer. I was sitting in the recliner with a big bandage on the top of my head.

Doktor Michael erschien am folgenden Samstag mit einer Flasche Wein und einer Tüte voller Salzbrezeln. Ingrid führte ihn in unser Wohnzimmer. Alle Möbel waren wieder an ihrem gewohnten Platz. Ernst und Karl, zwei andere Freunde aus meiner Hochschulzeit, saßen schon mit einem Bier auf der Couch. Mit einem großen Verband am Kopf saß ich im Lehnsessel.

"What happened to you?" Michael asked.

»Was ist mit dir passiert?« fragte Michael.

"You did this to me," I said. "Consider yourself lucky I don't sue you for malpractice."

»Das hast du mir angetan«, sagte ich. »Du kannst froh sein, dass ich dich nicht wegen Behandlungsfehler verklage.«

"How did *I* do it?"

»Was soll ich denn verbrochen haben?«

Dumbbells Everywhere

»Michael, du musst die ganze Geschichte hören«, sagte Ingrid.
'mɪçaːeːl duː mʊst diː 'gantsə gə'ʃɪçtə 'høːʁən 'zaktə 'ɪŋgʁɪt
Michael you you have to the whole story to hear she said Ingrid

"You need to hear the whole story, Michael," Ingrid said.

»Da werde ich mich lieber vorher mit etwas Wein stärken.«
daː 'veːɐdə ɪç mɪç 'liːbɐ 'foːɐheːɐ mɪt 'ɛtvas vaɪn 'ʃtɛʁkən
then I will I myself rather first with some wine to fortify

"I better fortify myself with some wine."

Er setzte sich und entfernte den Schraubverschluss der Weinflasche.
eːɐ 'zɛtstə zɪç ʊnt ɛnt'fɛʁntə deːn 'ʃʁaʊpfɛɐˌʃlʊs deːɐ 'vaɪnˌflaʃə
he he sat down and he removed the screw cap of the wine bottle

He sat down and unscrewed the cap on the wine bottle.

»Kannst du dir keinen Wein mit Korkverschluss leisten?«, fragte Ernst.
kanst duː diːɐ 'kaɪnən vaɪn mɪt 'kɔʁkfɛɐˌʃlʊs 'laɪstən 'fʁaːktə ɛʁnst
can you you → not a wine with cork closure ← to afford he asked Ernst

"Can't you afford wine that comes in bottles with corks?" asked Ernst.

»Das ist ein ausgezeichneter Wein«, antwortete Michael. »Und so es ist wesentlich leichter, die Flasche zu öffnen.«
das ɪst aɪn 'aʊsgəˌtsaɪçnətɐ vaɪn 'antvɔʁtətə 'mɪçaːeːl ʊnt zoː ɛs ɪst 've:zəntlɪç 'laɪçtɐ diː 'flaʃə tsuː 'œfnən
this it is an excellent wine he responded Michael and this way it it is substantially easier the bottle to to open

"This is very good wine," Michael responded. "And it's a lot easier to open the bottle."

Michael nahm ein leeres Weinglas vom Couchtisch, schenkte ein und reichte Ingrid das halbvolle Glas.
'mɪçaːeːl naːm aɪn 'leːʁəs 'vaɪnˌglaːs fɔm 'kaʊtʃˌtɪʃ 'ʃɛŋktə aɪn ʊnt 'ʁaɪçtə 'ɪŋgʁɪt das 'halpˌfɔlə glaːs
Michael he took an empty wine glass from the coffee table he poured and he handed Ingrid the half-full glass

Michael picked up an empty wine glass from the coffee table, poured, and handed the half-full glass to Ingrid.

»Danke Michael, woher hast du gewusst, dass ich das jetzt brauche?«
'daŋkə 'mɪçaːeːl vo'heːɐ hast duː gə'vʊst das ɪç das jɛtst 'bʁaʊxə
thank you Michael from where → hast you ← you knew that I this now I need

"Thank you, Michael. How did you know I needed this?"

»Wenn ich Klaus' Kopfverband sehe und erfahre, das es eine Geschichte dazu gibt, dann weiß ich, dass du wahrscheinlich eine
vɛn ɪç klaʊs 'kɔpfˌfɛɐbant 'zeːə ʊnt ɛɐ'faːʁə das ɛs 'aɪnə gə'ʃɪçtə da'tsuː gɪpt dan vaɪs ɪç das duː vaːɐ'ʃaɪnlɪç 'aɪnə
when I Klaus's head bandage I see and I learn that there is → a story to it ← then I know I that you probably a

"When I see a bandage on Klaus's head and find out that there's a story behind it, I know that you have probably had a difficult week," he said.

89

Story 8

	schwierige Woche hinter dir hast«, sagte er.
	ˈʃviːʁɪɡə ˈvɔxə ˈhɪntɐ diːɐ hast ˈzaktə eːɐ
	difficult week behind you you have he said he

He poured another glass for himself, sat down, and looked at me.	Er schenkte ein weiteres Glas für sich selbst ein, setzte sich und
	eːɐ ˈʃɛŋktə aɪn ˈvaɪtəʁəs glaːs fyːɐ zɪç zɛlpst aɪn ˈzɛtstə zɪç ʊnt
	he he poured→ an additional glass for himself ← he sat down and

	schaute mich an.
	ˈʃaʊtə mɪç an
	he looked→ me ←

"Tell me the story."	»Erzähle mir die Geschichte.«
	ɛɐˈtsɛːlə miːɐ diː ɡəˈʃɪçtə
	tell me the story

"Ten minutes until the game starts," said Karl. "Tell it quickly."	»Noch zehn Minuten, bis das Spiel beginnt«, sagte Karl. »Erzähl
	nɔx tseːn mɪˈnuːtən bɪs das ʃpiːl bəˈɡɪnt ˈzaktə kaʁl ɛɐˈtseːl
	still ten minutes until the game it starts he said Karl tell

	es schnell.«
	ɛs ʃnɛl
	it quickly

"Wait a minute," said Michael. "What happened to the ceiling?" He pointed to a big hole in the ceiling above the couch.	»Moment mal«, sagte Michael. »Was ist mit der Decke passiert?«
	moːˈmɛnt maːl ˈzaktə ˈmɪçaːeːl vas ɪst mɪt deːɐ ˈdɛkə paˈsiːɐt
	moment ! he said Michael what → with the ceiling ←it happened

	Er deutete auf ein großes Loch in der Decke über der Couch.
	eːɐ ˈdɔɪtətə aʊf aɪn ˈɡʁoːsəs lɔx ɪn deːɐ ˈdɛkə ˈyːbɐ deːɐ kaʊtʃ
	he he pointed to a big hole in the ceiling over the couch

"It's part of the story," said Karl. "Klaus didn't want to tell us until you got here."	»Das ist Teil der Geschichte«, sagte Karl. »Klaus wollte es uns
	das ɪst taɪl deːɐ ɡəˈʃɪçtə ˈzaktə kaʁl klaʊs ˈvɔltə ɛs ʊns
	that it is part of the story he said Karl Klaus he wanted it to us

	nicht erzählen, bevor ihr da seid.«
	nɪçt ɛɐˈtseːlən bəˈfoːɐ iːɐ daː zaɪt
	not to tell before you here you are

I was just about to explain everything when Ingrid interrupted. "I need more wine."	Ich wollte gerade alles erklären, doch Ingrid unterbrach mich.
	ɪç ˈvɔltə ɡəˈʁaːdə ˈaləs ɛɐˈklɛːʁən dɔx ˈɪŋɡʁɪt ʊntɐˈbʁaːx mɪç
	I I wanted just everything to explain but Ingrid she interrupted me

	»Ich brauche mehr Wein.«
	ɪç ˈbʁaʊxə meːɐ vaɪn
	I I need more wine

She grabbed the bottle and refilled her glass.	Sie ergriff die Flasche und füllte ihr Glas nach.
	ziː ɛɐˈɡʁɪf diː ˈflaʃə ʊnt ˈfʏltə iːɐ ɡlaːs naːx
	she she grabbed the bottle and she refilled→ her glass ←

"This will help me listen to the story again without throwing the remote control at Klaus," she said to my friends.	»Das wird mir helfen, die Geschichte nochmals anzuhören, ohne
	das vɪʁt miːɐ ˈhɛlfən diː ɡəˈʃɪçtə ˈnɔxmaːls ˈantsuˌhøːʁən ˈoːnə
	this it will me to help the story again to listen without

Dumbbells Everywhere

dass	ich	die	Fernbedienung	auf	Klaus	werfe«,	sagte	sie	zu	meinen
das	ɪç	diː	ˈfɛʁnbəˌdiːnʊŋ	aʊf	klaʊs	ˈvɛʁfə	ˈzaktə	ziː	tsuː	ˈmaɪnən
that	I	the	remote control	at	Klaus	to throw	she said	she	to	my

Freunden.
ˈfʁɔɪndən
friends

4

Einen kurzen Moment fragte ich mich, warum meine Frau einen kleinen, harten Gegenstand auf mich schleudern wollte. Ich beschloss, ihre Bemerkung zu übersehen, und erzählte meine Geschichte.

For a brief moment I wondered why my wife would want to hurl a small, hard object at me. I decided to overlook her comment and told my story.

»Ich kaufte mir das Buch, das du mir verschrieben hast, dazu ein paar Hanteln und fing an zu trainieren.«

"I bought the book you prescribed, bought some weights, and started exercising."

»Prima«, sagte Michael.

"Great," said Michael.

»Nicht so prima«, sagte Ingrid. »Er entschied sich, in diesem Zimmer zu trainieren, am Abend während des Fernsehens.«

"Not so great," said Ingrid. "He decided he could exercise in this room while he was watching television at night."

Michaels Augen weiteten sich. »Oh«, sagte er. »Plötzlich wird mir alles klar.«

Michael's eyes opened wide. "Ahhh," he said. "Suddenly things are becoming clear."

»Eine der Übungen verlangte von mir, auf der Stelle zu treten und

"One of the workout routines required me to march in place and pump the weights with my arms. I decided to

Story 8

combine the exercise with some step aerobics, so I put a small stool on the floor."

dabei	die	Gewichte	mit	den	Armen	auf- und abzubewegen.
da'baɪ	diː	gə'vɪçtə	mɪt	deːn	'aʁmən	aʊf ʊnt 'apˌtsuːbəˈveːgən
at the same time	the	weights	with	the	arms	to move up and down

Ich	beschloss	die	Übung	mit	etwas	Step-Aerobic	zu	kombinieren,
ɪç	bə'ʃlɔs	diː	'yːbʊŋ	mɪt	'ɛtvas	ʃtɛp-ɛ'ʁoːbɪk	tsuː	kɔmbiˈniːʁən
I	I decided	the	exercise	with	some	step-aerobics	to	to combine

und	stellte	einen	kleinen	Hocker	auf	den	Boden.«
ʊnt	'ʃtɛltə	'aɪnən	'klaɪnən	'hɔkɐ	aʊf	deːn	'boːdən
and	I put	a	small	stool	on	the	floor

"He was watching one of those reality shows," interrupted Ingrid.

»Er	schaute	sich	gerade	eine	von	diesen	Realityshows	an«,
eːɐ	'ʃaʊtə	zɪç	gə'ʁaːdə	'aɪnə	fɔn	'diːzən	ʁiˈɛlitiˌʃoːs	an
he	he watched →		at the time	one	of	those	reality shows	←

unterbrach	Ingrid.
ʊntɐ'bʁaːx	'ɪŋgʁɪt
she interrupted	Ingrid

"I didn't even realize that I was swinging those weights right up to the ceiling," I continued.

»Mir	war	gar	nicht	bewusst,	dass	ich	die	Gewichte	bis	zur	Decke
miːɐ	vaːɐ	gaːɐ	nɪçt	bə'vʊst	das	ɪç	diː	gə'vɪçtə	bɪs	tsuːɐ	'dɛkə
→		not at all		← I was aware	that	I	the	weights		up to the	ceiling

schwang«,	fuhr	ich	fort.
ʃvaŋ	fuːɐ	ɪç	fɔʁt
I swung	I continued →	I	←

"He stepped on the stool and punched a one and a half kilo dumbbell through the ceiling," Ingrid concluded.

»Er	stieg	auf	den	Hocker	und	schlug	eine	Hantel	von	anderthalb
eːɐ	ʃtiːk	aʊf	deːn	'hɔkɐ	ʊnt	ʃluːk	'aɪnə	'hantl	fɔn	'andɐt'halp
he	he stepped up		the	stool	and	he punched	a	dumbbell	of	one and a half

Kilo	durch	die	Decke«,	schloss	Ingrid.
'kiːlo	dʊʁç	diː	'dɛkə	ʃlɔs	'ɪŋgʁɪt
kilo	through	the	ceiling	she concluded	Ingrid

Michael, Ernst, and Karl started laughing at me.

Michael,	Ernst	und	Karl	fingen an,	mich	auszulachen.
'mɪçaːˌeːl	ɛʁnst	ʊnt	kaʁl	'fɪŋən an	mɪç	'aʊstsuˌlaxn
Michael	Ernst	and	Karl	they started	me	to laugh at

"Who is telling this story?" I demanded.

»Wer	erzählt	hier	die	Geschichte?«,	wollte	ich	wissen.
veːɐ	ɛɐ'tsɛːlt	hiːɐ	diː	gə'ʃɪçtə	'vɔltə	ɪç	'vɪsən
who	he tells	here	the	story	I wanted	I	to know

"I was on our bed watching a good medical drama," said Ingrid. "There was a big noise, and suddenly Klaus's hand was sticking through the floor."

»Ich	lag	auf	unserem	Bett	und	schaute	mir	gerade	einen	gutes
ɪç	laːk	aʊf	'ʊnzəʁəm	bɛt	ʊnt	'ʃaʊtə miːɐ		gə'ʁaːdə	'aɪnən	'guːtəs
I	I lay	on	our	bed	and	I watched →		just	a	good

Ärztedrama	an«,	sagte	Ingrid.	»Da	hörte	ich	einen	Riesenkrach
'ɛːɐtstəˌdʁaːma	an	'zaktə	'ɪŋgʁɪt	daː	'høːɐtə	ɪç	'aɪnən	'ʁiːznˌkʁaːx
medical drama	←	she said	Ingrid	there	I heard	I	a	giant crash

und	plötzlich	schaute	die	Hand	von	Klaus	aus	dem	Boden
ʊnt	'plœtslɪç	'ʃaʊtə	diː	hant	fɔn	klaʊs	aʊs	deːm	'boːdən
and	suddenly	it poked out →	the	hand	of	Klaus	from	the	floor

heraus.«
hɛ'ʁaʊs
←

Dumbbells Everywhere

Die Jungs lachten noch lauter.
di: jʊŋs laxtən nɔx ˈlaʊtɐ
the guys they laughed still louder

The guys laughed harder.

»Das ist eine Übertreibung«, schrie ich.
das ɪst ˈaɪnə yːbɐˈtʁaɪbʊŋ ʃʁiː ɪç
that it is an exaggeration I yelled I

"That's an exaggeration," I yelled.

Ingrid ergriff die Fernbedienung und warf mir einen bösen Blick zu. Ich hielt besser meinen Mund.
ˈɪŋɡʁɪt ɛɐ̯ˈɡʁɪf diː ˈfɛʁnbəˌdiːnʊŋ ʊnt vaʁf miːɐ̯ ˈaɪnən ˈbøːzən blɪk tsuː ɪç hiːlt ˈbɛsɐ ˈmaɪnən mʊnt
Ingrid she grabbed the remote control and she threw→ to me an angry look ← I I shut better my mouth

Ingrid picked up the remote control and gave me an evil look. I decided to quiet down.

Michael hob seine Hand hoch. »Ist dir ein Teil der Decke auf den Kopf gefallen?«
ˈmɪçaeˌl hoːp ˈzaɪnə hant hoːx ɪst diːɐ̯ aɪn taɪl deːɐ̯ ˈdɛkə aʊf deːn kɔpf ɡəˈfalən
Michael he held up→ his hand ← → onto you a piece of the ceiling on the head ←it fell

Michael held up his hand. "Did a piece of the ceiling fall on your head?"

»Ingrid wollte nicht, dass ich die Gewichte nochmals verwende, also wählte ich eine andere Trainingsübung aus dem Buch.«
ˈɪŋɡʁɪt ˈvɔltə nɪçt das ɪç diː ɡəˈvɪçtə ˈnɔxmaːls fɛɐ̯ˈvɛndə ˈalzo ˈvɛːltə ɪç ˈaɪnə ˈandəʁə ˈtʁɛːnɪŋsˌyːbʊŋ aʊs deːm buːx
Ingrid she wanted not that I the weights again I use so I chose I another exercise routine out of the book

"Ingrid wouldn't let me use the weights again, so I picked another exercise routine from the book."

»Eine Aerobic-Übung, bei der man die Knie hochzieht und dann mit den Füßen tritt«, fügte Ingrid hinzu.
ˈaɪnə ɛˈʁoːbɪkˈyːbʊŋ baɪ deːɐ̯ man diː kniː ˈhoːxˌtsiːt ʊnt dan mɪt deːn ˈfyːsn tʁɪt ˈfyːktə ˈɪŋɡʁɪt hɪnˈtsuː
an aerobic exercise in which one the knees he raises and then with the feet one kicks she added→ Ingrid ←

"An aerobics exercise that called for knee lifts and kicks," Ingrid added.

»Es war ein sehr gutes Training«, sagte ich.
ɛs vaːɐ̯ aɪn zeːɐ̯ ˈɡuːtəs ˈtʁɛːnɪŋ ˈzaktə ɪç
it it was a very good workout I said I

"It was a pretty good workout," I said.

»Bis er zu nah an den Fernseher gelangte«, sagte Ingrid.
bɪs eːɐ̯ tsuː naː an deːn ˈfɛʁnˌzeːɐ̯ ɡəˈlaŋtə ˈzaktə ˈɪŋɡʁɪt
until he too close to the television he got to she said Ingrid

"Until he got too close to the television," said Ingrid.

»Hör auf, mich zu unterbrechen«, beschwerte ich mich.
høːɐ̯ aʊf mɪç tsuː ʊntɐˈbʁɛçn̩ bəˈʃveːɐ̯tə ɪç mɪç
stop me to to interrupt I complained→ I ←

"Quit interrupting," I complained.

»Er rammte seinen Fuß direkt durch den Fernseher«, sagte Ingrid.
eːɐ̯ ˈʁamtə ˈzaɪnən fuːs diˈʁɛkt dʊʁç deːn ˈfɛʁnˌzeːɐ̯ ˈzaktə ˈɪŋɡʁɪt
he he rammed his foot directly through the TV she said Ingrid

"He put his foot right through the TV," said Ingrid.

Story 8

Now my three college friends were howling. Ernst was holding his knees, rocking from side to side. Tears were coming from Karl's eyes.

Jetzt	johlten	meine	drei	Uni-Freunde.	Ernst	hielt	sich	an	den
jɛtst	'joːltən	'maɪnə	dʁaɪ	'ʊniˑ'fʁɔɪndə	ɛʁnst	hiːlt	zɪç	an	deːn
now	they howled	my	three	university friends	Ernst	he held	himself	on	the

Knien	und	schaukelte	nach	beiden	Seiten.	Aus	Karls	Augen	kamen
'kniːən	ʊnt	'ʃaʊkəltə	naːx	'baɪdən	'zaɪtən	aʊs	kaʁls	'aʊɡən	'kaːmən
knees	and	he rocked	to	both	sides	from	Karl's	eyes	they came

Tränen.
'tʁɛːnən
tears

I fumed in silence. What could I say?

Ich	kochte	innerlich.	Was	hätte	ich	sagen	sollen?
ɪç	'kɔxtə	'ɪnɐlɪç	vas	'hɛtə	ɪç	'zaːɡən	'zɔlən
I	I boiled	inwardly	what	→	I	←I should have said	

"I had to go to the store on Tuesday to get a new TV for today's game. Klaus was too ashamed," Ingrid concluded.

»Ich	musste	am Dienstag	in	den	Laden	gehen,	um	einen
ɪç	'mʊstə	am 'diːnsˌtak	ɪn	deːn	'laːdən	'ɡeːən	ʊm	'aɪnən
I	I had to	on Tuesday	into	the	store	to go	in order to	a

neuen	Fernseher	für	das	heutige	Spiel	zu	holen.	Es	war	Klaus	zu
'nɔɪən	'fɛʁnˌzeːɐ	fyːɐ	das	'hɔɪtɪɡə	ʃpiːl	tsuː	'hoːlən	ɛs	vaːɐ	klaʊs	tsuː
new	TV	for	the	today's	game	to	to get	it	it was	to Klaus	too

peinlich«,	erzählte	Ingrid	zu	Ende.
'paɪnˌlɪç	ɛɐ'tsɛːltə	'ɪŋɡʁɪt	tsuː	'ɛndə
embarrassing	she told	Ingrid	to	end

It took a few minutes for my friends to get control of themselves.

Es	dauerte	ein paar	Minuten,	bis	meine	Freunde	ihre	Fassung
ɛs	'daʊɐtə	aɪn paːɐ	mɪ'nuːtən	bɪs	'maɪnə	'fʁɔɪndə	'iːʁə	'fasʊŋ
it	it took	a few	minutes	until	my	friends	their	composure

wieder	fanden.
'viːdɐ	'fandən
again	they found

"You still haven't told me how you hurt your head," Michael asked.

»Du	hast	mir	immer	noch	nicht	erzählt,	wie	du	dir	den	Kopf
duː	hast	miːɐ	'ɪmɐ	nɔx	nɪçt	ɛɐ'tsɛːlt	viː	duː	diːɐ	deːn	kɔpf
you	→	me	still		not	←you told	how	you	yourself	the	head

verletzt	hast«,	fragte	Michael.
fɛɐ'lɛtst	hast	'fʁaːktə	'mɪçaˑeːl
you injured		he asked	Michael

"Ingrid told me I had to exercise in a spot that was far away from the new television. I moved to the side of the room over there," I pointed to a spot near the fireplace.

»Ingrid	sagte	mir,	ich	müsse	an	einer	Stelle	trainieren,	die	vom
'ɪŋɡʁɪt	'zaktə	miːɐ	ɪç	'mʏsə	an	'aɪnɐ	'ʃtɛlə	tʁɛ'niːʁən	diː	fɔm
Ingrid	he told	to me	I	I had to	in	a	spot	to exercise	that	from the

neuen	Fernseher	weit	entfernt	sei.	Deshalb	zog	ich	zu	der
'nɔɪən	'fɛʁnˌzeːɐ	vaɪt	ɛnt'fɛʁnt	zaɪ	'dɛshalp	tsoːk	ɪç	tsuː	deːɐ
new	television	far	away	it was	so	I moved→	I	to	that

Seite	des	Zimmers	dort	um«,	ich	zeigte	auf	eine	Stelle	neben
'zaɪtə	dɛs	'tsɪmɐs	dɔʁt	ʊm	ɪç	'tsaɪktə	aʊf	'aɪnə	'ʃtɛlə	'neːbən
side	of the	room	there	←	I	I pointed	at	a	spot	next to

dem	offenen	Kamin.
deːm	'ɔfənən	ka'miːn
the		fireplace

Dumbbells Everywhere

»Außerdem wechselte ich die Trainingsübung.«
ˈaʊsɐdeːm ˈvɛkslətə ɪç diː ˈtʁɛːnɪŋsyːbʊŋ
apart from that I switched I the exercise routine

"I also picked a different exercise routine."

»Hampelmannsprünge«, sagte Ingrid.
ˈhamplmanʃpʁʏŋə ˈzaktə ˈɪŋgʁɪt
jumping jacks she said Ingrid

"Jumping jacks," said Ingrid.

»Wie hast du dich beim Hampelmannspringen verletzt?«, fragte Michael.
viː hast duː dɪç baɪm ˈhampɛlmanʃpʁɪŋən fɛɐˈlɛtst ˈfʁaːktə ˈmɪçaːˌeːl
how → you yourself with the (doing of) jumping jacks ← you injured he asked Michael

"How did you injure yourself doing jumping jacks?" asked Michael.

»Wir hatten eine hübsche Glaslampe an der Decke montiert, um diesen Bereich des Zimmers zu beleuchten«, sagte Ingrid.
viːɐ ˈhatən ˈaɪnə ˈhyːpʃə ˈglaːslampə an deːɐ ˈdɛkə mɔnˈtiːɐt ʊm ˈdiːzən bəˈʁaɪç dɛs ˈtsɪmɐs tsuː bəˈlɔɪçtən ˈzaktə ˈɪŋgʁɪt
we → a pretty glass light on the ceiling ← we had mounted in order to this area of the room to to illuminate she said Ingrid

"We used to have a pretty, glass light mounted on the ceiling to illuminate that part of the room," said Ingrid.

Sie zeigte auf zwei elektrische Drähte, die jetzt einsam von der Decke neben der Kaminverkleidung baumelten.
ziː ˈtsaɪktə aʊf tsvaɪ eːˈlɛktʁɪʃə ˈdʁɛːtə diː jɛtst ˈaɪnzam fɔn deːɐ ˈdɛkə ˈneːbən deːɐ kaˈmiːnfɛɐˈklaɪdʊŋ ˈbaʊməltən
she she pointed to two electrical wires that now forlornly from the ceiling next to the mantelpiece they dangled

She pointed to two electrical wires that were now dangling forlornly from the ceiling near the fireplace mantle.

»Er hat doch nicht etwa … «, sagte Michael zu ihr.
eːɐ hat dɔx nɪçt ˈɛtva ˈzaktə ˈmɪçaːˌeːl tsuː iːɐ
he he did *not* he said Michael to her

"He didn't..." Michael said to her.

»Er schaute diese Serie mit den Vampiren«, erwiderte sie.
eːɐ ˈʃaʊtə ˈdiːzə ˈzeːʁiə mɪt deːn vamˈpiːʁən ɛɐˈviːdɐtə ziː
he he watched that TV series with the vampires she replied she

"He was watching that show with the vampires," she replied.

»Diese Serie, in der die Brüste der Vampirfrauen gezeigt werden«, fügte ich hinzu in der Hoffnung, es würde erklären, warum ich ein drittes Mal versagte.
ˈdiːzə ˈzeːʁiə ɪn deːɐ diː ˈbʁʏstə deːɐ vamˈpiːɐfʁaʊən gəˈtsaɪkt ˈveːɐdən ˈfyːktə ɪç hɪnˈtsuː ɪn deːɐ ˈhɔfnʊŋ ɛs ˈvʏʁdə ɛɐˈklɛːʁən vaˈʁʊm ɪç aɪn ˈdʁɪtəs maːl fɛɐˈzaːktə
that TV show in which the breasts of the vampire ladies they are shown I added→ I ← in the hope it it would to explain why I a third time I screwed up

"The one where they show the breasts of the lady vampires," I added, hoping to explain why I had screwed up a third time.

»Er war so von den Brüsten vereinnahmt, dass er nicht merkte,
eːɐ vaːɐ zoː fɔn deːn ˈbʁʏstən fɛɐˈaɪnˌnaːmt das eːɐ nɪçt ˈmɛʁktə
he he was so by the breasts engrossed that he not he noticed

"He was so engrossed in the breasts that he didn't realize he was jumping closer to the light," said Ingrid.

Story 8

	wie er immer näher zur Lampe hüpfte«, sagte Ingrid. viː eːɐ ˈɪmɐ ˈnɛːɐ tsuːɐ ˈlampə ˈhʏpftə ˈzaktə ˈɪŋɡʁɪt how he nearer and nearer to the lamp he jumped she said Ingrid
"He clapped his hands together and demolished the ceiling light," concluded Michael.	»Er schlug seine Hände zusammen und zerbrach dabei die eːɐ ʃluːk ˈzaɪnə ˈhɛndə tsuˈzamən ʊnt tsɛɐˈbʁaːx daˈbaɪ diː he he slapped his hands together and he shattered in the process the Deckenleuchte«, sagte Michael abschließend. ˈdɛkənˌlɔɪçtə ˈzaktə ˈmɪçaːeːl ˈapʃliːsənt ceiling light he said Michael concluding
"Large pieces of glass dropped onto his head," said Ingrid.	»Große Glasscherben fielen auf seinen Kopf herunter«, sagte ˈɡʁoːsə ˈɡlasˌʃɛɐbn̩ ˈfiːlən aʊf ˈzaɪnən kɔpf hɛˈʁʊntɐ ˈzaktə large pieces of broken glass they fell down→ on his head ← he said Ingrid. ˈɪŋɡʁɪt Ingrid
"Next thing I knew, I was getting ten stitches at the hospital," I said.	»Das Nächste, woran ich mich erinnere, ist, dass die Wunde mit das ˈnɛçstə voˈʁan ɪç mɪç ɛɐˈɪnəʁə ɪst das diː ˈvʊndə mɪt the next thing of what I I remember it is that the wound with zehn Stichen im Krankenhaus genäht wurde«, sagte ich. tsɛːn ˈʃtɪçən ɪm ˈkʁaŋkn̩ˌhaʊs ɡəˈnɛːt ˈvʊʁdə ˈzaktə ɪç ten stitches in the hospital it was being stitched I said I
They kept laughing at me through the entire first half of the game. During a time out, Michael said to me: "Seriously, you can't keep trying to exercise in this room. You could break everything."	Sie lachten über mich während der ganzen ersten Spielhälfte. ziː ˈlaxtən ˈyːbɐ mɪç ˈvɛːʁənt deːɐ ˈɡantsən ˈeːɐstn̩ ˈʃpiːlˌhɛlftə they they laughed at me during the entire first half Während einer Pause sagte Michael zu mir: »Ganz im Ernst, du ˈvɛːʁənt ˈaɪnɐ ˈpaʊzə ˈzaktə ˈmɪçaːeːl tsuː miːɐ ɡants ɪm ɛʁnst duː during a break he said Michael to me seriously you kannst in diesem Zimmer nicht weitertrainieren. Du könntest kanst ɪn ˈdiːzəm ˈtsɪmɐ nɪçt ˈvaɪtɐtʁɛˌniːʁən duː ˈkœntəst you can in this room not to keep exercising you you could alles zertrümmern.« ˈaləs tsɛɐˈtʁʏmɐn everything to smash
"Ingrid told me I have to spend my lunch hours with her at the gym. That way she can keep an eye on me and make sure I eat a lot of yogurt."	»Ingrid sagte mir, dass ich meine Mittagspause mit ihr im ˈɪŋɡʁɪt ˈzaktə miːɐ das ɪç ˈmaɪnə ˈmɪtaːksˌpaʊzə mɪt iːɐ ɪm Ingrid she told to me that I my lunch hour with her in the Fitnessstudio verbringen müsse. Auf diese Weise kann sie mich ˈfɪtnɛsˌʃtuːdjo fɛɐˈbʁɪŋən ˈmʏsə aʊf ˈdiːzə ˈvaɪzə kan ziː mɪç gym to spend I would have to this way she can she me im Auge behalten und sicherstellen, dass ich viel Joghurt esse.« ɪm ˈaʊɡə bəˈhaltən ʊnt ˈzɪçɐˌʃtɛlən das ɪç fiːl ˈjoːɡʊʁt ˈɛsə to keep an eye on and to make sure that I a lot yogurt I eat
"Excellent plan," everyone agreed.	»Ausgezeichneter Plan«, stimmten alle zu. ˈaʊsɡəˌtsaɪçnətɐ plaːn ˈʃtɪmtən ˈalə tsuː excellent plan they agreed→ everyone ←

STORY 9

In Good Repair

»Wir müssen einen Klempner anrufen«, sagte meine Frau Ingrid zu mir.

"We need to call a plumber," my wife Ingrid said to me.

»Warum?«

"Why?"

»Der Abfallzerkleinerer ist kaputt.«

"The garbage disposal is broken."

»Klempner sind teuer«, erwiderte ich. »Wahrscheinlich kann ich einen neuen Zerkleinerer kaufen und selbst einbauen.«

"Plumbers are expensive," I replied. "I can probably buy a new disposal and install it myself."

»Klaus, ich denke, dass du die Arbeit von einem Fachmann machen lassen solltest.«

"Klaus, I think you should let a professional do the work."

»Hast du denn kein Vertrauen in die handwerklichen Fähigkeiten deines Ehemannes?«, fragte ich.

"Don't you have faith in your husband's mechanical abilities?" I asked.

»Du bist gut im Heckenschneiden und im Rasenmähen«, sagte sie zu mir.

"You're good at cutting the hedges and mowing the lawn," she said to me.

Story 9

"I can do technical work, too," I insisted.

»Ich kann auch handwerkliche Arbeit verrichten«, versicherte ich.
ɪç kan aʊx ˈhantvɛʁklɪçə ˈaʁbaɪt fɛɐ̯ˈʁɪçtn̩ fɛɐ̯ˈzɪçɐtə ɪç
I I can also technical work to perform I assured I

"What about the light pole that you replaced in the front yard?" she asked.

»Wie war das doch mit dem Laternenpfahl, den du vorne im
viː vaːɐ̯ das dɔx mɪt deːm laˈtɛʁnənˌpfaːl deːn duː ˈfoːʁnə ɪm
how it was that ! with the lamp post that you (in the) front in the

Garten ausgetauscht hast?«, fragte sie.
ˈɡaʁtn̩ ˈaʊsɡəˌtaʊʃt hast ˈfʁaːktə ziː
yard you replaced she asked she

"It works great."

»Er funktioniert doch prima.«
eːɐ̯ fʊŋktsjoˈniːɐ̯t dɔx ˈpʁiːma
it it works ! great

"It leans fifteen centimeters to the left," she said.

»Er steht schräg und neigt sich ungefähr fünfzehn Zentimeter
eːɐ̯ ʃteːt ʃʁɛːk ʊnt naɪkt zɪç ˈʊŋɡəfɛːɐ̯ ˈfʏnftseːn tsɛntiˈmeːtɐ
it it stands slanting and it leans about fifteen centimeter

nach links«, sagte sie.
naːx lɪŋks ˈzaktə ziː
to the left she said she

"That way you get more light on the driveway."

»Dadurch fällt mehr Licht auf die Einfahrt.«
daˈdʊʁç fɛlt meːɐ̯ lɪçt aʊf diː ˈaɪnfaːɐ̯t
thereby it falls more light on the driveway

"And the fuse blows out if we turn on the television while the front light is shining."

»Und die Sicherung brennt durch, wenn wir das Fernsehgerät
ʊnt diː ˈzɪçəʁʊŋ bʁɛnt dʊʁç vɛn viːɐ̯ das ˈfɛʁnzeːɡəˌʁɛːt
and the fuse it blows out if we the television set

einschalten, während das Gartenlicht an ist.«
ˈaɪnˌʃaltən ˈvɛːʁənt das ˈɡaʁtn̩ˌlɪçt an ɪst
to turn on while the garden light on it is

"Blame the electrician who wired the house," I said. "He overloaded the circuit."

»Dafür ist der Elektriker verantwortlich, der die Leitungen
daˈfyːɐ̯ ɪst deːɐ̯ eˈlɛktʁɪkɐ fɛɐ̯ˈantvɔʁtlɪç deːɐ̯ diː ˈlaɪtʊŋən
for that he is the electrician responsible who the wires

gelegt hat«, sagte ich. »Er hat den Stromkreis überlastet.«
ɡəˈleːkt hat ˈzaktə ɪç eːɐ̯ hat deːn ˈʃtʁoːmˌkʁaɪs yːbɐˈlastət
he laid I said I he → the circuit ← he overloaded

"I still think you should call a plumber."

»Ich glaube immer noch, dass wir den Klempner anrufen sollten.«
ɪç ˈɡlaʊbə ˈɪmɐ nɔx das viːɐ̯ deːn ˈklɛmpnɐ ˈanˌʁuːfən ˈzɔltən
I I think still that we the plumber to call we should

I didn't argue with Ingrid any further. Secretly, I planned to do the work myself. I would show her how easy it is to fix things around the house.

Ich debattierte mit Ingrid nicht mehr weiter. Insgeheim plante ich,
ɪç debaˈtiːɐ̯tə mɪt ˈɪŋɡʁɪt nɪçt meːɐ̯ ˈvaɪtɐ ɪnsɡəˈhaɪm ˈplaːntə ɪç
I I argued with Ingrid no longer secretly I planned I

die Arbeit selbst zu verrichten. Ich würde ihr zeigen, wie einfach
diː ˈaʁbaɪt zɛlpst tsuː fɛɐ̯ˈʁɪçtn̩ ɪç ˈvʏʁdə iːɐ̯ ˈtsaɪɡən viː ˈaɪnfax
the work myself to to do I I would her to show how easy

In Good Repair

es	ist,	verschiedene	Sachen	am Haus	selbst	zu	reparieren.
ɛs	ɪst	fɛɐˈʃiːdənə	ˈzaxən	am haʊs	zɛlpst	tsuː	ʁepaˈʁiːʁən
it	it is	different	things	around the house	oneself	to	to fix

―――――― 2 ――――――

Es	ist	Samstag.	Die	Kinder	verbringen	das	Wochenende	bei	meinen		It's Saturday. The kids are spending
ɛs	ɪst	ˈzamstaːk	diː	ˈkɪndɐ	fɛɐˈbʁɪŋən	das	ˈvɔxnˌɛndə	baɪ	ˈmaɪnən		the weekend with my parents. Ingrid
it	it is	Saturday	the	kids	they spend	the	weekend	with	my		just left to visit some friends from her

Eltern.	Ingrid	ist	gerade	los,	um	ein paar	Freunde	aus	ihrer	college days. I will be alone for at least
ˈɛltɐn	ˈɪŋɡʁɪt	ɪst	ɡəˈʁaːdə	loːs	ʊm	aɪn paːɐ	ˈfʁɔɪndə	aʊs	ˈiːɐɐ	six hours. Time to put my plan into
parents	Ingrid	she is	just	gone	in order to	some	friends	from	her	action. I called my next door neighbor

Studienzeit	zu	besuchen.	Ich	werde	mindestens	sechs	Stunden	Jürgen, a retired engineer.
ˈʃtuːdiənˌtsaɪt	tsuː	bəˈzuːxən	ɪç	ˈveːɐdə	ˈmɪndəstəns	zɛks	ˈʃtʊndən	
college time	to	to visit	I	I will	at least	six	hours	

alleine	sein.	Zeit,	mein	Vorhaben	in die Tat	umzusetzen.	Ich	rief
aˈlaɪnə	zaɪn	tsaɪt	maɪn	ˈfoːɐˌhaːbn	ɪn diː taːt	ˈʊmtsuˌzɛtsən	ɪç	ʁiːf
alone	to be	time	my	plan	to put into action		I	I called→

meinen	Nachbarn	Jürgen	an,	einen	pensionierten	Ingenieur,	der
ˈmaɪnən	ˈnaxbaːɐn	ˈjʏʁɡn	an	ˈaɪnən	pãzjoˈniːɐtn	ɪnʒeˈnjøːɐ	deːɐ
my	neighbor	Jürgen	←	a	retired	engineer	who

gleich	neben	mir	wohnt.
ɡlaɪç	ˈneːbən	miːɐ	voːnt
right	next to	me	he lives

»Kannst	du	mir	heute	helfen,	einen	neuen	Abfallzerkleinerer	"Can you help me put in a new
kanst	duː	miːɐ	ˈhɔɪtə	ˈhɛlfən	ˈaɪnən	ˈnɔɪən	ˈapfalˌtsɛɐˈklaɪnəʁɐ	garbage disposal today?"
can you	you	me	today	to help	a	new	garbage disposal	

einzubauen?«
ˈaɪntsuˌbaʊən
to install

»Sicher.«	"Sure."
ˈzɪçɐ	
sure	

»Komm	gleich	rüber.	Ich	habe	den	neuen	Zerkleinerer	schon	"Come right over. I already bought a
kɔm	ɡlaɪç	ˈʁyːbɐ	ɪç	ˈhaːbə	deːn	ˈnɔɪən	tsɛɐˈklaɪnəʁɐ	ʃoːn	new disposal. It's hidden in the base-
come	right	over	I	→	the	new	disposal	already	ment."

besorgt.	Er	ist	im	Keller	versteckt.«
bəˈzɔʁkt	eːɐ	ɪst	ɪm	ˈkɛlɐ	fɛɐˈʃtɛkt
←I procured	it	it is	in the	basement	hidden

»Ingrid	will	nicht,	dass	du	diese	Arbeit	ausführst,	nicht wahr?«	"Ingrid doesn't want you doing this
ˈɪŋɡʁɪt	vɪl	nɪçt	das	duː	ˈdiːzə	ˈaʁbaɪt	ˈaʊsˌfyːɐst	nɪçt vaːɐ	work, does she?"
Ingrid	she wants	not	that	you	this	work	you perform	right	

»Warum	sagst	du	das?«	"Why do you say that?"
vaˈʁʊm	zaːkst	duː	das	
why	you say	you	that	

Story 9

"Because you had to hide the new disposal in the basement. Also, I remember the time you flooded your second floor bathroom when you tried to install a new cold water faucet in the sink."

»Weil du den neuen Zerkleinerer im Keller verstecken musstest. Ich erinnere mich auch daran, dass du einmal dein Badezimmer im Obergeschoss unter Wasser gesetzt hast, als du versucht hast, einen neuen Kaltwasserhahn am Waschbecken anzubringen.«

"That was an accident," I said.

»Das war ein Unfall«, sagte ich.

"You forgot to screw the handle into the pipe."

»Du hast vergessen, den Armaturengriff am Rohr festzuschrauben.«

"It wasn't my fault. I was interrupted by the kids."

»Das war nicht mein Fehler. Ich wurde durch die Kinder abgelenkt.«

"When you turned the main water valve to the house back on, the handle shot off the pipe so hard it wedged into the ceiling."

»Als du den Hauptanschluss im Haus wieder aufgedreht hast, wurde der Handgriff mit solcher Wucht vom Wasserrohr weggesprengt, dass er in der Decke stecken blieb.«

"Don't remind me."

»Erinnere mich bloß nicht daran.«

"Meanwhile, you were in the basement and didn't hear the water spraying all over the bathroom floor."

»Währenddessen warst du im Kellergeschoss und hast nicht gehört, wie das Wasser überall im Badezimmer auf den Boden

100

In Good Repair

spritzte.«
ˈʃpʁɪtstə
it sprayed

»Ich habe diese Geschichte längst vergessen.«
ɪç ˈhaːbə ˈdiːzə gəˈʃɪçtə lɛŋst fɛɐˈgɛsn
I → this story long ago ←I forgot

"I've put that episode behind me."

»Der Wasserschaden war so schlimm, dass du die Wohnzimmerdecke erneuern musstest«, sagte Jürgen.
deːɐ ˈvasɐˌʃaːdn vaːɐ zoː ʃlɪm das duː diː ˈvoːnˌtsɪmɐˌdɛkə ɛɐˈnɔɪɐn ˈmʊstɛst ˈzaktə ˈjʏʁgn
the water damage it was so bad that you the living room ceiling to replace you had to he said Jürgen

"The water damage was so bad you had to replace the ceiling above the living room," said Jürgen.

»Willst du mir helfen oder nicht?«
vɪlst duː miːɐ ˈhɛlfən ˈoːdɐ nɪçt
you want you me to help or not

"Do you want to help me or not?"

»Ich helfe dir schon. Ich sage ja nur, warum ich weiß, dass Ingrid nicht will, dass du diese Arbeit machst. Ich komme gleich rüber.«
ɪç ˈhɛlfə diːɐ ʃoːn ɪç ˈzaːgə jaː nuːɐ vaˈʁʊm ɪç vaɪs das ˈɪŋgʁɪt nɪçt vɪl das duː ˈdiːzə ˈaʁbaɪt maxst ɪç ˈkɔmə glaɪç ˈʁyːbɐ
I I help you ! I I say ! just how I I know that Ingrid not she wants that you this job you do I I come right over

"I'll be glad to help. I'm just explaining why I know Ingrid doesn't want you to do this job. I'll be right over."

---3---

Zwanzig Minuten später waren wir in meiner Küche und legten unsere Werkzeuge bereit. Jürgen nahm den neuen Abfallzerkleinerer aus seiner Verpackung.
ˈtsvantsɪç mɪˈnuːtən ˈʃpɛːtɐ ˈvaːʁən viːɐ ɪn ˈmaɪnɐ ˈkʏçə ʊnt ˈleːktən ˈʊnzəʁə ˈvɛʁkˌtsɔɪgə bəˈʁaɪt ˈjʏʁgn naːm deːn ˈnɔɪən ˈapfalˌtsɛɐˈklaɪnəʁɐ aʊs ˈzaɪnɐ fɛɐˈpakʊŋ
twenty minutes later we were we in my kitchen and we laid out→ our tools ← Jürgen he took the new garbage disposal out of its packaging

Twenty minutes later, we were in my kitchen laying out our tools. Jürgen took the new garbage disposal out of its packaging.

»Zuerst müssen wir den alten Zerkleinerer vom Strom nehmen«, sagte Jürgen.
tsuˈeːɐst ˈmʏsən viːɐ deːn ˈaltən tsɛɐˈklaɪnəʁɐ fɔm ʃtʁoːm ˈneːmən ˈzaktə ˈjʏʁgn
first we have to we the old disposal from the electricity to take he said Jürgen

"First we need to disconnect the old disposal," Jürgen said.

Er beugte seinen Kopf hinunter und steckte ihn in den Schrank
eːɐ ˈbɔɪktə ˈzaɪnən kɔpf hɪˈnʊntɐ ʊnt ˈʃtɛktə iːn ɪn deːn ʃʁaŋk
he he bent down→ his head ← and he stuck it in the cabinet

He ducked his head down and stuck it into the cabinet that was under the sink. We already took all the plastic

Story 9

bottles, cleaning supplies, and other assorted items out of the cabinet so they wouldn't be in our way. Jürgen spent a few minutes with his head inside the cabinet, doing something or other.

unter	dem	Spülbecken.	Wir	hatten	schon	alle	Plastikflaschen,
ˈʊntɐ	deːm	ˈʃpyːlbəkən	viːɐ	ˈhatn	ʃoːn	ˈalə	ˈplastɪkˌflaʃn
under	the	sink	we	→	already	all	plastic bottles

Reinigungsmittel	und	andere	verschiedene	Sachen	aus	dem
ˈʁaɪnɪgʊŋsˌmɪtl	ʊnt	ˈandəʁə	fɛɐˈʃiːdənə	ˈzaxən	aʊs	deːm
cleaning supplies	and	other	assorted	items	out of	the

Schrank	herausgenommen,	damit	sie	uns	nicht	im	Weg
ʃʁaŋk	hɛˈʁaʊsgəˌnɔmən	daˈmɪt	ziː	ʊns	nɪçt	ɪm	vɛk
cabinet	← we had taken out	so that	they	us	not	in the	way

sein	würden.	Mit	seinem	Kopf	im	Schrank	verbrachte	Jürgen
zaɪn	ˈvʏʁdn	mɪt	ˈzaɪnəm	kɔpf	ɪm	ʃʁaŋk	fɛɐˈbʁaxtə	ˈjʏʁgn
they would be	with	his	head	in the	cabinet	he spent	Jürgen

bereits	einige	Minuten	damit,	das ein oder andere zu richten.
bəˈʁaɪts	ˈaɪnɪgə	mɪˈnuːtən	daˈmɪt	das aɪn ˈoːdɐ ˈandəʁə tsuː ˈʁɪçtn
already	a few	minutes	with it	to fix one thing or another

Then he said, "Come look at this."

Dann	sagte	er:	»Komm	hier	herunter	und	schau	dir	das	an.«
dan	ˈzaktə	eːɐ	kɔm	hiːɐ	hɛˈʁʊntɐ	ʊnt	ʃaʊ	diːɐ	das	an
then	he said	he	come down →	here	←	and	look at →	this	←

I stuck my head into the cabinet.

Ich	steckte	meinen	Kopf	in	den	Schrank.
ɪç	ˈʃtɛktə	ˈmaɪnən	kɔpf	ɪn	deːn	ʃʁaŋk
I	I stuck	my	head	in	the	cabinet

"This is the drain pipe that I just detached from the disposal." He pointed to a white plastic pipe hanging near the disposal.

»Hier	ist	das	Abflussrohr,	das	ich	gerade	vom	Zerkleinerer
hiːɐ	ɪst	das	ˈapflʊsˌʁoːɐ	das	ɪç	gəˈʁaːdə	fɔm	tsɛɐˈklaɪnəʁɐ
here	it is	the	drain pipe	that	I	just	from the	disposal

entfernt	habe.«	Er	deutete	auf	ein	weißes	Kunststoffrohr,	das
ɛntˈfɛʁnt	ˈhaːbə	eːɐ	ˈdɔɪtətə	aʊf	aɪn	ˈvaɪsəs	ˈkʊnstʃtɔfˌʁoːɐ	das
I disconnected		he	he pointed	to	a	white	plastic pipe	that

neben	dem	Zerkleinerer	hing.
ˈneːbən	deːm	tsɛɐˈklaɪnəʁɐ	hɪŋ
next to	the	disposal	it hung

"The disposal is latched onto the bottom of the sink right here." He pointed to something different. A metal contraption of some kind. "Put your screwdriver on the latch right where it folds down and then tap it with a hammer to open the latch and loosen the disposal."

»Der	Zerkleinerer	ist	genau	hier	am	Boden	des	Beckens
deːɐ	tsɛɐˈklaɪnəʁɐ	ɪst	gəˈnaʊ	hiːɐ	am	ˈboːdən	dɛs	ˈbɛkəns
the	disposal	it is	right	here	on the	bottom	of the	sink

befestigt.«	Er	zeigte	auf	irgendetwas	anderes.	Eine	Art
bəˈfɛstɪçt	eːɐ	ˈtsaɪktə	aʊf	ˈɪʁgntˌɛtvas	ˈandəʁəs	ˈaɪnə	aʁt
attached	he	he pointed	at	something else		a	type

metallischer	Vorrichtung.	»Setze	deinen	Schraubenzieher	an	der
meˈtalɪʃɐ	ˈfoːɐˌʁɪçtʊŋ	ˈzɛtsə	ˈdaɪnən	ˈʃʁaʊbəntsiːɐ	an	deːɐ
metal	contraption	place on →	your	screwdriver	on	the

Verriegelung	an,	genau	dort,	wo	sie	gebogen	ist.	Dann	klopfe
fɛɐˈʁiːgəlʊŋ	an	gəˈnaʊ	dɔʁt	voː	ziː	gəˈboːgən	ɪst	dan	ˈklɔpfə
latch	←	right	there	where	it	bent	it is	then	tap

mit	dem	Hammer	leicht	darauf,	um	die	Verriegelung	zu	öffnen
mɪt	deːm	ˈhamɐ	laɪçt	daːˈʁaʊf	ʊm	diː	fɛɐˈʁiːgəlʊŋ	tsuː	ˈœfnən
with	the	hammer	lightly	on it	in order to	the	latch	to	to open

In Good Repair

und um den Zerkleinerer zu lösen.«
ʊnt ʊm deːn tsɛɐ̯ˈklainəʁɐ tsuː ˈløːzən
and in order to the disposal to to loosen

Ich tat was er sagte, aber nichts geschah.
ɪç taːt vas eːɐ̯ ˈzaktə ˈaːbɐ nɪçts gəˈʃaː
I I did what he he said but nothing it happened

I did what he said, but nothing happened.

»Die Verriegelung scheint festgerostet zu sein«, sagte ich.
diː fɛɐ̯ˈʁiːgəlʊŋ ʃaɪnt ˈfɛstgəˌʁɔstət tsuː zaɪn ˈzaktə ɪç
the latch it seems to be rusted tight I said I

"The latch seems to be rusted tight," I said.

Jürgen erhob sich. Es ist nicht leicht, sich zu bücken und
ˈjʏʁgn̩ ɛɐ̯ˈhoːp zɪç ɛs ɪst nɪçt laɪçt zɪç tsuː ˈbʏkən ʊnt
Jürgen he stood up it it is not easy to bend down and

dabei in den Schrank zu schauen.
daˈbaɪ ɪn deːn ʃʁaŋk tsuː ˈʃaʊən
at the same time in the cabinet to to look

Jürgen stood up. It's hard bending down looking into a cabinet.

»Schlage etwas fester drauf«, sagte er.
ˈʃlaːgə ˈɛtvas ˈfɛstɐ dʁaʊf ˈzaktə eːɐ̯
tap somewhat harder on it he said he

"Tap it harder," he said.

Ich versetzte dem Schraubenzieher einen mächtigen Schlag. Mit
ɪç fɛɐ̯ˈzɛtstə deːm ˈʃʁaʊbəntsiːɐ̯ ˈaɪnən ˈmɛçtɪgən ʃlaːk mɪt
I I gave the screwdriver a mighty whack with

Erfolg! Die Verriegelung löste sich. Der Abfallzerkleinerer fiel
ɛɐ̯ˈfɔlk diː fɛɐ̯ˈʁiːgəlʊŋ ˈløːstə zɪç deːɐ̯ ˈapfalˌtsɛɐ̯klainəʁɐ fiːl
success the latch it loosened the garbage disposal it fell

vom Haltering.
fɔm ˈhaltəʁɪŋ
from the mounting ring

I gave the screwdriver a mighty whack. Success! The latch came loose. The disposal fell from the mount ring.

»Was ist passiert?«, fragte Jürgen.
vas ɪst paˈsiːɐ̯t ˈfʁaːktə ˈjʏʁgn̩
what it happened he asked Jürgen

"What happened?" asked Jürgen.

»Du kannst dir gar nicht vorstellen, wie groß das Loch ist, wenn
duː kanst diːɐ̯ gaːɐ̯ nɪçt ˈfoːɐ̯ʃtɛlən viː gʁoːs das lɔx ɪst vɛn
you you can → not at all ←to imagine how big the hole it is when

ein Abfallzerkleinerer auf den Boden eines Küchenschränkchens
aɪn ˈapfalˌtsɛɐ̯klainəʁɐ aʊf deːn ˈboːdən ˈaɪnəs ˈkʏçnʃʁɛŋkçəns
a garbage disposal on the bottom of a kitchen cabinet

fällt«, antwortete ich.
fɛlt ˈantvɔʁtətə ɪç
it falls I responded I

"You can't believe what a big hole a heavy disposal can make when it falls onto the bottom of a kitchen cabinet," I responded.

»Ich hätte wohl den Zerkleinerer festhalten sollen, als du die
ɪç ˈhɛtə voːl deːn tsɛɐ̯ˈklainəʁɐ ˈfɛstˌhaltən ˈzɔlən als duː diː
I → probably the disposal ←I should have held on while you the

"I guess I should have held onto the disposal while you loosened the latch."

Story 9

I stood up so Jürgen could look into the cabinet.

"That's quite a big hole," he agreed. "It looks like a small cannon ball went through the floor of the cabinet. I have a small piece of plywood at home that we can use to fix that hole. Don't do anything until I get back."

While Jürgen was gone, I started to worry about what Ingrid would say when she got home. I needed a glass of water to clear my head. I turned on the cold water and let it run into the sink. After a few seconds the water was nice and cold. I filled a glass and sat at the kitchen table. Jürgen came back a few minutes later.

"I couldn't find that plywood. You'll have to buy a piece at the store," he said. "Hey, why is there a big puddle on the kitchen floor?"

Verriegelung gelockert hast.«
fɛɐ̯ˈʁiːɡəlʊŋ ɡəˈlɔkɐt hast
latch you loosened

Ich stand auf, damit Jürgen in das Schränkchen schauen konnte.
ɪç ʃtant aʊ̯f daˈmɪt ˈjʏʁɡn̩ ɪn das ˈʃʁɛŋkçən ˈʃaʊ̯ən ˈkɔntə
I I stood up so that Jürgen in the cabinet he could look

»Das ist ein ganz schön großes Loch«, stimmte er zu. »Es
das ɪst aɪ̯n ɡants ʃøːn ˈɡʁoːsəs lɔx ˈʃtɪmtə eːɐ̯ tsuː ɛs
that it is a quite big hole he agreed→ he ← it

sieht aus, als ob eine kleine Kanonenkugel den Boden des
ziːt aʊ̯s als ɔp ˈaɪ̯nə ˈklaɪ̯nə kaˈnoːnənˌkuːɡl̩ deːn ˈboːdən dɛs
it looks as if a small cannon ball the floor of the

Küchenschränkchens durchschlagen hätte. Ich habe ein kleines
ˈkʏçn̩ʃʁɛŋkçəns ˈdʊʁçʃluːk ˈhɛtə ɪç ˈhaːbə aɪ̯n ˈklaɪ̯nəs
kitchen cabinet it would have punched through I I have a small

Stück Sperrholz zu Hause. Wir können es zur Reparatur des
ʃtʏk ˈʃpɛʁˌhɔlts tsuː ˈhaʊ̯zə viːɐ̯ ˈkœnən ɛs tsuːɐ̯ ʁepaʁaˈtuːɐ̯ dɛs
piece plywood at home we we can it for the repair of the

Loches verwenden. Rühre nichts an, bis ich wieder da bin.«
ˈlɔxəs fɛɐ̯ˈvɛndən ˈʁyːʁə nɪçts an bɪs ɪç ˈviːdɐ daː bɪn
hole to use don't touch anything until I again there I am

Während Jürgen weg war, fing ich an, mir Sorgen
ˈvɛːʁənt ˈjʏʁɡn̩ vɛk vaːɐ̯ fɪŋ ɪç an miːɐ̯ ˈzɔʁɡən
while Jürgen away he was I started→ I ← myself worries

darüber zu machen, was wohl Ingrid sagen würde, wenn sie
daˈʁyːbɐ tsuː ˈmaxn̩ vas voːl ˈɪŋɡʁɪt ˈzaːɡən ˈvʏʁdə vɛn ziː
about it to to make what probably Ingrid she would say when she

nach Hause kommt. Ich brauchte ein Glass Wasser, um einen
naːx ˈhaʊ̯zə kɔmt ɪç ˈbʁaʊ̯xtə aɪ̯n ɡlaːs ˈvasɐ ʊm ˈaɪ̯nən
she gets home I I needed a glass water in order to a

klaren Kopf zu bekommen. Ich drehte das kalte Wasser auf und
ˈklaːʁən kɔpf tsuː bəˈkɔmən ɪç ˈdʁeːtə das ˈkaltə ˈvasɐ aʊ̯f ʊnt
clear head to to get I I turned on→ the cold water ← and

ließ es in das Becken laufen. Nach ein paar Sekunden war das
liːs ɛs ɪn das ˈbɛkən ˈlaʊ̯fən naːx aɪ̯n paːɐ̯ zeˈkʊndən vaːɐ̯ das
I let it in the sink to run after a few seconds it was the

Wasser angenehm kalt. Ich füllte ein Glas und setzte mich an den
ˈvasɐ ˈaŋɡəˌneːm kalt ɪç ˈfʏltə aɪ̯n ɡlaːs ʊnt ˈzɛtstə mɪç an deːn
water pleasantly cold I I filled a glass and I sat at the

Küchentisch. Jürgen kam ein paar Minuten später zurück.
ˈkʏçn̩ˌtɪʃ ˈjʏʁɡn̩ kaːm aɪ̯n paːɐ̯ mɪˈnuːtən ˈʃpɛːtɐ tsuˈʁʏk
kitchen table Jürgen he came back→ a few minutes later ←

»Ich konnte das Sperrholz nicht finden. Du musst ein Stück
ɪç ˈkɔntə das ˈʃpɛʁˌhɔlts nɪçt ˈfɪndən duː mʊst aɪ̯n ʃtʏk
I I could the plywood not to find you you have to a piece

im Geschäft kaufen«, sagte er. »Hey, warum ist da eine große
ɪm gəˈʃɛft ˈkaʊfən ˈzaktə eːɐ hɛɪ vaˈʁʊm ɪst daː ˈaɪnə ˈɡʁoːsə
in the store to buy he said he hey why it is there a big

Pfütze auf dem Küchenboden?«
ˈpfʏtsə aʊf deːm ˈkʏçənˌboːdən
puddle on the kitchen floor

»Welche Pfütze?« "What puddle?"
ˈvɛlçə ˈpfʏtsə
what puddle

Jürgen sah mein Glas Wasser. »Du hast doch nicht etwa Wasser   Jürgen saw my glass of water. "You
ˈjʏʁɡn zaː maɪn ɡlaːs ˈvasɐ duː hast dɔx nɪçt ˈɛtva ˈvasɐ   didn't run water into the sink, did
Jürgen he saw my glass water you → ! not some water   you?"

in den Ausguss laufen lassen, oder?«
ɪn deːn ˈaʊsˌɡʊs ˈlaʊfən ˈlasən ˈoːdɐ
in the sink ←you let run did you

Wir starrten beide in den Küchenschrank unter dem Spülbecken.   We both peered into the cabinet under
viːɐ ˈʃtaʁtn ˈbaɪdə ɪn deːn ˈkʏçənʃʁaŋk ˈʊntɐ deːm ˈʃpyːlˌbɛkən   the sink.
we we stared both into the kitchen cabinet under the kitchen sink

»Schau dir dieses Schlamassel an«, sagte Jürgen.   "Look at this mess," said Jürgen.
ʃaʊ diːɐ ˈdiːzəs ʃlaˈmasəl an ˈzaktə ˈjʏʁɡn
look→ this mess ← she said Jürgen

»Ich vergaß, dass das Abflussrohr entfernt war.«   "I forgot that the drain pipe was disconnected."
ɪç fɛɐˈɡaːs das das ˈapflʊsˌʁoːɐ ɛntˈfɛʁnt vaːɐ
I I forgot that the drain pipe disconnected it was

»Da müssen ein paar Liter Wasser aus dem Becken raus und   "There must be a few liters of water
daː ˈmʏsn aɪn paːɐ ˈliːtɐ ˈvasɐ aʊs deːm ˈbɛkən ʁaʊs ʊnt   that ran out of the sink and into that
there → a few liters water out→ the sink ←aus and   hole. Now it's leaking out onto the floor."

in das Loch rein gelaufen sein. Jetzt rinnt es auf den Boden
ɪn das lɔx ʁaɪn ɡəˈlaʊfən zaɪn jɛtst ʁɪnt ɛs aʊf deːn ˈboːdən
in→ the hole ←in ←they must have run now it leaks out→ it onto the floor

hinaus.«
hɪˈnaʊs
←

»Ich werde es aufwischen.«   "I'll clean it up."
ɪç ˈveːɐdə ɛs ˈaʊfˌvɪʃn
I I will it to wipe up

»Mach das nur. Gehe anschließend in den Laden und besorge   "You do that. Then go to the store and
max das nuːɐ ˈɡeːə ˈanʃliːsnt ɪn deːn ˈlaːdn ʊnt bəˈzɔʁɡə   buy a small piece of plywood. I'm going
do that just go subsequently into the store and procure   home to take a nap. Call me when you are back from the store."

ein kleines Stück Sperrholz. Ich gehe nach Hause und werde
aɪn ˈklaɪnəs ʃtʏk ˈʃpɛʁˌhɔlts ɪç ˈɡeːə naːx ˈhaʊzə ʊnt ˈveːɐdə
a small piece plywood I I go home and I will

Story 9

ein Nickerchen machen. Ruf mich an, wenn du vom Geschäft
aɪn ˈnɪkɐçən ˈmaxən ʁuːf mɪç an vɛn duː fɔm ɡəˈʃɛft
to take a nap call→ me ← when you from the store

zurück bist.«
tsuˈʁʏk bɪst
you are back

4

It took me more than an hour to clean up the kitchen and buy a small piece of wood to cover the hole in the cabinet. When I got home, I called Jürgen on the phone.

Ich verbrachte über eine Stunde damit, die Küche zu säubern
ɪç fɛɐˈbʁaxtə ˈyːbɐ ˈaɪnə ˈʃtʊndə daˈmɪt diː ˈkʏçə tsuː ˈzɔʏbɐn
I I spent over an hour with it the kitchen to to clean

und ein kleines Stück Holz zu kaufen, um das Loch im
ʊnt aɪn ˈklaɪnəs ʃtʏk hɔlts tsuː ˈkaʊfən ʊm das lɔx ɪm
and a small piece wood to to buy in order to the hole in the

Küchenschrank abzudecken. Als ich zu Hause war, rief ich
ˈkʏçənˌʃʁaŋk ˈaptsuˌdɛkən als ɪç tsuː ˈhaʊzə vaːɐ ʁiːf ɪç
kitchen cabinet to cover when I at home I was I called→ I

Jürgen an.
ˈjʏʁɡn̩ an
Jürgen ←

"Jürgen had to go to our son's house," his wife told me. "They needed someone to watch the baby while they went shopping."

»Jürgen musste zu unserem Sohn fahren«, sagte mir seine Frau.
ˈjʏʁɡn̩ ˈmʊstə tsuː ˈʊnzəʁəm zoːn ˈfaːʁən ˈzaktə miːɐ ˈzaɪnə fʁaʊ
Jürgen he had to to our son to go she told to me his wife

»Sie brauchten jemanden, der nach dem Baby schaut, während
ziː ˈbʁaʊxtən ˈjeːmandən deːɐ naːx deːm ˈbeːbi ʃaʊt ˈvɛːʁənt
they they needed someone who after the baby to look while

sie beim Einkaufen sind.«
ziː baɪm ˈaɪnˌkaʊfən zɪnt
they during the shopping they are

"He was supposed to help me fix something," I whined.

»Er sollte mir eigentlich bei einer Reparatur helfen«,
eːɐ ˈzɔltə miːɐ ˈaɪɡəntlɪç baɪ ˈaɪnɐ ʁepaʁaˈtuːɐ ˈhɛlfən
he he was supposed me actually with a repair to help

jammerte ich.
ˈjamɐtə ɪç
I whined I

"Grandchildren come first," she said to me. "Anyway, I thought you weren't allowed to fix things in the house any more."

»Enkelkinder gehen vor«, sagte sie zu mir. »Und außerdem, ich
ˈɛŋkəlˌkɪndɐ ˈɡeːən foːɐ ˈzaktə ziː tsuː miːɐ ʊnt ˈaʊsɐdeːm ɪç
grandchildren they come first she said she to me and besides I

dachte, du darfst nichts mehr im Haus reparieren.«
ˈdaxtə duː daʁfst nɪçts meːɐ ɪm haʊs ʁepaˈʁiːʁən
I thought you you are allowed nothing else in the house to fix

"I'd rather not talk about that."

»Darüber rede ich lieber nicht.«
daˈʁyːbɐ ˈʁeːdə ɪç ˈliːbɐ nɪçt
about that I talk I rather not

In Good Repair

»Ich erinnere mich an deinen Versuch, ein Loch im Dach über deinem Schlafzimmer abzudichten. Du bist das Dach hinunter gerutscht und beinahe in die Büsche gefallen.«

"I remember when you tried to seal that hole on the roof above your bedroom. You slid down the roof and right into the bushes."

»Das Dach war viel rutschiger, als ich dachte.«

"The roof was a lot more slippery than I expected."

»Wenigstens warst du klug genug, dich an einen Baum im Hinterhof zu binden, bevor du auf das Dach geklettert bist. Musstest du nicht eine Zeitlang am obersten Ast baumeln, bis der Polizist dich rettete?«

"At least you were smart enough to tie yourself to that tree in the backyard before you climbed onto the roof. Didn't you dangle from the top limb for a while until the police officer saved you?"

»Für ihn war es eine gute Trainingseinheit«, sagte ich. »Ich muss jetzt wirklich gehen.«

"It was a good training exercise for him," I said. "I really have to go now."

Ich legte den Hörer auf. Jetzt hatte ich ein Problem. Jürgen war weg und Ingrid würde in drei Stunden zu Hause sein.

I hung up the phone. Now I had a problem. Jürgen was away and Ingrid would be home in three hours.

»Es sieht ganz so aus, als ob ich die Arbeit selbst machen müsste«, sagte ich zum Hund, der dasaß und mich mit einem komischen Gesichtsausdruck betrachtete.

"Looks like I'll have to do the job myself," I said to the dog, who was sitting there watching me with a funny look on her face.

Story 9

I studied the installation instructions. They were written in Japanese. A quick search told me that there was no other instruction book. Panic started to rise in my stomach.

Ich studierte die Installationsanleitung. Sie war in Japanisch geschrieben. Eine eilige Suche ergab, dass es keine andere Anleitung gab. Ein Gefühl von Panik breitete sich in meinem Magen aus.

After five minutes of feverish thinking, I concluded that I had only one course of action. Reluctantly, I picked up the phone and dialed another number.

Nach fünf Minuten fieberhaften Grübelns kam ich zu dem Schluss, dass mir nur noch eine Vorgehensweise blieb. Zögernd hob ich den Hörer ab und wählte eine weitere Nummer.

The phone rang once. I dreaded having this conversation. It rang a second time. My self esteem was at its lowest ebb since seventh grade. A third ring sounded in my ear. Maybe nobody was home. Unfortunately, the call was answered.

Das Telefon läutete einmal. Ich fürchtete mich vor dieser Unterhaltung. Es klingelte ein zweites Mal. Mein Selbstwertgefühl war an seinem tiefsten Punkt seit der siebten Klasse. Ein drittes Klingeln war zu hören. Vielleicht war niemand zu Hause. Leider wurde der Anruf entgegengenommen.

"Hello," said a voice that had tormented me for years.

»Hallo«, sagte eine Stimme, die mich jahrelang gequält hatte.

"Hi Maria. I need a little help."

»Hallo Maria. Ich brauche etwas Hilfe.«

In Good Repair

»Klaus, das ist aber nett, dass du anrufst«, gurrte meine Schwester Maria ins Telefon. »Worum geht es denn?«

"Klaus, so nice to hear from you," my sister Maria cooed into the phone. "What is the problem?"

Ich schluckte meinen Stolz hinunter. »Kannst du mir am Telefon erklären, wie man einen Abfallzerkleinerer einbaut?«

I swallowed my pride. "Can you explain over the phone how to install a garbage disposal?"

»Wann hast du dich entschieden, Klempner zu werden?«

"When did you decide to be a plumber?"

»Seitdem Klempner teurere Autos als meins fahren.«

"Ever since plumbers started driving more expensive cars than mine."

»Erinnerst du dich noch daran, als du mir helfen wolltest, ein Bücherregal aufzubauen?«, fragte Maria.

"Do you remember that time you tried to help me build those bookshelves?" Maria asked.

Meine Schwester ist ein Jahr älter als ich. Sie war immer schon gut im Aufbauen und Reparieren von Dingen. Als wir Teenager waren, versuchte ich ein paar Mal, ihr zu helfen.

My sister is a year older than I am. She has always been able to build and fix things. When we were teenagers I tried to help her a few times.

»Erinnere mich nicht daran«, sagte ich.

"Don't remind me," I said.

»Du hast dir dauernd mit dem Hammer auf den Daumen geschlagen. Er schwoll so stark an, dass Mutti die Nägel für dich

"You kept hitting your thumb with the hammer. It got so swollen that mom had to hold the nails for you."

109

Story 9

"She only held one nail," I said.

»Sie hat nur einen Nagel gehalten«, sagte ich.
zi: hat nuɐ 'aɪnən 'na:gəl gə'haltən 'zaktə ɪç
she → only one nail ← she held I said I

halten musste.«
'haltən 'mʊstə
to hold she had to

"That's right," Maria laughed. "She quit when you hit her thumb, too."

»Richtig«, lachte Maria. »Sie gab auf, als du auch auf ihren
ʁɪçtɪç 'laxtə ma'ʁi:a zi: ga:p aʊf als du: aʊx aʊf 'i:ʁən
right she laughed Maria she she quit when you also on her

Daumen geschlagen hast.«
'daʊmən gə'ʃla:gən hast
thumb you hit

"I'm much better with hammers now," I said. "I could probably do the job myself, but the installation instructions are printed in Japanese."

»Ich kann jetzt mit dem Hammer viel besser umgehen«, sagte
ɪç kan jɛtst mɪt de:m 'hamɐ fi:l 'bɛsɐ ʊm'ge:ən 'zaktə
I I can now with the hammer much better to handle I said

ich. »Ich könnte die Arbeit wahrscheinlich selbst ausführen aber
ɪç ɪç 'kœntə di: 'aʁbaɪt va:ɐ'ʃaɪnlɪç zɛlpst 'aʊsˌfy:ʁən 'a:bɐ
I I I could the job probably myself to perform but

die Installationsanleitung ist auf Japanisch.«
di: ɪnstala'tsjo:nsˈanˌlaɪtʊŋ ɪst aʊf ja'pa:nɪʃ
the installation manual it is in Japanese

"Put the phone on speaker," my sister sighed. "I'll walk you through the whole thing."

»Stell das Telefon auf Lautsprecher«, seufzte meine Schwester.
ʃtɛl das te:le'fo:n aʊf 'laʊtˌʃpʁɛçɐ 'zɔɪftstə 'maɪnə 'ʃvɛstɐ
put the telephone on loudspeaker she sighed my sister

»Ich werde dich durch die ganze Angelegenheit leiten.«
ɪç 'veːɐdə dɪç dʊʁç di: 'gantsə 'angəˌleːgnhaɪt 'laɪtn
I I will you through the whole issue to guide

---6---

Ingrid arrived home just as I was putting the tools away.

Ich verstaute gerade die Werkzeuge, als Ingrid nach Hause kam.
ɪç fɛɐ'ʃtaʊtə gə'ʁa:də di: 'vɛʁkˌtsɔɪgə als 'ɪŋgʁɪt na:x 'haʊzə ka:m
I I put away just the tools as Ingrid she got home

"We have a new garbage disposal," I told her.

»Wir haben einen neuen Abfallzerkleinerer«, sagte ich zu ihr.
vi:ɐ 'ha:bn̩ 'aɪnən 'nɔɪən 'apfalˌtsɛɐˈklaɪnəʁɐ 'zaktə ɪç tsu: i:ɐ
we we have a new garbage disposal I said I to her

She went into the kitchen and looked under the sink.

Sie ging in die Küche und schaute unter das Spülbecken.
zi: gɪŋ ɪn di: 'kʏçə ʊnt 'ʃaʊtə 'ʊntɐ das 'ʃpy:lˌbɛkən
she she went in the kitchen and she looked under the sink

"It really is new," she said. "What plumber did you use?"

»Er ist wirklich neu«, sagte sie. »Welchen Klempner hast du
e:ɐ ɪst 'vɪʁklɪç nɔɪ 'zaktə zi: 'vɛlçən 'klɛmpnɐ hast du:
it it is really new she said she which plumber → you

angerufen?«
'angəˌʁu:fn̩
← you called

In Good Repair

»Ich habe es selbst gemacht.«
ɪç ˈhaːbə ɛs zɛlpst gəˈmaxt
I → it myself ←I did

"I did it myself."

»Nein, hast du nicht«, sagte meine reizende Frau. »In der Küche
naɪn hast duː nɪçt ˈzaktə ˈmaɪnə ˈʁaɪtsəndə fʁaʊ ɪn deːɐ ˈkʏçə
no you didn't she said my lovely wife in the kitchen

ist nichts kaputtgegangen.«
ɪst nɪçts kaˈpʊtˌgəˈgaŋən
→ nothing ←it got broken

"No you didn't," my lovely wife said. "Nothing in the kitchen is broken."

»Schau nochmals in das Küchenschränkchen«, sagte ich zu ihr.
ʃaʊ ˈnɔxmaːls ɪn das ˈkʏçnʃʁɛŋkçən ˈzaktə ɪç tsuː iːɐ
look again in the kitchen cabinet I said I to her

»Unter den Abfalleimer.«
ˈʊntɐ deːn ˈapfalˌaɪmɐ
under the garbage can

"Look in the cabinet again," I told her. "Under the garbage can."

»Schau nur, wie groß das Loch ist«, rief sie ein paar
ʃaʊ nuːɐ viː gʁoːs das lɔx ɪst ʁiːf ziː aɪn paːɐ
look just how big the hole it is she exclaimed she a few

Sekunden später. »Da passt ja ein Kürbis rein.«
zeˈkʊndən ˈʃpɛːtɐ daː past jaː aɪn ˈkʏʁbɪs ʁaɪn
seconds later there it fits ! a pumpkin inside

"Look at the size of this hole," she exclaimed a few seconds later. "You could fit a pumpkin into it."

»Ich wollte es mit einem Stück Sperrholz reparieren, aber ich
ɪç ˈvɔltə ɛs mɪt ˈaɪnəm ʃtʏk ˈʃpɛʁˌhɔlts ʁepaˈʁiːʁən ˈaːbɐ ɪç
I I intended it with a piece plywood to fix but I

hatte keine Zeit dazu.«
ˈhatə ˈkaɪnə tsaɪt daˈtsuː
I had not any time for it

"I was going to fix it with a piece of plywood, but I didn't have time."

»Wenn das der einzige Schaden ist, den du angerichtet hast, dann
vɛn das deːɐ ˈaɪntsɪgə ˈʃaːdən ɪst deːn duː ˈangəˌʁɪçtət hast dan
if this the only damage it is that you you caused then

bin ich beeindruckt«, sagte Ingrid. »Bist du sicher, dass dir sonst
bɪn ɪç bəˈaɪnˌdʁʊkt ˈzaktə ˈɪŋgʁɪt bɪst duː ˈzɪçɐ das diːɐ zɔnst
I am I impressed she said Ingrid you are you sure that your else

niemand geholfen hat?«
ˈniːmant gəˈhɔlfən hat
no one he helped

"If this is the only damage you did, then I'm impressed," said Ingrid. "Are you sure you didn't have any help?"

»Am Anfang war Jürgen hier, aber er musste weg.«
am ˈanˌfaŋ vaːɐ ˈjʏʁgn̩ hiːɐ ˈaːbɐ eːɐ ˈmʊstə vɛk
in the beginning he was Jürgen here but he he had to go

"Jürgen was here at the beginning but he had to leave."

»Das muss gefeiert werden. Lasst uns eine Flasche Wein öffnen.«
das mʊs gəˈfaɪɐt ˈveːɐdn̩ last ʊns ˈaɪnə ˈflaʃə vaɪn ˈœfnən
this calls for a celebration let's a bottle wine to open

"This calls for a celebration. Let's open a bottle of wine."

Story 9

She took a bottle of chardonnay out of the refrigerator and poured two glasses.

Sie	nahm	eine	Flasche	Chardonnay	aus	dem	Kühlschrank	und
ziː	naːm	ˈaɪnə	ˈflaʃə	ʃaʁdɔˈneː	aʊs	deːm	ˈkyːlʃʁaŋk	ʊnt
she	she took	a	bottle	chardonnay	out of	the	refrigerator	and

füllte	zwei	Gläser.
ˈfʏltə	tsvaɪ	ˈglɛːzɐ
she filled	two	glasses

We clinked the glasses together.

Wir	stießen	miteinander	an.
viːɐ	ˈʃtiːsən	ˈmɪtaɪˌnandɐ	an
we	we clinked glasses →	together	←

"A toast to my handyman," said Ingrid as we took a sip of the chardonnay.

»Einen	Toast	auf	meinen	Handwerker«,	sagte	Ingrid,	während
ˈaɪnən	toːst	aʊf	ˈmaɪnən	ˈhantˌvɛʁkɐ	ˈzaktə	ˈɪŋgʁɪt	ˈvɛːʁənt
a	toast	to	my	handyman	she said	Ingrid	as

wir	einen	kleinen	Schluck	Chardonnay	tranken.
viːɐ	ˈaɪnən	ˈklaɪnən	ʃluːk	ʃaʁdɔˈneː	ˈtʁaŋkən
we	a	small	sip	Chardonnay	we drank

We stayed in the kitchen, drinking the wine and preparing dinner. Ingrid did the cooking. I set the table and made a salad. Ingrid told me all about her college friends.

Wir	blieben	in	der	Küche,	tranken	Wein	und	bereiteten
viːɐ	ˈbliːbən	ɪn	deːɐ	ˈkʏçə	ˈtʁaŋkən	vaɪn	ʊnt	bəˈʁaɪtətən
we	we stayed	in	the	kitchen	we drank	wine	and	we prepared →

das	Abendessen	vor.	Ingrid	widmete sich	dem	Kochen.	Ich
das	ˈaːbntˌɛsn	foːɐ	ˈɪŋgʁɪt	ˈvɪtmətə zɪç	deːm	ˈkɔxən	ɪç
the	dinner	←	Ingrid	she applied herself to	the	cooking	I

deckte	den	Tisch	und	machte	einen	Salat.	Ingrid	erzählte	mir
ˈdɛktə	deːn	tɪʃ	ʊnt	ˈmaxtə	ˈaɪnən	zaˈlaːt	ˈɪŋgʁɪt	ɛɐˈtsɛːltə	miːɐ
I set the table			and	I made	a	salad	Ingrid	she told	me

alles	Mögliche	über	ihre	Schulfreunde.
ˈaləs	ˈmøːklɪçə	ˈyːbɐ	ˈiːʁə	ˈʃuːlˌfʁɔɪndə
everything	possible	about	her	schoolmates

"We went to the mall and ate sushi for lunch," she said.

»Wir	gingen	zum	Einkaufszentrum	und	haben	dort	Sushi
viːɐ	ˈgɪŋən	tsʊm	ˈaɪnkaʊfsˌtsɛntʁʊm	ʊnt	ˈhaːbn	dɔʁt	ˈzuːʃi
we	we went	to the	mall	and	→	there	sushi

zu Mittag	gegessen«,	sagte	sie.
tsuː ˈmɪtaːk	gəˈgɛsn	ˈzaktə	ziː
← we ate lunch		she said	she

"That's nice."

»Wie	schön.«
viː	ʃøːn
how	nice

Ingrid and I were on our third glass of wine by the time we sat down to dinner. I was feeling very relaxed.

Bis	wir	uns	endlich	zum Abendessen	setzten,	waren	Ingrid
bɪs	viːɐ	ʊns	ˈɛntlɪç	tsʊm ˈaːbntˌɛsn	ˈzɛtstən	ˈvaːʁən	ˈɪŋgʁɪt
by the time	we	→	finally	for dinner	← we sat	→	Ingrid

und	ich	schon	bei	unserem	dritten	Glas	Wein	angelangt.	Ich
ʊnt	ɪç	ʃoːn	baɪ	ˈʊnzəʁəm	ˈdʁɪtən	glaːs	vaɪn	ˈangəˌlaŋt	ɪç
and	I	already	on	our	third	glass	wine	← we got to	I

fühlte	mich	sehr	entspannt.
ˈfyːltə	mɪç	zeːɐ	ɛntˈʃpant
I felt		very	relaxed

In Good Repair

»So, hast du heute sonst noch mit jemand Interessantem, außer Jürgen gesprochen?«, fragte sie.

"So did you talk to anyone interesting today besides Jürgen?" she asked.

»Ich rief meine Schwester Maria an«, erwähnte ich.

"I called my sister Maria," I mentioned.

»Aha«, sagte Ingrid und zeigte mit dem Finger auf mich. »Maria hat dir geholfen.«

"Aha," Ingrid said as she pointed a finger at me. "Maria helped you."

»Unfair«, beschwerte ich mich. »Du hast mir Wein gegeben, um mir die Wahrheit zu entlocken.«

"No fair," I complained. "You gave me wine to sneak the truth out of me."

»Ich kann doch nichts dafür, das du keinen Wein verträgst«, kicherte sie.

"I can't help it if you have no tolerance for wine," she giggled.

»Du hast mich schamlos ausgenutzt«, beschwerte ich mich.

"You took unfair advantage of me," I complained.

»Du brauchst dich nicht zu schämen«, sagte Ingrid. »Es war schlau, jemanden um Hilfe zu bitten.«

"You don't have to feel ashamed," Ingrid said. "You were smart to ask someone for help."

»Die Installationsanleitung war auf Japanisch.«

"The installation instructions were in Japanese."

»Nicht jeder ist als Werkzeugfachmann und Mechaniker

"Not everyone was born to be an expert with tools and mechanical things," Ingrid said. "You have lots of other talents that your sister lacks."

113

Story 9

auf die Welt gekommen«, sagte Ingrid. »Du hast viele andere
aʊf diː vɛlt ɡəˈkɔmən ˈzaktə ˈɪŋɡʁɪt duː hast ˈfiːlə ˈandəʁə
← he was born she said Ingrid you you have many other

Talente, die deine Schwester nicht hat.«
taˈlɛntə diː ˈdaɪnə ˈʃvɛstɐ nɪçt hat
talents that your sister not she has

"Like what?"

»Was zum Beispiel?«
vas tsʊm ˈbaɪʃpiːl
what for example

She thought for a minute. "You are really good at rubbing my feet."

Sie dachte eine Minute nach. »Du kannst wirklich gut meine
ziː ˈdaxtə ˈaɪnə mɪˈnuːtə naːx duː kanst ˈvɪʁklɪç ɡuːt ˈmaɪnə
she she thought→ a minute ← you you can really well my

Füße massieren.«
ˈfyːsə maˈsiːʁən
feet to massage

"I don't want people to know about that. They might think I'm strange."

»Ich will nicht, dass jemand davon erfährt. Man könnte
ɪç vɪl nɪçt das ˈjeːmant daˈfɔn ɛɐ̯ˈfɛːɐ̯t man ˈkœntə
I I want not that anyone of that he finds out one he could

annehmen, ich hätte eine seltsame Neigung.«
ˈanˌneːmən ɪç ˈhɛtə ˈaɪnə ˈzɛltzaːmə ˈnaɪɡʊŋ
to assume I I had a weird inclination

"Your secret is safe with me. It's just that I'm much happier with a husband who rubs my feet than I would be with a husband who fixes things. You don't have to feel insecure about not being handy around the house. Let's hire people to do that stuff."

»Dein Geheimnis ist bei mir sicher. Ich bin einfach viel glücklicher
daɪn ɡəˈhaɪmnɪs ɪst baɪ miːɐ̯ ˈzɪçɐ ɪç bɪn ˈaɪnfax fiːl ˈɡlʏklɪçɐ
your secret it is with me safe I I am just much happier

mit einem Ehemann, der meine Füße massiert, als mit einem
mɪt ˈaɪnəm ˈeːəˌman deːɐ̯ ˈmaɪnə ˈfyːsə maˈsiːɐ̯t als mɪt ˈaɪnəm
with a husband who my feet he massages than with a

Ehemann, der Dinge repariert. Du brauchst dich nicht unsicher
ˈeːəˌman deːɐ̯ ˈdɪŋə ʁepaˈʁiːɐ̯t duː bʁaʊxst dɪç nɪçt ˈʊnzɪçɐ
husband who things he fixes you you need → not insecure

deswegen zu fühlen, weil du nicht so geschickt bist, was
ˈdɛsˌveːɡn̩ tsuː ˈfyːlən vaɪl duː nɪçt zoː ɡəˈʃɪkt bɪst vas
because of that to ←to feel because you not so handy you are what

Reparaturen am Haus angeht. Lass uns lieber Leute beauftragen,
ʁepaʁaˈtuːʁən am haʊs ˈanˌɡeːt las ʊns ˈliːbɐ ˈlɔɪtə bəˈʔaʊfˌtʁaːɡn̩
repairs on the house it concerns let's rather people to hire

die sich damit auskennen.«
diː zɪç daˈmɪt ˈaʊsˌkɛnən
who → about that ←they know about

"That sounds like a good plan," I said. "You don't know how stressful my day has been."

»Das klingt nach einer vernünftigen Lösung«, sagte ich. »Du
das klɪŋt naːx ˈaɪnɐ fɛɐ̯ˈnʏnftɪɡən ˈløːzʊŋ ˈzaktə ɪç duː
that it sounds like a wise solution I said I you

hast keine Ahnung, wie stressig mein Tag gewesen ist.«
hast ˈkaɪnə ˈaːnʊŋ viː ˈʃtʁɛsɪç maɪn taːk ɡəˈveːzən ɪst
you have not any idea how stressful my day it has been

STORY 10

All Inclusive

Wir	aßen	mit	Josef	und	Martina,	einem	netten	Paar	aus
viːɐ	ˈaːsn	mɪt	ˈjoːzɛf	ʊnt	maʁˈtiːna	ˈaɪnəm	ˈnɛtən	paːɐ	aʊs
we	we ate dinner→	with	Josef	and	Martina	a	nice	couple	from

Bremen,	zu Abend.	Wir	hatten	sie	zuvor	am Nachmittag	am
ˈbʁeːmən	tsuːˈaːbənt	viːɐ	ˈhatən	ziː	tsuˈfoːɐ	am ˈnaːxmɪˌtaːk	am
Bremen	←	we	→	them	earlier	in the afternoon	at the

Pool	an	der	Insel-Bar	getroffen.	Sie	waren	so	unterhaltsame
puːl	an	deːɐ	ˈɪnzl̩-baːɐ	ɡəˈtʁɔfən	ziː	ˈvaːʁən	zoː	ʊntɐˈhaltzaːmə
pool	at	the	island-bar	←we had met	they	they were	such	enjoyable

Leute,	dass	wir	sie	fragten,	ob	sie	uns	nicht	zum	Abendessen
ˈlɔɪtə	das	viːɐ	ziː	ˈfʁaːktn̩	ɔp	ziː	ʊns	nɪçt	tsʊm	ˈaːbnt̩ˌɛsn̩
people	that	we	them	we asked	if	they	us	not	for the	dinner

Gesellschaft	leisten	möchten.
ɡəˈzɛlʃaft	ˈlaɪstən	ˈmœçtn̩
company	to provide	they would like

We were having dinner with Josef and Martina, a nice couple from Bremen. We had met them at the pool swim up bar earlier in the afternoon. They were such fun people that we asked them to join us for dinner.

»So,	was	habt	ihr	zwei	heute	gemacht?«,	fragte	Josef.
zoː	vas	haːpt	iːɐ	tsvaɪ	ˈhɔɪtə	ɡəˈmaxt	ˈfʁaːktə	ˈjoːzɛf
so	what	→	you	two	today	←you did	he asked	Josef

"So what did you two do today?" asked Josef.

»Klaus	hat	zehn	Margaritas	getrunken	und	ist	am	Strand
klaʊs	hat	tseːn	maʁɡaˈʁiːtas	ɡəˈtʁʊŋkən	ʊnt	ɪst	am	ʃtʁant
Klaus	→	ten	margaritas	←he drank	and	→	on the	beach

eingeschlafen«,	sagte	Ingrid.	»Jetzt	hat	er	einen	schlimmen
ˈaɪnɡəʃlaːfən	ˈzaktə	ˈɪŋɡʁɪt	jɛtst	hat	eːɐ	ˈaɪnən	ˈʃlɪmən
←he fell asleep	she said	Ingrid	now	he has	he	a	bad

Sonnenbrand.«
ˈzɔnənˌbʁant
sunburn

"Klaus drank ten margaritas and fell asleep on the beach," Ingrid said. "Now he has a bad sunburn."

Martina	schaute	mich	an.	»Du	bist	tatsächlich	etwas	rot«,
maʁˈtiːna	ˈʃaʊtə	mɪç	an	duː	bɪst	taˈtzɛçlɪç	ˈɛtvas	ʁoːt
Martina	she looked at→	me	←	you	you are	actually	somewhat	red

bemerkte	sie.
bəˈmɛʁktə	ziː
she remarked	she

Martina looked at me. "You do look a little red," she remarked.

»Die	Sonne	hier	in	Cancun	ist	wirklich	stark.	Du	musst
diː	ˈzɔnə	hiːɐ	ɪn	kanˈkʊn	ɪst	ˈvɪʁklɪç	ʃtaʁk	duː	mʊst
the	sun	here	in	Cancun	it is	really	strong	you	you have to

"The sun here in Cancun is really powerful. You have to be careful," said Josef. "Have a few more margaritas and you'll feel better."

Story 10

»vorsichtig sein«, sagte Josef. »Trink noch ein paar Margaritas und du wirst dich besser fühlen.«

"This place is so great," Martina said. "We can eat and drink as much as we want, and it's all included in the price. Plus they have great water sports, kayaks, sailboats, and snorkeling right here at the resort."

»Dieser Ort ist so großartig«, sagte Martina. »Wir können essen und trinken, soviel wir wollen, und es ist alles im Preis inbegriffen. Außerdem gibt es ein großartiges Wassersportangebot mit Kajaks, Segelbooten und Schnorcheln direkt hier im Resort.«

"I hope my mother is doing alright watching the kids," Ingrid said.

»Ich hoffe, meiner Mutter geht es gut bei der Kinderbetreuung«, sagte Ingrid.

"She'll be fine," I said.

»Sie kommt schon klar«, sagte ich.

"What if something happens?"

»Was ist, wenn etwas passiert?«

"Nothing bad will happen," I said. "But your mother has the telephone number of the hotel. She can always call that number and ask them to find us."

»Es wird nichts Schlimmes passieren«, sagte ich. »Aber deine Mutter hat die Telefonnummer des Hotels. Sie kann dort jederzeit anrufen und uns suchen lassen.«

"The water aerobics was a strenuous workout," Ingrid mentioned. "Klaus tried it, but he couldn't keep up the pace."

»Die Wassergymnastik war ein anstrengendes Fitnesstraining«, erwähnte Ingrid. »Klaus hat es auch ausprobiert, aber er konnte

All Inclusive

mit dem Tempo nicht mithalten.«
mɪt deːm ˈtɛmpoː nɪçt ˈmɪtˌhaltən
with the pace not to keep up with

»War das vor oder nach dem Trinkgelage?«, fragte Josef.
vaːʁ das foːʁ ˈoːdɐ naːx deːm ˈtʁɪŋkɡəˌlaːɡə ˈfʁaːktə ˈjoːzɛf
it was this before or after the drinking spree he asked Josef

"Was this before or after the heavy drinking?" Josef asked.

»Vorher«, sagte ich. »Otto leitet die Aerobic-Kurse. Er ist wie
ˈfoːʁheːʁ ˈzaktə ɪç ˈɔto ˈlaɪtət diː ɛˈʁoːbɪkˈkʊʁzə eːʁ ɪst viː
before I said I Otto he leads the aerobic classes he he is like

ein militärischer Ausbilder. Ich verstehe nicht, wie die Frauen alle
aɪn miliˈtɛːʁɪʃɐ ˈaʊsˌbɪldɐ ɪç fɛʁˈʃteːə nɪçt viː diː ˈfʁaʊən ˈalə
a military instructor I I understand not how the women all

im Schwimmbad eine ganze Stunde lang ihre Arme schwingen
ɪm ˈʃvɪmbaːt ˈaɪnə ˈɡantsə ˈʃtʊndə laŋ ˈiːʁə ˈaʁmə ˈʃvɪŋən
in the swimming pool a whole hour long their arms to swing

und mit ihren Beinen pumpen konnten.«
ʊnt mɪt ˈiːʁən ˈbaɪnən ˈpʊmpən ˈkɔntən
and with their legs to pump they could

"Before," I said. "Otto runs the aerobics classes. He's like an army drill sergeant. I don't know how all those women at the pool could swing their arms and pump their legs for a full hour."

»Außerdem gibt Otto täglich um vier Uhr Salsa-Unterricht«,
ˈaʊsɐdeːm ɡiːpt ˈɔto ˈtɛːklɪç ʊm fiːʁ uːʁ ˈzaltsaˈʊntɐˌʁɪçt
in addition he gives Otto daily at four o'clock salsa instruction

sagte Ingrid. »Als Klaus am Strand schnarchte, hat er mir eine
ˈzaktə ˈɪŋɡʁɪt als klaʊs am ʃtʁant ˈʃnaʁçtə hat eːʁ miːʁ ˈaɪnə
she said Ingrid while Klaus on the beach he snored → he to me a

Stunde gegeben.«
ˈʃtʊndə ɡəˈɡeːbən
lesson ←he gave

"Otto also gives salsa lessons at four o'clock every day," Ingrid said. "He gave me a lesson while Klaus was snoring on the beach."

»Du hast mir nichts davon gesagt, das Otto dir eine Tanzstunde
duː hast miːʁ nɪçts daˈfɔn ɡəˈzaːkt das ˈɔto diːʁ ˈaɪnə ˈtantsʃtʊndə
you → to me not about that ←you told that Otto to you a dance lesson

gegeben hat«, sagte ich. »Ich glaube nicht, das mir das gefällt.«
ɡəˈɡeːbən hat ˈzaktə ɪç ɪç ˈɡlaʊbə nɪçt das miːʁ das ɡəˈfɛlt
he gave I said I I think not that to me that it pleases

"You didn't tell me that Otto gave you a dance lesson," I said. "I'm not sure I like that."

»Und mir gefällt es nicht, wie du die beiden jungen Mädchen in
ʊnt miːʁ ɡəˈfɛlt ɛs nɪçt viː duː diː ˈbaɪdən ˈjʊŋən ˈmɛːtçən ɪn
and to me it pleases it not how you the two young girls in

ihren Tangabikinis angestarrt hast, als sie ihre Wassergymnastik
ˈiːʁən ˈtaŋɡabiˈkiːnis ˈaŋɡəʃtaʁt hast als ziː ˈiːʁə ˈvasɐˌɡʏmˈnastɪk
their thong bikinis you stared while they their aquarobics

machten«, sagte Ingrid.
ˈmaxtən ˈzaktə ˈɪŋɡʁɪt
they did she said Ingrid

"And I don't like the way you were staring at those two young girls in the thong bikinis during the water aerobics," Ingrid said.

Ich schloss meine Augen und erinnerte mich an die zwei
ɪç ʃlɔs ˈmaɪnə ˈaʊɡən ʊnt ɛʁˈɪnɐtə mɪç an diː tsvaɪ
I I closed my eyes and I remembered the two

I closed my eyes and remembered the two gorgeous young women Ingrid was talking about. They had perfect

Story 10

tans, a few classy tattoos, and brightly polished fingernails. The thought of them was enough to make the sunburn pain stop for a few seconds.

wunderschönen	jungen	Frauen,	die	Ingrid	erwähnte.	Sie	hatten
vʊndɐˈʃøːnən	ˈjʊŋən	ˈfʁaʊən	diː	ˈɪŋɡʁɪt	ɛɐ̯ˈvɛːntə	ziː	ˈhatən
gorgeous	young	women	who	Ingrid	she alluded to	they	they had

eine	perfekte	Bräune,	ein paar	stilvolle	Tätowierungen	und
ˈaɪnə	pɛɐ̯ˈfɛktə	ˈbʁɔʏnə	aɪn paːɐ̯	ˈʃtiːlfɔlə	tɛtoˈviːʁʊŋən	ʊnt
a	perfect	tan	a few	classy	tattoos	and

glänzend	polierte	Fingernägel.	Allein	der	Gedanke	an	sie
ˈɡlɛntsənt	poˈliːɐ̯tə	ˈfɪŋɐˌnɛːɡl	aˈlaɪn	deːɐ̯	ɡəˈdaŋkə	an	ziː
brightly	polished	fingernails	alone	the	thought	of	them

ließ	meine	Sonnenbrandschmerzen	für	ein paar	Sekunden	lang
liːs	ˈmaɪnə	ˈzɔnənˌbʁantˈʃmɛɐ̯tsn̩	fyːɐ̯	aɪn paːɐ̯	zeˈkʊndən	laŋ
it let	my	sunburn pain	for	a few	seconds	long

verschwinden.
fɛɐ̯ˈʃvɪndən
to disappear

"They had really pretty belly button rings," I sighed.

»Sie	hatten	wirklich	hübsche	Bauchnabelpiercings«,	seufzte	ich.
ziː	ˈhatən	ˈvɪʁklɪç	ˈhʏpʃə	ˈbaʊxˌnaːbl̩ˈpiːɐ̯sɪŋs	ˈzɔɪftstə	ɪç
they	they had	really	pretty	belly button rings	I sighed	I

Ingrid punched me. "You must have gotten a real close look to know that," she said.

Ingrid	schlug	mich.	»Da	musst	du	ja	wirklich	sehr
ˈɪŋɡʁɪt	ʃluːk	mɪç	daː	mʊst	duː	jaː	ˈvɪʁklɪç	zeːɐ̯
Ingrid	she punched	me	!	you must	you	!	really	very

genau	hingeschaut haben,	um	das	zu	wissen«,	sagte	sie.
ɡəˈnaʊ	ˈhɪnɡəˌʃaʊt ˈhaːbn̩	ʊm	das	tsuː	ˈvɪsən	ˈzaktə	ziː
you looked closely		in order to	that	to	to know	she said	she

"I know the girls you mean," Martina interrupted. "I have shoes older than them."

»Ich	kenne	die	Mädchen,	die	du	meinst«,	unterbrach	Martina.
ɪç	ˈkɛnə	diː	ˈmɛːtçən	diː	duː	maɪnst	ʊntɐˈbʁaːx	maʁˈtiːna
I	I know	the	girls	that	you	you mean	she interrupted	Martina

»Ich	habe	Schuhe,	die	älter	sind	als	sie.«
ɪç	ˈhaːbə	ˈʃuːə	diː	ˈɛltɐ	zɪnt	als	ziː
I	I have	shoes	that	older	they are	than	them

"Did you notice two guys in cowboy hats standing in the pool the entire afternoon?" asked Josef.

»Hast	du	die	zwei	Jungs	in	Cowboyhüten	gesehen,	die	den	ganzen
hast	duː	diː	tsvaɪ	jʊŋs	ɪn	ˈkaʊbɔɪˌhyːtn̩	ɡəˈzeːən	diː	deːn	ˈɡantsən
→	you	the	two	guys	in	cowboy hats	←you saw	who	the	whole

Nachmittag	im	Schwimmbad	standen?«,	fragte	Josef.
ˈnaːxmɪˌtaːk	ɪm	ˈʃvɪmbaːt	ˈʃtandən	ˈfʁaːktə	ˈjoːzɛf
afternoon	in the	swimming pool	they stood	he asked	Josef

"They were at the water aerobics," Ingrid said. "Drinking beer out of large insulated mugs in one hand and doing the exercises with the other. It was so funny."

»Sie	waren	beim	Wasser-Aerobic«,	sagte	Ingrid.	»Sie	tranken
ziː	ˈvaːʁən	baɪm	ˈvasɐ-ɛˈʁoːbɪk	ˈzaktə	ˈɪŋɡʁɪt	ziː	ˈtʁaŋkən
they	they were	at the	water aerobics	she said	Ingrid	they	they drank

mit	einer	Hand	Bier	aus	großen	Thermosbechern	und	machten
mɪt	ˈaɪnɐ	hant	biːɐ̯	aʊs	ˈɡʁoːsən	ˈtɛʁmosˌbɛçɐn	ʊnt	ˈmaxtən
with	one	hand	beer	out of	large	insulated mugs	and	they did

Übungen	mit	der	anderen.	Es	war	so	lustig.«
ˈyːbʊŋən	mɪt	deːɐ̯	ˈandəʁən	ɛs	vaːɐ̯	zoː	ˈlʊstɪç
exercises	with	the	other	it	it was	so	funny

All Inclusive

»Hört ihr euch die Band an, die heute Abend hier spielt?«, fragte Josef.

"Are you going to listen to the band that is playing here tonight?" asked Josef.

»Ich denke, dass wir auf dem Zimmer bleiben und lesen. Mein Sonnenbrand bringt mich um. Viel Spaß euch zweien«, sagte ich.

"I think we'll stay in the room and read. My sunburn is killing me. You two have fun," I said.

―― 2 ――

Zur Cocktailparty des Managers kamen wir um fünf Uhr an. Josef und Martina saßen schon in der Nähe der Bar. Wir leisteten ihnen bei ein paar Drinks Gesellschaft.

We arrived for the manager's cocktail party at five o'clock. Josef and Martina were already sitting near the bar. We joined them for a few drinks.

»Du siehst nicht sehr gut aus«, sagte ich zu Josef.

"You don't look too good," I said to Josef.

»Er hat gestern Abend ein paar Iren in der Karaokebar kennengelernt«, sagte Martina. »Sie haben Bier getrunken und bis Mitternacht gesungen.«

"He met some Irish guys at the karaoke bar last night," said Martina. "They drank shots and sang songs until midnight."

»Und wir mussten heute wirklich früh für einen Tauchgang draußen am Riff aufstehen«, sagte Josef.

"And we had to get up really early for a dive out at the reef today," Josef added.

»Der Alkohol, das Tauchen, und das Boot, das auf dem Wasser

"The alcohol, the diving, and the boat bouncing up and down on the water made Josef very ill," Martina said.

Story 10

	auf- und abschaukelte,	machten	Josef	ganz	krank«,	sagte	Martina.
	aʊf ʊnt 'apʃaʊkəltə	'maxtən	'joːzɛf	gants	kʁaŋk	'zaktə	maʁ'tiːna
	it bobbed up and down	they made	Josef	quite	ill	she said	Martina

"They're probably still cleaning up the boat," Josef said.

»Wahrscheinlich	sind	sie	immer noch	dabei,	das	Boot
vaːʁˈʃaɪnlɪç	zɪnt	ziː	'ɪmɐ nɔx	da'baɪ	das	boːt
probably	they are	they	still	at it	the	boat

sauber zu machen«,	sagte	Josef.
'zaʊbɐ tsuː 'maxən	'zaktə	'joːzɛf
to clean up	he said	Josef

"The captain banned us from his boat for the rest of the week," Martina complained. "Now we can't go diving anymore."

»Der	Kapitän	hat	uns	aus	seinem	Boot	verbannt,	für	den	Rest	der
deːɐ	kapiˈtɛːn	hat	ʊns	aʊs	'zaɪnəm	boːt	fɛɐˈbant	fyːɐ	deːn	ʁɛst	deːɐ
the	captain	→	us	from	his	boat	← he banned	for	the	rest	of the

Woche«,	beschwerte	sich	Martina.	»Jetzt	können	wir	nicht	mehr
'vɔxə	bəˈʃveːɐtə	zɪç	maʁˈtiːna	jɛtst	'kœnən	viːɐ	nɪçt	meːɐ
week	she complained		Martina	now	we can	we	not	anymore

tauchen	gehen.«
'taʊxən	'geːən
to dive	to go

"Couldn't you hang your head over the side?" I asked.

»Hättest	du	deinen	Kopf	nicht	über	den	Bootsrand
'hɛtəst	duː	'daɪnən	kɔpf	nɪçt	'yːbɐ	deːn	'boːtsˌʁant
→	you	your	head	not	over	the	boat edge

hinauslehnen	können?«,	fragte	ich.
hɪˈnaʊsˌleːnən	'kœnən	'fʁaːktə	ɪç
← you could have leaned out		I asked	I

"I tried to, but I didn't make it."

»Ich	habe	es	versucht,	aber	nicht	geschafft.«
ɪç	'haːbə	ɛs	fɛɐˈzuːxt	'aːbɐ	nɪçt	gəˈʃaft
I	→→	it	← I tried	but	not	← I managed

"So what are you drinking now?" Ingrid asked.

»Also,	was	trinkst	du	jetzt?«,	fragte	Ingrid.
'alzo	vas	tʁɪŋkst	duː	jɛtst	'fʁaːktə	'ɪŋgʁɪt
so	what	you drink	you	now	she asked	Ingrid

"Just a beer. I'm hoping more alcohol will settle my stomach."

»Bloß	Bier.	Ich	hoffe,	mehr	Alkohol	wird	meinen	Magen
bloːs	biːɐ	ɪç	'hɔfə	meːɐ	'alkohoːl	vɪʁt	'maɪnən	'maːgən
just	beer	I	I hope	more	alcohol	it will	my	stomach

beruhigen.«
bəˈʁuːɪgən
to settle

"What did you guys do today?" asked Martina.

»Was	habt	ihr	heute	gemacht?«,	fragte	Martina.
vas	haːpt	iːɐ	'hɔɪtə	gəˈmaxt	'fʁaːktə	maʁˈtiːna
what	→	you	today	← you did	she asked	Martina

"Klaus learned how to put our rental car into reverse gear," Ingrid said proudly.

»Klaus	lernte,	wie	man	bei	unserem	Mietwagen	den
klaʊs	'lɛʁntə	viː	man	baɪ	'ʊnzəʁəm	'miːtˌvaːgən	deːn
Klaus	he learned	how	one	in	our	rental car	the

All Inclusive

Rückwärtsgang einlegt«, sagte Ingrid voller Stolz.
reverse gear he engages she said Ingrid full of pride

Josef und Martina schauten mich leicht befremdet an.
Josef and Martina they looked at me slightly strangely

Josef and Martina looked at me a little strangely.

»Wir sind nach Tulum gefahren, um die Ruinen zu sehen«, sagte ich. »Auf dem Weg dorthin hielten wir bei einem Geschäft an und ich parkte das Auto dem Geschäft zugewandt. Als wir wegfahren wollten, konnte ich beim Auto den Rückwärtsgang nicht einlegen.«

we to Tulum we drove in order to the ruins to to see I said I on the way there we stopped we at a store and I I parked the car to the store facing when we to drive off we wanted I could I with the car the reverse gear not to engage

"We drove to Tulum to see the ruins," I said. "On the way we stopped at a convenience store and I parked the car with the front facing the store. When we tried to leave I couldn't put the car into reverse."

»Warum nicht?«
why not

"Why not?"

»Ich wusste nicht, wie. Der Schalthebelkopf zeigte die Position des Rückwärtsgangs an, aber ich schaffte es nicht, den Schaltknüppel in diese Position zu bewegen.«

I I knew not how the shift knob it displayed the position of the reverse gear but I I managed it not the gear stick in this position to to move

"I didn't know how. The shift knob showed me where reverse was located but the stick wouldn't move into that position."

»Wir haben einen netten jungen Mann dafür bezahlt, es uns zu zeigen«, sagte Ingrid.

we a nice young man for it we paid it to show us she said Ingrid

"We paid a nice young man to show us," Ingrid said.

»Zehn Pesos, um uns zu zeigen, wie die Gänge geschaltet werden, und dreißig Pesos dafür, dass er mich nicht

ten pesos in order to to show us how the gears they are shifted and thirty pesos for it that he me not

"Ten pesos for showing us how to work the gears and thirty pesos for not laughing at me," I said.

121

Story 10

	auslacht«, sagte ich.
	ˈaʊsˌlaxt ˈzaktə ɪç
	he laughs at I said I

"Haven't you ever driven a manual transmission before?" Martina asked.

»Bist du vorher noch nie mit einem Handschaltgetriebe
bɪst du: ˈfoːɐheːɐ nɔx niː mɪt ˈaɪnəm ˈhantʃaltgəˌtʁiːbə
→ you previously never before with a manual transmission

gefahren?«, fragte Martina.
gəˈfaːʁən ˈfʁaːktə maʁˈtiːna
← you drove she asked Martina

"Yes, but this car had a little ring at the bottom of the shift knob. I had to pull up the ring to engage reverse gear," I said.

»Doch, aber dieses Auto hatte einen kleinen Ring unterhalb
dɔx ˈaːbɐ ˈdiːzəs ˈaʊto ˈhatə ˈaɪnən ˈklaɪnən ʁɪŋ ˈʊntɐhalp
yes but this car it had a small ring under

des Ganghebels. Ich musste den Ring hochziehen, um den
dɛs ˈgaŋˌheːbls ɪç ˈmʊstə deːn ʁɪŋ ˈhoxtsiːən ʊm deːn
the gear stick I I had to the ring to pull up in order to the

Rückwärtsgang einzulegen«, sagte ich.
ˈʁʏkvɛʁtsˌgaŋ ˈaɪntsuˌleːgn ˈzaktə ɪç
reverse gear to engage I said I

"That's a new trick," Josef said.

»Das ist ein neuer Trick«, sagte Josef.
das ɪst aɪn ˈnɔɪɐ tʁɪk ˈzaktə ˈjoːzɛf
that it is a new trick he said Josef

"Are you going to dinner at the buffet tonight?" Ingrid asked Martina.

»Geht ihr heute zum Abendessen ans Buffet?«, fragte Ingrid
geːt iːɐ ˈhɔɪtə tsʊm ˈaːbntˌɛsn ans bʏˈfeː ˈfʁaːktə ˈɪŋgʁɪt
you go you today to dinner at the buffet she asked Ingrid

Martina.
maʁˈtiːna
Martina

"We decided to order room service, in case Josef gets ill again. We'll probably see you tomorrow sometime."

»Wir haben beschlossen, den Zimmerservice zu nutzen, falls Josef
viːɐ ˈhaːbn bəˈʃlɔsn deːn ˈtsɪmɐˌsœʁvɪs tsuː ˈnʊtsən fals ˈjoːzɛf
we we decided the room service to to use in case Josef

wieder krank wird. Wir werden euch dann wahrscheinlich
ˈviːdɐ kʁaŋk vɪʁt viːɐ ˈveːɐdn ɔɪç dan vaːɐˈʃaɪnlɪç
again ill he becomes we we will you then probably

irgendwann morgen sehen.«
ˈɪʁgn̩tˈvan ˈmɔʁgn̩ ˈzeːən
sometime tomorrow to see

---— 3 —---

"What were you thinking?" Ingrid yelled at me.

»Was hast du dir denn dabei gedacht?«, schrie mich Ingrid an.
vas hast du: diːɐ dɛn daˈbaɪ gəˈdaxt ʃʁiː mɪç ˈɪŋgʁɪt an
what → ! with it ← you thought she yelled at → me Ingrid ←

"It wasn't my fault," I said.

»Es war nicht meine Schuld«, sagte ich.
ɛs vaːɐ nɪçt ˈmaɪnə ʃʊlt ˈzaktə ɪç
it it was not my fault I said I

All Inclusive

»Du weißt doch nicht einmal, wie man mit einem Spielzeugboot in unserer Badewanne segelt. Wie kommst du darauf, eines der Segelboote des Resorts in einen aufgewühlten Ozean zu steuern?«

"You don't even know how to sail a toy boat in our tub. Why would you take out one of the resort sailboats into a choppy ocean?"

»Es hat so leicht ausgeschaut. Die anderen Feriengäste schienen alle mit ihren Segelbooten zurechtzukommen.«

"It looked so easy. All the other guests seemed to be able to handle the sailboats."

»Aber du hast es geschafft, dein Boot komplett zu zerstören.«

"But you somehow wrecked your boat."

»Die Leute, die an dem Wassersporttresen arbeiten, waren sehr freundlich. Niemand hat mich angeschrien. Weshalb bist du so sauer?«

"The people working at the water sports counter were very friendly. Nobody screamed at me. How come you are so angry?"

»Weil wir dem Resort ein neues Segel bezahlen müssen.«

"Because we have to pay the resort for a new sail."

»Können die das Loch nicht einfach wieder zunähen?«

"Can't they just sew up the hole in the sail?"

»Dieses Loch war größer als unser Mietwagen.«

"That hole was bigger than our rental car."

Ingrid spazierte ein paar Stunden zuvor an der Küste entlang, als sie auf mein armes Segelboot stieß, welches flach im

Ingrid was walking down the beach a few hours earlier when she came upon my poor sailboat, laying flat in the water. I was standing on the jetty, watching the water sports employees unhook the sail from the mast. The sail was impaled on a large pole embedded in the rocks on the jetty. The two girls with the polished nails, tattoos, and

123

Story 10

tiny bathing suits were standing next to me. Ingrid figured correctly that I had taken the ladies on a pleasure ride that ended badly. She has been mad at me ever since.

Wasser lag. Ich stand am Steg und sah den Mitarbeitern der
ˈvasɐ laːk ɪç ʃtant am ʃteːk ʊnt zaː deːn ˈmɪtaʁˌbaɪtɐn deːɐ
water it lay I I stood on the jetty and I watched→ the employees of the

Wassersportabteilung zu, wie sie das Segel vom Mast entfernten.
ˈvasɐʃpɔʁtapˈtaɪlʊŋ tsuː viː ziː das ˈzeːɡl̩ fɔm mast ɛntˈfɛʁntən
water sports department ← as they the sail from the mast they removed

Aufgespießt an einer langen Stange, lag das Segel zwischen den
ˈaʊfɡəˌʃpiːst an ˈaɪnɐ ˈlaŋən ˈʃtaŋə laːk das ˈzeːɡl̩ ˈtsvɪʃən deːn
impaled by a long pole it lay the sail between the

Felsen beim Bootssteg. Die zwei Mädchen mit den lackierten
ˈfɛlzən baɪm ˈboːtsˌʃteːk diː tsvaɪ ˈmɛːtçən mɪt deːn laˈkiːɐtn̩
rocks near the landing stage the two girls with the polished

Fingernägeln, Tätowierungen und knappen Badeanzügen standen
ˈfɪŋɐˌnɛːɡl̩n tɛtoˈviːʁʊŋən ʊnt ˈknapən ˈbaːdəˌantsyːɡn̩ ˈʃtandən
fingernails tattoos and tiny swimsuits they stood

neben mir. Ingrid erkannte richtigerweise, dass ich die Damen
ˈneːbən miːɐ ˈɪŋɡʁɪt ɛɐˈkantə ˈʁɪçtɪɡɐˌvaɪzə das ɪç diː ˈdaːmən
next to me Ingrid she figured correctly that I the ladies

auf eine Vergnügungsfahrt mitgenommen hatte, eine Fahrt, die
aʊf ˈaɪnə fɛɐˈɡnyːɡʊŋsˌfaːɐt ˈmɪtɡəˌnɔmən ˈhatə ˈaɪnə faːɐt diː
on a joyride I had taken for a ride a ride that

unglücklich endete. Seitdem ist sie sauer auf mich.
ˈʊnˌɡlʏklɪç ˈɛndətə zaɪtˈdeːm ɪst ziː ˈzaʊɐ aʊf mɪç
unfortunately it ended ever since she is she angry at me

She smacked me in the back of the head. "Why did you tell the water sports staff that you were an expert sailor?"

Sie schlug mir auf den Hinterkopf. »Warum hast du den Leuten
ziː ʃluːk miːɐ aʊf deːn ˈhɪntɐˌkɔpf vaˈʁʊm hast duː deːn ˈlɔɪtn̩
she she smacked me on the back of the head why → you the people

der Wassersportabteilung gesagt, dass du ein erfahrener Segler
deːɐ ˈvasɐʃpɔʁtapˈtaɪlʊŋ ɡəˈzaːkt das duː aɪn ɛɐˈfaːʁənɐ ˈzeːɡlɐ
of the water sports department ←you told that you an expert sailor

seist?«
zaɪst
you are

"I wanted to impress the girls," I admitted.

»Ich wollte die Mädchen beeindrucken«, gab ich zu.
ɪç ˈvɔltə diː ˈmɛːtçən bəˈaɪnˌdʁʊkən ɡaːp ɪç tsuː
I I wanted the girls to impress I admitted→ I ←

"And why were you sailing with two girls who are too young to vote, instead of with your wife?"

»Und warum bist du mit zwei Mädchen, die noch nicht mal
ʊnt vaˈʁʊm bɪst duː mɪt tsvaɪ ˈmɛːtçən diː nɔx nɪçt maːl
and why → you with two girls who not yet !

wählen dürfen, Segeln gegangen, anstatt mit deiner Frau?«
ˈvɛːlən ˈdʏʁfn̩ ˈzeːɡl̩n ɡəˈɡaŋən anˈʃtat mɪt ˈdaɪnɐ fʁaʊ
to vote they are allowed ←you went sailing instead of with your wife

"You wouldn't have gone unless we asked one of the staff members to help me sail the boat," I muttered.

»Du wärst nicht gegangen, außer wir hätten jemanden vom
duː vɛːɐst nɪçt ɡəˈɡaŋən ˈaʊsɐ viːɐ ˈhɛtn̩ ˈjeːmandən fɔm
you you would not have gone unless we → someone from the

124

All Inclusive

Personal gebeten, mir beim Segeln zu helfen«,
(pɛʁzoˈnaːl / ɡəˈbeːtən / miːɐ̯ / baɪ̯m / ˈzeːɡl̩n / tsuː / ˈhɛlfən)
staff / ←we would have asked / me / with the / sailing / to / to help

murmelte ich vor mich hin.
(ˈmʊʁml̩tə / ɪç / foːɐ̯ / mɪç / hɪn)
I muttered to myself

»Na so etwas. Ich glaube, du hattest die Hilfe nötig,
(na zoː ˈɛtvas / ɪç / ˈɡlaʊ̯bə / duː / ˈhatəst / diː / ˈhɪlfə / ˈnøːtɪç)
such a thing / I / I think / you / you needed→ / the / help / ←

oder etwa nicht?«
(ˈoːdɐ ˈɛtva nɪçt)
didn't you

"Well duh. I guess you needed the help, didn't you."

Glücklicherweise saßen wir an der Theke der zentralen Bar im
(ɡlʏklɪçɐˈvaɪ̯zə / ˈzaːsən / viːɐ̯ / an / deːɐ̯ / ˈteːkə / deːɐ̯ / tsɛnˈtʁaːlən / baːɐ̯ / ɪm)
luckily / we sat / we / at / the / counter / of the / main / bar / in the

Resort. In zwei Minuten sollte ein Kurs beginnen. Wir sollten
(ʁɪˈzoːɐ̯ / ɪn / tsvaɪ̯ / mɪˈnuːtən / ˈzɔltə / aɪ̯n / kʊʁs / bəˈɡɪnən / viːɐ̯ / ˈzɔltn̩)
resort / in / two / minutes / it should / a / lesson / it begins / we / we would

lernen, wie man Martinis macht.
(ˈlɛʁnən / viː / man / maʁˈtiːnɪs / maxt)
to learn / how / one / martinis / he makes

Luckily we were sitting at the main bar inside the resort. In two minutes a class was starting. We were going to learn how to make martinis.

»Lass uns die Vergangenheit vergessen«, sagte ich zu Ingrid. »Ich
(las ʊns / diː / fɛɐ̯ˈɡaŋənhaɪ̯t / fɛɐ̯ˈɡɛsn̩ / ˈzaktə / ɪç / tsuː / ˈɪŋɡʁɪt / ɪç)
let's / the / past / to forget / I said / I / to / Ingrid / I

kann es nicht abwarten zu lernen, wie man Martinis macht.«
(kan / ɛs / nɪçt / ˈapˌvaʁtən / tsuː / ˈlɛʁnən / viː / man / maʁˈtiːnɪs / maxt)
I can / it / not / to wait / to / to learn / how / one / martinis / he makes

"Let's forget about the past," I said to Ingrid. "I can't wait to learn how to make martinis."

Sie schlug mir noch einmal auf den Hinterkopf, um mir
(ziː / ʃluːk / miːɐ̯ / nɔx / ˈaɪ̯nmaːl / aʊ̯f / deːn / ˈhɪntɐˌkɔpf / ʊm / miːɐ̯)
she / she smacked / me / again / on / the / back of the head / in order to / to me

sozusagen Glück zu wünschen. Der Klaps war jedoch nicht so
(zoːtsuˈzaːɡn̩ / ɡlʏk / tsuː / ˈvʏnʃən / deːɐ̯ / klaps / vaːɐ̯ / jeˈdɔx / nɪçt / zoː)
so to say / luck / to / to wish / the / smack / it was / however / not / so

heftig wie beim letzten Mal, was ich so auslegte, dass sie
(ˈhɛftɪç / viː / baɪ̯m / ˈlɛtstən / maːl / vas / ɪç / zoː / ˈaʊ̯sˌleːktə / das / ziː)
hard / as / with the / last / time / which / I / thus / I interpreted / that / she

nicht mehr so böse auf mich sei. Ich hoffte, nach ein paar
(nɪçt meːɐ̯ / zoː / ˈbøːzə / aʊ̯f / mɪç / zaɪ̯ / ɪç / ˈhɔftə / naːx / aɪ̯n paːɐ̯)
no longer / so / angry / at / me / she was / I / I hoped / after / a few

Martinis würde sie den ganzen Vorfall vergessen.
(maʁˈtiːnɪs / ˈvʏʁdə / ziː / deːn / ˈɡantsən / ˈfoːɐ̯fal / fɛɐ̯ˈɡɛsn̩)
minutes / she would / she / the / whole / incident / to forget

She smacked me in the back of the head one more time for good luck. But not as hard as the last smack, which I interpreted to mean that she was not as angry. I hoped that after she had a few martinis, she would forget about this whole episode.

Alle Plätze in der Bar waren belegt. Um vier Uhr erschien Otto
(ˈalə / ˈplɛtsə / ɪn / deːɐ̯ / baːɐ̯ / ˈvaːʁən / bəˈleːkt / ʊm / fiːɐ̯ uːɐ̯ / ɛɐ̯ˈʃiːn / ˈɔto)
all / seats / in / the / bar / they were / occupied / at / four o'clock / it appeared / Otto

All the seats at the bar were filled. At four o'clock, Otto appeared next to Lukas, our favorite bartender.

125

Story 10

	mit Lukas, unserem Lieblingsbarkeeper.
	mɪt ˈluːkas ˈʊnzɐʁəm ˈliːplɪŋsˈbaːɐ̯ˌkiːpɐ
	with Lukas our favorite bartender

"Is everyone ready to learn about martinis?" Otto yelled.

»Seid ihr alle bereit, etwas über Martinis zu lernen?«, schrie Otto.
zaɪt iːɐ ˈalə bəˈʁaɪt ˈɛtvas ˈyːbɐ maʁˈtiːnis tsuː ˈlɛʁnən ʃʁiː ˈɔto
are you you all ready something about martinis to to learn he yelled Otto

"Yes!" we all yelled back.

»Jawohl!«, brüllten wir alle zurück.
jaˈvoːl ˈbʁʏltən viːɐ ˈalə tsuˈʁʏk
yes! we yelled back→ we all ←

He walked down the length of the bar. When he saw Ingrid, he picked up her hand and kissed the back of her hand.

Er ging an der ganzen Bar entlang. Als er Ingrid sah,
eːɐ gɪŋ an deːɐ ˈgantsən baːɐ ɛntˈlaŋ als eːɐ ˈɪŋgʁɪt zaː
he he walked along→ on the whole bar ← when he Ingrid he saw

hob er ihre Hand auf und küsste ihren Handrücken.
hoːp eːɐ ˈiːʁə hant aʊf ʊnt ˈkʏstə ˈiːʁən ˈhantˌʁʏkn
he picked up→ he her hand ← and he kissed her back of her hand

"Are all aerobics instructors this friendly?" I asked.

»Sind alle Aerobic-Lehrer so freundlich?«, fragte ich.
zɪnt ˈalə ɛˈʁoːbɪkˈleːʁɐ zoː ˈfʁɔɪntlɪç ˈfʁaːktə ɪç
are they all aerobics instructors so friendly I asked I

"It was a kiss of pity. He heard about the hopeless man I married."

»Das war ein Kuss aus Mitleid. Er hat von dem hoffnungslosen
das vaːɐ aɪn kʊs aʊs ˈmɪtˌlaɪt eːɐ hat fɔn deːm ˈhɔfnʊŋsloːzən
that it was a kiss out of pity he → of the hopeless

Mann gehört, mit dem ich verheiratet bin.«
man gəˈhøːɐ̯t mɪt deːm ɪç fɛɐ̯ˈhaɪʁaːtət bɪn
man ←he heard with whom I married I am

"Let's focus on the martinis," I said.

»Wir sollten uns auf die Martinis konzentrieren«, sagte ich.
viːɐ ˈzɔltən ʊns aʊf diː maʁˈtiːnis kɔntsɛnˈtʁiːʁən ˈzaktə ɪç
we should on the martinis to focus I said I

We learned how to make more martinis than I knew existed. Otto did not kiss Ingrid's hand again. I think he saw me glowering at him.

Wir lernten, eine Vielfalt an Martinis zuzubereiten, die ich nicht
viːɐ ˈlɛʁntən ˈaɪnə ˈfiːlˌfalt an maʁˈtiːnis ˈtsuːtsubəˌʁaɪtn diː ɪç nɪçt
we we learned a variety of martinis to prepare that I not

für möglich hielt. Otto gab Ingrid keinen Handkuss mehr. Ich
fyːɐ ˈmøːklɪç hiːlt ˈɔto gaːp ˈɪŋgʁɪt ˈkaɪnən ˈhantkʊs meːɐ ɪç
I considered possible Otto he gave Ingrid not a hand kiss more I

glaube, er bemerkte meinen finsteren Blick.
ˈglaʊbə eːɐ bəˈmɛʁktə ˈmaɪnən ˈfɪnstəʁən blɪk
I think he he noticed my glowering look

All Inclusive

»Komm, wir paddeln mit dem Kajak hinunter zum nächsten Resort«, sagte Josef zu mir.

"Let's paddle in a kayak down to the next resort," Josef said to me.

»Ich sitze ganz gerne hier am Ozean und schlürfe diese Piña Colada«, sagte ich. »Wieso sollte ich mich zu so etwas Schweißtreibendem hinreißen lassen?«

"I like sitting here by the ocean sipping this piña colada," I said. "Why would I want to work up a sweat?"

»Ich habe gehört, dass man in diesem Resort nackt sein darf. Dann können wir all die nackten Leute abchecken.«

"I heard that clothing is optional at that resort. We can check out all the naked people."

»Wer hat dir das gesagt?«

"Who told you?"

»Die Jungs mit den Cowboyhüten«, sagte Josef.

"The guys with the cowboy hats," Josef said.

»Die sind doch seit vier Tagen nicht aus dem Pool herausgekommen. Woher sollten die das wissen?«

"They haven't gotten out of the pool in four days. How would they know?"

»Ihre Frauen arbeiten beim Reisebüro. Sie wissen alles über diese Gegend.«

"Their wives work at a travel agency. They know everything about this area."

»Können wir nicht einfach die Küste hinuntergehen?«

"Can't we just walk down the beach?"

Story 10

"There is a big fence blocking the way," Josef said.

»Es gibt da einen großen Zaun, der den Weg versperrt«, sagte Josef.
ɛs giːpt daː ˈaɪnən ˈɡʁoːsən tsaʊn deːɐ deːn veːk fɛɐˈʃpɛʁt ˈzaktə ˈjoːzɛf
there is there a big fence that the way it blocks he said Josef

I put my drink down. "A little exercise wouldn't hurt me."

Ich stellte meinen Drink hin. »Ein wenig Bewegung würde mir nicht schaden.«
ɪç ˈʃtɛltə ˈmaɪnən dʁɪŋk hɪn aɪn ˈveːnɪç bəˈveːɡʊŋ ˈvʏʁdə miːɐ nɪçt ˈʃaːdən
I I put down→ my drink ← a little exercise it would me not to hurt

Ten minutes later Josef and I were paddling our kayaks furiously toward the next resort. When we got there, we had a major disappointment.

Zehn Minuten später paddelten Josef und ich unsere Kajaks wie besessen in Richtung des benachbarten Resorts. Als wir dort ankamen, erlebten wir eine große Enttäuschung.
tseːn mɪˈnuːtən ˈʃpɛːtɐ ˈpadltn ˈjoːzɛf ʊnt ɪç ˈʊnzəʁə ˈkaːjaks viː bəˈzɛsən ɪn ˈʁɪçtʊŋ dɛs bəˈnaxbaːɐtn ʁɪˈzoːɐs als viːɐ dɔʁt ˈanˌkaːmən ɛɐˈleːptən viːɐ ˈaɪnə ˈɡʁoːsə ɛntˈtɔʏʃʊŋ
ten minutes later we paddled Josef and I our kayaks furiously in direction of the neighboring resorts when we there we arrived we experienced we a major disappointment

"They have a big screen set up in front of the naked part of the beach," Josef said.

»Die haben einen großen Sichtschutz genau vor dem FKK-Strand aufgebaut«, sagte Josef.
diː ˈhaːbn ˈaɪnən ˈɡʁoːsən ˈzɪçtʃʊts ɡəˈnaʊ foːɐ deːm ɛfkaːˈkaː-ʃtʁant ˈaʊfɡəˌbaʊt ˈzaktə ˈjoːzɛf
they → a big screen right in front of the nudist beach ←they built he said Josef

"No fair. I busted a gut paddling against the wind to get down here and now I can't see any skin," I added.

»Das ist ungerecht. Um bis hierher gegen den Wind zu paddeln, habe ich mich totgeschuftet und jetzt sehe ich kein bisschen nackte Haut«, fügte ich hinzu.
das ɪst ˈʊnɡəˌʁɛçt ʊm bɪs ˈhiːɐˈheːɐ ˈɡeːɡən deːn vɪnt tsuː ˈpadln ˈhaːbə ɪç mɪç ˈtoːtɡəˌʃʊftət ʊnt jɛtst ˈzeːə ɪç kaɪn ˈbɪsçən ˈnaktə haʊt ˈfyːktə ɪç hɪnˈtsuː
that it is unfair up to here against the wind to to paddle I worked myself to death and now I see I none naked skin I added→ I ←

We sat in the water, thirty meters from shore, bobbing up and down in our kayaks.

Wir saßen im Wasser, dreißig Meter vom Strand entfernt, und schaukelten in unseren Kajaks auf und ab.
viːɐ ˈzaːsən ɪm ˈvasɐ ˈdʁaɪsɪç ˈmeːtɐ fɔm ʃtʁant ɛntˈfɛɐnt ʊnt ˈʃaʊkltn ɪn ˈʊnzəʁən ˈkaːjaks aʊf ʊnt ap
we we sat in the water thirty meter from the beach away and we bobbed up and down→ in our kayaks ←

"Let's land the kayaks," I suggested.

»Komm, ziehen wir die Kajaks an Land«, schlug ich vor.
kɔm ˈtsiːən viːɐ diː ˈkaːjaks an lant ʃluːk ɪç foːɐ
come we pull we the kayaks on land I suggested→ I ←

All Inclusive

Josef zögerte noch.
'jo:zɛf 'tsø:gɐtə nɔx
Josef he hesitated still

Josef hesitated.

»Ich bin nicht sicher, dass ich mich ausziehen will«, sagte er.
ɪç bɪn nɪçt 'zɪçɐ das ɪç mɪç 'aʊsˌtsi:ən vɪl 'zaktə e:ɐ
I I am not sure that I to take my clothes off I want he said he

"I'm not sure I want to get naked," he said.

»Es sind nicht alle nackt in dem Resort. Die Leute vor dem
ɛs zɪnt nɪçt 'alə nakt ɪn de:m ʁɪ'zo:ɐ di: 'lɔɪtə fo:ɐ de:m
they are not everyone naked at the resort the people in front of the

Sichtschutz tragen Badeanzüge.«
'zɪçtʃʊts 'tʁa:gən 'ba:dəˌantsy:gə
screen they wear swimsuits

"Not everyone at the resort is naked. The people in front of the screen are wearing bathing suits."

Ich konnte sehen wie Josef überlegte.
ɪç 'kɔntə 'ze:ən vi: 'jo:zɛf y:bɐ'le:ktə
I I could to see how Josef he contemplated

I could see Josef thinking things over.

»Da drüben am Strand neben den Stühlen liegt schon ein
da: 'dʁy:bən am 'ʃtʁant 'ne:bn de:n 'ʃty:lən li:kt ʃo:n am
over there on the beach by the chairs it lies already a

Zweierkajak«, sagte ich. »Wir können unsere gleich daneben
'tsvaɪɐˌka:jak 'zaktə ɪç vi:ɐ 'kœnən 'ʊnzɐə glaɪç da'ne:bən
double kayak I said I we we can ours right next to it

hinziehen.«
'hɪnˌtsi:ən
to pull

"There's a double kayak pulled up on the beach over by those chairs," I said. "We can pull ours right next to that one."

»Das Kajak ist von unserem Resort«, sagte Josef. »Es hat
das 'ka:jak ɪst fɔn 'ʊnzɐəm ʁɪ'zo:ɐ 'zaktə 'jo:zɛf ɛs hat
the kayak it is from our resort he said Josef it it has

dieselben Markierungen und dieselbe Farbe.«
di:'zɛlbən maʁ'ki:ʁʊŋən ʊnt di:'zɛlbə 'faʁbə
the same markings and the same color

"That kayak is from our resort," Josef said. "It has the same markings and color."

»Siehst du, wir sind nicht die einzigen, die diese Idee haben. Es
zi:st du: vi:ɐ zɪnt nɪçt di: 'aɪntsɪgən di: 'di:zə i'de: 'ha:bn ɛs
you see you we we are not the only who this idea who have it

wird schon gut gehen. Komm, los geht's!«
vɪʁt ʃo:n gu:t 'ge:ən kɔm lo:s ge:ts
it will all right to go come let's go

"You see, we're not the only ones with this idea. It will be fine. Come on, let's go!"

Es dauerte noch weitere fünf Minuten, bis Josef den nötigen
ɛs 'daʊɐtə nɔx 'vaɪtɐə fʏnf mɪ'nu:tən bɪs 'jo:zɛf de:n 'nø:tɪgən
it it took yet another five minutes until Josef the necessary

Mut fand, sein Kajak an Land zu bringen.
mʊt fant zaɪn 'ka:jak an lant tsu: 'bʁɪŋən
courage he found his kayak on land to to bring

It took five more minutes for Josef to get brave enough to land his kayak.

Story 10

"I wish I'd had a few more drinks," he said as we pulled our kayaks out of the water.

»Ich wünschte, ich hätte etwas mehr getrunken«, sagte er, als wir unsere Kajaks aus dem Wasser zogen.

"So, do we take off our suits or leave them on?" I asked.

»Also, sollen wir unsere Badehosen ausziehen oder anlassen?«, fragte ich.

After some debate, we decided to leave our suits on. We sauntered behind the screen that had been set up on the beach. There were ten or fifteen old men and old ladies lying on sun loungers. Some had bathing suits, but most were completely naked.

Nach einigem Hin und Her entschieden wir uns, die Badehosen anzulassen. Wir schlenderten hinter dem Sichtschutz herum, der am Strand aufgebaut war. Da lagen zehn oder fünfzehn alte Männer und Damen auf ihren Liegestühlen. Einige hatten Badeanzüge an, aber die meisten waren vollkommen nackt.

"Look at all the wrinkles on those people," Josef whispered.

»Schau dir bloß all die Falten dieser Leute an«, flüsterte Josef.

Older people do not look very sexy when they are naked. I made a mental note to wear lots of clothes when I turn seventy.

Ältere Menschen wirken nicht sehr sexy, wenn sie nackt sind. Ich machte mir im Geiste eine Notiz davon, möglichst viel anzuziehen, wenn ich einmal siebzig bin.

"Let's try the hot tub," I said.

»Komm, wir probieren den Whirlpool aus«, sagte ich.

We walked over to a large hot tub that was located just off the beach. There were at least twenty people already in

Wir gingen zu einem großen Whirlpool, der gleich am Strand

All Inclusive

lag, hinüber. Darin waren mindestens schon zwanzig Leute, die sich unterhielten und entspannten. Alle waren noch ziemlich faltenfrei. Die meisten von ihnen waren nackt. Mir fielen ein paar außerordentlich gutaussehende Leute auf.

the hot tub, talking and relaxing. They all looked fairly wrinkle free. Most of them were naked. I noticed a few exceptional looking people.

»Das wird der Hammer!«, sagte ich, als wir leger ins Wasser stiegen und uns hinsetzten.

"This is going to be so good!" I said as we casually entered the water and sat down.

Als ich anfing, die anderen Badegäste zu mustern, begann Josef plötzlich, an meine Schulter zu klopfen.

As I started to check out our fellow bathers, Josef started poking me on the shoulder.

»Was ist los?«, sagte ich, indem ich mich ihm zuwandte.

"What?" I said, as I looked over at him.

Er starrte auf zwei Frauen, die mit entblößten Brüsten ungefähr drei Meter vom Whirlpool entfernt in der Sonne saßen. Ich folgte seinem Blick und musste tief Luft holen. Ingrid und Martina hielten Drinks in den Händen und starrten uns entgegen.

He was staring at two bare chested women sitting in the sun about three meters from the hot tub. I followed his eyes and took a big gulp of air. Ingrid and Martina were holding drinks and staring back at us.

———5———

»Du bist so ein Perversling«, sagte Ingrid zu mir, als unser

"You are such a pervert," Ingrid said to me as our plane took off from the Cancun airport.

131

Story 10

	Flugzeug	vom	Flughafen	in	Cancun	abhob.
	ˈfluːkˌtsɔɪk	fɔm	ˈfluːkˌhaːfən	ɪn	kanˈkʊn	ˈapho:p
	airplane	from the	airport	in	Cancun	it took off

"Wait a minute. You were there, too. Topless, I might add."

»Moment mal. Du warst schließlich auch dort. Oben ohne, wenn ich hinzufügen darf.«
moˈmɛnt maːl duː vaːɐst ˈʃliːslɪç aʊx dɔɐt ˈoːbən ˈoːnə vɛn ɪç hɪnˈtsuːˌfyːɡn̩ daɐf
moment ! you you were in the end also there topless if I to add I may

"I went there to work on my tan. You just wanted to see naked girls."

»Ich ging nur zum Bräunen dorthin. Du wolltest nur nackte Mädchen sehen.«
ɪç ɡɪŋ nuːɐ tsʊm ˈbʁɔʏnən ˈdɔɐthɪn duː ˈvɔltɛst nuːɐ ˈnaktə ˈmɛːtçən ˈzeːən
I I went only to the tanning there you you wanted just naked girls to see

"Yesterday you thought it was pretty funny."

»Gestern warst du noch der Meinung, dass es ganz lustig wäre.«
ˈɡəstɐn vaːɐst duː nɔx deːɐ ˈmaɪnʊŋ das ɛs ɡants ˈlʊstɪç ˈvɛːʁə
yesterday you were you still of the opinion that it quite funny it was

She giggled and kissed my cheek. "I'm just teasing you."

Sie kicherte und küsste mich auf die Wange. »Ich ärgere dich nur.«
ziː ˈkɪçɐtə ʊnt ˈkʏstə mɪç aʊf diː ˈvaŋə ɪç ˈɛʁɡəʁə dɪç nuːɐ
she she giggled and she kissed me on the cheek I I tease you just

"You didn't mind Josef seeing your chest?" I asked.

»Hat es dir nichts ausgemacht, dass Josef deine Brust gesehen hat?«, fragte ich.
hat ɛs diːɐ nɪçts ˈaʊsɡəˌmaxt das ˈjoːzɛf ˈdaɪnə bʁʊst ɡəˈzeːən hat ˈfʁaːktə ɪç
→ it you not ← it bothered that Josef your chest he saw I asked I

"Not really. I lost my shyness when I was breast feeding the kids."

»Eigentlich nicht. Ich habe meine Scheu verloren, als ich meine Kinder gestillt habe.«
ˈaɪɡəntlɪç nɪçt ɪç ˈhaːbə ˈmaɪnə ʃɔɪ fɛɐˈloːʁən als ɪç ˈmaɪnə ˈkɪndɐ ɡəˈʃtɪlt ˈhaːbə
not really I → my shyness ← I lost when I my kids I breast fed

"Martina looked very nice without her bikini top," I said.

»Martina sah sehr hübsch aus ohne ihr Bikinioberteil«, sagte ich.
maɐˈtiːna zaː zeːɐ hypʃ aʊs ˈoːnə iːɐ biˈkiːniˌoːbɐˌtaɪl ˈzaktə ɪç
Martina she looked → very nice ← without her bikini top I said I

132

All Inclusive

Ingrid	lachte	und	schlug	mich	auf	den	Arm.	Meine	Frau
'ɪŋɡʁɪt	'laxtə	ʊnt	ʃluːk	mɪç	aʊf	deːn	aʁm	'maɪnə	fʁaʊ
Ingrid	she laughed	and	she punched	me	on	the	arm	my	wife

Ingrid laughed and punched me in the arm. My wife had hit me more times this week than the entire rest of our married life.

schlug	mich	diese	Woche	öfter	als	die	ganze	übrige	Zeit
ʃluːk	mɪç	'diːzə	'vɔxə	'œftɐ	als	diː	'ɡantsə	'yːbʁɪɡə	tsaɪt
she hit	me	this	week	more often	than	the	entire	remaining	time

unserer	Ehe.
'ʊnzəʁɐ	'eːə
our	marriage

Ich	lehnte	mich	in	meinem	Sitz	zurück	und	blickte	aus	dem
ɪç	'leːntə	mɪç	ɪn	'maɪnəm	zɪts	tsu'ʁʏk	ʊnt	'blɪktə	aʊs	deːm
I	I leaned back →		in	my	seat	←	and	I looked	out of	the

I sat back in my seat and looked out the window. The Yucatan Peninsula receded from my view as the plane headed out over the Gulf of Mexico.

Fenster.	Die	Halbinsel	Yucatan	verschwand	aus	meinem	Blickfeld,
'fɛnstɐ	diː	'halpˌɪnzl̩	juka'tan	fɛɐ'ʃvant	aʊs	'maɪnəm	'blɪkˌfɛlt
window	the	peninsula	Yucatan	it disappeared	from	my	field of view

als	sich	das	Flugzeug	in	Richtung	Golf	von	Mexiko	entfernte.
als	zɪç	das	'fluːkˌtsɔɪk	ɪn	'ʁɪçtʊŋ	ɡɔlf	fɔn	'mɛksiko:	ɛnt'fɛʁntə
as	→	the	airplane	in	direction	gulf	of	Mexico	←it departed

»Trotz	all	der	verrückten	Sachen,	die	so	passierten,	war	es	ein
tʁɔts	al	deːɐ	fɛɐ'ʁʏktn̩	'zaxən	diː	zoː	pa'siːɐtən	vaːɐ	ɛs	aɪn
despite	all	the	crazy	things	that	so	they happened	it was	it	a

"It was a pretty good vacation, despite all the crazy things that happened," I said.

ganz	netter	Urlaub«,	sagte	ich.
ɡants	'nɛtɐ	'uːɐˌlaup	'zaktə	ɪç
quite	nice	vacation	I said	I

STORY 11

Murder Mystery in L.A.

»Das ist eine schlechte Idee«, schreie ich in Karls Ohr.
das ist 'aɪnə 'ʃlɛçtə i'de: ʃʁaɪə ɪç ɪn kaʁls o:ɐ
that it is a bad idea I yell I into Karl's ear

"This is a bad idea," I yell into Karl's ear.

»In einer Bar etwas trinken?«, fragt er.
ɪn 'aɪnɐ ba:ɐ 'ɛtvas 'tʁɪŋkn fʁa:kt e:ɐ
in a bar something to drink he asks he

"Drinking in a bar?" he asks.

»In einer Bar etwas trinken macht mir nichts aus«, sage ich ihm.
ɪn 'aɪnɐ ba:ɐ 'ɛtvas 'tʁɪŋkn maxt mi:ɐ nɪçts aʊs 'za:gə ɪç i:m
in a bar something to drink I don't mind I tell I him

"I don't mind drinking in a bar," I tell him. "Just not this bar."

»Nur nicht in dieser Bar.«
nu:ɐ nɪçt ɪn 'di:zɐ ba:ɐ
just not in this bar

Ernst kommt mit zwei Bier und einem Glas Wein für mich zurück.
ɛʁnst kɔmt mɪt tsvaɪ bi:ɐ ʊnt 'aɪnəm gla:s vaɪn fy:ɐ mɪç tsu'ʁʏk
Ernst he comes back→ with two beer and a glass wine for me ←

Ernst comes back with two beers and a glass of wine for me.

»Da sind jede Menge Leute mit großen Plastik-Käsedreiecken auf ihren Köpfen«, brüllt er.
da: zɪnt 'je:də 'mɛŋə 'lɔɪtə mɪt 'gʁo:sən 'plastɪk-'kɛ:zə,dʁai̯ˌɛkn aʊf 'i:ʁən 'kœpfən bʁʏlt e:ɐ
there they are loads of people with big plastic cheese wedges on their heads he yells he

"There are a lot of people with big plastic cheese wedges on their heads," he yells.

Eine Band bestehend aus Jugendlichen ist auf der Bühne und macht mehr Lärm, als mein Trommelfell ertragen kann. Mir ist leicht schwindelig bei dem Sound. Es fällt schwer, den Worten der anderen zu folgen.
'aɪnə bant bə'ʃte:ənt aʊs 'ju:gəntlɪçn ɪst aʊf de:ɐ 'by:nə ʊnt maxt me:ɐ lɛʁm als maɪn 'tʁɔml̩ˌfɛl ɛɐ'tʁa:gn kan mi:ɐ ɪst laɪçt 'ʃvɪndəlɪç baɪ de:m zaʊnt ɛs fɛlt ʃve:ɐ de:n 'vɔʁtn de:ɐ 'andəʁən tsu: 'fɔlgn
a band composed of teenagers it is on the stage and it makes more noise than my eardrum to stand they can to me it is slightly dizzy by the sound it it is difficult the words of the others to to follow

A band of teenagers on stage is making more noise than my eardrums can handle. I feel slightly dizzy with the sound. It's hard to hear anyone talking.

135

Story 11

"That's why I don't want to drink in this bar," I yell back. "Let's find a neutral site."

»Gerade deshalb will ich in dieser Bar nichts trinken«, schreie ich zurück. »Lasst uns einen neutraleren Ort aufsuchen.«

Twenty minutes later we walk through the warm night air of California. We are trying to find a bar that isn't packed with people from the state of Wisconsin.

Zwanzig Minuten später spazieren wir durch die warme Abendluft von Kalifornien. Wir versuchen, eine Bar zu finden, die nicht mit Leuten aus Wisconsin überfüllt ist.

"Why do they always wear those fake plastic cheese wedges on their heads before a big football game?" I ask.

»Warum müssen die immer vor einem großen Footballspiel diese künstlichen Plastik-Käsedreiecke auf dem Kopf tragen?«, frage ich.

"What?" Karl and Ernst say. Our ears are still ringing from the loud noises the band was making.

»Was?«, sagen Karl und Ernst. Wir haben immer noch Ohrensausen von dem Krach, den die Band gemacht hat.

"I said I'm too old to listen to bad rock and roll anymore," I yell at them.

»Ich sagte, ich bin zu alt dafür, um mir schlechten Rock 'n' Roll anzuhören«, rufe ich ihnen zu.

The three of us are vacationing with our wives in Los Angeles for a week. The kids are home with their grandparents. Tonight, the ladies were too tired to go out after dinner. Karl, Ernst, and I decided to hit the bars and have some fun. We didn't realize that the University of Wisconsin football team is playing the University of California tomorrow. Half the state

Wir drei machen alle mit unseren Frauen eine Woche Ferien in Los Angeles. Die Kinder sind zu Hause bei ihren Großeltern. Heute Abend waren die Damen zu müde, nach dem Abendessen

136

Murder Mystery in L.A.

auszugehen. Karl, Ernst und ich entschieden uns, ein paar Bars zu besuchen und uns zu vergnügen. Wir wussten nicht, dass morgen das Footballteam der Uni Wisconsin gegen die Universität von Kalifornien spielt. Halb Wisconsin hat Los Angeles überfallen, um bei dem Spiel dabei zu sein. Wohin man auch blickt, sieht man Leute mit milchig weißer Haut und Plastik-Käsedreiecken auf dem Kopf.

»Die bekommen nicht viel Sonne oben in Wisconsin, oder?«, fragt Ernst.

»Ich glaube, ihre Haut ist so blass, weil die ersten Siedler Wikinger waren«, sagt Karl. »Schaut nur, wie groß diese Leute sind.«

Tatsächlich, es scheint, als wären die Durchschnittsgröße und das Gewicht eines Menschen aus Wisconsin im Vergleich zu einer typischen Person aus Los Angeles doppelt so groß.

of Wisconsin has invaded Los Angeles for the game. Everywhere we look, we see people with milky white skin and plastic cheese wedges on their heads.

"They don't get a lot of sun in Wisconsin, do they?" Ernst asks.

"I think their skin is so pale because the original settlers were Vikings," Karl says. "Look at the size of these people."

Indeed, it seems like the average height and weight of a person from Wisconsin is double that of the typical person from Los Angeles.

Story 11

"That last bar was crazy," Ernst says. "I was in the men's room and two Wisconsin supporters were holding a guy with a University of California shirt. They kept dunking his head in the toilet and singing."

»Die letzte Bar war verrückt«, sagt Ernst. »Ich war auf der Herrentoilette und zwei Wisconsin-Fans hielten einen Burschen fest mit einem T-Shirt der Universität von Kalifornien. Sie tauchten seinen Kopf in die Toilette und sangen dazu.«

"Sports fans are crazy," I tell them. "Here's a bar that seems pretty quiet."

»Sportfans spinnen einfach«, sage ich zu ihnen. »Da ist eine Bar, die ziemlich ruhig aussieht.«

We walk into a dimly lit pub. Five people sit at the bar talking in low tones. The rest of the place is empty.

Wir gehen in ein spärlich beleuchtetes Lokal hinein. Fünf Leute sitzen an der Theke und unterhalten sich mit gedämpfter Stimme. Die übrigen Plätze sind leer.

We sit at the bar and order a round of drinks. "This place is much less stressful," I say.

Wir sitzen an der Bar und bestellen eine Runde Getränke. »Dieses Lokal ist viel weniger stressig«, sage ich.

We talk about our next day's activities. The wives want to go to the Los Angeles Museum of Art. We want to go to the La Brea tar pits.

Wir unterhalten uns über unsere Pläne für den nächsten Tag. Die Frauen wollen ins Kunstmuseum ›Los Angeles Museum of Art‹ gehen. Wir wollen die La Brea Tar Pits besuchen.

I notice a puddle on the floor near where we are sitting.

Mir fällt eine Pfütze am Boden auf, gleich neben der Stelle, wo

Murder Mystery in L.A.

wir sitzen.
viːɐ ˈzɪtsən
we   we sit

»Da ist etwas am Boden«, sage ich zum Barkeeper.
daː ɪst ˈɛtvas am ˈboːdən ˈzaːgə ɪç tsʊm ˈbaːɐˌkiːpɐ
there it is something on the floor I tell I to the bartender

"There is something on the floor," I tell the bartender.

»Keine Sorge, es ist schon trocken«, sagt er.
ˈkaɪnə ˈzɔʁgə ɛs ɪst ʃoːn ˈtʁɔkən zakt eːɐ
not a worry it it is already dry he says he

"Don't worry, it's dry," he says.

»Was ist das?«, frage ich.
vas ɪst das ˈfʁaːgə ɪç
what it is that I ask I

"What is it?" I ask.

»Blut. Irgendein Kerl wurde hier vor einer Stunde erschossen. Er
bluːt ˈɪʁgntˈaɪn kɛɐl ˈvʊʁdə hiːɐ foːɐ ˈaɪnɐ ˈʃtʊndə ɛɐˈʃɔsn eːɐ
blood some guy → here ago an hour ←he was shot he

saß auf Ihrem Barhocker.«
zaːs aʊf ˈiːʁəm ˈbaːɐˌhɔkɐ
he sat on your barstool

"Blood. Some guy got shot here an hour ago. He was sitting on your stool."

»Das erklärt, warum das Lokal so ruhig ist«, sagt Karl.
das ɛɐˈklɛːɐt vaˈʁʊm das loˈkaːl zoː ˈʁuːɪç ɪst zakt kaʁl
that it explains why the place so quiet it is he says Karl

"That explains why the place is so quiet," Karl says.

»Wie stehen die Chancen, dass hier heute Abend noch eine
viː ˈʃteːən diː ˈʃɑ̃ːsn das hiːɐ ˈhɔɪtə ˈaːbənt nɔx ˈaɪnə
what are the odds that here tonight another

Schießerei stattfindet?«, fragt Ernst.
ʃiːsəˈʁaɪ ˈʃtatˌfɪndət fʁaːkt ɛʁnst
shooting it takes place he asks Ernst

"What are the odds there will be another shooting here tonight?" Ernst asks.

»Wahrscheinlich bei Null. Wir sollten hierbleiben«, sage ich.
vaːɐˈʃaɪnlɪç baɪ nʊl viːɐ ˈzɔltən ˈhiːɐˌblaɪbn ˈzaːgə ɪç
probably at zero we we should to stay here I say I

"Probably zero. We should stay," I say.

Ein paar Minuten später spüre ich jemanden auf meine Schulter
aɪn paːɐ mɪˈnuːtən ˈʃpɛːtɐ ˈʃpyːʁə ɪç ˈjeːmandən aʊf ˈmaɪnɐ ˈʃʊltɐ
a few minutes later I feel I somebody on my shoulder

klopfen. Ich drehe mich um und sehe eine umwerfend schöne Frau.
ˈklɔpfən ɪç ˈdʁeːə mɪç ʊm ʊnt ˈzeːə ˈaɪnə ˈʊmˌvɛʁfnt ˈʃøːnə fʁaʊ
to tap I I turn around and I see a drop-dead gorgeous woman

Sie reicht mir ein kleines Päckchen.
ziː ʁaɪçt miːɐ aɪn ˈklaɪnəs ˈpɛkçən
she she hands me a small package

A few minutes later someone taps on my shoulder. I look around and see a gorgeous woman. She hands me a package.

»Hier ist dein Geld und die Informationen zu deinem Ziel«, sagt
hiːɐ ɪst daɪn gɛlt ʊnt diː ɪnfɔʁmaˈtsjoːnən tsu ˈdaɪnəm tsiːl zakt
here it is your money and the information to your target she says

"Here is your money and the information about your target," she says, and she walks away.

Story 11

	sie	und	geht	davon.			
	zi:	ʊnt	ge:t	daˈfɔn			
	she	and	she goes away				

I am too amazed by the sight of this beautiful woman to react until she is almost out the door.

Ich	bin	zu	überrascht	vom	Anblick	dieser	wunderschönen	Frau,
ɪç	bɪn	tsu:	yːbɐˈʁaʃt	fɔm	ˈanˌblɪk	ˈdiːzɐ	vʊndɐˈʃøːnən	fʁaʊ
I	I am	too	amazed	from the	sight	of this	beautiful	woman

um	zu	reagieren,	bis	sie	fast	schon	aus	der	Tür	ist.
ʊm	tsu:	ʁeaˈgiːʁən	bɪs	zi:	fast	ʃoːn	aʊs	deːɐ	tyːɐ	ɪst
to	to	react	until	she	almost	already	out	the	door	she is

"Hey!" I yell. "What are you talking about?"

»Hallo!«,	rufe	ich.	»Wovon	reden	Sie	überhaupt?«
haˈlɔ	ˈʁuːfə	ɪç	voˈfɔn	ˈʁeːdn	zi:	yːbɐˈhaʊpt
hey	I shout	I	of what	you talk	you	actually

I open the envelope. It's stuffed with hundred dollar bills.

Ich	öffne	den	Umschlag.	Er	ist	mit	Einhundert-Dollar-Noten
ɪç	ˈœfnə	deːn	ˈʊmʃlaːk	eːɐ	ɪst	mɪt	ˈaɪnˌhʊndɐt-ˈdɔlaʁ-ˌnoːtən
I	I open	the	envelope	it	it is	with	one hundred dollar bills

vollgestopft.							
ˈfɔlgəˌʃtɔpft							
stuffed							

"Look at this, guys. We can drink free all night."

»Schaut	mal	her,	Leute.	Wir	können	die	ganze	Nacht	umsonst
ʃaʊt	maːl	heːɐ	ˈlɔɪtə	viːɐ	ˈkœnən	diː	ˈgantsə	naːxt	ʊmˈzɔnst
look		here	people	we	we can	the	whole	night	free

trinken.«
ˈtʁɪŋkn
to drink

We pull out the money. In addition, there are pictures of some nasty looking person with a scar on his cheek and a printout with personal information about the guy.

Wir	nehmen	das	Geld	heraus.	Außerdem	gibt	es	Bilder	eines
viːɐ	ˈneːmən	das	gɛlt	hɛˈʁaʊs	ˈaʊsɐdeːm	gɪpt	ɛs	ˈbɪldɐ	ˈaɪnəs
we	we take out →	the	money	←	in addition	there are		pictures	of a

wirklich	fies	aussehenden	Typen	mit	einer	Narbe	an	der	Wange
ˈvɪʁklɪç	fiːs	ˈaʊsˌzeːəndən	ˈtyːpn	mɪt	ˈaɪnɐ	ˈnaʁbə	an	deːɐ	ˈvaŋə
really	nasty	looking	guy	with	a	scar	on	the	cheek

und	einem	Ausdruck	mit	den	persönlichen	Daten	dieses	Kerls.
ʊnt	ˈaɪnəm	ˈaʊsˌdʁʊk	mɪt	deːn	pɛʁˈzøːnlɪçən	ˈdaːtən	ˈdiːzəs	kɛʁls
and	a	printout	with	the	personal	information	of this	guy

"What is this?" Karl asks.

»Was	ist	das?«,	fragt	Karl.
vas	ɪst	das	fʁaːkt	kaʁl
what	it is	this	he asks	Karl

And then, the police burst through the door.

Und	dann	stürmt	die	Polizei	durch	die	Tür.
ʊnt	dan	ʃtyʁmt	diː	poliˈtsaɪ	dʊʁç	diː	tyːɐ
and	then	the police storm			through	the	door

Murder Mystery in L.A.

»Ich war mir ziemlich sicher, dass Sie keine professionellen Auftragsmörder sind, als Sie zu heulen angefangen haben«, sagt der Kriminalbeamte zu uns.

"I was pretty sure you guys weren't professional hit men when you started crying," the detective tells us.

»Und warum hat es dann vier Stunden lang gedauert und fünftausend Dollar Anwaltsgebühren gekostet, bis wir gehen durften?«, fragt Karl.

"So why did it take four hours and five thousand dollars worth of lawyer fees before you let us go?" Karl asks.

Wir holen unsere persönlichen Habseligkeiten, Gürtel und Schuhbänder am Empfang irgendeines Hochsicherheitstraktes der Polizei in der Nähe von Hollywood ab.

We are retrieving our personal effects, belts, and shoelaces at the front desk of some maximum security police facility near Hollywood.

»Der Bezirksanwalt war auf einer Party. Er hat keine Entlassungspapiere unterschrieben, bevor die vorbei war.«

"The District Attorney was at a party. He wouldn't sign any release papers until it was over."

»Wie lautet seine Adresse?«, frage ich. »Ich möchte ihm ein Weihnachtsgeschenk schicken.«

"What's his address?" I ask. "I'd like to send him a Christmas present."

»Werden Sie nicht frech«, sagt der Polizist am Empfang. »Wir hätten Sie die ganze Nacht hierbehalten können.«

"Don't get smart," the cop at the front desk says. "We could have kept you all night."

Story 11

"We just got tired of hearing you scream that the other inmates scared you," the detective says.

»Wir konnten Ihr Gekreische, dass die anderen Insassen Ihnen Angst machen, einfach nicht mehr hören«, sagt der Polizeibeamte.

"You put us in a holding cell with two drug dealers, a crazy biker, and a guy who just bit someone's ear off," Ernst says.

»Sie haben uns in eine Zelle mit zwei Drogenhändlern, einem verrückten Motorradfahrer und einem Burschen gesteckt, der gerade jemandem das Ohr vom Kopf abgebissen hat«, sagt Ernst.

"We don't have special accommodations for nerds from Germany," the desk cop says. "At least you didn't get thrown into the cell with those crazy people with cheese on their heads."

»Wir haben keine Sonderunterkünfte für Langweiler aus Deutschland«, sagt der Polizist vom Empfang. »Wenigstens sind Sie nicht in die Zelle mit den Verrückten mit Käse auf dem Kopf, geworfen worden.«

"When you put it that way, we were lucky," I tell the cops.

»Von dieser Seite betrachtet haben wir Glück gehabt«, sage ich zu den Polizisten.

"What about the money?" I ask.

»Wie steht es mit dem Geld?«, frage ich.

"That's not yours. It was intended for the real hit man."

»Das gehört nicht Ihnen. Das sollte der echte Auftragsmörder bekommen.«

Murder Mystery in L.A.

»Das muss der Kerl gewesen sein, der erschossen wurde, bevor
das mʊs deːɐ kɛɐl ɡəˈveːzən zaɪn deːɐ ɛɐˈʃɔsn̩ ˈvʊɐdə bəˈfoːɐ
that → the guy ← it must have been who (he) was shot before

wir in der Bar eintrafen«, sagt Ernst.
viːɐ ɪn deːɐ baːɐ ˈaɪnˌtʁaːfən zakt ɛɐnst
we at the bar we came in he says Ernst

"He must have been the guy who was shot before we arrived at the bar," Ernst says.

»Wenn Ihre Geheimagenten die Bar beobachtet haben, warum
vɛn ˈiːʁə ɡəˈhaɪmaˌɡɛntən diː baːɐ bəˈoːbaxtət ˈhabn̩ vaˈʁʊm
if your undercover agents the bar they monitored why

haben Sie dann von der vorangegangenen Schießerei nichts
ˈhabn̩ ziː dan fɔn deːɐ foːɐˈaŋɡəˌɡaŋənən ʃiːsəˈʁaɪ nɪçts
→ you then of the preceding shooting nothing

gewusst?«, fragt Karl.
ɡəˈvʊst fʁaːkt kaʁl
← you knew he asks Karl

"If your undercover agents had the bar staked out, why didn't you know about the earlier shooting?" asks Karl.

»Wir haben die Bar nicht beobachtet. Wir sind der Frau gefolgt.
viːɐ ˈhabn̩ diː baːɐ nɪçt bəˈoːbaxtət viːɐ zɪnt deːɐ fʁaʊ ɡəˈfɔlkt
we → the bar not ← we monitored we → the woman ← we followed

Die vorausgegangene Schießerei hat niemand gemeldet. Wir
diː foːɐˈaʊsɡəˌɡaŋənə ʃiːsəˈʁaɪ hat ˈniːmant ɡəˈmɛldət viːɐ
the preceding shooting → nobody ← he reported we

verhörten den Barmann zwei Stunden lang, bis er endlich zugab,
fɛɐˈhøːɐtən deːn ˈbaːɐˌman tsvaɪ ˈʃtʊndən laŋ bɪs eːɐ ˈɛntlɪç ˈtsuːˌɡaːp
we questioned the bartender two hours long until he finally he admitted

den Typen einfach in den Müllcontainer geworfen zu haben.«
deːn ˈtyːpən ˈaɪnfax ɪn deːn ˈmʏlkɔnˌteːnɐ ɡəˈvɔɐfən tsuː ˈhabn̩
the guy just in the dumpster having thrown

"We didn't have the bar staked out. We were following the woman. And nobody reported the earlier shooting. We questioned the bartender for two hours before he admitted that he just threw the guy into a dumpster."

»Was sind das bloß für Leute, die in dieser Stadt wohnen?«,
vas zɪnt das bloːs fyːɐ ˈlɔɪtə diː ɪn ˈdiːzɐ ʃtat ˈvoːnən
→ they are that ! ← what type of people who in this town they live

frage ich. »Jemand wird vor ihren Augen erschossen und sie
ˈfʁaːɡə ɪç ˈjeːmant vɪɐt foːɐ ˈiːʁən ˈaʊɡən ɛɐˈʃɔsn̩ ʊnt ziː
I ask I someone → before their eyes ← he gets shot and they

trinken einfach weiter, während der Barmann die Leiche in einem
ˈtʁɪŋkn̩ ˈaɪnfax ˈvaɪtɐ ˈvɛːʁənt deːɐ ˈbaːɐˌman diː ˈlaɪçə ɪn ˈaɪnəm
they drink simply onward while the bartender the body in a

Müllcontainer entsorgt und dann den Boden putzt.«
ˈmʏlkɔnˌteːnɐ ɛntˈzɔʁkt ʊnt dan deːn ˈboːdən pʊtst
dumpster he disposes and then the floor he cleans

"What kinds of people live in this town?" I ask. "Someone gets shot in front of them and they continue drinking while the bartender throws the body in a dumpster and washes the floor."

»Das waren wahrscheinlich arbeitslose Schauspieler«, sagt der
das ˈvaːʁən vaːɐˈʃaɪnlɪç ˈaʁbaɪtsloːzə ˈʃaʊʃpiːlɐ zakt deːɐ
these they were probably unemployed actors he says the

Kriminalbeamte.
kʁimiˈnaːlbəˌamtə
(police) detective

"They were probably unemployed actors," the detective says.

Story 11

"How about the woman you followed?"

»Und was ist mit der Frau, die Sie verfolgt haben?«
ʊnt vas ɪst mɪt deːɐ fʁaʊ diː ziː fɛɐˈfɔlkt ˈhaːbn
and what about the woman that you you followed

"We lost her when the police charged into the bar."

»Wir haben sie verloren, als die Polizei in die Bar eindrang.«
viːɐ ˈhaːbn ziː fɛɐˈloːʁən als diː poliˈtsaɪ ɪn diː baːɐ ˈaɪnˌdʁaŋ
we → her ←we lost when the police in the bar it entered

"Great," I say.

»Großartig«, sage ich.
ˈɡʁoːsˌaːɐtɪç ˈzaːɡə ɪç
great I say I

We leave the police station and try to get a taxi. It's four thirty in the morning, so we don't have much luck. As we wait in the street, I get another tap on my shoulder. The gorgeous woman again.

Wir verlassen die Polizeistation und versuchen, ein Taxi zu finden.
viːɐ fɛɐˈlasən diː poliˈtsaɪstaˌtsjoːn ʊnt fɛɐˈzuːxən aɪn ˈtaksi tsuː ˈfɪndən
we we leave the police station and we try a taxi to to find

Es ist halb fünf Uhr morgens und wir haben kein großes Glück.
ɛs ɪst halp fʏnf uːɐ ˈmɔʁɡns ʊnt viːɐ ˈhaːbn kaɪn ˈɡʁoːsəs ɡlʏk
it it is 4:30 a.m. and we we have no good luck

Als wir auf der Straße warten, spüre ich nochmals ein Klopfen
als viːɐ aʊf deːɐ ˈʃtʁaːsə ˈvaʁtən ˈʃpyːʁə ɪç ˈnɔxmaːls aɪn ˈklɔpfən
as we in the street we wait I feel I again a tap

auf meiner Schulter. Es ist wieder diese umwerfende Frau.
aʊf ˈmaɪnɐ ˈʃʊltɐ ɛs ɪst ˈviːdɐ ˈdiːzə ˈʊmˌvɛʁfndə fʁaʊ
on my shoulder it it is again this stunning woman

This time I have the presence of mind to grab her. She sticks a small gun in my face and I let go.

Dieses Mal habe ich die Geistesgegenwart und halte sie fest. Sie
ˈdiːzəs maːl ˈhaːbə ɪç diː ˈɡaɪstəsˌɡeːɡnvaʁt ʊnt ˈhaltə ziː fɛst ziː
this time I have I the presence of mind and I grab→ her ← she

richtet eine kleine Pistole auf mein Gesicht und ich lasse sie los.
ˈʁɪçtət ˈaɪnə ˈklaɪnə pɪsˈtoːlə aʊf maɪn ɡəˈzɪçt ʊnt ɪç ˈlasə ziː loːs
she points a small gun at my face and I I let go→ her ←

"Big Sam says you have to give the money back by noon, or you're toast," she says.

»Big Sam sagt, dass ihr das Geld bis Mittag zurückgeben müsst,
bɪk saːm zakt das iːɐ das ɡɛlt bɪs ˈmɪtaːk tsuˈʁʏkˌɡeːbən mʏst
Big Sam he says that you the money until noon to give back you have to

oder ihr seid geliefert«, sagt sie.
ˈoːdɐ iːɐ zaɪt ɡəˈliːfɐt zakt ziː
or you you are done for she says she

The three of us stare at her. She backs into a waiting car and it drives off.

Alle drei starren wir sie an. Sie geht rückwärts in ein
ˈalə dʁaɪ ˈʃtaʁən viːɐ ziː an ziː ɡeːt ˈʁʏkˌvɛʁts ɪn aɪn
all three we stare at→ we her ← she she walks backwards into a

wartendes Auto und fährt davon.
ˈvaʁtəndəs ˈaʊto ʊnt fɛːɐt daˈfɔn
waiting car and it drives off

"We are really in trouble now," Ernst says.

»Jetzt sind wir echt in Schwierigkeiten«, sagt Ernst.
jɛtst zɪnt viːɐ ɛçt ɪn ˈʃviːʁɪçkaɪtən zakt ɛʁnst
now we are we really in trouble he says Ernst

Murder Mystery in L.A.

Zwei Stunden später verlassen wir die Polizeistation zum zweiten Mal.
tsvaɪ 'ʃtʊndən 'ʃpɛːtɐ fɛɐ'lasən viːɐ diː poliˈtsaɪʃtaˌtsjoːn tsʊm 'tsvaɪtən maːl
two hours later we leave we the police station for the second time

Two hours later we leave the police station for the second time.

»Ich kann es nicht fassen, dass sie uns nicht glauben«, sage ich.
ɪç kan ɛs nɪçt 'fasn das ziː ʊns nɪçt 'glaʊbən 'zaːgə ɪç
I I can it not to grasp that they us not they believe I say I

"I can't believe they don't believe us," I say.

»Ich kann es kaum glauben, dass uns eine Frau mit einer Pistole direkt vor der Polizeistation bedroht hat und niemand hat es gesehen«, sagt Ernst.
ɪç kan ɛs kaʊm 'glaʊbən das ʊns 'aɪnə fʀaʊ mɪt 'aɪnɐ pɪs'toːlə dɪ'ʀɛkt foːɐ deːɐ poliˈtsaɪʃtaˌtsjoːn bə'dʀoːt hat ʊnt 'niːmant hat ɛs gə'zeːən zakt ɛʀnst
I I can it hardly to believe that us a woman with a gun directly in front of the police station she threatened and nobody → it ← he saw he says Ernst

"I can't believe a lady pulled a gun on us right in front of their station and nobody saw it," Ernst says.

»Das erinnert mich an einen wirklich schlechten Film«, sagt Karl.
das ɛɐ'ɪnɐt mɪç an 'aɪnən 'vɪʀklɪç 'ʃlɛçtən fɪlm zakt kaʀl
this it reminds me of a really bad movie he says Karl

"This reminds me of a really bad movie," Karl says.

»Glaubst du, dass dieser Typ, Big Sam, uns Schwierigkeiten bereiten wird?«, fragt Ernst.
glaʊpst duː das 'diːzɐ tyːp bɪk saːm ʊns 'ʃviːʀɪçkaɪtən bə'ʀaɪtən vɪʀt fʀaːkt ɛʀnst
you think you that this guy Big Sam us trouble to cause he will he asks Ernst

"Do you think this Big Sam guy is going to give us trouble?" Ernst asks.

»Wir sagen einfach, dass die Frau den falschen Leuten das Geld gegeben hat. Sie ist schuld«, sage ich.
viːɐ 'zaːgən 'aɪnfax das diː fʀaʊ deːn 'falʃən 'lɔɪtən das gɛlt gə'geːbən hat ziː ɪst ʃʊlt 'zaːgə ɪç
we we say just that the woman the wrong people the money she gave it's her fault I say I

"We'll just explain that the woman gave the money to the wrong people. It's her fault," I say.

Unser einziges Glück ist, dass die Taxis um halb sieben wieder auf den Straßen sind. Ein schläfriger Fahrer bringt uns in unser Hotel zurück und wir schließen einen Pakt, unseren Frauen
'ʊnzɐ 'aɪntsɪgəs glʏk ɪst das diː 'taksɪs ʊm halp 'ziːbən 'viːdɐ aʊf deːn 'ʃtʀaːsən zɪnt aɪn 'ʃlɛːfʀɪgɐ 'faːɐɐ bʀɪŋt ʊns ɪn 'ʊnzɐ hoːˈtɛl tsuˈʀʏk ʊnt viːɐ 'ʃliːsən 'aɪnən pakt 'ʊnzəʀən 'fʀaʊən
our only luck it is that the taxis at half seven again on the streets they are a sleepy driver he brings back → us into our hotel ← and we we make a pact our wives

Our only good luck is that taxis are back on the street at six thirty in the morning. As a sleepy driver takes us back to our hotel, we make a pact not to tell our wives anything. I sneak into my hotel room just as Ingrid wakes up from a refreshing night's sleep.

145

Story 11

überhaupt nichts davon zu erzählen. Gerade als Ingrid aus einem
erholsamen Schlaf erwacht, schleiche ich mich ins Hotelzimmer.

"Did you have a good time, Klaus?" Ingrid asks.

»Hast du es dir gut gehen lassen, Klaus?«, fragt Ingrid.

"You can't even imagine."

»Das kannst du dir gar nicht vorstellen.«

I am too tired to argue with Ingrid about what sights to see, which is why I find myself standing next to her a few hours later, viewing three hundred year old paintings. Ernst and Karl and their wives are with us.

Ich bin zu müde, um mit Ingrid darüber zu diskutieren, welche Sehenswürdigkeiten wir anschauen sollen. Aus diesem Grund stehe ich ein paar Stunden später neben ihr und betrachte dreihundert Jahre alte Gemälde. Ernst, Karl und deren Frauen sind ebenfalls bei uns.

"Isn't this art museum so much nicer than those tar pits?" Ingrid asks me.

»Ist dieses Kunstmuseum nicht viel schöner als diese Teergruben?«, fragt mich Ingrid.

I barely mumble a response. I'm having a hard enough time keeping my eyes open, much less talk. I notice that Ernst and Karl are having similar problems.

Ich schaffe es gerade noch, eine Antwort zu murmeln. Es fällt mir schwer genug, die Augen offen zu halten, geschweige denn zu reden. Ich bemerke, das Ernst und Karl

Murder Mystery in L.A.

ähnliche Probleme haben.
ˈɛːnlɪçə pʁoˈbleːmə ˈhaːbn
similar problems they have

Die Damen beschließen, dass wir im Museum zu Mittag essen.
diː ˈdaːmən bəˈʃliːsn das viːɐ ɪm muˈzeːʊm tsuː ˈmɪtaːk ˈɛsən
the ladies they decide that we in the museum to eat lunch

The ladies decide that we should eat our lunch at the museum.

»Schau mal, die Kantine hat eine vegetarische Speisekarte«, sagt Karls Frau.
ʃaʊ maːl diː kanˈtiːnə hat ˈaɪnə vegeˈtaːʁɪʃə ˈʃpaɪzəˌkaʁtə zakt kaʁls fʁaʊ
look ! the cafeteria it has a vegetarian menu she says Karl's wife

"Look, they have a vegetarian menu in the cafeteria," Karl's wife says.

»Ihr Männer seid heute so ruhig«, sagt Ernsts Frau, während wir unsere Tofuburger essen. »Was habt ihr eigentlich so spät noch gemacht?«
iːɐ ˈmɛnɐ zaɪt ˈhɔɪtə zoː ˈʁuːɪç zakt ɛʁnsts fʁaʊ ˈvɛːʁənt viːɐ ˈʊnzəʁə ˈtoːfuˌbʊʁgɐ ˈɛsən vas haːpt iːɐ ˈaɪgəntlɪç zoː ʃpɛːt nɔx gəˈmaxt
you men you are today so quiet she says Ernst's wife as we our tofu burgers to eat what → you actually so late ! ← you did

"You are so quiet today," Ernst's wife says as we eat our tofu burgers. "What were you doing out so late, anyway?"

»Wir hatten einfach Spaß«, murmle ich.
viːɐ ˈhatən ˈaɪnfax ʃpaːs ˈmʊʁmlə ɪç
we → just ← we had fun I murmur I

"Having fun," I murmur.

»Das ist schon deine dritte Tasse Kaffee«, sagt Karls Frau zu ihm. »Du wirst heute Nacht nicht schlafen können.«
das ɪst ʃoːn ˈdaɪnə ˈdʁɪtə ˈtasə ˈkafeː zakt kaʁls fʁaʊ tsuː iːm duː vɪʁst ˈhɔɪtə naːxt nɪçt ˈʃlaːfən ˈkœnən
that it is already your third cup coffee she says Karl's wife to him you you will tonight not to sleep to be able

"That's your third cup of coffee," Karl's wife tells him. "You won't be able to sleep tonight."

»Ich versuche doch bloß, den Tag zu bewältigen«, sagt er.
ɪç fɛɐˈzuːxə dɔx bloːs deːn taːk tsuː bəˈvɛltɪgən zakt eːɐ
I I try just the day to to cope with he says he

"I'm just trying to get through the day," he says.

Nach dem Mittagessen sagen wir unseren Frauen, dass wir auf die Toilette müssen.
naːx deːm ˈmɪtaːkˌɛsn ˈzaːgən viːɐ ˈʊnzəʁən ˈfʁaʊən das viːɐ aʊf diː toaˈlɛtə ˈmʏsən
after the lunch we tell we our wives that we to the toilet we have to

After lunch, we tell the wives we have to visit the restroom.

»Dann treffen wir uns in der Ausstellung nahöstlicher Keramik«,
dan ˈtʁɛfən viːɐ ʊns ɪn deːɐ ˈaʊsʃtɛlʊŋ ˈnaːœstlɪçɐ keˈʁaːmɪk
then we meet up in the exhibit middle eastern pottery

"Meet us in the Middle Eastern pottery exhibit," Ingrid says.

Story 11

	sagt	Ingrid.
	zakt	'ɪŋgʁɪt
	she says	Ingrid

We splash water on our faces in an effort to keep awake.

Um	uns wach zu halten,	bespritzen	wir	unsere	Gesichter	mit
ʊm	ʊns vax tsu: 'haltən	bə'ʃpʁɪtsn	vi:ɐ	'ʊnzəʁə	gə'zɪçtɐ	mɪt
in order to	to keep ourselves awake	we splash	we	our	faces	with

Wasser.
'vasɐ
water

Before we can leave, two nasty looking men walk in and block our exit.

Bevor	wir	hinausgehen	können,	kommen	zwei	widerlich
bə'fo:ɐ	vi:ɐ	hɪ'naʊsˌge:ən	'kœnən	'kɔmən	tsvaɪ	'vi:dɐlɪç
before	we	to leave	we can	they come	two	nasty

aussehende	Männer	in	den	Raum	und	blockieren	den	Ausgang.
'aʊsˌze:əndə	'mɛnɐ	ɪn	de:n	ʁaʊm	ʊnt	blɔ'ki:ʁən	de:n	'aʊsˌgaŋ
looking	men	in	the	room	and	they block	the	exit

"Where's the money?" the taller one says.

»Wo	ist	das	Geld?«,	sagt	der	Größere	von	ihnen.
vo:	ɪst	das	gɛlt	zakt	de:ɐ	'gʁø:səʁə	fɔn	'i:nən
where	it is	the	money	he says	the	taller	of	them

"The police took it as evidence," I whine. "They wouldn't give it back to us."

»Die	Polizei	hat	es	als	Beweismittel	beschlagnahmt«,	jammere
di:	poli'tsaɪ	hat	ɛs	als	bə'vaɪsˌmɪtl	bə'ʃla:kˌna:mt	'jamɐə
the	police	→	it	as	evidence	← they confiscated	I whine

ich.	»Sie	wollten	es	uns	nicht	wiedergeben.«
ɪç	zi:	'vɔltən	ɛs	ʊns	nɪçt	'vi:dɐˌge:bn
I	they	they would	it	to us	not	to give back

"Big Sam is not going to like this," he says.

»Big Sam	wird	das	nicht	gefallen«,	sagt	er.
bɪk sa:m	vɪʁt	das	nɪçt	gə'falən	zakt	e:ɐ
Big Sam	he will	that	not	to like	he says	he

"The guy who was supposed to get the money was shot an hour before we got to the bar," Karl says. "That woman made a mistake and gave Big Sam's money to the wrong people."

»Der	Kerl,	der	das	Geld	erhalten	sollte,	wurde	eine	Stunde,
de:ɐ	kɛʁl	de:ɐ	das	gɛlt	ɛɐ'haltn	'zɔltə	'vʊʁdə	'aɪnə	'ʃtʊndə
the	guy	who	the	money	to receive	he was supposed	→	an	hour

bevor	wir	in	die	Bar	kamen,	erschossen«,	sagt	Karl.	»Diese
bə'fo:ɐ	vi:ɐ	ɪn	di:	ba:ɐ	'ka:mən	ɛɐ'ʃɔsn	zakt	kaʁl	'di:zə
before	we	in	the	bar	we came	← he got shot	he says	Karl	that

Frau	machte	einen	Fehler	und	gab	Big Sams	Geld	den	falschen
fʁaʊ	'maxtə	'aɪnən	'fe:lɐ	ʊnt	ga:p	bɪk sa:ms	gɛlt	de:n	'falʃən
woman	she made	a	mistake	and	she gave	Big Sam's	money	to the	wrong

Leuten.«
'lɔɪtən
people

"Why would a professional hit man allow himself to be gunned down while he was waiting for his money?" the smaller man sneered.

»Warum	sollte	sich	ein	professioneller	Killer	niederschießen
va'ʁʊm	'zɔltə	zɪç	aɪn	pʁofɛsjo'nɛlɐ	'kɪlɐ	'ni:dɐˌʃi:sn
why	he should	himself	a	professional	killer	to shoot

Murder Mystery in L.A.

lassen,	während	er	auf	sein	Geld	wartet?«,	spottete	der	kleinere
ˈlasən	ˈvɛːʁənt	eːɐ	aʊf	zaɪn	gɛlt	ˈvaʁtət	ˈʃpɔtətə	deːɐ	ˈklaɪnəʁə
to let	while	he	on	his	money	he waited	he sneered	the	smaller

Mann.
man
man

»Offenbar	passieren	solche	Sachen	in	Los	Angeles	andauernd«,
ˈɔfnbaːɐ	paˈsiːʁən	ˈzɔlçə	ˈzaxən	ɪn	lɔs	ˈændʒəlɪs	ˈanˌdaʊɐnt
apparently	they happen	such	things	in	Los	Angeles	constantly

"Apparently, things like this happen in Los Angeles all the time," Ernst responds.

antwortet	Ernst.
ˈantvɔʁtət	ɛʁnst
he responds	Ernst

»Ihr	könnt	froh	sein,	dass	sie	das	Geld	dem	Falschen
iːɐ	kœnt	fʁoː	zaɪn	das	ziː	das	gɛlt	deːm	ˈfalʃən
you	you can	happy	to be	that	she	the	money	to the	wrong person

"You're lucky she gave the money to the wrong guy," I tell them. "The police were tailing her. If they had grabbed the real hit man he would have told them all about Big Sam. On the other hand, we know nothing about Big Sam, so things worked out pretty well for him."

gegeben	hat«,	sage	ich	zu	ihm.	»Die	Polizei	hatte	sie	beschattet.
gəˈgeːbn hat		ˈzaːgə	ɪç	tsuː	iːm	diː	poliˈtsaɪ	ˈhatə	ziː	bəˈʃatət
she gave		I tell	I	to	them	the	police	→	her	← it had tailed

Wenn	sie	den	richtigen	Killer	erwischt	hätten,	hätte	er
vɛn	ziː	deːn	ˈʁɪçtɪgən	ˈkɪlɐ	ɛɐˈvɪʃt	ˈhɛtən	ˈhɛtə	eːɐ
if	they	the	correct	killer	they caught		→	he

ihnen	wahrscheinlich	alles	über	Big Sam	erzählt.	Wir
ˈiːnən	vaːɐˈʃaɪnlɪç	ˈaləs	ˈyːbɐ	bɪk saːm	ɛɐˈtsɛːlt	viːɐ
them	probably	everything	about	Big Sam	← he would have told	we

hingegen	wissen	nichts	über	Big Sam.	So gesehen	ist	es	für
ˈhɪnˌgeːgən	ˈvɪsən	nɪçts	ˈyːbɐ	bɪk saːm	zoː gəˈzeːən	ɪst	ɛs	fyːɐ
on the other hand	we know	nothing	about	Big Sam	looking at it that way	→	it	for

ihn	gut gelaufen.«
iːn	guːt gəˈlaʊfən
him	← it worked out

»Ich	rufe	besser	Big Sam	an«,	sagt	der	größere	Bursche.	»Ihr
ɪç	ˈʁuːfə	ˈbɛsɐ	bɪk saːm	an	zakt	deːɐ	ˈgʁøːsəʁə	ˈbʊʁʃə	iːɐ
I	I call →	better	Big Sam	←	he says	the	bigger	guy	you

"I better call Big Sam," the taller fellow says. "You guys stay right where you are."

bleibt	genau,	wo	ihr	seid.«
blaɪpt	gəˈnaʊ	voː	iːɐ	zaɪt
you stay	right	where	you	you are

Er	geht	hinaus,	um	seinen	Anruf	zu	tätigen,	während	sein
eːɐ	geːt	hɪˈnaʊs	ʊm	ˈzaɪnən	ˈanˌʁuːf	tsuː	ˈtɛːtɪgən	ˈvɛːʁənt	zaɪn
he	he goes out		in order to	his	call	to	to carry out	while	his

He goes outside to make a call while his partner stays in the bathroom with us. We take the opportunity to sit in three separate stalls and get some rest.

Partner	bei	uns	in	der	Toilette	bleibt.	Wir	nutzen	die	Gelegenheit
ˈpaʁtnɐ	baɪ	ʊns	ɪn	deːɐ	toaˈlɛtə	blaɪpt	viːɐ	ˈnʊtsən	diː	gəˈleːgənhaɪt
partner	with	us	in	the	toilet	he stays	we	we use	the	opportunity

und	setzen	uns	in	drei	verschiedene	Toilettenkabinen	um	uns
ʊnt	ˈzɛtsən	ʊns	ɪn	dʁaɪ	fɛɐˈʃiːdənə	toaˈlɛtnkaˌbiːnən	ʊm	ʊns
and	we sit		in	three	separate	toilet cubicles	in order to	→

Story 11

	etwas	auszuruhen.
	'ɛtvas	'aʊstsuˌʁuːən
	some	←to have a rest

After five minutes, the tall guy comes back in.

Nach	fünf	Minuten	kommt	der	Große	zurück.
naːx	fʏnf	mɪˈnuːtən	kɔmt	deːɐ	ˈɡʁoːsə	tsuˈʁʏk
after	five	minutes	he comes back→	the	tall (one)	←

"You guys come with us. Big Sam wants to see you."

»Ihr	kommt	mit	uns.	Big Sam	möchte	euch	sehen.«
iːɐ	kɔmt	mɪt	ʊns	bɪk saːm	ˈmœçtə	ɔɪç	ˈzeːən
you	you come	with	us	Big Sam	he would like	you	to see

We hesitate, but the two of them show us the pistols in their shoulder holsters, so we leave the bathroom with them.

Wir	zögern,	aber	die beiden	zeigen	uns	ihre	Pistolen	in	den
viːɐ	ˈtsøːɡɐn	ˈaːbɐ	diː ˈbaɪdən	ˈtsaɪɡən	ʊns	ˈiːʁɐ	pɪsˈtoːlən	ɪn	deːn
we	we hesitate	but	the two of them	they show	us	their	guns	in	the

Schulterhalftern,	also	verlassen	wir	die	Toilette	mit	ihnen.
ˈʃʊltɐˌhalftɐn	ˈalzo	fɛɐˈlasən	viːɐ	diː	toaˈlɛtə	mɪt	ˈiːnən
shoulder holsters	so	we leave	we	the	bathroom	with	them

Four senior citizens are lined up waiting to get into the bathroom.

Vier	Senioren	stehen Schlange,	um	auf	die	Toilette	zu	gehen.
fiːɐ	zeˈnjoːʁən	ˈʃteːən ˈʃlaŋə	ʊm	aʊf	diː	toaˈlɛtə	tsuː	ˈɡeːən
four	senior citizens	they stand in line	in order to	in	the	bathroom	to	to go

"It's about time you guys finished cleaning the place," one of them says. "Our tour bus is about to leave and we have to wait ten minutes for the bathroom. It's not right."

»Es wurde ja langsam Zeit,	dass	Sie	mit	dem	Saubermachen	fertig
ɛs ˈvʊʁdə ja: ˈlaŋˌzaːm tsaɪt	das	ziː	mɪt	deːm	ˈzaʊbɐˌmaxən	ˈfɛʁtɪç
it's about time	that	you	with	the	cleaning	finished

sind«,	sagt	einer	von	ihnen.	»Unser	Reisebus	fährt	gleich	ab
zɪnt	zakt	ˈaɪnɐ	fɔn	ˈiːnən	ˈʊnzɐ	ˈʁaɪzəˌbʊs	fɛːɐt	ɡlaɪç	ap
you are	he says	one	of	them	our	tour bus	it leaves→	shortly	←

und	wir	müssen	hier	zehn	Minuten	auf	die	Benutzung	der
ʊnt	viːɐ	ˈmʏsən	hiːɐ	tseːn	mɪˈnuːtən	aʊf	diː	bəˈnʊtsʊŋ	deːɐ
and	we	we have to	here	ten	minutes	for	the	use	of the

Toilette	warten.	Das	ist	nicht	richtig.«
toaˈlɛtə	ˈvaʁtən	das	ɪst	nɪçt	ˈʁɪçtɪç
toilet	to wait	that	it is	not	right

"Who said we were cleaning?" I ask.

»Wer	hat	gesagt,	wir	hätten	sauber gemacht«,	frage	ich.
veːɐ	hat	ɡəˈzaːkt	viːɐ	ˈhɛtn	ˈzaʊbɐ ɡəˈmaxt	ˈfʁaːɡə	ɪç
who	he said		we		we were cleaning	I ask	I

"The tall fellow," another senior answers.

»Der	Große	da«,	antwortet	einer der	Senioren.
deːɐ	ˈɡʁoːsə	da:	ˈantvɔʁtət	ˈaɪnɐ deːɐ	zeˈnjoːʁən
the	tall (one)	there	he answers	one of the	senior citizens

"He lied to you," Karl yells.

»Er	hat	Sie	angelogen«,	schreit	Karl.
eːɐ	hat	ziː	ˈaŋəˌloːɡən	ʃʁaɪt	kaʁl
he	→	you	←he lied to	he yells	Karl

Suddenly, the four seniors with full bladders attack Big Sam's men.

Urplötzlich	greifen	die	vier	Senioren	mit	vollen	Harnblasen
ˈuːɐˌplœtslɪç	ˈɡʁaɪfən	diː	fiːɐ	zeˈnjoːʁən	mɪt	ˈfɔlən	ˈhaʁnblaːzən
all of a sudden	they attack→	the	four	senior citizens	with	full	bladders

Murder Mystery in L.A.

Big Sams Leute an.
bɪk saːms lɔɪtə an
Big Sam's people ←

»Ich weiß zwar nicht, was diese Typen für eine Reise
ɪç vaɪs tsvaːɐ nɪçt vas ˈdiːzə ˈtyːpən fyːɐ ˈaɪnə ˈʁaɪzə
I I know ! not what kind of→ these guys ← a tour

machen, aber sie beherrschen alle Judo«, sagt Karl.
ˈmaxn̩ ˈaːbɐ ziː bəˈhɛʁʃən ˈalə ˈjuːdo zakt kaʁl
they do but they they are proficient all judo he says Karl

"I don't know what tour these guys are with, but they all know judo," says Karl.

»Erinnere mich bitte von nun an daran etwas netter zu alten
ɛɐˈɪnəʁə mɪç ˈbɪtə fɔn nuːn an daˈʁan ˈɛtvas ˈnɛtɐ tsuː ˈaltən
remind me please from now on on it somewhat nicer to old

Leuten zu sein«, sagt Ernst, während wir einen Herrn mit
ˈlɔɪtən tsuː zaɪn zakt ɛʁnst ˈvɛːʁənt viːɐ ˈaɪnən hɛɐn mɪt
people to to be he says Ernst as we a gentleman with

Gehgestell beobachten, wie er Big Sams kleineren Gangster im
ˈgeːgəˌʃtɛl bəˈoːbaxtən viː eːɐ bɪk saːms ˈklaɪnəʁən ˈgɛŋstɐ ɪm
walker we watch as he Big Sam's smaller gunman in the

Würgegriff festhält.
ˈvyʁgəˌgʁɪf ˈfɛstˌhɛlt
choke hold he holds

"Remind me to be nice to older people from now on," Ernst tells me as we watch a guy with a walker grab Big Sam's shorter gunman in a choke hold.

Innerhalb von zwei Minuten sind die Bösewichte bewusstlos und
ˈɪnɐhalp fɔn tsvaɪ mɪˈnuːtən zɪnt diː ˈbøːzəˌvɪçtə bəˈvʊstloːs ʊnt
within two minutes they are the bad guys unconscious and

in Handschellen gelegt.
ɪn ˈhantʃɛlən gəˈleːkt
handcuffed

Within two minutes, the bad guys are unconscious and handcuffed.

---4---

Heute besuchen unsere Frauen Pasadena. Ernst, Karl und ich
ˈhɔɪtə bəˈzuːxən ˈʊnzəʁə ˈfʁaʊən pɛsəˈdiːnə ɛʁnst kaʁl ʊnt ɪç
today they visit our wives Pasadena Ernst Karl and I

schlafen bis etwa elf Uhr und anschließend essen wir mit
ˈʃlaːfən bɪs ˈɛtva ɛlf uːɐ ʊnt ˈanʃliːsənt ˈɛsən viːɐ mɪt
we sleep until about eleven o'clock and afterwards we eat lunch→ we with

unserem Bekannten von der Kripo zu Mittag.
ˈʊnzəʁəm bəˈkantən fɔn deːɐ ˈkʁiːpo tsuː ˈmɪtaːk
our acquaintance from the detective police ←

Today our wives are visiting Pasadena. Ernst, Karl, and I sleep until about eleven and have lunch with our police detective acquaintance.

»Wir wussten nicht, das Sie uns gestern gefolgt sind«, sagt Karl.
viːɐ ˈvʊstən nɪçt das ziː ʊns ˈgɛstɐn gəˈfɔlkt zɪnt zakt kaʁl
we we knew not that you us yesterday you followed he says Karl

"We didn't know you were following us yesterday," Karl says.

»Big Sams Leute wussten es ebenso wenig. Daher war es so
bɪk saːms ˈlɔɪtə ˈvʊstən ɛs ˈeːbənzoː ˈveːnɪç ˈdaːhɛɐ vaːɐ ɛs zoː
Big Sam's people they knew it just as little that's why it was it so

"Neither did Big Sam's men. That's why it was so easy to arrest them outside the bathroom."

151

Story 11

einfach,	sie	vor der	Toilette	zu	verhaften.«
ˈaɪnfax	ziː	foːɐ deːɐ	toaˈlɛtə	tsuː	fɛɐˈhaftən
easy	them	outside the	toilet	to	to arrest

"Your men had good disguises," I say.

»Ihre Leute haben sich gut verkleidet«, sage ich.
ˈiːʁə ˈlɔɪtə ˈhaːbn zɪç guːt fɛɐˈklaɪdət ˈzaːgə ɪç
your people → themselves well ←they disguised I say I

"Actually, we just used some of the guys who are near retirement," he says.

»Um ehrlich zu sein, wir haben ein paar Leute eingesetzt, die kurz
ʊm ˈeːɐlɪç tsuː zaɪn viːɐ ˈhaːbn aɪn paːɐ ˈlɔɪtə ˈaɪngəˌzɛtst diː kʊʁts
to be honest we → a few people ←we used who shortly

vor der Pensionierung stehen«, sagt er.
foːɐ deːɐ pɛnzjoˈniːʁʊŋ ˈʃteːən zakt eːɐ
before the retirement they stand he says he

"So what about Big Sam?" Ernst wants to know.

»Und was ist nun mit Big Sam?«, will Ernst wissen.
ʊnt vas ɪst nuːn mɪt bɪk saːm vɪl ɛʁnst ˈvɪsn
and how is it now with Big Sam he wants Ernst to know

"The District Attorney made a deal with one of Sam's men. He told us where Big Sam was hiding and admitted that Sam had put a contract on one of his competitors. We arrested Sam this morning, along with the woman who gave you the money."

»Der Staatsanwalt hat mit einem von Sams Männern
deːɐ ˈʃtaːtsanˌvalt hat mɪt ˈaɪnəm fɔn sams ˈmɛnɐn
the district attorney → with one of Sam's men

eine Vereinbarung getroffen. Dieser sagte uns, wo sich Big Sam
ˈaɪnə fɛɐˈaɪnbaːʁʊŋ gəˈtʁɔfən ˈdiːzɐ ˈzaktə ʊns voː zɪç bɪk saːm
←he reached an agreement this one he told us where → Big Sam

versteckt hielt und gab zu, dass Sam den Auftrag erteilt hatte,
fɛɐˈʃtɛkt hiːlt ʊnt gaːp tsuː das saːm deːn ˈaʊfˌtʁaːk ɛɐˈtaɪlt ˈhatə
←he hid out and he admitted that Sam the order he had issued

einen seiner Mitbewerber zu töten. Wir haben heute Morgen Sam
ˈaɪnən ˈzaɪnɐ ˈmɪtbəˌvɛʁbɐ tsuː ˈtøːtən viːɐ ˈhaːbn ˈhɔɪtə ˈmɔʁgn saːm
one of his competitors to to kill we → today morning Sam

mitsamt der Frau, die Ihnen das Geld gegeben hat, verhaftet.«
mɪtˈzamt deːɐ fʁaʊ diː ˈiːnən das gɛlt gəˈgeːbən hat fɛɐˈhaftət
together with the woman who you the money she gave ←we arrested

"That's a relief," I say. "Now we can finish enjoying our vacation without our wives seeing us get strangled or run over by a bulldozer."

»Das ist aber eine Erleichterung«, sage ich. »Jetzt können wir
das ɪst ˈaːbɐ ˈaɪnə ɛɐˈlaɪçtəʁʊŋ ˈzaːgə ɪç jɛtst ˈkœnən viːɐ
that it is ! a relief I say I now we can we

unsere Ferien zu Ende genießen und unsere Frauen müssen nicht
ˈʊnzəʁə ˈfeːʁiən tsuː ˈɛndə gəˈniːsn ʊnt ˈʊnzəʁə ˈfʁaʊən ˈmʏsən nɪçt
our vacation to finish enjoying and our wives they have to not

dabei zusehen, wie wir erwürgt oder von einer Planierraupe
daˈbaɪ ˈtsuːzeːən viː viːɐ ɛɐˈvʏʁkt ˈoːdɐ fɔn ˈaɪnɐ plaˈniːɐˌʁaʊpə
at it to see how we we get strangled or by a bulldozer

überrollt werden.«
yːbɐˈʁɔlt ˈveːɐdn
to get run over

"Just promise that you take your next vacation in some other place," the detective says.

»Versprechen Sie mir nur, dass Sie Ihre nächsten Ferien an
fɛɐˈʃpʁɛçn ziː miːɐ nuːɐ das ziː ˈiːʁə ˈnɛːçstən ˈfeːʁiən an
promise me just that you your next vacation in

Murder Mystery in L.A.

einem	anderen	Ort	verbringen werden«,	sagt	der	Kriminalbeamte.	
ˈaɪnəm	ˈandəʁən	ɔʁt	fɛɐ̯ˈbʁɪŋən ˈveːɐ̯dn	zaːkt	deːɐ̯	kʁimiˈnaːlbəˌamtə	
another		place	you will spend	he says	the	detective	

»Vielleicht probieren wir es in Wisconsin«, sagt Karl. »Die Leute   "Maybe we'll try Wisconsin," Karl
fiˈlaɪçt pʁoˈbiːʁən viːɐ̯ ɛs ɪn wɪsˈkɔnsɪn zaːkt kaʁl diː ˈlɔɪtə   says. "The people seem to be reason-
maybe we try we it in Wisconsin he says Karl the people   ably normal."

dort scheinen zumindest halbwegs normal zu sein.«
dɔʁt ˈʃaɪnən tsuˈmɪndəst ˈhalpveːks nɔʁˈmaːl tsuː zaɪn
there they seem at least reasonably normal to to be

STORY 12

Mommy and Me

»Sie müssen ihr Einhalt gebieten, Herr Dietrich.«
zi: ˈmʏsən iːɐ ˈaɪnhalt ɡəˈbiːtən hɛʁ ˈdiːtʁɪç
you you have to her to order a stop to Mr. Dietrich

"You have to stop her, Mr. Dietrich."

»Was genau macht meine Mutter?«
vas ɡəˈnaʊ maxt ˈmaɪnə ˈmʊtɐ
what exactly she does my mother

"What is my mother doing, exactly?"

»Helga erzählt allen in ihrem Altersheim, dass sie zwei Stunden
ˈhɛlɡa ɛɐˈtsɛːlt ˈalən ɪn ˈiːʁəm ˈaltɐsˌhaɪm das ziː tsvaɪ ˈʃtʊndən
Helga she tells everyone in her retirement home that she two hours

lang an einen Tisch gefesselt gewesen sei und es ihr nicht gestattet
laŋ an ˈaɪnən tɪʃ ɡəˈfɛsəlt ɡəˈveːzn̩ zaɪ ʊnt ɛs iːɐ nɪçt ɡəˈʃtatət
long on a table strapped she had been and it her not allowed

gewesen sei, zur Toilette zu gehen.«
ɡəˈveːzn̩ zaɪ tsuːɐ toaˈlɛtə tsuː ˈɡeːən
she had not been to the toilet to to go

"Helga is telling everyone in her retirement community that she was strapped to a table for two hours and wasn't allowed to go to the bathroom."

Es klang, als ob Dr. Christa Weber, meine Zahnärztin, am
ɛs klaŋ als ɔp ˈdɔktoːɐ ˈkʁɪsta ˈveːbɐ ˈmaɪnə ˈtsaːnˌɛɐtstɪn am
it it sounded as if Doctor Christa Weber my dentist on the

Hörer herumnagte, als sie mit mir sprach. Vielleicht knirschte
ˈhøːʁɐ hɛˈʁʊmˌnaːktə als ziː mɪt miːɐ ʃpʁaːx fiːˈlaɪçt ˈknɪʁʃtə
receiver she gnawed as she with me she spoke maybe she ground

sie mit den Zähnen. Ich wollte ihr schon sagen, das diese
ziː mɪt deːn ˈtsɛːnən ɪç ˈvɔltə iːɐ ʃoːn ˈzaːɡən das ˈdiːzə
she with the teeth I I wanted her ! to tell that this

Angewohnheit für ihre Zähne schlecht ist, aber das wusste sie
ˈanɡəˌvoːnhaɪt fyːɐ ˈiːʁə ˈtsɛːnə ʃlɛçt ɪst ˈaːbɐ das ˈvʊstə ziː
habit for her teeth bad it is but that she knew she

wahrscheinlich schon.
vaːɐˈʃaɪnlɪç ʃoːn
probably already

It sounded like Dr. Christa Weber, my dentist, was gnawing on the phone as she was speaking. Maybe she was grinding her teeth. I was tempted to tell her that these actions are bad for the teeth, but she probably knew that already.

Stattdessen sagte ich: »Sie war an keinem Tisch gefesselt. Sie
ʃtatˈdɛsn̩ ˈzaktə ɪç ziː vaːɐ an ˈkaɪnəm tɪʃ ɡəˈfɛsəlt ziː
instead I said I she she was on not a table strapped she

saß in ihrem Behandlungsstuhl. Sie ließen sie nach einer Stunde
zaːs ɪn ˈiːʁəm bəˈhandlʊŋsˌʃtuːl ziː ˈliːsən ziː naːx ˈaɪnɐ ˈʃtʊndə
she sat in her dentist's chair you you let her after an hour

Instead I said, "She wasn't strapped to a table. She was sitting in your dental chair. You let her get up after an hour to go to the bathroom."

Story 12

"I know. But Helga is telling her neighbors that I tortured her. Four people from the retirement village have already called to cancel their appointments. One lady said she heard I didn't even have a license."

»Ich weiß. Aber Helga erzählt ihren Nachbarn, dass ich sie gefoltert hätte. Vier Leute aus dem Altersheim riefen bereits an, um ihre Termine abzusagen. Eine Dame sagte, sie habe gehört, dass ich keine Zulassung hätte.«

Dr. Weber sounded desperate. Half of her patients lived in my mother's community. If they believed the things my mother was saying, Dr. Weber would lose a lot of business.

Dr. Weber hörte sich verzweifelt an. Die Hälfte ihrer Patienten wohnte im selben Heim wie meine Mutter. Wenn die glaubten, was meine Mutter erzählte, hätte Dr. Weber sehr viele Einbußen zu befürchten.

Helga Dietrich, my mother, is eighty-eight years old. She doesn't suffer from any diseases. She walks without a cane. Her mind is still sharp. She has a few minor medical problems, but she is in great physical shape for her age.

Helga Dietrich, meine Mutter, ist achtundachtzig Jahre alt. Sie hat keine Krankheiten. Sie kann ohne Stock gehen. Ihr geistiger Zustand ist sehr gut. Sie hat ein paar kleinere gesundheitliche Probleme, doch sie ist in großartiger körperlicher Verfassung für ihr Alter.

Unfortunately, mom is unhappy with her life. She believes that if she is not happy, then nobody else should be happy. Therefore, she goes out of her

Unglücklicherweise ist meine Mutter mit ihrem Leben nicht

Mommy and Me

zufrieden.	Sie	bildet	sich	ein,	dass	wenn	sie	nicht	glücklich
tsuˈfʁiːdən	ziː	ˈbɪldət	zɪç	aɪn	das	vɛn	ziː	nɪçt	ˈɡlʏklɪç
happy	she	she imagines			that	if	she	not	happy

sein	könne,	auch	alle	anderen	nicht	zufrieden	sein	sollten.	Deshalb
zaɪn	ˈkœnə	aʊx	ˈalə	ˈandəʁən	nɪçt	tsuˈfʁiːdən	zaɪn	ˈzɔltn̩	ˈdɛshalp
she can be		also	all	others	not	content		they should be	therefore

macht	sie	alles,	um	allen	anderen	das	Leben	schwer	zu
maxt	ziː	ˈaləs	ʊm	ˈalən	ˈandəʁən	das	ˈleːbən	ʃveːʁ	tsuː
she does	she	everything	in order to	for all	others	the	life	difficult	to

machen.	Im	Moment	lässt	sie	Dr.	Weber	ihren	Unmut	spüren.
ˈmaxn̩	ɪm	moˈmɛnt	lɛst	ziː	ˈdɔktoːʁ	ˈveːbɐ	ˈiːʁən	ˈʊnˌmuːt	ˈʃpyːʁən
to make	at the moment		she makes	she	doctor	Weber	her	displeasure	to feel

"Way to make everyone else's life miserable. Now it was Dr. Weber's turn to feel her wrath."

»Ich	werde	Mama	sofort	anrufen«,	sagte	ich.
ɪç	ˈveːɐ̯də	ˈmama	zoˈfɔʁt	ˈanˌʁuːfən	ˈzaktə	ɪç
I	I will	mom	immediately	to call	I said	I

"I'll call mom right now," I said.

»Ich	habe	es	schon	versucht.	Ihr	Telefon	ist	besetzt.	Könnten	Sie
ɪç	ˈhaːbə	ɛs	ʃoːn	fɛɐ̯ˈzuːxt	iːɐ̯	teˈleˌfoːn	ɪst	bəˈzɛtst	ˈkœntən	ziː
I	→	it	already	←I tried	her	telephone	it is	busy	could you	you

zu	ihr	fahren	und	mit	ihr	reden?	Bitte.«
tsuː	iːɐ̯	ˈfaːʁən	ʊnt	mɪt	iːɐ̯	ˈʁeːdən	ˈbɪtə
to	her	to drive	and	with	her	to speak	please

"I already tried. Her telephone line is busy. Could you drive over there and talk with her? Please."

Ich	legte	auf	und	sprang	in	mein	Auto.	Während	der	drei
ɪç	ˈleːktə	aʊf	ʊnt	ʃpʁaŋ	ɪn	maɪn	ˈaʊto	ˈvɛːʁənt	deːɐ̯	dʁaɪ
I	I hung up		and	I jumped	into	my	car	as	the	three

Kilometer	langen	Fahrt	zur	Wohnung	meiner	Mutter	fühlte	ich,
kiloˈmeːtɐ	ˈlaŋən	faːɐ̯t	tsuːɐ̯	ˈvoːnʊŋ	ˈmaɪnɐ	ˈmʊtɐ	ˈfyːltə	ɪç
kilometer	long	drive	to the	apartment	of my	mother	I felt	I

wie	mich	Schuldgefühle	überkamen.	Es	war	meine	Schuld,	dass
viː	mɪç	ˈʃʊltɡəˌfyːlə	yːbɐˈkaːmən	ɛs	vaːɐ̯	ˈmaɪnə	ʃʊlt	das
how	me	feelings of guilt	they overcame	it	it was	my	fault	that

Dr.	Weber	dieses	Problem	hatte.
ˈdɔktoːɐ̯	ˈveːbɐ	ˈdiːzəs	pʁoˈbleːm	ˈhatə
doctor	Weber	this	problem	she had

I hung up my phone and jumped into my car. As I drove the three kilometers to my mother's apartment, I could feel the guilt descending on me. It was my fault that Dr. Weber was having this big problem.

Vor	ein	paar	Wochen	hatte	meine	Mutter	starke	Zahnschmerzen.
foːɐ̯	aɪn	paːɐ̯	ˈvɔxən	ˈhatə	ˈmaɪnə	ˈmʊtɐ	ˈʃtaʁkə	ˈtsaːnʃmɛʁtsən
ago	a few		weeks	she had	my	mother	intense	toothache

Sie	hatte	schon	seit	Jahren	keinen	Zahnarzt	mehr	besucht.
ziː	ˈhatə	ʃoːn	zaɪt	ˈjaːʁən	ˈkaɪnən	ˈtsaːnˌaʁtst	meːɐ̯	bəˈzuːxt
she	→	!	since	years	not a	dentist	more	←she had visited

A few weeks ago, mom's teeth started giving her a lot of pain. She hadn't seen a dentist in years.

»Wieso	soll	ich	für	meine	Zähne	Geld	ausgeben?	In	ein	paar
viˈzoː	zɔl	ɪç	fyːɐ̯	ˈmaɪnə	ˈtsɛːnə	ɡɛlt	ˈaʊsˌɡeːbən	ɪn	aɪn	paːɐ̯
why	I should	I	for	my	teeth	money	to spend	in		a few

Jahren	bin	ich	sowieso	tot«,	sagte	sie	dauernd.
ˈjaːʁən	bɪn	ɪç	zoviˈzoː	toːt	ˈzaktə	ziː	ˈdaʊɐnt
years	I am	I	anyway	dead	she said	she	constantly

"Why spend money on my teeth? I'll be dead in a few years," she kept telling me.

157

Story 12

I insisted that she go to see my dentist, Dr. Weber.

Ich bestand darauf, dass sie meine Zahnärztin Dr. Weber sehen solle.
ɪç bəˈʃtant daˈʁaʊf das ziː ˈmaɪnə ˈtsaːnˌɛːɐtstɪn ˈdɔktoːɐ ˈveːbɐ ˈzeːən ˈzɔlə
I I insisted that she my dentist doctor Weber to see she should

"I'll go, but no x-rays," she said to me.

»Ich werde hingehen, aber ich will keine Röntgenaufnahmen«, sagte sie zu mir.
ɪç ˈveːɐdə ˈhɪnˌgeːən ˈaːbɐ ɪç vɪl ˈkaɪnə ˈʁœntgnaʊfˌnaːmən ˈzaktə ziː tsuː miːɐ
I I will to go there but I I want not any x-ray pictures she said she to me

"Dr. Weber has to take x-rays so she can see if there are any hidden problems," I told her.

»Dr. Weber muss Aufnahmen machen, damit sie sehen kann, ob
ˈdɔktoːɐ ˈveːbɐ mʊs ˈaʊfnaːmən ˈmaxn̩ daˈmɪt ziː ˈzeːən kan ɔp
doctor Weber she has to to take (x-ray) pictures so that she to see she can if

es irgendwelche versteckten Probleme gibt«, sagte ich zu ihr.
ɛs ˈɪʁgntvɛlçə fɛɐˈʃtɛktn̩ pʁoˈbleːmə giːpt ˈzaktə ɪç tsuː iːɐ
there are → some hidden problems ← I told I to her

"How much will the x-rays cost?" she asked.

»Wie viel werden die Röntgenaufnahmen kosten?«, fragte sie.
viː fiːl ˈveːɐdn̩ diː ˈʁœntgnaʊfˌnaːmən ˈkɔstn̩ ˈfʁaːktə ziː
how much they will the x-ray pictures to cost she asked she

"It doesn't matter. You need them."

»Das spielt keine Rolle. Du brauchst sie.«
das ʃpiːlt ˈkaɪnə ˈʁɔlə duː ˈbʁaʊxst ziː
that (it) doesn't matter you you need them

"I can't afford x-rays."

»Ich kann mir keine Röntgenaufnahmen leisten.«
ɪç kan miːɐ ˈkaɪnə ˈʁœntgnaʊfˌnaːmən ˈlaɪstn̩
I I can → no (x-ray) pictures ← to afford

"You've got plenty of money."

»Du hast genügend Geld.«
duː hast gəˈnyːgənt gɛlt
you you have enough money

"You don't know how much money I have," Mom said.

»Du weißt nicht, wie viel Geld ich habe«, sagte Mama.
duː vaɪst nɪçt viː fiːl gɛlt ɪç ˈhaːbə ˈzaktə ˈmama
you you know not how much money I I have she said mom

"I know all about your finances. I pay your bills."

»Ich kenne deine finanzielle Situation. Ich zahle deine
ɪç ˈkɛnə ˈdaɪnə finanˈtsiɛlə zituaˈtsjoːn ɪç ˈtsaːlə ˈdaɪnə
I I know your financial situation I I pay your

Rechnungen.«
ˈʁɛçnʊŋən
bills

Mom tried a new argument.

Mama erhob einen neuen Einwand.
ˈmama ɛɐˈhoːp ˈaɪnən ˈnɔɪən ˈaɪnˌvant
mom she raised a new objection

Mommy and Me

»Ich brauche das Geld für den Fall, dass ich in ein Pflegeheim muss.«

"I need the money in case I have to go into a nursing home."

»Aber du sollst auch dein Essen ohne Schmerzen kauen können«, sagte ich zu ihr.

"You also need to be able to chew your food without pain," I told her.

Schließlich schaffte ich es, meine Mutter zu Dr. Weber zu bringen. Mama benötigte eine Wurzelbehandlung und eine Krone auf einem ihrer Schneidezähne. Drei andere Zähne hatten Löcher, die behandelt werden mussten.

Eventually, I dragged mom to see Dr. Weber. She needed a root canal and a cap on one of her incisors. Three other teeth had cavities that needed to be fixed.

Vor zwei Tagen arbeitete Dr. Weber an der Wurzelbehandlung und versah Mamas Schneidezahn mit einer vorläufigen Krone. Die ganze Behandlung dauerte zwei Stunden. Mama musste noch zweimal kommen, bis die endgültige Krone eingepasst werden konnte.

Two days ago, Dr. Weber did the root canal and put a temporary cap on mom's front tooth. The whole process took two hours. Mom needed to go back twice more before a permanent cap was in place.

Jetzt erzählte Mama den Leuten, dass Dr. Weber ihre Patienten foltere. Wenn ich Mama nicht zu meiner Zahnärztin

Now mom was telling people that Dr. Weber tortures her patients. If I hadn't dragged mom to my dentist, this problem never would have happened. Yes, I felt a lot of guilt.

159

Story 12

gebracht	hätte,	wäre	dieses	Problem	nie	entstanden. Jawohl,
gəˈbʁaxt	ˈhɛtə	ˈvɛːʁə	ˈdiːzəs	pʁoˈbleːm	niː	ɛntˈʃtandən jaˈvoːl
I had brought		→	this	problem	never	← it would have arisen yes indeed

ich	fühlte mich	sehr	schuldig.
ɪç	ˈfyːltə mɪç	zeːɐ	ˈʃʊldɪç
I	I felt	very	guilty

―――――― 2 ――――――

As I walked into Mom's apartment, she was on the phone.

Als ich Mamas Wohnung betrat, war sie gerade am Telefon.
als ɪç ˈmamas ˈvoːnʊŋ bəˈtʁaːt vaːɐ ziː gəˈʁaːdə am teːleˈfoːn
as I mom's apartment I entered she was she currently on the telephone

"I'm telling you, she strapped me to a table for two hours. Imagine what it did to my back. I still can't move my legs properly," Mom was telling someone.

»Und ich sage dir, sie band mich zwei Stunden lang an
ʊnt ɪç ˈzaːgə diːɐ ziː bant mɪç tsvaɪ ˈʃtʊndən laŋ an
And I I tell to you she she strapped me two hours long to

einen Tisch. Stell dir vor, was das meinem Rücken antat. Ich kann
ˈaɪnən tɪʃ ʃtɛl diːɐ foːɐ vas das ˈmaɪnəm ˈʁʏkən ˈanˌtaːt ɪç kan
a table imagine what that my back it did I I can

immer noch nicht meine Beine richtig bewegen«, erzählte Mama
ˈɪmɐ nɔx nɪçt ˈmaɪnə ˈbaɪnə ˈʁɪçtɪç bəˈveːgən ɛɐˈtsɛːltə ˈmama
still not my legs correctly to move she told mom

irgendjemandem.
ˈɪʁgntˌjeːmandəm
to somebody

"Hang up the phone Mom!" I yelled.

»Leg den Hörer auf, Mama!«, rief ich.
leːk deːn ˈhøːʁɐ aʊf ˈmama ʁiːf ɪç
hang up → the receiver ← mom I yelled I

She jumped a little at the sound of my voice.

Sie hüpfte beinahe hoch beim Klang meiner Stimme.
ziː ˈhʏpftə ˈbaɪnaːə hoːx baɪm klaŋ ˈmaɪnɐ ˈʃtɪmə
she she jumped nearly up at the sound of my voice

"My son just arrived for a visit," she said into the phone. "Thanks for calling."

»Mein Sohn ist gerade zu Besuch gekommen«, sagte sie in den
maɪn zoːn ɪst gəˈʁaːdə tsuː bəˈzuːx gəˈkɔmən ˈzaktə ziː ɪn deːn
my son → just for a visit ← he arrived she said she into the

Hörer. »Danke für deinen Anruf.«
ˈhøːʁɐ ˈdaŋkə fyːɐ ˈdaɪnən ˈanˌʁuːf
handset thanks for your call

"That was one of my neighbors," she said as she put her phone back onto its stand. "She wanted to know all about my cap."

»Das war eine meiner Nachbarinnen«, sagte sie, während sie das
das vaːɐ ˈaɪnə ˈmaɪnɐ ˈnaxbaːʁɪnən ˈzaktə ziː ˈvɛːʁənt ziː das
that it was one of my neighbors she said she as she the

Telefon in seine Halterung zurückstellte. »Sie wollte alles über
teːleˈfoːn ɪn ˈzaɪnə ˈhaltəʁʊŋ tsuˈʁʏkʃtɛltə ziː ˈvɔltə ˈaləs ˈyːbɐ
telephone in its holder she put back she she wanted all about

meine Krone wissen.«
ˈmaɪnə ˈkʁoːnə ˈvɪsn
my crown to know

Mommy and Me

»Wieso erzählst du den Leuten, dass du dich beim Zahnarzt auf einen Tisch hättest legen müssen?«

"Why are you telling people that the dentist made you lie on a table?"

»Weil ich genau das tun musste. Mein Rücken bringt mich um.«

"Because that's exactly what I had to do. My back is killing me."

»Du hast in einem Behandlungsstuhl gesessen. Sie hat ihn nur nach hinten gekippt.«

"You were sitting in a dental chair. She just had it tilted backwards."

»Woher willst du das wissen?«, fragte Mama mit einer gewissen Verärgerung.

"How do you know?" Mom asked with annoyance.

»Ich war dabei. Erinnerst du dich nicht daran, dass ich dich zur Zahnarztpraxis gefahren habe und dort die ganze Zeit blieb?«

"I was there. Don't you remember that I drove you to the dentist's office and stayed for the whole visit?"

Sie zog ihr Gesicht in Falten und versuchte, sich zu erinnern. Mama ist klein. Wenn sie ihr Gesicht so verzieht, sieht sie aus wie Yodas ältere Schwester. Ihre lockigen, weißen Haare sind kurz geschnitten. Jede achtzigjährige Frau, die ich je gesehen habe, hat kurzes, lockiges Haar. Vielleicht ist das so etwas wie eine Vorschrift.

She scrunched up her face, trying to remember. Mom is very short. When she does that thing with her face, she looks like Yoda's older sister. Her curly white hair is cut short. Every eighty year old woman I have ever seen has short, curly hair. Maybe it's a rule.

Story 12

Mom also wears large glasses that turn purple in the sunlight. They hide most of her features. When she's outside, all you see is the white curly hair and a purple face. It's quite interesting.

Mama	trägt	auch	eine	große	Brille,	deren	Farbe	im	Sonnenlicht
ˈmama	tʁɛkt	aʊx	ˈaɪnə	ˈɡʁoːsə	ˈbʁɪlə	ˈdeːʁən	ˈfaʁbə	ɪm	ˈzɔnənlɪçt
mom	she wears	also	a	large	glasses	of which	color	in the	sunlight

zu	lila	wechselt.	Sie	versteckt	nahezu	alle	ihre	Gesichtszüge.
tsuː	ˈliːla	ˈvɛkslt	ziː	fɛɐ̯ˈʃtɛkt	ˈnaːətsu	ˈalə	ˈiːʁə	ɡəˈzɪçtsˌtsyːɡə
to	purple	it changes	they	they hide	nearly	all	of her	facial features

Wenn	sie	draußen	ist,	kann	man	nur	die	weißen,	lockigen
vɛn	ziː	ˈdʁaʊsən	ɪst	kan	man	nuːɐ̯	diː	ˈvaɪsən	ˈlɔkɪɡən
when	she	outside	she is	one is able	one	only	the	white	curly

Haare	und	ein	lilafarbenes	Gesicht	sehen.	Das	ist	recht	interessant.
ˈhaːʁə	ʊnt	aɪn	ˈliːlaˌfaʁbnəs	ɡəˈzɪçt	ˈzeːən	das	ɪst	ʁɛçt	ɪntəʁɛˈsant
hair	and	a	purple-colored	face	to see	that	it is	quite	interesting

I watched her think for a few seconds. Finally she said, "You weren't there."

Ich	beobachtete	sie	beim	Überlegen.	Schließlich	sagte	sie:	»Du
ɪç	bəˈoːbaxtətə	ziː	baɪm	yːbɐˈleːɡn	ˈʃliːslɪç	ˈzaktə	ziː	duː
I	I watched	her	at the	thinking	finally	she said	she	you

warst	nicht	dabei.«
vaːɐ̯st	nɪçt	daˈbaɪ
you were	not	there

"Yes I was. There was no torture table. And Dr. Weber let you go to the bathroom after an hour."

»Doch,	war	ich.	Es gab	keinen	Foltertisch	und	Dr.	Weber
dɔx	vaːɐ̯	ɪç	ɛs ɡaːp	ˈkaɪnən	ˈfɔltɐˌtɪʃ	ʊnt	ˈdɔktoːɐ̯	ˈveːbɐ
on the contrary	I was	I	there was	not a	torture table	and	doctor	Weber

ließ	dich	nach	einer	Stunde	auf	die	Toilette	gehen.«
liːs	dɪç	naːx	ˈaɪnɐ	ˈʃtʊndə	aʊf	diː	toaˈlɛtə	ˈɡeːən
she let	you	after	an	hour	to	the	toilet	to go

"No she didn't. She kept me strapped to that thing for two hours."

»Nein,	ließ	sie	mich	nicht.	Sie	hatte	mich	zwei	Stunden	lang	an
naɪn	liːs	ziː	mɪç	nɪçt	ziː	ˈhatə	mɪç	tsvaɪ	ˈʃtʊndən	laŋ	an
no	she let	she	me	not	she	→		two	hours	long	on

dieses	Ding	angebunden.«
ˈdiːzəs	dɪŋ	ˈanɡəˌbʊndən
that	thing	←she had me strapped down

"I helped you walk to the bathroom."

»Ich	habe	dir	geholfen,	zur	Toilette	zu	gehen.«
ɪç	ˈhaːbə	diːɐ̯	ɡəˈhɔlfən	tsuːɐ̯	toaˈlɛtə	tsuː	ˈɡeːən
I	→	you	←I helped	to the	toilet	to	to walk

"She put a big piece of concrete on my chest."

»Sie	legte	mir	ein	großes	Stück	Beton	auf	die	Brust.«
ziː	ˈleːktə	miːɐ̯	aɪn	ˈɡʁoːsəs	ʃtʏk	beˈtɔː	aʊf	diː	bʁʊst
she	she placed	on me	a	big	piece	concrete	on	the	chest

"That was a lead vest to protect you from the x-rays."

»Das	war	eine	Bleiweste,	um	dich	vor	den	Röntgenstrahlen
das	vaːɐ̯	ˈaɪnə	ˈblaɪˌvɛstə	ʊm	dɪç	foːɐ̯	deːn	ˈʁœntɡnˌʃtʁaːlən
that	it was	a	lead vest	in order to	you	from	the	x-rays

zu	schützen.«
tsuː	ˈʃʏtsən
to	to protect

Mommy and Me

Mama machte ein zorniges Gesicht. Sie kann es nicht leiden, wenn man ihr widerspricht.

Mom made an angry face. She hates it when anyone contradicts with her.

»Du musst aufhören, den Leuten zu erzählen, dass Dr. Weber dich gefoltert habe«, fuhr ich fort. »Die haben bereits ihre Termine abgesagt.«

"You have to stop telling people that Dr. Weber tortured you," I continued. "They have been canceling their appointments."

»Ich habe es nur drei oder vier Leuten erzählt.«

"I only told three or four people."

»Schlechte Nachrichten verbreiten sich schnell in deinem Altersheim. Morgen wird sogar der Bürgermeister deine Geschichte kennen, wenn du nicht alle wieder anrufst und ihnen sagst, dass du übertrieben hast.«

"Bad news travels fast in your retirement village. By tomorrow even the mayor will know your story if you don't call everyone back and tell them you exaggerated."

Mama wechselte das Thema. »Die Zahnärztin soll mir ja keine große Rechnung schicken.«

Mom changed the topic. "The dentist better not send me a big bill."

»Sie hat dir bereits einen Ausdruck davon gegeben, wie viel alles kosten wird.«

"She already gave you a printout of what everything would cost."

»Warum will sie, dass ich nächste Woche wiederkomme? Ich

"Why is she making me go back next week? I already have my new tooth."

Story 12

	habe	doch	bereits	meinen	neuen	Zahn.«
	ˈhaːbə	dɔx	bəˈʁaɪts	ˈmaɪnə	ˈnɔɪən	tsaːn
	I have	!	already	my	new	tooth

"That's a temporary tooth. You have to go back a few more times until the permanent cap is in place. She told you that."

»Das	ist	nur	ein	provisorischer	Zahn.	Du	musst	noch	ein paar
das	ɪst	nuːɐ	aɪn	pʁoviˈzoːʁɪʃɐ	tsaːn	duː	mʊst	nɔx	aɪn paːɐ
that	it is	only	a	temporary	tooth	you	you have to	still	a few

Mal	hingehen,	bis	die	endgültige	Krone	gemacht wird.	Sie	hat	dir
maːl	ˈhɪnˌgeːən	bɪs	diː	ˈɛntgʏltɪgə	ˈkʁoːnə	gəˈmaxt vɪʁt	ziː	hat	diːɐ
time	to go there	until	the	final	crown	it is done	she	→	you

das	bereits	gesagt.«
das	bəˈʁaɪts	gəˈzaːkt
that	already	←she told

"No she didn't. She just wants more money!"

»Hat	sie	nicht.	Sie	will	bloß	mehr	Geld	haben!«
hat	ziː	nɪçt	ziː	vɪl	blɔs	meːɐ	gɛlt	ˈhaːbn
	she	didn't	she	she wants	just	more	money	to have

"I was there when she told you."

»Ich	war	dabei,	als	sie	es	dir	sagte.«
ɪç	vaːɐ	daˈbaɪ	als	ziː	ɛs	diːɐ	ˈzaktə
I	I was	there	when	she	it	to you	she told

"Next time, I want Ursula to take me."

»Nächstes	Mal	möchte	ich,	dass	Ursula	mich	hinbringt.«
ˈnɛːçstəs	maːl	ˈmøçtə	ɪç	das	ˈʊʁzula	mɪç	ˈhɪnˌbʁɪŋt
next	time	I would like	I	that	Ursula		she takes me there

"No. I was the one who convinced you to go to the dentist. I will take you to your appointments."

»Nein,	ich	habe	dich	davon	überzeugt,	zum	Zahnarzt	zu	gehen.
naɪn	ɪç	ˈhaːbə	dɪç	daˈfɔn	yːbɐˈtsɔɪkt	tsʊm	ˈtsaːnˌaʁtst	tsuː	ˈgeːən
no	I	→	you	of it	←I convinced	to the	dentist	to	to go

Ich	werde	dich	zu	deinen	Terminen	begleiten.«
ɪç	ˈveːɐdə	dɪç	tsuː	ˈdaɪnən	tɛʁˈmiːnən	bəˈglaɪtn
I	I will	you	to	your	appointments	to accompany

"You were always a bad son," she told me. This was her favorite expression.

»Du	warst	immer	schon	ein	schlimmer	Sohn«,	sagte	sie	zu	mir.
duː	vaːɐst	ˈɪmɐ	ʃoːn	aɪn	ˈʃlɪmɐ	zoːn	ˈzaktə	ziː	tsuː	miːɐ
you	you were	always		a	bad	son	she said	she	to	me

Das	war	ihr	Lieblingsausspruch.
das	vaːɐ	iːɐ	ˈliːplɪŋsˈaʊsˌʃpʁʊx
this	it was	her	favorite expression

I stayed at mom's apartment for about an hour while she called all of her acquaintances and told them that she had exaggerated her story about the dentist.

Ich	blieb	ungefähr	eine	Stunde	in	der	Wohnung	meiner	Mutter,
ɪç	bliːp	ˈʊngəfɛːɐ	ˈaɪnə	ˈʃtʊndə	ɪn	deːɐ	ˈvoːnʊŋ	ˈmaɪnɐ	ˈmʊtɐ
I	I stayed	roughly	an	hour	in	the	apartment	of my	mother

während	sie	alle	ihre	Bekannten	anrief	und	ihnen	sagte,	dass	sie
ˈvɛːʁənt	ziː	ˈalə	ˈiːʁə	bəˈkantən	ˈanˌʁiːf	ʊnt	ˈiːnən	ˈzaktə	das	ziː
while	she	all	her	friends	she called	and	them	she told	that	she

mit	ihrer	Geschichte	über	die	Zahnärztin	übertrieben	hätte.
mɪt	ˈiːʁɐ	gəˈʃɪçtə	ˈyːbɐ	diː	ˈtsaːnˌɛːɐtstɪn	yːbɐˈtʁiːbən	hɛtə
with	her	story	about	the	dentist	she had exaggerated	

Mommy and Me

Sie	fragen	sich	wahrscheinlich,	wer	Ursula	ist.	Ist	sie
ziː	ˈfʁaːgn̩	zɪç	vaːɐ̯ˈʃaɪnlɪç	veːɐ̯	ˈʊʁzula	ɪst	ɪst	ziː
you	you wonder		probably	who	Ursula	she is	she is	she

eine	Verwandte?	Eine	Sozialarbeiterin?	Nein.	Ursula	ist	ein
ˈaɪnə	fɛɐ̯ˈvantə	ˈaɪnə	zoˈtsjaːlaɐ̯ˌbaɪtəʁɪn	naɪn	ˈʊʁzula	ɪst	aɪn
a	relative	a	social worker	no	Ursula	she is	a

fünfundsiebzig	Jahre	altes	Energiebündel.
ˈfʏnfʊntˌziːptsɪç	ˈjaːʁə	ˈaltəs	enɛʁˈgiːˌbʏndl̩
seventy-five	year	old	bundle of energy

You are probably wondering about Ursula. Is she a relative? A social worker? No. Ursula is a seventy-five year old bundle of energy.

Sie	verbringt	die	meiste	Zeit	damit,	in	der	Stadt	Besorgungen	für
ziː	fɛɐ̯ˈbʁɪŋt	diː	ˈmaɪstə	tsaɪt	daˈmɪt	ɪn	deːɐ̯	ʃtat	bəˈzɔʁgʊŋən	fyːɐ̯
she	she spends	the	most	time	with it	in	the	town	errands	for

die	älteren	Leute,	die	in	der	Seniorenwohnanlage	meiner	Mutter
diː	ˈɛltəʁən	ˈlɔɪtə	diː	ɪn	deːɐ̯	zeˈnjoːʁənˌvoːnanlaːɡə	ˈmaɪnɐ	ˈmʊtɐ
the	older	people	who	in	the	retirement home	of my	mother

wohnen,	zu	machen.	Was	es	auch	sei,	sie	besorgt	es.	Sie	fährt
ˈvoːnən	tsuː	ˈmaxn̩	vas	ɛs	aʊx	zaɪ	ziː	bəˈzɔʁkt	ɛs	ziː	fɛːɐ̯t
they live	to	to do	whatever it may be				she	she gets	it	she	she drives

die	Senioren	zu	Geschäften,	Arztpraxen	und	Krankenhäusern.
diː	zeˈnjoːʁən	tsuː	ɡəˈʃɛftən	ˈaːɐ̯tstˌpʁaksn̩	ʊnt	ˈkʁaŋkn̩ˌhɔʏzɐn
the	seniors	to	stores	doctor's practices	and	hospitals

Sie	kauft	Lebensmittel	für	Leute	ein,	die	selbst	nicht	mehr
ziː	kaʊft	ˈleːbn̩sˌmɪtl̩	fyːɐ̯	ˈlɔɪtə	aɪn	diː	zɛlpst	nɪçt	meːɐ̯
she	she buys→	groceries	for	people	←	who	themselves	no longer	

einkaufen	können.	Dann	hört	sie	ihnen	zu,	wenn	sie
ˈaɪnˌkaʊfən	ˈkœnən	dan	høːɐ̯t	ziː	ˈiːnən	tsuː	vɛn	ziː
to buy	they can	then	she listens→	she	to them	←	when	they

sich	beschweren,	dass	sie	die	falsche	Dosengröße	der	Bohnen
zɪç	bəˈʃveːʁən	das	ziː	diː	ˈfalʃə	ˈdoːzn̩ˌɡʁøːsə	deːɐ̯	ˈboːnən
they complain		that	she	the	wrong	can size	of the	beans

gekauft	habe	oder,	dass	die	Bananen	zu	teuer	seien.
ɡəˈkaʊft	ˈhaːbə	ˈoːdɐ	das	diː	baˈnaːnən	tsuː	ˈtɔɪɐ	ˈzaɪən
she bought		or	that	the	bananas	too	expensive	they are

She spends most of her time running around town doing errands for the older people who live in my mother's retirement community. You name it, she does it. She drives the senior citizens to stores, doctor offices, and hospitals. She buys groceries for the people who can't shop for themselves. Then she listens to them complain that she bought the wrong size can of peas or the bananas are too expensive.

Manchmal	nimmt	Ursula	sogar	die	Wäsche	eines	Kranken
ˈmançmaːl	nɪmt	ˈʊʁzula	zoˈɡaːɐ̯	diː	ˈvɛʃə	ˈaɪnəs	ˈkʁaŋkən
sometimes	she takes along→	Ursula	even	the	laundry	of a	sick person

mit	nach	Hause	und	wäscht	sie	dort.
mɪt	naːx	ˈhaʊzə	ʊnt	vɛʃt	ziː	dɔʁt
←		home	and	she washes	it	there

Sometimes Ursula even brings a sick person's clothes to her house and washes them.

Ursula	erhält	nicht	viel	Dank	für	ihre	guten	Taten.	Besonders
ˈʊʁzula	ɛɐ̯ˈhɛlt	nɪçt	fiːl	daŋk	fyːɐ̯	ˈiːʁə	ˈɡuːtən	ˈtaːtn̩	bəˈzɔndɐs
Ursula	she gets	not	much	thanks	for	her	good	deeds	especially

nicht	von	Leuten	wie	meiner	Mutter,	die	glauben,	diese	guten
nɪçt	fɔn	ˈlɔɪtən	viː	ˈmaɪnɐ	ˈmʊtɐ	diː	ˈɡlaʊbən	ˈdiːzə	ˈɡuːtən
not	from	people	like	my	mother	who	they think	these	good

Ursula doesn't get a lot of thanks for all her good work. Especially from people like my mother, who seem to think they are entitled to these acts of kindness. Just last week I had the following conversation with mom.

Story 12

Taten stünden ihnen ohnehin zu. Erst letzte Woche hatte
ˈtaːtən ʃtʏndn ˈiːnən ˈoːnəhɪn tsuː eːɐst ˈlɛtstə ˈvɔxə ˈhatə
deeds they are entitled to→ them anyway ← only last week I had

ich folgende Unterhaltung mit Mama.
ɪç ˈfɔlɡəndə ʊntɐˈhaltʊŋ mɪt ˈmama
I following conversation with mom

"Ursula came to visit this morning. She screwed up my whole day."

»Ursula besuchte mich heute Morgen. Sie hat mir den ganzen
ˈʊʁzula bəˈzuːxtə mɪç ˈhɔɪtə ˈmɔʁɡn ziː hat miːɐ deːn ˈɡantsən
Ursula she visited me today morning she → to me the whole

Tag durcheinander gebracht.«
taːk dʊʁçaɪˈnandɐ ɡəˈbʁaxt
day ←she messed up

"How did she do that?"

»Wie denn das?«
viː dɛn das
how ! that

"She sat there for an hour talking to me," Mom said.

»Sie saß hier und redete eine Stunde mit mir«, sagte Mama.
ziː zaːs hiːɐ ʊnt ˈʁeːdətə ˈaɪnə ˈʃtʊndə mɪt miːɐ ˈzaktə ˈmama
she she sat here and she talked an hour with me she said mom

"It's good you had a visitor. Hardly anyone ever comes to your apartment."

»Es ist gut, dass du Besuch hattest. Es kommt ja kaum jemand
ɛs ɪst ɡuːt das duː bəˈzuːx ˈhatəst ɛs kɔmt jaː kaʊm ˈjeːmant
it it is good that you visit you had it it comes ! hardly anyone

zu dir in die Wohnung.«
tsuː diːɐ ɪn diː ˈvoːnʊŋ
to you in the apartment

"She never listens to me."

»Sie hört mir nie zu.«
ziː høːɐt miːɐ niː tsuː
she she listens→ to me never ←

"Why do you say that?"

»Wieso sagt du das?«
viˈzoː zakt duː das
why you say you that

"I mentioned the heart attack I had last Sunday, and she said it was nothing. How does she know?"

»Ich erwähnte meinen Herzinfarkt, den ich vergangenen Sonntag
ɪç ɛɐˈvɛːntə ˈmaɪnən ˈhɛʁtsɪnˌfaʁkt deːn ɪç fɛɐˈɡaŋənən ˈzɔnˌtaːk
I I mentioned my heart attack that I last Sunday

hatte, und sie meinte es wäre nichts gewesen. Woher will sie
ˈhatə ʊnt ziː ˈmaɪntə ɛs ˈvɛːʁə nɪçts ɡəˈveːzən voˈheːɐ vɪl ziː
I had and she she said it → nothing ←it had been from where she wants she

das wissen?«
das ˈvɪsən
that to know

"She's a nurse, mom."

»Sie ist eine Krankenschwester, Mama.«
ziː ɪst ˈaɪnə ˈkʁaŋkənˌʃvɛstɐ ˈmama
she she is a nurse mom

Mommy and Me

»Na und? Sie ist kein Arzt.«
"So what? She's not a doctor."

»Sogar ich wusste, dass du keinen Herzinfarkt hattest. Weißt du noch, als du mich Sonntagnachmittag angerufen und mir deine Symptome beschrieben hast?«
"Even I know you didn't have a heart attack. Remember you called me Sunday afternoon and told me your symptoms?"

»Ja.«
"Yes."

»Verstopfung und Magenschmerzen sind keine Symptome eines Herzinfarktes.«
"Constipation and stomach ache are not the symptoms of a heart attack."

»Es war mehr als das. Ich hatte auch Brustschmerzen.«
"It was more than that. I had chest pains, too."

»Das hast du dazuerfunden. Ich fragte dich nach Brustschmerzen, als du mich angerufen hast, und du hast gesagt, dass deine Brust in Ordnung wäre.«
"You're making that up. I asked you about chest pains when you called me and you said that your chest was fine."

»Nun, sie sollte mir trotzdem nicht sagen, ich wäre bei guter Gesundheit. Sie kennt schließlich nicht alle meine Beschwerden und Schmerzen.«
"Well, she still shouldn't tell me that I have good health. She doesn't know all my aches and pains."

167

Story 12

"Yes she does," I said. "She's takes you to the doctor and sits in the examining room with you."

»Kennt sie schon«, sagte ich. »Sie bringt dich zum Arzt und sitzt mit dir im Untersuchungszimmer.«

"She talks so much to the doctor that he charges extra money for the visit. I keep telling her not to say anything to him, but she won't listen."

»Sie redet so viel mit dem Arzt, dass er mir für den Besuch mehr berechnet. Ich sage ihr immer schon, nichts mehr zu ihm zu sagen, aber sie hört nicht auf mich.«

"That's because when you go to the doctor, you forget to tell him all your medical problems, so Ursula has to tell him."

»Sie macht das, weil du beim Arzt vergisst, ihm von all deinen Gesundheitsbeschwerden zu erzählen. Deshalb muss Ursula ihm davon erzählen.«

"Well then, she should pay for the extra time that he charges me."

»Na dann soll auch sie für den zusätzlichen Zeitaufwand bezahlen, den er mir in Rechnung stellt.«

"Mom, Ursula is the nicest person in the world. Don't ask her to pay for part of your doctor visit. She might be offended."

»Mama, Ursula ist der netteste Mensch auf dieser Welt. Verlange nicht von ihr, für einen Teil deiner Arztbesuche aufzukommen. Sie könnte es als Beleidigung auffassen.«

"Maybe I'll ask her to start doing my wash," she continued.

»Vielleicht sollte ich sie fragen, ob sie meine Wäsche machen kann«, fuhr sie fort.

Mommy and Me

Mama nahm es ihr wirklich übel, dass Ursula nie angeboten hat, ihre Wäsche zu machen. Sie fühlte sich übergangen.

Mom really resented that Ursula had never offered to do her wash. She felt snubbed.

»Sie wäscht nur für Leute, die wirklich krank sind. Du bist nicht wirklich krank. Du kannst deinen Wagen zum Waschraum rollen und deine Wäsche selbst machen«, sagte ich.

"She only does the wash for people who are really sick. You're not really sick. You can wheel your cart to the laundry room and do your own wash," I said.

»Ich bin praktisch körperbehindert. Du hast keine Ahnung, was für Schmerzen ich in meinen Knien habe.«

"I'm practically disabled. You don't know how much pain I have in my knees."

»Deine Knie sind vollkommen in Ordnung«, sagte ich zu ihr.

"Your knees are totally fine," I said to her.

»Du warst immer schon ein schlimmer Sohn!«, sagte sie.

"You were always a bad son!" she said.

Und da war er wieder, ihr Lieblingsausspruch.

There it was again. Her favorite expression.

Sechs Wochen später ...

Six weeks later ...

Freitagabend ist reine Männersache. Und genau das habe ich gemacht. Poker spielen mit meinen Nachbarn Thomas, Ben und Günter. Wir hingen ab, entspannten uns, tranken Bier und

Friday night is male bonding time. That's what I was doing. Playing poker with my neighbors Thomas, Ben, and Günter. We were hanging out, relaxing, drinking beer, and talking.

Story 12

Life has been pretty stressful for me and my mom. It took four more dental visits over a period of four weeks before mom had a permanent cap on her bad tooth and new fillings in three other teeth. Twenty-eight days of listening to her complain about what a bad job the dentist was doing and how much the whole thing was going to cost. At least she wasn't calling any other people in town and accusing Dr. Weber of practicing voodoo.

"How's your mom doing?" my buddy Günter asked.

"She keeps telling me she wants to live at my house," I said.

"Somebody please deal the cards," Ben said. "I feel lucky."

Mommy and Me

Glück versuchen.«
glʏk   fɛɐˈzuːxn
luck   to try

»Ziehst du wirklich in Betracht, deine Mutter bei dir wohnen
tsiːst   duː   ˈvɪʁklɪç   ɪn bəˈtʁaxt   ˈdaɪnə   ˈmʊtɐ   baɪ   diːɐ   ˈvoːnən
you consider→   you   really   ←   your   mother   with   you   to live

zu lassen?«, fragte Günter.
tsuː   ˈlasən   ˈfʁaːktə   ˈɡʏntɐ
to   to let   he asked   Günter

"Are you actually considering letting your mother live in your house?" Günter asked.

Ich schüttelte meinen Kopf. »Auf keinen Fall. Meine Ehe könnte
ɪç   ˈʃʏtəltə   ˈmaɪnən   kɔpf   aʊf ˈkaɪnən fal   ˈmaɪnə   ˈeːə   ˈkœntə
I   I shook   my   head   no way   my   marriage   it could

dieser Belastung nicht standhalten. Außerdem würde sie mich
ˈdiːzɐ   bəˈlastʊŋ   nɪçt   ˈʃtantˌhaltn   ˈaʊsɐdeːm   ˈvʏʁdə   ziː   mɪç
this   strain   not   to withstand   furthermore   she would   she   me

verrückt machen. Ich sage ihr das jedes Mal, wenn sie das Thema
fɛɐˈʁʏkt   ˈmaxn   ɪç   ˈzaːɡə   iːɐ   das   ˈjeːdəs   maːl   vɛn   ziː   das   ˈteːma
crazy   to make   I   I tell   her   that   every   time   when   she   the   topic

anschneidet.«
ˈanˌʃnaɪdət
she brings up

I shook my head from side to side. "No way. My marriage can't take the strain. Plus, she would drive me crazy. I tell her that every time she brings up the subject."

»Ich wusste nicht, dass deine Mutter so schwierig ist«, sagte
ɪç   ˈvʊstə   nɪçt   das   ˈdaɪnə   ˈmʊtɐ   zoː   ˈʃviːʁɪç   ɪst   ˈzaktə
I   I knew   not   that   you   mother   so   difficult   she is   he said

Günter.
ˈɡʏntɐ
Günter

"I didn't know your mother was so difficult," said Günter.

»Das liegt daran, dass du noch neu hier bist«, sagte Thomas.
das liːkt daˈʁan   das   duː   nɔx   nɔɪ   hiːɐ   bɪst   ˈzaktə   ˈtoːmas
that is because   that   you   still   new   here   you are   he said   Thomas

"That's because you're new in town," said Thomas.

»Es gibt viele Leute, die Helga-Geschichten zu erzählen haben«,
ɛs ɡiːpt   ˈfiːlə   ˈlɔɪtə   diː   ˈhɛlɡa-ɡəˈʃɪçtən   tsuː   ɛɐˈtsɛːlən   ˈhaːbn
there are   many   people   who   Helga stories   to   to tell   they have

sagte Günter. »Sie ist eine echte Last.«
ˈzaktə   ˈɡʏntɐ   ziː   ɪst   ˈaɪnə   ˈɛçtə   last
he said   Günter   she   she is   a   real   burden

"There are lots of people who have Helga stories," Günter said. "She's a real pain."

»Erinnerst du dich noch an die Party bei Jörg vergangenen
ɛɐˈɪnɐst duː dɪç   nɔx   an   diː   ˈpaːɐti   baɪ jœʁk   fɛɐˈɡaŋənən
you remember→   still   ←   the   party   at Jörg's   last

Sommer?«, lachte Ben. »Helga schrie uns an, weil wir
ˈzɔmɐ   ˈlaxtə   bɛn   ˈhɛlɡa   ʃʁiː   ʊns   an   vaɪl   viːɐ
summer   he laughed   Ben   Helga   she yelled at→   us   ←   because   we

so viel gegessen hatten.«
zoː   fiːl   ɡəˈɡɛsn ˈhatn
so   much   we had eaten

"Remember that party at Jörg's house last summer?" laughed Ben. "Helga started yelling at us for eating so much."

Story 12

"She wanted to take the leftovers home," added Thomas. "She made my wife put some potato salad back in the bowl."

»Sie wollte die Reste mit nach Hause nehmen«, fügte Thomas hinzu. »Sie forderte meine Frau auf, den Kartoffelsalat in die Schüssel zurückzutun.«

"You must have so much guilt, telling her she can't live with you," Günter said as he raked in a pot.

»Du musst dich so schuldig fühlen, wenn du ihr sagst, dass sie nicht bei dir wohnen kann«, sagte Günter als er die Gewinneinsätze einstrich.

"I've had guilt for years. Nothing I do is good enough for her. If I call five times a week, she complains that my wife Ingrid doesn't call. If I visit twice a week, she tells me that her neighbors' kids see them every day."

»Ich hatte jahrelang Schuldgefühle. Alles, was ich mache, ist nicht gut genug für sie. Wenn ich fünf Mal in der Woche anrufe, beschwert sie sich, dass meine Frau Ingrid nie anruft. Wenn ich sie zwei Mal die Woche besuche, sagt sie mir, dass die Kinder ihres Nachbarn sie jeden Tag sehen.«

"How would she know about what other people's kids do?" asked Ben.

»Woher will sie wissen, was anderer Leute Kinder machen?« fragte Ben.

"Everyone in her retirement village lies to each other about how well their children take care of them. They also brag about their genius grandchildren," I said. "It's a competition to see who has the best relatives."

»Jeder in ihrem Altersheim belügt den anderen damit, wie sehr seine Kinder sich um ihn kümmern. Außerdem geben alle mit

Mommy and Me

ihren Genie-Enkeln an«, sagte ich. »Es ist ein Wettbewerb darüber, wer die besten Verwandten hat.«

»Genug geredet«, unterbrach Günter. »Teil die Karten aus.«

"Enough talking," Günter interrupted. "Deal the cards."

Ich teilte eine neue Runde aus. Ich schaute auf meine Karten. Zwei Könige. Vielleicht gewinne ich endlich einmal den Pott.

I dealt another hand. I looked at my cards. Two kings. Maybe I'd win a pot for once.

Ich habe diese Runde tatsächlich gewonnen, indem ich noch den dritten König zog. Trotzdem kam ich am Ende des Abends mit weniger Geld nach Hause. Ich gewinne einfach nie beim Poker.

I actually won that hand by drawing a third king. Still, at the end of the night, I returned home with less money. I never win at poker.

---------5---------

Zwei Wochen später ...

Two weeks later ...

»Wissen Sie, dass Helga die Blumen auf dem Parkplatzgelände abgeschnitten hat?«

"You know that Helga cut the flowers in the parking lot."

Ich hörte Monika zu, der Leiterin der Seniorenwohnanlage, wie sie sich über meine Mutter beschwerte.

I was listening to Monika, the director of the retirement community, complain about my mother.

Story 12

"How could she do that?" I asked. "Mom can't bend over without falling on her face. Anyway, she says she wasn't there."

»Wie hat sie das geschafft?«, fragte ich. »Mutter kann sich nicht bücken, ohne dass sie auf ihr Gesicht fällt. Wie dem auch sei, sie behauptet, dass sie nicht dort gewesen sei.«

"She managed somehow. There are eight witnesses. They were just coming out of the weekly Bingo game as she was putting the flowers into a cardboard box. At least she only cut the flowers right next to the curb."

»Irgendwie muss sie es doch geschafft haben. Es gibt acht Augenzeugen. Die kamen gerade von ihrem wöchentlichen Bingospiel, als sie gerade die Blumen in eine Pappschachtel packte. Wenigstens hat sie nur die Blumen direkt neben dem Randstein abgeschnitten.«

"Can't we pretend she was helping the garden club by pruning some of the plants?" I asked.

»Können wir nicht einfach so tun, als ob sie dem Gartenverein geholfen hätte, indem sie einige Pflanzen zurechtstutzte?«, fragte ich.

"I don't think the garden club is going to support that excuse. Their president fainted when she saw the damage this morning. We had to call an ambulance."

»Ich glaube nicht, dass der Gartenverein diese Ausrede unterstützen wird. Die Vorsitzende fiel in Ohnmacht, als sie den Schaden heute Morgen sah. Wir mussten den Notarzt rufen.«

"At least mom's apartment is decorated nicely. You should see the floral arrangements she made," I said.

»Immerhin ist Mamas Wohnung hübsch dekoriert. Sie sollten die

Mommy and Me

Blumengestecke sehen, die sie gemacht hat«, sagte ich.

»Helga hatte letzte Woche außerdem ein Missgeschick in der Küche«, fuhr Monika fort.

"Helga also had an accident in the kitchen last week," Monika continued.

»Sie vergaß schlichtweg, den Herd auszuschalten. Ich bedaure sehr, dass die Feuerwehr kommen musste.«

"She just forgot to turn off the stove. I'm really sorry about the fire department showing up."

»Sie wird zur Gefahr für die Allgemeinheit«, sagte Monika.

"She's becoming a danger to the community," Monika said.

»Niemand kam zu Schaden. Bitte geben Sie Mama noch eine Chance.«

"Nobody was hurt. Please give mom another chance."

Sie seufzte und rieb sich die Stirn. Es muss schwierig sein, ein Heim voll alter Leute zu leiten.

She sighed and rubbed her forehead. It must be tough running a place filled with old people.

»Einverstanden, Herr Dietrich. Aber ich bestehe darauf, dass Ihre Mutter nicht mehr kocht. Sie kann jeden Abend in unserem Hauptspeisesaal zu Abend essen. Es kostet nur sieben Euro und das Essen ist sehr gut.«

"OK, Mr. Dietrich. But I insist that your mother stop cooking. She can have dinner in our main dining room every night. It only costs seven Euro, and the food is very good."

175

Story 12

"No more cooking or cutting flowers," I promised.

»Kein Kochen oder Blumenabschneiden mehr«, versprach ich.
kaɪn ˈkɔxən ˈoːdɐ ˈbluːmənapˌʃnaɪdn meːɐ fɛɐˈʃpʁaːx ɪç
not any cooking or flower cutting more I promised I

———————————— 6 ————————————

I headed to mom's apartment and told her about my meeting with Monika.

Ich ging zu Mutters Wohnung und erzählte ihr von meinem
ɪç gɪŋ tsuː ˈmʊtɐs ˈvoːnʊŋ ʊnt ɛɐˈtsɛːltə iːɐ fɔn ˈmaɪnəm
I I went to mother's apartment and I told her about my

Treffen mit Monika.
ˈtʁɛfən mɪt ˈmoːnika
meeting with Monika

"She doesn't like me," Mom said. "Ever since I whacked her puppy with Ilse's cane."

»Sie kann mich nicht leiden«, sagte Mutter. »Seitdem ich ihr
ziː kan mɪç nɪçt ˈlaɪdən ˈzaktə ˈmʊtɐ zaɪtˈdeːm ɪç iːɐ
she she can't stand me she said mother ever since I her

Hündchen mit Ilses Gehstock schlug.«
ˈhʏntçən mɪt ˈɪlzəs ˈgeːʃtɔk ʃluːk
puppy dog with Ilse's cane I whacked

"Please don't tell me that you hurt her cute little dog," I said.

»Sag mir bitte nicht, dass du ihrem niedlichen, kleinen Hund
zaːk miːɐ ˈbɪtə nɪçt das duː ˈiːʁəm ˈniːtlɪçən ˈklaɪnən hʊnt
tell me please not that you her cute little dog

wehgetan hast«, sagte ich.
ˈveːgəˌtaːn hast ˈzaktə ɪç
you hurt I said I

"I just wanted it to stop yapping. It was a love tap."

»Ich wollte, dass er zu kläffen aufhört. Es war ein
ɪç ˈvɔltə das eːɐ tsuː ˈklɛfn ˈaʊfˌhøːɐt ɛs vaːɐ aɪn
I I wanted that it to to yap it stops it it was a

kleiner Schubser.«
ˈklaɪnɐ ˈʃʊpsɐ
love tap

"Did she see you do it?"

»Hat sie gesehen, dass du es warst?«
hat ziː gəˈzeːən das duː ɛs vaːɐst
→ she ←she saw that you it it was

"No. I blamed Ilse. It's her cane."

»Nein, ich habe Ilse beschuldigt. Es ist ja ihr Stock.«
naɪn ɪç ˈhaːbə ˈɪlzə bəˈʃʊldɪçt ɛs ɪst jaː iːɐ ʃtɔk
no I → Ilse ←I blamed it it is ! her cane

"So you got Ilse in trouble."

»Demnach hast du Ilse in Schwierigkeiten gebracht.«
ˈdeːmnaːx hast duː ˈɪlzə ɪn ˈʃviːʁɪçkaɪtən gəˈbʁaxt
therefore → you Ilse in trouble ←you brought

"Monika didn't believe me. She said Ilse is too weak to swing her cane. We had a big argument."

»Monika hat mir nicht geglaubt. Sie meinte Ilse sei zu
ˈmoːnika hat miːɐ nɪçt gəˈglaʊpt ziː ˈmaɪntə ˈɪlzə zaɪ tsuː
Monika → me not ←she believed she she said Ilse she is too

schwach, ihren Stock zu schwingen. Wir hatten eine große
ʃvax ˈiːʁən ʃtɔk tsuː ˈʃvɪŋən viːɐ ˈhatən ˈaɪnə ˈgʁoːsə
weak her cane to to swing we we had a big

Mommy and Me

Auseinandersetzung.«
  aʊsaɪˈnandɐˌzɛtsʊŋ
  argument

»Vergessen wir Ilse und den Hund. Ich habe Monika versprochen,
  fɛɐˈɡɛsn viːɐ ˈɪlzə ʊnt deːn hʊnt ɪç ˈhaːbə ˈmoːnika fɛɐˈʃpʁɔxən
  let's forget Ilse and the dog   I   →   Monika   ←I promised

dass du jeden Abend im Hauptgebäude essen wirst. Das bedeutet,
  das duː ˈjeːdən ˈaːbənt ɪm ˈhaʊptɡəˌbɔʏdə ˈɛsən vɪʁst das bəˈdɔɪtət
  that you every night in the main building to eat you will that it means

es wird nicht mehr gekocht. Du wirst auch keine Blumen oder
  ɛs vɪʁt nɪçt meːɐ ɡəˈkɔxt duː vɪʁst aʊx ˈkaɪnə ˈbluːmən ˈoːdɐ
  it →   no longer ← it is cooked you you will also no flowers or

Büsche mehr abschneiden. Und keine Bäume fällen.«
  ˈbʏʃə meːɐ ˈapˌʃnaɪdən ʊnt ˈkaɪnə ˈbɔʏmə ˈfɛlən
  bushes anymore to cut and no trees to chop down

"Let's forget Ilse and the dog. I promised Monika you would eat dinner at the hall each night. That means no more cooking. No cutting up the flowers or the bushes either. No chopping down trees."

»Sei nicht albern, ich habe doch gar keine Axt. Hallo, ich kann
  zaɪ nɪçt ˈalbɐn ɪç ˈhaːbə dɔx ɡaːɐ ˈkaɪnə akst haˈlɔ ɪç kan
  be not silly   I I have ! not any   axe   hey I I can

mir doch nicht jedes Mal sieben Euro für ein Abendessen leisten.
  miːɐ dɔx nɪçt ˈjeːdəs maːl ˈziːbən ˈɔɪʁo fyːɐ aɪn ˈaːbəntˌɛsn ˈlaɪstən
  →   !   not every time seven Euro for a dinner   ← I afford

Ich bin arm.«
  ɪç bɪn aʁm
  I I am poor

"Don't be so silly. I don't even own an axe. Hey, I can't afford seven Euro every night for dinner. I'm poor."

Die nächsten fünf Minuten hatten wir eine hitzige Diskussion.
  diː ˈnɛçstən fʏnf mɪˈnuːtən ˈhatən viːɐ ˈaɪnə ˈhɪtsɪɡə dɪskʊˈsjoːn
  the next   five minutes   we had we   a   heated discussion

Mutter stimmte schließlich den Bedingungen von Monika zu, aber
  ˈmʊtɐ ˈʃtɪmtə ˈʃliːslɪç deːn bəˈdɪŋʊŋən fɔn ˈmoːnika tsuː ˈaːbɐ
  mother she agreed→ eventually the terms of Monika ← but

ich musste versprechen, für sie das Abendessen im Hauptgebäude
  ɪç ˈmʊstə fɛɐˈʃpʁɛçən fyːɐ ziː das ˈaːbntˌɛsn ɪm ˈhaʊptɡəˌbɔʏdə
  I I had to to promise for her the dinner in the main building

zu bezahlen. Es war mir sieben Euro pro Abend wert, denn
  tsuː bəˈtsaːlən ɛs vaːɐ miːɐ ˈziːbən ˈɔɪʁo pʁoː ˈaːbənt veːɐt dɛn
  to   to pay   it → to me seven   Euro per night ← it was worth because

so musste ich mich nicht darüber sorgen, dass Mama ihr
  zoː ˈmʊstə ɪç mɪç nɪçt daˈʁyːbɐ ˈzɔʁɡən das ˈmama iːɐ
  that way I had to I → not about it ← to worry that mom her

Wohngebäude niederbrennt.
  ˈvoːnɡəˌbɔʏdə ˈniːdɐˌbʁɛnt
  apartment building she burns down

We had a heated discussion for the next five minutes. Mom eventually agreed to Monika's terms, but I had to promise to pay for her meals at the hall. It was worth seven Euro a night so I didn't have to worry about mom burning down her apartment building.

Mama schaute auf eine Liste, die auf ihrem Küchentisch lag. Sie
  ˈmama ˈʃaʊtə aʊf ˈaɪnə ˈlɪstə diː aʊf ˈiːʁəm ˈkʏçnˌtɪʃ laːk ziː
  mom she looked at a list that on her kitchen table it lay she

Mom looked at a list that was sitting on her kitchen table. She frequently made lists of things to complain about.

177

Story 12

machte öfters eine Auflistung von Beschwerdepunkten.
'maxtə 'œftɐs 'amə 'aʊfˌlɪstʊŋ fɔn bəˈʃveːɐdəˌpʊŋktn̩
she made quite often a list of complaints

"You never take me anyplace."
»Du fährst nie mit mir irgendwohin.«
duː ˈfɛːɐst niː mɪt miːɐ ˈɪɐgn̩tvoˈhɪn
you you go never with me anywhere

I thought for a minute.
Ich dachte ein wenig nach.
ɪç ˈdaxtə aɪn ˈveːnɪç naːx
I I thought→ a bit ←

"Why don't we go to the movies?"
»Warum gehen wir nicht ins Kino?«
vaˈʁʊm ˈgeːən viːɐ nɪçt ɪns ˈkiːnoː
why we go we not to the cinema

"That last movie we went to was disgusting. You should be ashamed of yourself."
»Der letzte Film, den wir angesehen haben, war widerlich. Du
deːɐ ˈlɛtstə fɪlm deːn viːɐ ˈangəˌzeːən ˈhaːbn̩ vaːɐ ˈviːdɐlɪç duː
the last movie that we we watched it was disgusting you

solltest dich schämen.«
ˈzɔltɛst dɪç ˈʃɛːmən
you should to be ashamed of yourself

"It's not my fault they say bad words in movies," I answered.
»Es ist doch nicht meine Schuld, dass man in Filmen schlimme
ɛs ɪst dɔx nɪçt ˈmaɪnə ʃʊlt das man ɪn ˈfɪlmən ˈʃlɪmə
it it is ! not my fault that one in movies bad

Wörter benutzt«, antwortete ich.
ˈvœʁtɐ bəˈnʊtst ˈantvɔʁtətə ɪç
words one uses I answered I

"Let's go to the park. We can sit on a bench and watch the birds."
»Komm, wir gehen in den Park. Wir können auf einer Bank
kɔm viːɐ ˈgeːən ɪn deːn paʁk viːɐ ˈkœnən aʊf ˈaɪnɐ baŋk
come we we go to the park we we can on a bench

sitzen und Vögel beobachten.«
ˈzɪtsən ʊnt ˈføːgəl bəˈoːbaxtən
to sit and birds to watch

"Okay, that sounds good."
»Prima, das hört sich gut an.«
ˈpʁiːma das ˈhøːɐt zɪç guːt an
great that it sounds→ good ←

It took her ten minutes to get ready, have a couple sips of water, and hit the bathroom just in case. We drove to a local park. It wasn't a long walk from the parking lot to a bench that was shaded by trees. Mom needed to hold on to me the whole time.

Sie brauchte zehn Minuten, um sich fertig zu machen, noch
ziː ˈbʁaʊxtə tseːn mɪˈnuːtən ʊm zɪç ˈfɛʁtɪç tsuː ˈmaxn̩ nɔx
she she needed ten minutes in order to herself ready to to make still

ein paar Schluck Wasser zu trinken und für alle Fälle auf die
aɪn paːɐ ʃlʊk ˈvasɐ tsuː ˈtʁɪŋkn̩ ʊnt fyːɐ ˈalə ˈfɛlə aʊf diː
a few sip water to to drink and just in case to the

Toilette zu gehen. Wir fuhren zu einem Park in der Nähe. Es war
toaˈlɛtə tsuː ˈgeːən viːɐ ˈfuːʁən tsuː ˈaɪnəm paʁk ɪn deːɐ ˈnɛːə ɛs vaːɐ
toilet to to go we we drove to a park nearby it it was

Mommy and Me

kein	allzu	langer	Spaziergang	vom	Parkplatz	zu	einer	Bank
kaɪn	ˈaltsuː	ˈlaŋɐ	ʃpaˈtsiːɐˌɡaŋ	fɔm	ˈpaʁkˌplats	tsuː	ˈaɪnə	baŋk
not a	excessively	long	walk	from the	parking lot	to	a	bench

im	Schatten	der	Bäume.	Mama	musste	sich	die	ganze	Zeit	bei
ɪm	ˈʃatən	deːɐ	ˈbɔʏmə	ˈmama	ˈmʊstə	zɪç	diː	ˈɡantsə	tsaɪt	baɪ
in the	shade	of the	trees	mom	she had to	→	the	whole	time	on

mir	festhalten.
miːɐ	ˈfɛstˌhaltən
me	← to hold on to

Von	der	Bank	aus	konnten	wir	einen	kleinen	Teich	sehen.	Neben
fɔn	deːɐ	baŋk	aʊs	ˈkɔntən	viːɐ	ˈaɪnən	ˈklaɪnən	taɪç	ˈzeːən	ˈneːbən
from →	the	bench	←	we could	we	a	small	pond	to see	next to

We could see a little pond from the bench. Next to the pond was a playground. A little kid was chasing ducks near the water.

dem	Teich	war	ein	Spielplatz.	Ein	kleines	Kind	verfolgte	die
deːm	taɪç	vaːɐ	aɪn	ˈʃpiːlˌplats	aɪn	ˈklaɪnəs	kɪnt	fɛɐˈfɔlktə	diː
the	pond	it was	a	playground	a	little	kid	he chased	the

Enten	nahe	dem	Wasser.
ˈɛntən	ˈnaːə	deːm	ˈvasɐ
ducks	near	the	water

»Hier	ist	es	schön«,	sagte	ich.
hiːɐ	ɪst	ɛs	ʃøːn	ˈzaktə	ɪç
here	it is	it	nice	I said	I

"This is nice," I said.

»Wen	interessieren	schon	Enten?«,	sagte	Mutter.	»Meine
veːn	ɪntəʁɛˈsiːʁən	ʃoːn	ˈɛntən	ˈzaktə	ˈmʊtɐ	ˈmaɪnə
who	they care about	!	ducks	she said	mother	my

"Who cares about ducks?" Mom said. "My health insurance hasn't paid for my last doctor visit."

Krankenversicherung	hat	den	letzten	Arztbesuch	nicht	bezahlt.«
ˈkʁaŋknfɛɐˌzɪçəʁʊŋ	hat	deːn	ˈlɛtstən	ˈaːɐtstbəˌzuːx	nɪçt	bətsaːlt
health insurance	→	the	last	doctor visit	not	← they paid

Ich	seufzte.	»Wir	haben	uns	darüber	schon	einige	Male
ɪç	ˈzɔɪftstə	viːɐ	ˈhaːbn	ʊns	daˈʁyːbɐ	ʃoːn	ˈaɪnɪɡə	ˈmaːlə
I	I sighed	we	→		about this	already	a few	times

I sighed. "We talked about this a few times," I reminded her. "Your insurance sent you a statement that said the cost of the visit was applied to your deductible."

unterhalten«,	erinnerte	ich	sie.	»Deine	Versicherung	hat	dir
ʊntɐˈhaltən	ɛɐˈʔɪnɐtə	ɪç	ziː	ˈdaɪnə	fɛɐˈzɪçəʁʊŋ	hat	diːɐ
← we talked	I reminded	I	her	your	insurance	→	to you

eine	Abrechnung	geschickt,	die	besagt,	dass	die	Kosten	des
ˈaɪnə	ˈapˌʁɛçnʊŋ	ɡəˈʃɪkt	diː	bəˈzaːkt	das	diː	ˈkɔstən	dɛs
a	bill	← it sent	that	it said	that	the	cost	of the

Besuches	mit	der	Selbstbeteiligung	verrechnet	wurden.«
bəˈzuːxəs	mɪt	deːɐ	ˈzɛlpstbəˌtaɪlɪɡʊŋ	fɛɐˈʁɛçnət	ˈvʊʁdn
visit	with	the	deductible	it was charged to	

»Was	ist	eine	Selbstbeteiligung?«
vas	ɪst	ˈaɪnə	ˈzɛlpstbəˌtaɪlɪɡʊŋ
what	it is	a	deductible

"What's a deductible?"

»Ich	habe	dir	schon	drei	Mal	erklärt,	was	eine
ɪç	ˈhaːbə	diːɐ	ʃoːn	dʁaɪ	maːl	ɛɐˈklɛːɐt	vas	ˈaɪnə
I	→	to you	already	three	time	← I have explained	what	a

"I've told you three times about deductibles. Why don't you write it down?"

179

Story 12

»... Selbstbeteiligung ist. Warum schreibst du es dir nicht auf?«

"You never told me about deductibles. What about my eye doctor? He just sent me a bill for ninety-five Euro. He's a thief."

»Du hast mir nichts von einer Selbstbeteiligung gesagt. Und was ist mit meinem Augenarzt los? Er hat mir gerade eine Rechnung über fünfundneunzig Euro geschickt. Er ist ein Dieb.«

"He gave you a complete checkup," I told her.

»Er machte eine komplette ärztliche Untersuchung«, sagte ich zu ihr.

"Some young girl did everything. She's probably just a nurse. I'm not paying."

»Irgendein junges Mädchen hat das alles gemacht. Sie ist wahrscheinlich nur eine Krankenschwester. Ich bezahle das nicht.«

"Ursula told me he did most of the work and the girl took notes," I said.

»Ursula sagte mir, dass er die meiste Arbeit machte und das Mädchen die Schreibarbeiten«, sagte ich.

"The doctor was eating a sandwich. He just watched. I'll sue him."

»Der Arzt hat ein Sandwich gegessen. Er hat nur zugeschaut. Ich werde ihn verklagen.«

My eye started to twitch. Heat started rising to my face. I took a few deep breaths. Miraculously, I was able to calm myself, even though she kept complaining about her doctors. After ten minutes she ran out of things to

Mein Auge fing an zu zucken. Die Hitze stieg mir ins Gesicht. Ich holte ein paar Mal tief Luft. Es war ein Wunder, dass ich

Mommy and Me

die Ruhe bewahren konnte,	obwohl	sie	sich	weiterhin	über	ihre	complain about.
diː ʁuːə bəˈvaːʁən ˈkɔntə	ɔpˈvoːl	ziː	zɪç	ˈvaɪtɐhɪn	yːbɐ	ˈiːʁə	
I could keep calm	even though	she	→	still	about	her	

Ärzte	beschwerte.	Nach	zehn	Minuten	wusste	sie	nichts	mehr,
ˈɛːɐtstə	bəˈʃveːɐtə	naːx	tsɛːn	mɪˈnuːtən	ˈvʊstə	ziː	nɪçts	meːɐ
doctors	←she complained	after	ten	minutes	she knew	she	nothing	more

worüber	sie	sich	beschweren	könnte.
voːˈʁyːbɐ	ziː	zɪç bəʃveːʁən	ˈkœntə	
about what	she	she could complain		

Wir	saßen	noch	eine	weitere	Stunde	auf	der	Bank,	genossen	die	We spent another hour sitting on the bench, enjoying the sun and talking about life.
viːɐ	ˈzaːsən	nɔx	ˈaɪnə	ˈvaɪtəʁə	ˈʃtʊndə	aʊf	deːɐ	baŋk	ɡəˈnɔsən	diː	
we	we sat	another	further	hour	on	the	bench	we enjoyed	the		

Sonne	und	unterhielten	uns	über	das	Leben.
ˈzɔnə	ʊnt	ʊntɐˈhiːltn	ʊns	ˈyːbɐ	das	
sun	and	we talked	about	the	life	

7

»Ich	war	ein	guter	Junge,	warum	also	tut	meine	Mutter	alles,	"I was a good child, so why is my mother trying so hard to make me miserable?"
ɪç	vaːɐ	aɪn	ˈɡuːtɐ	ˈjʊŋə	vaˈʁʊm	ˈalzo	tuːt	ˈmaɪnə	ˈmʊtɐ	ˈaləs	
I	I was	a	good	boy	why	so	she does	my	mother	everything	

nur	damit	ich	mich	elend	fühle?«
nuːɐ	daˈmɪt	ɪç	mɪç	ˈeːlɛnt	ˈfyːlə
just	so that	I	→	miserable	←I feel

»Sie	erinnert	sich	nicht mehr	daran,	was für	ein	wunderbares	Kind	"She doesn't remember what a wonderful child you were," Dr. Rosenberg said.
ziː	ɛɐˈɪnɐt zɪç	nɪçt meːɐ	daˈʁan	vas fyːɐ	aɪn	ˈvʊndɐbaːʁəs	kɪnt		
she	she remembers	no longer	on it	what a	a	wonderful	child		

Sie	waren«,	sagte	Dr.	Rosenberg.
ziː	ˈvaːʁən	ˈzaktə	ˈdɔktoːɐ	ˈʁoːzənbɛʁk
you	you were	he said	doctor	Rosenberg

Dr.	Rosenberg	ist	mein	Psychiater.	Ich	treffe	mich	jede	Woche	Dr. Rosenberg is my psychiatrist. I meet with him every week. He's been helping me deal with the problems I have with my mother.
ˈdɔktoːɐ	ˈʁoːzənbɛʁk	ɪst	maɪn	psyˈçjaːtɐ	ɪç	ˈtʁɛfə mɪç	ˈjeːdə	ˈvɔxə		
doctor	Rosenberg	he is	my	psychiatrist	I	I meet	every	week		

mit	ihm.	Er	hilft	mir	dabei,	mit	den	Problemen	umzugehen,	die
mɪt	iːm	eːɐ	hɪlft	miːɐ	daˈbaɪ	mɪt	deːn	pʁoˈbleːmən	ˈʊmtsuɡeːən	diː
with	him	he	he helps	me	with it	with	the	problems	to handle	that

ich	mit	meiner	Mutter	habe.
ɪç	mɪt	ˈmaɪnɐ	ˈmʊtɐ	ˈhaːbə
I	with	my	mother	I have

»Auf jeden Fall	habe	ich	sie	nicht	in	den	Teich	geworfen«,	sagte	"At least I didn't throw her into the pond," I said.
aʊf ˈjeːdən fal	ˈhaːbə	ɪç	ziː	nɪçt	ɪn	deːn	taɪç	ɡəˈvɔʁfən	ˈzaktə	
in any case	→	I	her	not	into	the	pond	←I threw	I said	

ich.
ɪç
I

Story 12

"That proves you are a wonderful child," he said.

»Das beweist, Sie sind ein großartiges Kind«, sagte er.

"She's just a mean person, isn't she?" I asked.

»Sie ist einfach nur eine gemeine Frau, nicht wahr?«, fragte ich.

"We've gone over this before. She's unhappy with her life and takes it out on anyone who comes near her."

»Wir sind das bereits durchgegangen. Sie ist mit ihrem Leben unglücklich und sie lässt es an jedem aus, der ihr nahekommt.«

"She'll never change," I said.

»Sie wird sich nie ändern«, sagte ich.

"This is why you are learning how to cope with her."

»Deshalb lernen Sie hier, wie Sie mit ihr zurechtkommen.«

"She still drives me crazy."

»Sie macht mich immer noch verrückt.«

"Yes, but you are handling it better. A year ago you couldn't sleep at night after you visited her. Yesterday you took all of the grief she gave you without pulling your hair out. Afterwards, you had a pleasant time with her. That shows major progress."

»Ja, aber Sie gehen damit besser um. Noch vor einem Jahr konnten Sie nach einem Besuch bei ihr nachts nicht schlafen. Den ganzen Kummer, den sie Ihnen gestern bereitete, haben Sie überstanden, ohne sich die Haare auszureißen. Anschließend haben Sie noch eine schöne Zeit mit ihr verbracht. Das zeugt schon von einem gewaltigen Fortschritt.«

Mommy and Me

»Ja, wir hatten eine ganz nette Zeit miteinander, nachdem sie aufgehört hatte, über die Ärzte zu meckern.«

"Yeah, we had a pretty nice time after she stopped yelling about doctors."

»Worüber haben Sie sich unterhalten?«

"What did you talk about?"

»Angenehme Sachen. Die Größe und Form ihres Stuhlgangs am Morgen. Den überschüssigen Schleim, der sich in ihrer Nase bildet. Die Nachbarin, die zum kostenlosen, wöchentlichen Mittagessen in der Seniorenwohnanlage geht und dabei möglichst viel Essen für später in ihre Handtasche schaufelt.«

"Nice things. The size and shape of her bowel movements that morning. The excess mucus that builds up in her nose. The lady next door who goes to the free weekly lunches at her retirement community and shovels as much extra food as possible into her purse."

»Hat das nicht Spaß gemacht?«, fragte Dr. Rosenberg.

"Wasn't that fun?" asked Dr. Rosenberg.

---8---

»Du machst Fortschritte, weil du deine Mutter im Park nicht erwürgt hast und weil du dich nicht betrunken hast, als du nach Hause gekommen bist?«, fragte Ingrid.

"You're making progress because you didn't strangle your mother at the park and didn't get drunk when you came home?" Ingrid asked.

»Das hat Dr. Rosenberg gesagt.«

"That's what Dr. Rosenberg said."

»Das ist ein Grund zum Feiern. Wir sollten deine Mutter

"This is a cause for celebration. Let's invite your mom over for dinner."

183

Story 12

	zum Abendessen einladen.«
	tsʊm 'a:bnt͜ˌɛsn 'aɪnˌla:dən
	for dinner to invite
"Not tonight."	»Nicht heute Abend.«
	nɪçt 'hɔɪtə 'a:bənt
	not tonight
"Does she know that you are seeing a psychiatrist because she's so malicious toward you?"	»Weiß sie, dass du zu einem Psychiater gehst, weil sie dir gegenüber so bösartig ist?«
	vaɪs zi: das du: tsu: 'aɪnəm psy'çja:tɐ ge:st vaɪl zi: di:ɐ ge:gn'y:bɐ zo: 'bø:sˌaˑɐtɪç ɪst
	she knows she that you to a psychiatrist you go because she to you toward so malicious she is
"What good would it do to tell her? She thinks she's nice to everyone."	»Was brächte es, wenn man es ihr sagen würde? Sie glaubt, sie wäre zu allen nett.«
	vas 'bʀɛçtə ɛs vɛn man ɛs iːɐ 'za:gn 'vʏʀdə zi: glaʊpt zi: 'vɛːʀə tsu: 'alən nɛt
	what it would bring it if one it her he would tell she she thinks she she would be to everyone nice
"So what are you going to do?"	»Also, was wirst du tun?«
	'alzo vas vɪʀst du: tu:n
	so what you will you to do
"What I've been doing. Spend time with her, listen to her complaints, try to make her unhappy life a little better, resist the urge to bury her alive."	»Was ich bisher getan habe. Ich verbringe Zeit mit ihr, höre mir ihre Beschwerden an, versuche, ihr unglückliches Leben etwas besser zu machen, und widersetze mich dem Drang, sie lebendig zu begraben.«
	vas ɪç bɪs'heːɐ gə'ta:n 'ha:bə ɪç fɛɐ'bʀɪŋə tsaɪt mɪt iːɐ 'høːʀə miːɐ 'iːʀə bə'ʃveːɐdn an fɛɐ'zu:xə iːɐ 'ʊnˌglʏklɪçəs 'le:bən 'ɛtvas 'bɛsɐ tsu: 'maxn ʊnt viːdɐ'zɛtsə mɪç de:m dʀaŋ zi: le'bɛndɪç tsu: bə'gʀa:bən
	what I so far I have done I I spend time with her I listen to → her complaints ← I try her unhappy life somewhat better to to make and I resist the urge her alive to to bury
"Do you still need to see the psychiatrist?"	»Musst du immer noch zum Psychiater?«
	mʊst du: 'ɪmɐ nɔx tsum psy'çja:tɐ
	you have to you still to the psychiatrist
"I'll probably have to meet with him every week until she is dead."	»Ich werde wahrscheinlich jede Woche zu ihm müssen, bis sie tot ist.«
	ɪç 'veːɐdə vaːɐ'ʃaɪnlɪç 'jeːdə 'vɔxə tsu: iːm 'mʏsn bɪs zi: to:t ɪst
	I I will probably every week to him to have to until she dead she is

Mommy and Me

»Sie wird noch weitere zwanzig Jahre leben!«
zi: vɪʁt nɔx ˈvaɪtəʁə ˈtsvantsɪç ˈjaːʁə ˈleːbən
she she will still another twenty years to live

"She'll live for another twenty years!"

»Das hoffe ich. Kannst du mich bis dahin ertragen?«, fragte ich.
das ˈhɔfə ɪç kanst duː mɪç bɪs daˈhɪn ɛɐ̯ˈtʁaːgn̩ ˈfʁaːktə ɪç
that I hope I can you you me until then to tolerate I asked I

"I hope so. Can you tolerate me until then?" I asked.

Ingrid schauderte.
ˈɪŋgʁɪt ˈʃaʊdɐtə
Ingrid she shuddered

Ingrid shuddered.

»Ich denke, du bist es wert«, sagte sie.
ɪç ˈdɛŋkə duː bɪst ɛs veːɐ̯t ˈzaktə ziː
I I think you you are it worth she said she

"I guess you're worth it," she said.

STORY 13

Evolution

»Ich glaube an Gott, aber ich denke nicht, dass er zu sehr in unseren Alltag eingebunden ist. Er hat das Universum erschaffen und die Dinge vor ein paar Milliarden Jahren in Bewegung gebracht. Dann hat er sich zurückgelehnt, um zu beobachten.«

"I believe in God but I don't think he gets too involved in our daily lives. He created the universe and set things in motion a few billion years ago. And then he sat back to watch."

Ich denke einen Moment nach und dann fahre ich fort.

I think for a few seconds and then continue.

»Die Evolution ist Gottes Weg, die Ordnung in der Welt aufrechtzuerhalten. Wenn etwas anfängt, schief zu laufen, findet die Evolution einen Weg. Manchmal dauert es ein oder zwei Jahrhunderte, aber letztendlich hilft die Evolution der Welt ihre Probleme zu lösen.«

"Evolution is God's way of keeping order in the world. If something starts to go wrong, evolution finds an answer. Sometimes it takes a century or two, but eventually evolution helps the world solve its problems."

Ich schaue den Mann an, mit dem ich rede. Er scheint nicht interessiert zu sein.

I look at the guy I am talking to. He doesn't seem interested.

Story 13

"Centuries ago," I continue, "people worried about dying from plague. Even longer ago, humans couldn't digest animals milk. Then evolution stepped into the picture. Our genetics changed bit by bit. In addition, new technologies have boosted our evolutionary response. Eventually, we will be more resistant to diseases that are killing us today. These are great examples of how evolution creates solutions to problems."

»Vor Jahrhunderten«, fahre ich fort, »machten sich die Menschen Sorgen, an der Pest zu sterben. Sogar noch länger ist es her, dass Menschen keine Milch von Tieren verdauen konnten. Dann trat die Evolution ins Geschehen ein. Unsere Erbanlagen veränderten sich Stück für Stück. Zusätzlich haben neue Technologien unsere evolutionäre Reaktion verstärkt. Letztendlich werden wir resistenter gegen Krankheiten sein, die heute tödlich für uns sind. Das sind großartige Beispiele dafür, wie die Evolution Problemlösungen findet.«

The man is still unresponsive.

Der Mann reagiert immer noch nicht.

"I know what you are thinking," I tell him. "Deadly diseases are not a good example, because now many people are dying of AIDS, malaria, or cholera. But I am sure that evolution will figure out how to combat these diseases, too."

»Ich weiß, was Sie denken«, sage ich zu ihm. »Tödliche Krankheiten sind kein gutes Beispiel, da ja heutzutage viele Menschen an AIDS, Malaria oder Cholera sterben. Aber ich bin sicher, dass die Evolution einen Weg finden wird, wie man auch diese Krankheiten bekämpfen kann.«

Evolution

Ich ziehe eine Wasserflasche aus meiner Jackentasche und nehme ein paar Schlucke.

»Hier ist ein weiteres Beispiel dafür, wie die Evolution ein Problem löst«, sage ich zu dem Mann. »Sie sind ein Parasit, der anderen Menschen Elend und Leiden verursacht. Die Evolution hat dafür ein Heilmittel gefunden. Nämlich mich!«

Ich begreife, dass ich meine Zeit vergeude. Am Ende kümmert sich dieser Mann doch nicht um meine Weltanschauung. Er hat immerhin drei Schüsse ins Herz abbekommen!

I pull a bottle of water out of my jacket pocket and take a few sips.

"Here's another example of evolution solving a problem," I say to the man. "You are a parasite who causes misery and suffering for other people. Evolution developed a cure. That would be me!"

I realize that I'm wasting my time. After all, this guy doesn't care about my theory of the universe. He's got three bullet holes in his heart!

---—2—---

Ein paar Tage zuvor ...

Ich lehne mich in meinem Drehstuhl zurück und schaue aus dem Bürofenster. Es ist ein schöner Herbstmorgen. Alles ist friedlich und ruhig.

Da höre ich schwere Schritte im Gang. Die Tür öffnet sich und

A few days earlier ...

I lean back in my swivel chair and look out of the office window. It's a pretty autumn morning. Everything is peaceful and quiet.

Then I hear heavy footsteps in the hallway. The door opens and a large, square man walks in. He looks at me like I am a lower life form that he

Story 13

wanted to dissect.

ein großer, vierschrötiger Mann kommt herein. Er blickt mich
aɪn ˈɡʁoːsɐ fiːɐ̯ˈʃʁøːtɪɡɐ man kɔmt heˈʁaɪn eːɐ̯ blɪkt mɪç
a large square man he comes in he he looks at →

an, als ob ich eine untergeordnete Lebensform wäre, die er nun
an als ɔp ɪç ˈaɪnə ʊntɐɡəˈʔɔʁdnətə ˈleːbənsfɔʁm ˈvɛːʁə diː eːɐ̯ nuːn
← as if I an inferior life form I was that he now

sezieren wollte.
zeˈtsiːʁən ˈvɔltə
to dissect he wanted

"Would you like to apply for a life insurance policy?" I ask him. "If you are in good health and don't smoke you can qualify for at least a million Euro in coverage. I can get you great rates."

»Möchten Sie eine Lebensversicherung beantragen?«, frage ich
ˈmœçtən ziː ˈaɪnə ˈleːbənsfɛɐ̯ˌzɪçəʁʊŋ bəˈʔantʁaːɡən ˈfʁaːɡə ɪç
would you like you a life insurance policy to apply for I ask I

ihn. »Wenn Sie gesund sind und nicht rauchen, wären Sie
iːn vɛn ziː ɡəˈzʊnt zɪnt ʊnt nɪçt ˈʁaʊxən ˈvɛːʁən ziː
him if you healthy you are and not to smoke you would be you

für eine Deckungssumme von mindestens einer Million Euro
fyːɐ̯ ˈaɪnə ˈdɛkʊŋsˌzʊmə fɔn ˈmɪndəstəns ˈaɪnɐ mɪlˈjoːn ˈɔɪʁo
for a coverage of at least a million Euro

qualifiziert. Ich kann Ihnen sehr günstige Beiträge anbieten.«
kvalifiˈtsiːɐ̯t ɪç kan ˈiːnən zeːɐ̯ ˈɡʏnstɪɡə ˈbaɪtʁɛːɡə ˈanbiːtən
qualified I I can you very low-priced premiums to offer

His gaze wanders from my expensive furniture to the fancy pictures on the wall.

Sein Blick wandert nun von meinen teuren Möbeln zu den
zaɪn blɪk ˈvandɐt nuːn fɔn ˈmaɪnən ˈtɔɪʁən ˈmøːbəln tsuː deːn
his gaze it wanders now from my expensive furniture to the

extravaganten Bildern an der Wand.
ˈɛkstʁavaɡantn̩ ˈbɪldɐn an deːɐ̯ vant
fancy pictures on the wall

"Nice office," he says.

»Schönes Büro«, sagt er.
ˈʃøːnəs byˈʁoː zakt eːɐ̯
nice office he says he

"Yes it is. I have a new coffee maker. You want some decaf? Where did you get all those scars and that crooked nose? If you work in a hazardous profession, you have to state that on the application."

»Ja, das stimmt. Ich habe eine neue Kaffeemaschine. Möchten
jaː das ʃtɪmt ɪç ˈhaːbə ˈaɪnə ˈnɔɪə ˈkafeːmaˌʃiːnə ˈmœçtən
yes that is true I I have a new coffee machine would you like

Sie einen koffeinfreien Kaffee haben? Woher haben Sie all diese
ziː ˈaɪnən kɔfeˈiːnˌfʁaɪən ˈkafe ˈhaːbn̩ voˈheːɐ̯ ˈhaːbn̩ ziː al ˈdiːzə
you a caffeine-free coffee to have from where you have you all those

Narben und diese schiefe Nase? Wenn Sie einen risikoreichen
ˈnaʁbən ʊnt ˈdiːzə ˈʃiːfə ˈnaːzə vɛn ziː ˈaɪnən ˈʁiːzikoˌʁaɪçn̩
scars and that crooked nose if you a hazardous

Beruf ausüben, müssen Sie dies in Ihrem Antrag angeben.«
bəˈʁuːf ˈaʊsˌyːbn̩ ˈmʏsən ziː diːs ɪn ˈiːʁəm ˈantʁaːk ˈanˌɡeːbn̩
profession to perform you have to you this in your application to state

"Stop talking about life insurance," he says to me.

»Hören Sie auf, von der Lebensversicherung zu reden«, sagt er
ˈhøːʁən ziː aʊf fɔn deːɐ̯ ˈleːbənsfɛɐ̯ˌzɪçəʁʊŋ tsuː ˈʁɛːdən zakt eːɐ̯
stop about the life insurance policy to to talk he says he

zu mir.
tsu: miːɐ
to me

»Ich kann ihren Akzent nicht zuordnen«, erwähne ich. »Russland?
ɪç kan ˈiːʁən akˈtsɛnt nɪçt tsuːˈɔʁdnən ɛɐˈvɛːnə ɪç ˈʁʊslant
I   I can your accent   not   to place   I mention I Russia

Der Balkan vielleicht?«
deːɐ balˈkaːn fiˈlaɪçt
the Balkans maybe

"I can't place the accent." I mention. "Russia? The Balkans, maybe?"

»Ich komme aus Leipzig.«
ɪç ˈkɔmə aʊs ˈlaɪptsɪç
I   I come from Leipzig

"I am from Leipzig."

Er steckt die Hand in seine Tasche und zieht ein kleines Bild
eːɐ ʃtɛkt di: hant ɪn ˈzaɪnə ˈtaʃə ʊnt tsiːt aɪn ˈklaɪnəs bɪlt
he he puts the hand in his   pocket and he pulls out→ a small picture

heraus. Er legt es auf meinen Tisch. Ich schaue es mir an und
hɛˈʁaʊs eːɐ leːkt ɛs aʊf ˈmaɪnən tɪʃ ɪç ˈʃaʊə ɛs miːɐ an ʊnt
←   he he places it on my   desk I   I look at it and

sehe eine junge Frau, etwa vierundzwanzig oder fünfundzwanzig
ˈzeːə ˈaɪnə ˈjʊŋə fʁaʊ ˈɛtva ˈfiːɐʊntˌtsvantsɪç ˈoːdɐ ˈfʏnfʊntˌtsvantsɪç
see   a   young woman about twenty-four   or   twenty-five

Jahre alt.
ˈjaːʁə alt
years old

He puts his hand into his pocket, brings out a small picture, and puts it on my desk. I look at it and see a young woman, maybe twenty-four or twenty-five years old.

»Sie ist sehr hübsch, Ihre Tochter, nicht wahr?«, fragt er.
ziː ɪst zeːɐ hyːpʃ ˈiːʁə ˈtɔxtɐ nɪçt vaːɐ fʁaːkt eːɐ
she she is very pretty your daughter right   he asks he

"She is very pretty, your daughter, yes?" he asks.

Mir wird klar, dass es sich hier um einen ernstzunehmenden
miːɐ vɪʁt klaːɐ das ɛs zɪç hiːɐ ʊm ˈaɪnən ˈɛʁnsttsuˌneːməndn
to me it becomes clear that it → here about a serious

Besuch handelt. Wir starren uns gegenseitig ein paar Sekunden
bəˈzuːx ˈhandəlt viːɐ ˈʃtaʁən ʊns ˈgeːgnˌzaɪtɪç aɪn paːɐ zeˈkʊndən
visit   ←it is about we   we stare at each other→   a few   seconds

lang an.
laŋ an
long ←

I realize that this is a serious visit. We stare at each other for a few seconds.

»Auf einmal sind Sie ja ganz still?«, fragt er. »Weil Sie nämlich
aʊf ˈaɪnmaːl zɪnt ziː jaː gants ʃtɪl fʁaːkt eːɐ vaɪl ziː ˈnɛːmlɪç
suddenly   you are you !   completely quiet he asks he because you in fact

Ihre Tochter lieben und nicht möchten, dass ihr etwas zustößt.«
ˈiːʁə ˈtɔxtɐ ˈliːbən ʊnt nɪçt ˈmœçtən das iːɐ ˈɛtvas tsuːˈʃtøːst
your daughter you love and not you would like that to her something it happens to

"You are not talking so much now, are you?" he asks. "That is because you love your daughter and do not want to see anything happen to her."

Story 13

"Are you threatening me?" I ask.

»Soll das eine Drohung sein?«, frage ich.
zɔl das 'aɪnə 'dʁoːʊŋ zaɪn 'fʁaːgə ɪç
it is supposed that a threat to be I ask I

"No. I am saying you would do anything to protect your daughter."

»Nein, ich sage nur, dass Sie alles tun würden, um Ihre
naɪn ɪç 'zaːgə nuːɐ das ziː 'aləs tuːn 'vʏʁdən ʊm 'iːʁə
no I I say only that you anything to do you would in order to your

Tochter zu beschützen.«
'tɔxtɐ tsu bə'ʃʏtsən
daughter to to protect

He gives me a piece of paper. On it is written: "Be ready. Two days. Small unmarked bills."

Er gibt mir ein Stück Papier. Darauf steht geschrieben:
eːɐ giːpt miːɐ aɪn ʃtʏk pa'piːɐ da'ʁaʊf ʃteːt gə'ʃʁiːbən
he he gives to me a piece paper on it it stands written

»Seien Sie bereit. In zwei Tagen. Kleine, unmarkierte Geldscheine.«
'zaɪən ziː bə'ʁaɪt ɪn tsvaɪ 'taːgən 'klaɪnə ʊnmaʁ'kiːɐtə 'gɛltʃaɪnə
be ready in two days small unmarked banknotes

There is also a large amount of money written on the note. Then he gets up and walks out.

Zudem ist noch ein großer Geldbetrag auf das Papier geschrieben.
'tsuːdeːm ɪst nɔx aɪn 'gʁoːsɐ 'gɛltbə‿tʁaːk aʊf das pa'piːɐ gə'ʃʁiːbən
in addition it is also a large amount of money on the paper written

Dann steht er auf und geht hinaus.
dan ʃteːt eːɐ aʊf ʊnt geːt hɪ'naʊs
then he stands up and he walks out

———3———

Nobody in my local police department wants to hear about my problem. They don't have the resources to deal with this type of crime. At least they are nice enough to give me the phone number for the State Police.

Bei der örtlichen Polizei will niemand etwas von meinen
baɪ deːɐ 'œʁtlɪçn̩ poli'tsaɪ vɪl 'niːmant 'ɛtvas fɔn 'maɪnən
at the local police it wants nobody anything of my

Problemen hören. Sie hat keine Möglichkeiten, sich mit derartigen
pʁo'bleːmən 'høːʁən ziː hat 'kaɪnə 'møːklɪçkaɪtən zɪç mɪt 'deːɐaːɐtɪgn̩
problems to hear it it has not any possibilities → with such

Straftaten zu befassen. Wenigstens sind sie so nett, mir die
'ʃtʁaːfˌtaːtən tsu bə'fasən 've:nɪçstəns zɪnt ziː zoː nɛt miːɐ diː
crimes to ←to deal at least they are they so nice to me the

Telefonnummer der Landespolizei zu geben.
telə'foːnˌnʊmɐ deːɐ 'landəspoliˌtsaɪ tsu 'geːbən
telephone number of the state police to to give

I dial the number in my cell phone and spend ten minutes selecting options from various menus on the State Police answering system.

Ich wähle die Nummer auf meinem Handy und brauche zehn
ɪç 'vɛːlə diː 'nʊmɐ aʊf 'maɪnəm 'hɛndi ʊnt 'bʁaʊxə tseːn
I I dial the number on my cell phone and I need ten

Minuten, um die Antworten aus den verschiedenen Menüs
mɪ'nuːtən ʊm diː 'antvɔʁtən aʊs deːn fɛɐ'ʃiːdənən me'nyːs
minutes in order to the answers from the different menus

des Antwortsystems der Landespolizei auszuwählen.
dɛs 'antvɔʁtzʏsˌteːms deːɐ 'landəspoliˌtsaɪ 'aʊstsuˌvɛːlən
of the answering system of the state police to select

Evolution

Dann	spreche	ich	mit	jemandem,	der	mich	mit	jemand	anderem
dan	ˈʃpʁɛçə	ɪç	mɪt	ˈjeːmandəm	deːɐ	mɪç	mɪt	ˈjeːmant	ˈandəʁəm
then	I talk	I	with	someone	who	me	with	someone	else

verbindet,	welcher	mich	wiederum	mit	dem	Kriminalbeamten
fɛɐˈbɪndət	ˈvɛlçɐ	mɪç	ˈviːdəʁʊm	mɪt	deːm	kʁimiˈnaːlbəˌamtn̩
he connects	who	me	in turn	with	the	detective

Frank	Müller	verbindet.	Er	arbeitet	in	der	Abteilung,	die	sich	mit
fʁaŋk	ˈmʏlɐ	fɛɐˈbɪndət	eːɐ	ˈaʁbaɪtət	ɪn	deːɐ	ˈaptaɪlʊŋ	diː	zɪç	mɪt
Frank	Müller	he connects	he	he works	in	the	division	that	→	

Erpressungsfällen	befasst.	Ich	erzähle	ihm	meine	Geschichte.
ɛɐˈpʁɛsʊŋsˌfɛlən	bəˈfast	ɪç	ɛɐˈtsɛːlə	iːm	ˈmaɪnə	gəˈʃɪçtə
extortion cases	←they deal with	I	I tell	him	my	story

Als	ich	fertig	bin,	stelle	ich	ihm	einige	Fragen.
als	ɪç	ˈfɛʁtɪç	bɪn	ˈʃtɛlə	ɪç	iːm	ˈaɪnɪgə	ˈfʁaːgən
when	I	finished	I am	I ask	I	him	a few	questions

Then I talk to someone who connects me to someone else, who connects me to Detective Sergeant Frank Müller. He works in the division that handles extortion cases. I tell him my story. When I am done, I ask him a few questions.

»Haben	Sie	jemanden,	der	ermitteln	wird?«,	frage	ich.
ˈhaːbn̩	ziː	ˈjeːmandən	deːɐ	ɛɐˈmɪtln̩	vɪʁt	ˈfʁaːgə	ɪç
you have	you	someone	who	to investigate	he will	I say	I

"Do you have someone who will investigate?" I ask.

»Auf	jeden	Fall.«
aʊf	ˈjeːdən	fal
		absolutely

"Absolutely."

»Ich	habe	gehört,	es	gibt	da	mindestens	drei	weitere
ɪç	ˈhaːbə	gəˈhøːɐt	ɛs	gɪpt	daː	ˈmɪndəstəns	dʁaɪ	ˈvaɪtəʁə
I	I heard		there were	there	at least	three	additional	

Versicherungsleute	wie	mich,	die	in	den	letzten	sechs	Monaten
fɛɐˈzɪçəʁʊŋsˌlɔɪtə	viː	mɪç	diː	ɪn	deːn	ˈlɛtstən	zɛks	ˈmoːnatən
insurance people	like	me	who	in	the	last	six	months

Opfer	einer	Erpressung	wurden.	Ermittelt	Ihre	Abteilung	in	diesen
ˈɔpfɐ	ˈaɪnɐ	ɛɐˈpʁɛsʊŋ	ˈvʊʁdən	ɛɐˈmɪtlt	ˈiːʁə	ˈaptaɪlʊŋ	ɪn	ˈdiːzən
victims	of a	extortion	they became	it investigates	your	department	in	those

Fällen?«
ˈfɛlən
cases

"I've heard that there were at least three other insurance people like me who have been victims of extortion in the last six months. Is your department investigating those cases?"

»Ja.«
jaː
yes

"Yes."

»Weshalb	haben	Sie	noch	niemanden	verhaftet?«
vɛsˈhalp	ˈhaːbn̩	ziː	nɔx	ˈniːmandən	fɛɐˈhaftət
why	→	you	still	nobody	←you have arrested

"How come you haven't arrested anyone yet?"

»Wir	verfolgen	einige	wertvolle	Hinweise.«
viːɐ	fɛɐˈfɔlgn̩	ˈaɪnɪgə	ˈveːɐtˌfɔlə	ˈhɪnvaɪzə
we	we follow	some	valuable	leads

"We have a number of strong leads."

Story 13

"Weren't two of the victims shot to death?" I ask.

»Wurden nicht zwei der Opfer erschossen?«, frage ich.
'vʊʁdən nɪçt tsvaɪ deːɐ 'ɔpfɐ ɛɐ'ʃɔsn̩ 'fʁaːɡə ɪç
they were not two of the victims shot dead I ask I

"Yes," he says.

»Ja«, sagt er.
jaː zakt eːɐ
yes he says he

"And wasn't the wife of the third victim killed with the same gun?"

»Und wurde nicht die Ehefrau des dritten Opfers mit derselben Waffe getötet?«
ʊnt 'vʊʁdə nɪçt diː 'eːəfʁaʊ dɛs 'dʁɪtən 'ɔpfɐs mɪt deːɐ'zɛlbn̩ 'vafə ɡə'tøːtət
and → the wife of the third victim with the same gun ←wasn't she killed

"Yes. All of this was reported by the media."

»Ja, das wurde alles in den Medien berichtet.«
jaː das 'vʊʁdə 'aləs ɪn deːn 'meːdjən bə'ʁɪçtət
yes this → all in the media ←it was reported

"Why don't you have any suspects?"

»Warum haben Sie denn überhaupt keine Verdächtigen?«
va'ʁʊm 'haːbn̩ ziː dɛn yːbɐ'haʊpt 'kaɪnə fɛɐ'dɛçtɪɡən
why you have you ! at all not any suspects

"I can't talk about an ongoing investigation."

»Über eine laufende Ermittlung kann ich nicht sprechen.«
'yːbɐ 'aɪnə 'laʊfəndə ɛɐ'mɪtlʊŋ kan ɪç nɪçt 'ʃpʁɛçən
about an ongoing investigation I can I not to talk

"Mr. Müller, I'm worried that these criminals are smarter than the State Police."

»Herr Müller, ich befürchte, dass diese Verbrecher schlauer sind als die Landespolizei.«
hɛʁ 'mʏlɐ ɪç bə'fʏʁçtə das 'diːzə fɛɐ'bʁɛçɐ 'ʃlaʊɐ zɪnt als diː 'landəspoliˌtsaɪ
Mr. Müller I I worry that these criminals smarter they are than the state police

"I can't comment."

»Ich kann dazu nichts sagen.«
ɪç kan da'tsuː nɪçts 'zaːɡən
I I can to that nothing to say

"Maybe I should pay them what they want. I can afford it."

»Vielleicht sollte ich ihnen zahlen, was sie verlangen. Ich kann es mir leisten.«
fiˈlaɪçt 'zɔltə ɪç 'iːnən 'tsaːlən vas ziː fɛɐ'laŋən ɪç kan ɛs miːɐ 'laɪstən
maybe I should I them to pay what they they demand I I can it to afford

"Two people did that. They were killed by the gang anyway."

»Zwei Leute haben das gemacht. Sie wurden von der Bande trotzdem umgebracht.«
tsvaɪ 'lɔɪtə 'haːbn̩ das ɡə'maxt ziː 'vʊʁdən fɔn deːɐ 'bandə 'tʁɔtsdeːm 'ʊmɡəˌbʁaxt
two people → that ←they did they → by the gang anyway ←they were killed

»Vielleicht	wurden sie getötet,	weil	sie	beschlossen,	mit	der	"Maybe they were killed because they decided to cooperate with the police and the criminals found out."
fiˈlaɪçt	ˈvʊʁdən ziː ɡəˈtøːtət	vaɪl	ziː	bəˈʃlɔsn	mɪt	deːɐ̯	
maybe	they were killed	because	they	they decided	with	the	

Polizei	zusammenzuarbeiten,	und	die	Verbrecher	haben	das
poliˈtsaɪ	tsuˈzamən̩tsuːˌaʁbaɪtn̩	ʊnt	diː	fɛɐ̯ˈbʁɛçɐ	ˈhaːbn̩	das
police	to cooperate	and	the	criminals	→	that

| herausgefunden.« |
| hɛˈʁausɡəˌfʊndn̩ |
| ← they found out |

»Dazu	kann	ich	nichts	sagen.«	"I can't comment about that."
daˈtsuː	kan	ɪç	nɪçts	ˈzaːɡən	
to that	I can	I	nothing	to say	

»Das	hilft mir	nicht	weiter.	Jedes	Mal	wenn	ich	etwas	"You aren't helping. Every time I mention something important you tell me that you can't comment."
das	hɪlft miːɐ̯	nɪçt	ˈvaɪtɐ	ˈjeːdəs	maːl	vɛn	ɪç	ˈɛtvas	
that	it helps me →	not	←	every	time	when	I	something	

Wesentliches	erwähne,	antworten	Sie	mir,	dass	Sie	dazu	nichts
ˈveːzəntlɪçəs	ɛɐ̯ˈvɛːnə	ˈantvɔʁtən	ziː	miːɐ̯	das	ziː	daˈtsuː	nɪçts
important	I mention	you answer	you	to me	that	you	to that	nothing

sagen	können.«
ˈzaːɡən	ˈkœnən
you can say	

»Meine	Abteilung	arbeitet	rund um die Uhr,	um	diese	Bande	"My department is working around the clock to find this gang. You can help us by working with me. Can I come to your office and look for fingerprints?"
ˈmaɪnə	ˈaptaɪlʊŋ	ˈaʁbaɪtət	ʁʊnt ʊm diː uːɐ̯	ʊm	ˈdiːzə	ˈbandə	
my	department	it works	around the clock	in order to	this	gang	

zu	finden.	Sie	können	uns	helfen,	indem	Sie	mit	mir
tsuː	ˈfɪndən	ziː	ˈkœnən	ʊns	ˈhɛlfən	ˈɪndəm	ziː	mɪt	miːɐ̯
to	to find	you	you can	us	to help	by	you	with	me

zusammenarbeiten.	Kann	ich	in	Ihr	Büro	kommen	und	nach
tsuˈzamənˌaʁbaɪtn̩	kan	ɪç	ɪn	iːɐ̯	byˈʁoː	ˈkɔmən	ʊnt	naːx
to work together	can I	I	in	your	office	to come	and	for

Fingerabdrücken	suchen?«
ˈfɪŋɐˌapdʁʏkən	ˈzuːxən
fingerprints	to look for

»Er	hatte	Handschuhe	an«,	sage	ich.	"He wore gloves," I say.
eːɐ̯	ˈhatə	ˈhantʃuːə	an	ˈzaːɡə	ɪç	
he	he wore →	gloves	←	I say	I	

»Na gut,	dann	treffen Sie sich	wenigstens	mit	mir	und	machen	"Well, at least meet with me and make a formal complaint."
na ɡuːt	dan	ˈtʁɛfən ziː zɪç	ˈveːnɪçstəns	mɪt	miːɐ̯	ʊnt	ˈmaxən	
well	then	meet	at least	with	me	and	make	

eine	formale	Beschwerde.«
ˈaɪnə	fɔʁˈmaːlə	bəˈʃveːɐ̯də
a	formal	complaint

»Ich	bin	mir	nicht	sicher,	ob	ich	das	will.	Drei	Leute	"I'm not sure I want to do that. Three people are dead and you don't appear to be making any progress."
ɪç	bɪn	miːɐ̯	nɪçt	ˈzɪçɐ	ɔp	ɪç	das	vɪl	dʁaɪ	ˈlɔɪtə	
I	I am	myself	not	sure	if	I	that	I want (to do)	three	people	

Evolution

Story 13

sind tot und es hat nicht den Anschein, dass Sie irgendwelche
zɪnt toːt ʊnt ɛs hat nɪçt deːn ˈanʃaɪn das ziː ˈɪʁgnˌtvɛlçə
they are dead and it it has not the appearance that you any

Fortschritte machen.«
ˈfɔʁtʃʁɪtə ˈmaxən
progress you make

"Then why did you call?"

»Warum haben Sie dann angerufen?«
vaˈʁʊm ˈhaːbn ziː dan ˈangəʁuːfən
why → you then ←you called

"That's a good question. Let me think about my situation and get back to you."

»Das ist eine gute Frage. Lassen Sie mich meine Situation
das ɪst ˈaɪnə ˈguːtə ˈfʁaːgə ˈlasən ziː mɪç ˈmaɪnə zituaˈtsjoːn
that it is a good question let me my situation

überdenken und dann werde ich mich wieder an Sie wenden.«
yːbɐˈdɛŋkən ʊnt dan ˈveːɐdə ɪç mɪç ˈviːdɐ an ziː ˈvɛndən
to think over and then → again to you ←I will contact

Five minutes after my conversation with Sergeant Müller, I call Joseph Graf. He is the insurance agent whose wife was murdered five months ago. I ask him to meet me for lunch the next day.

Fünf Minuten nach meiner Unterhaltung mit dem Kriminalbeamten
fynf mɪˈnuːtən naːx ˈmaɪnɐ ˈʊntɐhaltʊŋ mɪt deːm kʁimiˈnaːlbəˌamtn
five minutes after my conversation with the detective

Müller rufe ich Joseph Graf an. Er ist der Versicherungsagent,
ˈmylɐ ˈʁuːfə ɪç ˈjoːzɛf gʁaːf an eːɐ ɪst deːɐ fɛɐˈzɪçəʁʊŋsaˌgɛnt
Müller I call→ I Joseph Graf ← he he is the insurance agent

dessen Frau vor fünf Monaten ermordet wurde. Ich bitte ihn, sich
ˈdɛsən fʁaʊ foːɐ fynf ˈmoːnatən ɛɐˈmɔʁdət ˈvʊʁdə ɪç ˈbɪtə iːn zɪç
whose wife ago five months she was murdered I I ask him →

mit mir am nächsten Tag zum Mittagessen zu treffen.
mɪt miːɐ am ˈnɛçstən taːk tsʊm ˈmɪtaːkˌɛsn tsuː ˈtʁɛfən
with me on the next day for lunch to ←to meet

4

Joseph Graf looks terrible. His face is gaunt. His beard is ragged. He has trouble focusing on the lunch menu.

Joseph Graf sieht furchtbar aus. Sein Gesicht ist ausgemergelt.
ˈjoːzɛf gʁaːf ziːt ˈfʊʁçtbaːɐ aʊs zaɪn gəˈzɪçt ɪst ˈaʊsgəˌmɛʁglt
Joseph Graf he looks→ terrible ← his face it is gaunt

Sein Bart ist struppig. Er hat Probleme, sich auf die Speisekarte
zaɪn baːɐt ɪst ˈʃtʁʊpɪç eːɐ hat pʁoˈbleːmə zɪç aʊf diː ˈʃpaɪzəˌkaʁtə
his beard it is ragged he he has problems → on the menu

zu konzentrieren.
tsuː kɔntsɛnˈtʁiːʁən
to ←to concentrate

"The medication makes it hard for me to be more active," he says. "I'm sleepy all the time."

»Die Medikamente machen es mir schwer, aktiv am Leben
diː mediˈkamɛntə ˈmaxən ɛs miːɐ ʃveːɐ akˈtiːf am ˈleːbn
the medication they make it for me hard actively at the life

teilzunehmen«, sagt er. »Ich bin immer müde.«
ˈtaɪltsuˌneːmən zakt eːɐ ɪç bɪn ˈɪmɐ ˈmyːdə
to take part he says he I I am always tired

Evolution

Wir unterhalten uns darüber, wie traurig er ist, seitdem seine Frau
viːɐ   ʊntɐˈhaltən ʊns   daˈʁyːbɐ   viː   ˈtʁaʊʁɪç   eːɐ ɪst   ˈzaɪtdeːm ˈzaɪnə fʁaʊ
we   we converse   about it   how   sad   he   he is since   his   wife

ermordet wurde. Ich wechsle das Thema nach ein paar Minuten
ɛɐˈmɔʁdət ˈvʊʁdə   ɪç   ˈvɛkslə das ˈteːma naːx aɪn paːɐ mɪˈnuːtən
she was murdered   I   I change the subject after a few   minutes

und erkläre, dass dieselbe Verbrecherbande nun meine Tochter
ʊnt ɛɐˈklɛːʁə   das   diːˈzɛlbə   fɛɐˈbʁɛçɐbandə   nuːn   ˈmaɪnə   ˈtɔxtɐ
and I explain   that the same   criminal gang   now   my   daughter

bedroht.
bəˈdʁoːt
it threatens

We talk about how sad he has been since his wife was killed. I change the subject after a few minutes and explain that the same group of criminals is threatening my daughter.

»Soll ich die Polizei einschalten?«, frage ich.
zɔl   ɪç   diː poliˈtsaɪ ˈaɪnʃaltən   ˈfʁaːɡə ɪç
should I I   the police   to involve   I ask   I

"Should I get the police involved?" I ask.

»Nein, zahlen Sie ihnen das Geld.«
naɪn   ˈtsaːlən ziː ˈiːnən das ɡɛlt
no   pay   them   the   money

"No. Pay them."

»Wie lange soll das gehen?«
viː   ˈlaŋə   zɔl   das   ˈɡeːən
how   long   it should that   to go

"For how long?"

»Sie haben mir gesagt, sie würden mich nach einem Jahr in
ziː   ˈhaːbn̩   miːɐ ɡəˈzaːkt   ziː   ˈvyʁdən   mɪç   naːx   ˈaɪnəm   jaːɐ   ɪn
they →   me   ←they told they they would me   after   a   year   in

Ruhe lassen«, sagt er.
ˈʁuːə   ˈlasən   zaːkt   eːɐ
peace   to leave   he says   he

"They told me they would leave me alone after I paid for one year," he says.

»Haben Sie ihnen geglaubt?«
ˈhaːbn̩   ziː   ˈiːnən   ɡəˈɡlaʊpt
→   you   them   ←you believed

"Did you believe them?"

»Nein, deshalb ging ich zur Polizei.«
naɪn   ˈdɛshalp   ɡɪŋ   ɪç   tsuːɐ   poliˈtsaɪ
no   so   I went I   to the   police

"No. So I went to the police."

»Warum wurde Ihre Frau ermordet?«, frage ich.
vaˈʁʊm   ˈvʊʁdə   ˈiːʁə   fʁaʊ   ɛɐˈmɔʁdət   ˈfʁaːɡə   ɪç
why   →   your   wife   ←she was murdered I ask   I

"Why was your wife murdered?" I ask.

»Irgendwoher wussten die Gauner, dass ich mit der Polizei
ˈɪʁɡəntvoˌheːɐ   ˈvʊstən   diː   ˈɡaʊnɐ   das   ɪç mɪt deːɐ   poliˈtsaɪ
from somewhere   they knew the   criminals   that I   with the   police

kooperierte.«
koˌopəˈʁiːɐtə
I cooperated

"Somehow, the criminals knew I was working with the police."

197

Story 13

"How did they know that?"

»Wie haben die das erfahren?«
viː ˈhaːbn̩ diː das ɛɐˈfaːʁən
how → they that ←they found out

"My next payment was supposed to be made at a gas station near the highway. A few detectives followed me. They wore regular clothes so they would blend in with the people at the gas station. The criminals must have seen them, because nobody showed up to take the money."

»Meine nächste Zahlung sollte an einer Tankstelle
ˈmaɪnə ˈnɛçstə ˈtsaːlʊŋ ˈzɔltə an ˈaɪnɐ ˈtaŋkʃtɛlə
my next payment it was supposed at a gas station

in der Nähe der Autobahn gemacht werden. Ein paar
ɪn deːɐ ˈnɛːə deːɐ ˈaʊtoˌbaːn gəˈmaxt ˈveːɐdn̩ aɪn paːɐ
near the highway to have been made a few

Kriminalbeamte folgten mir. Sie trugen normale Kleidung, damit
kʁimiˈnaːlbəˌamtə ˈfɔlktən miːɐ ziː ˈtʁuːgən nɔʁˈmaːlə ˈklaɪdʊŋ daˈmɪt
detectives they followed me they they wore normal clothes so that

sie unter den Leuten an der Tankstelle nicht auffielen. Die
ziː ˈʊntɐ deːn ˈlɔɪtən an deːɐ ˈtaŋkʃtɛlə nɪçt ˈaʊfˌfiːlən diː
they among the people at the gas station not they stood out the

Verbrecher müssen sie gesehen haben, da niemand kam, um
fɛɐˈbʁɛçɐ ˈmʏsən ziː gəˈzeːən ˈhaːbn̩ daː ˈniːmant kaːm ʊm
criminals they must have seen them because nobody he came in order to

das Geld abzuholen.«
das gɛlt ˈaptsuˌhoːlən
the money to pick up

He waits a moment and takes a few sips of coffee.

Er wartet eine Minute and nimmt ein paar Schlückchen Kaffee.
eːɐ ˈvaʁtət ˈaɪnə mɪˈnuːtə ʊnt nɪmt aɪn paːɐ ˈʃlʏkçən ˈkafe
he he waits a minute and he takes a few sips coffee

"A few days later my wife was shot at close range. It was a professional hit."

»Ein paar Tage später wurde meine Frau aus unmittelbarer Nähe
aɪn paːɐ ˈtaːgə ˈʃpɛːtɐ ˈvʊʁdə ˈmaɪnə fʁaʊ aʊs ˈʊnˌmɪtlbaːʁɐ ˈnɛːə
a few days later → my wife at close range

erschossen. Es war ein Auftragsmord.«
ɛɐˈʃɔsn̩ ɛs vaːɐ aɪn ˈaʊftʁaːksˌmɔʁt
←she was shot it it was a hit job

He starts to cry.

Er fängt an zu weinen.
eːɐ fɛŋt an tsuː ˈvaɪnən
he he starts to to cry

"She would still be alive if I had not gone to the police."

»Sie wäre noch am Leben, wenn ich nicht zur Polizei
ziː ˈvɛːʁə nɔx am ˈleːbən vɛn ɪç nɪçt tsuːɐ poliˈtsaɪ
she she would be still alive if I not to the police

gegangen wäre.«
gəˈgaŋən ˈvɛːʁə
I had gone

After our depressing lunch I drive him back to his house.

Nach unserem deprimierenden Mittagessen fahre ich ihn zurück
naːx ˈʊnzəʁəm depʁiˈmiːʁəndn̩ ˈmɪtaːkˌɛsn̩ ˈfaːʁə ɪç iːn tsuˈʁʏk
after our depressing lunch I drive I him back

zu seinem Haus.
tsuː ˈzaɪnəm haʊs
to his house

Evolution

»Ich gehe nicht mehr ins Büro«, sagt er mir. »Ich bin zu
ɪç ˈgeːhə nɪçt meːɐ ɪns byˈʁoː zakt eːɐ miːɐ ɪç bɪn tsuː
I   I go   no longer into the office he says he to me   I   I am   too
deprimiert zum Arbeiten.«
depʁiˈmiːɐt tsʊm ˈaʁbaitn
depressed   to work

"I don't go to the office any more," he tells me. "I'm too depressed to work."

»Sie sollten einen Job bei einer großen Agentur annehmen«, sage
ziː ˈzɔltən ˈaɪnən dʒɔp baɪ ˈaɪnɐ ˈgʁoːsən agɛnˈtuːɐ ˈanˌneːmən ˈzaːgə
you you should a   job with a   big   agency to accept   I say
ich zu ihm. »Die meisten wären froh, wenn ein so erfolgreicher
ɪç tsuː iːm diː ˈmaɪstən ˈvɛːʁən fʁoː vɛn aɪn zoː ɛɐˈfɔlkʁaɪçɐ
I to him most   they would be happy if a so   successful
Verkäufer bei ihnen arbeiten würde. Außerdem wäre es gut für
fɛɐˈkɔyfɐ baɪ ˈiːnən ˈaʁbaitn ˈvʏʁdə ˈaʊsɐdeːm ˈvɛːʁə ɛs guːt fyːɐ
salesman with them he would work   in addition it would be it good for
Sie, unter Leuten zu sein.«
ziː ˈʊntɐ ˈlɔytən tsuː zaɪn
you among people to to be

"You should take a job with a big agency," I tell him. "Most places would love to have a successful salesman like you working with them. Plus, it will do you good to be with people."

Er antwortet nur mit einem niedergeschlagenen Achselzucken.
eːɐ ˈantˌvɔʁtət nuːɐ mɪt ˈaɪnəm ˈniːdɐgəˌʃlaːgənən ˈakslˌtsʊkn
he he answers   just with a   low-spirited   shrug

He gives me a defeated shrug.

»Sprechen Sie wenigstens mit einem professionellen
ˈʃpʁɛçən ziː ˈveːnɪçstəns mɪt ˈaɪnəm pʁofɛsjoˈnɛlən
speak   at least   with a   professional
Trauerbegleiter«, sage ich.
ˈtʁaʊɐbəˌglaɪtɐ ˈzaːgə ɪç
grief counselor I say I

"At least meet with a professional grief counselor," I say.

Ich steuere das Auto in seine Einfahrt.
ɪç ˈʃtɔɪəʁə das ˈaʊto ɪn ˈzaɪnə ˈaɪnfaːɐt
I I steer   the car into his   driveway

I pull the car into his driveway.

Er steigt aus dem Auto aus, winkt mir zaghaft zu und
eːɐ ʃtaɪkt aʊs deːm ˈaʊtoː aʊs vɪŋkt miːɐ ˈtsaːkˌhaft tsuː ʊnt
he he gets out→ out of the car   ←   he waves→ to me   timidly   ←   and
schlurft in sein Haus. Ich kehre zurück in mein Büro und
ʃlʊʁft ɪn zaɪn haʊs ɪç ˈkeːʁə tsuˈʁʏk ɪn maɪn byˈʁoː ʊnt
he shuffles into   his house I   I return   to   my   office   and
mache ein Nickerchen. Für die Pokerrunde muss ich frisch sein.
ˈmaxə aɪn ˈnɪkɐçən fyːɐ diː ˈpoːkɐˌʁʊndə mʊs ɪç fʁɪʃ zaɪn
I take a nap   for the poker game   I have to I fresh to be

He gets out of the car, gives me a little wave, and shuffles into his home. I go back to my office and take a nap. I have to be fresh for the poker game.

---------5---------

Mein Blick wandert durch die Runde am Tisch von Mitspieler
maɪn blɪk ˈvandɐt dʊʁç diː ˈʁʊndə am tɪʃ fɔn ˈmɪtˌʃpiːlɐ
my   gaze it wanders through the company at the table from other player

I look around the table at the other players. Max, the drug dealer, sits on my right. He smells like hair gel and

199

Story 13

aftershave. His girlfriend stands behind him, leaning down and kissing his ear. I have a hard time looking at my cards.

zu	Mitspieler.	Max,	der	Drogenhändler,	sitzt	zu	meiner	Rechten.
tsuː	ˈmɪtˌʃpiːlɐ	maks	deːɐ	ˈdʁoːgnˌhɛndlɐ	zɪtst	tsuː	ˈmaɪnɐ	ˈʁɛçtən
to	other player	Max	the	drug dealer	he sits	to	my	right (side)

Er	riecht	nach	Haargel	und	Rasierwasser.	Seine	Freundin	steht
eːɐ	ʁiːçt naːx		ˈhaːɐˌɡəl	ʊnt	ʁaˈziːɐˌvasɐ	ˈzaɪnə	ˈfʁɔɪndɪn	ʃteːt
he	he smells of		hair gel	and	aftershave	his	girlfriend	she stands

hinter	ihm,	beugt	sich	nieder	und	küsst	sein	Ohr.	Ich	habe
ˈhɪntɐ	iːm	bɔɪkt	zɪç	ˈniːdɐ	ʊnt	kʏst	zaɪn	oːɐ	ɪç	ˈhaːbə
behind	him	she bends down			and	she kisses	his	ear	I	I have

Schwierigkeiten,	auf	meine	Karten	zu	schauen.
ˈʃviːʁɪçkaɪtən	aʊf	ˈmaɪnə	ˈkaʁtən	tsuː	ˈʃaʊən
troubles	on	my	cards	to	to look

Johann, an accountant, sits across from me. His suit is wrinkled, his tie is crooked and the top two buttons on his shirt are open. His bottle of whiskey is already half empty and we haven't played for more than an hour.

Johann,	ein	Buchhalter,	sitzt	mir	gegenüber.	Sein	Anzug	ist
ˈjoːhan	aɪn	ˈbuːxˌhaltɐ	zɪtst	miːɐ ɡeˈɡnyːbɐ		zaɪn	ˈanˌtsuːk	ɪst
Johann	an	accountant	he sits	across from me		his	suit	it is

zerknittert,	seine	Krawatte	sitzt	schief	und	die	obersten	zwei
tsɛɐˈknɪtɐt	ˈzaɪnə	kʁaˈvatə	zɪtst	ʃiːf	ʊnt	diː	ˈoːbɐstən	tsvaɪ
wrinkled	his	tie	it sits	crooked	and	the	topmost	two

Knöpfe	an	seinem	Hemd	sind	offen.	Seine	Whiskyflasche	ist
ˈknœpfə	an	ˈzaɪnəm	hɛmt	zɪnt	ˈɔfən	ˈzaɪnə	ˈvɪskiˌflaʃə	ɪst
buttons	on	his	shirt	they are	open	his	whiskey bottle	it is

bereits	halbleer	und	wir	haben	noch	nicht	einmal	länger	als	eine
bəˈʁaɪts	ˈhalpˌleːɐ	ʊnt	viːɐ	ˈhaːbn	nɔx	nɪçt	ˈaɪnmaːl	ˈlɛŋɐ	als	ˈaɪnə
already	half-empty	and	we	→	still	not	even	longer	than	an

Stunde	gespielt.
ˈʃtʊndə	ɡəˈʃpiːlt
hour	← we have played

"Hard day at the office, Johann?" I ask him.

»Schwerer	Tag	im	Büro,	Johann?«,	frage	ich	ihn.
ˈʃveːʁɐ	taːk	ɪm	byˈʁoː	ˈjoːhan	ˈfʁaːɡə	ɪç	iːn
hard	day	at the	office	Johann	I ask	I	him

"Some government lawyers are making my life very difficult," he answers.

»Einige	Regierungsanwälte	machen	mir	das	Leben	sehr	schwer«,
ˈaɪnɪɡə	ʁeˈɡiːʁʊŋsˌanvɛltə	ˈmaxən	miːɐ	das	ˈleːbən	zeːɐ	ʃveːɐ
some	government lawyers	they make	to me	the	life	very	difficult

antwortet	er.
ˈantˌvɔʁtət	eːɐ
he answers	he

Reinhold, the fourth member of our group, is on my left. Reinhold lends money to people who cannot get loans from banks. He charges very high interest rates. If his clients don't pay the loans back on time, his assistant breaks their legs.

Reinhold,	das	vierte	Mitglied	unserer	Gruppe,	sitzt	zu	meiner
ˈʁaɪnhɔlt	das	ˈfiːɐtə	ˈmɪtˌɡliːt	ˈʊnzəʁɐ	ˈɡʁʊpə	zɪtst	tsuː	ˈmaɪnɐ
Reinhold	the	fourth	member	of our	group	he sits	to	my

Linken.	Reinhold	verleiht	Geld	an	Leute,	die	keine	Darlehen	von
ˈlɪŋkən	ˈʁaɪnhɔlt	fɛɐˈlaɪt	ɡɛlt	an	ˈlɔɪtə	diː	ˈkaɪnə	ˈdaːɐleːən	fɔn
left (side)	Reinhold	he lends	money	to	people	who	not any	loans	from

Banken	bekommen	können.	Er	verlangt	sehr	hohe	Zinsen.	Wenn
ˈbaŋkən	bəˈkɔmən	ˈkœnən	eːɐ	fɛɐˈlaŋt	zeːɐ	hoːə	ˈtsɪnzən	vɛn
banks	to get	they can	he	he charges	very	high	interest rates	if

Evolution

seine Klienten die Darlehen nicht rechtzeitig zurückzahlen, bricht
ihnen sein Assistent die Beine.

'zaɪnə kliˈɛntən diː ˈdaʁleːən nɪçt ˈʁɛçtˌtsaɪtɪç tsuˈʁʏktsaːlən bʁɪçt
ˈiːnən zaɪn asɪsˈtɛnt diː ˈbaɪnə

his clients the loans not on time they pay back he breaks
them his assistant the legs

Reinholds Assistent sitzt in der Ecke und schaut fern auf einem Großbildschirm. Irgendeine Show über Hausverschönerungen.

ˈʁaɪnhɔlts asɪsˈtɛnt zɪtst ɪn deːʁ ˈɛkə ʊnt ʃaʊt fɛʁn aʊf ˈaɪnəm ˈɡʁoːsˈbɪltʃɪʁm ˈɪʁɡntaɪnə ʃoː ˈyːbɐ ˈhaʊsfɛɐʃøːnəʁʊŋən

Reinhold's assistant he sits in the corner and he watches TV on a big-screen some show about home improvements

Reinhold's assistant sits in the corner watching a big screen television. Some sort of show about home makeovers.

Wieso gefallen einem Typen, der als Lebensunterhalt Leute verprügelt, diese dummen Realityshows? Über Geschmack lässt sich nicht streiten.

viˈzoː ɡəˈfalən ˈaɪnəm ˈtyːpən deːʁ als ˈleːbnsˌʊntɐhalt ˈlɔɪtə fɛɐˈpʁyːɡəlt ˈdiːzə ˈdʊmən ʁiˈɛlitiʃoːs ˈyːbɐ ɡəˈʃmak lɛst zɪç nɪçt ˈʃtʁaɪtən

why they appeal to a guy who as livelihood people he beats those silly reality shows about taste it is not debatable

Why does a guy who beats on people for a living enjoy those silly reality shows? There is no accounting for taste.

Wir spielen Poker in einem Raum des Feuerwehrhauses der freiwilligen Feuerwehr Wedding. Der Feuerwehrhauptmann teilt die Karten aus und kassiert fünf Prozent Provision von jedem Pott. Nach den schönen Möbeln im Feuerwehrhaus zu urteilen, hat diese Provision über die Jahre ganz schön viel Geld für das Feuerwehrhaus eingebracht. Ich frage mich, wie viel der Feuerwehrhauptmann davon für sich behält.

viːʁ ˈʃpiːlən ˈpoːkɐ ɪn ˈaɪnəm ʁaʊm dɛs ˈfɔɪɐveːɐˌhaʊzəs deːʁ ˈfʁaɪˌvɪlɪɡn̩ ˈfɔɪɐˌveːɐ ˈvɛdɪŋ deːʁ ˈfɔɪɐveːɐˌhaʊptman taɪlt diː ˈkaʁtən aʊs ʊnt kaˈsiːɐt fʏnf pʁoˈtsɛnt pʁoviˈzjoːn fɔn ˈjeːdəm pɔt naːx deːn ˈʃøːnən ˈmøːbəln ɪm ˈfɔɪɐveːɐˌhaʊs tsuː ˈuːɐˌtaɪlən hat ˈdiːzə pʁoviˈzjoːn ˈyːbɐ diː ˈjaːʁə gants ʃøːn fiːl gɛlt fyːʁ das ˈfɔɪɐveːɐˌhaʊs ˈaɪŋəbʁaxt ɪç ˈfʁaːɡə mɪç viː fiːl deːʁ ˈfɔɪɐveːɐˌhauptman daˈfɔn fyːʁ zɪç bəˈhɛlt

we we play poker in a room of the fire station of the volunteer Wedding fire department the fire chief he deals out→ the cards ← and he collects five percent commission from each pot by the nice furniture in the firehouse to to judge → this commission over the years quite a lot of money for the firehouse ←it brought in I I wonder how much the fire chief from it for himself he keeps

We are playing poker in a room of a volunteer fire station in Wedding. The fire chief deals the cards for us and takes a five percent commission from every pot. Judging by the nice furniture in the firehouse, that commission has brought a lot of money into the firehouse over the years. I wonder how much the fire chief keeps for himself.

Meine Kollegin Lina sitzt auf einem Sofa in der Nähe des

ˈmaɪnə kɔˈleːɡɪn ˈliːna zɪtst aʊf ˈaɪnəm ˈzoːfa ɪn deːʁ ˈnɛːə dɛs

my associate Lina she sits on a couch near the

My associate, Lina, sits on a couch near the television. She is reading a book by Stephen Hawking. Something about the stars and planets.

201

Story 13

Johann keeps glancing over at Lina. Max would look too, except his girlfriend was blocking his view. Reinhold doesn't look. He appears focused on his hand. The fire chief keeps his eyes on the cards and the money.

Fernsehers.	Sie	liest	ein	Buch	von	Stephen	Hawking.	Irgendetwas
ˈfɛʁnˌzeːɐs	ziː	liːst	aɪn	buːx	fɔn	ˈstiːvən	ˈhɔkɪŋ	ˈɪʁɡntˌɛtvas
television	she	she reads	a	book	by	Stephen	Hawking	something

über	Sterne	und	Planeten.
ˈyːbɐ	ˈʃtɛʁnə	ʊnt	plaˈneːtən
about	stars	and	planets

Johann	schaut	immer wieder	kurz	auf	Lina.	Max	würde
ˈjoːhan	ʃaʊt	ˈɪmɐ ˈviːdɐ	kʊʁts	aʊf	ˈliːna	maks	ˈvʏʁdə
Johann	he looks	over and over	briefly	at	Lina	Max	he would

auch	schauen,	wenn	ihm	seine	Freundin	nicht	den	Blick
aʊx	ˈʃaʊən	vɛn	iːm	ˈzaɪnə	ˈfʁɔɪndɪn	nɪçt	deːn	blɪk
also	to look	if	him	his	girlfriend	not	the	view

versperren	würde.	Reinhold	schaut	nicht.	Er	scheint	auf	sein	Blatt
fɛɐˈʃpɛʁən	ˈvʏʁdə	ˈʁaɪnhɔlt	ʃaʊt	nɪçt	eːɐ	ʃaɪnt	aʊf	zaɪn	blat
she was blocking		Reinhold	he looks	not	he	he appears	on	his	hand

konzentriert	zu	sein.	Der	Feuerwehrhauptmann	behält	die
kɔntsɛnˈtʁiːɐt	tsuː	zaɪn	deːɐ	ˈfɔɪɐveːɐˌhauptman	bəˈhɛlt	diː
focused	to	to be	the	fire chief	he keeps an eye on →	the

Karten	und	das	Geld	im	Auge.
ˈkaʁtən	ʊnt	das	ɡɛlt	ɪm	ˈaʊɡə
cards	and	the	money	←	

Lina is maybe five centimeters shorter than me, which puts her at about one meter eighty. She has medium length brown hair. Her forehead wrinkles slightly as she concentrates on the book she is reading. She wears a comfortable track suit, but no makeup or jewelry.

Lina	ist	vielleicht	fünf	Zentimeter	kleiner	als	ich	und	damit	etwa
ˈliːna	ɪst	fiːˈlaɪçt	fʏnf	tsɛntiˈmeːtɐ	ˈklaɪnɐ	als	ɪç	ʊnt	daˈmɪt	ˈɛtva
Lina	she is	maybe	five	centimeter	shorter	than	me	and	therefore	about

einen	Meter	achtzig	groß.	Sie	hat	mittellange,	braune	Haare.
ˈaɪnən	ˈmeːtɐ	ˈaxtsɪç	ɡʁoːs	ziː	hat	ˈmɪtlˌlaŋə	ˈbʁaʊnə	ˈhaːʁə
one	meter	eighty	tall	she	she has	medium length	brown	hair

Auf	ihrer	Stirn	bilden	sich	leichte	Falten,	während	sie	sich	auf
aʊf	ˈiːʁɐ	ʃtɪʁn	ˈbɪldən	zɪç	ˈlaɪçtə	ˈfaltən	ˈvɛːʁənt	ziː	zɪç	aʊf
on	her	forehead	they form		light	wrinkles	as	she	→	on

das	Buch,	das	sie	liest,	konzentriert.	Sie	trägt	einen	bequemen
das	buːx	das	ziː	liːst	kɔntsɛnˈtʁiːɐt	ziː	tʁɛkt	ˈaɪnən	bəˈkveːmən
the	book	that	she	she reads	← she concentrates	she	she wears	a	comfortable

Trainingsanzug,	jedoch	weder	Schmuck	noch	Schminke.
ˈtʁɛnɪŋsˌantsuːk	jeˈdɔx	ˈveːdɐ	ʃmʊk	nɔx	ˈʃmɪŋkə
tracksuit	but	neither	jewelry	nor	makeup

"She's not your girlfriend," Reinhold says. "Why did you bring her?"

»Sie	ist	doch	nicht	deine	Freundin«,	sagt	Reinhold.	»Warum
ziː	ɪst	dɔx	nɪçt	ˈdaɪnə	ˈfʁɔɪndɪn	zaːkt	ˈʁaɪnhɔlt	vaˈʁʊm
she	she is	!	not	your	girlfriend	he says	Reinhold	why

hast	du	sie	mitgebracht?«
hast	duː	ziː	ˈmɪtɡəˌbʁaxt
→	you	her	← you brought

"For luck," I tell him. "I need lots of luck tonight. Let's hope I win big money."

»Als	Glücksbringer«,	sage	ich	zu	ihm.	»Ich	brauche	heute	Abend
als	ˈɡlʏksˌbʁɪŋɐ	ˈzaːɡə	ɪç	tsuː	iːm	ɪç	ˈbʁaʊxə	ˈhɔɪtə	ˈaːbənt
as	lucky charm	I say	I	to	him	I	I need		tonight

viel Glück. Hoffentlich gewinne ich viel Geld.«

"Let's hope you don't," says Reinhold.

»Hoffentlich gewinnst du nicht«, sagt Reinhold.

»Wie geht es deiner Frau, Johann?«, frage ich.

"How's your wife doing, Johann?" I ask.

»Gut.«

"Fine."

Johanns Frau ist die Tochter eines bekannten Berliner Gangsters. Sein Schwiegervater wird ›Alex die Axt‹ genannt. Johann erledigt die finanziellen Angelegenheiten für Alex' Geschäfte.

Johann's wife is the daughter of a well-known gangster from Berlin. His father-in-law is called 'Alex the Ax'. Johann does all the financial work for Alex's businesses.

»Hat irgendjemand das Spiel am letzten Samstag angeschaut?«, frage ich.

"Anyone watch the game last Saturday?" I ask.

Als Antwort erhalte ich ein paar Grummellaute und Flüche. Das ist keine freundliche Gruppe.

I'm answered with a few grunts and curses. This is not a friendly group.

Max schiebt seine Freundin sanft von sich. »Sandra, ich kann nicht nachdenken, wenn du dauernd an mir klebst. Geh und schau fern.«

Max gently pushes his girlfriend away. "Sandra, I can't think with you hanging all over me. Go watch TV."

Story 13

She glides away and sits next to Lina.

Sie	gleitet	davon	und	setzt	sich	neben	Lina.
zi:	ˈglaɪtət	daˈfɔn	ʊnt	zɛtst	zɪç	ˈneːbən	ˈliːna
she	she glides	off	and	she sits down		next to	Lina

"Any of you guys ever have dealings with the police?" I ask them.

»Hat	jemand	von	euch	schon	mal	mit	der	Polizei	zu tun gehabt?«,
hat	ˈjeːmant	fɔn	ɔɪç	ʃoːn maːl		mɪt	deːɐ	poliˈtsaɪ	tsuː tuːn gəˈhaːpt
he has	anyone	of	you	ever before		with	the	police	you had to deal

frage	ich.
ˈfʁaːgə	ɪç
I ask	I

"Who hasn't?" asks Reinhold.

»Wer	denn	nicht?«,	fragt	Reinhold.
veːɐ	dɛn	nɪçt	fʁaːkt	ˈʁaɪnhɔlt
who	!	not	he asks	Reinhold

"I have something going on right now," I tell them. "Do you know if any of the top people are willing to do favors for guys like us?"

»Ich	habe	da	gerade	eine	Sache	laufen«,	sage	ich	zu	ihnen.
ɪç	ˈhaːbə	daː	gəˈʁaːdə	ˈaɪnə	ˈzaxə	ˈlaʊfən	ˈzaːgə	ɪç	tsuː	ˈiːnən
I	I have	here	just	a	thing	to be in progress	I tell	I	to	them

»Wisst	ihr,	ob	jemand	aus	den	oberen	Rängen	Leuten	wie	uns
vɪst	iːɐ	ɔp	ˈjeːmant	aʊs	deːn	ˈoːbəʁən	ˈʁɛŋən	ˈlɔɪtn	viː	ʊns
you know	you	if	anybody	from	the	upper	ranks	for people	like	us

einen	Gefallen	tun	würde?«
ˈaɪnən	gəˈfalən	tuːn	ˈvʏʁdə
a	favor		he would do

We play cards for a few more minutes.

Wir	spielen	noch ein paar	Minuten	Karten.
viːɐ	ˈʃpiːlən	nɔx aɪn paːɐ	mɪˈnuːtən	ˈkaʁtən
we	we play	a few more	minutes	cards

"If the price is right, you can convince someone to do something," Reinhold says.

»Wenn	der	Preis	stimmt,	überzeugst	du	die	Leute	davon,	etwas
vɛn	deːɐ	pʁaɪs	ʃtɪmt	yːbɐˈtsɔɪkst	duː	diː	ˈlɔɪtə	daˈfɔn	ˈɛtvas
if	the	price	it is right	you convince	you	the	people	with it	something

für	dich	zu	tun«,	sagt	Reinhold.
fyːɐ	dɪç	tsuː	tuːn	zakt	ˈʁaɪnhɔlt
for	you	to	to do	he says	Reinhold

"Who?"

»Wen?«
veːn
who

"It depends on what you want."

»Das	kommt darauf an,	was	du	willst.«
das	kɔmt daˈʁaʊf an	vas	duː	vɪlst
that	it depends on	what	you	you want

"I want to stop an investigation," I say.

»Ich	möchte	eine	Ermittlung	stoppen«,	sage	ich.
ɪç	ˈmøçtə	ˈaɪnə	ɛɐˈmɪtlʊŋ	ˈʃtɔpən	ˈzaːgə	ɪç
I	I would like	an	investigation	to stop	I say	I

"I might have a name. Give me your cell phone number."

»Vielleicht	hätte	ich	da	jemanden.	Gib	mir	deine
fiˈlaɪçt	ˈhɛtə	ɪç	daː	ˈjeːmandən	giːp	miːɐ	ˈdaɪnə
maybe	I would have	I	there	someone	give	me	your

Evolution

Handynummer.«
    ˈhɛndɪˌnʊmɐ
    cell phone number

Ich	schreibe	meine	Telefonnummer	auf	ein	Stück	Papier	und
ɪç	ˈʃʁaɪbə	ˈmaɪnə	teləˈfoːnˌnʊmɐ	aʊf	aɪn	ʃtʏk	paˈpiːɐ	ʊnt
I	I write	my	telephone number	on	a	piece	paper	and

I write my phone number on a piece of paper and slide it over to him.

schiebe	es	zu	ihm	hinüber.
ˈʃiːbə	ɛs	tsuː	iːm	hɪnˈyːbɐ
I push over→	it	to	him	←

»Lass	mir	ein paar	Tage	Zeit«,	sagt	er.
las	miːɐ	aɪn paːɐ	ˈtaːɡə	tsaɪt	zakt	eːɐ
allow	me	a few	days	time	he says	he

"Give me a few days," he says.

»Du	hast	was	gut	bei	mir«,	sage	ich	zu	ihm.
duː	hast	vas	ɡuːt	baɪ	miːɐ	ˈzaːɡə	ɪç	tsuː	iːm
you	you have	something	good	with	me	I say	I	to	him

"I owe you," I tell him.

Johann	wirft	seine	Karten	auf	den	Tisch	und	steigt aus,	ich
ˈjoːhan	vɪʁft	ˈzaɪnə	ˈkaʁtən	aʊf	deːn	tɪʃ	ʊnt	ˈʃtaɪkt aʊs	ɪç
Johann	he throws	his	cards	on	the	table	and	he folds	I

Johann throws his cards on the table and folds. I do, too. Reinhold and Max draw some cards.

ebenso.	Reinhold	und	Max	ziehen	ein paar	Karten.
ˈeːbənzoː	ˈʁaɪnhɔlt	ʊnt	maks	ˈtsiːən	aɪn paːɐ	ˈkaʁtən
also	Reinhold	and	Max	they draw	a few	cards

»Möchte	jemand	ein	Bier?«,	frage	ich.
ˈmœçtə	ˈjeːmant	aɪn	biːɐ	ˈfʁaːɡə	ɪç
he wants	anyone	a	beer	I ask	I

"Anyone want a beer?" I ask.

Max	nickt	mir	zu.	Ich	gehe	zum	Kühlschrank	und	hole	zwei
maks	nɪkt	miːɐ	tsuː	ɪç	ˈɡeːə	tsʊm	ˈkyːlʃʁaŋk	ʊnt	ˈhoːlə	tsvaɪ
Max	he nods→	to me	←	I	I walk	to the	refrigerator	and	I fetch	two

Max gives me a nod. I walk to the refrigerator and get two bottles of beer. When I get back to the table, Max is raking in the chips.

Flaschen	Bier.	Als	ich	zum	Tisch	zurückkomme,	schaufelt	Max
ˈflaʃən	biːɐ	als	ɪç	tsʊm	tɪʃ	tsuˈʁʏkˌkɔmə	ˈʃaʊfəlt	maks
bottles	beer	when	I	to the	table	I come back	he shovels in→→	Max

sich	die	Chips	ein.
zɪç	diː	tʃɪps	aɪn
←	the	chips	←

»Wir	haben	ein	mäßiges	Spiel	heute	Abend«,	sagt	Reinhold.
viːɐ	ˈhaːbn	aɪn	ˈmɛːsɪɡəs	ʃpiːl	ˈhɔɪtə	ˈaːbənt	zakt	ˈʁaɪnhɔlt
we	we have	a	mediocre	game		tonight	he says	Reinhold

"The cards are cold tonight," says Reinhold.

Der	Feuerwehrhauptmann	teilt	neue	Karten	aus.	Wir
deːɐ	ˈfɔɪɐveːɐˌhaʊptman	taɪlt	ˈnɔɪə	ˈkaʁtən	aʊs	viːɐ
the	fire chief	he deals out→	new	cards	←	we

The fire chief deals a new hand. We start talking about basketball. Four hours later, I decide to call it a night.

fangen an,	uns	über	Basketball	zu	unterhalten.	Vier	Stunden
ˈfaŋən an	ʊns	ˈyːbɐ	ˈbaskətˌbal	tsuː	ʊntɐˈhaltn	fiːɐ	ˈʃtʊndən
we start	→	about	basketball	to	←to talk	four	hours

205

Story 13

später beschließe ich, nach Hause zu gehen.
'ʃpɛːtɐ   bə'ʃliːsə   ɪç   naːx 'haʊzə   tsuː   'geːən
later   I decide   I   home   to   to go

"You've won a lot of money," Johann says as Lina and I turn to leave. "Stick around so we can get some of it back."

»Du hast einen Haufen Geld gewonnen«, sagt Johann, als Lina
duː hast 'aɪnən 'haʊfən gɛlt gə'vɔnən   zakt 'joːhan als 'liːna
you →   a   heap   money ←you won   he says Johann as   Lina

und ich aufbrechen. »Bleib noch hier, damit wir etwas davon
ʊnt ɪç 'aʊf‿bʁɛçn̩   blaɪp nɔx   hiːɐ   da'mɪt   viːɐ   'ɛtvas   da'fɔn
and I   we set out   stay   still here so that   we   some   of it

zurückgewinnen können.«
tsu'ʁʏkgə‿vɪnən   'kœnən
to win back   we can

"Thanks, Johann, but I need the money right now for something else."

»Danke, Johann, aber ich brauche das Geld gerade für etwas
'daŋkə 'joːhan   'aːbɐ   ɪç   'bʁaʊxə   das   gɛlt   gə'ʁaːdə   fyːɐ   'ɛtvas
thanks Johann   but   I   I need   the   money right now for   something

anderes.«
'andəʁəs
else

"Right. That thing about the ongoing police investigation," he says.

»Ach ja, die Sache mit der laufenden Polizeiermittlung«, sagt er.
ax jaː   diː   'zaxə   mɪt deːɐ   'laʊfəndən   poli'tsaɪ‿ɐ‿'mɪtlʊŋ   zakt   eːɐ
oh right the   thing   with the   ongoing   police investigation he says he

We walk out of the firehouse and down the street to our car. On our way we pass by a long, tall hedge. I search in my pocket for the car remote.

Wir verlassen das Feuerwehrhaus und gehen die Straße
viːɐ   fɛɐ'lasn̩   das   'fɔɪɐveːɐ‿haʊs   ʊnt   'geːən   diː   'ʃtʁaːsə
we   we exit   the   firehouse   and   we walk down→ the street

hinunter zu unserem Auto. Auf unserem Weg kommen wir an
hɪ'nʊntɐ   tsuː   'ʊnzəʁəm   'aʊto   aʊf   'ʊnzəʁəm   veːk   'kɔmən   viːɐ   an
←   to   our   car   on   our   way   we pass by→

einer langen, hohen Hecke vorbei. Ich suche in meiner Tasche
'aɪnɐ   'laŋən   'hoːən   'hɛkə   fɔːɐ'baɪ   ɪç   'zuːxə   ɪn   'maɪnɐ   'taʃə
a   long   tall   hedge   ←   I   I search in   my   pocket

nach der Fernbedienung fürs Auto.
naːx   deːɐ   'fɛʁnbə‿diːnʊŋ   fyːɐs   'aʊto
for   the   remote   for the car

Suddenly, Lina spins on her left foot. She smashes her right foot into the face of a big guy who appeared from behind the hedge. He drops the club he is holding and falls backwards onto his butt.

Plötzlich wirbelt Lina auf ihrem linken Fuß herum. Sie tritt
'plœtslɪç   'vɪʁbl̩t   'liːna   aʊf   'iːʁəm   'lɪŋkən   fuːs   hɛ'ʁʊm   ziː   tʁɪt
suddenly   she spins around→ Lina on   her   left   foot   ←   she she kicks

mit ihrem Fuß in das Gesicht eines großen Burschen, der plötzlich
mɪt   'iːʁəm   fuːs   ɪn   das   gə'zɪçt   'aɪnəs   'gʁoːsən   'bʊʁʃən   deːɐ   'plœtslɪç
with her   foot   in   the   face   of a   big   guy   who   suddenly

hinter der Hecke hervorgekommen ist. Der Schlagstock, den er
'hɪntɐ   deːɐ   'hɛkə   hɛɐ'foːɐgə‿kɔmən   ɪst   deːɐ   'ʃlaːkʃtɔk   deːn   eːɐ
behind   the   hedge   he appeared from   the   club   that   he

hält, fällt ihm aus der Hand und er fällt rückwärts auf seinen
hɛlt   fɛlt   iːm   aʊs   deːɐ   hant   ʊnt   eːɐ   fɛlt   'ʁʏkvɛʁts   aʊf   'zaɪnən
he holds it falls him   out of the   hand   and   he   he falls   backwards on   his

Evolution

Hintern.
'hɪntɐn
buttocks

Ich	lehne mich	am	Auto	an,	als	zwei	weitere	Männer	aus
ɪç	'le:nə mɪç	am	'aʊto	an	als	tsvaɪ	'vaɪtəʁə	'mɛnɐ	aʊs
I	I lean against→	on the	car	←	as	the	other	men	out of

der	Dunkelheit	herausspringen.	Der	eine	hält	einen	kleinen
de:ɐ	'dʊŋkəlhaɪt	hɛʁ'aʊsʃpʁɪŋən	de:ɐ	'aɪnə	hɛlt	'aɪnən	'klaɪnən
the	darkness	they jump out	the	one	he holds	a	small

Schlagstock	in	der	Hand.	Der	andere	hat	ein	Messer.	Sie	sind
'ʃla:kʃtɔk	ɪn	de:ɐ	hant	de:ɐ	'andəʁə	hat	aɪn	'mɛsɐ	zi:	zɪnt
club	in	the	hand	the	other	he has	a	knife	they	they are

jung,	etwa	neunzehn	oder	zwanzig	Jahre	alt.	Sie	sind	etwas
jʊŋ	'ɛtva	'nɔɪntsɛn	'o:dɐ	'tsvantsɪç	'ja:ʁə	alt	zi:	zɪnt	'ɛtvas
young	about	nineteen	or	twenty	years	old	they	they are	somewhat

kleiner	als	ich,	aber	wahrscheinlich	wiegen	sie	fünfzehn	Kilogram
'klaɪnɐ	als	ɪç	'a:bɐ	va:ɐ̯'ʃaɪnlɪç	'vi:gən	zi:	'fʏnftse:n	'kɪlogʁam
shorter	than	me	but	probably	they weigh	they	fifteen	kilogram

mehr	als	ich.
me:ɐ	als	ɪç
more	than	me

I lean against the car, as two other men spring out of the darkness. One holds a small club. The other has a knife. They are young - maybe 19 or 20 years old. A little shorter than me, but they probably weigh fifteen kilograms more than me.

Lina	steht	ihnen	gegenüber.	Ihre	Knie	sind	leicht	gebeugt.
'li:na	ʃte:t	'i:nən	ge:gn'y:bɐ	'i:ʁə	kni:	zɪnt	laɪçt	gə'bɔɪkt
Lina	she stands facing→	them	←	her	knees	they are	slightly	bent

Die	Unterarme	sind	nach oben	gerichtet	und	die	Ellbogen	am
di:	'ʊntɐˌa:ɐ̯mə	zɪnt	na:x 'o:bən	gə'ʁɪçtət	ʊnt	di:	'ɛlˌbo:gn	am
the	forearms	they are	up	directed	and	the	elbows	on the

Körper	angelegt.	Ihre	Fäuste	sind	leicht	geballt.	Der	linke
'kœɐ̯pɐ	'angəˌle:kt	'i:ʁə	'fɔʏstə	zɪnt	laɪçt	gə'balt	de:ɐ	'lɪŋkə
body	they rest against	her	fists	they are	slightly	clenched	the	left

Fuß	steht	vorne	und	die	rechten	Zehen	zeigen	nach außen.
fu:s	ʃte:t	'fɔʁnə	ʊnt	di:	'ʁɛçtən	'tse:ən	'tsaɪgən	na:x 'aʊsən
foot	it stands	in front	and	the	right	toes	they point	outwards

Beide	Fersen	sind	vom	Boden	gelöst.	Das	ist	die	traditionelle
'baɪdə	'fɛʁzən	zɪnt	fɔm	'bo:dən	gə'lø:st	das	ɪst	di:	tʁadɪtsjo:'nɛlə
both	heels	they are	from the	ground	removed	this	it is	the	traditional

Muay-Thai-Kampfhaltung.
mɔɪ-taɪ-'kampfˌhaltʊŋ
muay thai fighting stance

Lina stands facing them. Her knees are slightly bent. The forearms are up and the elbows are in. Her fists are loosely clenched. The left foot is forward, and the right toes are pointing to the side. Both heels are off the ground. This is the traditional Muay Thai fighting stance.

Die	zwei	harten	Kerle	schauen	zu	ihrem	Freund,	der	am	Boden
di:	tsvaɪ	'haʁtən	'kɛʁlə	'ʃaʊən	tsu:	'i:ʁəm	fʁɔɪnt	de:ɐ	am	'bo:dən
the	two	tough	guys	they look	at	their	friend	who	on the	ground

sitzt.	Er	hält	seine	Hände	vor	das	Gesicht.	Blut	quillt
zɪtst	e:ɐ	hɛlt	'zaɪnə	'hɛndə	fo:ɐ	das	gə'zɪçt	blu:t	kvɪlt
he sits	he	he holds	his	hands	in front of	the	face	blood	it gushes→

The two tough guys look at their friend sitting on the ground. He has his hands up to his face. Blood is spurting out between his fingers.

Story 13

	zwischen	seinen	Fingern	hervor.
	ˈtsvɪʃən	ˈzaɪnən	ˈfɪŋɐn	hɛɐˈfoːɐ
	between	his	fingers	←

They hesitate and Lina attacks. The guy holding the club tries to swing it. Too late.

Sie	zögern	und	Lina	greift an.	Der	Typ	mit	dem	Schlagstock
ziː	ˈtsøːɡɐn	ʊnt	ˈliːna	ɡʁaɪft an	deːɐ	tyːp	mɪt	deːm	ˈʃlaːkʃtɔk
they	they hesitate	and	Lina	she attacks	the	guy	with	the	club

versucht	auszuholen.	Zu	spät.
fɛɐˈzuːxt	ˈaʊstsuˌhoːlən	tsuː	ʃpɛːt
he tries	to take a swing	too	late

Lina's elbow smashes his nose, and her left leg sweeps his feet out from under him before the club moves five centimeters.

Linas	Ellbogen	zertrümmert	seine	Nase	und	ihr	linkes	Bein
ˈliːnas	ˈɛlˌboːɡn̩	tsɛɐˈtʁʏmɐt	ˈzaɪnə	ˈnaːzə	ʊnt	iːɐ	ˈlɪŋkəs	baɪn
Lina's	elbow	it smashes	his	nose	and	her	left	leg

zieht	ihm	die	Füße	unter	sich	weg,	bevor	sich	sein	Schläger
tsiːt	iːm	diː	ˈfyːsə	ˈʊntɐ	zɪç	vɛk	bəˈfoːɐ	zɪç	zaɪn	ˈʃlɛːɡɐ
it pulls away→	him	the	feet	under	him	←	before	→	his	club

auch	nur	fünf	Zentimeter	bewegt.
aʊx	nuːɐ	fʏnf	tsɛntiˈmeːtɐ	bəˈveːkt
even	just	five	centimeter	←it moves

As he falls, she dances clear of a knife thrust from the second man. He stabs too hard and winds up off balance. Lina closes in before he can recover.

Als	er	hinfällt,	weicht	sie	tänzerisch	einem	Messerstich	des
als	eːɐ	ˈhɪnfɛlt	vaɪçt	ziː	ˈtɛntsəʁɪʃ	ˈaɪnəm	ˈmɛsɐʃtɪç	dɛs
as	he	he falls down	she avoids→	she	dancing	a	knife thrust	of the

zweiten	Mannes	aus.	Er	sticht	zu	fest	zu	und	verliert	dabei
ˈtsvaɪtn̩	ˈmanəs	aʊs	eːɐ	ʃtɪçt	tsuː	fɛst	tsuː	ʊnt	fɛɐˈliːɐt	daˈbaɪ
second	man	←	he	he stabs→	too	hard	←	and	he loses	in the process

das	Gleichgewicht.	Lina		geht		schon	zum Angriff über,	
das	ˈɡlaɪçɡəˌvɪçt	ˈliːna		ɡeːt		ʃoːn	tsʊm ˈanˌɡʁɪf ˈyːbɐ	
the	balance	Lina	she launches an attack→			already	←	

bevor	er	sich	fangen	konnte.
bəˈfoːɐ	eːɐ	zɪç	ˈfaŋən	ˈkɔntə
before	he	he could recover		

She knees him in the kidney and punches the side of his jaw with a hard jab. His body buckles from the force of the strike.

Sie	stößt	ihm	ihr	Knie	in	die	Niere	und	schlägt	ihm	seitlich
ziː	ʃtøːst	iːm	iːɐ	kniː	ɪn	diː	ˈniːʁə	ʊnt	ʃlɛːkt	iːm	ˈzaɪtlɪç
she	she thrusts	him	her	knee	into	the	kidney	and	she punches	him	sideways

auf	den	Kiefer	mit	einer	harten,	kurzen	Geraden.	Sein	Körper
aʊf	deːn	ˈkiːfɐ	mɪt	ˈaɪnɐ	ˈhaʁtən	ˈkʊʁtsən	ɡəˈʁaːdən	zaɪn	ˈkœʁpɐ
onto	the	jaw	with	a	hard	short	jab	his	body

sackt	durch	die	Wucht	des	Schlages	zu	Boden.
zakt	dʊʁç	diː	vʊxt	dɛs	ˈʃlaːɡəs	tsuː	ˈboːdn̩
it sags	from	the	force	of the	strike	to	ground

As he falls, she dances over to the guy with the club and stomps on his crotch. He whimpers and passes out.

Als	er	hinfällt,	tänzelt	sie	zum	Kerl	mit	dem	Schlagstock	und
als	eːɐ	ˈhɪnfɛlt	ˈtɛntsəlt	ziː	tsʊm	kɛʁl	mɪt	deːm	ˈʃlaːkʃtɔk	ʊnt
as	he	he falls down	she prances	she	to the	guy	with	the	club	and

stampft	ihm	in	den	Schritt.	Er	wimmert	und	wird ohnmächtig.
ʃtampft	iːm	ɪn	deːn	ʃʁɪt	eːɐ	ˈvɪmɐt	ʊnt	vɪʁt ˈoːnˌmɛçtɪç
she stomps	him	in	the	crotch	he	he whimpers	and	he passes out

Dann schlurft sie zurück zu dem Mann mit dem Messer, der nun am Boden liegt. Sie tritt ihm gegen den Kopf. Er lässt das Messer fallen und bleibt reglos liegen.

Then she shuffles back to the guy with the knife who is now on the ground. She kicks him in the head. He drops the knife and lays still.

Inzwischen hat sich unser erster Angreifer wieder auf die Beine gestellt. Er fummelt an einer Pistole herum, die in seiner Hosentasche steckt. Seine Hände sind glitschig von dem Blut aus seiner Nase und seinem Mund. Das macht es schwierig für ihn, die Pistole zu fassen.

By this time, our first assailant has pulled himself back onto his feet. He fumbles with a gun that is stuck in his pants pocket. His hands are slippery with the blood from his nose and mouth, which makes it hard for him to grab the gun.

Ich schlage ihm lässig mit einem kleinen Knüppel aus meiner Tasche auf die Kopfseite. Er sackt auf dem Pflaster in sich zusammen.

I casually swat him on the side of the head with a little club that I keep in my pocket. He crumbles back onto the pavement.

»Du brauchst ein Schulterhalfter«, sage ich zu dem bewusstlosen Mann. »Das erleichtert das Ziehen der Pistole.«

"You need a shoulder holster," I tell the unconscious man. "Makes it easier to pull the gun."

»Er kann dich nicht hören«, sagt Lina.

"He can't hear you," Lina says.

Sie ist nicht einmal außer Atem. Wir setzen uns beide in mein

She isn't even breathing hard. The two of us get into my car and drive off.

Story 13

	Auto	und	fahren	davon.
	ˈaʊto	ʊnt	ˈfaːʁən	daˈfɔn
	car	and		we drive off

"How did they know about the poker game?" she asks.

»Woher	wussten	sie	von	dem	Pokerspiel?«,	fragt	sie.
voˈheːɐ	ˈvʊstən	ziː	fɔn	deːm	ˈpoːkɐˌʃpiːl	fʁaːkt	ziː
from where	they knew	they	about	the	poker game	she asks	she

"Maybe they are members of the volunteer fire department," I say.

»Vielleicht	sind	sie	Mitglieder	der	freiwilligen	Feuerwehr«,	sage	ich.
fiˈlaɪçt	zɪnt	ziː	ˈmɪtˌgliːdɐ	deːɐ	ˈfʁaɪˌvɪlɪgn	ˈfɔʏɐveːɐ	ˈzaːgə	ɪç
maybe	they are	they	members	of the	volunteer	fire department	I say	I

6

The man from Leipzig with the funny accent calls me the next morning. On my cell phone! How did he get that number?

Der	Mann	aus	Leipzig	mit	dem	komischen	Akzent	ruft	mich
deːɐ	man	aʊs	ˈlaɪptsɪç	mɪt	deːm	ˈkoːmɪʃən	akˈtsɛnt	ʁuːft	mɪç
the	man	from	Leipzig	with	the	funny	accent	he calls →	me

am	nächsten	Morgen	an.	Auf	meinem	Handy!	Wie	hat	er	diese
am	ˈnɛçstən	ˈmɔʁgn̩	an	aʊf	ˈmaɪnəm	ˈhɛndɪ	viː	hat	eːɐ	ˈdiːzə
on the	next	morning	←	on	my	cell phone	how	→	he	this

Nummer	bekommen?
ˈnʊmɐ	bəˈkɔmən
number	← he got

"You will bring my gift to the Treptower Park parking lot at two o'clock," he says.

»Sie	werden	mein	Geschenk	um	zwei	Uhr	zum	Parkplatz	am
ziː	ˈveːɐdn̩	maɪn	gəˈʃɛŋk	ʊm	tsvaɪ	uːɐ	tsʊm	ˈpaʁkˌplats	am
you	you will	my	gift	at		two o'clock	to the	parking lot	at the

Treptower	Park	bringen«,	sagt	er.
ˈtʁɛːptoɐ paʁk		ˈbʁɪŋən	zaːkt	eːɐ
Treptower Park		to bring	he says	he

"No," I answer.

»Nein«,	antworte	ich.
naɪn	ˈantvɔʁtə	ɪç
no	I answer	I

There is a pause on the line.

Schweigen	in	der	Leitung.
ˈʃvaɪgn̩	ɪn	deːɐ	ˈlaɪtʊŋ
silence	on	the	line

"You don't have the gift?" he asks.

»Sie	haben	das	Geschenk	nicht?«,	fragt	er.
ziː	ˈhaːbn̩	das	gəˈʃɛŋk	nɪçt	fʁaːkt	eːɐ
you	you have	the	gift	not	he asks	he

"I have it, but I'm not driving all the way down there to meet you."

»Ich	habe	es,	aber	ich	fahre	nicht	den	ganzen	Weg	dort
ɪç	ˈhaːbə	ɛs	ˈaːbɐ	ɪç	ˈfaːʁə	nɪçt	deːn	ˈgantsən	vɛk	dɔʁt
I	I have	it	but	I	I drive down →	not	the	whole	way	there

hinunter,	um	Sie	zu	treffen.«
hɪnˈʊntɐ	ʊm	ziː	tsuː	ˈtʁɛfən
←	in order to	you	to	to meet

Evolution

»Ich mache keine Witze. Sie müssen tun, was ich sage.« — "I'm not joking. You must do what I say."

»Wenn Sie Ihr Geld haben wollen, dann werde ich es Ihnen an einem Ort geben, den ich vorschlage.« — "If you want your money, I'll give it to you at a place that I pick."

Er denkt ein paar Sekunden nach. — He thinks for a few seconds.

»Wenn die Polizei dort ist, werde ich es wissen. Ich bin sehr vorsichtig.« — "If the police are there, I will know. I am very careful."

»Keine Sorge«, sage ich zu ihm, »die Polizei wird nicht dort sein.« — "Don't worry," I tell him, "the police won't be there."

Nach zwanzig Sekunden Stillschweigen sagt er: »In Ordnung, wohin wollen Sie das Geschenk bringen?« — After twenty seconds of silence he says, "Okay, where do you want to bring the gift?"

»Ich werde Sie am U-Bahnhof Kottbusser Tor in Neukölln treffen. Das ist ein schöner, offener Platz.« — "I'll meet you at the Kottbusser Tor subway station in Neukölln. That's a nice public place."

»Haben Sie Angst, dass ich Ihnen etwas antun könnte?« — "Are you worried that I will do something to you?"

»Ich will Zeugen haben.« — "I want to have witnesses."

Story 13

"Remember," he tells me, "if the police show up, I will know."

»Denken Sie daran«, sagt er zu mir, »wenn die Polizei kommt,
ˈdɛŋkn̩ ziː daˈʁan   zakt eːɐ tsuː miːɐ   vɛn   diː poliˈtsai kɔmt
remember   he says he to   me   if   the police   it comes

werde ich es wissen.«
ˈveːɐdə ɪç ɛs ˈvɪsən
I will   I   it to know

"Understood," I say.

»Verstanden«, sage ich.
fɛɐˈʃtandn̩   ˈzaːgə ɪç
understood   I say   I

"By the way, do you accept checks?"

»Wo wir gerade dabei sind, nehmen Sie auch Schecks?«
voː viːɐ gəˈʁaːdə daˈbai zɪnt   ˈneːmən ziː aux ʃɛks
while we're at it   you take you also checks

He doesn't even chuckle.

Nicht einmal ein Kichern ist zu hören.
nɪçt ˈainmaːl ain ˈkɪçɐn ɪst tsuː ˈhøːʁən
not even   a   chuckle it is to   to hear

A few hours later I am standing at Kottbusser Gate Station reading a newspaper. A train stops and ten people get off. Then the train rumbles onward. Nobody pays any attention to me. My new friend walks down the platform and stands in front of me.

Ein paar Stunden später stehe ich am Bahnhof Kottbusser Tor und
ain paːɐ ˈʃtʊndən ˈʃpɛːtɐ ˈʃteːə ɪç   am ˈbaːnˌhoːf ˈkɔtˌbʊsɐ toːɐ ʊnt
     a few hours   later   I stand I   at Kottbusser Tor station   and

lese eine Zeitung. Ein Zug hält und zehn Leute steigen aus.
ˈleːsə ˈainə ˈtsaitʊŋ   ain tsuːk hɛlt ʊnt tseːn ˈlɔitə ˈʃtaigən aus
I read   a   newspaper a   train it stops and ten   people they get out

Dann rumpelt der Zug weiter. Niemand beachtet mich. Mein
dan   ˈʁʊmpəlt deːɐ tsuːk ˈvaitɐ   ˈniːmant bəˈaxtət mɪç   main
then it rumbles the   train onward   nobody   he pays attention to me my

neuer Freund geht die Plattform hinunter und steht
ˈnɔiɐ fʁɔint geːt diː ˈplatfɔʁm hɪnˈʊntɐ ʊnt ʃteːt
new   friend he walks down→ the platform   ←   and he stands

vor mir.
foːɐ miːɐ
in front of me

"Where is my gift?" he asks.

»Wo ist mein Geschenk?«, fragt er.
voː ɪst main gəˈʃɛŋk   fʁaːkt eːɐ
where it is my   gift   he asks he

This is a good question, since I don't have a suitcase or backpack with me.

Das ist eine gute Frage, da ich ja keinen Koffer oder Rucksack
das ɪst ˈainə ˈguːtə ˈfʁaːgə daː ɪç jaː ˈkainən ˈkɔfɐ ˈoːdɐ ˈʁʊkˌzak
this it is a   good   question since I   !   not a   suitcase or   backpack

dabei habe.
daˈbai ˈhaːbə
with me I have

"It's nearby," I say. "Before I get it, can we make some kind of deal?"

»Es ist in der Nähe«, sage ich. »Bevor ich es hole, können wir
ɛs   ɪst ɪn deːɐ ˈnɛːə   ˈzaːgə ɪç   bəˈfoːɐ ɪç   ɛs   ˈhoːlə   ˈkœnən viːɐ
it   it is nearby   I say   I   before   I   it   I get   we can   we

212

eine Art Vereinbarung treffen?«
'aɪnə aʁt   fɛɐ̯'aɪnbaːʁʊŋ 'tʁɛfən
some kind of   to strike a deal

Er wirkt amüsiert. — He looks amused.
eːɐ̯ vɪʁkt amyˈziːɐ̯t
he he looks amused

»Ziehen Sie Ihre Jacke aus«, sagt er. — "Take off your jacket," he says.
ˈtsiːən ziː iːʁə ˈjakə aʊs zakt eːɐ̯
take off→ your jacket ← he says he

Nachdem ich das getan habe, klopft er mir mit seinen Händen
naːxˈdeːm ɪç das gəˈtaːn ˈhaːbə klɔpft eːɐ̯ miːɐ̯ mɪt ˈzaɪnən ˈhɛndən
after I that I did he pats→ he me with his hands

die Brust, den Bauch, Rücken und die Oberschenkel ab. Nach
diː bʁʊst deːn baʊx ˈʁʏkən ʊnt diː ˈoːbɐʃɛŋkəl ap naːx
the chest the stomach back and the thighs ← after

ein paar Minuten hört er auf.
aɪn paːɐ̯ mɪˈnuːtən høːɐ̯t eːɐ̯ aʊf
a few minutes he stops→ he ←

After I did that, he pats his hands around my chest, stomach, back, and thighs. After a few minutes, he stops.

»Sie tragen keine Abhörgeräte. Jetzt können wir uns unterhalten.
ziː ˈtʁaːgn̩ ˈkaɪnə ˈaphøːɐ̯gəˌʁɛːtə jɛtst ˈkœnən viːɐ̯ ʊns ʊntɐˈhaltn̩
you you wear not a listening devices now we can we to talk

Die Vereinbarung lautet, dass Sie mir jeden Monat etwas
diː fɛɐ̯ˈaɪnbaːʁʊŋ ˈlaʊtət das ziː miːɐ̯ ˈjeːdən ˈmoːnat ˈɛtvas
the agreement it is that you to me every month something

bezahlen müssen.«
bəˈtsaːlən ˈmʏsn̩
to pay you must

"You are not wearing any listening devices. We can talk. The deal is that you must pay me every month."

»Das ist eine Menge Geld«, sage ich. »Können wir Ihren Boss
das ɪst ˈaɪnə ˈmɛŋə gɛlt ˈzaːgə ɪç ˈkœnən viːɐ̯ ˈiːʁən bɔs
that it is a lots of Money I say I can we we your boss

anrufen und etwas anderes vereinbaren?«
ˈanˌʁuːfən ʊnt ˈɛtvas ˈandəʁəs fɛɐ̯ˈaɪnbaːʁən
to call and something else to arrange

"That's a lot of money," I say. "Can we call your boss and negotiate something different?"

»Mein Boss verhandelt nicht.« — "The boss doesn't make deals."
maɪn bɔs fɛɐ̯ˈhandlt nɪçt
my boss he negotiates not

»Besteht die Möglichkeit, dass ich einen Prozentsatz meines
bəˈʃteːt diː ˈmøːklɪçkaɪt das ɪç ˈaɪnən pʁoˈtsɛntˌzats ˈmaɪnəs
it exists the possibility that I a percentage of my

Einkommens zahlen könnte? Ich verdiene nicht jeden Monat
ˈaɪnˌkɔmən̩s ˈtsaːlən ˈkœntə ɪç fɛɐ̯ˈdiːnə nɪçt ˈjeːdn̩ ˈmoːnat
income to pay I could I I earn not every month

"Is there a way I could pay a percentage of my income? Some months I don't make as much as others."

Story 13

"No more talking. Take me to the money," he responds.

»Schluss mit dem Gerede. Bringen Sie mich zum Geld«, antwortet er.
ʃlʊs mɪt deːm ɡəˈʁeːdə ˈbʁɪŋən ziː mɪç tsʊm ɡɛlt ˈantˌvɔʁtət eːɐ̯
finish with the talking bring me to the money he responds he

gleich viel.«
ɡlaɪç fiːl
equal amounts

The guy seems determined, so I lead him behind the station and down a stairway. Halfway down the stairs a backpack lays on the floor. An electric box is attached to the wall about two meters above the steps. As he looks at the backpack, I grab a gun from the top of the electric box and shoot him three times in the heart.

Der Kerl scheint entschlossen zu sein. Also führe ich ihn hinter den Bahnsteig und die Stufen hinunter. Auf halbem Weg liegt ein Rucksack auf den Stufen. Ein elektrischer Verteilerkasten ist an der Wand ungefähr zwei Meter über den Stufen angebracht. Als er auf den Rucksack blickt, greife ich nach der Pistole, die oben auf dem Verteilerkasten liegt, und schieße ihm dreimal ins Herz.

deːɐ̯ kɛʁl ʃaɪnt ɛntˈʃlɔsən tsuː zaɪn ˈalzo ˈfyːʁə ɪç iːn ˈhɪntɐ deːn ˈbaːnˌʃtaɪk ʊnt diː ˈʃtuːfən hɪnˈʊntɐ aʊf ˈhalbəm vɛk liːkt aɪn ˈʁʊkˌzak aʊf deːn ˈʃtuːfən aɪn eːˈlɛktʁɪʃɐ fɛɐ̯ˈtaɪlɐˌkastn̩ ɪst an deːɐ̯ vant ˈʊnɡəfɛːɐ̯ tsvaɪ ˈmeːtɐ ˈyːbɐ deːn ˈʃtuːfən ˈanɡəbʁaxt als eːɐ̯ aʊf deːn ˈʁʊkˌzak blɪkt ˈɡʁaɪfə ɪç naːx deːɐ̯ pɪsˈtoːlə diː ˈoːbən aʊf deːm fɛɐ̯ˈtaɪlɐˌkastn̩ liːkt ʊnt ˈʃiːsə iːm ˈdʁaɪmaːl ɪns hɛʁts

the guy he seems determined to to be so I lead I him behind the station platform and the steps downstairs halfway it lays a backpack on the steps an electric junction box it is on the wall about two meter above the steps affixed as he at the backpack he looks I reach for → I ← the gun that on top of the junction box it lays and I shoot him three times in the heart

"You should have taken that life insurance policy," I say to his corpse.

»Sie hätten die Lebensversicherung abschließen sollen«, sage ich zu seiner Leiche.
ziː ˈhɛtn̩ diː ˈleːbn̩sfɛɐ̯ˌzɪçəʁʊŋ ˈapˌʃliːsn̩ ˈzɔlən ˈzaːɡə ɪç tsuː ˈzaɪnɐ ˈlaɪçə
you → the life insurance policy ← you should have closed I say I to his corpse

―――― 7 ――――

The gun is silenced, so nobody rushes down the stairs to see what happened. I make a quick call to Lucia.

Die Pistole hat einen Schalldämpfer, damit niemand die Treppen hinunter eilt, um zu sehen, was passiert ist. Ich rufe Lucia
diː pɪsˈtoːlə hat ˈaɪnən ˈʃalˌdɛmpfɐ daˈmɪt ˈniːmant diː ˈtʁɛpən hɪnˈʊntɐ aɪlt ʊm tsuː ˈzeːən vas paˈsiːɐ̯t ɪst ɪç ˈʁuːfə luˈtsia
the gun it has a silencer so that nobody the stairs down he rushes in order to to to see what it happened I I call → Lucia

214

Evolution

kurz an.
kʊʁts an
quickly ←

»Es ist erledigt«, sage ich zu ihr.
ɛs ɪst ɛɐ̯'le:dɪçt 'za:gə ɪç tsu: i:ɐ̯
it it is done I tell I to her

"It's done," I tell her.

Zwanzig Sekunden später höre ich rasselnde Geräusche. Die
'tsvantsɪç ze:'kʊndən 'ʃpɛ:tɐ 'hø:ʁə ɪç 'ʁasəlndə gə'ʁɔʏʃə di:
twenty seconds later I hear I rattling sounds the

Mitglieder meines Teams verschließen die Türen oberhalb und
'mɪt‚gliːdɐ 'maɪnəs ti:ms fɛɐ̯'ʃliːsən di: 'ty:ʁən 'o:bɐhalp ʊnt
members of my team they seal off the doors above and

unterhalb der Treppe mit einer Kette. Das gibt mir Zeit
'ʊntɐhalp deːɐ̯ 'tʁɛpə mɪt 'aɪnɐ 'kɛtə das gi:pt mi:ɐ̯ tsaɪt
below the staircase with a chain that it gives me time

zum Nachforschen. Ich sehe in seinen Taschen nach. Nichts.
tsʊm 'na:x‚fɔʁʃn ɪç 'ze:ə ɪn 'zaɪnən 'taʃən na:x nɪçts
for investigating I I check→ in his pockets ← nothing

Ich ziehe seine Kleider aus und suche nach Tätowierungen oder
ɪç 'tsi:ə 'zaɪnə 'klaɪdɐ aʊs ʊnt 'zu:xə na:x tɛto'vi:ʁʊŋən 'o:dɐ
I I take off→ his clothes ← and I search for tattoos or

Narben. Nichts.
'naʁbən nɪçts
scars nothing

Twenty seconds later I hear clanging sounds. The members of my team are chaining shut the doors at the top and the bottom of the stairway. This gives me time to investigate. I check his pockets. Nothing. I take his clothes off and look for tattoos or scars. Nothing.

Währenddessen erkläre ich ihm meine Evolutionstheorie. Sie
vɛ:ʁənt'dɛsn ɛɐ̯'klɛ:ʁə ɪç i:m 'maɪnə evoluts'jo:nsteo‚ʁi: zi:
during that I explain I to him my theory of evolution you

erinnern sich doch noch an den Monolog zu Beginn dieser
ɛɐ̯'ɪnɐn zɪç dɔx nɔx an de:n mono'lo:k tsu: bə'gɪn 'di:zɐ
you remember ! still on the monologue at the beginning of this

Geschichte, oder?
gə'ʃɪçtə 'o:dɐ
story right

While I do these things, I explain my theory of evolution to him. You remember that monologue from the beginning of this story, don't you?

Ich hacke seine Finger ab und stecke sie in eine Plastiktüte. Es
ɪç 'hakə 'zaɪnə 'fɪŋɐ ap ʊnt 'ʃtɛkə zi: ɪn 'aɪnə 'plastɪk‚ty:tə ɛs
I I chop off→ his fingers ← and I put them in a plastic bag it

ist viel einfacher, Fingerabdrücke von den abgehackten Fingern
ɪst fi:l 'aɪnfaxɐ 'fɪŋɐ‚apdʁʏkə fɔn de:n 'apgə‚haktn 'fɪŋɐn
it is much easier fingerprints from the chopped-off fingers

zu machen und DNA daraus zu gewinnen, als die ganze Leiche
tsu: 'maxn ʊnt de:ɛn'a: da'ʁaʊs tsu: gə'vɪnən als di: 'gantsə 'laɪçə
to to make and DNA from them to to obtain than the whole body

zu transportieren.
tsu: tʁanspɔʁ'ti:ʁən
to to transport

I chop off his fingers and put them in a plastic bag. We can get prints and DNA from the fingers, and they are a lot easier to carry than the whole body.

215

Story 13

I walk down the stairs and knock on the closed door at the bottom. Anja unlocks a chain and opens the door. She chains the door shut again and we head to her car. With any luck, the body won't be discovered for a few weeks. After all, this is Neukölln.

Ich	gehe	die	Treppen	hinunter	und	klopfe	unten	an	die
ɪç	ˈgeːhə	diː	ˈtʁɛpən	hɪˈnʊntɐ	ʊnt	ˈklɔpfə	ˈʊntən	an	diː
I	I walk down→	the	stairs	←	and	I knock	downstairs	on	the

verschlossene	Tür.	Anja	öffnet	eine	Kette	und	macht	die	Tür
fɛɐˈʃlɔsənə	tyːɐ	ˈanja	ˈœfnət	ˈaɪnə	ˈkɛtə	ʊnt	maxt	diː	tyːɐ
closed	door	Anja	she unlocks	the	chain	and	she opens→	the	door

auf.	Sie	versperrt	die	Tür	wieder	mit	der	Kette	und	wir	gehen	zu
aʊf	ziː	fɛɐˈʃpɛʁt	diː	tyːɐ	ˈviːdɐ	mɪt	deːɐ	ˈkɛtə	ʊnt	viːɐ	ˈgeːən	tsuː
←	she	she locks up	the	door	again	with	the	chain	and	we	we go	to

ihrem	Auto.	Mit	etwas	Glück	wird	die	Leiche	ein paar	Wochen
ˈiːʁəm	ˈaʊto	mɪt	ˈɛtvas	glʏk	vɪʁt	diː	ˈlaɪçə	aɪn paːɐ	ˈvɔxən
her	car	with	any	luck	it will	the	corpse	a few	weeks

lang	nicht	entdeckt	werden.	Schließlich	sind	wir	hier	in	Neukölln.
laŋ	nɪçt	ɛntˈdɛkt	ˈveːɐdn	ˈʃliːslɪç	zɪnt	viːɐ	hiːɐ	ɪn	nɔɪˈkœln
long	not	to be discovered		after all	we are	we	here	in	Neukölln

---
8

Anja drives us away from the train station. She's wearing a business suit. Her ponytail has been replaced with a more mature looking hairstyle.

Anja	fährt	uns	vom	Bahnhof	weg.	Sie	trägt	einen
ˈanja	feːɐt	ʊns	fɔm	ˈbaːnhoːf	vɛk	ziː	tʁɛkt	ˈaɪnən
Anja	she drives away→	us	from the	train station	←	she	she wears	a

Businessanzug.	Ihr	Pferdeschwanz	ist	durch	eine	etwas	reifer
ˈbɪznɪsˌanˌtsuːk	iːɐ	ˈpfeːɐdəʃvants	ɪst	dʊʁç	ˈaɪnə	ˈɛtvas	ˈʁaɪfɐ
business suit	her	ponytail	→	by	a	somewhat	more mature

wirkende	Frisur	ersetzt worden.
ˈvɪʁkndə	fʁiˈzuːɐ	ɛɐˈzɛtst ˈvɔʁdən
looking	hairstyle	← it was replaced

"Why are you wearing that suit?" I ask her.

»Wieso	trägst	du	diesen	Anzug«,	frage	ich	sie.
viˈzoː	tʁɛːkst	duː	ˈdiːzən	ˈanˌtsuːk	ˈfʁaːgə	ɪç	ziː
why	you wear	you	that	suit	I ask	I	her

"I'm blending in with the commuters," she answers.

»Ich	gleiche	mich	den	Pendlern	an«,	sagt	sie.
ɪç	ˈglaɪçə	mɪç	deːn	ˈpɛndlɐn	an	zakt	ziː
I	I blend in with→		the	commuters	←	she says	she

"Drop me off at the insurance office. I've got an appointment at four thirty. You can take the fingers back to headquarters. Take the gun, too. Tell Lucia to get rid of it."

»Lass	mich	beim	Versicherungsbüro	raus.	Ich	habe	um	halb	fünf
las	mɪç	baɪm	fɛɐˈzɪçəʁʊŋsbyˌʁoː	ʁaʊs	ɪç	ˈhaːbə	ʊm	halp	fʏnf
let me out→		at the	insurance office	←	I	I have	at	4:30	

einen	Termin.	Du	kannst	die	Finger	zum	Hauptquartier
ˈaɪnən	tɛɐˈmiːn	duː	kanst	diː	ˈfɪŋɐ	tsʊm	ˈhaʊptkvaɐˌtiːɐ
an	appointment	you	you can	the	fingers	to the	headquarters

mitnehmen.	Nimm	auch	die	Pistole.	Sag	Lucia,	sie	soll	sie
ˈmɪtˌneːmən	nɪm	aʊx	diː	pɪsˈtoːlə	zaːk	luˈtsia	ziː	zɔl	ziː
to take with	take	also	the	gun	tell	Lucia	she	she should	it

beseitigen.«
bəˈzaɪtɪgən
to get rid of

»Hast du bei dem Kerl im Treppenhaus eine Bewusstseinsbeeinflussung durchgeführt?«

"Did you mind fog the guy in the stairwell?"

»Ich tat es, als wir am Bahnsteig waren. Was glaubst du, wieso er mir freiwillig folgte?«

"I did it while we were on the platform. Why do you think he was willing to follow me?"

»Und das machte es leichter für dich, ihn zu erschießen.«

"And that made it easy for you to shoot him."

»Sicher. Ich gab ihm den Denkanstoß, auf den Rucksack zu schauen. Er hat mich nicht einmal bemerkt, als ich nach der Pistole griff. Aber ich hätte es wahrscheinlich auch machen können, ohne sein Bewusstsein zu trüben.«

"Sure. I gave him a mental push to look at the backpack. He didn't even notice me grab the gun. But I probably could have done it without fogging him."

»Ich weiß, wie schnell du bist«, sagt sie.

"I know how fast you are," she says.

»Ich bin mit dem Alter nicht langsamer geworden«, erinnere ich sie.

"I haven't slowed down with age," I remind her.

»Da hat aber jemand schlechte Laune.«

"Somebody is in a bad mood."

»Ich hasse es einfach, Leute zu erschießen.«

"I just hate shooting people."

Story 13

"But you still do it."

»Aber du machst es trotzdem.«
ˈaːbɐ duː makst ɛs ˈtʁɔtsdeːm
but you you do it anyway

"I'm the field agent, remember? Somebody has to do the dirty work."

»Vergiss nicht, ich bin doch der Agent im Außeneinsatz. Jemand muss die Drecksarbeit machen.«
fɛɐ̯ˈɡɪs nɪçt ɪç bɪn dɔx deːɐ̯ aˈɡɛnt ɪm ˈaʊsnˌaɪnzats ˈjeːmant mʊs diː ˈdʁɛksaɐ̯ˌbaɪt ˈmaxn̩
forget not I I am ! the agent in the field somebody he has to the dirty work to do

"Tell me again why everyone thinks you're a real insurance agent," she says.

»Sag mir nochmal warum alle glauben, dass du ein Versicherungsagent wärst«, sagt sie.
zaːk miːɐ̯ ˈnɔxmaːl vaˈʁʊm ˈalə ˈɡlaʊbən das duː aɪn fɛɐ̯ˈzɪçəʁʊŋsaˌɡɛnt vɛːɐ̯st zaːkt ziː
tell me again why everyone they believe that you an insurance agent you are she says she

"My special ability can manifest in a few different ways. I can fog a person's mind so that they don't know what is happening. I can change their memories of recent events. I can persuade them to do simple things like look at a backpack or drop a gun. And I can make them believe I am someone else."

»Meine besondere Fähigkeit offenbart sich auf verschiedene Weise. Ich kann die Psyche einer Person so beeinflussen, dass sie nicht weiß, was vor sich geht. Ich kann ihr Kurzzeitgedächtnis ändern. Ich kann sie zu einfachen Handlungen veranlassen, wie zum Beispiel auf einen Rucksack zu schauen oder eine Pistole fallen zu lassen. Und ich kann sie in den Glauben versetzen, das ich jemand anders wäre.«
ˈmaɪnə bəˈzɔndəʁə ˈfɛːɪçkaɪt ɔfnˈbaːɐ̯t zɪç aʊf fɛɐ̯ˈʃiːdənə ˈvaɪzə ɪç kan diː ˈpsyːçə ˈaɪnɐ pɛɐ̯ˈzoːn zoː bəˈaɪnˌflʊsn̩ das ziː nɪçt vaɪs vas foːɐ̯ zɪç ɡeːt ɪç kan iːɐ̯ ˈkʊɐ̯tststsaɪtɡəˌdɛçtnɪs ˈɛndɐn ɪç kan ziː tsuː ˈaɪnfaçən ˈhandlʊŋən fɛɐ̯ˈanlasn̩ viː tsʊm ˈbaɪʃpiːl aʊf ˈaɪnən ˈʁʊkˌzak tsuː ˈʃaʊən ˈoːdɐ ˈaɪnə pɪsˈtoːlə ˈfalən tsuː ˈlasn̩ ʊnt ɪç kan ziː ɪn deːn ˈɡlaʊbən fɛɐ̯ˈzɛtsn̩ das ɪç ˈjeːmant ˈandɐs ˈvɛːʁə
my special ability it shows itself in different ways I I can the mind of a person in such a way to manipulate that she (the person) not (person) knows what it happens I I can their short-term memory to change I I can them to simple actions to induce like for example at a backpack to to look or a gun to drop and I I can them in the belief to transfer that I someone else I am

"Can you hypnotize a whole room?" she asks.

»Kannst du einen ganzen Raum voller Menschen hypnotisieren?«, fragt sie.
kanst duː ˈaɪnən ˈɡantsən ʁaʊm ˈfɔlɐ ˈmɛnʃən hʏpnotiˈziːʁən fʁaːkt ziː
can you you an entire room full of people to hypnotize she asks she

"It's not hypnosis. I don't even know how to describe my talent, but it only works on individuals and small

»Es ist keine Hypnose. Ich weiß nicht einmal, wie ich meine
ɛs ɪst ˈkaɪnə hʏpˈnoːzə ɪç vaɪs nɪçt ˈaɪnmaːl viː ɪç ˈmaɪnə
it it is not a hypnosis I I know not even how I my

Fähigkeit beschreiben soll, aber sie funktioniert nur bei einzelnen Personen und bei kleinen Gruppen.« — "groups."

»Wo ist die Person, als die du dich ausgibst?«, fragt Anja. — "Where is the person you've been impersonating?" Anja asks.

»Ich habe ihn und seine Tochter für ein paar Wochen auf eine nette Reise nach Spanien geschickt. Sie sind gerne gegangen, nachdem ich ihm erklärt hatte, dass unser Top-Analytiker meinte, er wäre das nächste Anschlagsziel.« — "I sent him and his daughter on a nice trip to Spain for a few weeks. They were happy to go when I explained to him that our top analyst thought he would be the next target."

»Wer ist dein Top-Analytiker?« — "Who is your top analyst?"

»Roland.« — "Roland."

»Nicht ich?« — "Not me?"

»Du bist die ranghöchste Analytikerin.« — "You are the top senior analyst."

»Gut«, sagt sie. — "Good," she says.

Ein Augenblick der Stille stellt sich ein, als ich das schöne Stadtzentrum Neuköllns bewundere. — There is a minute of quiet as I admire beautiful downtown Neukölln.

Story 13

"I hope you are not actually selling insurance policies," Anja says.

»Ich hoffe, dass du nicht wirklich Versicherungen verkaufst«, sagt Anja.

"I haven't sold one yet. People don't believe me when I explain the benefits of life insurance. Apparently I don't have an honest face."

»Ich habe noch nicht eine verkauft. Die Leute glauben mir nicht, wenn ich ihnen die Vorteile einer Lebensversicherung erkläre. Anscheinend habe ich kein ehrliches Gesicht.«

There is another minute of silence as we merge onto the highway.

Wir schweigen noch eine Minute, als wir auf die Autobahn auffahren.

"You are asking a lot of questions today," I tell Anja.

»Du stellst heute eine Menge Fragen«, sage ich zu Anja.

"I'm practicing my conversation skills."

»Ich übe meine Kommunikationsfähigkeiten.«

"Are you planning to become a lawyer?"

»Denkst du daran, Rechtsanwältin zu werden?«

"No, I'm just trying to be a better member of the team."

»Nein, ich versuche nur, ein besseres Mitglied unserer Einheit zu sein.«

"Did Lucia say anything to you?"

»Hat Lucia irgendetwas zu dir gesagt?«

"She mentioned that I need to work on my people skills."

»Sie erwähnte, dass ich an meiner Sozialkompetenz arbeiten

müsse.«
ˈmʏsə
I need to

»Weil du den Bildschirm auf Roland geworfen hast?«
vaɪl duː deːn ˈbɪltʃɪʁm aʊf ˈʁoːlant ɡəˈvɔʁfən hast
because you the monitor at Roland you threw

"Because you threw that monitor at Roland?"

»Er kann manchmal so nerven.«
eːɐ kan ˈmançmaːl zoː ˈnɛʁfn̩
he he can sometimes really to get on one's nerves

"He is so annoying sometimes."

Ich muss kichern.
ɪç mʊs ˈkɪçɐn
I I have to to chuckle

I chuckle.

»Was glaubst du, für wen der Tote gearbeitet hat?«, fragt sie.
vas ɡlaʊbst duː fyːɐ veːn deːɐ ˈtoːtə ɡəˈaʁbaɪtət hat fʁaːkt ziː
what you think you for whom the dead person he worked she asks she

"Who do you think the dead guy worked for?" she asks.

»Roland ist ziemlich sicher, dass es ein hohes Tier von der Landespolizei ist.«
ˈʁoːlant ɪst ˈtsiːmlɪç ˈzɪçɐ das ɛs aɪn ˈhoːəs tiːɐ fɔn deːɐ ˈlandəspoliˌtsaɪ ɪst
Roland she is pretty sure that it a bigwig from the state police it is

"Roland is pretty sure it's someone high up in the State Police department."

»Und du glaubst ihm?«
ʊnt duː ɡlaʊbst iːm
and you you believe him

"And you believe him?"

»Er lag niemals daneben mit all seinen anderen Prognosen. Einer der Typen, mit denen ich Poker spiele, wird mir ein paar Namen senden, die ich mir ansehen werde.«
eːɐ laːk ˈniːmaːls daˈneːbən mɪt al ˈzaɪnən ˈandəʁən pʁoɡˈnoːzən ˈaɪnɐ deːɐ ˈtyːpən mɪt ˈdeːnən ɪç ˈpoːkɐ ˈʃpiːlə vɪʁt miːɐ aɪn paːɐ ˈnaːmən ˈzɛndən diː ɪç miːɐ ˈanzeːən ˈveːɐdə
he he was never wrong with all his other predictions one of the guys with whom I poker I play he will to me a few names to send that I I will look at

"He's never been wrong with any of his other predictions. One of the guys I play poker with is going to send me a few names to look into."

»Wieso lassen dich diese Gangster beim Poker mitspielen?«
viˈzoː ˈlasən dɪç ˈdiːzə ˈɡaŋstɐ baɪm ˈpoːkɐ ˈmɪtʃpiːlən
why they let you those gangsters at the poker to play with

"Why do those gangsters let you play poker with them?"

»Ich habe einmal eine Menge Arbeit als Freiberufler gemacht. Manchmal erledigte ich Jobs für Kriminelle. Die kennen meinen
ɪç ˈhaːbə ˈaɪnmaːl ˈaɪnə ˈmɛŋə ˈaʁbaɪt als ˈfʁaɪbəˌʁuːflɐ ɡəˈmaxt ˈmançmaːl ɛɐˈleːdɪçtə ɪç dʒɔps fyːɐ kʁiːmiːˈnɛlə diː ˈkɛnən ˈmaɪnən
I → once a great deal of work as freelancer ←I did sometimes I handled I jobs for criminals they they know my

"I used to do a lot of freelance work. Sometimes I did jobs for criminals. They know my reputation."

221

Story 13

"Since you can mind fog people, how come you don't win big piles of money every time you play poker?"

»Da du doch die Psyche von Leuten beeinflussen kannst, wieso gewinnst du dann nicht jedes Mal einen Haufen Geld, wenn du Poker spielst?«

da: du: dɔx di: 'psy:çə fɔn 'lɔɪtən bə'aɪnˌflʊsn̩ kanst vi'zo: gə'vɪnst du: dan nɪçt 'je:dəs ma:l 'aɪnən 'haʊfən gɛlt vɛn du: 'po:kɐ ʃpi:lst

since you ! the mind of people to influence you can why you win you then not every time piles of money when you poker you play

"I don't want to."

»Weil ich nicht will.«
vaɪl ɪç nɪçt vɪl
because I not I want

"Why not?"

»Wieso nicht?«
vi'zo: nɪçt
why not

"I play poker with those guys to collect information, not to win money. That's why I play in different locations with different groups of people. I usually try to win a little bit or lose a little bit. The thing I don't want to do is call a lot of attention to myself by winning all the time."

»Ich spiele mit diesen Typen, um Informationen zu sammeln, nicht, um Geld zu gewinnen. Deshalb spiele ich an verschiedenen Orten mit verschiedenen Gruppen. Ich versuche normalerweise, ein bisschen zu gewinnen und ein bisschen zu verlieren. Was ich auf keinen Fall will, ist, die ganze Aufmerksamkeit auf mich zu ziehen, indem ich dauernd gewinne.«

ɪç 'ʃpi:lə mɪt 'di:zən 'ty:pən ʊm ɪnfɔʁma'tsjo:nən tsu: 'zamln nɪçt ʊm gɛlt tsu: gə'vɪnən 'dɛs'halp 'ʃpi:lə ɪç an fɛɐ'ʃi:dənən 'ɔʁtn̩ mɪt fɛɐ'ʃi:dənən 'gʁʊpən ɪç fɛɐ'zu:xə nɔʁ'ma:lɐvaɪzə aɪn 'bɪsçən tsu: gə'vɪnən ʊnt aɪn 'bɪsçən tsu: fɛɐ'li:ʁən vas ɪç aʊf 'kaɪnən fal vɪl ɪst di: 'gantsə 'aʊfˌmɛʁkza:mkaɪt aʊf mɪç tsu: 'tsi:ən ɪn'dɛm ɪç 'daʊɐnt gə'vɪnə

I I play with those guys in order to information to to gather not in order to money to to win this I play I in different places with different groups I I try usually a little to to win and a little to to lose what I in no case I want it is the entire attention on me to to draw by I constantly I win

"You won a lot of money yesterday night."

»Gestern Abend hast du eine Menge Geld gewonnen.«
'gɛstɐn 'a:bənt hast du: 'aɪnə 'mɛŋə gɛlt gə'vɔnən
last night → you a lot of money ←you won

"I got carried away. I was trying to impress this girl who was there."

»Ich habe mich hinreißen lassen. Ich versuchte, auf das Mädchen, das dort war, Eindruck zu machen.«
ɪç 'ha:bə mɪç 'hɪnˌʁaɪsn̩ 'lasən ɪç fɛɐ'zu:xtə aʊf das 'mɛ:tçən das dɔʁt va:ɐ 'aɪndʁʊk tsu: maxən
I I got carried away I I tried on the girl that there she was impression to to make

Ruf.«
ʁu:f
reputation

Evolution

»Auf Linα?«
aʊf 'liːna
on Lina

"Lina?"

»Auf jemand anderen. Die war vielleicht heiß.«
aʊf 'jeːmant 'andəʁən diː vaːʁ fiˈlaɪçt haɪs
on someone else that one she was ! hot

"Someone else. She was hot."

»So genau wollte ich das gar nicht wissen!«, schreit mich
zoː gəˈnaʊ ˈvɔltə ɪç das gaʁ nɪçt ˈvɪsən ʃʁaɪt mɪç
so precisely I wanted I that not at all to know she shouted at→ me

Anja an.
ˈanja an
Anja ←

"Too much information!" Anja yells at me.

Es wird wieder ruhig im Auto. Anja übt ihre Fertigkeiten
ɛs vɪʁt ˈviːdɐ ˈʁuːɪç ɪm ˈaʊto ˈanja yːpt ˈiːʁə ˈfɛʁtɪçkaɪtən
it it becomes again quiet in the car Anja she practices her skills

im dichten Auffahren und Fahrspurwechseln. Einige Autos
ɪm ˈdɪçtən ˈaʊfˌfaːʁən ʊnt ˈfaːʁʃpuːʁˌvɛksəln ˈaɪnɪɡə ˈaʊtos
in the tailgating and lane changing a few cars

hupen uns an.
ˈhuːpən ʊns an
they honk at→ us ←

The car becomes quiet again. Anja practices her tailgating and lane changing skills. A few drivers honk at us.

»Winke ihnen doch mit der Pistole zu«, sagt sie zu mir.
ˈvɪŋkə ˈiːnən dɔx mɪt deːʁ pɪsˈtoːlə tsuː zakt ziː tsuː miːʁ
wave→ to them ! with the gun ← she says she to me

"Wave your gun at them," she tells me.

»Das ist Neukölln. Die haben vermutlich größere Waffen.«
das ɪst nɔʏˈkœln diː ˈhaːbn fɛʁˈmuːtlɪç ˈɡʁøːsəʁə ˈvafən
this it is Neukölln they they have probably bigger guns

"This is Neukölln. They probably have bigger guns."

»Hast du dem Toten deine Evolutionstheorie erzählt?«, fragt
hast duː deːm ˈtoːtən ˈdaɪnə evolutsˈjoːnsteoˌʁiː ɛʁˈtsɛːlt fʁaːkt
→ you the dead person your theory of evolution ←you told she asks

sie.
ziː
she

"Did you tell the corpse your theory about evolution?" she asks.

»Ich erklärte ihm meine Theorie, als ich seine Kleider
ɪç ɛʁˈklɛːʁtə iːm ˈmaɪnə teoˈʁiː als ɪç ˈzaɪnə ˈklaɪdɐ
I I explained to him my theory while I his clothes

durchsuchte.«
dʊʁçˈzuːxtə
I searched through

"I explained my theory to him while I was searching his clothing."

»Glaubst du nicht, dass es etwas komisch ist, Toten etwas
ɡlaʊpst duː nɪçt das ɛs ˈɛtvas ˈkoːmɪʃ ɪst ˈtoːtən ˈɛtvas
you think you not that it somewhat strange it is dead person something

"Don't you think it's a little strange to talk to dead people?" she asks.

223

Story 13

                                    zu erzählen?«, fragt   sie.
                                    tsuː ɛɐ̯ˈtsɛːlən   fʁaːkt ziː
                                    to   to tell   she asks she

"Everyone who visits a cemetery talks   »Jeder, der   einen   Friedhof   besucht,   spricht   zu   den   Toten«,   sage
to dead people," I say.   ˈjeːdɐ   deːɐ̯   ˈaɪnən   ˈfʁiːtˌhoːf bəˈzuːxt   ʃpʁɪçt   tsuː deːn   ˈtoːtən   ˈzaːɡə
                                          everyone who   a   cemetery   he visits he talks to   the   dead people I say

                                    ich.
                                    ɪç
                                    I

"That's different. They aren't explain-   »Das   ist   etwas   anderes.   Die   erklären   nicht   ihre   Weltanschauung.
ing their view of the universe. Any-   das   ɪst   ˈɛtvas   ˈandəʁəs   diː   ɛɐ̯ˈklɛːʁən nɪçt   ˈiːʁə   ˈvɛltanʃaʊʊŋ
way, we didn't get our special powers   that   it is something different they   they explain not   their   world-view
from evolution."
                                    Wie   auch   immer,   wir   haben   unsere   besonderen   Kräfte   nicht   durch
                                    viː   aʊx   ˈɪmɐ   viːɐ̯ ˈhaːbn̩ ˈʊnzəʁə bəˈzɔndəʁən   ˈkʁɛftə nɪçt   dʊʁç
                                    anyway   we   →   our   special   powers   not   through

                                    die   Evolution   erhalten.«
                                    diː   eːvoluˈtsjoːn   ɛɐ̯ˈhaltn̩
                                    the   evolution   ←we got

"Then how did we get these strange   »Wie   haben   wir   diese   sonderbaren   Gaben   dann   erhalten?«
talents?"   viː   ˈhaːbn̩ viːɐ̯ ˈdiːzə   ˈzɔndɐˌbaːʁən ˈɡaːbən   dan   ɛɐ̯ˈhaltn̩
                                      how   →   we   these   strange   talents   then   ←we got

"Aliens from outer space added their »Außerirdische   aus   dem   Weltall   haben   ihre   DNA   bereits
DNA to human chromosomes back in   ˈaʊsɐˌɪʁdɪʃə   aʊs deːm ˈvɛltˌal   ˈhaːbn̩   ˈiːʁə   deːˈɛnˈaː   bəˈʁaɪts
the stone age. Every few generations   aliens   from outer space   →   their   DNA   already
after that, something unusual pops
out - like us."   in   der   Steinzeit   den   menschlichen   Chromosomen
                                    ɪn   deːɐ̯   ˈʃtaɪntsaɪt   deːn   ˈmɛnʃlɪçən   kʁomoˈzoːmən
                                    in   the   stone age   the   human   chromosomes

                                    hinzugefügt.   In   der   Folge   kommt   alle   paar   Generationen   dabei
                                    hɪnˈtsuːɡəˌfyːkt   ɪn   deːɐ̯   ˈfɔlɡə   kɔmt   ˈalə   paːɐ̯   ɡenəʁaˈtsjoːnən daˈbaɪ
                                    ←they added in   subsequently   it comes out→   every few   generations   with it

                                    etwas   Ungewöhnliches   heraus   -   wie   wir.«
                                    ˈɛtvas   ˈʊnɡəˌvøːnlɪçəs   hɛˈʁaʊs   viː   viːɐ̯
                                    something unusual   ←   like   us

"That's silly," I say.   »Das   ist   albern«,   sage   ich.
                                     das   ɪst   ˈalbɐn   ˈzaːɡə   ɪç
                                     that   it is   silly   I say   I

"Not as silly as you believing in a god   »Nicht   so   albern   wie   dein   Glaube   an   einen   Gott,   der   nicht
who doesn't exist."   nɪçt   zoː ˈalbɐn   viː   daɪn ˈɡlaʊbə   an   ˈaɪnən   ɡɔt   deːɐ̯   nɪçt
                                            not   so   silly   like   your   belief   in   a   god   that   not

                                    existiert.«
                                    ɛksɪsˈtiːɐ̯t
                                    it exists

»Ich	kann	es	kaum	glauben,	ich	arbeite	mit	einer	Atheistin«,
ıç	kan	ɛs	kaʊm	ˈglaʊbən	ɪç	ˈaʁbaɪtə	mɪt	ˈaɪnɐ	ateˈɪstn
I	I can	it	hardly	to believe	I	I work	with	an	atheist

"I can't believe I work with an atheist," I exclaim. "The rest of The Squad will hear about this."

rufe	ich	aus.	»Der	Rest	des	Kommandos	wird	davon	hören.«
ˈʁuːfə	ɪç	aʊs	deːɐ	ʁɛst	dɛs	kɔˈmandos	vɪʁt	daˈfɔn	ˈhøːʁən
I exclaim→	I	←	the	rest	of the	squad	it will	about that	to hear

»Niemand	hat	gesagt,	dass	wir	unser	Team	›Das	Kommando‹
ˈniːmant	hat	gəˈzaːkt	das	viːɐ	ˈʊnzɐ	tiːm	das	kɔˈmando
nobody		he said	that	we	our	team	the	squad

"Nobody agreed to call our team 'The Squad'," she says.

nennen«,	sagt	sie.
ˈnɛnən	zakt	ziː
to name	she says	she

»Aber	es	hatte	auch	niemand	etwas	dagegen.«
ˈaːbɐ	ɛs	ˈhatə	aʊx	ˈniːmant	ˈɛtvas	daˈgeːgən
but	it	he had	also	nobody	anything	against it

"Nobody disagreed either."

»Wir	wollten	dich	nicht	kränken.	Es	ist	ein	bescheuerter	Name.«
viːɐ	ˈvɔltən	dɪç	nɪçt	ˈkʁɛŋkən	ɛs	ɪst	aɪn	bəˈʃɔɪɐtɐ	ˈnaːmə
we	we wanted	you	not	to hurt feelings	it	it is	a	stupid	name

"We didn't want to hurt your feelings. It's a stupid name."

»Mir	gefällt	er.	Vielleicht	können	wir	Jacken	bestellen,	wo	am
miːɐ	gəˈfɛlt	eːɐ	fiˈlaɪçt	ˈkœnən	viːɐ	ˈjakən	bəˈʃtɛlən	voː	am
I like		it	maybe	we can	we	jackets	to order	where	on the

"I like it. Maybe we can order jackets with 'The Squad' written on the back."

Rücken	›Das	Kommando‹	draufsteht.«
ˈʁʏkən	das	kɔˈmando	ˈdʁaʊfʃteːt
back	the	squad	it is on

»Ich	finde,	wir	sollten	über	den	Namen	abstimmen«,	sagt	sie.
ɪç	ˈfɪndə	viːɐ	ˈzɔltən	ˈyːbɐ	deːn	ˈnaːmən	ˈapʃtɪmən	zakt	ziː
I	I find	we	we should	about	the	name	to vote	she says	she

"I think we should vote on the name," she says.

»Wir	werden	sehen.«
viːɐ	ˈveːɐdn	ˈzeːən
we	we will	to see

"We'll see."

9

Am	selben	Abend	läutet	das	Telefon.	Ich	hebe	ab	und	höre	wieder
am	ˈzɛlbən	ˈaːbənt	ˈlɔʏtət	das	ˈteːleˌfoːn	ɪç	ˈheːbə	ap	ʊnt	ˈhøːʁə	ˈviːdɐ
on the	same	evening	it rings	the	phone	I	I pick up		and	I hear	again

That evening the cell phone rings. I pick up and hear another voice with a strange accent.

eine	Stimme	mit	einem	fremden	Akzent.
ˈaɪnə	ˈʃtɪmə	mɪt	ˈaɪnəm	ˈfʁɛmdən	akˈtsɛnt
a	voice	with	a	strange	accent

»Wo	ist	er?«
voː	ɪst	eːɐ
where	he is	he

"Where is he?"

Story 13

"Who is this?"

»Wer ist da?«
veːɐ ɪst daː
who it is there

"Don't act stupid. I'll ask again - where is he?"

»Stellen Sie sich nicht so bescheuert an. Ich frage nochmal - wo ist er?«
ʃtɛlən ziː zɪç nɪçt zoː bəˈʃɔɪɐt an ɪç ˈfʁaːɡə ˈnɔxmaːl voː ɪst eːɐ
act→ not so stupid ← I I ask again where he is he

"Are you talking about the guy I was supposed to meet today?" I ask.

»Reden Sie von einem Typen, den ich heute treffen sollte?«, frage ich.
ˈʁeːdn̩ ziː fɔn ˈaɪnəm ˈtyːpən deːn ɪç ˈhɔɪtə ˈtʁɛfən ˈzɔltə ˈfʁaːɡə ɪç
you talk you about a guy that I today to meet I was supposed I ask I

"Stop wasting time. Answer the question."

»Hören Sie auf mit der Zeitverschwendung. Beantworten Sie die Frage.«
ˈhøːʁən ziː aʊf mɪt deːɐ ˈtsaɪtfɐˌʃvɛndʊŋ bəˈʔantvɔʁtn̩ ziː diː ˈfʁaːɡə
stop with the waste of time answer the question

"I don't know," I say. "I spent half an hour at the train station in Neukölln, praying I wouldn't get mugged by some commuter, and your man never showed."

»Ich weiß nicht«, sage ich. »Ich war eine halbe Stunde lang am Bahnhof in Neukölln, betete, dass ich nicht von irgendeinem Pendler ausgeraubt werde, und Ihr Mann ist nie aufgetaucht.«
ɪç vaɪs nɪçt ˈzaːɡə ɪç ɪç vaːɐ ˈaɪnə ˈhalbə ˈʃtʊndə laŋ am ˈbaːnhoːf ɪn nɔɪˈkœln ˈbeːtətə das ɪç nɪçt fɔn ˈɪʁɡn̩taɪnəm ˈpɛndlɐ ˈaʊsɡəˌʁaʊpt ˈveːɐdə ʊnt iːɐ man ɪst niː ˈaʊfɡəˌtaʊxt
I I know not I say I I I was a half hour long at the train station in Neukölln I prayed that I not by some commuter I will be robbed and your man → never ←he showed up

"He was there. What happened to him?"

»Er war dort. Was ist mit ihm passiert?«
eːɐ vaːɐ dɔʁt vas ɪst mɪt iːm paˈsiːɐt
he he was there what → with him ←it happened

"I don't know?"

»Ich weiß nicht?«
ɪç vaɪs nɪçt
I I know not

This went on for a few minutes. He kept claiming that I did something, and I kept telling him that I did nothing. I was lying, but the guy on the phone didn't know that. Finally he decided I was telling the truth. After all, who would believe that someone with my sunny personality could shoot somebody in the heart and chop

So ging es einige Minuten weiter. Er behauptete dauernd, ich hätte etwas getan, und ich sagte ihm dauernd, dass ich nichts
zoː ɡɪŋ ɛs ˈaɪnɪɡə miˈnuːtn̩ ˈvaɪtɐ eːɐ bəˈhaʊptətə ˈdaʊɐnt ɪç ˈhɛtə ˈɛtvas ɡəˈtaːn ʊnt ɪç ˈzaːktə iːm ˈdaʊɐnt das ɪç nɪçts
like this it went it a few minutes further he he claimed constantly I → something ←I had done and I I told him constantly that I nothing

226

getan habe. Ich habe gelogen, aber der Typ am Telefon wusste das nicht. Schließlich entschied er, dass ich die Wahrheit sagte. Wer würde denn schließlich annehmen, dass jemand mit meinem sonnigen Gemüt jemandem ins Herz schießen und seine Finger abhacken könnte.

off his fingers?

»Ich komme auf dich zurück«, sagt er.

"I'll get back to you," he says.

»Das bekomme ich oft von Mädchen zu hören«, sage ich, als er den Anruf beendet.

"I hear that from a lot of girls," I say, as he disconnects the call.

Am nächsten Tag lese ich in der Zeitung, dass der Mann, den ich erschossen hatte, bereits gefunden wurde. Irgendein emsiger Hausmeister sägte die Kette durch, welche die Tür verschloss, und entdeckte die Leiche.

The next day, I read in the newspaper that the man I shot has already been found. Some industrious janitor sawed off the chain that kept the door closed and discovered the body.

Im Bericht wird vermutet, dass es sich um eine Hinrichtung der Mafia handele. Ich möchte am liebsten die Reporterin anrufen, um die Geschichte richtigzustellen, aber dann

The story suggests that this murder is a mafia execution. I think about calling the reporter to correct her story, but decide against it. She wouldn't believe me.

Story 13

	entscheide ich mich dagegen. Sie würde mir nicht glauben.
	ɛntˈʃaɪdə ɪç mɪç daˈgeːgən ziː ˈvʏʁdə miːɐ nɪçt ˈglaʊbən
	I decide against it she she would me not to believe

Later that day I amble over to a local restaurant for lunch.

Später schlendere ich zum Mittagessen in ein örtliches Restaurant.
ˈʃpeːtɐ ˈʃlɛndəʁə ɪç tsʊm ˈmɪtaˌkɛsn̩ ɪn aɪn ˈœʁtlɪçəs ʁɛstoˈʁɑ̃ː
later I amble I for lunch in a local restaurant

A ninety year old waitress comes over to take my order.

Eine neunzig Jahre alte Kellnerin kommt herüber, um meine
ˈaɪnə ˈnɔɪntsɪç ˈjaːʁə ˈaltə ˈkɛlnəʁɪn kɔmt hɛˈʁyːbɐ ʊm ˈmaɪnə
a ninety year old waitress she comes over in order to my

Bestellung aufzunehmen.
bəˈʃtɛlʊŋ ˈaʊftsuˌneːmən
order to take down

"What is today's special?" I ask.

»Was gibt es heute als Tagesgericht?«, frage ich.
vas giːpt ɛs ˈhɔɪtə als ˈtaːgəsɡəˌʁɪçt ˈfʁaːɡə ɪç
what is there today as dish of the day I ask I

"Onion soup and lamb sausage."

»Zwiebelsuppe und Wurst vom Lamm.«
ˈtsviːblˌzʊpə ʊnt vʊʁst fɔm lam
onion soup and sausage from lamb

"Is it good?"

»Schmeckt es gut?«
ʃmɛkt ɛs guːt
it tastes it good

"How should I know? I don't eat here."

»Woher soll ich das wissen? Ich esse hier nicht.«
voˈheːɐ zɔl ɪç das ˈvɪsən ɪç ˈɛsə hiːɐ nɪçt
from where I should I that to know I I eat here not

"Why not?"

»Wieso nicht?«
viˈzoː nɪçt
why not

"I have to watch my cholesterol."

»Ich muss auf mein Cholesterin achten.«
ɪç mʊs aʊf maɪn kolɛsteˈʁiːn ˈaxtən
I I have to → my cholesterol ← to pay attention to

"Are you still serving breakfast?"

»Servieren Sie noch Frühstück?«
zɛʁˈviːʁən ziː nɔx ˈfʁyːʃtʏk
you serve you still breakfast

"No breakfast after eleven o'clock. It says so right on the menu."

»Kein Frühstück mehr nach elf Uhr. So steht es auch auf der
kaɪn ˈfʁyːʃtʏk meːɐ naːx ɛlf uːɐ zoː ʃteːt ɛs aʊx aʊf deːɐ
no breakfast more after eleven o'clock so it stands it also on the

Speisekarte.«
ˈʃpaɪzəˌkaʁtə
menu

"I'm thinking about the tuna salad. Is it fresh?"

»Ich denke gerade an den Thunfischsalat. Ist er frisch?«
ɪç ˈdɛŋkə ɡəˈʁaːdə an deːn ˈtuːnfɪʃzaˌlaːt ɪst eːɐ fʁɪʃ
I I'm just thinking about the tuna fish salad is it it fresh

»Werden Sie heute noch etwas bestellen, oder sind Sie hier,
'veːɐdn ziː 'hɔɪtə nɔx 'ɛtvas bə'ʃtɛlən 'oːdɐ zɪnt ziː hiːɐ
will you you today still something to order or are you you here

um eine Meinungsumfrage zu machen?«
ʊm 'aɪnə 'maɪnʊŋsˌʊmfʁaːɡə tsuː 'maxən
in order to a opinion survey to to do

"Are you going to order something today, or are you here to take a survey?"

»Ich dachte, Sie würden sich über etwas Unterhaltung
ɪç 'daxtə ziː 'vʏʁdən zɪç 'yːbɐ 'ɛtvas ʊntɐ'haltʊŋ
I I thought you you would → some conversation

freuen«, sage ich zu ihr. »Schließlich ist hier nicht
'fʁɔɪən 'zaːɡə ɪç tsuː iːɐ 'ʃliːslɪç ɪst hiːɐ nɪçt
← to be pleased about I say I to her after all it is going on→ here not

gerade sehr viel los.«
ɡə'ʁaːdə zeːɐ fiːl loːs
exactly very much ←

"I thought you would enjoy some conversation," I tell her. "After all, the place isn't very busy."

»Nun, meine Füße tun mir weh«, sagt sie zu mir, »also
nuːn 'maɪnə 'fyːsə tuːn miːɐ veː zakt ziː tsuː miːɐ 'alzɔ
well my feet they hurt me she tells she to me so

beeilen Sie sich und bestellen Sie etwas.«
bə'aɪlən ziː zɪç ʊnt bə'ʃtɛlən ziː 'ɛtvas
hurry and order something

"Well, my feet hurt," she tells me, "so hurry up and order something."

»Ich nehme einen Hamburger und eine Cola.«
ɪç 'neːmə 'aɪnən 'hamˌbʊʁɡɐ ʊnt 'aɪnə 'koːla
I I take a hamburger and a Coke

"I'll take a hamburger and a Cola."

Die Kellnerin schreibt meine Bestellung auf ihren Notizblock
diː 'kɛlnəʁɪn ʃʁaɪpt 'maɪnə bə'ʃtɛlʊŋ aʊf 'iːʁən no'tiːtsˌblɔk
the waitress she writes my order in her notepad

und geht weg. Zehn Minuten später setzt sich ein hässlicher Typ
ʊnt ɡeːt vɛk tseːn mi'nuːtən 'ʃpeːtɐ zɛtst zɪç aɪn 'hɛslɪçɐ tyːp
and she walks away ten minutes later he sits an ugly guy

genau neben mich an die Theke. Das ist ungewöhnlich, da es
ɡə'naʊ 'neːbən mɪç an diː 'teːkə das ɪst ʊnɡə'vøːnlɪç daː ɛs
right next to me at the counter this it is unusual since there are→

noch jede Menge freier Hocker gibt. Die Leute in Berlin wollen
nɔx 'jeːdə 'mɛŋə 'fʁaɪɐ 'hɔkɐ ɡiːpt diː 'lɔɪtə ɪn bɛʁ'liːn 'vɔlən
still plenty free stools ← the people in Berlin they want

normalerweise nicht unmittelbar neben jemandem sitzen, wenn es
nɔʁ'maːlɐvaɪzə nɪçt 'ʊnˌmɪtlbaːɐ 'neːbən 'jeːmandəm 'zɪtsən vɛn ɛs
normally not directly next to someone to sit if it

sich vermeiden lässt.
zɪç fɛɐ'maɪdn lɛst
it can be avoided

The waitress writes my order onto her notepad and walks away. Ten minutes later an ugly guy sits next to me at the counter. This is unusual, since there are plenty of empty stools. People in Berlin don't normally want to sit right next to each other if they can avoid it.

»Nächste Woche zahlst du das Zweifache«, sagt er zu
'nɛçstə 'vɔxə tsaːlst duː das 'tsvaɪfaxə zakt eːɐ tsuː
next week you pay you twice as much he says he to

"Next week you pay double," he says to me. "I will be at your office on Tuesday. No changes in location."

Story 13

	mir.	»Ich	werde	am Dienstag	in	deinem	Büro	sein.	Keine
	miːɐ	ɪç	ˈveːɐdə	am ˈdiːnstak	ɪn	ˈdaɪnəm	byˈʁoː	zaɪn	ˈkaɪnə
	me	I	I will	on Tuesday	in	your	office	to be	no

Treffpunktänderungen.«
ˈtʁɛfˌpʊŋktˈɛndəʁʊŋən
changes in meeting place

Then he leaves. I talk into a tiny microphone on my jacket.

Dann	geht	er.	Ich	spreche	in	ein	Ansteckmikrofon	an	meiner
dan	geːt	eːɐ	ɪç	ˈʃpʁɛçə	ɪn	aɪn	ˈanʃtɛkmikʁoˈfoːn	an	ˈmaɪnɐ
then	he leaves	he	I	I talk	into	a	clip-on microphone	on	my

Jacke.
ˈjakə
jacket

"He's on his way out. Brown hair, one meter eighty-five, weighs about ninety-five kilos. He is wearing a dark jacket and jeans. Looks like he lost a fight with a train."

»Er	ist	auf	dem	Weg	nach draußen.	Braune	Haare,	einen	Meter
eːɐ	ɪst	aʊf	deːm	vɛk	naːx ˈdʁaʊsən	ˈbʁaʊnə	ˈhaːʁə	ˈaɪnən	ˈmeːtɐ
he	he is	on	the	way	outside	brown	hair	one	meter

fünfundachzig,	wiegt	ungefähr	fünfundneunzig	Kilo.	Er	trägt
ˈfʏnfʊntˌaxtsɪç	viːkt	ˈʊŋɡəfɛːɐ	ˈfʏnfʊntˌnɔɪntsɪç	ˈkiːlo	eːɐ	tʁɛːkt
eighty-five	he weighs	about	ninety-five	kilogram	he	he wears

eine	dunkle	Jacke	und	Jeans.	Sieht aus,	als	ob	er	eine	Rauferei
ˈaɪnə	ˈdʊŋklə	ˈjakə	ʊnt	dʒiːns	ziːt aʊs	als	ɔp	eːɐ	ˈaɪnə	ˈʁaʊfəʁaɪ
a	dark	jacket	and	jeans	he looks like	as	if	he	a	brawl

mit	einem	Zug	verloren hätte.«
mɪt	ˈaɪnəm	tsuːk	fɛɐˈloːʁən ˈhɛtə
with	a	train	he had lost

I have a small receiver in my ear so I can hear the person on the other end. A private investigator who has been following me since yesterday.

Ich	habe	einen	kleinen	Empfänger	in	meinem	Ohr,	damit	ich	die
ɪç	ˈhaːbə	ˈaɪnən	ˈklaɪnən	ˈɛmpfɛŋɐ	ɪn	ˈmaɪnəm	oːɐ	daˈmɪt	ɪç	diː
I	I have	a	small	receiver	in	my	ear	so that	I	the

Person	am	anderen	Ende	hören	kann.	Ein	Privatdetektiv,	der
pɛɐˈzoːn	am	ˈandəʁən	ˈɛndə	ˈhøːʁən	kan	aɪn	pʁiˈvaːtdetɛkˌtiːf	deːɐ
person	on the	other	end	to hear	I can	a	private investigator	who

mich	seit	gestern	unauffällig	begleitet.
mɪç	zaɪt	ˈɡəstɐn	ˈʊnˌaʊfɛlɪç	bəˈɡlaɪtət
me	since	yesterday	inconspicuously	he accompanies

"I've got him," the private investigator reports. "I'll call you later and tell you where he ends up."

»Ich	habe	ihn«,	berichtet	der	Privatdetektiv.	»Ich	rufe	dich	später
ɪç	ˈhaːbə	iːn	bəˈʁɪçtət	deːɐ	pʁiˈvaːtdetɛkˌtiːf	ɪç	ˈʁuːfə	dɪç	ˈʃpɛːtɐ
I	I have	him	he reports	the	private investigator	I	I call →	you	later

an	und	sage	dir,	wo	er	hingefahren ist.«
an	ʊnt	ˈzaːɡə	diːɐ	voː	eːɐ	ˈhɪnɡəˌfaːʁən ɪst
←	and	I tell	you	where	he	he went

Just then the waitress brings my hamburger. It is delicious. I leave a nice tip when I leave.

Gerade	jetzt	bringt	die	Kellnerin	meinen	Hamburger.	Er	schmeckt
ɡəˈʁaːdə	jɛtst	bʁɪŋt	diː	ˈkɛlnəʁɪn	ˈmaɪnən	ˈhamˌbœʁɡɐ	eːɐ	ʃmɛkt
just	now	she brings	the	waitress	my	hamburger	it	it tastes

köstlich.	Ich	hinterlasse	ein	ordentliches	Trinkgeld,	bevor	ich	gehe.
ˈkœstlɪç	ɪç	hɪntɐˈlasə	aɪn	ˈɔʁdəntlɪçəs	ˈtʁɪŋkˌɡɛlt	bəˈfoːɐ	ɪç	ˈɡeːə
delicious	I	I leave behind	a	decent	tip	before	I	I go

Evolution

Der	Rest	des	Tages	verläuft	ohne	besondere	Ereignisse.	Ich	lese
deːɐ̯	ʁɛst	dɛs	ˈtaːɡəs	fɛɐ̯ˈlɔyft	ˈoːnə	bəˈzɔndəʁə	ɛɐ̯ˈaiɡnɪsə	ɪç	ˈleːsə
the	rest	of the	day	it proceeds	without	special	events	I	I read

ein	paar	Handbücher	darüber,	wie	man	Zahnversicherungen	an
ain	paːɐ̯	ˈhantbyːçɐ	daˈʁyːbɐ	viː	man	ˈtsaːnfɛɐ̯ˌzɪçɐʁʊŋən	an
a	few	handbooks	about it	how	one	dental insurance	to

Leute	verkauft,	die	sie	nicht	wollen.	Ich	spiele	ein	paar	Spiele	am
ˈlɔytə	fɛɐ̯ˈkauft	diː	ziː	nɪçt	ˈvɔlən	ɪç	ˈʃpiːlə	ain	paːɐ̯	ˈʃpiːlə	am
people	one sells	who	they	not	they want	I	I play	a few		games	on the

Bürocomputer.	Dann	mache	ich	ein	Kreuzworträtsel.	Als	nächstes
byˈʁoːkɔmˌpjuːtɐ	dan	ˈmaxə	ɪç	ain	ˈkʁɔytsvɔʁtˌʁɛːtsl̩	als	ˈnɛçstəs
office computer	then	I do	I	a	crossword puzzle		next

mache	ich	ein	Nickerchen.	Schließlich	gehe	ich	online	und
ˈmaxə	ɪç	ain	ˈnɪkɛɐ̯çən	ˈʃliːslɪç	ˈɡeːə	ɪç	ˈɔnlain	ʊnt
I do	I	a	nap	finally	I go	I	online	and

lese	Klatschgeschichten	über	Hollywoods	Berühmtheiten.	Tausende
ˈleːsə	ˈklatʃɡəˌʃɪçtn̩	ˈyːbɐ	ˈhɔliwʊts	bəˈʁyːmtˌhaitən	ˈtauzndə
I read	gossip	about	Hollywood's	celebrities	thousands of

Webseiten	sind	dem	gewidmet.
vɛpˈzaitn̩	zɪnt	deːm	ɡəˈvɪtmət
websites	they are	to that	dedicated

Um	halb	sieben	ruft	meine	Privatdetektivin	zurück.
ʊm	halp	ˈziːbən	ʁuːft	ˈmainə	pʁiˈvaːtdetɛkˌtiːvɪn	tsuˈʁʏk
at	half	seven	he calls back →	my	private investigator	←

»Der	Typ	ging	zu	einem	alten	Wohnblock	in	Kreuzberg,
deːɐ̯	tyːp	ɡɪŋ	tsuː	ˈainəm	ˈaltən	ˈvoːnblɔk	ɪn	ˈkʁɔytsˌbɛʁk
the	guy	he went	to	an	old	apartment building	in	Kreuzberg

holte	seine	Wäsche	ab	und	hat	sie	in	einem	Waschsalon
ˈhoːltə	ˈzainə	ˈvɛʃə	ap	ʊnt	hat	ziː	ɪn	ˈainəm	ˈvaʃzaˌlõː
he picked up →	his	laundry	←	and	→	it	in	a	laundromat

in	der	Nähe	gewaschen.«
ɪn deːɐ̯		ˈnɛːə	ɡəˈvaʃən
nearby			← he washed

»Ist	dir	aufgefallen,	ob	auf	irgendeinem	der	Schlafanzüge,	die	er
ɪst diːɐ̯		ˈaufɡəˌfalən	ɔp	auf	ˈɪʁɡntainəm	deːɐ̯	ˈʃlaːfanˌtsyːɡə	diː	eːɐ̯
did you notice			if	on	any	of the	pajamas	that	he

gewaschen	hat,	Kaninchen	waren?«
ɡəˈvaʃən hat		kaˈniːnçən	ˈvaːʁən
he washed		bunnies	they were

»Kaninchen?«
kaˈniːnçən
bunnies

»Ja,	junge	Kaninchen.	Ich	liebe	Schlafanzüge	mit	Kaninchen.«
jaː	ˈjʊŋə	kaˈniːnçən	ɪç	ˈliːbə	ˈʃlaːfanˌtsyːɡə	mɪt	kaˈniːnçən
yes	young	rabbits	I	I love	pajamas	with	bunnies

The rest of my day is uneventful. I read a few manuals about how to sell dental insurance to people who don't want it. I play a few games on the office computer. Then I do a crossword puzzle. Next I take a nap. Finally, I go online to read gossip about Hollywood celebrities. There are thousands of websites devoted to this.

At six thirty the private investigator calls back.

"The guy went to an old apartment building in Kreuzberg, picked up his laundry, and did some wash at a nearby laundromat."

"Did you notice if any of the pajamas he washed had bunnies on them?"

"Bunnies?"

"Yeah. Baby rabbits. I love pajamas with bunnies."

Story 13

"I didn't get that close."

»So nahe bin ich nicht herangekommen.«
zo: 'na:ə bɪn ɪç nɪçt hɛˈʁaŋəˌkɔmən
so close → I not ←I approached

"You are supposed to notice these things. I plan to send a complaint letter to your supervisor."

»Solche Sachen sollten dir auffallen. Ich habe vor, deinem
ˈzɔlçə ˈzaxən ˈzɔltən diːɐ ˈaʊfˌfalən ɪç ˈhaːbə foːɐ ˈdaɪnəm
such things they are supposed to catch your eye I I plan your

Vorgesetzten einen Beschwerdebrief zu senden.«
ˈfoːɐɡəˌzɛtstn̩ ˈaɪnən bəˈʃveːɐdəˌbʁiːf tsuː ˈzɛndən
supervisor a letter of complaint to to send

"Paul, I don't have a supervisor."

»Paul, ich habe keinen Vorgesetzten.«
paʊl ɪç ˈhaːbə ˈkaɪnən ˈfoːɐɡəˌzɛtstn̩
Paul I I have not a supervisor

"I forgot. Where is the guy now?"

»Das habe ich vergessen. Wo ist dieser Typ jetzt?«
das ˈhaːbə ɪç fɛɐˈɡɛsən voː ɪst ˈdiːzɐ tyːp jɛtst
that → I ←I forgot where he is this guy now

"He is drinking at a restaurant in Friedrichshain."

»Er trinkt gerade etwas in einem Restaurant in Friedrichshain.«
eːɐ ˈtʁɪŋkt ɡəˈʁaːdə ˈɛtvas ɪn ˈaɪnəm ʁɛstoˈʁãː ɪn ˈfʁiːdʁɪçsˌhaɪn
he he drinks right now something in a restaurant in Friedrichshain

"Give me the address. I'll be there in half an hour."

»Gib mir die Adresse. Ich werde in einer halben Stunde dort
ɡiːp miːɐ diː aˈdʁɛsə ɪç ˈveːɐdə ɪn ˈaɪnɐ ˈhalbən ˈʃtʊndə dɔɐt
give me the address I I will in a half hour there

sein.«
zaɪn
to be

"Do you need directions?"

»Brauchst du eine Wegbeschreibung?«
bʁaʊxst duː ˈaɪnə ˈveːkbəˌʃʁaɪbʊŋ
you need you directions

"Of course not. I have GPS."

»Natürlich nicht, ich habe ein Navi.«
naˈtyːɐlɪç nɪçt ɪç ˈhaːbə aɪn ˈnavi
of course not I I have a GPS

When I get to the restaurant I see my man sitting at the end of the bar. I take the seat next to him. He looks at me. I smile. He doesn't recognize me. As I mentioned earlier, my special ability allows me to control what people see and hear.

Als ich zum Restaurant komme, sehe ich meinen Mann, wie er
als ɪç tsʊm ʁɛstoˈʁãː ˈkɔmə ˈzeːə ɪç ˈmaɪnən man viː eːɐ
when I to the restaurant I arrive I see I my man as he

am Ende der Bar sitzt. Ich setze mich auf den Platz neben ihm.
am ˈɛndə deːɐ baːɐ zɪtst ɪç ˈzɛtsə mɪç aʊf deːn plats ˈneːbən iːm
at the end of the bar he sits I I take a seat on the seat next to him

Er sieht mich an. Ich lächle. Er erkennt mich nicht. Wie ich
eːɐ ziːt mɪç an ɪç ˈlɛçlə eːɐ ɛɐˈkɛnt mɪç nɪçt viː ɪç
he he looks at→ me ← I smile he he recognizes me not as I

zuvor schon erwähnte, gibt mir meine besondere Fähigkeit die
tsuˈfoːɐ ʃoːn ɛɐˈvɛːntə ɡiːpt miːɐ ˈmaɪnə bəˈzɔndɐə ˈfɛːɪçkaɪt diː
earlier already I mentioned it gives me my special ability the

Kontrolle darüber, was Leute sehen und hören.

»Sind diese Navigationssysteme nicht erstaunlich?«, frage ich den Typen. — "Aren't those GPS systems amazing?" I ask the guy.

»Lassen Sie mich in Ruhe«, brummelt er. — "Leave me alone," he mutters.

»Mein Navi hat einen österreichischen Akzent. Ich tue gerne so, als ob ich mit Arnold Schwarzenegger fahren würde.« — "My GPS has an Austrian accent. I like to pretend I'm driving with Arnold Schwarzenegger."

»Wenn Sie mich nochmal anreden werde ich Ihnen eine reinhauen.« — "If you talk to me again I will punch you."

In diesem Moment richte ich meine ganze Kraft auf ihn, um sein Bewusstsein zu trüben. — At this point, I hit him with a full blast of my mental fog.

»Warum trinken Sie Ihr Glas nicht aus und dann machen wir eine kleine Fahrt«, sage ich zu ihm. — "Why don't you finish that drink and we'll take a ride," I say to him.

Er schüttet das restliche Bier hinunter und folgt mir hinaus zu meinem Auto. — He gulps the rest of his beer and follows me outside to my car.

Story 13

"Get in and relax," I tell him. "I'll drive."

»Setzen Sie sich rein und entspannen Sie sich«, sage ich zu ihm.
ˈzɛtsn̩ ziː zɪç ʁaɪn ʊnt ɛntˈʃpanən ziː zɪç ˈzaːɡə ɪç tsuː iːm
sit inside and relax I tell I to him

»Ich werde fahren.«
ɪç ˈveːɐ̯də ˈfaːʁən
I I will to drive

I handcuff the gentleman to the passenger side door and call Lucia. We agree to meet at a deserted construction site near the airport. Twenty minutes later, the guy's head is clear, but his hands and feet are tied.

Ich fessele den Herrn mit Handschellen an die Beifahrertür
ɪç ˈfɛsələ deːn hɛʁn mɪt ˈhantʃɛlən an diː ˈbaɪfaːɐ̯ɐˌtyːɐ̯
I I handcuff the gentleman with handcuffs to the door on passenger's side

und rufe Lucia an. Wir vereinbaren, uns an einer verlassenen
ʊnt ˈʁuːfə luˈtsia an viːɐ̯ fɛɐ̯ˈaɪnbaːʁən ʊns an ˈaɪnɐ fɛɐ̯ˈlasənən
and I call→ Lucia ← we we agree → on an abandoned

Baustelle in der Nähe des Flughafens zu treffen. Zwanzig
ˈbaʊˌʃtɛlə ɪn deːɐ̯ ˈnɛːə dɛs ˈfluːkˌhaːfn̩s tsuː ˈtʁɛfən ˈtsvantsɪç
construction site near the airport to ←to meet twenty

Minuten später ist der Kopf des Typen wieder klar, aber seine
mɪˈnuːtən ˈʃpɛːtɐ ɪst deːɐ̯ kɔpf dɛs ˈtyːpn̩ ˈviːdɐ klaːɐ̯ ˈaːbɐ ˈzaɪnə
minutes later it is the head of the guy again clear but his

Hände und Füße sind gefesselt.
ˈhɛndə ʊnt ˈfyːsə zɪnt ɡəˈfɛsəlt
hands and feet they are handcuffed

Lucia is speaking with him. Lucia has this interesting ability. She talks with people and they tell her whatever she wants to know. She can't explain how she does it, just like I don't know how my mental fog works. But it's a great talent.

Lucia spricht mit ihm. Lucia hat diese interessante Fähigkeit.
luˈtsia ʃpʁɪçt mɪt iːm luˈtsia hat ˈdiːzə ɪntəʁɛˈsantə ˈfɛːɪçkaɪt
Lucia she talks to him Lucia she has this interesting ability

Sie unterhält sich mit Leuten und die erzählen ihr alles, was
ziː ʊntɐˈhɛlt zɪç mɪt ˈlɔɪtən ʊnt diː ɛɐ̯ˈtsɛːlən iːɐ̯ ˈaləs vas
she she talks with people and they they tell her everything that

sie wissen will. Sie kann nicht erklären, wie sie es macht,
ziː ˈvɪsən vɪl ziː kan nɪçt ɛɐ̯ˈklɛːʁən viː ziː ɛs maxt
she to know she wants she she can not to explain how she it she does

genau wie ich nicht weiß, wie meine Bewusstseinsverwirrung
ɡəˈnaʊ viː ɪç nɪçt vaɪs viː ˈmaɪnə bəˈvʊstzaɪnsfɛɐ̯ˈvɪʁʊŋ
just like I not I know how my mental fogging

funktioniert. Aber es ist eine großartige Gabe.
fʊŋktsjoˈniːɐ̯t ˈaːbɐ ɛs ɪst ˈaɪnə ˈɡʁoːsˌaːɐ̯tɪɡə ˈɡaːbə
it works but it it is a great talent

Unfortunately, this guy doesn't know much. Lucia finds out his name, that he comes from the Ukraine and that he arrived in Germany ten months ago on an Aeroflot jet. He tells her that there are a few more Ukrainians working with him, but he doesn't know their names. He gives her three apartment addresses where his associates might be staying, but he doesn't know who is running the operation.

Unglücklicherweise weiß dieser Typ nicht viel. Lucia findet
ˌʊnɡlʏklɪçɐˈvaɪzə vaɪs ˈdiːzɐ tyːp nɪçt fiːl luˈtsia ˈfɪndət
unfortunately he knows this guy not much Lucia she finds out→

seinen Namen heraus, dass er aus der Ukraine kommt und dass
ˈzaɪnən ˈnaːmən hɛˈʁaʊs das eːɐ̯ aʊs deːɐ̯ ukʁaˈiːnə kɔmt ʊnt das
his name ← that he from the Ukraine he comes and that

er vor zehn Monaten in Deutschland mit einem Aeroflot-Flugzeug
eːɐ̯ foːɐ̯ tseːn ˈmoːnatən ɪn ˈdɔɪtʃlant mɪt ˈaɪnəm aːɛʁoˈfloːt-ˈfluːktsɔɪk
he ago ten months in Germany with an Aeroflot airplane

234

angekommen ist. Er erzählt ihr, dass da noch ein paar weitere Ukrainer mit ihm arbeiten, aber er kennt ihre Namen nicht. Er gibt ihr drei Adressen von Wohnungen, wo seine Kollegen möglicherweise sind, aber er weiß nicht, wer die Operation leitet.

»Er erhält alle seine Anweisungen über ein Handy«, sagt mir Lucia, nachdem sie ihr Verhör beendet hat.

"He gets all his instructions through a cell phone," Lucia tells me when she's completed her interrogation.

»Was sollen wir mit ihm machen?«, frage ich.

"What should we do with him?" I ask.

»Lass wieder die Bewusstseinseintrübung über ihn kommen. Mach, dass er die letzten paar Stunden vergisst.«

"Throw the mind haze at him again. Make him forget the last few hours."

Lucia gibt mir eine Pistole mit einem Schalldämpfer.

Lucia hands me a gun with a silencer.

»Das ist die Waffe, mit der du den ersten Ukrainer erschossen hast«, sagt Lucia zu mir. »Gib sie diesem Typen und setz ihn in der Nähe einer Polizeistation ab.«

"This is the gun you used to shoot the first Ukrainian," Lucia tells me. "Give it to the guy and drop him off near a police station."

»Großartige Idee. Es wäre am besten, wenn er nackt wäre,

"Great idea. It would be best if he's naked, so that the police notice him right away."

235

Story 13

damit	die	Polizei	ihn	sofort	bemerkt.«
da'mɪt	di:	poli'tsaɪ	i:n	zo:'fɔʁt	bə'mɛʁkt
so that	the	police	him	right away	it notices

"Sounds good to me," Lucia says.

»Das	hört	sich	gut	an«,	sagt	Lucia.
das	høːʁt	zɪç	guːt	an	zakt	lu'tsia
that	it sounds→		good	←	she says	Lucia

Lucia heads back to our home base. I put the man to sleep in the back of my car and write a confession for him. Then I strip off his clothes, tape the confession to his chest, and drive him to a police station in the next town.

Lucia	fährt	zu	unserer	Zentrale	zurück.	Ich lasse den Mann
lu'tsia	feːʁt	tsu:	'ʊnzəʁɐ	tsɛn'tʁaːlə	tsu'ʁʏk	ɪç 'lasə deːn man
Lucia	she drives back→	to	our	main office	←	I I let the man

auf	dem	Rücksitz	meines	Wagens	in	einen	Schlaf	versinken	und
aʊf	deːm	'ʁʏkˌzɪts	'maɪnəs	'vaːɡəns	ɪn	'aɪnən	ʃlaːf	fɛɐ'zɪŋkən	ʊnt
in	the	back seat	of my	car	in	a	sleep	to sink	and

schreibe	ein	Geständnis	für	ihn.	Dann	entferne	ich	seine	Kleidung,
'ʃʁaɪbə	aɪn	ɡə'ʃtɛntnɪs	fyːɐ	iːn	dan	ɛnt'fɛʁnə	ɪç	'zaɪnə	'klaɪdʊŋ
I write	a	confession	for	him	then	I take off	I	his	clothes

klebe	ihm	das	Geständnis	auf	die	Brust	und	fahre	ihn	zu	einer
'kleːbə	iːm	das	ɡə'ʃtɛntnɪs	aʊf	diː	bʁʊst	ʊnt	'faːʁə	iːn	tsu:	'aɪnɐ
I tape	on him	the	confession	to	the	chest	and	I drive	him	to	a

Polizeistation	im	nächsten	Ort.
poli'tsaɪʃtaˌtsjoːn	ɪm	'nɛçstən	ɔʁt
police station	in the	next	town

I stop in front of the building and tell him to get out of the car. He's groggy, but manages to hold the gun as he walks naked into the station to talk to the friendly policemen. Sometimes I just love my work!

Ich	halte	vor	dem	Gebäude	und	sage	ihm,	dass	er	aus	dem
ɪç	'haltə	foːɐ	deːm	ɡə'bɔʏdə	ʊnt	'zaːɡə	iːm	das	eːɐ	aʊs	deːm
I	I stop	in front of	the	building	and	I tell	him	that	he	out of	the

Auto	aussteigen	soll.	Er	ist	angeschlagen,	aber	schafft	es,	die
'aʊto	'aʊsˌʃtaɪɡn̩	zɔl	eːɐ	ɪst	'anɡəʃlaːɡn̩	'aːbɐ	ʃaft	ɛs	diː
car	to get out	he should	he is		groggy	but	he manages	it	the

Pistole	zu	halten,	als	er	nackt	in	die	Station	hineingeht,	um
pɪs'toːlə	tsuː	'haltən	als	eːɐ	nakt	ɪn	diː	ʃta'tsjoːn	hɪ'naɪnˌɡeːt	ʊm
gun	to	to hold	as	he	naked	in	the	station	he goes in	in order to

mit	den	freundlichen	Polizisten	zu	reden.	Manchmal	liebe	ich
mɪt	deːn	'fʁɔʏntlɪçn̩	poli'tsɪstən	tsuː	'ʁeːdən	'mançmaːl	'liːbə	ɪç
with	the	friendly	policemen	to	to talk	sometimes	I love	I

einfach	meine	Arbeit.
'aɪnfax	'maɪnə	'aʁbaɪt
just	my	work

---10---

"I thought this was all settled," I say to Roland over the phone. "I want us to call ourselves 'The Squad'."

»Ich	dachte,	das	wäre	alles	geregelt«,	sage	ich	zu	Roland	am
ɪç	'daxtə	das	'vɛːʁə	'aləs	ɡə'ʁeːɡəlt	'zaːɡə	ɪç	tsuː	'ʁoːlant	am
I	I thought	this	it was	all	settled	I say	I	to	Roland	on the

Telefon.	»Ich	will	uns	›Das	Kommando‹	nennen.«
'teːleˌfoːn	ɪç	vɪl	ʊns	das	kɔ'mando	'nɛnən
phone	I	I want	us	the	squad	to call

236

»Anja überzeugte Lucia, dass wir über einen Namen abstimmen sollten«, sagt er zu mir.

"Anja convinced Lucia that we should vote for a name," he tells me.

»Wie wäre es mit ›Männer in Schwarz‹.«

"How about 'Men in Black'?"

»Sehen Lucia, Anja und Lina aus wie Männer?«

"Do Lucia, Anja, and Lina look like men?"

»Eher nicht.«

"I guess not."

Roland entschließt sich, das Thema zu wechseln.

Roland decides to change the subject.

»Wo ist das Geld, das du beim Pokerspiel gewonnen hast?«

"Where is that money you won at the poker game?"

»Es liegt auf meinem Bürotisch. Ich hatte noch keine Zeit, es zur Bank zu bringen.«

"It's on my office desk. I haven't had time to deposit it at the bank."

»Lucia sorgt sich darüber, dass du es dazu verwenden könntest, um Ferien zu machen.«

"Lucia is worried you'll use it to go on vacation."

Lucia ist die Chefin, aber manchmal glaube ich, dass sie sich zu viel Sorgen ums Geld macht.

Lucia is the boss, but sometimes I think she worries about money too much.

»Sag ihr, sie soll sich entspannen«, sage ich.

"Tell her to relax," I say.

Story 13

"You know I've been studying accounting online," Roland says.

»Du weißt, dass ich Buchhaltung online lerne«, sagt Roland.

"I'm sure you are learning a lot."

»Ich bin sicher, du lernst sehr viel.«

"Lucia is letting me help with our corporate finances," he says.

»Lucia lässt mich bei den finanziellen Angelegenheiten der Firma mithelfen«, sagt er.

"Why do I need to know about this?" I ask him.

»Warum sollte ich davon wissen?«, frage ich ihn.

"She put me in charge of the expense reports. I need to keep track of your poker winnings."

»Sie hat mir die Verantwortung für die Kostenabrechnung übertragen. Ich muss deine Pokergewinne nachverfolgen können.«

"I have a special system," I tell him. "When I win at poker I keep the money and use it for my business related expenses. That way I don't have to file another expense report until the money runs out."

»Ich habe ein besonderes System«, sage ich zu ihm. »Wenn ich beim Poker gewinne, behalte ich das Geld und benutze es für meine geschäftlichen Ausgaben. Auf diese Art brauche ich keine weitere Kostenabrechnung auszufüllen bis das Geld alle ist.«

"That's not how you're supposed to do it," Roland says.

»So sollst du es nicht machen«, sagt Roland.

"Why not? It's simple and it saves time."

»Warum nicht? Es ist einfach und es spart Zeit.«

"But we don't see your actual expenses. All we know is that you win money in a poker game and you spend it on business related activities over the next few weeks. We don't know

»Aber wir sehen dann nicht deine tatsächlichen Ausgaben. Alles, was wir wissen, ist, dass du Geld in einem Pokerspiel gewinnst und es dann während der nächsten paar Wochen für geschäftliche Zwecke ausgibst. Wir wissen nicht, wie viel du gewinnst oder wohin das Geld tatsächlich geht.«

how much money you win or where the money actually goes."

»Glaube mir, du willst das nicht wissen.«

"Trust me, you don't want to know."

»Lucia will es aber.«

"Lucia does."

»Sag Lucia, dass ich Außenagent bin und kein Buchhalter.«

"Tell Lucia I'm a field agent, not an accountant."

»Ich sage ihr überhaupt nichts. Du redest mit ihr«, sagt Roland.

"I'm not telling her anything. You talk to her," Roland says.

»Hat Lucia die Adressen geprüft, die wir von dem Ukrainer erhalten haben?«

"Did Lucia check those addresses we got from the Ukrainian?"

»Ja, aber die Wohnungen waren leer.«

"Yeah, but the apartments were vacant."

Ich lege auf, als Roland versucht, mich daran zu erinnern, wann die nächste Kostenabrechnung fällig ist. Warum muss es so kompliziert sein, ein kleines Unternehmen wie das unsere zu

I disconnect as Roland tries to remind me when the next expense report is due. Why does running a small business like ours have to be so complicated? I call Lucia a minute later.

Story 13

	führen.	Eine	Minute	später	rufe	ich	Lucia	an.
	ˈfyːʁən	ˈaɪnə	mɪˈnuːtə	ˈʃpɛːtɐ	ˈʁuːfə	ɪç	luˈtsia	an
	to manage	one	minute	later	I call→	I	Lucia	←

"Roland is bothering me about expense reports."

»Roland	belästigt	mich	wegen	der	Kostenabrechnungen.«
ˈʁoːlant	bəˈlɛstɪçt	mɪç	ˈveːgən	deːɐ	ˈkɔstn̩ˌapʁɛçnʊŋən
Roland	he bothers	me	about	the	expense reports

"Give him what he wants."

»Gib	ihm,	was	er	haben	will.«
giːp	iːm	vas	eːɐ	ˈhaːbn̩	vɪl
give	him	what	he	to have	he wants

"I like this job," I tell her. "The work is exciting. It's safer than the freelance work I used to do. The pay isn't bad, and we get excellent health care benefits. That's always good to have, just in case a bullet penetrates my internal organs."

»Ich	mag	diese	Arbeit«,	sage	ich	zu	ihr.	»Die	Arbeit	ist
ɪç	mak	ˈdiːzə	ˈaʁbaɪt	ˈzaːgə	ɪç	tsuː	iːɐ	diː	ˈaʁbaɪt	ɪst
I	I like	this	job	I say	I	to	her	the	work	it is

aufregend.	Sie	ist	sicherer	als	die	freiberufliche	Arbeit,	die	ich
ˈaʊfˌʁeːgn̩t	ziː	ɪst	ˈzɪçəʁɐ	als	diː	ˈfʁaɪbəˌʁuːflɪçə	ˈaʁbaɪt	diː	ɪç
exciting	it	it is	safer	than	the	freelance	work	that	I

gemacht	habe.	Die	Bezahlung	ist	nicht	schlecht	und	wir	bekommen
gəˈmaxt	ˈhaːbə	diː	bəˈtsaːlʊŋ	ɪst	nɪçt	ʃlɛçt	ʊnt	viːɐ	bəˈkɔmən
I had done		the	pay	it is	not	bad	and	we	we get

ausgezeichnete	Krankenversicherungsleistungen.	Die	sind	immer
ˈaʊsgəˌtsaɪçnətə	ˈkʁaŋknfɛɐˌzɪçəʁʊŋsˌlaɪstʊŋən	diː	zɪnt	ˈɪmɐ
excellent	health insurance benefits	they	they are	always

von	Vorteil	für	den	Fall,	dass	eine	Kugel	meine	inneren	Organe
fɔn	ˈfoːɐˌtaɪl	fyːɐ	deːn	fal	das	ˈaɪnə	ˈkuːgəl	ˈmaɪnə	ˈɪnəʁən	ɔʁˈgaːnə
	beneficial	in case		that		a	bullet	my	inner	organs

durchdringt.«
ˈdʊʁçˌdʁɪŋt
it penetrates

"In addition, we work with a team of great people," she reminds me.

»Außerdem	darfst	du	mit	einem	Team	ausgezeichneter	Leute
ˈaʊsɐdeːm	daʁfst	duː	mɪt	ˈaɪnəm	tiːm	ˈaʊsgəˌtsaɪçnətɐ	ˈlɔɪtə
in addition	you may	you	with	a	team	excellent	people

zusammenarbeiten«,	erinnert	sie	mich.
tsuˈzamənˌaʁbaitn	ɛɐˈɪnɐt	ziː	mɪç
to work together	she reminds	she	me

"I was going to say that," I respond. "I was also going to say my job description does not say anything about expense reports."

»Ich	wollte	das	gerade	sagen«,	antworte	ich.	»Ich	wollte
ɪç	ˈvɔltə	das	gəˈʁaːdə	ˈzaːgən	ˈantvɔʁtə	ɪç	ɪç	ˈvɔltə
I	I wanted	that	just	to say	I respond	I	I	I wanted

auch	gerade	sagen,	dass	meine	Stellenbeschreibung	nichts	von
aʊx	gəˈʁaːdə	ˈzaːgən	das	ˈmaɪnə	ˈʃtɛlənbəˌʃʁaɪbʊŋ	nɪçts	fɔn
also	just	to say	that	my	job description	nothing	of

Kostenabrechnungen	erwähnt.«
ˈkɔstn̩ˌapʁɛçnʊŋən	ɛɐˈvɛːnt
expense reports	it mentions

"We don't have a job description for what you do," Lucia reminds me.

»Wir	haben	keine	Stellenbeschreibung	für	das,	was	du	machst«,
viːɐ	ˈhaːbn̩	ˈkaɪnə	ˈʃtɛlənbəˌʃʁaɪbʊŋ	fyːɐ	das	vas	duː	makst
we	we have	not a	job description	for	that	what	you	you do

erinnert mich Lucia.
ɛɐ'ɪnɐt mɪç lu'tsia
she reminds me Lucia

»Wenn du eine schreibst, dann stelle sicher, dass ich keine
vɛn du: 'aɪnə ʃʁaɪpst dan 'ʃtɛlə 'zɪçɐ das ɪç 'kaɪnə
when you one you write then make sure that I not any

"When you write one, make sure it says that I don't have to submit expense reports."

Kostenabrechnungen abgeben muss.«
'kɔstn̩ˌapʁɛçnʊŋən 'apˌge:bn̩ mʊs
expense reports to submit I have to

Ich höre sie seufzen.
ɪç 'hø:ʁə zi: 'zɔɪftsn̩
I I hear she to sigh

I hear her sigh.

»Können wir später darüber sprechen?«, fragt sie mich.
'kœnən vi:ɐ 'ʃpɛ:tɐ da'ʁy:bɐ 'ʃpʁɛçən fʁa:kt zi: mɪç
can we we later about it to talk she asks she me

"Can we talk about this later?" she asks me.

»Okay, denk einfach daran, dass ich meine Meinung nicht ändern
o'ke: dɛŋk 'aɪnfax da'ʁan das ɪç 'maɪnə 'maɪnʊŋ nɪçt 'ɛndɐn
okay just remember that I my mind not to change

"OK. Just remember I am not going to change my mind."

werde.«
've:ɐdə
I will

---11---

Am nächsten Tag sitze ich im Versicherungsbüro. Nachdem ich
am 'nɛçstən ta:k 'zɪtsə ɪç ɪm fɛɐ'zɪçəʁʊŋsby,ʁo: na:x'de:m ɪç
the next day I sit I in the insurance office after I

I sit in the insurance office the next day. After ten minutes reading an article about Long Term Disability Insurance I am so sleepy I almost fall off my chair. I hit the speed dial on my cell phone to talk to Lucia.

zehn Minuten lang einen Artikel über Invaliditätsversicherungen
tsɛ:n mɪ'nu:tən laŋ 'aɪnən aʁ'ti:kəl 'y:bɐ ɪnvalidi'tɛ:tsfɛɐˌzɪçəʁʊŋən
ten minutes long an article about long-term disability insurance

gelesen habe, bin ich so müde, dass ich fast von meinem Stuhl
gə'le:zən 'ha:bə bɪn ɪç zo: 'my:də das ɪç fast fɔn 'maɪnəm ʃtʊl
I read I am I so tired that I almost from my chair

falle. Ich drücke die Kurzwahl auf meinem Handy, um mit
'falə ɪç 'dʁʏkə di: 'kʊʁtsˌva:l aʊf 'maɪnəm 'hɛndi ʊm mɪt
I fall I I press the speed dial on my cell phone in order to with

Lucia zu sprechen.
lu'tsia tsu: 'ʃpʁɛçən
Lucia to to talk

»Was ist los?«
vas ɪst lo:s
what's up

"What's up?"

»Ist unsere Privatdetektivin in der Nähe?«
ɪst 'ʊnzəʁə pʁi'va:tdetɛkˌti:vɪn ɪn de:ɐ 'nɛ:ə
she is our private investigator nearby

"Is our private investigator nearby?"

Story 13

"Yes."

»Ja.«
ja:
yes

"Remind me why I need a baby sitter."

»Sag mir nochmals, warum ich einen Babysitter brauche.«
zaːk miːɐ ˈnɔxmaːls vaˈʁʊm ɪç ˈaɪnən ˈbɛɪbiˌsɪtɐ ˈbʁaʊxə
tell me again why I a babysitter I need

"You need backup in case the bad guys send a small army after you."

»Du brauchst Rückendeckung für den Fall, dass die Bösen eine
duː bʁaʊxst ˈʁʏknˌdɛkʊŋ fyːɐ deːn fal das diː ˈbøːzən ˈaɪnə
you you need backup in case that the bad people a

kleine Armee zu dir schicken.«
ˈklaɪnə aʁˈmeː tsuː diːɐ ˈʃɪkən
small army to you they send

"Did you get my email today? Reinhold came through with a few names."

»Hast du heute meine E-Mail erhalten? Reinhold hatte mit
hast duː ˈhɔɪtə ˈmaɪnə ˈiːmeːl ɛɐˈhaltn̩ ˈʁaɪnhɔlt ˈhatə mɪt
→ you today my email ← you received Reinhold he had with

ein paar Namen Erfolg.«
aɪn paːɐ ˈnaːmən ɛɐˈfɔlk
a few names success

"Anja and Roland are researching those names right now."

»Anja und Roland überprüfen diese Namen gerade.«
ˈanja ʊnt ˈʁoːlant yːbɐˈpʁyːfən ˈdiːzə ˈnaːmən ɡəˈʁaːdə
Anja and Roland they are checking those names right now

"Why don't we grab the people Reinhold told me about, throw them in those holding cells in the office basement, and you pull the truth out of them. That's easier than Anja and Roland doing computer research."

»Warum schnappen wir uns nicht diese Leute, die mir Reinhold
vaˈʁʊm ˈʃnapən viːɐ ʊns nɪçt ˈdiːzə ˈlɔɪtə diː miːɐ ˈʁaɪnhɔlt
why we snap up not these people that to me Reinhold

genannt hat, werfen sie in einer der Arrestzellen im Bürokeller
ɡəˈnant hat ˈvɛʁfən ziː ɪn ˈaɪnə deːɐ aˈʁɛstˌtsɛlən ɪm byˈʁoːˌkɛlɐ
he named we throw them into one of the holding cells in the office basement

und du holst die Wahrheit aus ihnen heraus. Das ist
ʊnt duː hɔlst diː ˈvaːɐhaɪt aʊs ˈiːnən hɛˈʁaʊs das ɪst
and you you pump information → the truth out of them ← that it is

leichter als eine Computerrecherche durch Anja und Roland.«
ˈlaɪçtɐ als ˈaɪnə kɔmˈpjuːtɐʁeˌʃɛʁʃ dʊʁç ˈanja ʊnt ˈʁoːlant
easier than a computer research by Anja and Roland

"You want to kidnap senior officers of the police?"

»Du willst ranghohe Beamte der Polizei entführen?«
duː vɪlst ˈʁaŋˌhoːə bəˈamtə deːɐ poliˈtsaɪ ɛntˈfyːʁən
you you want high-ranking officers of the police to kidnap

"Sure. I can hit them with mind mojo so they don't remember what we look like."

»Sicher, ich kann sie mit einem Bewusstseinszauber beeinflussen,
ˈzɪçɐ ɪç kan ziː mɪt ˈaɪnəm bəˈvʊstzaɪnsˌtsaʊbɐ bəˈaɪnˌflʊsn̩
sure I I can them with a mind mojo to influence

damit sie sich nicht daran erinnern, wie wir aussehen.«
daˈmɪt ziː zɪç nɪçt daˈʁan ɛɐˈɪnɐn viː viːɐ ˈaʊsˌzeːən
so that they → not on it ← they remember what we look like

Evolution

»Ich ziehe eine unauffälligere Arbeitsweise vor«, sagt Lucia.

"I prefer to be more subtle," Lucia says.

»Brauchen die Kinder Unterstützung bei ihren Nachforschungen?«

"Do the kids need help with the research?".

»Nein, bleib dort und tu so, als ob du ein Versicherungsvertreter wärst. Rufe potentielle Kunden an.«

"No. Stay there and pretend to be an insurance agent. Make telephone calls to potential clients."

»Ich hasse diese Tätigkeit. Alle schreien mich an und legen auf.«

"I hate doing that. Everyone yells at me and hangs up."

»Du musst an deinen Verkaufsfähigkeiten arbeiten.«

"You need to work on your sales skills."

»Ich habe nicht einmal eine Zulassung, Versicherungen zu verkaufen. Was passiert, wenn jemand eine Police von mir kaufen will?«

"I don't even have an insurance license. What if someone wants to buy a policy from me?"

»Ich glaube nicht, dass du dich darum sorgen musst.«

"I don't think you'll have to worry about that."

Ich verbringe den Rest des Tages damit, auf ein Dutzend bewaffneter Männer zu warten, die durch meine Tür hereinstürmen, aber nichts passiert. Verdeckte Aufklärungsarbeit ist nicht immer spannend.

I spent the rest of the day waiting for a dozen armed men to crash through my door, but nothing happens. Undercover work is not always exciting.

Story 13

Finally, five o'clock rolls around. I need coffee, so I head for a nearby cafe. The private investigator is probably close behind. I order a latte with extra foam, pay the lady three Euro, and I sit down.

Schließlich	geht	es	auf	fünf Uhr	zu.	Ich	brauche	einen
ˈʃliːslɪç	geːt	ɛs	aʊf	fynf uːɐ	tsuː	ɪç	ˈbʁaʊxə	ˈaɪnən
finally	it approaches →	it	towards	five o'clock	←	I	I need	a

Kaffee	und	gehe	daher	zu	einem	nahegelegenen	Café.	Meine
ˈkafe	ʊnt	ˈgeːə	ˈdaːheːɐ	tsuː	ˈaɪnəm	ˈnaːəgəˌleːgnən	kaˈfeː	ˈmaɪnə
coffee	and	I go	therefore	to	a	nearby	cafe	my

Privatdetektivin	ist	wahrscheinlich	gleich	hinter	mir.	Ich	bestelle
pʁiˈvaːtdetɛkˌtiːvɪn	ɪst	vaːɐˈʃaɪnlɪç	glaɪç	ˈhɪntɐ	miːɐ	ɪç	bəˈʃtɛlə
private investigator	she is	probably	right	behind	me	I	I order

einen	Latte	mit	extra	Schaum,	zahle	der	Dame	drei	Euro	und
ˈaɪnən	ˈlatə	mɪt	ˈɛkstʁa	ʃaʊm	ˈtsaːlə	deːɐ	ˈdaːmə	dʁaɪ	ˈɔɪʁo	ʊnt
a	latte	with	extra	foam	I pay	the	lady	three	Euro	and

setze	mich	hin.
ˈzɛtsə	mɪç	hɪn
		I sit down

I reflect on the high cost of coffee in Berlin when someone holding a newspaper sits on the armchair next to mine. He leans forward and gives me a fierce look.

Ich	denke	gerade	über	die	hohen	Kosten	von	Kaffee	in	Berlin
ɪç	ˈdɛŋkə	gəˈʁaːdə	ˈyːbɐ	diː	ˈhoːən	ˈkɔstən	fɔn	ˈkafe	ɪn	bɛʁˈliːn
I	I think →	just	about	the	high	costs	of	coffee	in	Berlin

nach,	als	sich	jemand	mit	einer	Zeitung	in	der	Hand	in	den
naːx	als	zɪç	ˈjeːmant	mɪt	ˈaɪnɐ	ˈtsaɪtʊŋ	ɪn	deːɐ	hant	ɪn	deːn
←	when →		someone	with	a	newspaper	in	the	hand	in	the

Sessel	neben	mir	hinsetzt.	Er	lehnt	sich	vor	und	sieht	mich
ˈzɛsəl	ˈneːbən	miːɐ	ˈhɪnˌzɛtst	eːɐ	leːnt	zɪç	foːɐ	ʊnt	ziːt	mɪç
armchair	next to	me	← he sits down	he	he leans forward			and	he looks at →	me

mit	grimmiger	Miene	an.
mɪt	ˈgʁɪmɪgɐ	ˈmiːenə	an
with	fierce	expression	←

I let my cup tremble a little bit and spill some of the drink onto the table. Just to let him know that his scowl is working.

Ich	lasse	meine	Tasse	etwas	zittern	und	verschütte	etwas
ɪç	ˈlasə	ˈmaɪnə	ˈtasə	ˈɛtvas	ˈtsɪtɐn	ʊnt	fɛɐˈʃʏtə	ˈɛtvas
I	I let	my	cup	somewhat	to tremble	and	I spill	some

von	dem	Getränk	auf	den	Tisch.	Das	jedoch	nur,	um
fɔn	deːm	gəˈtʁɛŋk	aʊf	deːn	tɪʃ	das	jeˈdɔx	nuːɐ	ʊm
of	the	drink	on	the	table	this	though	only	in order to

ihn	wissen	zu	lassen,	dass	sein	finsterer	Blick	eine	Wirkung	hat.
iːn	ˈvɪsən	tsuː	ˈlasən	das	zaɪn	ˈfɪnstəʁɐ	blɪk	ˈaɪnə	ˈvɪʁkʊŋ	hat
	to let him know			that	his		scowl	an	impact	it has

"I told the other guy I would bring the money on Tuesday," I whisper.

»Ich	sagte	dem	anderen	Typ,	dass	ich	das	Geld	am Dienstag
ɪç	ˈzaktə	deːm	ˈandəʁən	tyːp	das	ɪç	das	gɛlt	am ˈdiːnstak
I	I told	the	other	guy	that	I	the	money	on Tuesday

bringen	würde«,	flüstere	ich.
ˈbʁɪŋən	ˈvʏʁdə	ˈflʏstəʁə	ɪç
to bring	I would	I whisper	I

The guy looks at me with a bemused expression and shows me a handgun he is hiding under his newspaper.

Der	Kerl	schaut	mich	mit	einem	verwirrten	Ausdruck	an	und
deːɐ	kɛʁl	ʃaʊt	mɪç	mɪt	ˈaɪnəm	fɛɐˈvɪʁtn	ˈaʊsdʁʊk	an	ʊnt
the	guy	he looks at →	me	with	a	bemused	expression	←	and

Evolution

zeigt mir eine Pistole, die er unter der Zeitung versteckt hält.
'tsaɪkt miːɐ 'aɪnə pɪsˈtoːlə diː eːɐ 'ʊntɐ deːɐ 'tsaɪtʊŋ fɛɐˈʃtɛkt hɛlt
he shows to me a gun that he under the newspaper hidden he holds

»Der andere Mann wurde nackt vor einer Polizeistation gefunden. Er wurde festgenommen und ich glaube, Sie hatten etwas damit zu tun.«
deːɐ 'andəʁə man 'vʊʁdə nakt foːɐ 'aɪnɐ poliˈtsaɪʃtaˌtsjoːn gəˈfʊndən eːɐ 'vʊʁdə 'fɛstgəˌnɔmən ʊnt ɪç 'glaʊbə ziː 'hatn 'ɛtvas daˈmɪt tsuː tuːn
the other man naked in front of a police station ←he was found he he was arrested and I I think you you had something with it to to do

"The other man was found naked outside of a police station. He has been arrested. I think you had something to do with that."

Ich blicke ihn nichtssagend an.
ɪç 'blɪkə iːn 'nɪçtsˌzaːgnt an
I I gaze at→ him expressionless ←

I give him a blank look.

»Ich habe ihn nicht ausgezogen, falls Sie das meinen«, sage ich zu ihm.
ɪç 'haːbə iːn nɪçt 'aʊsgəˌtsoːgn fals ziː das 'maɪnən 'zaːgə ɪç tsuː iːm
I → him not ←I undressed in case you that you mean I say I to him

"I didn't take his clothes off, if that's what you mean," I say to him.

»Lassen Sie uns irgendwo hingehen, wo wir ungestört reden können«, sagt er. »Sie werden mir alles erzählen.«
'lasn ziː ʊns 'ɪʁgəntvoː 'hɪnˌgeːən voː viːɐ 'ʊngəˌʃtøːɐt 'ʁeːdən 'kœnən zakt eːɐ ziː 'veːɐdn miːɐ 'aləs ɛɐˈtsɛːlən
let's somewhere to go where we undisturbed to talk we can he says he you you will to me everything to tell

"Let's go somewhere to talk in private," he says. "You will tell me everything."

Ich werfe ihm einen besorgten Blick zu und sage: »Bitte tun Sie mir nicht weh.«
ɪç 'vɛʁfə iːm 'aɪnən bəˈzɔʁktən blɪk tsuː ʊnt 'zaːgə 'bɪtə tuːn ziː miːɐ nɪçt veː
I I throw→ him a worried look ← and I say please hurt→ me not ←

I give him a worried look and say, "Please don't hurt me."

»Wir werden einen Spaziergang machen«, sagt er. »Lassen Sie das Getränk stehen.«
viːɐ 'veːɐdn 'aɪnən ʃpaˈtsiːɐˌgaŋ 'maxən zakt eːɐ 'lasn ziː das gəˈtʁɛnk 'ʃteːən
we we will to go for a walk he says he leave→ the drink ←

"We will take a walk," he says. "Leave the drink."

Ich schaffe es, ein oder zwei Zitterbewegungen vorzutäuschen,
ɪç 'ʃafə ɛs aɪn 'oːdɐ tsvaɪ 'tsɪtɐbəˌveːgʊŋən 'foːɐtsuˌtɔʏʃn
I I manage it one or two trembles to put on

I manage a tremble or two as we exit the coffee shop. We walk into the parking lot. Sarah, the private investigator, leans against a car reading a magazine.

Story 13

	als wir das Café verlassen. Wir gehen zum Parkplatz. Sarah, die
	als viːɐ das kaˈfeː fɛɐˈlasən viːɐ ˈgeːən tsʊm ˈpaʁkˌplats ˈzaːʁa diː
	as we the cafe to leave we we walk to the parking lot Sarah the

Privatdetektivin, lehnt an einem Auto und liest ein Magazin.
pʁiˈvaːtdetɛkˌtiːvɪn leːnt an ˈaɪnəm ˈaʊto ʊnt liːst aɪn magaˈtsiːn
private investigator she leans on a car and she reads a magazine

I hit the guy with a full brain fog just as we reach Sarah. He stops walking and puts his hands down. I take his gun and help him into the front seat of the car.

Ich überwältige den Typ mit einer vollen Bewusstseinstrübung,
ɪç yːbɐˈvɛltɪɡə deːn tyːp mɪt ˈaɪnɐ ˈfɔlən bəˈvʊstˌzaɪnsˌtʁyːbʊŋ
I I subdue the guy with a full mind fog

gerade als wir Sarah erreichen. Er bleibt stehen und senkt seine
ɡəˈʁaːdə als viːɐ ˈzaːʁa ɛɐˈʁaɪçn̩ eːɐ blaɪpt ˈʃteːən ʊnt zɛŋkt ˈzaɪnə
just as we Sarah we reach he he stops and he lowers his

Hände. Ich nehme die Pistole und helfe ihm in den Vordersitz
ˈhɛndə ɪç ˈneːmə diː pɪsˈtoːlə ʊnt ˈhɛlfə iːm ɪn deːn ˈfoːɐdɐˌzɪts
hands I I take the gun and I help him into the front seat

des Wagens.
dɛs ˈvaːɡəns
of the car

Sarah gets into the driver's side while I cuff him to the passenger door. I jump in the back and away we go.

Sarah nimmt auf dem Fahrersitz Platz, während ich ihn an der
ˈzaːʁa nɪmt aʊf deːm ˈfaːʁɐˌzɪts plats ˈvɛːʁənt ɪç iːn an deːɐ
Sarah she takes a seat→ the driver seat ← while I him to the

Beifahrertür mit Handschellen anhänge. Ich springe auf den
ˈbaɪfaːʁɐˌtyːɐ mɪt ˈhantˌʃɛlən ˈanˌhɛŋə ɪç ˈʃpʁɪŋə aʊf deːn
door on passenger's side with handcuffs I attach I I jump in the

Rücksitz und wir fahren weg.
ˈʁʏkˌzɪts ʊnt viːɐ ˈfaːʁən vɛk
back seat and we we drove off

"You look very nice in that trench coat," I say to Sarah.

»Du siehst sehr hübsch in deinem Trenchcoat aus«, sage ich
duː ziːst zeːɐ hyːpʃ ɪn ˈdaɪnəm ˈtʁɛntʃˌkoːt aʊs ˈzaːɡə ɪç
you you appear→ very nice in your trench coat ← I say I

zu Sarah.
tsuː ˈzaːʁa
to Sarah

"I'm glad you like it," she says. "How come this man let us take him without a fight?"

»Ich bin froh, dass er dir gefällt«, sagt sie. »Wieso lässt sich
ɪç bɪn fʁoː das eːɐ diːɐ ɡəˈfɛlt zaːkt ziː ˈviːzoː lɛst zɪç
I I am happy that it you it pleases she says she how come he lets

der Mann von uns kampflos mitnehmen?«
deːɐ man fɔn ʊns ˈkampfloːs ˈmɪtˌneːmən
the man by us without a fight to take with

"I put something into his drink back in the coffee shop."

»Ich habe etwas in sein Getränk getan, als wir in dem Café
ɪç ˈhaːbə ˈɛtvas ɪn zaɪn ɡəˈtʁɛŋk ɡəˈtaːn als viːɐ ɪn deːm kaˈfeː
I → some in his drink ←I put when we in the cafe

waren.«
ˈvaːʁən
we were

Es ist besser, wenn Sarah nicht weiß, dass ich besondere Fähigkeiten besitze. Wir fahren ein paar Minuten lang stillschweigend.

Sarah is better off not knowing about my special abilities. We drive in silence for a few minutes.

»Musst du Kostenabrechnungen ausfüllen?«, frage ich sie.

"Do you have to fill out expense reports?" I ask her.

»Wenn ich für Lucia einen Job erledige, muss ich immer eine Kostenabrechnung und ein Zeitprotokoll einreichen. Lucia besteht darauf.«

"When I'm doing a job for Lucia I always have to provide an expense report and a time log. Lucia insists on it."

»Wie steht es mit den Leuten von der Sicherheit?«, frage ich.

"What about the security guys?" I ask.

»Ich zahle ihnen einen festen Preis für jeden Einsatz. Sie geben mir die Quittungen für irgendwelche speziellen Dinge, die sie kaufen müssen.«

"I pay them a fixed price for each assignment. They give me receipts for any special items they had to buy."

Meiner Gruppe gehört die Sicherheitsfirma einer Briefkastengesellschaft. Sarah leitet die Firma und ist die einzige Vollzeitangestellte. Die Sicherheitsfirma stellt Arbeitskräfte und Ausrüstung, um spezielle Aufgaben für

My group owns a security company through a shell corporation. Sarah manages the company and is the only full time employee. The security company provides manpower and equipment to do special jobs for our clients. Sarah has a long list of mercenaries and ex-armed forces personnel that she can hire for any particular assignment, depending on the skills we need.

Story 13

unsere Kunden zu erledigen. Sarah hat eine lange Liste von Söldnern und ehemaligen Mitgliedern der Streitkräfte, die sie für jegliche Einsätze anheuern kann, je nach den benötigten Kenntnissen.

"Roland is starting to help Lucia with the office accounting," I tell her. "He's already bugging me about sending in my paperwork on time."

»Roland fängt an, Lucia bei der Bürobuchhaltung zu helfen«, sage ich zu ihr. »Er geht mir jetzt schon auf die Nerven, damit ich meinen Papierkram rechtzeitig abgebe.«

"That's what grown-ups do," Sarah says. "They fill out their paperwork."

»So etwas machen Erwachsene nun einmal«, sagt Sarah. »Sie erledigen ihren Schreibkram.«

"Don't start telling me about adult responsibilities," I say to her. "I'm not even sure you are old enough to drink."

»Fang bloß du nicht an, mir von der Verantwortung Erwachsener zu erzählen«, sage ich zu ihr. »Ich bin mir nicht einmal ganz sicher, ob du alt genug bist, Alkohol trinken zu dürfen.«

Sarah is the same age as Roland. They were childhood friends. Her parents were both private investigators, and she grew up helping them with their investigations. She took over the family business when they retired.

Sarah ist im gleichen Alter wie Roland. Sie sind seit ihrer Kindheit befreundet. Ihre Eltern waren beide Privatdetektive und als sie aufwuchs, half sie ihnen bei den Ermittlungen.

Sie übernahm das Familienunternehmen, als sie in Rente gingen. Roland stellte sie kurz danach Lucia vor. Über die nächsten Jahre beauftragte Lucia Sarah mit einer Reihe besonderer Aufgaben. Sarah erwies sich als großartige Detektivin. Innerhalb weniger Jahre wurde unser Team zum wichtigsten Kunden von Sarah.

Shortly after that Roland introduced her to Lucia. Lucia entrusted Sarah with a number of special jobs over the next few years. Sarah turned out to be a great detective. Within a few years, our team became Sarah's main client.

Schließlich bat Lucia sie, die Sicherheitsabteilung zu leiten. Sarah arbeitet immer noch für andere Kunden, aber widmet den größten Teil ihrer Zeit der Hilfe unseres Teams.

Finally, Lucia asked her to run the security operation. Sarah still does work for other clients, but spends most of her time helping our team.

»Warum hast du mich heute gebraucht?«, fragt Sarah. »Alles, was wir gemacht haben, war, einen harmlosen Kerl ins Auto zu setzen.«

"Why did you need me today?" Sarah asks. "All we did was put a harmless guy into the car."

»Wir waren nicht sicher, was geschehen würde«, sage ich ihr. »Es hätten fünf Männer mit Kampfhunden und Panzerfäusten sein können. Es hat sich herausgestellt, dass du entbehrlich

"We weren't sure what would happen," I tell her. "There could have been five men with attack dogs and bazookas. It turns out you were superfluous, but it's always a good idea to be safe."

Story 13

	warst, aber es ist immer gut, auf Nummer sicher zu gehen.«	
	vaʁst 'aːbɐ ɛs ɪst 'ɪmɐ guːt aʊf 'nʊmɐ 'zɪçɐ tsuː 'geːən	
	you were but it it is always good to play it safe	

"Nice word," she tells me. "Superfluous. Where did you learn that one?"

»Nettes Wort«, sagt sie zu mir. »Entbehrlich. Wo hast du das
'nɛtəs vɔʁt zakt ziː tsuː miːɐ ɛntˈbeːɐlɪç voː hast duː das
nice word she says she to me superfluous where → you that

gelernt?«
gəˈlɛʁnt
← you learned

"I always like to surprise people with my vocabulary skills."

»Ich überrasche Leute immer gerne mit meinem breiten
ɪç yːbɐˈʁaʃə ˈlɔɪtə ˈɪmɐ ˈgɛʁnə mɪt ˈmaɪnəm ˈbʁaɪtn
I I surprise people always like to with my broad

Wortschatz.«
ˈvɔʁtʃats
vocabulary

Sarah drives and we talk a little about the local soccer teams.

Während Sarah fährt, reden wir ein bisschen über die örtlichen
ˈvɛːʁənt ˈzaːʁa fɛːɐt ˈʁeːdn viːɐ aɪn ˈbɪsçən ˈyːbɐ diː ˈœʁtlɪçən
as Sarah she drives we talk we a little about the local

Fußballmannschaften.
ˈfuːsbalˌmanʃaftn
soccer teams

Sarah pulls the car into a small parking area next to a warehouse in the neighborhood of Marzahn. Lucia is waiting by an open metal door. A high fence makes it impossible for anyone to see the parking area from the street.

Sarah steuert den Wagen auf einen kleinen Parkplatz neben
ˈzaːʁa ˈʃtɔʁt deːn ˈvaːgən aʊf ˈaɪnən ˈklaɪnən ˈpaʁkˌplats ˈneːbən
Sarah she steers the car in a small parking area next to

einem Lagerhaus im Ortsteil Marzahn. Lucia wartet neben
ˈaɪnəm ˈlaːgɐˌhaʊs ɪm ˈɔʁtsˌtaɪl maʁˈtsaːn luˈtsia ˈvaʁtət ˈneːbən
a warehouse in the neighborhood Marzahn Lucia she waits next to

einer offenen Metalltür. Ein hoher Zaun macht es für jeden
ˈaɪnɐ ˈɔfənən meˈtalˌtyːɐ aɪn ˈhoːɐ tsaʊn maxt ɛs fyːɐ ˈjeːdən
an open metal door a high fence it makes it for everyone

unmöglich, das Parkplatzgelände von der Straße aus zu sehen.
ʊnˈmøːklɪç das ˈpaʁkˌplatsgəˌlɛndə fɔn deːɐ ˈʃtʁaːsə aʊs tsuː ˈzeːən
impossible the parking area from→ the street ← to to see

I unlock our captive's handcuffs. Lucia leads him into the building. By the time the mind fog wears off, he'll be in a holding cell in the basement of the warehouse.

Ich schließe die Handschellen unseres Gefangenen auf. Lucia führt
ɪç ˈʃliːsə diː ˈhantˌʃɛlən ˈʊnzəʁəs gəˈfaŋənən aʊf luˈtsia fyːɐt
I I unlock→ the handcuffs of our captive ← Lucia she leads

ihn in das Gebäude. Bis die Bewusstseinstrübung abklingt,
iːn ɪn das gəˈbɔʏdə bɪs diː bəˈvʊstzaɪnsˌtʁyːbʊŋ ˈapˌklɪŋt
him in the building by the time the mind fog it wears off

wird er in einer Sicherungszelle im Keller des Lagerhauses sein.
vɪʁt eːɐ ɪn ˈaɪnɐ ˈzɪçəʁʊŋsˌtsɛlə ɪm ˈkɛlɐ dɛs ˈlaːgɐˌhaʊzəs zaɪn
he will he in a holding cell in the basement of the warehouse to be

So why is the headquarters located in Marzahn? Lucia probably got a good deal on the building.

Nun, warum ist das Hauptquartier in Marzahn? Wahrscheinlich
nuːn vaˈʁʊm ɪst das ˈhaʊptkvaʁˌtiːɐ ɪn maʁˈtsaːn vaːɐˈʃaɪnlɪç
well why it is the headquarters in Marzahn probably

hat Lucia einen Vorzugspreis für das Gebäude bekommen.
hat lu'tsia 'aınən 'foːɐ̯ˌtsuːksˌpʁaɪs fyːɐ̯ das gə'bɔʏdə bə'kɔmən
→ Lucia a good price for the building ← she got

»Du musst mir einen Gefallen tun«, sagt Sarah zu mir, als   "I need a favor," Sarah says to me as we
duː mʊst miːɐ̯ 'aınən gə'falən tuːn zakt 'zaːʁa tsuː miːɐ̯ als   drive away.
you you have to me a favor to do she says Sarah to me as
wir wegfahren.
viːɐ̯ 'vɛkˌfaːʁən
we we drive away

»Willst du, dass ich dir einen guten Tätowierer empfehle?«   "You want me to recommend a good
vɪlst duː das ɪç diːɐ̯ 'aınən 'guːtən tɛto'viːʁɐ ɛm'pfeːlə   tattoo artist?"
you want you that I to you a good tattoo artist I recommend

»Nein, danke.«   "No, thank you."
naın 'daŋkə
no thanks

»Was kann ich sonst noch für dich tun?«   "What else can I do for you?"
vas kan ɪç zɔnst nɔx fyːɐ̯ dɪç tuːn
what I can I else for you to do

»Ich habe einen neuen Kunden. Die Leute, gegen die ich für   "I have a new client. The people he
ɪç 'haːbə 'aınən 'nɔɪən 'kʊndən diː 'lɔɪtə 'geːgən diː ɪç fyːɐ̯   wants me to investigate are very dan-
I I have a new client the people against whom I for   gerous. Can you help me?"
ihn ermitteln soll, sind sehr gefährlich. Kannst du mir helfen?«
iːn ɛɐ̯'mɪtln zɔl zɪnt zeːɐ̯ gə'fɛːʁlɪç kanst duː miːɐ̯ 'hɛlfən
him to investigate I should they are very dangerous can you you me to help

»Wieso ich?«   "Why me?"
vi'zoː ɪç
why me

»Weil du wirklich gut bist, wenn es um Gewalttätigkeit geht.«   "Because you are really good at vio-
vaıl duː 'vɪʁklɪç guːt bɪst vɛn ɛs ʊm gə'valtˌtɛːtɪçkaıt geːt   lence."
because you really good you are when it comes to → violence ←

»Lina ist eine bessere Kämpferin«, sage ich zu ihr.   "Lina is a better fighter," I tell her.
'liːna ɪst 'aınə 'bɛsəʁə 'kɛmpfəʁın 'zaːgə ɪç tsuː iːɐ̯   "Don't get me wrong, I'm pretty good
Lina she is a better fighter I say I to her   at knocking people around. But she's
»Verstehe mich nicht falsch, ich kann ganz gut Leute verprügeln,   better."
fɛɐ̯'ʃteːə mɪç nɪçt falʃ ɪç kan gants guːt 'lɔɪtə fɛɐ̯'pʁyːgəln
don't get me wrong I I can quite well people to beat
aber sie ist besser.«
'aːbɐ ziː ɪst 'bɛsɐ
but she she is better

»In diesem Fall könnte es sein, dass geschossen werden muss.«   "This case might require some shoot-
ɪn 'diːzəm fal 'kœntə ɛs zaın das gə'ʃɔsən 've:ɐ̯dn mʊs   ing."
in this case it could it to be that there will have to be shooting

Story 13

---- 12 ----

"Tell me the details," I say.

»Erzähle mir die Einzelheiten«, sage ich.
ɛɐˈtseːlə miːɐ diː ˈaɪntsəlhaɪtən ˈzaːgə ɪç
tell me the details I say I

Two days later ...

Zwei Tage später ...
tsvaɪ ˈtaːgə ˈʃpɛːtɐ
two days later

"I count one vote to name ourselves 'The Squad' and four votes against having a name," Lucia says.

»Ich zähle eine Stimme dafür, uns ›Das Kommando‹ zu nennen,
ɪç ˈtseːlə ˈaɪnə ˈʃtɪmə daˈfyːɐ ʊns das kɔˈmando tsuː ˈnɛnən
I I count one vote for it ourselves the squad to to name

und vier Stimmen dagegen«, sagt Lucia.
ʊnt fiːɐ ˈʃtɪmən daˈgeːgən zakt luˈtsia
and four votes against it she says Lucia

"I want a recount," I tell her.

»Ich will die Stimmen nochmals zählen«, sage ich zu ihr.
ɪç vɪl diː ˈʃtɪmən ˈnɔxmaːls ˈtseːlən ˈzaːgə ɪç tsuː iːɐ
I I want the votes again to count I say I to her

"Paul, there are only five votes. I'm not going to count them again."

»Paul, es gibt nur fünf Stimmen. Ich werde sie nicht noch einmal
paʊl ɛs giːpt nuːɐ fynf ˈʃtɪmən ɪç ˈveːɐdə ziː nɪçt nɔx ˈaɪnmaːl
Paul there are only five votes I I will them not again

zählen.«
ˈtseːlən
to count

"But every good team needs a name."

»Aber jede gute Mannschaft braucht einen Namen.«
ˈaːbɐ ˈjeːdə ˈguːtə ˈmanʃaft bʁaʊxt ˈaɪnən ˈnaːmən
but every good team it needs a name

"Looks like you lose again," says Anja. "Just like when you wanted us to buy a cat for a mascot. That vote was four against one also. I think I detect a pattern."

»Es sieht so aus, als würdest du wieder verlieren«, sagt Anja.
ɛs ziːt zoː aʊs als ˈvʏʁdəst duː ˈviːdɐ fɛɐˈliːʁən zakt ˈanja
it seems as if you would you again to lose she says Anja

»Genau wie du damals wolltest, dass wir eine Katze als
gəˈnaʊ viː duː ˈdaːmaːls ˈvɔltɛst das viːɐ ˈaɪnə ˈkatsə als
just like you back then you wanted that we a cat as

Maskottchen kaufen. Diese Abstimmung war auch vier zu eins.
masˈkɔtçən ˈkaʊfən ˈdiːzə ˈapʃtɪmʊŋ vaːɐ aʊx fiːɐ tsuː aɪns
mascot to buy that vote it was also four to one

Ich glaube, ich sehe da ein Muster.«
ɪç ˈglaʊbə ɪç ˈzeːə daː aɪn ˈmʊstɐ
I I think I I see there a pattern

Anja is our information expert. She spends her time analyzing tons of data, looking for patterns. When she finds something unusual, she asks Roland for help. He looks at the data and makes predictions.

Anja ist unsere Informationsexpertin. Sie verbringt ihre Zeit
ˈanja ɪst ˈʊnzəʁə ɪnfɔʁmaˈtsjoːnsˌɛksˈpɛʁtɪn ziː fɛɐˈbʁɪŋt ˈiːʁə tsaɪt
Anja she is our information expert she she spends her time

damit, eine Menge von Daten zu analysieren, um nach
daˈmɪt ˈaɪnə ˈmɛŋə fɔn ˈdaːtən tsuː analyˈziːʁən ʊm naːx
with that quite a lot of data to to analyze in order to after

Verhaltensmustern zu suchen. Wenn sie etwas Ungewöhnliches findet, bittet sie Roland um Hilfe. Er sieht sich die Daten an und macht Voraussagen.

Anja hat sich alle Daten rund um die Verbrechen gegen bekannte Versicherungsvertreter in Berlin angeschaut und entdeckte ein paar interessante Muster. Roland überprüfte die Muster und sagte uns, der Verantwortliche für die Erpressungsoperation sei vermutlich an der Spitze der Polizeibehörde zu finden gewesen. Er fand ebenso heraus, wer das nächste Opfer sein würde. Diese Informationen werden unsere Arbeit sicherlich beschleunigen.

Anja examined all the data surrounding the crimes against prominent insurance agents in Berlin and detected a few interesting patterns. Roland reviewed the patterns and told us that the person running the extortion operation was probably high up in the Police Department. He also figured out who the next target would be. That kind of information certainly speeds up our work.

Anja und Roland verwalten auch die Anlagenportfolios unserer Gruppe und sie verdienen dabei jede Menge Geld. Lucia verwendet dieses zusätzliche Geld, um neue technische Spielereien und Waffen zu kaufen.

Anja and Roland also manage our group's investment portfolio, and they make lots of money doing this. Lucia uses the extra money to buy new gadgets and weapons.

Roland hat noch ein Talent. Er ist ein sagenhafter Hacker. Kein

Roland has another talent. He is an awesome hacker. No computer or network is safe when Roland decides he wants to look for a certain piece of in-

Story 13

formation.

Computer oder Netzwerk ist sicher, wenn Roland sich entschließt,
kɔmˈpjuːtɐ ˈoːdɐ ˈnɛtsˌvɛʁk ɪst ˈzɪçɐ vɛn ˈʁoːlant zɪç ɛntˈʃliːst
computer   or   network   it is safe when Roland he decides

eine bestimmte Information zu suchen.
ˈaɪnə bəˈʃtɪmtə ɪnfɔʁmaˈtsjoːn tsuː ˈzuːxən
a   certain   information   to   to look for

You already know that Lina is a great fighter. Her reflexes are faster than a cobra strike and she can learn any kung fu or karate move in a matter of seconds. In addition, she's also a competitive cake decorator.

Sie wissen ja bereits, dass Lina eine großartige Kämpferin ist.
ziː ˈvɪsən jaː bəˈʁaɪts das ˈliːna ˈaɪnə ɡʁoːsˌaʁtɪɡə ˈkɛmpfəʁɪn ɪst
you you know ! already that Lina   a   great   fighter   she is

Ihre Reflexe sind schneller als die einer Kobra und sie kann jede
ˈiːʁə ʁɛˈflɛksə zɪnt ˈʃnɛlɐ als diː ˈaɪnɐ ˈkoːbʁa ʊnt ziː kan ˈjeːdə
her   reflexes they are faster than those of a cobra and she she can any

Kung-Fu- oder Karatebewegung innerhalb von Sekunden erlernen.
kʊŋ-fuː- ˈoːdɐ kaˈʁaːtəbəˌveːɡʊŋ ˈɪnɐhalp fɔn zeˈkʊndən ɛɐ̯ˈlɛʁnən
kung fu   or   karate move   in the space of seconds   to learn

Zusätzlich nimmt sie auch an Tortendekorationswettbewerben
ˈtsuːˌzɛtslɪç nɪmt ziː aʊx an ˈtɔʁtn̩dekoʁaˈtsjoːnsˌvɛtbəˌvɛʁbn̩
in addition   she takes part→ she also at cake decoration competitions

teil.
taɪl
←

Lucia spent twenty five years working for various law enforcement agencies. As I mentioned, she has the special ability of making people tell the truth. During her career, she used this talent to solve some very high profile cases. It was difficult, but she managed to do this without anyone realizing that she had "extra" abilities.

Lucia arbeitete fünfundzwanzig Jahre lang für verschiedene
luˈtsia ˈaʁbaɪtətə ˈfʏnfʊntˌtsvantsɪç ˈjaːʁə laŋ fyːɐ̯ fɛɐ̯ˈʃiːdənə
Lucia   she worked twenty-five   years long for different

Vollzugsbehörden. Wie ich schon erwähnte, hat sie die besondere
fɔlˈtsuːksbəˌhøːɐ̯dn̩ viː ɪç ʃoːn ɛɐ̯ˈvɛːntə hat ziː diː bəˈzɔndəʁə
law enforcement agencies as I already I mentioned she has she the special

Gabe, Leute dazu zu bringen, dass sie die Wahrheit sagen.
ˈɡaːbə ˈlɔɪtə daˈtsuː tsuː ˈbʁɪŋən das ziː diː ˈvaːɐ̯haɪt ˈzaːɡən
gift   people to it   to   to bring that they the truth   they tell

Während ihrer Karriere benutzte sie diese Gabe, um einige
ˈvɛːʁənt ˈiːʁɐ kaˈʁieːʁə bəˈnʊtstə ziː ˈdiːzə ˈɡaːbə ʊm ˈaɪnɪɡə
during   her   career   she used   she this   gift   in order to some

bedeutende Fälle zu lösen. Es war schwierig, aber sie schaffte
bəˈdɔɪtəndə ˈfɛlə tsuː ˈløːzən ɛs vaːɐ̯ ˈʃviːʁɪç ˈaːbɐ ziː ˈʃaftə
high profile cases to to solve it it was difficult but she she managed

es, ohne dass jemand ihre besondere Gabe bemerkte.
ɛs ˈoːnə das ˈjeːmant ˈiːʁə bəˈzɔndəʁə ˈɡaːbə bəˈmɛʁktə
it without that anyone   her   special   gift   he noticed

Lucia retired five years ago, when she reached the age of fifty. Rather than learn how to garden, she started to put our team together.

Lucia ging vor fünf Jahren, als sie fünfzig Jahre alt wurde,
luˈtsia ɡɪŋ foːɐ̯ fʏnf ˈjaːʁən als ziː ˈfʏnftsɪç ˈjaːʁə alt ˈvʊʁdə
Lucia she retired→ ago five years when she fifty   years old she became

in Rente. Anstatt das Gärtnern zu erlernen, begann sie, unser
ɪn ˈʁɛntə ˈanʃtat das ˈɡɛʁtnɐn tsuː ɛɐ̯ˈlɛʁnən bəˈɡan ziː ˈʊnzɐ
←   instead of the gardening to to learn   she started she our

Evolution

Team zu formieren.
ti:m tsu: fɔʁˈmiːʁən
team to to form

Während ihrer Karriere hielt Lucia Augen und Ohren offen,
ˈvɛːʁənt ˈiːʁɐ kaˈʁieːʁɐ hiːlt luˈtsia ˈaʊɡən ʊnt ˈoːʁən ˈɔfən
during her career she kept Lucia eyes and ears open

um andere mit besonderen Talenten zu finden. Zum Zeitpunkt
ʊm ˈandəʁɐ mɪt bəˈzɔndəʁən taˈlɛntən tsu: ˈfɪndən tsʊm ˈtsaɪtˌpʊŋkt
in order to others with special talents to to find at the time

ihres Renteneintritts hatte sie eine Liste von zehn möglichen
ˈiːʁəs ˈʁɛntnˌaɪntʁɪts ˈhatə ziː ˈaɪnə ˈlɪstə fɔn tseːn ˈmøːklɪçən
of her start of retirement she had she a list of ten possible

Kandidaten für das Team. Sechs dieser Kandidaten stellten sich als
kandiˈdaːtən fyːɐ das tiːm zɛks ˈdiːzɐ kandiˈdaːtən ˈʃtɛltən zɪç als
candidates for the team six of these candidates they turned out to be →

Leute mit normalen Fähigkeiten heraus. Vier von uns waren
ˈlɔɪtə mɪt nɔʁˈmaːlən ˈfɛːɪçkaɪtn hɛˈʁaʊs fiːɐ fɔn ʊns ˈvaːʁən
people with normal abilities ← four of us we were

etwas Besonderes. Ich war der Erste auf ihrer Liste.
ˈɛtvas bəˈzɔndəʁəs ɪç vaːɐ deːɐ ˈeːɐstə aʊf ˈiːʁɐ ˈlɪstə
something special I I was the first on her list

During her career, Lucia kept her eyes and ears open to find others with special talents. By the time she retired, she had a list of ten possible candidates for the team. Six of these prospects turned out to be people with normal abilities. Four of us were special. I was the first person on her list.

Als sie mit mir sprach, sagte ich zu ihr, dass sie zu viele
als ziː mɪt miːɐ ʃpʁaːx ˈzaktə ɪç tsu: iːɐ das ziː tsu: ˈfiːlə
when she with me she spoke I told I to her that she too many

Comicbücher gelesen habe. Aber sie überzeugte mich, wir würden
ˈkɔmɪkˌbyːçɐ ɡəˈleːzən ˈhaːbə ˈaːbɐ ziː yːbɐˈtsɔɪktə mɪç viːɐ ˈvʏʁdən
comic books she has read but she she convinced me we we would

Spaß haben, gute Taten vollbringen, ein paar Leute erschießen
ʃpaːs ˈhaːbn ˈɡuːtə ˈtaːtən fɔlˈbʁɪŋən aɪn paːɐ ˈlɔɪtə ɛɐˈʃiːsn
fun to have good deeds to perform a few people to shoot

und viel Geld verdienen. Somit unterschrieb ich. Das war vor
ʊnt fiːl ɡɛlt fɛɐˈdiːnən zoːˈmɪt ʊntɐˈʃʁiːp ɪç das vaːɐ foːɐ
and a lot of money to earn thus I signed up I that it was ago

vier Jahren.
fiːɐ ˈjaːʁən
four years

When she talked to me, I told her that she had been reading too many comic books. But she convinced me that we would have fun, do good deeds, shoot some people, and make a lot of money. So I signed up. That was four years ago.

Als Nächstes rekrutierte sie Anja von einer Expertenkommission
als ˈnɛçstəs ʁekʁuˈtiːɐtə ziː ˈanja fɔn ˈaɪnɐ ɛksˈpɛɐtnkɔmɪˌsjoːn
next she recruited she Anja from a think-tank

der Regierung. Roland kam zu uns als Computerspezialist vom
deːɐ ʁeˈɡiːʁʊŋ ˈʁoːlant kaːm tsu: ʊns als kɔmˈpjuːtɐʃpetsjaˌlɪst fɔm
of the government Roland he came to us as computer specialist from the

BND. Lina war die letzte Rekrutin. Sie trainierte LKA-Agenten
beːɛnˈdeː ˈliːna vaːɐ diː ˈlɛtstə ʁeˈkʁuːtɪn ziː tʁɛˈniːɐtə ɛlkaːˈaːaˈɡɛntən
BND Lina she was the last recruit she she trained LKA agents

Next, she recruited Anja from a government think-tank. Roland came to us from a job as a computer specialist at the BND. Lina was the last recruit. She trained LKA agents in self defense techniques.

Story 13

in Selbstverteidigungstechniken.

But I digress. Back to the actual story.

Aber ich schweife ab. Zurück zur eigentlichen Geschichte.

We are meeting in our gorgeous home base. It used to be a plumbing supply warehouse. There are still rusted pieces of pipes and elbow joints scattered around in some of the unused rooms.

Wir treffen uns in unserer großartigen Basis. Sie war früher ein Vorratslager für Klempnerbedarf. Es liegen immer noch verrostete Rohr- und Eckstücke in einigen der ungenutzten Räume verstreut.

"How is our prisoner?" I ask.

»Wie geht es unserem Gefangenen?«, frage ich.

"Homeland Security has him."

»Er ist bei den Sicherheitsbehörden.«

"Why?"

»Warum?«

"It turns out he is a Russian who has been here illegally for a few years," Lucia tells me.

»Es hat sich herausgestellt, dass er ein Russe ist, der seit ein paar Jahren illegal hier ist«, sagt Lucia.

"He doesn't know a thing about the Ukrainians. Someone called him a few days ago and hired him to torture you until you told him what happened with the first two men."

»Er weiß nichts über die Ukrainer. Jemand rief ihn vor ein paar Tagen an und heuerte ihn an, dich zu foltern, bis du ihm sagst, was mit den ersten zwei Männern passiert ist.«

Evolution

»Können wir das Gespräch nachverfolgen?«
ˈkœnən viːɐ das gəˈʃpʀɛːç ˈnaːxfɛɐˌfɔlgn
can we we the call to trace back

"Can we trace the phone call?"

»Der Anruf wurde von einem Einwegtelefon gemacht. Derjenige,
deːɐ ˈanʀuːf ˈvʊʀdə fɔn ˈaınəm ˈaınveːkˌteːleˈfoːn gəˈmaxt deːɐˌjeːnɪgə
the call → from a disposable phone ← it was made the one

der den Einsatz leitet, ist ganz schön schlau.«
deːɐ deːn ˈaınˌzats ˈlaıtət ɪst gants ʃøːn ʃlaʊ
who the operation he leads he is quite ! smart

"The call was made from a disposable phone. The person running this operation is pretty smart."

Während Lucia und ich miteinander sprechen, beginnen Anja
ˈvɛːʀənt luˈtsia ʊnt ɪç ˈmɪtaıˌnandɐ ˈʃpʀɛçən bəˈgınən ˈanja
while Lucia and I with each other we speak they begin Anja

und Roland eine Diskussion darüber, ob Mendelejew besondere
ʊnt ˈʀoːlant ˈaınə dɪskʊˈsjoːn daˈʀyːbɐ ɔp mendeˈlejev bəˈzɔndəʀə
and Roland a discussion about it if Mendeleev special

evolutionäre Kräfte hatte oder nicht. Ich frage Lina, ob Mendelejew
evolutsjoˈnɛːʀə ˈkʀɛftə ˈhatə ˈoːdɐ nɪçt ɪç ˈfʀaːgə ˈliːna ɔp mendeˈlejev
evolutionary powers he had or not I I ask Lina if Mendeleev

der Premierminister von Russland ist.
deːɐ pʀəˈmjeːmɪˌnɪstɐ fɔn ˈʀʊslant ɪst
the prime minister from Russia he is

While Lucia and I are talking, Anja and Roland start discussing whether or not Mendeleev had special evolutionary powers. I ask Lina if Mendeleev is the prime minister of Russia.

»Nein, er erfand das Periodensystem, damals im 19.
naın eːɐ ɛɐˈfant das peːɐˈjoːdnzʏsˌteːm ˈdaːmaːls ɪm ˈnɔɪnˌtseːntən
no he he invented the periodic table back then in the 19th

Jahrhundert«, sagt sie zu mir. »Er sagte auch die
ˈjaːɐˌhʊndɐt zakt ziː tsuː miːɐ eːɐ ˈzaktə aʊx diː
century she says she to me he he predicted→ also the

Eigenschaften von Elementen voraus, die noch nicht entdeckt
ˈaıgənˌʃaftən fɔn eləˈmɛntn foˈʀaʊs diː nɔx nıçt ɛntˈdɛkt
properties of elements ← that not yet discovered

waren.«
ˈvaːʀən
they were

"No, he invented the periodic table, back in the 19th century," she tells me. "He also predicted the properties of elements that hadn't even been discovered yet."

Roland und Anja debattieren ein paar Minuten. Dann fangen
ˈʀoːlant ʊnt ˈanja debaˈtiːʀən aın paːɐ mɪˈnuːtən dan ˈfaŋən
Roland and Anja they argue a few minutes then they started→

sie an, sich anzuschreien. Dann fangen sie an, miteinander zu
ziː an zıç ˈantsuʃʀaıən dan ˈfaŋən ziː an ˈmɪtaıˌnandɐ tsuː
they ← they yell then they started→ they ← with each other to

kämpfen.
ˈkɛmpfən
to fight

Roland and Anja argue for a few minutes. Then they start yelling. Then they are wrestling with each other.

»Kämpft, kämpft, kämpft«, feuere ich sie an.
kɛmpft kɛmpft kɛmpft ˈfɔıʀə ıç ziː an
fight fight fight I cheered on→ I them ←

"Fight, fight, fight," I chant.

Story 13

Lina stands up and whacks Anja and Roland on the legs a few times with a wood staff that she likes to carry.

Lina	steht	auf	und	schlägt	Anja	und	Roland	ein paar	Mal	mit
ˈliːna	ʃteːt	aʊf	ʊnt	ʃlɛːkt	ˈanja	ʊnt	ˈʁoːlant	aɪn paːɐ̯	maːl	mɪt
Lina	she stands up	and		she whacks	Anja	and	Roland	a few	time	with

einem	Holzstab,	den	sie	gerne	mit sich herumträgt,	auf	die	Beine.
ˈaɪnəm	ˈhɔltsʃtaːp	deːn	ziː	ˈɡɛʁnə mɪt zɪç hɛˈʁʊmˌtʁɛːkt		aʊf	diː	ˈbaɪnə
a	wood staff	that	she	she likes to carry around with her		on	the	legs

"Ow. Stop. That hurts," says Roland.

»Au,	hör auf.	Das	tut weh«,	sagt	Roland.
aʊ	høːɐ̯ aʊf	das	tuːt veː	zakt	ˈʁoːlant
ow	stop	that	it hurts	he says	Roland

"Let's finish the meeting," Lina says.

»Lasst uns	die	Besprechung	beenden«,	sagt	Lina.
last ʊns	diː	bəˈʃpʁɛçʊŋ	bəˈɛndən	zakt	ˈliːna
let's	the	meeting	to finish	she says	Lina

Anja and Roland get off the floor rubbing their shins. They sit down in their seats. Now that she has our attention, Lucia continues talking.

Anja	und	Roland	stehen	vom	Boden	auf	und	reiben	sich	die
ˈanja	ʊnt	ˈʁoːlant	ˈʃteːən	fɔm	ˈboːdən	aʊf	ʊnt	ˈʁaɪbən	zɪç	diː
Anja	and	Roland	they get up →	from the	floor	←	and	they rub		their

Schienbeine.	Sie	setzen sich auf	ihre	Plätze.	Jetzt,	nachdem	sie
ˈʃiːnˌbaɪnə	ziː	ˈzɛtsən zɪç aʊf	ˈiːʁə	ˈplɛtsə	jɛtst	naːxˈdeːm	ziː
shins	they	they sit down on	their	seats	now	after	she

wieder	unsere	Aufmerksamkeit	hat,	spricht	Lucia	weiter.
ˈviːdɐ	ˈʊnzəʁə	ˈaʊfˌmɛʁkzaːmkaɪt	hat	ʃpʁɪçt	ˈluːtsia	ˈvaɪtɐ
again	our	attention	she has	she keeps speaking →	Lucia	←

"Arno is still checking the DNA and fingerprints to try to pinpoint where the Ukrainians come from. Maybe that will give us a lead."

»Arno	überprüft	immer noch	die	DNA	und	die	Fingerabdrücke,
ˈaʁno	yːbɐˈpʁyːft	ˈɪmɐ nɔx	diː	deːʔɛnˈaː	ʊnt	diː	ˈfɪŋɐˌapdʁʏkə
Arno	he checks	still	the	DNA	and	the	fingerprints

um	die	Herkunft	der	Ukrainer	festzustellen.	Vielleicht
ʊm	diː	ˈheːɐ̯ˌkʊnft	deːɐ̯	ukʁaˈiːnɐ	ˈfɛsttsuˌʃtɛlən	fiˈlaɪçt
in order to	the	origin	of the	Ukrainians	to determine	maybe

ergibt sich	daraus	ein	Anhaltspunkt.«
ɛɐ̯ˈɡiːpt zɪç	daˈʁaʊs	aɪn	ˈanhaltsˌpʊŋkt
it results	from this	a	lead

Arno is a friend of Anja's. I think she likes him. They met while she was studying for her PhD. At that time, Arno already had a doctorate in chemistry and was an expert in proteins and things like that. We set Arno up in his own research facility a few years ago and funded some of his projects. In return, he acts as our own private forensics lab.

Arno	ist	ein	Freund	von	Anja.	Ich	glaube,	sie	mag	ihn.	Sie
ˈaʁno	ɪst	aɪn	fʁɔɪnt	fɔn	ˈanja	ɪç	ˈɡlaʊbə	ziː	mak	iːn	ziː
Arno	he is	a	friend	of	Anja	I	I think	she	she likes	him	they

haben sich kennengelernt,	als	sie	an	ihrer	Promotion	arbeitete.
ˈhaːbn̩ zɪç ˈkɛnəŋɡəˌlɛʁnt	als	ziː	an	ˈiːʁɐ	pʁomoˈtsjoːn	ˈaʁbaɪtətə
they met each other	while	she	for	her	doctorate	she worked

Zu dieser Zeit	hatte	Arno	bereits	einen	Doktortitel	in	Chemie	und
tsuː ˈdiːzɐ tsaɪt	ˈhatə	ˈaʁno	bəˈʁaɪts	ˈaɪnən	ˈdɔktoːɐ̯ˌtiːtl̩	ɪn	çeˈmiː	ʊnt
at this time	he had	Arno	already	a	doctorate	in	chemistry	and

war	ein	Experte	für	Proteine	und	Ähnliches.	Vor	ein paar	Jahren
vaːɐ̯	aɪn	ɛksˈpɛʁtə	fyːɐ̯	pʁoteˈiːnə	ʊnt	ˈɛːnlɪçəs	foːɐ̯	aɪn paːɐ̯	ˈjaːʁən
he was	an	expert	for	proteins	and	similar things	ago	a few	years

haben	wir	Arno	in	seinem	eigenen	Forschungslabor	ausgerüstet
ˈhaːbn̩	viːɐ̯	ˈaʁno	ɪn	ˈzaɪnəm	ˈaɪɡənən	ˈfɔʁʃʊŋslaboːɐ̯	ˈaʊsɡəˌʁʏstət
→	we	Arno	in	his	own	research lab	← we equipped

und förderten einige seiner Projekte. Als Gegenleistung agiert er als unser eigenes, privates, kriminaltechnisches Labor.

»Irgendwelche Fortschritte mit den Namen, die ich von Reinhold bekommen habe?«, frage ich.

"Any progress with those names that I got from Reinhold?" I ask.

»Noch nicht«, antwortet Roland. »Ich schreibe gerade ein paar Spezialprogramme, um Informationen über Ukrainer, die nach Deutschland gekommen sind, ans Licht zu bringen. Ich schaue mir auch alle von den Landespolizisten bearbeiteten Transaktionen an, von denen Pauls Freund sagt, dass sie gewillt seien, Schmiergelder anzunehmen. Ich werde so viele Jahre zurückgehen wie ich kann, um zu sehen, ob es dort irgendwelche Zusammenhänge gibt.«

"Not yet," Roland answers. "I'm writing a few special programs to try to uncover information about Ukrainians who have been coming to Germany. I'm also looking into all the transactions processed by the state police people who Paul's friend says are willing to take payoffs. I'll go back as many years as I can to see if there are any connections."

»Reinhold ist nicht gerade mein Freund«, sage ich.

"Reinhold isn't exactly my friend," I say.

»Haben wir einen Kunden, der für diesen Fall zahlt?«, fragt Lina.

"Do we have a client that is paying for this case?" Lina asks.

»Nein«, sagt Lucia. »Wir zahlen dafür aus eigener Tasche.«

"No," Lucia says. "We're paying for this with our own money."

»Wie rechtfertigen wir die Kosten?«, fragt Roland.

"How do we justify the expense?" Roland asks.

Story 13

"Sometimes we do things because they need to be done," answers Lucia. "This is one of those times."

»Manchmal tun wir etwas, weil es getan werden muss«, antwortet Lucia. »Und das ist jetzt der Fall.«

"I was just asking," Roland says.

»Ich habe doch nur gefragt«, sagt Roland.

"Well, now you know."

»Nun, jetzt weißt du es.«

We talk about other issues for a few minutes. Roland gets bored and starts to play a computer game. Ten minutes later Anja calls over to him.

Wir unterhalten uns ein paar Minuten lang über etwas anderes. Roland wird es langweilig und er fängt mit einem Computerspiel an. Zehn Minuten später ruft Anja zu ihm hinüber.

"Roland, did you hear the last thing Lucia said?"

»Roland, hast du verstanden, was Lucia zuletzt gesagt hat?«

"I'm on level ten right now," he mumbles.

»Ich bin gerade bei Level zehn«, murmelt er.

Anja tries to push the 'off' button on Roland's laptop. He pushes her away with one hand and continues to type with his other hand. She pulls him out of his seat.

Anja versucht, den Aus-Knopf auf Rolands Laptop zu drücken. Er schubst sie mit einer Hand weg und tippt mit der anderen Hand weiter. Sie zieht ihn von seinem Platz.

"Just once I would like to have a meeting where nobody has a fight," Lucia says to me.

»Ich möchte nur einmal eine Besprechung erleben, wo sich niemand streitet«, sagt Lucia zu mir.

Evolution

»Sie streiten sich nicht wirklich«, sage ich zu ihr.   "They're not really fighting," I tell her.

»Es ist deine Schuld«, sagt sie.   "This is your fault," she says.

»Wieso beschuldigst du mich?«   "Why are you blaming me?"

»Du reichst deine Berichte nicht ordnungsgemäß ein, du feuerst diese Kinder an, wenn sie verrückt spielen und du beschwerst dich, weil du in Marzahn arbeiten musst. Ich kann zehn andere Fälle benennen, wo du ein schlechtes Beispiel darstellst.«   "You don't file your reports properly, you encourage the kids when they start to act up, you complain about working in Marzahn. I can name other ways that you set a bad example."

Plötzlich bemerken wir, dass uns die anderen drei beobachten.   Suddenly we realize the other three are watching us.

»Okay, Papa und Mama haben eine kleine Auseinandersetzung. Aber macht euch keine Sorgen, wir haben euch noch lieb«, sage ich zu ihnen.   "OK, dad and mom are having a little fight. But don't worry, we still love you," I tell them.

Sie rollen die Augen.   They roll their eyes.

»Nur noch eine geschäftliche Angelegenheit«, sage ich, »und   "One more piece of business," I say, "and then you can continue the fight."

261

Story 13

	dann	könnt	ihr	weiterstreiten.«
	dan	kœnt	iːɐ	ˈvaɪtɐˌʃtʁaɪtən
	then	you can	you	to continue fighting

"What?" asks Anja.

	»Worum	geht es?«,	fragt	Anja.
	voˈʁʊm	geːt ɛs	fʁaːkt	ˈanja
	what's the issue		she asks	Anja

"Sarah has a case that she can't handle by herself."

»Sarah	hat	einen	Fall,	den	sie	alleine	nicht	bearbeiten	kann.«
ˈzaːʁa	hat	ˈaɪnən	fal	deːn	ziː	aˈlaɪnə	nɪçt	bəˈaʁbaitn	kan
Sarah	she has	a	case	that	she	alone	not	to handle	she can

"Tell us about it," says Lucia.

»Erzähle	uns	davon«,	sagt	Lucia.
ɛɐˈtsɛːlə	ʊns	daˈfɔn	zakt	luˈtsia
tell	us	about it	she says	Lucia

───────────── 13 ─────────────

"Sarah has to investigate a motorcycle club."

»Sarah	muss	gegen	einen	Motorradclub	ermitteln.«
ˈzaːʁa	mʊs	ˈgeːgən	ˈaɪnən	ˈmoːtoːɐˌʁaːtˈklʊp	ɛɐˈmɪtln
Sarah	she has to	→	a	motorcycle club	← to investigate

"Cool," Lina says.

»Geil«,	sagt	Lina.
gaɪl	zakt	ˈliːna
cool	she says	Lina

"Who hired her?" Lucia asks.

»Wer	hat	sie	angeheuert?«,	fragt	Lucia.
veːɐ	hat	ziː	ˈangəˌhɔʁɐt	fʁaːkt	luˈtsia
who	→	her	← he hired	she asks	Lucia

"The president of the club. One of his gang is stealing from them. He wants Sarah to watch his people and find out who is taking money."

»Der	Vorsitzende	des	Clubs.	Einer	in	seiner	Gang	bestiehlt	sie.
deːɐ	ˈfoːɐˌzɪtsndə	dɛs	klʊps	ˈaɪnɐ	ɪn	ˈzaɪnɐ	gaŋ	bəˈʃtiːlt	ziː
the	president	of the	club	one person	in	his	gang	he steals from	them

Er	möchte,	dass	Sarah	seine	Leute	beobachtet	und	herausfindet,
eːɐ	ˈmœçtə	das	ˈzaːʁa	ˈzaɪnə	ˈlɔɪtə	bəˈoːbaxtət	ʊnt	hɛˈʁaʊsˌfɪndət
he	he would like	that	Sarah	his	people	she watches	and	she finds out

wer	das	Geld	nimmt.«
veːɐ	das	gɛlt	nɪmt
who	the	money	he takes

"How does he know that money is missing?" Lucia asks.

»Woher	weiß	er,	dass	Geld	fehlt?«,	fragt	Lucia.
voˈheːɐ	vaɪs	eːɐ	das	gɛlt	feːlt	fʁaːkt	luˈtsia
from where	he knows	he	that	money	it is missing	she asks	Lucia

"The club president keeps a monthly log of their income. The income this year was lower than it was last year, even though prices are higher."

»Der	Clubpräsident	führt	monatliche	Aufzeichnungen	über	ihre
deːɐ	ˈklʊpˌpʁɛziˈdɛnt	fyːɐt	ˈmoːnatlɪçə	ˈaʊftsaɪçnʊŋən	ˈyːbɐ	ˈiːʁə
the	club president	he keeps	monthly	records	about	their

Einkommen.	Die	Einnahmen	in	diesem	Jahr	waren	niedriger	als
ˈaɪnˌkɔmən	diː	ˈaɪnˌnaːmən	ɪn	ˈdiːzəm	jaːɐ	ˈvaːʁən	ˈniːdʁɪgɐ	als
income	the	revenues	in	this	year	they were	lower	than

im letzten Jahr, obwohl die Preise höher sind.«
im 'lɛtstən ja:ɐ ɔp'vo:l di: 'pʁaɪzə 'hø:ɐ zɪnt
in the last year even though the prices higher they are

»Klingt nach einer ganzen Menge Spaß«, sagt Anja. »Ich
klɪŋt na:x 'aɪnɐ 'gantsən 'mɛŋə ʃpas zakt 'anja ɪç
it sounds like a great deal of fun she says Anja I

"This sounds like fun," Anja says. "I always wanted to ride around on a big Harley Davidson."

wollte schon immer einmal auf einer großen Harley Davidson
'vɔltə ʃo:n 'ɪmɐ 'aɪnma:l aʊf 'aɪnɐ 'gʁo:sən 'haʁli: 'dɛvɪdzo:n
I wanted always once on a big Harley Davidson

herumfahren.«
hɛ'ʁʊm'fa:ʁən
to drive around

»Da ist ein großes Motorradtreffen nächste Woche oben an
da: ɪst aɪn 'gʁo:səs 'mo:to:ɐ̯ʁa:t'tʁɛfn̩ 'nɛçstə 'vɔxə 'o:bən an
there it is a big motorcycle rally next week up on

"There's a huge motorcycle rally up at the Baltic Sea next week," I tell them. "The gang will be there, doing a lot of illegal things. Sarah thinks that is the best place to find the thief."

der Ostsee«, erzähle ich ihnen. »Die Gang wird dort sein und
de:ɐ 'ɔst,ze: ɛɐ̯'tsɛ:lə ɪç 'i:nən di: gaŋ vɪɐ̯t dɔɐ̯t zaɪn ʊnt
the Baltic Sea I tell I them the gang it will there to be and

eine Menge illegaler Sachen machen. Sarah denkt, das sei der
'aɪnə 'mɛŋə 'ɪlega:lɐ 'zaxən 'maxən 'za:ʁa dɛŋkt das zaɪ de:ɐ
a lot of illegal things to do Sarah she thinks that it is the

beste Ort, den Dieb zu finden.«
'bəstə ɔʁt de:n di:p tsu: 'fɪndən
best place the thief to to find

»Gehen wir alle hin?«, fragt Anja.
'ge:ən vi:ɐ 'alə hɪn fʁa:kt 'anja
we go there→ we all ← she asks Anja

"Do we all go?" Anja asks.

»Ja, ich habe Sarah klargemacht, dass sie nicht alle Gangmitglieder
ja: ɪç 'ha:bə 'za:ʁa 'kla:ɐ̯gə,maxt das zi: nɪçt 'alə gaŋ'mɪt,gli:dɐ
yes I → Sarah ←I made clear that she not all gang members

"Yes. I convinced Sarah that she couldn't keep track of all the gang members by herself. So we'll all go to help. I knew you would like a field trip."

beaufsichtigen kann. Daher werden wir alle hingehen und helfen.
bə'aʊfzɪçtɪgən kan 'da:he:ɐ 've:ɐ̯dn̩ vi:ɐ 'alə 'hɪn,ge:ən ʊnt 'hɛlfən
to monitor she can so we will we all to go there and to help

Ich wusste, dass euch ein Ausflug gefallen wird.«
ɪç 'vʊstə das ɔɪç aɪn 'aʊs,flu:k gə'falən vɪɐ̯t
I I knew that you a field trip it would please you

»Juhu, ein Wochenende an der Ostsee«, sagt Lina.
ju'hu: aɪn 'vɔxn̩,ɛndə an de:ɐ 'ɔst,ze: zakt 'li:na
yay a weekend at the Baltic Sea she says Lina

"Yay, a weekend at the Baltic Sea," Lina says.

---14---

Ein paar Tage später ...
aɪn pa:ɐ 'ta:gə 'ʃpɛ:tɐ
a few days later

A few days later ...

Story 13

"It's Thursday," Lina reminds us. "Time to go to the Baltic Sea."

»Es ist Donnerstag«, erinnert uns Lina. »Zeit, an die Ostsee zu fahren.«
ɛs ɪst ˈdɔnɐsˌtaːk ɛɐˈɪnɐt ʊns ˈliːna tsaɪt an diː ˈɔstˌzeː tsu ˈfaːʁən
it it is Thursday she remind us Lina time to the Baltic Sea to to go

"Isn't it a little early?" I ask. "We just finished lunch."

»Ist es nicht ein bisschen zu früh?«, frage ich. »Wir haben gerade zu Mittag gegessen.«
ɪst ɛs nɪçt aɪn ˈbɪsçən tsuː fʁyː ˈfʁaːɡə ɪç viːɐ ˈhaːbn̩ ɡəˈʁaːdə tsuː ˈmɪtaːk ɡəˈɡɛsən
is it it not a little too early i ask I we → just now ← we ate lunch

"We want to walk around the fair grounds and check out the things the vendors are selling," Lina says.

»Wir wollen auf dem Ausstellungsgelände herumgehen und die Sachen ansehen, die von den Händlern angeboten werden«, sagt Lina.
viːɐ ˈvɔlən aʊf deːm ˈaʊsʃtɛlʊŋsɡəˌlɛndə hɛˈʁʊmˌɡeːən ʊnt diː ˈzaxən ˈanzeːən diː fɔn deːn ˈhɛndlɐn ˈanɡəˌboːtn̩ ˈveːɐdn̩ zakt ˈliːna
we we want on the fair grounds to walk around and the thing to look at that from the traders they are offering she says Lina

Anja holds up a shiny black leather jacket. It has fringes on the sleeves.

Anja hält eine glänzende, schwarze Lederjacke hoch. Sie hat Fransen an den Ärmeln.
ˈanja hɛlt ˈaɪnə ˈɡlɛntsəndə ˈʃvaʁtsə ˈleːdɐˌjakə hoːx ziː hat ˈfʁaːnzən an deːn ˈɛʁməln
Anja she holds up→ a shiny black leather jacket ← it it has fringes on the sleeves

"These are excellent," she tells Lucia.

»Die sind ausgezeichnet«, sagt sie zu Lucia.
diː zɪnt ˈaʊsɡəˌtsaɪçnət zakt ziː tsuː luˈtsia
they they are excellent she says she to Lucia

"They would be a lot better if we had a team name on the back," I say.

»Die wären noch viel besser, wenn wir einen Teamnamen am Rücken hätten«, sage ich.
diː ˈvɛːʁən nɔx fiːl ˈbɛsɐ vɛn viːɐ ˈaɪnən ˈtiːmˌnaːmən am ˈʁʏkən ˈhɛtən ˈzaːɡə ɪç
they they would be even much better if we a team name on the back we had I say I

"It's time for you to give up that idea," Roland says.

»Es wird Zeit, dass du diese Idee aufgibst«, sagt Roland.
ɛs vɪʁt tsaɪt das duː ˈdiːzə iˈdeː ˈaʊfˌɡiːpst zakt ˈʁoːlant
it's time that you that idea you give up he says Roland

"Have we found any more clues that could help us track the extortionists?" Lina asks.

»Haben wir noch irgendwelche Hinweise gefunden, die uns bei
ˈhaːbn̩ viːɐ nɔx ˈɪʁɡn̩tvɛlçə ˈhɪnvaɪzə ɡəˈfʊndən diː ʊns baɪ
→ we yet any clues ←we found that us with

264

German	IPA	English
der Verfolgung der Erpresser helfen könnten?«, fragt Lina.	deːɐ fɛɐˈfɔlgʊŋ deːɐ ɛɐˈpʁɛsɐ ˈhɛlfən ˈkœntn̩ fʁaːkt ˈliːna	the tracking of the extortionists to help they could she asks Lina

»Nein«, sagt Anja, »Rolands Programme haben uns noch keine Resultate geliefert.«

"No," Anja says, "Roland's programs haven't given us any results yet."

»Während der nächsten paar Tage sollten wir uns über die Ukrainer keine Gedanken machen und uns auf die Motorradgang konzentrieren«, sagt Sarah zu uns.

"For the next few days we should not worry about the Ukrainians and focus on the motorcycle gang," Sarah tells us.

Sie kam vor ein paar Minuten an und trug einen kleinen Koffer mit Kleidung für das Wochenende.

She arrived a few minutes ago, carrying a small suitcase of clothes for the weekend.

»Wo werden wir unterkommen?«, fragt Anja.

"Where are we staying?" Anja asks.

»Ich habe das Hotelbuchungssystem gehackt«, sagt Roland. »Die haben ein Hotel ungefähr acht Kilometer von dem Ort entfernt, wo das Treffen abgehalten wird. Ich habe die Namen von sechs bestehenden Reservierungen gelöscht und mit unseren Namen ersetzt. Wir haben schöne Zimmer, aber so manches Gangmitglied wird bitterböse sein, wenn er versucht, einzuchecken.«

"I hacked the hotel reservation system," Roland says. "They have a hotel about eight kilometers from the place where the rally is being held. I deleted the names on six existing reservations and replaced them with our names. We've got nice rooms, but a few of the motorcycle people are going to be very upset when they try to check in."

Evolution

265

Story 13

"Is the equipment ready?" Lucia asks me.

»Ist die Ausrüstung fertig?«, fragt mich Lucia.

"The weapons are clean, the communications equipment is working well, the computers are functional, and the van is packed. All we need to do is load our suitcases."

»Die Waffen sind sauber, die Kommunikationsausrüstung ist einsatzbereit, die Computer funktionieren und der Lieferwagen ist beladen. Alles, was wir noch tun müssen, ist unsere Koffer einzuladen.«

"Anja and Roland have already identified the four members of the motorcycle club who are most likely to be stealing," Lucia says. "One runs the drug selling business. Another is in charge of the gang's gun smuggling operation. The third leads the gang's efforts to hijack trucks, and the fourth operates their prostitution business. These are the men we will be following."

»Anja und Roland haben bereits die vier Mitglieder des Motorradclubs identifiziert, die höchstwahrscheinlich klauen«, sagt Lucia. »Einer leitet den Drogenverkauf. Ein anderer ist für die Waffenschmuggel-Transaktionen der Gang verantwortlich. Der Dritte leitet die Gangaktivitäten in Sachen LKW-Entführungen und der Vierte organisiert das Prostitutionsgeschäft. Das sind die Männer, denen wir folgen werden.«

"We went over this yesterday when you handed out our assignments and gave us pictures of each target," Roland reminds her.

»Wir sind das gestern durchgegangen, als du uns die Aufträge ausgehändigt hast und uns die Bilder von jeder Zielperson gegeben hast«, erinnert sie Roland.

Evolution

»Es kann nicht schaden, das Ganze nochmal fünf Minuten durchzugehen«, sagt sie zu ihm.

"It can't hurt to spend five minutes going over things again," she tells him.

Alle stöhnen, als sie weitermacht und alles wiederholt, was sie uns am Tag vorher bereits gesagt hat. Lucia erwischt mich dabei, wie ich Grimassen hinter ihrem Rücken schneide.

Everyone groans as she proceeds to repeat everything she told us the day before. Lucia catches me making faces behind her back.

»Au«, sage ich, als sie mir auf die Schläfe schlägt.

"Ow," I say when she smacks me in the temple.

»Habt ihr alle die Wegbeschreibung zum Hotel und zum Ausstellungsgelände?«, fragt Lucia.

"Do you all have directions to the hotel and the fair grounds?" Lucia asks.

»Ich habe sie ausgedruckt, nur für den Fall, dass unsere Handys keinen Empfang haben«, sagt Roland.

"I printed them out, just in case our cell phones lose signal," Roland says.

Er gibt jedem von uns eine Kopie. Wir schnappen unser Gepäck und gehen durch die Hintertür des Lagerhauses. Drei glänzende Motorräder und ein großer Lieferwagen stehen auf dem Parkplatzgelände.

He gives each of us a copy. We pick up our luggage and walk out the back door of the warehouse. Three shiny motorcycles and a large van sit in the parking lot.

Der Lieferwagen sieht eher wie ein Lastwagen aus. In den

The van looks more like a small truck. There are storage panels in the side walls of the truck where all our equip-

Story 13

ment is stored. The middle section has three chairs and a small desk bolted to the floor. We can use it as an office when we are parked. The front cab has space for four people.

Seitenwänden	des	Lasters	befinden sich	Storäume,	wo	alle
ˈzaɪtnˌvɛndn	dɛs	ˈlastɐs	bəˈfɪndən zɪç	ˈʃtaʊˌʁɔʏmə	voː	ˈalə
side walls	of the	truck	they are situated	storage space	where	all

unsere	Geräte	gelagert	sind.	Im	mittleren	Bereich	sind	drei
ˈʊnzəʁə	gəˈʁɛːtə	gəˈlaːgɐt	zɪnt	ɪm	ˈmɪtləʁən	bəˈʁaɪç	zɪnt	dʁaɪ
our	equipment	stored	they are	in the	middle	section	they are	three

Stühle	und	eine	kleiner	Tisch	am	Boden	festgeschraubt.	Wir
ˈʃtyːlə	ʊnt	ˈaɪnə	ˈklaɪnɐ	tɪʃ	am	ˈboːdən	ˈfɛstgəʃʁaʊpt	viːɐ
chairs	and	a	small	table	on the	floor	bolted down	we

können	ihn	als	Büro	benutzen,	sobald	wir	geparkt	sind.	Das
ˈkœnən	iːn	als	byˈʁoː	bəˈnʊtsən	zoˈbalt	viːɐ	gəˈpaʁkt	zɪnt	das
we can	it	as	office	to use	once	we	parked	we are	the

Führerhaus	hat	Platz	für	vier	Personen.
ˈfyːʁɐˌhaʊs	hat	plats	fyːɐ	fiːɐ	pɛʁˈzoːnən
driver's cab	it has	space	for	four	people

I rented all the vehicles a few days earlier. Lucia locks up the building while the kids load our luggage into the van. Anja, Roland, and Lina put on their leather jackets, jump on their motorcycles, and roar away. Sarah, Lucia, and I follow in the van. We are all excited about our trip.

Ich	habe	alle	Fahrzeuge	ein paar	Tage	vorher	gemietet.	Lucia
ɪç	ˈhaːbə	ˈalə	ˈfaːɐˌtsɔɪgə	aɪn paːɐ	ˈtaːgə	ˈfoːɐhɛɐ	gəˈmiːtət	ˈluːtsia
I →	all	vehicles	a few	days	previously	←I rented	Lucia

sperrt	das	Gebäude	ab,	während	die	Kinder	unser	Gepäck	in
ʃpɛʁt	das	gəˈbɔʏdə	ap	ˈvɛːʁənt	diː	ˈkɪndɐ	ˈʊnzɐ	gəˈpɛk	ɪn
she locks up →	the	building	←	while	the	kids	our	luggage	into

den	Lieferwagen	bringen.	Anja,	Roland	und	Lina	ziehen	ihre
deːn	ˈliːfɐˌvaːgn	ˈbʁɪŋən	ˈanja	ˈʁoːlant	ʊnt	ˈliːna	ˈtsiːən	ˈiːʁə
the	van	they bring	Anja	Roland	and	Lina	they put on →	their

Lederjacken	an,	schwingen sich	auf	ihre	Motorräder	und	donnern
ˈleːdɐˌjakən	an	ˈʃvɪŋən zɪç	aʊf	ˈiːʁə	ˈmoːtoːɐˌʁɛːdɐ	ʊnt	ˈdɔnɐn
leather jackets	←	they swing	onto	their	motorcycles	and	they roar

davon.	Sarah,	Lucia	und	ich	folgen	ihnen	im	Lieferwagen.	Wir
daˈfɔn	ˈzaːʁa	ˈluːtsia	ʊnt	ɪç	ˈfɔlgən	ˈiːnən	ɪm	ˈliːfɐˌvaːgn	viːɐ
off	Sarah	Lucia	and	I	we follow	them	in the	van	we

sind	alle	begeistert	über	den	Ausflug.
zɪnt	ˈalə	bəˈgaɪstɐt	ˈyːbɐ	deːn	ˈaʊsfluːk
we are	all	excited	about	the	trip

Later that afternoon we drive into the fair grounds where the rally is being held. We spend the next few hours checking out the concession booths set up around four large tents. For dinner, we buy an assortment of bratwursts, popcorn, and soft drinks.

Später	am	Nachmittag	fahren	wir	auf	das	Ausstellungsgelände,
ˈʃpɛːtɐ	am	ˈnaːxmɪˌtaːk	ˈfaːʁən	viːɐ	aʊf	das	ˈaʊsʃtɛlʊŋsgəˌlɛndə
later	in the	afternoon	we drive	we	to	the	fair grounds

wo	das	Treffen	stattfindet.	Die	nächsten	paar	Stunden	verbringen
voː	das	ˈtʁɛfən	ˈʃtatˌfɪndət	diː	ˈnɛçstən	paːɐ	ˈʃtʊndən	fɛɐˈbʁɪŋən
where	the	rally	it takes place	the	next	few	hours	we spend

wir	damit,	die	Imbissbuden	zu	überprüfen,	die	rings um	vier	große
viːɐ	daˈmɪt	diː	ˈɪmbɪsˌbuːdn	tsu	yːbɐˈpʁyːfən	diː	ʁɪŋs ʊm	fiːɐ	ˈgʁoːsə
we	with it	the	snack stalls	to	to check out	that	encircling	four	large

Zelte	aufgebaut sind.	Zum Abendessen	kaufen	wir	eine	Auswahl
ˈtsɛltə	ˈaʊfgəˌbaʊt zɪnt	tsʊm ˈaːbntˌɛsn	ˈkaʊfən	viːɐ	ˈaɪnə	ˈaʊsvaːl
tents	they were built	for dinner	we buy	we	an	assortment

Evolution

an	Bratwürsten,	Popcorn	und	Erfrischungsgetränken.
an	ˈbʁaːtˌvʏʁstən	ˈpɔpkɔʁn	ʊnt	ɛɐ̯ˈfʁɪʃʊŋsɡəˌtʁɛŋkn̩
of	bratwursts	popcorn	and	soft drinks

Motorradfahrer	von	überallher	beginnen	bereits	einzutreffen.	Sie
moˈtoːɐ̯ˌʁaːtˈfaːʁɐ	fɔn	yːbɐˈalˌheːɐ̯	bəˈɡɪnən	bəˈʁaɪts	ˈaɪntsuˌtʁɛfən	ziː
bikers	from	all over	they start	already	to arrive	they

Bikers from all around have already started to arrive. They look mean. I'm glad my gun is fully loaded.

sehen	gemein	aus.	Ich	bin	froh,	dass	meine	Knarre	voll	geladen
ˈzeːən	ɡəˈmaɪn	aʊs	ɪç	bɪn	fʁoː	das	ˈmaɪnə	ˈknaːʁə	fɔl	ɡəˈlaːdən
they look→	mean	←	I	I am	happy	that	my	gun	fully	loaded

ist.
ɪst
it is

Um	neun Uhr	donnern	unser	Kunde	und	seine	Gruppe
ʊm	nɔɪn uːɐ̯	ˈdɔnɐn	ˈʊnzɐ	ˈkʊndə	ʊnt	ˈzaɪnə	ˈɡʁʊpə
at	nine o'clock	they roar	our	client	and	his	group

At nine o'clock, our client and his group of scoundrels roar into the fair grounds. There are twenty of them. Nasty, ugly looking people.

von	Schurken	in	das	Ausstellungsgelände.	Ekelhafte,	hässlich
fɔn	ˈʃʊʁkən	ɪn	das	ˈaʊsˌʃtɛlʊŋsɡəˌlɛndə	ˈeːkəlhaftə	ˈhɛslɪç
of	scoundrels	into	the	fair grounds	nasty	ugly

aussehende Leute.
ˈaʊsˌzeːəndə ˈlɔɪtə
looking people

───── 15 ─────

Wir	teilen	uns	auf,	um	unsere	vier	Zielpersonen	zu
viːɐ̯	ˈtaɪlən	ʊns	aʊf	ʊm	ˈʊnzɐʁə	fiːɐ̯	ˈtsiːlpɛɐ̯ˌzoːnən	tsuː
we	we split up→	ourselves	←	in order to	our	four	targets	to

We split up to follow our four targets. My guy is pretty boring. I watch him drink a lot of beer and argue with his girlfriend as they walk around the fairgrounds. At about eleven o'clock, I hear a familiar voice behind me. I turn around and see Anja and Roland leaning against a concession stand.

verfolgen.	Mein	Typ	ist	ganz	schön	langweilig.	Ich	beobachte	ihn
fɛɐ̯ˈfɔlɡn̩	maɪn	tyːp	ɪst	ɡants	ʃøːn	ˈlaŋvaɪlɪç	ɪç	bəˈoːbaxtə	iːn
to follow	my	guy	he is	completely		boring	I	I watch	him

dabei,	wie	er	eine	Menge	Bier	trinkt	und	mit	seiner	Freundin
daˈbaɪ	viː	eːɐ̯	ˈaɪnə	ˈmɛŋə	biːɐ̯	tʁɪŋkt	ʊnt	mɪt	ˈzaɪnɐ	ˈfʁɔɪndɪn
at it	as	he		loads of	beer	he drinks	and	with	his	girlfriend

streitet,	während	sie	auf	dem	Ausstellungsgelände	herumgehen.
ˈʃtʁaɪtət	ˈvɛːʁənt	ziː	aʊf	deːm	ˈaʊsˌʃtɛlʊŋsɡəˌlɛndə	hɛˈʁʊmˌɡeːən
he argues	as	they	on	the	fair ground	they walk around

Ungefähr	um	elf Uhr	höre	ich	eine	bekannte	Stimme	hinter	mir.
ˈʊnɡəfɛːɐ̯	ʊm	ɛlf uːɐ̯	ˈhøːʁə	ɪç	ˈaɪnə	bəˈkantə	ˈʃtɪmə	ˈhɪntɐ	miːɐ̯
about	at	eleven o'clock	I hear	I	a	familiar	voice	behind	me

Ich	drehe	mich	um	und	sehe	Anja	und	Roland,	wie	sie	an	einer
ɪç	ˈdʁeːə	mɪç	ʊm	ʊnt	ˈzeːə	ˈanja	ʊnt	ˈʁoːlant	viː	ziː	an	ˈaɪnɐ
I	I turn around			and	I see	Anja	and	Roland	as	they	on	a

Imbissbude lehnen.
ˈɪmbɪsˌbuːdə ˈleːnən
snack stall they lean

Story 13

"Roland, don't eat so much cotton candy," Anja says.

»Roland, iss nicht so viel Zuckerwatte«, sagt Anja.
ʁoːlant ɪs nɪçt zoː fiːl ˈtsʊkɐˌvatə zakt ˈanja
Roland eat not so much cotton candy she says Anja

"You're not my mother," Roland tells her.

»Du bist nicht meine Mutter«, sagt Roland zu ihr.
duː bɪst nɪçt ˈmamə ˈmʊtɐ zakt ˈʁoːlant tsuː iːɐ
you you are not my mother he says Roland to her

I slide over to them.

Ich gleite zu ihnen hinüber.
ɪç ˈɡlaɪtə tsuː ˈiːnən hɪˈnyːbɐ
I I slide over→ to them ←

"I don't think you need the sunglasses, since it's already dark," I say.

»Ich glaube nicht, dass ihr Sonnenbrillen braucht, da es schon
ɪç ˈɡlaʊbə nɪçt das iːɐ ˈzɔnənˌbʁɪlən bʁaʊxt daː ɛs ʃoːn
I I think not that you sunglasses you need since it already

dunkel ist«, sage ich.
ˈdʊŋkəl ɪst ˈzaːɡə ɪç
dark it is I say I

"Yeah, but we look so cool in them," Anja responds.

»Ja schon, aber damit sehen wir so cool aus!«, antwortet Anja.
jaː ʃoːn ˈaːbɐ daˈmɪt ˈzeːən viːɐ zoː kuːl aʊs ˈantˌvɔʁtət ˈanja
yes ! but with it we look→ we so cool ← she responds Anja

"Has your guy done anything suspicious?" Roland asks.

»Hat dein Typ irgendetwas Verdächtiges gemacht?«, fragt Roland.
hat daɪn tyːp ˈɪʁɡntˌɛtvas fɛɐˈdɛçtɪɡəs ɡəˈmaxt fʁaːkt ˈʁoːlant
→ your guy anything suspicious ←he did he asks Roland

"Nothing unusual so far. He just got rid of his girlfriend and walked over to the man you are following."

»Nichts Ungewöhnliches soweit. Er ist gerade seine Freundin
nɪçts ˈʊŋɡəˌvøːnlɪçəs zoːˈvaɪt eːɐ ɪst ɡəˈʁaːdə ˈzaɪnə ˈfʁɔɪndɪn
nothing unusual so far he → just his girlfriend

losgeworden und ging hinüber zu dem Mann, dem du folgst.«
ˈlɔsɡəˌvɔʁdən ʊnt ɡɪŋ hɪˈnyːbɐ tsuː deːm man deːm duː fɔlkst
←he got rid of and he went over to the man that you you follow

"Hey, there's a member of another gang going over to talk with them," Roland says.

»He, da geht ein Mitglied einer anderen Gang hinüber,
heː daː ɡeːt aɪn ˈmɪtɡliːt ˈaɪnɐ ˈandəʁən ɡaŋ hɪˈnyːbɐ
hey there he goes over→ a member of another gang ←

um mit ihnen zu reden«, sagt Roland.
ʊm mɪt ˈiːnən tsuː ˈʁɛːdən zakt ˈʁoːlant
in order to with them to to talk he says Roland

"I'm going to get closer," Anja says.

»Ich gehe ein bisschen näher ran«, sagt Anja.
ɪç ˈɡeːə aɪn ˈbɪsçən ˈnɛːɐ ʁan zakt ˈanja
I I am going up to→ a little closer ← she says Anja

"No need," I say. "We can listen to them from here."

»Nicht notwendig«, sage ich. »Wir können ihnen von hier aus
nɪçt ˈnoːtvɛndɪç ˈzaːɡə ɪç viːɐ ˈkœnən ˈiːnən fɔn hiːɐ aʊs
not necessary I say I we we can them from here

zuhören.«
ˈtsuːˌhøːʁən
to listen to

Evolution

Ich ziehe ein kleines Gerät aus meiner Tasche und richte es auf die drei Motorradfahrer.

»Das ist das Neueste in der Mikrofontechnik«, sage ich zu ihnen, als ich mir einen kleinen Ohrhörer ins linke Ohr stecke.

»Was sagen sie?«, fragt Anja mich.

»Es scheint nicht zu funktionieren.«

»Ich dachte, du hast alle Geräte geprüft?«

»Na gut, ich habe die meisten geprüft.«

»So viel zur modernsten Technik«, sagt Anja. »Ich gehe näher ran. Schaut mal, wie ich mit der Umgebung verschmelze.«

»Ich glaube nicht, dass sie gut dazupasst«, sage ich zu Roland, als sich Anja von uns wegbewegt. »Sie hat noch alle ihre Zähne, riecht gut und ihre Fingernägel sind sauber. Sie sieht aus wie eine Fußballmutti in Lederjacke.«

I pull a small gadget out of my pocket and aim it at the three bikers.

"This is the latest in microphone technology," I tell them as I plug a little earphone into my left ear.

"What are they saying?" Anja asks me.

"It doesn't seem to be working."

"I thought you tested all the equipment."

"Well, I tested most of it."

"So much for high technology," Anja says. "I'm getting closer. Watch me blend in with the surroundings."

"I don't think she will blend in well," I tell Roland as Anja moves away from us. "She has all her teeth, smells nice, and her fingernails are clean. She looks like a soccer mom in a leather jacket."

Story 13

The bikers are standing in front of a concession booth that sells bracelets and earrings. Anja casually walks up to within a meter of the bikers and pretends to look at some of the goods. Within several minutes, the three men are staring at her. One biker says something. The others laugh. She ignores them. A second biker grabs her arm and says something else. She slaps him.

Die Motorradfahrer stehen vor einem Verkaufsstand, wo
di: ˈmoːtoːɐ̯ˌʁaːtˈfaːɐ̯ɐ ˈʃteːən foːɐ̯ ˈaɪnəm fɛɐ̯ˈkaʊfsˌʃtant voː
the bikers they stand in front of a sales stand where

Armbänder und Ohrringe verkauft werden. Anja geht lässig
ˈaʁmˌbɛndɐ ʊnt ˈoːɐ̯ˌʁɪŋə fɛɐ̯ˈkaʊft ˈveːɐ̯dn ˈanja ɡeːt ˈlɛsɪç
bracelets and earrings they are being sold Anja she walks casually

bis auf einen Meter Entfernung zu den Motorradfahrern und
bɪs aʊf ˈaɪnən ˈmeːtɐ ɛntˈfɛʁnʊŋ tsuː deːn ˈmoːtoːɐ̯ˌʁaːtˈfaːʁɐn ʊnt
to within a meter distance to the bikers and

tut so, als ob sie einige Artikel betrachten würde. Binnen einiger
tuːt zoː als ɔp ziː ˈaɪnɪɡə aʁˈtiːkəl bəˈtʁaxtn̩ ˈvʏʁdə ˈbɪnən ˈaɪnɪɡɐ
she pretends she some product she was looking at within several

Minuten starren die drei Männer sie an. Einer der Biker sagt
mɪˈnuːtən ˈʃtaʁən diː dʁaɪ ˈmɛnɐ ziː an ˈaɪnɐ deːɐ̯ ˈbaɪkɐ zakt
minutes they stare at→ the three men her ← one of the bikers he says

irgendetwas. Die anderen lachen. Ein zweiter Biker packt sie am
ˈɪʁɡn̩tˌɛtvas diː ˈandəʁən ˈlaxən aɪn ˈtsvaɪtɐ ˈbaɪkɐ pakt ziː am
something the others they laugh a second biker he grabs her on the

Arm und sagt etwas anderes. Sie klatscht ihm eine.
aʁm ʊnt zakt ˈɛtvas ˈandəʁəs ziː klatʃt iːm ˈaɪnə
arm and he says something else she she slaps him one

"Stay here," Roland says.

»Bleib hier«, sagt Roland.
blaɪp hiːɐ̯ zakt ˈʁoːlant
stay here he says Roland

He walks over to the three bikers and tries to pull Anja away. Two of them grab him. The three bikers push and pull my two partners into a nearby tent. The vendor sees what is happening, but does nothing.

Er geht hinüber zu den drei Bikern und versucht, Anja
eːɐ̯ ɡeːt hɪˈnyːbɐ tsuː deːn dʁaɪ ˈbaɪkɐn ʊnt fɛɐ̯ˈzuːxt ˈanja
he he walks over to the three bikers and he tries Anja

wegzuziehen. Zwei von ihnen halten ihn fest. Die drei Biker
ˈvɛktsuˌtsiːən tsvaɪ fɔn ˈiːnən ˈhaltən iːn fɛst diː dʁaɪ ˈbaɪkɐ
to pull away two of them they grab→ him ← the three bikers

schubsen und ziehen meine zwei Partner in ein nahegelegenes
ˈʃʊbsən ʊnt ˈtsiːən ˈmaɪnə tsvaɪ ˈpaʁtnɐ ɪn aɪn ˈnaːəɡəˌleːɡnəs
they shove and they pull my two partners in a nearby

Zelt. Der Verkäufer sieht, was passiert, aber tut nichts.
tsɛlt deːɐ̯ fɛɐ̯ˈkɔyfɐ ziːt vas paˈsiːɐ̯t ˈaːbɐ tuːt nɪçts
tent the vendor he sees what it happens but he does nothing

I walk into the tent ten seconds later.

Zehn Sekunden später gehe ich in das Zelt.
tseːn zeˈkʊndən ˈʃpɛːtɐ ˈɡeːə ɪç ɪn das tsɛlt
ten seconds later I walk I into the tent

The tent is empty except for a few musicians warming up for their next performance. One of them sees Anja and Roland struggling and yells at the bikers. The biker holding Anja lets go of her with one hand. He turns away from her to give the musician his mid-

Außer ein paar Musikern, die sich für ihre nächste Vorstellung
ˈaʊsɐ aɪn paːɐ̯ ˈmuːzɪkɐn diː zɪç fyːɐ̯ ˈiːʁə ˈnɛçstə ˈfoːɐ̯ˌʃtɛlʊŋ
except for a few musicians who → for their next performance

aufwärmen, ist das Zelt leer. Einer von ihnen sieht, wie sich Anja
ˈaʊfˌvɛʁmən ɪst das tsɛlt leːɐ̯ ˈaɪnɐ fɔn ˈiːnən ziːt viː zɪç ˈanja
←they warm up it is the tent empty one of them he sees how → Anja

Evolution

und Roland abplagen, und schreit die Biker an. Der Biker, der Anja festhält, lässt sie mit einer Hand los. Er dreht sich von ihr weg und zeigt dem Musiker den Mittelfinger. Das ist ein Fehler.

and they struggle, and they yell at the bikers. The biker who holds onto Anja lets go of her with one hand. He turns away from her and he shows the musician the middle finger. This is a mistake.

Sie holt einen kleinen Schlagstock aus ihrer Tasche hervor und schwingt ihn auf das Bein des Mannes. Der Schlagstock trifft sein Schienbein. Der Kerl brüllt und fällt auf den Boden.

She whips a little club out of her jacket pocket and swings it at the man's leg. The club smacks against his shinbone. The guy howls and drops to the ground.

Anja schwingt den Schlagstock zurück und lässt ihn auf einen der Männer sausen, der Roland festhält. Er versucht, sich zu ducken, aber Roland wehrt sich so sehr, dass er Mühe hat, auszuweichen. Der Schlagstock trifft ihn direkt an der Stirn. Er zerbröselt wie ein alter Keks.

Anja reverses her swing and whistles the club toward one of the men who is holding Roland. He tries to duck but Roland is struggling so much he has trouble moving out of the way. The club hits him directly on the forehead. He crumbles like an old cookie.

Anja dreht sich zum ersten Mann um. Er liegt am Boden und hält sein Bein. Sie stampft ihm mit ihrem Biker Stiefel auf das andere Knie und er schreit.

Anja turns back to the first man. He is on the ground holding his leg. She stomps on his other knee with her biker boots and he screams.

Story 13

The third man grabs Anja and tries to pull her away before she can do any more damage. Suddenly he falls down. He lies on the ground, twitching. I notice that Roland is holding a stun gun. Roland kicks two of the bikers as he and Anja walk away from them.

Der dritte Mann greift Anja und versucht, sie wegzuziehen, bevor sie noch mehr Schaden anrichtet. Plötzlich fällt er hin. Er liegt zuckend am Boden. Ich bemerke, dass Roland eine Elektroschockpistole in der Hand hält. Roland gibt zwei Bikern einen Fußtritt, als er und Anja sich von ihnen entfernen.

"Well, I think your cover is blown," I tell them. "Why don't you go to the food court and blend in over there."

»Nun, ich denke, ihr seid aufgeflogen«, sage ich zu ihnen. »Warum geht ihr nicht in den Essbereich und mischt euch dort unter.«

"That was great," Roland says.

»Das war großartig«, sagt Roland.

"Thanks for your help," Anja tells him, "but I had it covered."

»Danke für deine Hilfe«, sagt Anja zu ihm, »aber ich hatte es unter Kontrolle.«

As they walk away, they start arguing about whether Anja could have handled all three bikers by herself. I amble over to the musicians and introduce myself.

Als sie weggehen, fangen sie an darüber zu streiten, ob Anja alle drei Biker alleine geschafft hätte. Ich schlendere hinüber zu den Musikern und stelle mich vor.

"You guys almost had a little trouble here," I say.

»Ihr hättet beinahe ein bisschen Ärger bekommen«, sage ich.

"I hate these gigs," the guitar player says. "The bikers always make trouble."

»Ich hasse diese Auftritte«, sagt der Gitarrenspieler. »Die Biker

Evolution

fangen immer an, Ärger zu machen.«
'faŋən 'ɪmɐ an 'ɛʁgɐ tsu: 'maxən
they start → always ← trouble to to make

»Aber die Bezahlung ist gut und an der Ostsee ist es schön um
'a:bɐ di: bə'tsa:lʊŋ ɪst gu:t ʊnt an de:ɐ 'ɔstˌze: ɪst ɛs ʃøːn ʊm
but the pay it is good and on the Baltic Sea it is it nice at

diese Jahreszeit«, sagt der Schlagzeuger.
'di:zə 'ja:ʁəsˌtsaɪt zakt de:ɐ 'ʃlaːktsɔɪgɐ
this time of year he says the drummer

"But the pay is good, and the Baltic Sea is nice at this time of the year," the drummer says.

»Was passiert mit den drei Kerlen, die da drüben am Boden
vas pa'siːɐt mɪt deːn dʁaɪ 'kɛʁlən di: da'dʁyːbən am 'boːdən
what it happens with the three guys who over there on the ground

liegen?«, frage ich.
'liːgən 'fʁaːgə ɪç
they lie I ask I

"What will happen to the three guys on the ground over there?" I ask.

»Die werden irgendwann aufstehen und dann in den Wald gehen,
diː 'veːɐdn 'ɪʁgəntvan 'aʊfʃteːən ʊnt dan ɪn deːn valt 'geːən
they they will eventually to get up and then in the woods to go

um high zu werden.«
ʊm haɪ tsuː 'veːɐdn
in order to to get high

"Eventually they'll get up and go off into the woods to get high."

»Einer von ihnen ist total weg«, erwähne ich.
'aɪnɐ fɔn 'iːnən ɪst to'taːl vɛk ɛɐ'vɛːnə ɪç
one of them he is totally gone I mention I

"One of them is out cold," I mention.

»Es fährt so jede halbe Stunde ein Wagen vom
ɛs fɛːɐt zoː 'jeːdə 'halbə 'ʃtʊndə aɪn 'vaːgn fɔm
it it drives by → so every half hour a vehicle from the

Sicherheitsdienst vorbei. Wenn er dann noch immer dort ist,
'zɪçɐhaɪtsˌdiːnst foːɐ'baɪ vɛn eːɐ dan nɔx 'ɪmɐ dɔʁt ɪst
security agency ← if he then still there he is

werden sie ihn zur Erste-Hilfe-Station mitnehmen.«
'veːɐdn ziː iːn tsuːɐ 'eːɐstə-'hɪlfə-ʃta'tsjoːn 'mɪtˌneːmən
they will they him to the first aid station to take with

"There is a security vehicle that swings by every half hour. If he's still here, they'll take him for first aid."

»Ich glaube, ich werde über das Mädchen mit dem Schlagstock ein
ɪç 'glaʊbə ɪç 'veːɐdə 'yːbɐ das 'mɛːtçən mɪt deːm 'ʃlaːkˌʃtɔk aɪn
I I think I I will about the girl with the club a

Lied schreiben«, sagt der Schlagzeuger. »Sie war erstaunlich.«
liːt 'ʃʁaɪbən zakt de:ɐ 'ʃlaːktsɔɪgɐ ziː va:ɐ ɛɐ'ʃtaʊnlɪç
song to write he says the drummer she she was amazing

"I think I'm going to write a song about that girl with the club," the drummer says. "She was amazing."

—16—

Am nächsten Morgen vergleichen wir unsere Notizen.
am 'nɛçstən 'mɔʁgn fɛɐ'glaɪçən viːɐ 'ʊnzəʁə no'tiːtsən
on the next morning we compare we our notes

The next morning we compare notes.

Story 13

"The guy in charge of the drug sales is not stealing," Sarah says.

»Der Kerl, der für den Drogenverkauf verantwortlich ist, klaut nicht«, sagt Sarah.

"How do you know?" Lucia asks.

»Woher weißt du das?«, fragt Lucia.

"Lina and I checked out the operation last night. He's a good manager. Two men keep a log of how much they give to each runner and how much cash the runner brings back. It would be impossible for anyone involved to steal anything."

»Lina und ich überprüften gestern Abend den Arbeitsablauf. Er ist ein guter Manager. Zwei Männer führen Buch darüber, wie viel sie jedem Drogenkurier geben und wie viel Bargeld der Drogenkurier zurückbringt. Es wäre für jeden, der in der Sache involviert ist, unmöglich, auch nur irgendetwas zu stehlen.«

"Anja and Roland put their man in the hospital with a broken kneecap. And they gave my man a concussion. Those men didn't do any stealing last night," I say.

»Anja und Roland schickten ihren Mann mit einer gebrochenen Kniescheibe ins Krankenhaus. Dazu verpassten sie meinem Mann eine Gehirnerschütterung. Diese Männer haben gestern Abend nichts gestohlen«, sage ich.

Lucia has already forgiven Anja and Roland for their fight with the bikers. She blames me for the whole thing. Just because that microphone didn't work.

Lucia hat Anja und Roland bereits für ihren Kampf mit den Bikern verziehen. Sie gibt mir die Schuld an allem. Bloß weil das Mikrofon nicht funktionierte.

Evolution

»Der Mann, den ich verfolgte, ist der Dieb«, sagt Lucia. »Er ist für das Prostitutionsgeschäft zuständig.«

"The man I followed is the thief," Lucia says. "He's in charge of the prostitution business."

»Ich habe keine Prostituierten gesehen«, sagt Roland.

"I didn't see any prostitutes," Roland says.

»Sie kamen in einem separaten Kleinbus. Die Gang hat fünfzehn Zelte hinten im Wald aufgestellt. Die Mädchen haben von den Zelten aus gearbeitet. Sie machten ein florierendes Geschäft.«

"They arrived in a separate minivan. The gang set up fifteen tents back in the woods. The girls operated out of the tents. They did a booming business."

»Wieso hat mir niemand etwas von diesen Zelten gesagt?«, will ich wissen.

"Why wasn't I told about these tents?" I demand to know.

»Woher willst du wissen, dass der Zuständige gestohlen hat?«, fragt Sarah.

"How do you know the man in charge was stealing?" Sarah asks.

»Ich habe die Anzahl der Männer und Frauen gezählt, die in die jeweiligen Zelte gingen«, sagt Lucia. »Ich schätzte den Gesamtbetrag, den die Prostituierten verdienten, indem ich die Zahl der Kunden mit den Kosten jeder Transaktion multiplizierte. Der Mann, der die Operation leitet, hat weniger als fünfzig Prozent

"I counted the number of men and women who went into each tent," Lucia says. "I estimated the total amount of money the prostitutes earned by multiplying the number of customers by the cost of each transaction. The man who runs the operation turned in less than fifty percent of my estimate."

277

Story 13

	meiner Schätzung abgeliefert.«	
	'maɪnɐ ˈʃɛtsʊŋ 'apgəˌliːfɐt	
	of my estimate ←he turned in	

"Why couldn't the president of the club figure this out?" I ask.

»Wieso konnte der Geschäftsführer des Clubs das nicht
viˈzoː ˈkɔntə deːɐ gəˈʃɛftsˌfyːɐɐ dɛs klʊps das nɪçt
why   he could the   manager   of the club that not

herausfinden?«, frage ich.
hɛˈʁaʊsˌfɪndn̩ ˈfʁaːgə ɪç
to figure out   I ask   I

"He was dead drunk an hour after the gang arrived. There was no way he could know how many customers were serviced."

»Er war eine Stunde, nachdem die Gang angekommen war,
eːɐ vaːɐ ˈaɪnə ˈʃtʊndə naːxˈdeːm diː gaŋ ˈangəˌkɔmən vaːɐ
he   he was an   hour   after   the gang they had arrived

total blau. Er hätte niemals wissen können, wie viele Kunden
toˈtaːl blaʊ eːɐ ˈhɛtə ˈniːmaːls ˈvɪsən ˈkœnən viː ˈfiːlə ˈkʊndən
totally drunk he   →   never   ←he could have known how many clients

bedient wurden.«
bəˈdiːɛnt ˈvʊʁdən
they were serviced

A few hours later, I throw a mind haze at the man in charge of the prostitutes and pull him into our van. Lucia talks with him for ten minutes and records his answers.

Ein paar Stunden später verpasse ich dem Mann, der für die
aɪn paːɐ ˈʃtʊndən ˈʃpɛːtɐ fɛɐˈpasə ɪç deːm man deːɐ fyːɐ diː
a few   hours   later   I inflict I   the   man   who   for   the

Prostituierten verantwortlich ist, eine Bewusstseinstrübung und
pʁɔstituˈiːɐtn̩ fɛɐˈantvɔʁtlɪç ɪst ˈaɪnə bəˈvʊstˌzaɪnstʁyːbʊŋ ʊnt
prostitutes   resposible   he is a   mind fog   and

ziehe ihn in unseren Lieferwagen. Lucia spricht mit ihm zehn
ˈtsiːə iːn ɪn ˈʊnzəʁən ˈliːfɐˌvaːgn̩ luˈtsia ʃpʁɪçt mɪt iːm tseːn
I pull him into our   van   Lucia   she speaks with him ten

Minuten lang und zeichnet seine Antworten auf.
mɪˈnuːtən laŋ ʊnt ˈtsaɪçnət ˈzaɪnə ˈantvɔʁtən aʊf
minutes   long and she records→ his   answers   ←

Remember I told you that she can get the truth out of anyone? The man tells her how long he has been stealing, how much he has stolen, and the location of the safe deposit box where he keeps the money.

Erinnern Sie sich noch daran, dass sie die Wahrheit aus jedem
ɛɐˈɪnɐn ziː zɪç nɔx daˈʁan das ziː diː ˈvaːɐhaɪt aʊs ˈjeːdəm
you remember still on it   that she the truth   out of anyone

herausbekommen kann? Der Mann sagt ihr, wie lange er schon
hɛˈʁaʊsbəˌkɔmən kan deːɐ man zaːkt iːɐ viː ˈlaŋə eːɐ ʃoːn
to pull out   she can the man he tells her how   long he already

stiehlt, wie viel er gestohlen hat und wo sich das Tresorfach
ʃtiːlt viː fiːl eːɐ gəˈʃtoːlən hat ʊnt voː zɪç das tʁeˈzoːɐˌfax
he steals how much he he stole   and where → the safe deposit box

befindet, in dem er das Geld aufbewahrt.
bəˈfɪndət ɪn deːm eːɐ das gɛlt ˈaʊfbəˌvaːɐt
←it is located in   which he the money he keeps

After the interrogation, I eliminate Lucia's voice from the recording. Then I make two copies so that Sarah can

Nach dem Verhör entferne ich Lucias Stimme von der
naːx deːm fɛɐˈhøːɐ ɛntˈfɛʁnə ɪç luˈtsias ˈʃtɪmə fɔn deːɐ
after the interrogation I eliminate I Lucia's voice from the

278

Evolution

German	IPA	Gloss
Aufzeichnung.	ˈaʊfˌtsaɪçnʊŋ	recording
Dann	dan	then
mache	ˈmaxə	I make
ich	ɪç	I
zwei	tsvaɪ	two
Kopien,	koˈpiːən	copies
damit	daˈmɪt	so that
Sarah	ˈzaːʁa	Sarah
eine davon	aɪnə daˈfɔn	one of them
ihrem	ˈiːʁəm	to her
Kunden	ˈkʊndən	clients
geben	ˈgeːbən	to give
kann.	kan	she can
Schließlich	ˈʃliːslɪç	finally
bringe	ˈbʁɪŋə	I muddle →
ich	ɪç	I
das	das	the
Gedächtnis	gəˈdɛçtnɪs	memory
des	dɛs	of the
Bikers	ˈbaikɐs	biker
durcheinander	dʊʁçaɪˈnandɐ	←
und	ʊnt	and
dann	dan	then
lasse	ˈlasə	I get
ich	ɪç	
ihn	iːn	him
einschlafen.	ˈaɪnˌʃlaːfn	to go to sleep

give one to her client. Finally, I scramble the biker's memory, and then I put him to sleep.

German	IPA	Gloss
Wenn	vɛn	when
er	eːɐ	he
aufwacht,	ˈaʊfˌvaxt	he wakes up
wird	vɪʁt	he will
er	eːɐ	he
denken,	ˈdɛŋkən	to think
ein	aɪn	a
furchterregender	ˈfʊʁçtɐˌʁeːgəndɐ	scary
Kerl	kɛʁl	guy
mittleren	ˈmɪtləʁən	middle
Alters	ˈaltɐs	aged
hätte	ˈhɛtə	→ → →
ihn	iːn	him
in	ɪn	in
einen	ˈaɪnən	a
Lieferwagen	ˈliːfɐˌvaːgn	van
gezerrt,	gəˈtsɛʁt	← he would have dragged
gefesselt	gəˈfɛslt	← he would have tied up
und	ʊnt	and
gedroht,	gəˈdʁoːt	← he would have threatened
ihm	iːm	him
ein	aɪn	a
Messer	ˈmɛsɐ	knife
in	ɪn	in
den	deːn	the
Augapfel	ˈaʊkˌapfl	eyeball
zu	tsuː	to
stoßen,	ˈʃtoːsən	to thrust
wenn	vɛn	if
er	eːɐ	he
kein	kaɪn	not a
volles	ˈfɔləs	full
Geständnis	gəˈʃtɛntnɪs	confession
ablegen	ˈapˌleːgn	he would confess
würde.	ˈvʏʁdə	

When he wakes up, he will think that some scary middle aged dude dragged him into a van, tied him up and threatened to stick a knife into his eyeball unless he made a full confession.

German	IPA	Gloss
Lucia	ˈluːtsia	Lucia
entfernt sich	ɛntˈfɛʁnt zɪç	she takes off
und	ʊnt	and
ich	ɪç	I
rufe	ˈʁuːfə	I call →
Sarah	ˈzaːʁa	Sarah
am	am	on the
Handy	ˈhɛndi	cell phone
an.	an	←
Ein paar	aɪn paːɐ	a few
Minuten	mɪˈnuːtən	minutes
später	ˈʃpɛːtɐ	later
bringt	bʁɪŋt	she brings
sie	ziː	she
den	deːn	the
Vorsitzenden	ˈfoːɐˌzɪtsndən	president
des	dɛs	of the
Motorradclubs	ˈmoːtoːɐˌʁaːtˌklʊps	motorcycle club
in	ɪn	into
den	deːn	the
Lieferwagen.	ˈliːfɐˌvaːgn	van

Lucia takes off, and I call Sarah on the cell phone. A few minutes later she brings the president of the motorcycle club into the van.

German	IPA	Gloss
»Wer	veːɐ	who
ist	ɪst	he is
dieser	ˈdiːzɐ	this
Typ?«,	tyːp	guy
fragt	fʁaːkt	he asks
er,	eːɐ	he
als	als	when
er	eːɐ	he
mich	mɪç	me
sieht.	ziːt	he sees

"Who is this guy?" he asks when he sees me.

German	IPA	Gloss
»Ich	ɪç	I
bin	bɪn	I am
ihr	iːɐ	her
angeheuerter	ˈangəˌhɔɪɐtɐ	hired
Schläger«,	ˈʃlɛːgɐ	puncher
sage	ˈzaːgə	I say
ich	ɪç	I
zu	tsuː	to
ihm.	iːm	him

"I'm her hired muscle," I tell him.

German	IPA	Gloss
»Du	duː	you
siehst	ziːst	you look →
nicht	nɪçt	not
so	zoː	so
hart	haʁt	tough
aus.«	aʊs	←

"You don't look so tough."

German	IPA	Gloss
»Aber	ˈaːbɐ	but
immerhin	ˈɪmɐˌhɪn	at least
hart	haʁt	tough
genug,	gəˈnuːk	enough
um	ʊm	in order to
ein	aɪn	a
volles	ˈfɔləs	full
Geständnis	gəˈʃtɛntnɪs	confession
von	fɔn	from

"Tough enough to get a full confession from your man. Here's the recording."

Story 13

	deinem	Mann	zu	erhalten.	Hier	ist	die	Aufnahme.«
	ˈdaɪnəm	man	tsuː	ɛɐ̯ˈhaltn̩	hiːɐ̯	ɪst	diː	ˈaʊfˌnaːmə
	your	man	to	to obtain	here	it is	the	recording

He looks at his associate who is tied up and sleeping in the corner of the van.

Er	schaut	auf	seinen	Mitarbeiter,	der	gefesselt	ist,	und	in	der
eːɐ̯	ʃaʊt	aʊf	ˈzaɪnən	ˈmɪtaɐ̯ˌbaɪtɐ	deːɐ̯	ɡəˈfɛsəlt	ɪst	ʊnt	ɪn	deːɐ̯
he	he looks	at	his	associate	who	tied up	he is	and	in	the

Ecke	des	Wagens	schläft.
ˈɛkə	dɛs	ˈvaːɡəns	ʃlɛːft
corner	of the	van	he sleeps

"What did you do to him?"

»Was	habt	ihr	mit	ihm	gemacht?«
vas	haːpt	iːɐ̯	mɪt	iːm	ɡəˈmaxt
what	→	you	with	him	← you have done

"Trust me, you don't want to know."

»Glaub	mir,	das	willst	du	nicht	wissen.«
ɡlaʊp	miːɐ̯	das	vɪlst	duː	nɪçt	ˈvɪsən
trust	me	that	you want	you	not	to know

The head of the gang is very happy after he plays the recording. He pulls a wad of hundred Euro bills from his pocket and pays Sarah. Then he drags his man out of the van and gives him to a few associates. I notice Sarah crying a little bit after the bikers leave.

Der	Kopf	der	Bande	ist	sehr	glücklich,	nachdem	er	die	Aufnahme
deːɐ̯	kɔpf	deːɐ̯	ˈbandə	ɪst	zeːɐ̯	ˈɡlʏklɪç	naːxˈdeːm	eːɐ̯	das	ˈaʊfˌnaːmə
the	head	of the	gang	he is	very	happy	after	he	the	recording

abgespielt	hat.	Er	zieht	ein	Bündel	Hundert-Euro-Scheine	aus
ˈapɡəˌʃpiːlt hat		eːɐ̯	tsiːt	aɪn	ˈbʏndəl	ˈhʊndɐt-ˈɔɪʁo-ˌʃaɪnə	aʊs
he played		he	he pulls	a	wad	hundred Euro bills	out of

seiner	Tasche	und	bezahlt	Sarah.	Dann	schleppt	er	seinen	Mann
ˈzaɪnɐ	ˈtaʃə	ʊnt	bəˈtsaːlt	ˈzaʁa	dan	ʃlɛpt	eːɐ̯	ˈzaɪnən	man
his	pocket	and	he pays	Sarah	then	he drags	he	his	man

aus	dem	Lieferwagen	und	übergibt	ihn	ein	paar	Mitarbeitern.
aʊs	deːm	ˈliːfɐˌvaːɡn̩	ʊnt	yːbɐˈɡiːpt	iːn	aɪn	paːɐ̯	ˈmɪtaɐ̯ˌbaɪtɐn
out of	the	van	and	he gives over to	him	a few		associates

Ich	bemerke,	wie	Sarah	ein	wenig	weint,	als	die	Biker	uns
ɪç	bəˈmɛʁkə	viː	ˈzaʁa	aɪn	ˈveːnɪç	vaɪnt	als	diː	ˈbaɪkɐ	ʊns
I	I notice	how	Sarah	a	little	she cries	as	the	bikers	us

verlassen.
fɛɐ̯ˈlasən
they leave

"What's the matter?"

»Was	ist	los?«
vas	ɪst	loːs
what's the matter		

"They are going to kill that man. I should have turned him over to the police."

»Sie	werden	diesen	Mann	umbringen.	Ich	hätte	ihn	der	Polizei
ziː	ˈveːɐ̯dn̩	ˈdiːzən	man	ˈʊmˌbʁɪŋən	ɪç	ˈhɛtə	iːn	deːɐ̯	poliˈtsaɪ
they	they will	the	guy	to kill	I	→	him	the	police

übergeben	sollen.«
yːbɐˈɡeːbn̩	ˈzɔlən
← I should have given over to	

»Wenn du ihn nicht der Gang überlassen hättest, hätten sie	vɛn du: i:n nɪçt deːɐ gaŋ yːbɐˈlasn ˈhɛtəst ˈhɛtən ziː	if you him not the gang you had delivered to → they
versucht, uns zu töten«, sage ich zu ihr. »Außerdem hat	fɛɐˈzuːxt ʊns tsuː ˈtøːtən ˈzaːgə ɪç tsuː iːɐ ˈaʊsɐdeːm hat	←the would have tried us to to kill I say I to her besides →
mir der Kerl während des Verhörs erzählt, dass er an einigen	miːɐ deːɐ kɛʁl ˈvɛːʁənt dɛs fɛɐˈhøːɐs ɛɐˈtsɛːlt das eːɐ an ˈaɪnɪgən	me the guy during the interrogation ←he told that he of a few
Morden schuld ist, wovon niemand etwas weiß.«	ˈmɔʁdən ʃʊlt ɪst voˈfɔn ˈniːmant ˈɛtvas vaɪs	murders guilty he is about which nobody anything he knows

"If you didn't give him to the gang, they would have tried to kill us," I tell her. "Besides, the guy told me during the interrogation that he was guilty of a few murders that nobody knows about. So he is getting a rough form of justice."

»Ich fühle mich immer noch nicht wohl dabei.«	ɪç ˈfyːlə mɪç ˈɪmɐ nɔx nɪçt voːl daˈbaɪ	I I feel still not well about it

"I still feel bad about it."

Gerade in diesem Moment kommen Lucia und der Rest unserer	gəˈʁaːdə ɪn ˈdiːzəm moˈmɛnt ˈkɔmən luˈtsia ʊnt deːɐ ʁɛst ˈʊnzəʁɐ	just in that moment she arrives Lucia and the rest of our
Gruppe. Roland trägt eine große Packung Popcorn und eine	ˈgʁʊpə ˈʁoːlant tʁɛkt ˈaɪnə ˈgʁoːsə ˈpakʊŋ ˈpɔpkɔʁn ʊnt ˈaɪnə	group Roland he carries a big package popcorn and a
große Flasche Coca-Cola.	ˈgʁoːsə ˈflaʃə ˈkoːkaˈkoːla	big bottle Coca Cola

Just then, Lucia and the rest of our group shows up. Roland is carrying a big bag of popcorn and a big bottle of Coca Cola.

»Können wir hier bleiben, bis das Bikertreffen vorbei ist?«, fragt	ˈkœnən viːɐ hiːɐ ˈblaɪbən bɪs das ˈbaɪkɐˌtʁɛfn foːɐˈbaɪ ɪst fʁaːkt	can we we here to stay until the biker rally over it is she asks
Lina.	ˈliːna	Lina

"Can we stay here for the rest of the rally?" Lina asks.

»Klar, gebt die Motorräder am Sonntag beim Verleih ab und	klaːɐ gəpt diː ˈmoːtoːɐˌʁɛːdɐ am ˈzɔntaːk baɪm fɛɐˈlaɪ ap ʊnt	sure drop off→ the motorcycles on Sunday at the rental shop ← and
wir holen euch dort ab«, sagt Lucia.	viːɐ ˈhoːlən ɔɪç dɔʁt ap zakt luˈtsia	we we pick up→ you there ← she says Lucia

"Sure, drop off the motorcycles at the rental shop on Sunday and we'll pick you up there," Lucia says.

Sarah unterhält sich mit Lucia ein paar Minuten lang und	ˈzaːʁa ʊntɐˈhɛlt zɪç mɪt luˈtsia aɪn paːɐ mɪˈnuːtən laŋ ʊnt	Sarah she talks with Lucia a few minutes long and
entschließt sich, ein Auto zu mieten und alleine wieder zurück	ɛntˈʃliːst zɪç aɪn ˈaʊto tsuː ˈmiːtən ʊnt aˈlaɪnə ˈviːdɐ tsuˈʁʏk	she decides a car to to rent and alone back
nach Berlin zu fahren.	naːx bɛɐˈliːn tsuː ˈfaːʁən	to Berlin to to drive

Sarah talks with Lucia for a few minutes and decides to rent a car and drive back to Berlin alone.

Story 13

"She needs some time to herself," Lucia tells me a few minutes later.

»Sie braucht etwas Zeit für sich selbst«, sagt mir Lucia ein paar
zi: bʁaʊxt ˈɛtvas tsaɪt fyːɐ zɪç zɛlpst zakt miːɐ luˈtsia aɪn paːɐ
she she needs some time for herself he tells to me Lucia a few

Minuten später.
mɪˈnuːtən ˈʃpɛːtɐ
minutes later

"It's not like she shot the guy in the head," I say. "She had to give him to the gang."

»Es ist ja nicht so, als hätte sie dem Typen in den Kopf
ɛs ɪst jaː nɪçt zoː als ˈhɛtə ziː deːm ˈtyːpən ɪn deːn kɔpf
it it is ! not as if → she the guy in the head

geschossen«, sage ich. »Sie musste ihn der Gang überlassen.«
ɡəˈʃɔsən ˈzaːɡə ɪç ziː ˈmʊstə iːn deːɐ ɡaŋ yːbɐˈlasn̩
← she would have shot I say I she she had to him to the gang to deliver

"But she is still very upset."

»Aber sie ist immer noch sehr beunruhigt.«
ˈaːbɐ ziː ɪst ˈɪmɐ nɔx zeːɐ bəˈʊnˌʁuːɪçt
but she she is still very upset

Lucia and I drive away in the van. We decide to spend the night at a little cute bed and breakfast in Neuruppin.

Lucia und ich fahren mit dem Lieferwagen davon.
luˈtsia ʊnt ɪç ˈfaːʁən mɪt deːm ˈliːfɐˌvaːɡn̩ daˈfɔn
Lucia and I we drive away→ with the van ←

Wir beschließen, die Nacht in einer kleinen, niedlichen
viːɐ bəˈʃliːsən diː naxt ɪn ˈaɪnɐ ˈklaɪnən ˈniːtlɪçn̩
we we decide the night in a little cute

Frühstückspension in Neuruppin zu verbringen.
ˈfʁyːʃtʏkspɑ̃ˌzjoːn ɪn nɔɪʁʊˈpiːn tsuː fɛɐˈbʁɪŋən
bed and breakfast in Neuruppin to to spend

"You know," I tell Lucia, "it would have been easier if you had just interrogated each of the four gang members in private. You could have got all the answers without us having to spend the weekend at the biker rally."

»Weißt du«, sage ich zu Lucia, »es wäre leichter gewesen,
vaɪst duː ˈzaːɡə ɪç tsuː luˈtsia ɛs ˈvɛːʁə ˈlaɪçtɐ ɡəˈveːzən
you know you I say I to Lucia it → easier ← it would have been

wenn du einfach jeden der vier Gangmitglieder unter vier Augen
vɛn duː ˈaɪnfax ˈjeːdən deːɐ fiːɐ ˈɡaŋˌmɪtɡliːdɐ ˈʊntɐ fiːɐ ˈaʊɡən
if you simply each of the four gang members in private

befragt hättest. Du hättest alle Antworten erhalten, ohne dass
bəˈfʁaːkt ˈhɛtəst duː ˈhɛtəst ˈalə ˈantvɔʁtən ɛɐˈhaltn̩ ˈoːnə das
you had interrogated you → all answers ← you could have got without that

wir das Wochenende auf dem Bikertreffen verbringen müssen.«
viːɐ das ˈvɔxn̩ˌɛndə aʊf deːm ˈbaɪkɐˌtʁɛfn̩ fɛɐˈbʁɪŋən ˈmʏsən
we the weekend at the biker rally to have to spend

"If I had done it that way, both Sarah and the gang leader would have realized that I have special abilities."

»Wenn ich das so gemacht hätte, hätten Sarah und
vɛn ɪç das zoː ɡəˈmaxt ˈhɛtə ˈhɛtən ˈzaːʁa ʊnt
if I that that way I had done → Sarah and

der Gangleiter alle beide bemerkt, dass ich besondere
deːɐ ˈɡaŋˌlaɪtɐ ˈalə ˈbaɪdə bəˈmɛʁkt das ɪç bəˈzɔndɐə
the gang leader both ← they would have noticed that I special

Fähigkeiten besitze.«
ˈfɛːɪçkaɪtən bəˈzɪtsə
abilities I possess

Evolution

»Stimmt«, sage ich.
ʃtɪmt ˈzaːɡə ɪç
right I say I

"Right," I say.

»Außerdem war es ein amüsantes Wochenende. Den Kindern
ˈaʊsɐdeːm vaːɐ ɛs aɪn amyˈzantəs ˈvɔxnˌɛndə deːn ˈkɪndɐn
in addition it was it an enjoyable weekend the kids

hat es viel Spaß gemacht, Lederjacken zu tragen und auf riesigen
hat ɛs fiːl ʃpas ɡəˈmaxt ˈleːdɐjakən tsuː ˈtʁaːɡən ʊnt aʊf ˈʁiːzɪɡən
it was lots of fun leather jackets to to wear and on giant

Motorrädern umherzufahren«, sagt Lucia.
ˈmoːtoːɐˌʁɛːdɐn ʊmˈheːɐtsuˌfaːʁən zakt luˈtsia
motorcycles to drive around on she says Lucia

"Plus, it was a fun weekend. The kids really enjoyed wearing leather jackets and driving around on giant motorcycles," Lucia says.

»Sarah behielt eine Kopie des Geständnisses für sich«, sagt mir
ˈzaːʁa bəˈhiːlt aɪnə koːˈpiː dɛs ɡəˈʃtɛntnɪsəs fyːɐ zɪç zakt miːɐ
Sarah she kept a copy of the confession for herself she tells me

Lucia ein paar Minuten später. »Sie hat vor, es der Polizei zu
luˈtsia aɪn paːɐ mɪˈnuːtən ˈʃpɛːtɐ ziː hat foːɐ ɛs deːɐ poliˈtsaɪ tsuː
Lucia a few minutes later she she plans it the police to

geben, mitsamt anderen Beweisen über illegale Tätigkeiten der
ˈɡeːbən mɪtˈzamt ˈandəʁən bəˈvaɪzən ˈyːbɐ ɪleˈɡaːlə ˈtɛːtɪçˌkaɪtn deːɐ
to give along with other evidence about illegal operations of the

Gang, die sie dieses Wochenende gesammelt hat.«
ɡaŋ diː ziː ˈdiːzəs ˈvɔxnˌɛndə ɡəˈzamlt hat
gang that she this weekend she collected

"Sarah kept a copy of the confession for herself," Lucia tells me a few minutes later. "She plans to give it to the police, along with other evidence of the gang's illegal activities that she collected this weekend."

»Achte darauf, dass sie ein paar Monate wartet und dass sie es
ˈaxtə daˈʁaʊf das ziː aɪn paːɐ ˈmoːnatə ˈvaʁtət ʊnt das ziː ɛs
make sure that she a few months she waits and that she it

so macht, dass die Gang es nicht zu ihr zurückverfolgen kann«,
zoː maxt das diː ɡaŋ ɛs nɪçt tsuː iːɐ tsuˈʁʏkfɛɐˌfɔlɡn kan
such she does that the gang it not to her to trace back it can

sage ich.
ˈzaːɡə ɪç
I say I

"Make sure she waits a few months and does it in a way that the gang can't trace it back to her," I say.

»Werde ich tun.«
ˈveːɐdə ɪç tuːn
I will I to do

"I will."

---17---

Der Mittwoch bringt gute Nachrichten.
deːɐ ˈmɪtˌvɔx bʁɪŋt ˈɡuːtə ˈnaːxˌʁɪçtn
Wednesday it brings good news

Wednesday brings good news.

»Roland fand die Namen und die Bilder von drei
ˈʁoːlant fant diː ˈnaːmən ʊnt diː ˈbɪldɐ fɔn dʁaɪ
Roland he found the names and the pictures of three

"Roland found the names and pictures of three additional Ukrainians who might be part of the extortion gang,"

Story 13

Anja says.

»weiteren Ukrainern, die möglicherweise in der Erpressungsgang involviert sind«, sagt Anja.

"How did he do that?" Lina asks.

»Wie hat er das gemacht?«, fragt Lina.

"He wrote a program that checked Aeroflot passenger records and compared them to Ukrainian police databases. The program identified four men with criminal records who flew into this country via Aeroflot in the last year. The man Lucia interrogated near the airport was one of them. The other three come from the same city."

»Er hat ein Programm geschrieben, welches die Daten von Aeroflot-Passagieren mit der Datenbank der ukrainischen Polizei abglich. Das Programm identifizierte vier vorbestrafte Männer, die mit Aeroflot letztes Jahr in dieses Land eingeflogen sind. Der Mann, den Lucia in der Nähe des Flughafens verhörte, war einer von ihnen. Die anderen drei kommen aus der gleichen Stadt.«

"Do we know what the three other men look like?" Lina asks.

»Wissen wir, wie die anderen drei Männer aussehen?«, fragt Lina.

"Yes," says Anja. "Luckily, Aeroflot documents every passenger's photo identification."

»Ja«, sagt Anja. »Glücklicherweise dokumentiert Aeroflot den Lichtbildausweis jedes Passagiers.«

"I'm really not looking forward to spending weeks showing pictures of these guys to people all over Berlin," I say.

»Ich freue mich nicht darauf, wochenlang die Bilder dieser Typen Leuten in ganz Berlin zu zeigen«, sage ich.

284

Evolution

»Die ukrainischen Einwanderer in Berlin sind in zwei sehr kleinen Gebieten konzentriert«, sagt Lucia zu mir. »Es wird nicht lange dauern, sie zu finden.«

"The Ukrainian immigrants in Berlin are concentrated in two very small areas," Lucia tells me. "It won't take too long to find them."

An diesem Abend fahren Lina, Sarah und ich in den ukrainischen Stadtteil. Wir fahren in separaten Autos.

That night, Lina, Sarah and I drive to the Ukrainian district. We drive in separate cars.

Lina treibt sich in Billardkneipen herum. Sarah überprüft die Lebensmittelgeschäfte und Waschsalons. Ich nehme mich der Bars und der Stripclubs an. In der ersten Nacht hatten wir kein Glück.

Lina hangs out in pool bars. Sarah checks the grocery stores and laundromats. I work the bars and strip clubs. No luck that first night.

»Ich traf in der Billardkneipe zwei Automechaniker, die mich heiraten wollen«, sagt mir Lina am Handy, als ich nach Hause fahre.

"I met two auto mechanics at the pool bar who want to marry me," Lina tells me on the cell phone as I drive home.

In der zweiten Nacht probieren wir dieselbe Gegend. Sarah ruft mich um zwei Uhr morgens an.

We try the same area the second night. Sarah calls me at two a.m.

»Hast du irgendwas gefunden?«, fragt sie.

"Did you find anything?" she asks.

»Niemand erkennt sie auf den Bildern«, sage ich zu ihr.

"Nobody recognizes them from the pictures," I tell her.

Story 13

"Did you get a lap dance?" she asks.

»Hast du einen Lapdance bekommen?«, fragt sie.
hast du: 'aɪnən 'lapˌdants bə'kɔmən fʁa:kt zi:
→ you a lap dance ←you got she asks she

"The ladies who dance in these clubs aren't my type," I tell her. "And a few bartenders offered to rearrange my nose if I didn't stop bothering their customers."

»Die Damen, die in diesen Klubs tanzen, sind nicht mein Typ«,
di: 'da:mən di: ɪn 'di:zən klʊps 'tantsən zɪnt nɪçt maɪn ty:p
the ladies who in these clubs they dance they are not my type

sage ich zu ihr. »Und einige Barkeeper drohten, sie würden
'za:gə ɪç tsu: i:ɐ ʊnt 'aɪnɪgə 'ba:ɐˌki:pɐ 'dʁo:tn zi: 'vyʁdn
I say I to her and a few bartenders they threatened they they would

mir die Nase umgestalten, wenn ich nicht aufhören würde, ihre
mi:ɐ di: 'na:zə 'ʊmgəˌʃtaltn vɛn ɪç nɪçt 'aʊfˌhø:ʁən 'vʏʁdə 'i:ʁə
for me the nose to rearrange if I not I would stop their

Kunden zu belästigen.«
'kʊndən tsu: bə'lɛstɪgən
customers to to bother

"How exciting," Sarah says.

»Wie aufregend«, sagt Sarah.
vi: 'aʊfˌʁe:gnt zakt 'za:ʁa
how exciting she says Sarah

"Where are you now?" I ask.

»Wo bist du gerade?«, frage ich.
vo: bɪst du: gə'ʁa:də 'fʁa:gə ɪç
where are you you currently I ask I

"Helping Lina show the pictures at the pool bars."

»Ich helfe Lina, die Bilder in den Billardkneipen herumzuzeigen.«
ɪç 'hɛlfə 'li:na di: 'bɪldɐ ɪn de:n 'bɪljaʁtˌknaɪpən hɛ'ʁʊmtsuˌtsaɪgn
I I help Lina the pictures in the pool bars to show around

"Are you having fun?"

»Amüsiert ihr euch?«
amy'zi:ɐt i:ɐ ɔɪç
you amuse you yourselves

"A guy named Georgi taught me to hold the cue."

»Ein Kerl mit dem Namen Georgi zeigte mir, wie man den
aɪn kɛʁl mɪt de:m 'na:mən ge'ɔʁgi: 'tsaɪktə mi:ɐ vi: man de:n
a guy with the name Georgi he showed to me how one the

Billardstock hält.«
'bɪljaʁtˌʃtɔk hɛlt
(pool) cue he holds

"Nice. You can go on tour in a few years."

»Schön, in ein paar Jahren kannst du auf Tour gehen.«
ʃø:n ɪn aɪn pa:ɐ 'ja:ʁən kanst du: aʊf tu:ɐ 'ge:ən
nice in a few years you can you on tour to go

"Georgi says I don't have enough concentration."

»Georgi sagt, dass ich mich nicht genügend konzentriere.«
ge'ɔʁgi: zakt das ɪç mɪç nɪçt gə'ny:gənt kɔntsɛn'tʁi:ʁə
Georgi he says that I → not enough ←I concentrate

"Are you feeling better about turning over the man who was stealing from the motorcycle gang?" I ask.

»Fühlst du dich besser wegen des Mannes, der die Bikergang
fy:lst du: dɪç 'bɛsɐ 've:gn dɛs 'manəs de:ɐ di: 'baɪkɐˌgaŋ
do you feel better because of the man who the biker gang

bestohlen hat und den du ausgeliefert hast?«, frage ich.
bəˈʃtoːlən hat ʊnt deːn duː ˈaʊsɡəˌliːfɐt hast ˈfʁaːɡə ɪç
he stole from and who you you delivered I ask I

»Ich denke, ich kann damit leben.«
ɪç ˈdɛŋkə ɪç kan daˈmɪt ˈleːbən
I I think I can with it to live

"I guess I can live with it."

»Gut.«
ɡuːt
good

"Good."

In der nächsten Nacht haben wir Glück. In einem Rattenloch,
ɪn deːɐ ˈnɛçstən naːxt ˈhaːbn̩ viːɐ ɡlʏk ɪn ˈaɪnəm ˈʁatənˌlɔx
in the next night we have we luck in a rat hole

einer Bar neben einer zugenagelten Tankstelle, treffe ich einen
ˈaɪnɐ baːɐ ˈneːbən ˈaɪnɐ ˈtsuːɡəˌnaːɡltn̩ ˈtaŋkˌʃtɛlə ˈtʁɛfə ɪç ˈaɪnən
a bar near a boarded-up gas station I meet I a

Kerl, der die Männer auf den Bildern erkennt, die ich ihm zeige.
kɛʁl deːɐ diː ˈmɛnɐ aʊf deːn ˈbɪldɐn ɛɐˈkɛnt diː ɪç iːm ˈtsaɪɡə
guy who the men on the pictures he recognizes that I him I show

The next night, we get lucky. I meet a guy at a hole-in-the-wall bar next to a boarded up gas station who recognizes the pictures I show him.

»Die leben alle in einer Wohnung in meinem Gebäude«, sagt er.
diː ˈleːbən ˈalə ɪn ˈaɪnɐ ˈvoːnʊŋ ɪn ˈmaɪnəm ɡəˈbɔʏdə zakt eːɐ
they they live all in an apartment in my building he says he

»Sehr schlimme Männer.«
zeːɐ ˈʃlɪmə ˈmɛnɐ
very bad men

"They all live in an apartment in my building," he says. "Very bad men."

---18---

Fünfunddreißig Minuten später treffen mich Lina und Sarah
ˈfʏnfʊntˌdʁaɪsɪç miˈnuːtən ˈʃpɛːtɐ ˈtʁɛfən mɪç ˈliːna ʊnt ˈzaːʁa
thirty-five minutes later they meet me Lina and Sarah

vor dem Gebäude, wo sich die Ukrainer befinden. Wir
foːɐ deːm ɡəˈbɔʏdə voː zɪç diː ukʁaˈiːnɐ bəˈfɪndən viːɐ
in front of the building where → the Ukrainians ← they are located we

setzen uns in mein Auto, um eine Telefonkonferenz mit Lucia
ˈzɛtsən ʊns ɪn maɪn ˈaʊto ʊm ˈaɪnə teːleˈfoːnkɔnfeˈʁɛnts mɪt ˈluːtsia
we sat down in my car in order to a conference call with Lucia

zu machen.
tsuː ˈmaxn̩
to to do

Thirty-five minutes later, Lina and Sarah meet me at the building where the three Ukrainians are staying. We get into my car to have a conference call with Lucia.

»Wir brauchen Gefangene«, sagt mir Lucia am Telefon.
viːɐ ˈbʁaʊxən ɡəˈfaŋənə zakt miːɐ ˈluːtsia am ˈteːləfoːn
we we need prisoners she tells me Lucia on the phone

»Erschießt sie nicht alle.«
ɛɐˈʃiːst ziː nɪçt ˈalə
shoot them not everyone

"We need prisoners," Lucia tells me over the phone. "Don't shoot everyone."

Story 13

"I'll stay outside in case anyone tries to come down the fire escape," Sarah says. "Plus, I can deal with the police if they show up unexpectedly."

»Ich bleibe draußen für den Fall, dass jemand versucht, über die Feuerleiter herunterzukommen«, sagt Sarah. »Außerdem kann ich mich so um die Polizei kümmern, sollte sie unerwartet auftauchen.«

I use a thin steel bar to break open the front door to the building. I don't make too much noise. Luckily, it's late at night. Everything is quiet as Lina and I creep up the stairs. My gun has a silencer. No sense waking people up.

Ich benutze eine dünne Stahlstange, um die Eingangstür des Gebäudes aufzubrechen. Ich mache nicht zu viel Lärm. Glücklicherweise ist es spät in der Nacht. Alles ist ruhig, als Lina und ich die Stufen hinaufschleichen. Meine Pistole hat einen Schalldämpfer. Es hat keinen Sinn, die Leute aufzuwecken.

Our strategy is simple. Lina will beat on the bad guys until they give up. If they don't give up, I will shoot them. Hopefully, one of them will live long enough for Lucia to talk to him.

Unsere Strategie ist einfach. Lina wird auf die Bösewichte einprügeln, bis sie aufgeben. Wenn sie nicht aufgeben, werde ich auf sie schießen. Hoffentlich wird einer von ihnen noch so lange leben, dass Lucia sich mit ihm unterhalten kann.

We sneak down the second floor hallway and listen outside the door to apartment 2. Through the door we hear the sound of heavy snoring. Snoring is good. Our opponents are sleeping.

Wir schleichen im ersten Stock den Flur entlang und lauschen an der Tür der Wohnung mit der Türnummer 2. Durch die Tür hören wir laute Schnarchgeräusche. Schnarchen ist gut. Unsere Widersacher schlafen.

Ich bemerke, wie Lina einen Schlagring auf ihre rechte Hand streift.

I notice Lina slipping brass knuckles onto her right hand.

»Wozu brauchst du denn den?«, frage ich.

"Why do you need those?" I ask.

»Ich will mir nicht die Fingernägel abbrechen. Ich habe sie gerade erst gemacht.«

"I don't want to chip my fingernails. I just did them."

»Ich glaube nicht, dass das funktioniert.«

"I'm not sure it will work."

Ich benutze meinen bewährten Dietrich, um die Tür zur Wohnung leise zu öffnen. Wir treten ein und sehen zwei schlafende Männer auf einem Sofa vor einem kleinen Fernseher. Ich schlage ihnen mit meinem Schlagstock auf den Kopf. Während ich ihnen Handschellen anlege, gleitet Lina den Flur entlang, um deren Kumpel zu finden.

I use my trusty lock pick to quietly open the door to the apartment. We step inside and see two men sleeping on a couch in front of a small television. I whack them over the head with my club. While I cuff them, Lina slides down the hall to find their buddy.

Unglücklicherweise haben sie eine Katze. Wer denkt schon daran,

Unfortunately, they have a cat. Who would expect that Ukrainian thugs like cats? The thing gives a yowl as

Story 13

Lina makes her way down the hall.

dass	ukrainische	Gauner	Katzen	mögen?	Das	Mistvieh	lässt
das	ukʁaˈiːnɪʃə	ˈgaʊnɐ	ˈkatsən	ˈmøːgən	das	ˈmɪstˌfiː	lɛst
that	Ukrainian	thugs	cats	they like	the	damn animal	it lets loose →

ein	Jaulen	los,	als	Lina	den	Flur	entlangläuft.
aɪn	ˈjaʊlən	loːs	als	ˈliːna	deːn	fluːɐ	ɛntlaŋˌlɔʏft
a	yowl	←	as	Lina	the	hallway	she walks along

As she gets to the bedroom door, it flies open. The third man, warned by the cat, jumps out at her. The guy is fast.

Als	sie	die	Schlafzimmertür	erreicht,	wird	diese	aufgestoßen.
als	ziː	diː	ˈʃlaːftsɪmɐˌtyːɐ	ɛɐˈʁaɪçt	vɪɐt	ˈdiːzə	ˈaʊfgəˌʃtoːsən
as	she	the	bedroom door	she reaches	→	this one	← it was pushed open

Der	dritte	Mann,	durch	die	Katze	gewarnt,	springt	Lina	an.
deːɐ	ˈdʁɪtə	man	dʊʁç	diː	ˈkatsə	gəˈvaʁnt	ʃpʁɪŋt	ˈliːna	an
the	third	man	by	the	cat	warned	he pounces on →	Lina	←

Der	Kerl	ist	schnell.
deːɐ	kɛʁl	ɪst	ʃnɛl
the	guy	he is	fast

He grabs Lina by the throat before she can move. He is five centimeters taller, and twenty kilograms heavier than Lina. He pushes her against the wall and starts to choke her. I sit on the couch and watch the fight.

Er	packt	Lina	an	der	Kehle,	bevor	sie	sich	bewegen	kann.	Er
eːɐ	pakt	ˈliːna	an	deːɐ	ˈkeːlə	bəˈfoːɐ	ziː	zɪç	bəˈveːgn̩	kan	eːɐ
he	he grabs	Lina	by	the	throat	before	she		to move	she can	he

ist	fünf	Zentimeter	größer	und	zwanzig	Kilogramm	schwerer	als
ɪst	fʏnf	tsɛntiˈmeːtɐ	ˈgʁøːsɐ	ʊnt	ˈtsvantsɪç	kiloˈgʁam	ˈʃveːʁɐ	als
he is	five	centimeter	taller	and	twenty	kilogram	heavier	than

Lina.	Er	stößt	sie	gegen	die	Wand	und	fängt	an,	sie	zu	würgen.
ˈliːna	eːɐ	ʃtøːst	ziː	ˈgeːgən	diː	vant	ʊnt	fɛŋt	an	ziː	tsuː	ˈvʏʁgən
Lina	he	he pushes	her	against	the	wall	and	he starts		her	to	to choke

Ich	sitze	auf	dem	Sofa	und	beobachte	den	Kampf.
ɪç	ˈzɪtsə	aʊf	deːm	ˈzoːfa	ʊnt	bəˈoːbaxtə	deːn	kampf
I	I sit	on	the	couch	and	I watch	the	fight

Lina crushes her knee into his groin. He lets go of her neck and she tries to break his nose with the palm of her hand. He blocks the blow with his forearm and swings an elbow at her cheek. She moves her head and the elbow pounds a hole in the wall behind her.

Lina	schmettert	ihr	Knie	in	seine	Leiste.	Er	lässt	ihren	Hals	los
ˈliːna	ˈʃmɛtɐt	iːɐ	kniː	ɪn	ˈzaɪnə	ˈlaɪstə	eːɐ	lɛst	ˈiːʁən	hals	loːs
Lina	she smashes	her	knee	into	his	groin	he	he lets go →	her	neck	←

und	sie	versucht,	ihm	die	Nase	mit	der	Handfläche	zu	brechen.
ʊnt	ziː	fɛɐˈzuːxt	iːm	diː	ˈnaːzə	mɪt	deːɐ	ˈhantˌflɛçə	tsuː	ˈbʁɛçən
and	she	she tries	him	the	nose	with	the	palm	to	to break

Er	blockiert	den	Schlag	mit	seinem	Unterarm	und	schwingt	den
eːɐ	blɔˈkiːɐt	deːn	ʃlaːk	mɪt	ˈzaɪnəm	ˈʊntɐˌaʁm	ʊnt	ʃvɪŋt	deːn
he	he blocks	the	punch	with	his	forearm	and	he swings	the

Ellbogen	auf	ihre	Wange	zu.	Sie	dreht	den	Kopf	zur	Seite
ˈɛlˌboːgn̩	aʊf	ˈiːʁə	ˈvaŋə	tsuː	ziː	dʁeːt	deːn	kɔpf	tsuːɐ	ˈzaɪtə
elbow	toward →	her	cheek	←	she	she turns	the	head	to the	side

und	der	Ellbogen	hämmert	hinter	ihr	ein	Loch	in	die	Wand.
ʊnt	deːɐ	ˈɛlˌboːgn̩	ˈhɛmɐt	ˈhɪntɐ	iːɐ	aɪn	lɔx	ɪn	diː	vant
and	the	elbow	it pounds	behind	her	a	hole	in	the	wall

Lina steps back into the living room to get more space. Her opponent is right on top of her. The knee to his groin hasn't slowed him down. This guy is

Lina	geht	zurück	ins	Wohnzimmer,	um	mehr	Platz	zu
ˈliːna	geːt	tsuˈʁʏk	ɪns	ˈvoːnˌtsɪmɐ	ʊm	meːɐ	plats	tsuː
Lina	she walks	back	into the	living room	in order to	more	space	to

haben. Ihr Gegner folgt ihr auf dem Fuße. Der Kniestoß in seine Leiste hat ihn nicht langsamer gemacht. Das ist ein harter Kerl.

tough.

Sie schwingt einen Aufwärtshaken mit der Schlagringfaust auf sein Kinn zu. Er blockiert den Schlag und rammt sie mit seinem Oberkörper. Lina hat die Balance einer Balletttänzerin. Sie hüpft einen halben Meter zurück und landet in perfekter Kampfhaltung.

She swings an uppercut to his chin with a brass knuckled fist. He blocks the punch and knocks into her with his upper body. Lina has the balance of a ballet dancer. She hops back half a meter and lands in perfect fighting position.

Er schwingt seine muskulöse Faust nach ihr. Sie wehrt sie mit dem Unterarm ab. Ich höre einen Knochen brechen. Er versucht, sie mit einem Roundhouse-Kick in die Seite zu treffen. Sie hebt ihr Bein und fängt den Stoß mit der Außenseite ihres Unterschenkels ab.

He swings his muscular fist at her. She blocks it with her forearm. I hear a bone break. He tries a roundhouse kick to her side. She lifts her leg and catches the kick on the outside of her lower leg.

Sie zuckt zusammen und springt einen weiteren Schritt zurück. Er schiebt sich nach vorne, täuscht an und schlägt zu. Dann tritt er schnell zurück und schwingt ein Bein auf

She winces and hops back another step. He shuffles forward, feinting and jabbing. Then he quickly steps back and swings a kick at her head. The kick is fast and ferocious. His leg is a blur as it speeds toward her.

Story 13

But Lina is an amazing fighter. She ducks under the kick and hammers his other knee with the brass knuckles. I hear a sound like ice being crushed and the guy grunts. Amazingly, he doesn't go down. He gets his other foot back onto the floor and backs up.

I don't know whether he trips over a rug on the floor or his cracked knee gives out. But he stumbles just a little bit, just enough to give Lina an opening. She moves in quickly and knees him in the groin again. Then she snaps his head back with an elbow to the chin. This leaves his neck exposed. She pounds his trachea with the brass knuckles.

---

ihren Kopf zu. Der Tritt ist schnell und heftig. Sein Bein wird ganz unscharf, als es auf sie zurast. Aber Lina ist eine erstaunliche Kämpferin. Sie duckt sich unter das Bein und hämmert mit dem Schlagring auf sein anderes Knie. Ich höre ein Geräusch, wie wenn Eis zerbricht, und der Typ ächzt. Erstaunlicherweise geht er nicht zu Boden. Er stellt seinen anderen Fuß zurück auf den Boden und weicht zurück. Ich weiß nicht, ob er über einen Teppich stolpert oder ob sein gebrochenes Knie nachgab. Aber er stolpert nur ein wenig, gerade genug, um Lina die Gelegenheit zu geben, einen neuen Angriff zu starten. Sie nähert sich sehr schnell und stößt ihm wieder mit dem Knie in die Leiste. Dann knickt sie seinen Kopf mit einem Ellbogenschlag gegen das Kinn zurück. Das lässt seinen Hals ungeschützt. Sie schlägt ihm mit dem Schlagring auf die Luftröhre.

Evolution

Der Kerl sackt zusammen. Ich gehe hinüber und sehe ihn an.
deːɐ kɛɐl zakt tsuˈzamən ɪç ˈgeːhə hɪˈnyːbɐ ʊnt ˈzeːə iːn an
the guy he slumps down I I go over and I look at→ him ←

Seine Kehle ist zerschlagen. Er ringt nach Atem, der niemals
ˈzaɪnə ˈkeːlə ɪst tsɛɐˈʃlaːgən eːɐ ʁɪŋt naːx ˈaːtəm deːɐ ˈniːmaːls
his throat it is crushed he he struggles for breath that never

kommen wird. Langsam verschwindet der Glanz aus seinen Augen.
ˈkɔmən vɪɐt ˈlaŋzaːm fɛɐˈʃvɪndət deːɐ glants aʊs ˈzaɪnən ˈaʊgən
to come it will slowly it fades away the shine from his eyes

The guy goes down. I walk over and look at him. His throat is crushed. He fights for breath that will never come. Slowly, the light fades from his eyes.

Ich schicke Sarah eine Nachricht mit meinem Handy und sie
ɪç ˈʃɪkə ˈzaːʁa ˈaɪnə ˈnaːxʁɪçt mɪt ˈmaɪnəm ˈhɛndi ʊnt ziː
I I send Sarah a message with my cell phone and she

kommt sofort mit Klebeband und Säcken herauf. Sarah und
kɔmt zoˈfɔɐt mɪt ˈkleːbəˌbant ʊnt ˈzɛkən hɛˈʁaʊf ˈzaːʁa ʊnt
she comes up→ immediately with duct tape and bags ← Sarah and

ich verbinden die zwei bewusstlosen Männer und stecken sie in
ɪç fɛɐˈbɪndən diː tsvaɪ bəˈvʊstloːzən ˈmɛnɐ ʊnt ˈʃtɛkən ziː ɪn
I we tie up the two unconscious guys and we stick them into

zwei große Säcke. Dann schleppen wir sie hinunter zu meinem
tsvaɪ ˈgʁoːsə ˈzɛkə dan ˈʃlɛpən viːɐ ziː hɪˈnʊntɐ tsuː ˈmaɪnəm
two big bags then we drag down→ we them ← to my

Auto.
ˈaʊto
car

I send Sarah a message with my cell phone and she comes right up with duct tape and bags. Sarah and I tape up the two unconscious guys and stuff them into two large bags. Then we drag them down to my car.

Während wir uns bemühen, die Kerle loszuwerden, durchsucht
ˈvɛːʁənt viːɐ ʊns bəˈmyːən diː ˈkɛɐlə ˈloːstsuˌveːɐdn dʊɐçˈzuːxt
while we we take pains the guys to get rid of she searches through

Lina die Wohnung. Sarah und ich laden die Männer in mein Auto
ˈliːna diː ˈvoːnʊŋ ˈzaːʁa ʊnt ɪç ˈlaːdən diː ˈmɛnɐ ɪn maɪn ˈaʊto
Lina the apartment Sarah and I we load the guys into my car

und ich laufe zurück, um Lina zu helfen. Sarah hilft
ʊnt ɪç ˈlaʊfə tsuˈʁʏk ʊm ˈliːna tsuː ˈhɛlfən ˈzaːʁa hɪlft
and I I run back in order to Lina to to help Sarah she helps down→

ihr die Treppen hinunter, während ich eine Tasche voller Sachen
iːɐ diː ˈtʁɛpən hɪˈnʊntɐ ˈvɛːʁənt ɪç ˈaɪnə ˈtaʃə ˈfɔlɐ ˈzaxn
her the steps ← while I a bag full things

trage, auf die wir Lina zufolge einen Blick werfen sollten. Linas
ˈtʁaːgə aʊf diː viːɐ ˈliːna tsuˈfɔlgə ˈaɪnən blɪk ˈvɛɐfən ˈzɔltən ˈliːnas
I carry on which we Lina according to to throw a look we should Lina's

Arm hängt an ihrer Seite herab.
aɐm hɛŋt an ˈiːʁɐ ˈzaɪtə hɛˈʁap
arm it dangles→ by her side ←

While we are taking pains to get rid of the guys, Lina checks the apartment. Sarah and I drop the guys into my car and run back upstairs to help Lina. Sarah helps her down the steps while I carry a bag full of things that Lina thought we might want to look at. Lina's left arm hangs by her side.

Auf unserem Weg hinunter begegnen wir einer anderen
aʊf ˈʊnzɐəm veːk hɪˈnʊntɐ bəˈgeːgnən viːɐ ˈaɪnɐ ˈandəʁən
on our way down we encounter we another

On our way down, we encounter one other resident of the building who was awakened by the noise. I throw a mind haze at her as we pass. We leave

Story 13

the dead man in the apartment. When we get to the cars I look through the things Lina threw into the bag.

> Bewohnerin des Gebäudes, die durch den Lärm aufwachte.
> bəˈvoːnəʁɪn dɛs ɡəˈbɔʏdəs diː dʊʁç deːn lɛʁm ˈaʊfˌvaxtə
> resident of the building who by the noise she woke up
>
> Beim Vorbeigehen setze ich eine Bewusstseinstrübung bei ihr
> baɪm foːɐ̯ˈbaɪˌɡeːən ˈzɛtsə ɪç ˈaɪnə bəˈvʊstˌzaɪnsˈtʁyːbʊŋ baɪ iːɐ̯
> while passing by I employ→ I a mind fog on her
>
> ein. Wir lassen den toten Mann in der Wohnung. Als wir beim
> aɪn viːɐ̯ ˈlasən deːn ˈtoːtən man ɪn deːɐ̯ ˈvoːnʊŋ als viːɐ̯ baɪm
> ← we we leave the dead man in the apartment when we at the
>
> Auto ankommen, werfe ich einen Blick auf die Sachen, die Lina
> ˈaʊto ˈanˌkɔmən ˈvɛʁfə ɪç ˈaɪnən blɪk aʊf diː ˈzaxn̩ diː ˈliːna
> cars we arrive I throw I a look at the things that Lina
>
> in die Tasche geworfen hat.
> ɪn diː ˈtaʃə ɡəˈvɔʁfən hat
> in the bag she threw

"A laptop, some cell phones, bills, and a checkbook. Maybe we have some evidence."

> »Einen Laptop, einige Handys, Rechnungen und ein Scheckheft.
> ˈaɪnən ˈlɛptɔp ˈaɪnɪɡə ˈhɛndis ˈʁɛçnʊŋən ʊnt aɪn ˈʃɛkˌhɛft
> a laptop some cell phones bills and a checkbook
>
> Vielleicht haben wir ein paar Beweise.«
> fiˈlaɪçt ˈhaːbn̩ viːɐ̯ aɪn paːɐ̯ bəˈvaɪzə
> maybe we have we some evidence

"I need to have my arm x-rayed," Lina says.

> »Ich muss meinen Arm röntgen lassen«, sagt Lina.
> ɪç mʊs ˈmaɪnən aʁm ˈʁœntɡən ˈlasən zakt ˈliːna
> I I must my arm to have x-rayed she says Lina

"Can you drive with one arm?" I ask.

> »Kannst du mit einem Arm fahren?«, frage ich.
> kanst duː mɪt ˈaɪnəm aʁm ˈfaːʁən ˈfʁaːɡə ɪç
> can you you with one arm to drive I ask I

"Sure," she answers.

> »Sicher«, antwortet sie.
> ˈzɪçɐ ˈantˌvɔʁtət ziː
> sure she answers she

I don't have to remind Lina to go to the private clinic our team uses for medical emergencies. It's run by a doctor who caters to people who pay in cash and don't use their real names. Before we drive away, Lina pulls me aside.

> Ich brauche Lina nicht daran zu erinnern, zu der Privatklinik
> ɪç ˈbʁaʊxə ˈliːna nɪçt daˈʁan tsuː ɛɐ̯ˈɪnɐn tsuː deːɐ̯ pʁiˈvaːtˌkliːnɪk
> I I need Lina not about it to to remind to the private clinic
>
> zu gehen, die unser Team für medizinische Notfälle benutzt. Sie
> tsuː ˈɡeːən diː ˈʊnzɐ tiːm fyːɐ̯ meːdiˈtsiːnɪʃə ˈnoːtˌfɛlə bəˈnʊtst ziː
> to to go that our team for medical emergencies it uses it
>
> wird von einem Arzt geleitet, der Leute versorgt, die bar zahlen
> vɪʁt fɔn ˈaɪnəm aːʁtst ɡəˈlaɪtət deːɐ̯ ˈlɔɪtə fɛɐ̯ˈzɔʁkt diː baːɐ̯ ˈtsaːlən
> → by a doctor ←it is headed who people he provides for the cash to pay
>
> und nicht ihre richtigen Namen verwenden. Bevor wir wegfahren,
> ʊnt nɪçt ˈiːʁə ˈʁɪçtɪɡən ˈnaːmən fɛɐ̯ˈvɛndən bəˈfoːɐ̯ viːɐ̯ ˈvɛkˌfaːʁən
> and not their proper names they use before we we drive away
>
> zieht mich Lina zur Seite.
> tsiːt mɪç ˈliːna tsuːɐ̯ ˈzaɪtə
> she pulls me Lina to the side

»Du hast diese Bewusstseinsbeeinflussung nicht bei dem Ukrainer benutzt, oder?«

"You didn't do that mind clouding thing on the Ukrainian, did you?"

»Auf keinen Fall«, sage ich. »Ich habe zur Abwechslung gerne einmal bei einem fairen Kampf zugeschaut. Du hast ihn ohne meine Hilfe besiegt.«

"No way," I say. "I liked watching a fair fight for once. You beat him without any help from me."

Sie nickt selbstgefällig. Lina ist sehr wetteifernd.

She nods to herself in satisfaction. Lina is very competitive.

---- 19 ----

Am nächsten Tag haben wir eine weitere Besprechung.

The next day, we have another meeting.

»Was hast du von unseren ukrainischen Gefangenen erfahren?«, frage ich Lucia.

"What did you get from our Ukrainian captives?" I ask Lucia.

»Sie haben mir von fünf weiteren Opfern erzählt, die ihnen eine Menge Geld bezahlten«, sagt sie.

"They told me about five other victims who paid them a lot of money," she says.

»Sie machen das schon länger, als wir dachten«, sage ich. »Waren die anderen Opfer Versicherungsagenten?«

"They've been doing this a lot longer than we thought," I say. "Were the other victims insurance agents?"

»Nein, sie waren unabhängige Finanzberater.«

"No, they were independent financial advisers."

Story 13

"That's pretty close," I say. "Do you know who the boss is?"

»Das ist beinahe das Gleiche«, sage ich. »Weißt du, wer der Boss ist?«
das ɪst ˈbaɪnaːə das ˈɡlaɪçə ˈzaːɡə ɪç vaɪst duː veːɐ deːɐ bɔs ɪst
that it is almost the same I say I you know you who the boss he is

"Not yet. Roland is still pulling information out of the computer you found at their apartment. These men were foolish enough to keep a log of all their activities. We know where they stayed, who they talked to, when they received phone calls from the boss, things like that. I'm hoping all this will help us somehow."

»Noch nicht. Roland zieht noch immer Informationen aus dem
nɔx nɪçt ˈʁoːlant tsiːt nɔx ˈɪmɐ ɪnfɔʁmaˈtsjoːnən aʊs deːm
not yet Roland he pulls still information out of the

Computer, den du in ihrer Wohnung gefunden hast. Diese Männer
kɔmˈpjuːtɐ deːn duː ɪn ˈiːɐɐ ˈvoːnʊŋ ɡəˈfʊndən hast ˈdiːzə ˈmɛnɐ
computer that you in their apartment you found these men

waren blöd genug, eine Liste ihrer Aktivitäten aufzubewahren.
ˈvaːʁən bløːt ɡəˈnuːk ˈaɪnə ˈlɪstə ˈiːɐɐ aktiviˈtɛːtn̩ ˈaʊftsubəˌvaːʁən
they were stupid enough a list of their activities to keep

Wir wissen, wo sie wohnten, mit wem sie gesprochen haben,
viːɐ ˈvɪsən voː ziː ˈvoːntən mɪt vem ziː ɡəˈʃpʁɔxən ˈhaːbn̩
we we know where they they live with whom they they spoke

wann sie Anrufe von ihrem Boss erhielten, solche Dinge halt. Ich
van ziː ˈanˌʁuːfə fɔn ˈiːʁəm bɔs ɛɐˈhiːltn̩ ˈzɔlçə ˈdɪŋə halt ɪç
when they calls from their boss they received such things I

hoffe, all das wird uns irgendwie helfen.«
ˈhɔfə al das vɪɐt ʊns ˈɪʁɡəntviː ˈhɛlfən
I hope all this it will us somehow to help

"So when do you think we'll know something solid?" Lina asks.

»Und wann glaubst du, werden wir etwas Konkretes wissen?«,
ʊnt van ɡlaʊpst duː ˈveːɐdn̩ viːɐ ˈɛtvas kɔnˈkʁeːtəs ˈvɪsən
and when you think you we will we something concrete to know

fragt Lina.
fʁaːkt ˈliːna
she asks Lina

She has a cast on her arm and is walking with a slight limp.

Sie hat einen Gips am Arm und humpelt etwas beim Gehen.
ziː hat ˈaɪnən ɡɪps am aʁm ʊnt ˈhʊmpəlt ˈɛtvas baɪm ˈɡeːən
she she has a cast on the arm and she hobbles somewhat while walking

"A few days, I hope."

»In ein paar Tagen, so hoffe ich.«
ɪn aɪn paːɐ ˈtaːɡən zoː ˈhɔfə ɪç
in a few days so I hope I

Anja calls me two days later.

Anja ruft mich zwei Tage später an.
ˈanja ʁuːft mɪç tsvaɪ ˈtaːɡə ˈʃpɛːtɐ an
Anja she calls→ me two days later ←

"We've got him," she says.

»Wir haben ihn«, sagt sie.
viːɐ ˈhaːbn̩ iːn zakt ziː
we we have him she says she

Evolution

»Nun, wer ist das große Verbrechergenie?«
nu:n veːɐ ɪst das ˈɡʁoːsə fɛɐˈbʁɛçɐˌɡeːniː
well who he is the great criminal genius

"So who is this great criminal mastermind?"

»Ein Hauptmann bei der Landespolizei mit dem Namen Philip Jung.«
aɪn ˈhaʊptman baɪ deːɐ ˈlandəspoliˌtsaɪ mɪt deːm ˈnaːmən ˈfɪlɪp jʊŋ
a captain with the state police with the name Philip Jung

"A captain in the State Police named Philip Jung."

»Wie habt ihr ihn gefunden?«
viː haːpt iːɐ iːn ɡəˈfʊndən
how → you him ← you found

"How did you find him?"

»Reinhold gab uns seinen Namen neben ein paar anderen. Wir prüften alle seine Kreditkartenquittungen und weißt du was?«
ˈʁaɪnhɔlt ɡaːp ʊns ˈzaɪnən ˈnaːmən ˈneːbən aɪn paːɐ ˈandəʁən viːɐ ˈpʁyːftən ˈalə ˈzaɪnə kʁeˈdiːtˌkaʁtn̩ˈkvɪtʊŋən ʊnt vaɪst duː vas
Reinhold he gave us his name along with a few others we we checked all his credit cards receipts and you know you what

"Reinhold gave us his name along with a few others. We looked at all of his credit card receipts and you know what?"

»Was?«
vas
what

"What?"

»Er bezahlte einen Zahnarzt dafür, einem der Ukrainer einen Zahn zu ziehen. Kannst du das glauben?«
eːɐ bəˈtsaːltə ˈaɪnən ˈtsaːnˌaːɐtst daˈfyːɐ ˈaɪnəm deːɐ ukʁaˈiːnɐ ˈaɪnən tsaːn tsuː ˈtsiːən kanst duː das ˈɡlaʊbən
he he paid a dentist for it one of the Ukrainians a tooth to to pull can you you that to believe

"He paid a dentist to pull a tooth for one of the Ukrainians. Can you believe that?"

»Ich bin überrascht, dass er nicht bar zahlte«, sage ich.
ɪç bɪn yːbɐˈʁaʃt das eːɐ nɪçt baːɐ ˈtsaːltə ˈzaːɡə ɪç
I I am surprised that he not cash he paid I say I

"I'm surprised he didn't pay in cash," I say.

»Das war sein einziger Fehler.«
das vaːɐ zaɪn ˈaɪntsɪɡɐ ˈfeːlɐ
that it was his only mistake

"That was his only mistake."

»Da habe ich also drei Nächte lang umsonst in Berlin Frauen mit Schnurrbärten beim Ausziehen beobachtet.«
daː ˈhaːbə ɪç ˈalzo dʁaɪ ˈnɛçtə laŋ ʊmˈzɔnst ɪn bɛɐˈliːn ˈfʁaʊən mɪt ˈʃnʊʁˌbɛːɐtn̩ baɪm ˈaʊsˌtsiːən bəˈʔoːbaxtət
there → I so three nights long for nothing in Berlin women with mustaches while undressing ← I watched

"So I spent three nights in Berlin watching women with mustaches take their clothes off for nothing?"

»Es war die Mühe wert, da wir den Rest der Gang
ɛs vaːɐ diː ˈmyːə veːɐt daː viːɐ deːn ʁɛst deːɐ ɡaŋ
it it was the effort worth because we the rest of the gang

"It was worth the effort because we found the rest of the gang."

Story 13

"What did Lucia do with the two captives?"

»Was hat Lucia mit den beiden Gefangenen gemacht?«

"Wrapped them up with a bow and sent them to some guy in the State Police Department named Müller. We also gave him the names of the other victims, the log the Ukrainians kept about their activities, and the fact that Captain Jung paid for the one man's dental work."

»Mit einer Schleife verpackt und zu einem Typen namens Müller bei der Landespolizei geschickt. Wir gaben ihm auch die Namen der anderen Opfer, die Auflistung der Aktivitäten, die die Ukrainer führten, und informierten ihn darüber, dass Hauptmann Jung die Zahnbehandlung für den einen bezahlte.«

"That should make him happy," I say.

»Das sollte ihn glücklich machen«, sage ich.

The following week, there is a big story in the newspapers. Captain Philip Jung of the State Police has been arrested and charged with running a large extortion operation in Berlin. The articles go into detail about all of the victims, and lists the names of the Ukrainian thugs who were hired to do all the dirty work.

In der folgenden Woche steht ein großer Bericht in der Zeitung. Hauptmann Philip Jung von der Landespolizei wurde festgenommen und angeklagt, eine große Erpressungsoperation in Berlin geleitet zu haben. Die Zeitung berichtet detailliert über die Opfer und listet die Namen der ukrainischen Gauner auf, die für die Drecksarbeit angeheuert wurden.

Two days later, there is another story in the newspapers. The investigators found a safe deposit box and two off-

Zwei Tage später steht noch ein Artikel in der Zeitung.

298

Die Ermittler fanden ein Bankschließfach und zwei Offshore-Bankkonten, die dem Hauptmann Jung gehören. Die Konten enthalten einige hunderttausend Euro. Das Schließfach ist voller ungeschliffener Diamanten.

shore bank accounts owned by Captain Jung. The accounts contain several hundred thousand Euro. The safe deposit box is full of uncut diamonds.

»Die hätten nie etwas über das Geld und das Schließfach herausgefunden, wenn ich nicht dem Kriminalbeamten Müller eine anonyme E-Mail geschickt hätte«, sagt Roland.

"They never would have found out about the money and the safe deposit box if I hadn't sent Detective Müller an anonymous email," Roland says.

»Ist nur schade, dass die Welt nie etwas von deinem Talent erfahren wird, Straftaten dank deiner Hackerfähigkeiten aufzudecken«, sage ich ihm.

"Too bad the world will never know your talent at uncovering crimes with your hacking skills," I tell him.

Die Kautionsanhörung von Hauptmann Jung wird von einem Richter geleitet, der ihm ein paar Gefälligkeiten schuldet. Er wird aus der Haft entlassen, nachdem er eine Kaution von einer halben Million Euro hinterlegt hat. So laufen die Dinge in Berlin, wenn man Freunde hat.

Captain Jung's bail hearing is presided over by a judge who owes him a few favors. He is released from detention after he posts bail for a half million Euro. That's how things work in Berlin if you have friends.

Story 13

Things quiet down for a few days while Roland and Anja look through the Ukrainians' computer for more evidence to send to Detective Müller. And then Captain Jung swallows half a bottle of poison and dies in his home. We have a team meeting the next day.

Die Angelegenheit beruhigt sich etwas, während Roland und Anja den Computer der Ukrainer nach weiteren Beweisen durchforsten, um sie an den Kriminalbeamten Müller zu senden. Und dann schluckt Hauptmann Jung eine halbe Flasche Gift und stirbt zu Hause. Wir haben am nächsten Tag eine Teambesprechung.

"Do you think the police had enough evidence to send Captain Jung to prison for a long time?" I ask Lucia.

»Glaubst du, die Polizei hatte genügend Beweise, um Hauptmann Jung auf lange Zeit ins Gefängnis zu schicken?«, frage ich Lucia.

"I don't think so. If he had hired a good lawyer, he would probably have served a few years at most."

»Ich glaube nicht. Wenn er einen guten Anwalt beauftragt hätte, hätte er bestenfalls ein paar Jahre absitzen müssen.«

"Then why would he kill himself? Roland, did you predict that?"

»Weshalb hätte er sich dann umbringen sollen? Roland, hast du das vorausgesehen?«

"If I thought he was going to take poison, I would have stopped searching for evidence a few days ago."

»Wenn ich gedacht hätte, dass er Gift nehmen würde, hätte ich vor ein paar Tagen bereits aufgehört, nach Beweisen zu suchen.«

300

Evolution

»Vielleicht müssen wir die Dinge aus einem anderen Blickwinkel betrachten«, schlug Lucia vor.

"Maybe we need to look at things from a different angle," Lucia suggests.

---20---

Zwei Wochen später ...

Two weeks later ...

»Sie sehen heute etwas besser aus«, sage ich zu Joseph Graf.

"You look a little better today," I say to Joseph Graf.

Wir essen belegte Brote, die ich ihm mit nach Hause gebracht habe.

We are eating sandwiches that I brought over to his house.

»Haben Sie aufgehört, die Medikamente zu nehmen?«

"Have you stopped taking that medication?"

»Ja«, sagt er zu mir. »Ich habe mit einer Trauerbegleiterin gesprochen, wie Sie bei unserem letzten Mittagessen vorgeschlagen haben. Sie hat mir geholfen, mich mit dem Verlust meiner Frau auseinanderzusetzen. Ich bekomme mein Leben endlich wieder in den Griff.«

"Yeah," he tells me. "I talked to a grief counselor, like you suggested at our last lunch. She has helped me to deal with the loss of my wife. I'm finally getting my life back together."

»Das ist großartig.«

"That's great."

Wir unterhalten uns etwas mehr über seine Therapiesitzungen.

We talk a little more about his therapy sessions. Due to my mind mojo, he still thinks I am his insurance friend.

301

Story 13

Finally, I get to the point.

Aufgrund	meiner	Bewusstseinszauberei	glaubt	er	immer noch,
aʊfgʀʊnt	ˈmaɪnɐ	bəˈvʊstzaɪnstsaʊbəˈʀaɪ	glaʊpt	eːɐ	ˈɪmɐ nɔx
due to	my	mind mojo	he thinks	he	still

dass	ich	ein	Freund	von	der	Versicherung	wäre.	Schließlich
das	ɪç	aɪn	fʀɔɪnt	fɔn	deːɐ	fɛɐˈzɪçəʀʊŋ	ˈvɛːʀə	ˈʃliːslɪç
that	I	a	friend	from	the	insurance	I was	finally

komme	ich	zur	Sache.
ˈkɔmmə	ɪç	tsuːɐ	ˈzaxə
	I get to the point		

"You almost succeeded," I tell him.

»Sie	haben	es	fast	geschafft«,	sage	ich	zu	ihm.
ziː	ˈhaːbn̩	ɛs	fast	gəˈʃaft	ˈzaːgə	ɪç	tsuː	iːm
you	→	it	almost	← you succeeded	I say	I	to	him

"Come again?" he asks.

»Wie	bitte?«,	fragt	er.
viː	ˈbɪtə	fʀaːkt	eːɐ
come again		he asks	he

"You know, the extortions, your wife's murder, and even the murder of Captain Jung."

»Sie	wissen	ja,	die	Erpressungen,	den	Mord	an	ihrer	Frau	und
ziː	ˈvɪsən	jaː	diː	ɛɐˈpʀɛsʊŋən	deːn	mɔʀt	an	ˈiːʀɐ	fʀaʊ	ʊnt
you	you know	!	the	extortions	the	murder	on	your	wife	and

sogar	die	Ermordung	von	Hauptmann	Jung.«
zoˈgaːɐ	diː	ɛɐˈmɔʀdʊŋ	fɔn	ˈhaʊptman	jʊŋ
even	the	murder	of	captain	Jung

"I don't know what you are talking about," he says.

»Ich	weiß	nicht,	wovon	Sie	sprechen«,	sagt	er.
ɪç	vaɪs	nɪçt	voˈfɔn	ziː	ˈʃpʀɛçən	zaːkt	eːɐ
I	I know	not	of what	you	you talk	he says	he

"Yes, you do know. We know you ran the whole extortion operation."

»Doch,	das	wissen	Sie.	Wir	wissen,	dass	Sie	die	ganze
dɔx	das	ˈvɪsən	ziː	viːɐ	ˈvɪsən	das	ziː	diː	ˈgantsə
on the contrary	that	you know	you	we	we know	that	you	the	whole

Erpressungsoperation	leiteten.«
ɛɐˈpʀɛsʊŋsopəʀaˈtsjoːn	ˈlaɪtətən
extortion operation	you led

"Are you with the police?" he asks.

»Sind	Sie	von	der	Polizei?«
zɪnt	ziː	fɔn	deːɐ	poliˈtsaɪ
are you	you	from	the	police

"I'm with a group that has spent the last fourteen days looking into every aspect of your life," I say. "You recruited Captain Jung to bring over the Ukrainians. You selected the extortion victims. You shot three people, one of them being your own wife. And you poisoned Captain Jung when things started to fall apart."

»Ich	gehöre	einer	Gruppe	an,	die	die	letzten	vierzehn	Tage
ɪç	gəˈhøːʀə	ˈaɪnɐ	ˈgʀʊpə	an	diː	diː	ˈlɛtstən	ˈfɪʀtseːn	ˈtaːgə
I	I belong to →	a	group	←	that	the	last	fourteen	days

damit	verbracht hat,	jeden	Aspekt	ihres	Lebens	zu	untersuchen«,
daˈmɪt	fɛɐˈbʀaxt hat	ˈjeːdən	asˈpɛkt	ˈiːʀəs	ˈleːbəns	tsuː	ʊntɐˈzuːxn̩
with it	it spent	every	aspect	of your	life	to	to examine

sage	ich.	»Sie	haben	Hauptmann	Jung	angeworben,	um	die
ˈzaːgə	ɪç	ziː	ˈhaːbn̩	ˈhaʊptman	jʊŋ	ˈangəˌvɔʀbn̩	ʊm	diː
I say	I	you	→	captain	Jung	← you recruited	in order to	the

Evolution

Ukrainer herüberzubringen. Sie wählten die Erpressungsopfer aus. Sie erschossen drei Leute, eine davon war ihre eigene Frau. Und Sie haben Hauptmann Jung vergiftet, als die Dinge langsam aus dem Ruder gerieten.«

»Sie sind verrückt«, sagt er zu mir. »Wo ist ihr Beweis?«

»Wir haben den Ort gefunden, wo Sie das Gift kauften. Die haben immer noch die Überwachungsvideos von allen Transaktionen, die an jenem Tag gemacht wurden. Ihr Gesicht ist in dem Video sehr klar zu erkennen. Außerdem erinnert sich der Kassierer an Sie.«

Herr Graf zieht eine Pistole aus der Tasche und richtet sie auf mich. Ich sitze ruhig da, als er um den Esstisch herum kommt und mich abtastet, um zu sehen, ob ich eine Waffe oder ein Abhörgerät bei mir trage. Dann setzt er sich hin und beißt ein weiteres Stück von seinem Truthahnbrot ab. Die Pistole ist

"You are insane," he tells me. "Where is your proof?"

"We found the place where you bought the poison. They still have a surveillance video of all the transactions that were made that day. Your face shows up very clearly on that video. Plus, the cashier remembers you."

Mr. Graf takes a gun out of his pocket and points it at me. I sit quietly as he comes around the dining room table and pats me to see if I am carrying a weapon or wearing an electronic listening device. Then he sits down and takes another bite out of his turkey sandwich. The gun still points my way.

Story 13

"You are very stupid to come here and say these things," he tells me. "Did you think I would pay you to keep quiet?"

»Es ist sehr dumm von Ihnen, hierherzukommen und diese Sachen zu sagen«, sagt er zu mir. »Haben Sie geglaubt, ich würde Sie bezahlen, damit Sie schweigen?«

"I just wanted the satisfaction of telling you face-to-face that you didn't get away with your crimes."

»Ich wollte nur die Genugtuung haben, Ihnen von Angesicht zu Angesicht zu sagen, dass Sie mit ihren Verbrechen nicht davongekommen sind.«

He laughs at me.

Er lacht mich aus.

"You have made a big mistake," he says.

»Sie haben einen schweren Fehler gemacht«, sagt er.

"Actually, Captain Jung made the mistake. If he hadn't paid for the Ukrainian's dental work with his credit card, both of you would be in the clear. We didn't have enough evidence to accuse anyone of anything until we found that credit card payment."

»Eigentlich machte Hauptmann Jung den Fehler. Wenn er nicht für die Zahnarztbehandlung des Ukrainers mit seiner Kreditkarte bezahlt hätte, wären Sie alle beide außer Verdacht. Wir hatten nicht genügend Beweise dafür, irgendjemanden wegen irgendetwas anzuklagen, bis wir die Kreditkartenzahlung fanden.«

"When you say 'we' who are you talking about?" he asks.

»Wenn Sie ›wir‹ sagen, von wem reden Sie dann eigentlich?«,

304

fragt er.
ˈfʁaːkt eːɐ
he asks he

»Meine Gruppe. Ich wollte uns ›Das Kommando‹ nennen, aber wir hatten eine Abstimmung und ich verlor. Deshalb nennen wir uns einfach das Team. Ich darf nicht einmal Teamjacken kaufen.«
ˈmaɪnə ˈɡʁʊpə ɪç ˈvɔltə ʊns das kɔˈmando ˈnɛnən ˈaːbɐ viːɐ ˈhatən ˈaɪnə ˈapʃtɪmʊŋ ʊnt ɪç fɛɐˈloːɐ ˈdɛsˈhalp ˈnɛnən viːɐ ʊns ˈaɪnfax das tiːm ɪç daʁf nɪçt ˈaɪnmaːl ˈtiːmjakən ˈkaʊfən
my group I I wanted us the squad to call but we we had a vote and I I lost thus we call we ourselves just the team I I am allowed not even team jackets to buy

"My group. I wanted to call us 'The Squad', but we had a vote and I lost. So we just call ourselves the team. I'm not even allowed to buy team jackets."

»Sind Sie high?«, fragt er mich. »Das ergibt doch keinen Sinn. Was für eine Abstimmung?«
zɪnt ziː haɪ ˈfʁaːkt eːɐ mɪç das ɛɐˈɡiːpt dɔx ˈkaɪnən zɪn vas fyːɐ ˈaɪnə ˈapʃtɪmʊŋ
are you you high he asks he me that it makes no sense what kind of a vote

"Are you high?" he asks me. "You aren't making any sense. What vote?"

»Das spielt keine Rolle.«
das ʃpiːlt ˈkaɪnə ˈʁɔlə
that it is irrelevant

"It's not important."

Joseph Graf seufzt.
ˈjoːzɛf ɡʁaːf zɔɪftst
Joseph Graf he sighs

Joseph Graf sighs.

»Sie werden mir von Ihrem Team erzählen.«
ziː ˈveːɐdn miːɐ fɔn ˈiːʁəm tiːm ɛɐˈtsɛːlən
you you will me about your team to tell

"You're going to tell me about your team."

»Nein, werde ich nicht.«
naɪn ˈveːɐdə ɪç nɪçt
no I will I not

"No, I'm not."

»Wenn Sie es nicht tun, werde ich Ihnen ins Knie schießen und dann ins andere Knie und dann in den Ellbogen, bis Sie es mir schließlich sagen.«
vɛn ziː ɛs nɪçt tuːn ˈveːɐdə ɪç ˈiːnən ɪns kniː ˈʃiːsən ʊnt dan ɪns ˈandəʁə kniː ʊnt dan ɪn deːn ˈɛlˌboːɡn bɪs ziː ɛs miːɐ ˈʃliːslɪç ˈzaːɡən
if you it not to do I will I you in the knee to shoot and then in the other knee and then in the elbow until you it me finally to tell

"If you don't, I'll shoot you in the knee, and then the other knee, and then the elbow, until you finally tell me."

Story 13

I hit him with a mind fog. He puts his arms down at his side. I take the gun and cuff him. Then I call Sarah on the cell phone. She shows up several minutes later.

Ich wende eine Bewusstseinstrübung auf ihn an. Er senkt seine Arme und lässt sie an der Seite herunterhängen. Ich nehme die Pistole und lege ihm Handschellen an. Dann rufe ich Sarah auf dem Handy an. Sie kreuzt einige Minuten später auf.

"Did you put a pill in his drink?" she asks.

»Hast du ihm Tabletten ins Getränk getan?«, fragt sie.

"What?" I say.

»Wie bitte?«, frage ich.

"He's almost asleep. How did you do that?"

»Er schläft beinahe. Wie hast du das geschafft?«

"I almost forgot. I spiked his drink."

»Ich habe es beinahe vergessen. Ich habe ihm etwas ins Getränk getan.«

"What next?" Sarah asks.

»Was machen wir nun?«, fragt Sarah.

"You tie him up. I'll plant enough evidence to involve him in every crime in the last ten years. Then I'll call the cops from Graf's cell phone."

»Du fesselst ihn. Ich platziere genügend Beweise, um ihn mit jedem Verbrechen der letzten zehn Jahre in Verbindung zu bringen. Dann rufe ich die Polizei von Grafs Handy aus an.«

---21---

"This is Detective Sergeant Frank Müller speaking to you on a recorded line. May I have your name, please?"

»Hier ist Kriminalbeamter Frank Müller, unser Gespräch

wird aufgezeichnet. Darf ich bitte Ihren Namen haben?«
vɪʁt ˈaʊfgəˌtsaɪçnət daʁf ɪç ˈbɪtə ˈiːʁən ˈnaːmən ˈhaːbn̩
it is being recorded may I I please your name to have

»Der ist unwichtig.«   "That's not important."
deːɐ ɪst ˈʊnvɪçtɪç
that it is unimportant

Ich spreche mit einer komischen Stimme, nur um ihn zu   I talk in a funny voice just to irritate him.
ɪç ˈʃpʁɛçə mɪt ˈaɪnɐ ˈkoːmɪʃən ˈʃtɪmə nuːɐ ʊm iːn tsuː
I I talk with a funny voice just in order to→ him ←

ärgern.
ˈɛʁgɐn
to annoy

»Sie sagten unserer Empfangsdame, dass Sie mir mit einigen   "You told our receptionist you want to help me with a few of my cases."
ziː ˈzaktən ˈʊnzɐʁɐ ɛmˈpfaŋsˌdaːmə das ziː miːɐ mɪt ˈaɪnɪgən
you you told our receptionist that you me with a few

meiner Fälle helfen wollen.«
ˈmaɪnɐ ˈfɛlə ˈhɛlfən ˈvɔlən
of my cases to help you want

»Ja, ich habe sie für Sie gelöst.«   "Yes. I solved them for you."
jaː ɪç ˈhaːbə ziː fyːɐ ziː gəˈløːst
yes I → them for you ←I solved

»Ich werde mit Ihnen nicht sprechen, es sei denn, Sie nennen mir   "I won't talk with you unless you tell me your name."
ɪç ˈveːɐdə mɪt ˈiːnən nɪçt ˈʃpʁɛçən ɛs zaɪ dɛn ziː ˈnɛnən miːɐ
I I will with you not to talk unless you you tell me

Ihren Namen.«
ˈiːʁən ˈnaːmən
your name

»Dann werden Sie aber wirklich dumm aussehen, wenn ich den   "Then you'll look really silly when I give the newspapers my information and mention that you weren't interested in listening."
dan ˈveːɐdən ziː ˈaːbɐ ˈvɪʁklɪç dʊm ˈaʊsˌzeːən vɛn ɪç deːn
then you will you ! really silly to look when I the

Zeitungen meine Information übermittle und erwähne, dass Sie
ˈtsaɪtʊŋən ˈmaɪnə ɪnfɔʁmaˈtsjoːn yːbɐˈmɪtlə ʊnt ɛɐˈvɛːnə das ziː
newspaper my information I pass on and I mention that you

nicht daran interessiert waren, mir zuzuhören.«
nɪçt daˈʁan ɪntəʁɛˈsiːɐt ˈvaːʁən miːɐ ˈtsuːtsuˌhøːʁən
not in it interested you were me to listen to

Ich höre ihn unter seinen Atemgeräuschen murmeln.   I hear him mutter under his breath.
ɪç ˈhøːʁə iːn ˈʊntɐ ˈzaɪnən ˈaːtəmgəˌʁɔʏʃn̩ ˈmʊʁmln̩
I I hear him under his breathing sounds to mutter

»Okay, reden Sie.«   "OK, talk to me."
oˈkeː ˈʁeːdən ziː
okay talk

Story 13

"A man named Joseph Graf murdered his wife about six months ago. You thought she was killed because of a botched extortion payoff, but he pulled the trigger."

»Ein Mann mit dem Namen Joseph Graf ermordete seine Frau vor etwa sechs Monaten. Sie dachten, sie sei wegen einer verpfuschten Erpresserzahlung umgebracht worden, jedoch hat er den Abzug betätigt.«

"And how do you know this?"

»Und woher wissen Sie das?«

"He never threw away the gun. Send someone to his house. You know where he lives. He's tied up and the gun is on the floor right next to him. His prints are all over it."

»Er hat die Pistole nie weggeworfen. Schicken Sie jemanden zu seinem Haus. Sie wissen doch, wo er wohnt. Er ist gefesselt und die Waffe liegt gleich neben ihm am Boden. Seine Fingerabdrücke sind überall darauf.«

Müller takes a few seconds to let that sink in.

Müller braucht ein paar Sekunden, um das sacken zu lassen.

"Can I put you on hold?" he asks.

»Können Sie einen Moment warten?«, fragt er.

"If you do that, I'll hang up and you won't know the whole story. By the way, I'm using Graf's cell phone."

»Wenn Sie das machen, werde ich auflegen und Sie werden nicht die ganze Geschichte kennen. Im Übrigen, ich benutze gerade Grafs Handy.«

"OK, keep talking."

»Okay, reden Sie weiter.«

Evolution

»Die zwei Versicherungsagenten wurden mit derselben Pistole
  di: tsvaɪ fɛɐ̯ˈzɪçəʁʊŋsaˌgɛntən ˈvʊʁdən   mɪt   deːɐ̯ˈzɛlbn   pɪsˈtoːlə
  the   two   insurance agents   →   with the same   gun
getötet, aber das wissen Sie schon.«
  gəˈtøːtət   ˈaːbɐ   das   ˈvɪsən   ziː   ʃoːn
  ← they were killed but   that you know you   already

"The same gun killed the two insurance agents, but you already know that."

»Ja.«
  jaː
  yes

"Yes."

»Herr Graf war der Drahtzieher hinter dem Erpressungsvorhaben.
  hɛʁ   gʁaːf vaːɐ̯ deːɐ̯ ˈdʁaːtˌtsiːɐ̯ ˈhɪntɐ deːm   ɛɐ̯ˈpʁɛsʊŋsˈfoːɐ̯ˌhaːbn
  Mr.   Graf   he was the   mastermind   behind   the   extortion enterprise
Er hat Hauptmann Philip Jung angeworben und ermordete ihn,
  eːɐ̯ hat ˈhaʊptman   ˈfilɪp   jʊŋ   ˈangəˌvɔʁbn   ʊnt   ɛɐ̯ˈmɔʁdətə   iːn
  he   →   captain   Philip   Jung ← he recruited and   he killed   him
als Hauptmann Jung auf Kaution frei war.«
  als   ˈhaʊptman   jʊŋ   aʊf kaʊˈtsjoːn   fʁaɪ   vaːɐ̯
  while captain   Jung   free on bail   he was

"Mr. Graf was the brains behind the extortion scheme. He recruited Captain Philip Jung and murdered him while Captain Jung was out on bail."

»Woher wissen Sie das?«
  voˈheːɐ̯   ˈvɪsən   ziː   das
  from where you know   you   this

"How do you know this?"

»Ich habe neben der Waffe einen Zettel hingelegt. Darin
  ɪç   ˈhaːbə   ˈneːbən   deːɐ̯   ˈvafə   ˈaɪnən   ˈtsɛtl   ˈhɪngəˌleːkt   daˈʁɪn
  I   →   next to   the   gun   a   note   ← I laid down therein
steht, wo das Gift gekauft wurde. Das Geschäft hat eine
  ʃteːt   voː   das   gɪft   gəˈkaʊft   ˈvʊʁdə   das   gəˈʃɛft   hat   aɪn
  it is stated where the   poison it was bought the   store   it has a
Überwachungskamera, deren Aufnahmen zeigen, wie Graf das
  yːbɐˈvaxʊŋsˌkameʁa   ˈdeːʁən   ˈaʊfnaːmən   ˈtsaɪgn   viː   gʁaːf   das
  surveillance camera   of which   recordings they show how   Graf   the
Gift kauft. Der Geschäftsführer wartet darauf, dass Sie das Band
  gɪft   ˈkaʊft   deːɐ̯   gəˈʃɛftsˌfyːʁɐ   ˈvaʁtət   daˈʁaʊf   das   ziː   das   bant
  poison he buys   the   store manager   he waits   for it   that   you   the   tape
abholen. Der Kassierer erinnert sich außerdem daran, wie Graf
  ˈapˌhoːlən   deːɐ̯   kaˈsiːʁɐ   ɛɐ̯ˈɪnɐt zɪç   ˈaʊsɐdeːm   daˈʁan   viː   gʁaːf
  to pick up   the   cashier   he remembers   also   on it   as   Graf
das Gift kaufte.«
  das   gɪft   ˈkaʊftə
  the   poison   he bought

"I left a note next to the gun. It tells you where the poison was purchased. The store has a surveillance camera that shows Graf buying the poison. The store manager is waiting for you to pick up the tape. Also, the cashier remembers Graf buying the poison."

»Was sonst noch?«, fragt er.
  vas   zɔnst   nɔx   fʁaːkt   eːɐ̯
  what   else   he asks   he

"What else?" he asks.

»Vergleichen Sie die Bankauszüge von Graf mit denen von
  fɛɐ̯ˈglaɪçən ziː   diː   ˈbaŋkˌaʊsˌtsyːgə   fɔn   gʁaːf   mɪt   ˈdeːnən   fɔn
  compare   the   bank statements   of   Graf   with   those   of

"Compare Graf's bank records against Captain Jung's records. You'll see that there are corresponding withdrawals

309

Story 13

and deposits."

Hauptmann	Jung.	Sie	werden	sehen,	dass	es	da
ˈhaʊptman	jʊŋ	ziː	ˈveːʁdn	ˈzeːən	das	ɛs	daː
captain	Jung	you	you will	to see	that	there are→	there

einander	entsprechende	Abbuchungen	und	Einzahlungen	gibt.«
aɪˈnandɐ	ɛntˈʃpʁeçəndə	ˈapˌbuːxʊŋən	ʊnt	ˈaɪnˌtsaːlʊŋən	ɡiːpt
corresponding		withdrawals	and	deposits	←

"Jung had offshore accounts. We couldn't trace the payments. Money seemed to get there from outer space," he says.

»Jung	hatte	Offshore-Konten.	Wir	konnten	die	Zahlungen	nicht
jʊŋ	ˈhatə	ˈɔfʃoːɐ-ˈkɔntn	viːɐ	ˈkɔntən	diː	ˈtsaːlʊŋən	nɪçt
Jung	he had	offshore accounts	we	we could	the	payments	not

verfolgen.	Das	Geld	schien	vom	Himmel	gefallen zu sein«,	sagt
fɛɐˈfɔlɡn	das	ɡɛlt	ʃiːn	fɔm	ˈhɪml	ɡəˈfalən tsuː zaɪn	zakt
to trace	the	money	it seemed	from the	sky	to have fallen	he says

er.
eːɐ
he

"You need a better hacker. My man will email you a detailed explanation of how the money was moved from one account into another. After you have all the records you will see that Jung and Graf were tied together like conjoined twins."

»Sie	brauchen	einen	besseren	Hacker.	Mein	Mann	wird	Ihnen
ziː	ˈbʁaʊxən	ˈaɪnən	ˈbɛsəʁən	ˈhakɐ	maɪn	man	vɪʁt	ˈiːnən
you	you need	a	better	hacker	my	man	he will	to you

eine	detaillierte	Erklärung	per	E-Mail	darüber	senden,	wie	das
ˈaɪnə	detaˈjiːɐtə	ɛɐˈklɛːʁʊŋ	pɛɐ	ˈiːmeːl	daˈʁyːbɐ	ˈzɛndən	viː	das
a	detailed	explanation	by	email	about it	to send	how	the

Geld	von	einem	Konto	zum	anderen	bewegt wurde.	Sobald	Sie
ɡɛlt	fɔn	ˈaɪnəm	ˈkɔntoː	tsʊm	ˈandəʁən	bəˈveːkt ˈvʊʁdə	zoˈbalt	ziː
money	from	one	account	to the	other	it was moved	once	you

alle	Unterlagen	vorliegen haben,	werden	Sie	sehen,	dass	Jung	und
ˈalə	ˈʊntɐlaːɡn	ˈfoːɐˌliːɡn ˈhaːbn	ˈveːʁdn	ziː	ˈzeːən	das	jʊŋ	ʊnt
all	documentation	you have on hand	you will	you	to see	that	Jung	and

Graf	wie	siamesische	Zwillinge	miteinander	verbunden	waren.«
ɡʁaːf	viː	ziaˈmeːzɪʃə	ˈtsvɪlɪŋə	ˈmɪtaɪˌnandɐ	fɛɐˈbʊndən	ˈvaːʁən
Graf	like		conjoined twins	with each other	connected	they were

"Who is this?"

»Wer	sind	Sie?«
veːɐ	zɪnt	ziː
who	are you	you

I hang up.

Ich	lege	auf.
ɪç	ˈleːɡə	aʊf
I	I hang up	

---22---

Five days later, the newspapers run a big story about Joseph Graf and Captain Philip Jung. Lina reads it to all of us.

Fünf	Tage	später	bringen	die	Zeitungen	einen	großen	Bericht
fynf	ˈtaːɡə	ˈʃpɛːtɐ	ˈbʁɪŋən	diː	ˈtsaɪtʊŋən	ˈaɪnən	ˈɡʁoːsən	bəˈʁɪçt
five	days	later	they bring	the	newspapers	a	big	story

über	Joseph	Graf	und	Hauptmann	Philip	Jung.	Lina	liest
ˈyːbɐ	ˈjoːzɛf	ɡʁaːf	ʊnt	ˈhaʊptman	ˈfɪlɪp	jʊŋ	ˈliːna	liːst
about	Joseph	Graf	and	captain	Philip	Jung	Lina	she reads aloud→

Evolution

ihn uns allen vor.
iːn ʊns ˈalən foːɐ̯
it to us all ←

»Du hast die Finger des ersten Ukrainers in Grafs Haus platziert«,
duː hast diː ˈfɪŋɐ dɛs ˈeːɐ̯stn ukʁaˈiːnɐs ɪn ɡʁaːfs haʊs plaˈtsiːɐ̯t
you → the fingers of the first Ukrainian in Graf's house ←you placed

sagt Anja. »Das ist widerlich!«
zakt ˈanja das ɪst ˈviːdɐlɪç
she says Anja that it is gross

"You put the first Ukranian's fingers in Graf's house," Anja says. "That's gross!"

»Ich fand es eine nette Geste«, sage ich.
ɪç fant ɛs ˈaɪnə ˈnɛtə ˈɡeːstə ˈzaːɡə ɪç
I I found it a nice touch I say I

"I thought it was a nice touch," I say.

»Die Polizei wird feststellen, dass Graf nicht die Finger seines
diː poliˈtsaɪ vɪʁt ˈfɛstʃtɛlən das ɡʁaːf nɪçt diː ˈfɪŋɐ ˈzaɪnəs
the police it will to realize that Graf not the fingers of his

eigenen Angestellten abschneiden würde«, sagt Roland.
ˈaɪɡənən ˈanɡəʃtɛltən ˈapʃnaɪdən ˈvʏʁdə zakt ˈʁoːlant
own employees he would cut off he says Roland

"The cops will realize that Graf wouldn't cut off his own employee's fingers," Roland says.

»Wahrscheinlich, aber es gibt den Reportern und Bloggern etwas,
vaːɐ̯ˈʃaɪnlɪç ˈaːbɐ ɛs ɡiːpt deːn ʁɛˈpɔʁtɐn ʊnt ˈblɔɡɐn ˈɛtvas
probably but it it gives the reporters and bloggers something

worüber sie sich auslassen können.«
voːˈʁyːbɐ ziː zɪç ˈaʊsˌlasn ˈkœnən
about which they they can spout off

"Probably, but it gives the reporters and bloggers something to shout about."

»Warum hat Graf seine Frau und die zwei Versicherungsleute
vaˈʁʊm hat ɡʁaːf ˈzaɪnə fʁaʊ ʊnt diː tsvaɪ fɛɐ̯ˈzɪçəʁʊŋsˌlɔɪtə
why → Graf his wife and the two insurance people

getötet?«, fragt Lina.
ɡəˈtøːtət fʁaːkt ˈliːna
←he killed she asks Lina

"Why did Graf kill his wife and the two insurance men?" Lina asks.

»Sie hat ihn dauernd angeschrien, den Toilettensitz unten zu
ziː hat iːn ˈdaʊɐnt ˈanɡəʃʁiːn deːn toaˈlɛtnˌzɪts ˈʊntən tsuː
she → him ←she kept yelling at the toilet seat down to

lassen«, scherzt Roland.
ˈlasən ˈʃɛʁtst ˈʁoːlant
to leave he jokes Roland

"She kept yelling at him to keep the toilet seat down," Roland jokes.

Ich schmunzle etwas.
ɪç ˈʃmʊntslə ˈɛtvas
I I chuckle somewhat

I chuckle a little bit.

»Das ist ein guter Witz.«
das ɪst aɪn ˈɡuːtɐ vɪts
that it is a good joke

"That's a pretty good one."

311

Story 13

"Could we please not make fun of murder victims?" Lucia asks.

»Könnten wir uns über Mordopfer bitte nicht lustig machen?«, bittet Lucia.

"He took out a ten million Euro life insurance policy on his wife a few years ago," Anja explains. "That's when he started thinking about how he could get rid of her without being caught. Which led to the whole extortion scheme."

»Vor ein paar Jahren hat er eine Lebensversicherung über zehn Millionen Euro auf seine Frau zu seinen Gunsten abgeschlossen«, erklärt Anja. »Damals fing er an, darüber nachzudenken, wie er sie loswerden könnte, ohne dabei erwischt zu werden. Was schließlich zu diesem ganzen Erpressungsplan führte.«

"Not a bad plan," Roland says. "He gets rid of his wife and eliminates himself as a suspect simultaneously."

»Kein schlechter Plan«, sagt Roland. »Er wird seine Frau los und schließt sich selbst gleichzeitig als Verdächtigen aus.«

"I don't know why he killed those two insurance men," I tell them. "I didn't bother asking him."

»Ich weiß nicht, warum er die beiden Versicherungsleute tötete«, sage ich zu ihnen. »Ich dachte nicht daran, ihn danach zu fragen.«

"Graf was a smart guy," Anja says. "We were lucky that Captain Jung made that one mistake."

»Graf war ein schlauer Bursche«, sagt Anja. »Wir hatten Glück, dass Hauptmann Jung den einen Fehler machte.«

"Do you think the police understand my email about the money transfers between Graf and Jung?" Roland asks.

»Meint ihr, die Polizei versteht meine E-Mail über den

Geldverkehr zwischen Graf und Jung?«, fragt Roland.

»Wahrscheinlich. Ich werde den Kriminalbeamten Müller in ein paar Tagen anrufen, um dem nachzugehen. Er wird wahrscheinlich wieder mit mir reden wollen.«

"Probably. I'll call Detective Müller in a few days to follow up. He probably wants to talk with me again."

»Warum?«, fragt Anja.

"Why?" Anja asks.

»Sarah ist hier nicht irgendwo im Büro, oder?«, frage ich.

"Sarah's not hanging around the office anywhere, is she?" I ask.

»Nein, sie arbeitet heute an einem anderen Fall«, sagt mir Lucia.

"No, she's working another case today," Lucia tells me.

»Gut. Um Anjas Frage zu beantworten, Sarah und ich haben Grafs Haus gesäubert, damit die Polizei unsere Fingerabdrücke nicht finden würde. Dann habe ich ein wenig Bewusstseinszauber bei Graf eingesetzt, um sicherzustellen, dass er sich nicht daran erinnern würde, uns jemals gesehen zu haben. Daher ist Müller wahrscheinlich sehr interessiert daran herauszufinden, wer ich bin und wie es mir möglich war, den Fall zu lösen.«

"Good. To answer Anja's question, Sarah and I sanitized Graf's house so the police wouldn't have our fingerprints. Then I worked a little mind mojo on Graf to make sure he wouldn't remember anything about ever seeing us. So Müller is probably very anxious to find out who I am and how I was able to solve the case."

»Von dem Geld und den Diamanten, die sie von Hauptmann Jung

"Between the money and diamonds they got from Captain Jung and whatever they find in Graf's accounts, the

Story 13

"victims will get most of their money back," Lucia says.

erhielten, und was auch immer sie in den Konten von Graf finden,
ɐɐˈhiːltn ʊnt vas aʊx ˈɪmɐ ziː ɪn deːn ˈkɔntən fɔn gʁaːf ˈfɪndən
they got and whatever else they in the accounts of Graf they find

werden die Opfer den Großteil ihres Geldes zurückbekommen«,
ˈveːɐdn diː ˈɔpfɐ deːn ˈgʁoːsˌtaɪl ˈiːʁəs ˈgɛldəs tsuˈʁʏkbəˌkɔmən
they will the victims the better part of their money to get back

sagt Lucia.
zakt luˈtsia
she says Lucia

"Do you think the evidence you left at the house is enough to convict him?" Anja asks.

»Glaubst du, dass die Beweise, die du im Haus hinterlassen hast,
glaʊpst duː das diː bəˈvaɪzə diː duː ɪm haʊs hɪntɐˈlasən hast
you think you that the evidence that you in the house you left behind

genug sind, um ihn zu überführen?«, fragt Anja.
gəˈnuːk zɪnt ʊm iːn tsuː yːbɐˈfyːʁən fʁaːkt ˈanja
enough they are in order to him to to convict she asks Anja

"I think so. Roland also fabricated a few financial transactions that link Graf to the Ukrainians. As the cops unravel Graf's bank records, those transactions will pop up like red flags," I tell her.

»Ich denke schon. Roland hat auch ein paar finanzielle
ɪç ˈdɛŋkə ʃoːn ˈʁoːlant hat aʊx aɪn paːɐ finanˈtsjɛlə
I I think so Roland → also a few financial

Transaktionen erfunden, die Graf mit den Ukrainern
tʁansakˈtsjoːnən ɐɐˈfʊndən diː gʁaːf mɪt deːn ukʁaˈiːnɐn
transactions ← he fabricated that Graf with the Ukrainians

in Verbindung bringen. Wenn die Polizei die Bankunterlagen
ɪn fɐɐˈbɪndʊŋ ˈbʁɪŋən vɛn diː poliˈtsaɪ diː ˈbaŋkʊntɐˌlaːgn
they link when the police the bank records

von Graf untersucht, werden ihnen diese Transaktionen wie
fɔn gʁaːf ʊntɐˈzuːxt ˈveːɐdn ˈiːnən ˈdiːzə tʁansakˈtsjoːnən viː
of Graf she (police) examines they will → these transactions like

Warnsignale ins Auge springen«, sage ich ihr.
ˈvaʁnzɪˌgnaːlə ɪns ˈaʊgə ˈʃpʁɪŋən ˈzaːgə ɪç iːɐ
warning signals ← to catch their eyes I say I to her

"You guys are so dishonest," Lina says.

»Ihr seid so unehrlich«, sagt Lina.
iːɐ zaɪt zoː ˈʊnˌeːɐlɪç zakt ˈliːna
you you are so dishonest she says Lina

That night, Lucia and I are in bed together. I rub her feet. She likes that. Lucia tells me that tomorrow she wants to look for a new location for our office.

Am selben Abend liegen Lucia und ich zusammen im Bett. Ich
am ˈzɛlbən ˈaːbənt ˈliːgən luˈtsia ʊnt ɪç tsuˈzamən ɪm bɛt ɪç
on the same night we lie Lucia and I together in bed I

reibe ihr die Füße. Sie mag das. Lucia sagt mir, dass sie morgen
ˈʁaɪbə iːɐ diː ˈfyːsə ziː mak das luˈtsia zakt miːɐ das ziː ˈmɔʁgn
I rub her the feet she she likes that Lucia she tells me that she tomorrow

einen neuen Standort für das Büro suchen wolle.
ˈaɪnən ˈnɔɪən ˈʃtantˌɔʁt fyːɐ das byˈʁoː ˈzuːxn ˈvɔlə
a new location for the office ← to look for she wants

"Why?" I ask.

»Warum?«, frage ich.
vaˈʁʊm ˈfʁaːgə ɪç
why I ask I

Evolution

»Wir können viel Geld verdienen, wenn wir die Marzahn-Immobilie in Wohnungen umwandeln und sie dann verkaufen. Der Immobilienmarkt erholt sich langsam«, sagt sie.
viːɐ ˈkœnən fiːl gɛlt fɛɐˈdiːnən vɛn viːɐ diː maɐˈtsaːn-ɪmoˈbiːljə ɪn ˈvoːnʊŋən ˈʊmˌvandəln ʊnt ziː dan fɛɐˈkaʊfən deːɐ ɪmoˈbiːljənˌmaɐkt ɛɐˈhoːlt zɪç ˈlaŋˌzaːm zaxt ziː
we we can a lot of money to earn if we the Marzahn property into apartments to convert and them then to sell the real estate market it is recovering slowly she says she

"We can make a lot of money converting the Marzahn property into condos and selling them. The real estate market is starting to come back," she says.

»Wo sollen wir uns umschauen?«, frage ich.
voː ˈzɔlən viːɐ ʊns ˈʊmʃaʊən ˈfʁaːgə ɪç
where should we we to look around I ask I

"Where should we look?" I ask.

»Ich dachte an Mariendorf. Das ist eine schöne kleine Gegend und liegt direkt an der Bahnstrecke nach Berlin. Außerdem gibt es dort großartige Restaurants. Du hattest nie eine Beziehung mit einer Maria, oder?«
ɪç ˈdaxtə an maˈʁiːənˌdɔɐf das ɪst ˈaɪnə ˈʃøːnə ˈklaɪnə ˈgeːgnt ʊnt liːkt diˈʁɛkt an deːɐ ˈbaːnˌʃtʁɛkə naːx bɛɐˈliːn ˈaʊsɐdeːm giːpt ɛs dɔɐt ˈgʁoːsˌaɐtigə ʁɛstoˈʁãːs duː ˈhatəst niː ˈaɪnə bəˈtsiːʊŋ mɪt ˈaɪnə maˈʁiːa ˈoːdɐ
I I thought about Mariendorf that it is a nice little neighborhood and it is located directly on the railway line to Berlin in addition there are there great restaurants you you had never a relationship with a Maria did you

"I was thinking of Mariendorf. It's a nice little neighborhood, and it's right on the train line for Berlin. Plus, there are great restaurants. You never dated anyone named Maria, did you?"

»Nicht, dass ich wüsste.«
nɪçt das ɪç ˈvʏstə
not that I I am aware of

"Not that I remember."

Ich reibe ihr die Füße noch etwas länger.
ɪç ˈʁaɪbə iːɐ diː ˈfyːsə nɔx ˈɛtvas ˈlɛŋɐ
I I rub her the feet a bit longer

I rub her feet some more.

»Ich brauche eine neue Pistole«, sage ich.
ɪç ˈbʁaʊxə ˈaɪnə ˈnɔɪə pɪsˈtoːlə ˈzaːgə ɪç
I I need a new gun I say I

"I need a new gun," I say.

»Reibst du mir deshalb die Füße?«
ʁaɪpst duː miːɐ ˈdɛsˌhalp diː ˈfyːsə
you rub you me that is why the feet

"Is that why you are rubbing my feet?"

»Vielleicht.«
fiˈlaɪçt
maybe

"Maybe."

»Wie wäre es, wenn du mir eine Weile den Rücken massierst.
viː ˈvɛːʁə ɛs vɛn duː miːɐ ˈaɪnə ˈvaɪlə deːn ˈʁʏkən maˈsiːɐst
how about if you me a while the back you massage

"How about massaging my back for a while. After that we can talk about guns."

Story 13

Danach können wir über Pistolen reden.«
daˈnaːx   ˈkœnən   viːɐ   ˈyːbɐ   pɪsˈtoːlən   ˈʁeːdən
after that we can   we   about   guns   to talk

Part II

STORIES IN GERMAN ONLY

STORY 1

Garden Variety

Einen Garten zu haben ist nicht der richtige Weg, Geld zu sparen. Man glaubt, dass all das selbst angebaute Gemüse Lebensmittelkosten verringern werde. Aber man vergisst die Kosten, die bei der Bewirtschaftung eines eigenen Gartens anfallen. Man sollte daher Gemüse nur wegen der psychologischen Vorteile anbauen.

Kaum zu glauben, wie sehr meine Frau ihren Garten liebt. Gemüse wachsen zu sehen, gibt ihr ein unglaubliches Gefühl von Zufriedenheit. Ich empfinde dagegen etwas anderes. Nämlich Schmerz!

Einen Garten einzuzäunen macht keinen Spaß. Es kostet ungefähr 250 Euro an Material, einen 5 mal 6 Meter großen Garten mit einem 2,5 Meter hohen Zaun einzuzäunen. Es braucht einen 2,5 Meter hohen Zaun, um die Rehe davon abzuhalten, den Garten in ein Salatbuffet zu verwandeln.

Und trotzdem können sie auf andere Art und Weise hineingelangen. Durch die Sträucher verdeckt, halten sie sich manchmal ganz in der Nähe der Gartentüre auf. Unbemerkt schlüpfen sie hinein, wenn man zum Unkrautjäten geht. Letzten Sommer versuchte ein Reh, mit einem Fallschirm im Garten zu landen. Glücklicherweise drehte der Wind und es blieb mit seinem Huf im Dach meines Nachbarn hängen.

Es ist keine leichte Angelegenheit, den Boden zu bestellen. Zuerst muss man zum örtlichen Geräteverleih gehen und eine Fräse finden, die in sein Fahrzeug passt. Wenn man nicht gerade einen Lastwagen mit Vierradantrieb hat, bleibt einem nur eine kleine Fräse.

Die Kleinen wiegen ungefähr ein Kilo und schlittern auf der Erdoberfläche nur so dahin. Das bedeutet, man muss die rotierenden Messer der Fräse in den harten Boden hineindrücken.

Bodenfräsen für zwei Stunden. Versuchen Sie das mal, wenn Ihre sonst üblichen Leibesübungen nur darin bestehen, ein Weinglas zu heben oder sich durch Fersehprogramme zu zappen.

Dann muss man seiner Frau helfen, die Löcher für die Samen zu buddeln. Zugegeben, es sind kleine Löcher. Aber Buddeln macht keinen Spaß, es sei denn, man findet einen vergrabenen Schatz.

Nach einigen Wochen, wenn es nicht zu viel und nicht zu wenig geregnet hat und die Hasen nicht durch den Zaun geschlüpft sind, darf man dann Unkraut zupfen und ein bisschen Gemüse ernten.

Ich versuche immer, zu verreisen, wenn das Unkraut aus dem Boden schießt, aber manchmal kann ich mir nicht freinehmen und dann lasse ich mich zum Jäten breitschlagen.

Dann verbringe ich einige Sitzungen beim Chiropraktiker, der dann meinen Rücken wieder so hinbiegt, dass ich normal stehen kann.

Die Erntearbeit erfordert viele Tätigkeiten in gebückter Haltung. Heben Sie nur einen Sack Bohnen auf und schon geht es wieder zum Chiropraktiker, der sich gerade eine kleine Jacht gekauft hat von den Gebühren, die ich ihm während der Gartensaison gezahlt habe.

Als die Kinder noch kleiner waren, hatten wir einen viel größeren Garten und pflanzten immer viel zu viel an. Jedes Jahr pflanzten wir vier Zucchinipflanzen. Welche normale Familie kann denn die Ernte von vier Zucchinipflanzen essen?

Wir hatten immer so viele Zucchini, dass wir sie verschenken mussten. Wir luden die Kinder in einen kleinen roten Leiterwagen, packten die Zucchini oben drauf, gaben ihnen Schnorchel, sodass sie nicht erstick-

Story 1

ten und marschierten die Straße hinunter.

Alle unsere Nachbarn bekamen Gemüse. Nach etwa ein bis zwei Wochen erkannten die Nachbarn das Quietschen unseres Leiterwagens, als wir unsere Runden machten. Sie zogen die Vorhänge zu und versperrten die Haustüren. Niemand war zu Hause in der gesamten Nachbarschaft.

Was soll mit den übrigen Zucchini geschehen? Wir errichteten einen Zucchini-Verkaufsstand in unserer Einfahrt. Selbst unsere Tochter, die jedem alles verkaufen kann, war nicht in der Lage, unsere Ware zu verkaufen.

Meine Frau entdeckte schließlich Rezepte für Zucchinisuppe, Zucchinikekse, Zucchinipopcorn, usw.

Nachts schlich ich in unseren Garten hinaus und gab den Zucchinipflanzen heimlich Tabletten zur Empfängnisverhütung. Ich versuchte einfach alles, damit die Vermehrung ein Ende habe.

Meine Frau pflanzte auch viele Auberginen. Ich hatte noch nie etwas von Auberginen gehört, bis ich von Berlin in die Eutiner Wildnis gezogen bin. Natürlich haben die meisten Leute in Eutin nicht gewusst, was eine Spezi ist, damit war ein gewisser Ausgleich gegeben.

Da meine Frau aus Hamburg stammt, habe ich keine Ahnung, wo sie jemals den Gedanken aufgriff, dass Auberginen etwas wären, was normale Menschen essen würden. Kein Mensch in Hamburg aß Auberginen.

Ich konnte mich mit der Idee, Auberginen anzupflanzen oder auch nur irgendetwas zu essen, das Auberginen enthält, nicht anfreunden. Sie hatten eine komische Farbe. Wer hat je von lilafarbenem Gemüse gehört? Sie waren zu matschig, wenn sie gekocht waren. Sie haben bei mir Cholera, Warzen oder ähnliche Sachen hervorgerufen.

Trotz allem bauten wir viele Auberginen an. Jeden Abend spielten wir »Verstecken«. Meine Frau versteckte irgendwo im Abendessen Auberginen und die Kinder und ich versuchten, sie zu finden, um sie dann auf den Boden fallen zu lassen.

Wir haben uns so oft beschwert, dass meine Frau in einen Kochstreik getreten ist. Das war nicht gut. Wir überlebten meine Kochkunst gerade drei Tage. Dann haben die Kinder das Handtuch geworfen. Ich hielt noch weitere zwanzig Minuten durch, um ihnen zu zeigen, was in mir steckt. Dann habe auch ich aufgegeben. Danach gab es Tag und Nacht Auberginen.

Die Tomaten waren der sogenannte Gnadenstoß in unserem Garten. Jedes Jahr haben wir zwölf, jawohl, ich sagte zwölf, Tomatenpflanzen angepflanzt.

Ich wollte sie einsperren. Ich dachte, das würde den Ertrag verringern. Aber diese Schmarotzer sind einfach zwischen den Stäben der Käfige hindurchgewachsen.

Jedes Jahr am dritten Donnerstag im August reiften alle Tomaten nacheinander im Abstand von acht Minuten. Dies bedeutete immer nur das eine – Tomatensauce. Ich hasse es, Tomatensauce zu machen. Das dauert ungefähr drei Tage.

Zuerst muss man ungefähr dreitausend Tomaten pflücken. Dann muss man sie in einen Topf mit kochendem Wasser werfen. Normalerweise machen wir ein Feuer unter dem Jacuzzi im Obergeschoss und benutzen ihn als Kochtopf.

Die Tomaten kreischen, wenn man sie hineinwirft. Es hört sich fürchterlich an. Naja, wenn ich darüber nachdenke, kommt der Lärm eigentlich von mir. Ich werfe die Tomaten immer etwas zu heftig in den Jacuzzi und bespritze mich dabei selbst mit dem kochend heißen Wasser. Das tut weh!

Nach ein paar Minuten muss man die Tomaten aus dem heißen Wasser herausnehmen und schälen. Sie lassen sich nicht gerne schälen. Sie winden sich und rutschen weg und versuchen zu entkommen.

Man darf sie nicht aus seinem Griff rutschen lassen, sonst wird man mit dem »bösen Blick« bestraft. Der böse Blick ist ein Gesichtsausdruck, mit dem mein Vater experimentierte und den meine Frau perfektionierte. Ich kann fühlen, wie der böse Blick mich durchdringt, wenn ich eine entschlüpfte, halbnackte Tomate ins Wohnzimmer verfolge.

Wenn die Tomaten alle geschält sind und zitternd am Jacuzzi liegen, muss man die Samen herausnehmen. Ich kann die Qualen, die ich dabei fühle, kaum beschreiben, während ich eines nach dem anderen dieser armen, kleinen Dinger nehme und drücke, bis ihre vielen kleinen Samen herausgequetscht sind. Ich kann kaum sagen, wie viele künftige Generationen dieser Tomaten von meinen schwieligen Fingern zerquetscht worden sind.

Schließlich püriert man die Tomaten in einem Mixer und übergibt sie seiner Frau, der Meisterin der Soßenherstellung. Ich weiß nicht, zu welchen unbeschreiblichen Handlungen sie von da an übergeht.

Nach dem Püree-Teil flüchte ich normalerweise aus der Küche. Da ich jedoch weiß, dass das Ergebnis sehr gut schmeckt, zerbreche ich mir darüber nicht allzu sehr den Kopf. Leider beträgt die Ausbeute aus tausenden Tomaten nach drei Tagen Arbeit ungefähr eine halbe Tasse Soße. Die Frucht dieser Arbeit ist also recht kurzlebig.

Während ich dies schreibe, erinnere ich mich an den Geruch der Tomatensoße, der aus der Küche kam. Es war ein wundervoller Geruch.

Heutzutage ist unser Garten viel kleiner. Gott sei Dank für diese kleinen, guten Taten.

Der Leiterwagen rostet im Keller vor sich hin und die Räder quietschen immer noch. Die Kinder sind nicht mehr hier, um »Aubergine-Verstecken« zu spielen. Die Nachbarn sind verreist, für den Fall, dass wir versuchen, mit ihnen unser Gemüse zu teilen.

Aber die Pflege des Gartens kostet immer noch weitaus mehr, als man beim Lebensmitteleinkauf spart.

Im letzten April habe ich den Garten für die Ernte dieses Jahres umgegraben und laufe immer noch herum wie jemand, der einen 20 Kilo schweren Stein auf seinem Rücken trägt. Ich muss wieder zurück zum Chiropraktiker!

STORY 2

A Good Sport

»Hört auf, Dreck aufeinander zu werfen!«, brüllte ich.

»Christian hat mich mit seiner Wasserflasche bespritzt.«

»Christian, hör auf!«

Christian, mein Sohn, sollte eigentlich ein gutes Beispiel für die anderen Jungen sein.

»Trainer Daniel, ich kann zum Spiel am Samstag nicht kommen«, sagte Peter. »Ich will nicht mehr trainieren.«

»Warum nicht?«, fragte ich.

»Ich mag Fußball nicht.«

»Warum bist du dann in die Mannschaft eingetreten?«

»Meine Mutter hat mich dazu gezwungen.«

In diesem Moment traf mich ein Dreckklumpen.

»Hört auf, Dreck zu werfen!«, schrie ich. »In zwei Tagen haben wir unser erstes Spiel. Jeder setzt sich jetzt und hört für ein paar Minuten zu.«

Endlich setzte sich meine Mannschaft, die aus neun- und zehnjährigen Jungen bestand, ins Gras. Sie waren sehr viel gelaufen und waren verschwitzt und müde.

Ich sprach schnell. Jungs können nicht allzu lange stillsitzen. Nachdem wir fünf Minuten lang die Vorgehensweise besprochen hatten, trainierten wir wieder.

Eine Stunde später war das Training vorbei. Ich musste zwanzig Minuten warten, bis die letzte Mutter erschien, um ihr Kind abzuholen.

»Wenn Sie nächstes Mal spät dran sind, werde ich ihn verkaufen«, sagte ich ihr.

―2―

Zu unserem ersten Spiel erschienen elf der insgesamt fünfzehn Spieler unserer Mannschaft.

»Wo sind sie denn alle?«, fragte meine Frau Ingrid.

»Das ist doch nur eine Ortsliga«, sagte einer der Väter. »Die Eltern und die Kinder nehmen es nicht ernst. Es ist für sie nur eine Samstagsbeschäftigung, wenn sie sonst nichts zu tun haben.«

»Es ist unfair gegenüber denjenigen, die kommen«, sagte ich.

Klaus kam während des Aufwärmens zu mir herüber.

»Ich will heute nicht spielen.«

»Warum nicht?«

»Der große Junge aus der anderen Mannschaft hat mir gesagt, dass er mich umhauen wird.«

»Hans wird dich beschützen.«

»Nein, werde ich nicht!«, schrie Hans.

Story 2

»Peter, warum ziehst du deine Stollenschuhe aus?«

»Ich will nicht spielen.«

Gerade in diesem Moment kam die Mutter von Peter und nahm ihm beim Ohr. Er begann, seine Stollenschuhe wieder anzuziehen.

Ein paar Minuten später fing das Spiel an. Prompt verließ Klaus den Platz und versteckte sich hinter einem Stuhl. Wir mussten daraufhin mit einem Mann weniger spielen.

Die Eltern unserer Spieler waren sehr ruhig. Die meiste Zeit saßen sie auf ihren Klappstühlen und redeten miteinander. Ich bemerkte, wie einige von ihnen etwa eine oder zwei Sekunden dem Spiel zusahen. Aber die meiste Zeit interessierten sie sich nicht zu sehr dafür. Sie ärgerten sich zur Halbzeit, da sie mit dem Plaudern aufhören mussten, um ihren Kindern einen Pausensnack zu geben.

»Die Sache hat auch etwas Positives«, sagte Ingrid. »Sie könnten ja auch wie die Eltern der Spieler der gegnerischen Mannschaft sein.«

»Diese Leute sind wirklich laut und nicht nett. Ich habe noch nie zuvor einen Vater gesehen, der wegen eines Handspiels einen Stuhl nach seinem eigenen Kind wirft.«

»Wir haben beim Freistoß ein Tor erzielt«, erinnerte mich Ingrid.

»Wird Christian in dieser Halbzeit wieder Torwart?«, fuhr sie fort.

»Nein.«

»Prima. Ich will nicht wieder dabei zusehen, wie sich seine Beine im Tornetz verfangen.«

»Wie hat er das bloß gemacht, ausgerechnet, als die andere Mannschaft einen Angriff startete?«

»Ich weiß es nicht, aber Gott sei Dank ist Dieter so schnell«, sagte Ingrid.

»Hätte er nicht den Stürmer eingeholt und den Ball ins Aus geschossen, hätte Christian traurig ausgesehen«, sagte ich.

———————3———————

Der große Junge der anderen Mannschaft war langsam. Irgendein Mann auf der anderen Seite des Fußballfeldes begann, entlang der Seitenlinie auf- und abzulaufen und rief ihm zu, schneller zu laufen.

»Wer ist dieser Spinner?«, fragte ich.

»Das ist sein Vater«, sagte Ingrid.

Nach zehn Minuten war der Junge so sauer, dass er das Feld verließ. Er setzte sich hin und weinte, während sich sein Vater und seine Mutter stritten.

»Da der Große ja aufgegeben hat, kann ich jetzt spielen«, sagte Klaus.

»Großartig. Geh rein als Innenverteidiger. Wir haben das ganze Spiel ohne einen gespielt.«

Zwei Minuten später bemerkte ich etwas.

»Niemand spielt in seiner Position«, sagte ich. »Die rennen alle einfach dem Ball nach.«

»Das kommt in dieser Liga oft vor«, sagte Martins Vater.

»Wie soll ich sie dazu bringen, damit aufzuhören?«

»Ich weiß nicht. Sie sind doch der Trainer.«

»Ingrid, lass Irma von der Leine.«

Irma war unser Hund. Wir hatten sie zum Spiel mitgebracht.

»Sie wird auf das Feld laufen und hinter dem Ball herrennen«, sagte Ingrid.

»Genau das soll sie machen. Der Schiedsrichter wird das Spiel unterbrechen und ich kann mit der Mannschaft reden.«

»Das ist nicht fair. Das mache ich nicht.«

»Sag einem der Kinder, es soll eine Verletzung vortäuschen«, schlug Martins Vater vor.

»Das ist auch nicht gerade nett«, sagte Ingrid.

»Das wird in der Europaliga immer so gemacht«, sagte ich ihr. »Einige Berufsfußballer machen das wirklich geschickt.«

»Aber das hier sind zehn Jahre alte Kinder. So etwas sollte man ihnen nicht beibringen, in ihren jungen Jahren.«

»Sicher nicht, aber sie wollen doch gewinnen.«

»Ihnen ist es egal, ob sie gewinnen«, sagte Ingrid. »Dir bedeutet es etwas.«

In diesem Moment erzielte die gegnerische Mannschaft ein Tor.

4

»War das nicht ein tolles Spiel?«, fragte ich Christian.

»Es hat wirklich Spaß gemacht«, antwortete er.

»Schade für den Trainer der anderen Mannschaft«, sagte Ingrid.

»Warum hat der Schiedsrichter ihn kurz vor dem Ende vom Platz geschickt?«, fragte Christian.

»Der Trainer war nicht davon überzeugt, dass der Schiedsrichter eine gute Arbeit geleistet hat«, sagte ich.

»Er benutzte viele schlimme Wörter, die man nicht in der Gegenwart anständiger Leute gebrauchen sollte«, fügte Ingrid hinzu.

»Wir haben nicht gewonnen«, sagte Christian. »Aber wir haben gut gespielt. Ein Unentschieden ist ziemlich gut.«

»Du hast lustig ausgesehen, als du nach dem Tor auf- und abgesprungen bist«, sagte Christian.

»Erinnerst du dich noch daran, was ich gerufen habe?«

»Bleibt auf eurer Position, bleibt auf eurer Position.«

»Richtig. Und in der verbleibenden Spielzeit habt ihr das alle beherzigt. Also hat sich das Herumhüpfen gelohnt.«

»Hat dir mein Kopfball gefallen?«

»Er war ziemlich gut. Das nächste Mal solltest du den oberen Teil deines Kopfes verwenden, nicht dein Gesicht.«

»Meine Nase tut immer noch weh.«

»Nach dem Eisessen wird es dir besser gehen.«

»Wann können wir nach Hause gehen?«

»Sobald die Schwellung zurückgeht und es aufhört, zu bluten«, sagte Ingrid. »Mama will nicht, das Blut auf den Teppich kommt.«

STORY 3

Truth Will Out

Ich habe Rolf, meinen Nachbarn und Börsenmakler, angerufen, um ihm ein paar Fragen über einen Investmentfonds, den er mir verkauft hat, zu stellen.

»Klaus, ich kann heute nicht mit dir sprechen«, sagte er zu mir.

»Warum nicht«, fragte ich.

»Ich nehme Medikamente gegen meine Rückenschmerzen. Sie haben eine sonderbare Nebenwirkung. Sie zwingen mich, die Wahrheit zu sagen.«

»Ist das so schlimm?«, fragte ich.

»Es ist das Schlimmste, was einem Börsenmakler passieren könnte. Wir erzählen nie die Wahrheit. Ups. Das hätte ich nicht sagen sollen. Siehst du, welche Wirkung diese Tabletten auf mich haben?«

»Ich bin dein Freund und Nachbar. Du kannst mir die Wahrheit erzählen.«

»Ich spreche mit niemandem, bis ich mit diesen Tabletten fertig bin. Es ist zu gefährlich. Der einzige Grund, weshalb ich diesen Anruf angenommen habe, ist, dass ich dachte, du willst dich mit mir zu einem Golfspiel verabreden. Alle anderen Anrufe werden direkt zur Mailbox weitergeleitet.«

Ich legte auf und ging in die Küche.

»Rolf will nicht mit mir reden«, sagte ich zu meiner Frau Ingrid.

»Das klingt aber komisch.«

»Er nimmt Tabletten für seinen Rücken und die zwingen ihn, immer nur die Wahrheit zu sagen«, sagte ich. »Daher hat er Angst, mit seinen Kunden zu sprechen.«

Ingrid saß am Küchentisch und aß ein Plätzchen. Sie runzelte die Stirn. Ich wusste, dass ihr etwas in den Sinn kam.

»Das wäre doch der richtige Zeitpunkt, herauszufinden, ob Rolf uns die richtigen Anlagen verkauft hat«, sagte sie.

Ich dachte eine Minute darüber nach.

»Du hast Recht«, sagte ich. »Besuchen wir ihn, wenn er heimkommt. Seine Frau ist auf einer Geschäftsreise und wird ihn nicht beschützen können.«

»Ich werde eine Babysitterin für die Kinder anrufen, damit wir uns nicht sorgen müssen, dass das Haus abbrennt, während wir Rolf zur Wahrheit zwingen«, sagte Ingrid.

Zwei Stunden später machte Rolf seine Haustür auf. Ingrid und ich traten hinter der großen Hecke neben der Tür hervor. Rolf sprang einen Meter hoch in die Luft. Dann erkannte er uns.

»Klaus, ich habe beinahe einen Herzinfarkt bekommen. Warum versteckst du dich mit Ingrid hinter dem Gebüsch?«

»Wir wollen dir ein paar Fragen über unsere Investitionen stellen«, sagte ich.

Ingrid öffnete die Tür und begleitete Rolf hinein.

»Setze dich da drüben hin, Rolf«, befahl Ingrid. Sie zeigte auf ein Sofa im Wohnzimmer.

»Vielleicht sollte ich mich hinlegen«, sagte Rolf. »Mein Rücken schmerzt so sehr.«

Story 3

»Nur zu«, sagte Ingrid.

»Wenn doch nur meine Frau hier wäre«, murmelte Rolf, als er sich hinlegte.

»Schau nicht so besorgt«, sagte ich. »Wir sind doch deine Freunde.«

»Hast du uns die richtigen Geldanlagen verkauft?«, verlangte Ingrid zu wissen.

»Ich sollte nicht über meine Arbeit sprechen, bis ich meine Tabletten alle genommen habe«, sagte Rolf.

Ingrid kniff ihre Augen zusammen, während sie unseren Nachbarn anstarrte.

»Wenn du nicht mitmachst, erzähle ich allen in der Nachbarschaft von deiner Nasenoperation und deinen Brustmuskelnimplantaten«, sagte Ingrid.

»Das ist Erpressung«, sagte Rolf.

»Du hast zwei Möglichkeiten«, sagte ich. »Entweder du redest mit uns oder die ganze Nachbarschaft wird dich auslachen.«

Ich bemerkte einen Ausdruck der Resignation in Rolfs Augen.

»Also gut, ich werde reden. Um eure Frage zu beantworten, ich verkaufe die Produkte, die mir die höchsten Provisionen einbringen. Mir ist es egal, ob das die richtigen Geldanlagen für euch sind.«

»Das haben wir davon, dass wir unseren Nachbarn vertrauen«, sagte Ingrid zu mir.

»Wer hat euch von meinen Schönheitsoperationen erzählt?«, fragte Rolf.

»Das ist mein Geheimnis«, sagte Ingrid. »Nach dem, was du mir erzählt hast, kannst du dich glücklich schätzen, dass deine neue Nase nicht gebrochen ist.«

Ingrid beugte sich über das Sofa und starrte in Rolfs Augen. Ich sah wie sich Schweißperlen auf seiner Stirn bildeten.

»Wie investieren wir am besten unser Geld?«, fragte Ingrid.

»Kauft einen Rentenfonds, einen Fonds der sich auf inländische Aktien spezialisiert, und einen anderen Fonds, der in ausländische Aktien investiert.«

»Wie viel Geld sollen wir in jeden Fonds einzahlen?«, fragte ich.

»In eurem Alter würde ich dreißig Prozent in Rentenfonds, fünfzehn Prozent in ausländische Aktienfonds und den Rest in inländische Aktienfonds investieren.«

Ingrid und ich verdauten diese neuen Informationen einige Minuten lang.

»Ich will wirklich keine Fragen mehr beantworten«, jammerte Rolf.

»Vielleicht sollte ich deiner Frau von den wöchentlichen Besuchen im Massagesalon in der Nähe deines Büros erzählen«, erwähnte Ingrid.

»Bist du mir etwa nachgeschlichen?«, keuchte Rolf.

Ingrid setzte ihr gnadenloses Verhör fort.

»Was sind die besten Geldanlagen, die wir kaufen können?«, fragte Ingrid.

»Preisgünstige Indexfonds.«

»Und die hast du auch selbst gekauft?«, fragte ich.

»Selbstverständlich. Alle Börsenmakler haben Indexfonds in ihrem eigenen Anlagenportfolio.«

»Wieso hast du uns das vorher nie erzählt?«, fragte ich.

»Ich verkaufe keine Indexfonds.«

Ingrid ergriff eine große Vase, die auf einem Tisch in der Nähe stand.

»Denk nicht mal daran, die auf seinem Kopf zu zertrümmern«, sagte ich zu ihr.

Rolf wirkte sehr unruhig, als Ingrid die Vase in der Hand hielt. Schließlich stellte sie sie zurück auf den Tisch.

»Sollen wir die Fonds jedes Jahr umschichten?«, fragte ich.

»Nein, die meisten Leute, die jedes Jahr ihr Geld umschichten, verlieren dabei Geld auf lange Sicht.«

»Und warum schiebst du dann unser Geld alle paar Monate von einem Fonds zum anderen?«, schrie Ingrid.

»Jedes Mal wenn ihr eine Transaktion durchführt, verdiene ich eine Provision. Je öfter ihr Aktien kauft oder verkauft, desto mehr verdiene ich.«

Ingrid wandte sich mir mit finsterer Miene zu: »Dein Freund wird gleich in seiner Unterwäsche an die Stoßstange unseres Wagens gebunden und durch die Stadt geschleift.«

»Bitte tut mir nicht weh«, sagte Rolf. »Ich versuche doch bloß, genug zu verdienen, um mir dieses schöne Haus hier, ein Ferienhaus in Florida und ein paar schicke Autos leisten zu können.«

Ingrids Gesicht lief nun rot an. Ihre Augen wurden blutunterlaufen. Es war erschreckend. Rolf und ich starrten sie an. Sie holte tief Luft, bis sie sich wieder unter Kontrolle hatte. Endlich konnte sie mit einer normalen Stimme sprechen.

»Ich gehe jetzt. Rolf, wenn ich dich wiedersehe, werde ich meine Initialen in eine deiner unechten Brustmuskeln ritzen.«

Dann stampfte sie durch die Haustür ins Freie.

»Du hattest Recht«, sagte ich zu Rolf. »Diese Tabletten sind wirklich gefährlich. Verlasse besser nicht das Haus, bis sie alle sind.«

»Woher weiß sie all diese Sachen von mir?«, fragte Rolf.

Ich hätte Rolf die Wahrheit sagen können. Dass Ingrids Schwester für Rolfs Schönheitschirurgen arbeitet und ihr Bruder der Inhaber des Massagesalons ist. Da Ingrid mit ihren Geschwistern ständig Kontakt hat, weiß sie, welche Nachbarn eine Bauchdeckenstraffung machen ließen und welche Massagen sie bevorzugen. Aber ich wollte, dass Rolf ein bisschen leidet.

»Sie arbeitet für den Geheimdienst«, erzählte ich ihm.

Ich machte mich auf den Weg zur Tür.

»Noch etwas«, sagte ich. »Ich werde mein ganzes Geld in preisgünstige Indexfonds umbuchen. Ich brauche dich nicht mehr als meinen Börsenmakler.«

STORY 4

Child's Play

»Worüber schimpfst du?«, fragt mich Ingrid.

»Das Internet funktioniert nicht.«

»Ist der Computer angeschlossen?«

»Laptops haben einen Akku. Im Gegensatz zu Toastern müssen sie nicht eingesteckt werden.«

»Klaus, du brauchst nicht sarkastisch zu sein. Ich versuche doch nur zu helfen. Warum rufst du nicht den technischen Kundendienst an?«

»Vielleicht kann Jörg mir helfen.«

»Das letzte Mal, als Jörg dir mit einem Computerproblem geholfen hat, hat er die Festplatte kaputtgemacht.«

»Ach, genau. Ich werde eines der Kinder bitten, das Problem zu beheben.«

»Ich will nicht, dass sie mit dem Computer herumspielen. Das letzte Mal, als du sie um Hilfe gebeten hast, hatten wir Disney-Prinzessinnen als Bildschirmhintergrund.«

»Ich werde die Computerfirma anrufen«, sage ich.

Ich warte zwanzig Minuten lang am Telefon auf den nächsten verfügbaren Techniker. Er lässt mich Schritt für Schritt alles wiederholen, was ich vorher schon versucht habe. Nach einigen Minuten finden wir das Problem.

»Ich werde per E-Mail einen Software-Download schicken, um das Problem zu korrigieren«, sagt er mir.

»Das wird nichts nützen, da ich nicht ins Internet komme.«

»Das habe ich vergessen«, sagt er.

»Da fällt mir ein, schicken Sie mir die E-Mail. Ich werde sie auf dem Computer meines Nachbarn öffnen und die Software auf einen USB-Stick kopieren, um sie dann auf meinem Computer zu installieren.«

»Ausgezeichnet.«

Ich laufe zu Jörgs Haus hinüber, um die E-Mail zu öffnen. Vierzig Minuten später ist mein Computer aktualisiert.

»Schau dir das an«, sage ich zu Ingrid.

»Funktioniert das Internet immer noch nicht?«

»Es läuft jetzt, aber ich habe gerade eine Meldung von Microsoft erhalten. Sie raten mir, ihr neuestes Software-Upgrade nicht herunterzuladen, weil es mit dem Internet nicht kompatibel ist.«

»Genau das hast du vor zwei Tagen gemacht.«

»Und das ist der Grund, warum das Internet nicht mehr funktioniert.«

»Möchtest du ein Glas Wein?«

»Ich denke schon.«

Story 4

Zwei Tage später rauft sich Ingrid die Haare.
»Der Drucker funktioniert nicht.«
»Hast du heute den Laptop vom Drucker getrennt?«
»Ja. Ich brauchte ihn in der Küche.«
»Manchmal entstehen dabei die Schwierigkeiten«, sage ich.
»Kannst du ihn in Ordnung bringen?«
»Ich habe dir schon einmal gezeigt, wie du genau dieses Problem beheben kannst.«
»Ich habe es vergessen.«
»Ich lese aber gerade«, sage ich ihr.
»Klaus, komm her und repariere den Drucker, sonst koche ich heute kein Abendessen.«
Ich behebe das Problem sofort. Ingrid ist eine ausgezeichnete Köchin. Ich will nicht, dass sie streikt.
»Warum kannst du es dir nie merken, wenn ich dir zeige, wie man kleinere Probleme mit dem Computer und Drucker korrigieren kann?«, frage ich Ingrid während des Abendessens.
»Das ist deine Aufgabe. Ich will mit der Reparatur von Elektrogeräten nichts zu tun haben.«
»Das ist nicht fair«, sage ich.
»Das Leben ist hart. Gewöhne dich daran.«

---3---

»Kannst du Onkel Friedrich zum Telefonbuch auf meinem Handy hinzufügen«, frage ich meinen sechs Jahre alten Sohn.
»Ich habe dir schon einmal gezeigt, wie man das macht«, sagt er zu mir.
»Zeig es mir noch einmal.«
»In deinem Schreibtisch ist eine Bedienungsanleitung«, sagt er.
»Mein Fuß tut weh. Ich kann nicht zum Schreibtisch gehen.«
»Sagst du das nur so?«, fragt er mich.
»Vielleicht.«
»Wenn du es nicht leiden kannst, dass Mama sich nicht an die Sachen erinnert, die du ihr am Computer zeigst, warum sollte ich dann dauernd erklären müssen, wie man seine Kontaktliste aktualisiert?«
Offensichtlich hat mein Sohn ein sehr gutes Gehör und ein ausgezeichnetes Gedächtnis. Ich mache mir eine geistige Notiz darüber, vorsichtig damit zu sein, was ich in Zukunft sage, wenn er in der Nähe ist.
»Weil ich dein Vater bin und dich immer zum Fußballtraining fahre«, sage ich zu ihm.
»Das ist das letzte Mal, dass ich das mache. Schau genau hin.«
Er fügt die Telefonnummer meines Bruders zu meiner Kontaktliste hinzu. Ich gebe vor, sehr aufmerksam zu sein. In Wahrheit fällt mir dabei nur auf, dass seine Fingernägel geputzt werden müssen. Es ist schlimm genug, ein Kind, das gerade einmal den Kindergarten abgeschlossen hat, bitten zu müssen, mir mit meinem Handy zu helfen. Aber es ist sogar noch schlimmer, dass ich ihn zwei Stunden später bitte, das Surround-Sound-System zu reparieren.
»Wo liegt das Problem?«, fragt er.
»Aus den vier zusätzlichen Lautsprechern kommt kein Ton«, sage ich.

Er zwängt sich hinter den Fernsehapparat in der Ecke unseres Wohnzimmers und betrachtet die vierhundert Kabel, die am Fernseher, DVD-Player, und der Kabel-TV-Box angeschlossen sind.

»Jemand hat diesen Knopf versehentlich gedrückt«, sagt er.

Ich luge hinter den Fernseher und sehe ihn in einem Nest aus Schnüren und Kabeln sitzen. Er zeigt auf einen kleinen Schalter auf der Rückseite der Kabel-TV-Box.

»Er steht auf ›Aus‹«, sagt er.

»Gut, dann schalte ihn an.«

Er drückt den Knopf und die vier zusätzlichen Lautsprecher erwachen lautstark zum Leben.

»Diesen Knopf ja nicht wieder anfassen«, sagt er.

»Ich habe ihn nicht angerührt.«

»Wenn du noch weitere Probleme hast, frag den Computerfreak«, sagt er zu mir.

»Hör auf, deine Schwester so zu nennen. Und überhaupt, warum sollte ich sie fragen?«

»Sie weiß mehr als ich. Herr Salzmann von nebenan bezahlt ihr zwanzig Euro pro Woche, damit sie sein Heimkino und seine Alarmanlage am Laufen hält.«

4

Etwas später am Abend sage ich zu Ingrid: »Der Fortschritt der Technologie geht uns einfach zu schnell.«

»Hast du wieder Probleme damit, den Wecker zu stellen?«, fragt sie mich.

»Ja. Warum haben wir dieses digitale Unding gekauft? Man braucht ja einen Meisterbrief in Elektronik, um es in Gang zu bringen.«

»Du ärgerst dich nur, dass die Kinder mehr Ahnung haben als du.«

»Unsere Tochter hat einen Technologie-Beratungsvertrag mit Herrn Salzmann.«

»Er hat keine Kinder, deshalb braucht er ihre Fachkenntnisse.«

Ich sitze im Bett und schüttle verwundert meinen Kopf.

»Der Taschenrechner, den sie im Matheunterricht benutzt, kann Gleichungen lösen«, sage ich zu Ingrid. »Ich wusste nicht einmal, wie man das Wort ›Gleichung‹ buchstabiert, als ich zehn war.«

»Unsere Kinder wachsen mit hochentwickelter Technologie auf«, sagt Ingrid. »Sie haben keine Angst vor all diesen Tasten und Knöpfen, und sie lernen viel schneller als wir.«

»Ich frage mich, wie die Senioren damit zurechtkommen«, sage ich.

»Sie rufen ihre Enkelkinder zu Hilfe oder sie halten sich mit diesen komplizierten Geräten erst gar nicht auf.«

»Genau wie deine Mutter, die sich weigert, einen Computer anzufassen, und sie wird auch nie ein Handy kaufen.«

»Genau«, sagt sie.

»Aber was ist, wenn sie eine Autopanne hat und einen Abschleppwagen rufen muss?«

»Sie fährt sowieso nicht mehr.«

»Stimmt, ich vergaß.«

»Was wirst du machen, wenn die Kinder ausziehen?«, fragt Ingrid.

»Die Hersteller werden bis dahin Geräte produzieren, die so einfach sind, das sie sogar ein Erwachsener bedienen kann. Andernfalls musst du noch ein paar Kinder zur Welt bringen.«

»Ich denke, zwei genügen«, sagt Ingrid.

STORY 5

Selling Out

Es ist Samstagmorgen um halb neun. Viel zu früh, um wach zu sein. Trotzdem bin ich hier mit meiner Ehefrau Ingrid und wir räumen mit Gerümpel beladene Tische von unserer Garage in unsere Einfahrt.

»Wie haben wir bloß dieses ganze Gerümpel angesammelt?«, fragt sie.

»Es ist ein Teufelskreis. Wir kaufen Dinge, die wir nicht brauchen, weil sie im Angebot sind. Schließlich verstauen wir die Sachen im Schuppen. Nach einigen Jahren ist der Schuppen voll. Wir veranstalten einen privaten Flohmarkt, um alles aus dem Schuppen loszuwerden. Und der Kreislauf beginnt von neuem.«

Plötzlich höre ich eine andere Stimme.

»Ich gebe Ihnen zwei Euro für diese Lampe.«

Ich drehe mich um. Eine kleine Frau mit grauem Haar und großer Brille steht neben einem der Tische, die wir aus der Garage geschleppt haben. Sie hält einen der Gegenstände, die wir verkaufen wollen, hoch.

»Es ist ein echte Tiffany-Lampe«, sage ich. »Der Preis dafür ist zwanzig Euro.«

»Zwanzig Euro werden Sie dafür nie bekommen. Wie wäre es mit fünf?«

»Meine Dame, der Verkauf beginnt in dreißig Minuten. Kommen Sie dann wieder und wir können darüber reden.«

»Das Stromkabel ist ausgefranst«, sagt sie.

Sie hält das Kabel mit ihrer linken Hand hoch und zeigt auf eine zerfranste Stelle.

»Das hat sie mit ihren Zähnen gemacht, während wir diesen Tisch herausgetragen haben«, sagt Ingrid. »Ich habe es gesehen.«

»Die Strafe für Manipulationen an der Ware ist eine Verdoppelung des ausgezeichneten Preises«, sage ich zu der Dame. »Vierzig Euro für die Lampe.«

Die Dame stampft, etwas vor sich her brummelnd, davon. Am Ende der Einfahrt tritt sie gegen unseren Laternenpfahl.

Zehn Minuten später kommt eine Gruppe Schnäppchenjäger in verschiedenen Fahrzeugen an. Sie durchstöbern den Klimperkram und die Kleingeräte, die Ingrid und ich auf den Tischen verteilt haben.

Ingrid schlendert zu zwei älteren Herren hinüber, die sich gerade über unsere Sachen bücken. »Ich habe gesehen, wie Sie die Preisschilder vertauscht haben«, sagt sie zu ihnen. Ihre Gesichter laufen rot an und sie gehen beschämt davon.

Nach einigem Feilschen verkaufe ich ein paar Sachen. Noch mehr Leute treffen ein.

Ingrid zerrt eine Jugendliche mit orangefarbener Stachelfrisur zu mir herüber. Das Mädchen hat ein paar Tätowierungen an den Armen und trägt schwarzen Lippenstift. Beide Augenbrauen sind mehrfach mit Ringen gepierct.

»Sie wollte diese CD in ihre Handtasche stecken«, berichtet mir Ingrid.

Ich schaue mir die CD an. »Das Beste der Beach Boys«, sage ich zu dem Mädchen. »Ist die nicht etwas zu heiter für dich?«

»Die ist für meinen Freund«, heult sie.

Story 5

»Ist er sechzig Jahre alt?«

»Er ist zwanzig. Er steht auf Surfmusik.«

»Geh und klau eine Rammstein-CD von einem Flohmarkt weiter unten an der Straße.«

»Lauf nach Hause, Sara, bevor ich deine Mutter anrufe«, sagt Ingrid.

»Kennen wir die?«, frage ich, während wir dem Mädchen nachschauen, wie es die Straße hinunterläuft.

»Sie hat immer auf unsere Kinder aufgepasst.«

»Wie unheimlich.«

Die nächsten zwanzig Minuten sind Ingrid und ich ganz schön beschäftigt. Unser Ramsch verkauft sich schneller als erwartet.

»Der Verkauf läuft so gut. Ich denke, ich werde die Preise für die übrigen Sachen um dreißig Prozent erhöhen«, sagt Ingrid, während sie einen Marker in die Hand nimmt.

»Lieber nicht«, sage ich zu ihr. »Die Leute befinden sich in einem Kaufrausch. Du könntest einen Aufstand verursachen, wenn du versuchst, mehr Geld aus ihnen herauszuquetschen.«

Ein gut gekleideter Herr kommt auf mich zu.

»Ich möchte den ausziehbaren Tisch kaufen«, sagt er mit einem leichten Akzent.

»Das macht zweiunddreißig Euro.«

»Könnten Sie ein ›Verkauft‹-Schild auf den Tisch stellen und ihn für mich reservieren, bis ich heute etwas später zurückkehre?«

»Klar, wenn Sie mir zweiunddreißig Euro bezahlen.«

»Ich gebe Ihnen eine Anzahlung über fünf Euro.«

»Nein. Sie zahlen mir jetzt den vollen Betrag, wenn ich den Tisch für Sie reservieren soll.«

»Aber ich muss doch nach Hause gehen, um mehr Geld zu holen.«

»Wollen Sie mir weismachen, dass Sie mit weniger als zweiunddreißig Euro auf einen Flohmarkt gekommen sind?«

»Ich habe nicht gedacht, dass ich irgendetwas Teures kaufen würde.«

»Ich kenne diesen Trick«, sage ich. »Ich reserviere Ihnen den Tisch bis zum Ende des Tages. Sie kommen dann zurück und wollen den vereinbarten Preis nicht bezahlen. Sie rechnen damit, ihn für zehn Euro stehlen zu können, weil dann eh schon alle Kunden weg sind. Das ist eine alte Masche. Verschwinden Sie.«

»Sie sind kein netter Mensch. Zu Ihrem nächsten Flohmarkt komme ich nicht.«

»Ich werde Sie von unserer Mailingliste streichen«, sage ich sarkastisch.

Der Mann geht weg und tritt gegen unseren Laternenpfahl. Ich mache eine Bekanntgabe.

»Wenn noch einer gegen meinen Laternenpfahl tritt, werde ich ihn eine Woche lang im Kofferraum meines Autos einsperren.«

Kein Mensch beachtet mich.

Eine Dame fragt Ingrid: »Kann ich diesen Toaster zurückbringen, wenn er mir nicht gefällt?«

»Es ist ein Toaster«, sagt Ingrid. »Entscheiden Sie jetzt, ob er Ihnen gefällt.«

»Vielleicht passt er nicht auf meine Küchentheke.«

»Jeder Verkauf ist endgültig, es gibt keine Rücknahmen.«

»Ich gebe Ihnen fünfzig Cent dafür.«

»Eher zertrümmere ich ihn mit einem Hammer und werfe ihn in den Abfall, als dass ich ihn für fünfzig Cent hergebe«, sagt Ingrid. »Der Preis beträgt fünf Euro.«

»Wie wäre es mit vier?«

Selling Out

»Verkauft. Nur Bargeld. Keine Schecks, bitte.«

Die Dame bezahlt mit einer Tasche voller Kleingeld. Sie geht mit ihrem Toaster davon. »Du bist eine sehr gute Verkäuferin«, sage ich zu Ingrid.

Sie strahlt vor Freude.

Gegen Ende des Tages sind nur noch ein paar Sachen übrig. Ingrid und ich sind hundemüde. Mit Kunden feilschen und sich mit Ladendieben anlegen ist harte Arbeit. Wir sind nahe am Zusammenbruch. Die Organisierung eines Flohmarktes könnte sogar den Buddha zum Mörder werden lassen.

Ein Kunde ist noch da.

»Ich gebe Ihnen drei Euro für diesen Bilderrahmen«, sagt er zu mir.

»Der Preis beträgt zwölf Euro. Da Sie der letzte Kunde sind, können Sie ihn für sechs haben.«

»Ich habe nur drei Euro.«

Ich überlege eine Sekunde lang. Ich sehne mich nach einer guten Flasche Wein. Vielleicht sollte ich einfach den Rahmen für drei Euro verkaufen und ich wäre diesen Kerl los.

»Einverstanden, drei Euro«, sagt Ingrid. Sie muss meine Gedanken gelesen haben.

»Sind Sie einverstanden, wenn ich mit Centstücken bezahle«, fragt er.

Ich entkorke den Wein, während Ingrid den Mann mit einer Schaufel die Straße hinunterjagt.

STORY 6

Don't Stop and Smell the Roses

»Ich habe noch drei getötet«, rief ich Ingrid zu.

»Kämpfe weiter und wir kommen hier eventuell lebend hinaus«, kreischte sie zurück.

Ich wandte mich für den Bruchteil einer Sekunde lang von meinen Angreifern ab und bemerkte, dass Ingrid vom Feind auf allen Seiten umzingelt war. Ich verlor keinen Gedanken über meine eigene Sicherheit und eilte ihr zu Hilfe.

»Kommt doch her, ihr Blutsauger«, schrie ich unsere Gegner an.

Rücken an Rücken standen wir und boxten und hauten auf unsere Gegner ein, während sie ihre Angriffe fortsetzten. Nach ein paar Minuten waren wir erschöpft. Unsere Feinde griffen ständig weiter an.

»Klaus, wir haben keine Wahl«, keuchte Ingrid. »Wir müssen die Giftstoffe einsetzen.«

»Es ist sehr wenig davon übrig.«

»Das ist die einzige Chance, die wir haben.« Die Verzweiflung in ihrer Stimme brachte mich dazu, mich umzudrehen, um einen Blick auf meine schöne Frau zu werfen. Ihre Augen waren mit Tränen gefüllt. Ihr Haar war zerzaust.

Ich zog die Mückenspraydose aus der Tasche meiner Shorts. Ich besprühte damit Ingrids nackte Arme und Beine. Den Rest sprühte ich auf mich selbst. Die Dose warf ich in den Schwarm der tödlichen kleinen Mörder, die unmittelbar vor uns schwebten.

Die Mücken zogen sich zurück, um ihre Angriffsreihen neu zu formieren. Sie waren klug genug, nicht auf der Haut zu landen, die gerade mit Insektenschutzmittel eingesprüht wurde. Ich konnte beobachten, wie die Mücken-Kommandanten ihre Truppen für einen neuen Angriff versammelten.

»Die Schutzwirkung hält nur ein paar Minuten an«, sagte Ingrid. »Lauf zum Auto so schnell du kannst.«

Wir waren zwei Kilometer vom Parkplatz entfernt, tief im Sumpfgebiet der Halbinsel Yucatan. Wir sahen ein kleines Holzschild mit einem Pfeil. Das Wort ›Salida‹ war darauf gemalt.

»Folge mir«, rief ich. Über das Gesumme von Millionen Mückenflügeln hinweg konnte ich mir nur mühsam Gehör verschaffen. Ich lief in die Richtung, die der Pfeil anzeigte. Ingrid war dicht hinter mir.

»Bedeutet ›Salida‹, dass das der Weg zum Parkplatz ist?«, keuchte sie.

»Es könnte bedeuten, dass wir zu einem großen Salat geführt werden«, antwortete ich. »Mein Spanisch ist nicht sehr gut.«

Zu Beginn unserer Wanderung war ich auf eine Baumwurzel getreten und hatte mir den Knöchel verdreht. Mein Fuß pochte vor Schmerz. Aber das konnte mich nicht davon abhalten, so schnell zu laufen, wie ich konnte, um zu entkommen.

Schweiß vermischt mit Sonnenmilch lief mir von der Stirn in die Augen, die zu brennen begannen. Ich fing an, den Urwald nur noch verschwommen zu sehen.

»Ich kann nichts sehen«, sagte ich zu Ingrid mit einer Stimme voller Panik. »Du gehst voran.«

Wir kamen an einem Mann vorbei, der auf einem Stuhl saß und Limonade aus einem bunten Wagen verkaufte.

Story 6

»Laufen Sie«, sagte ich zu ihm. »Sie sind direkt hinter uns.«

»Möchten Sie eine Cola kaufen?«, fragte der Mann.

Ich hatte keine Zeit für einen Verrückten, der sich nicht um seine eigene Sicherheit kümmerte. Wir ließen ihn zurück und liefen weiter.

Eine Gruppe von sieben Schulkindern und zwei Lehrern ging an uns vorbei. Während sie sich glücklich miteinander unterhielten, liefen sie in ihr sicheres Verderben.

Ingrid blieb einen Moment stehen und ergriff den Arm eines Lehrers. »Gehen Sie zurück. Kein Mensch kann im Sumpf überleben.«

Er musterte uns mit einem ruhigen Gesichtsausdruck. Vermutlich war er es gewohnt, verschwitzten Touristen mit irrem Gesichtsausdruck zu begegnen, bei denen sich abertausende Mückenstiche im Gesicht und auf den Armen und Beinen abzeichneten.

»Lass sie doch«, sagte ich zu Ingrid. »Vielleicht werden unsere Verfolger sie verschlingen. Dadurch gewinnen wir ein paar zusätzliche Sekunden, um zu unserem Mietauto zu gelangen.«

»Aber es sind doch Kinder«, weinte Ingrid.

»Entweder die oder wir«, sagte ich, während ich sie von den Schulkindern wegzog.

Nach einer Kurve wurde der steinige Feldweg zur Asphaltstraße.

»Da vorne ist ein Gebäude«, schrie Ingrid.

Wir rannten noch weitere zwanzig Meter, öffneten eine Fliegengittertür und taumelten in einen großen Raum. Sieben Leute befanden sich in diesem Raum. Sie blickten auf, als ich die Tür hinter uns zuschlug.

»Rufen Sie die Polizei und einen Krankenwagen«, sagte ich schwer atmend. »Wir brauchen medizinische und psychiatrische Hilfe.«

Ein älterer Mann schlenderte zu uns herüber.

»Sie haben Schwierigkeiten mit dem Ungeziefer«, sagte er in perfektem Englisch.

»Jawohl«, keuchte ich. »Wir wurden angegriffen, als wir den Kakteen- und Farnkrautbereich verließen.«

»Haben Sie kein Mückenspray mitgenommen?«, fragte er.

»Wir haben ein bisschen mitgenommen. Es sollte angeblich sechs Stunden wirken, aber es schreckte unseren Feind nur ein paar Minuten lang ab«, sagte ich. »Sie können sicher sein, dass ich dem Hersteller einen fiesen Brief schreiben und eine komplette Geldrückerstattung verlangen werde. Wir besprühten uns immer wieder, bis die Dose leer war. Dann rannten wir zum Parkplatz. Wir schafften es hierher, bevor der Schwarm uns wieder eingeholt hat.«

»Da draußen sind Kinder«, schluchzte Ingrid. »Jemand muss sie retten.«

»Es wird schon gut ausgehen«, erklärte der Mann. »Wir sind an diese Plagegeister gewöhnt.«

»Wo sind wir?«, fragte ich.

»Im Informationszentrum. Wir haben eine kleine Bücherei, wo Sie sich über die Sümpfe und die verschiedenen Arten der Flora in unseren Gärten informieren können. Der Parkplatz ist nur ein paar Meter von hier. Möchten Sie vielleicht etwas trinken?«

»Haben Sie irgendeinen Tequila?«

Er lachte. »Ihr Touristen seid vielleicht lustig. Wir haben Saft, Wasser, Tee und Kaffee.«

Ingrid und ich ließen uns auf den Hockern nieder, nippten an Wasserflaschen und versuchten, uns zusammenzureißen. Wir blätterten in einem Buch, das die verschiedenen Pflanzenarten im Botanischen Garten erläuterte. Meine Augen brannten immer noch und mein Knöchel begann, anzuschwellen.

»Wie konnten wir dieses Gebäude übersehen, als wir anfangs hier ankamen«, fragte Ingrid.

»Es gibt keine Beschilderung«, sagte ich. »Ich parkte das Auto am falschen Ende des Parkplatzes.«

»Wir hätten die Leute im Ferienort fragen sollen, ob sie eine Karte dieser Gegend haben«, sagte Ingrid.

»Kannst du zurückfahren?«, fragte ich sie.

»Ich weiß nicht, wie man mit Gangschaltung fährt«, sagte sie.

»Aber mein Fuß tut weh«, jammerte ich.

»Du kannst später ein Fußbad im Whirlpool nehmen.«

Nach einer Weile waren wir bereit, einen Fluchtversuch zu unserem Mietwagen zu machen.

»Ich gehe nicht über den ganzen Parkplatz«, sagte Ingrid. »Die Mücken haben uns wahrscheinlich irgendeine Falle gestellt.«

Ich stritt mit ihr darüber, aber es war umsonst. Wenn Ingrid sich einmal entschieden hat, wird sie ihre Meinung nicht ändern.

So schnell ich konnte sprang ich in unser Auto und hielt über meine Schulter Ausschau nach unseren Feinden. Glücklicherweise waren sie anderweitig beschäftigt. Wahrscheinlich zerlegten sie gerade die Leiche eines anderen Touristen, den sie im Sumpf erlegt hatten. Ich fuhr das Auto zum Eingang des Informationszentrums und Ingrid sprang rein.

Als wir zu unserem Hotel zurückrasten, versuchte Ingrid, die Anzahl der Stiche auf ihrem Körper zu zählen. Bei zweihundert hörte sie auf und schlug mir auf den Arm.

»Aua«, sagte ich. »Wofür war das denn?«

»Dafür, dass du mich in diesen bescheuerten Botanischen Garten geschleppt hast«, sagte sie.

»Du hast mich gezwungen, hierherzukommen«, sagte ich. »Ich wollte am Pool sitzen und Limonade trinken.«

»Das hätten wir tun sollen. Das ist deine Schuld.«

STORY 7

Fool's Gold

»Pass auf den Lastwagen auf!«, schrie meine Frau Ingrid.

»Ich sehe ihn. Willst du fahren?«

»Nein, Klaus, es macht mich nervös, in Manhattan zu fahren.«

»Gut, dann hör auf, Lärm zu machen. Du lenkst mich ab«, sagte ich, während ich einem Taxi auf der Tenth Avenue den Weg abschnitt.

»Der Taxifahrer hat eine obszöne Geste gemacht«, sagte Ingrid. »So ein unverschämter Mensch.«

»Er winkte nur zur Begrüßung.«

»Warum hupen denn alle? An jeder Ecke stehen Schilder, die besagen, dass das eine Dreihundertfünfzig-Dollar-Geldstrafe bedeutet.«

»Die Polizisten geben den einheimischen Fahrern keine Strafzettel. Da wir keine New Yorker Kennzeichen haben, bekämen wir einen Strafzettel. Ich garantiere dir, wenn ich einmal hupen würde, würde sich eine Horde von Polizisten auf uns stürzen und so viele Strafzettel schreiben, wie wir nur tragen könnten.«

»Wieso bleibt kein Autofahrer in seiner Spur«, fragte Ingrid.

»Sie sind zu beschäftigt damit, auf die gestrichelten Linien auf der Straße zu achten, weil sie Schlaglöchern, in zweiter Reihe geparkten Autos und diesen verrückten Fahrradfahrern ausweichen müssen.«

»Du bist gerade über Rot gefahren.«

»So wie die drei Autos hinter uns. Wenn ich gehalten hätte, wären wir gerammt worden.«

»Ich bin so froh, dass wir ein altes Auto fahren. Es hat so viele Dellen, dass jede weitere eine Verschönerung bedeuten würde.«

»Genau. Die Leute mit schicken, neuen Autos sind im Nachteil. Sie können es sich nicht leisten, aggressiv zu sein«, sagte ich.

»Warum hältst du an?«

»Ich will einen Hotdog.«

»Musst du das Auto nicht parken?«

»Alle Parkplätze sind besetzt. Man kann rechts neben dem Imbisswagen in zweiter Reihe parken.«

»Aber da warten schon zwei Busse und drei Lastwagen hinter uns und hupen. Werden die nicht sauer sein?«

»Wir sind hier in Manhattan. Sie müssen mit ein paar Verzögerungen rechnen«, sagte ich.

Ich öffnete mein Fenster. Der Geruch des Hotdogwagens breitete sich im Auto aus.

»Einen Hotdog mit Sauerkraut und Ketchup«, schrie ich auf Englisch über den Lärm der Presslufthämmer hinweg.

»Denkst du, das Essen ist unbedenklich?«, fragte Ingrid.

»Sicher. Das ist eine Baustelle. Nur den besten Hotdogverkäufern ist es erlaubt, ihr Essen hier zu verkaufen. Willst du etwas haben?«

»Ich denke, ich warte bis später.«

Story 7

»Du lässt dir hier einen wirklichen Leckerbissen entgehen«, sagte ich, während ich mein Essen von dem freundlichen Verkäufer entgegennahm und ihm vier Dollar gab.

»Der Busfahrer hinter uns steigt gerade aus und geht geradewegs auf dich zu«, sagte Ingrid ängstlich.

»Er will wahrscheinlich auch einen Hotdog haben«, sagte ich.

Genau in dem Moment, als der Busfahrer mein Fenster erreichte, trat ich auf das Gaspedal und fuhr weg.

»Er droht dir mit seiner Faust«, sagte Ingrid.

»Hör doch auf, durch das Rückfenster zu schauen«, sagte ich. »Du wirst dir noch einen steifen Hals holen.«

Ich aß meinen Hotdog, während ich mit nur einer Hand am Steuer die Tenth Avenue hinauffuhr. Ingrid stieß ein paar kleine Angstschreie aus. Ich weiß nicht, warum. Der Verkehr war heute ziemlich überschaubar. Ich bog unvermittelt nach links in die Neunundvierzigste Straße ein.

»Schau, wie die Leute uns aus dem Weg springen«, sagte Ingrid.

»Diese Nonnen sind ganz schön schnell. Sogar die Alte mit dem Spazierstock kann sich ganz schön schnell bewegen.«

Ich fuhr in ein Parkhaus. Es sah aus, als wäre es schon vor zehn Jahren außer Betrieb genommen worden, aber es hatte die besten Preise in New York City. Wir zahlten bei dem freundlichen russischen Parkwächter und gingen in östliche Richtung.

»Denkst du, dass wir in dieser Nachbarschaft sicher sind?«, fragte Ingrid.

»Mach dir keine Sorgen. Die Gauner in dieser Gegend arbeiten nur nachts«, sagte ich.

»Hast du das sarkastisch gemeint?«, fragte Ingrid.

»Ja.«

Zehn Minuten später waren wir im Diamond District. Siebenundvierzigste Straße, zwischen der Fifth und Sixth Avenue. Ich hielt an und lehnte mich an einen geparkten Lieferwagen.

»Warte einen Moment, damit ich Luft holen kann«, sagte ich zu Ingrid.

»Du bist wirklich nicht in Form«, sagte Ingrid.

»Wieso mussten wir den ganzen Weg von der Eighth Avenue bis hierher rennen«, fragte ich.

»Ich dachte, dass uns jemand verfolgt.«

»Ich wurde beinahe von einer Limousine angefahren, als wir über den Broadway sprinteten. Wir sollten eigentlich auf das grüne Licht warten.« Es dauerte eine Weile, bis ich meine Sätze hervorbrachte, da ich noch damit zu kämpfen hatte, Luft in meine Lungen zu bekommen.

»Hör mit dem Jammern auf«, sagte Ingrid. »Wir haben es bis hierher geschafft, ohne die Goldketten zu verlieren. Lass uns hinaufgehen und sehen, wie viel sie wert sind.«

Nach ein paar weiteren Minuten konnte ich wieder normal atmen. In der Mitte des Blocks betraten wir ein Gebäude mit zehn Stockwerken und fuhren mit dem Aufzug zum sechsten Stock. Zimmer 604 hatte ein Schild an der Tür mit dem Namen des Geschäfts in Gold eingraviert. Ein Türöffner ließ uns in ein kleines Empfangszimmer. Eine junge Dame saß an einem Schreibtisch hinter einer kugelsicheren Scheibe.

»Wir möchten ein paar goldene Halsketten verkaufen,« sagte Ingrid zu der Dame.

»Gehen Sie in die Kabine Nummer eins. Schließen Sie die Tür hinter sich und ich werde jemanden schicken.«

An einer Wand links von der Empfangsdame befanden sich drei nummerierte Türen. Wir gingen in die Tür mit der Nummer eins. Vor uns befand sich noch eine kugelsichere Scheibe. Innerhalb von drei Minuten erschien hinter der Scheibe ein kleiner, schlanker, junger Mann mit einem kleinen Schnurrbart.

»Hallo«, sagte er. »Sie haben Gold für mich?«

»Sie haben aber einen interessanten Akzent«, sagte ich, während Ingrid eine Plastiktüte aus ihrer Handtasche herausfischte. »Wo kommen Sie her?«

»Litauen«, antwortete er.

»Ist das in der Nähe von Chicago?«, fragte ich.

»Nein«, lachte er.

Ingrid holte ihre Tüte voller Goldketten hervor und schob sie durch einen Schlitz in der Glastrennwand, auf eine Ablage. Zwanzig Minuten später gingen wir mit vierhundert Dollar in bar hinaus.

»Sie gaben uns fünfzig Prozent mehr als die Juwelierläden in Brooklyn uns zahlen wollten«, sagte Ingrid. »Damit gönnen wir uns ein nettes Abendessen.«

»Wir sollten Hamburger essen gehen«, sagte ich. »Sonst geben wir am Ende unseren zusätzlichen Gewinn für unnötiges, teures Essen und Wein aus.«

»Ich habe eine Reservierung zum Abendessen gemacht, bevor wir das Hotel verlassen haben«, sagte Ingrid. »Es ist ein französisches Restaurant, nur zwei Kreuzungen von hier entfernt.«

Ich überlegte eine Minute.

»Dieses ganze Abenteuer war Teil eines raffinierten Plans, um in einem schicken Restaurant in Manhattan zu Abend zu essen, oder?«, sagte ich zu Ingrid.

»Was ist, wenn es so war?«

»Wir können dorthin gehen, solange du mich nicht zum Laufen zwingst«, sagte ich.

STORY 8

Dumbbells Everywhere

»Nimm etwas ab, Klaus.«

»Das ist alles?«, fragte ich. »Hundertfünfzehn Euro für eine komplette Untersuchung und alles, was du mir zu sagen hast, ist, dass ich abnehmen muss? Für so viel Geld hättest du mindestens vier weitere Beschwerden finden können. Ich möchte eine zweite Meinung einholen.«

»Okay«, sagte mein lieber Freund Dr. Michael Werner, »deine Nase sieht auch komisch aus.«

»Bist du freitagabends im Krankenhaus als Bühnenkomiker tätig?«, fragte ich.

»Hör zu«, sagte er, »wir kennen uns seit der Hochschulzeit. Du kannst mir vertrauen. Ich sage dir, du musst anfangen, jeden Tag Sport zu treiben.«

»Ich arbeite bereits fünfzig Stunden pro Woche«, sagte ich. »Ich habe drei kleine Kinder, mit denen ich versuche, Zeit zu verbringen. Und Ingrid, meine liebenswerte Frau, möchte sich mit mir auch hin und wieder unterhalten. Ich habe keine Zeit zum Sporttreiben.«

»Was machst du nach der Arbeit?«

»Ich hoffe, du hast nicht vor, mir diese Unterhaltung in Rechnung zu stellen«, sagte ich. »Ich habe gehört, dass Ärzte ihren Patienten einfache Gespräche berechnen.«

»Willst du, dass ich dir ein paar Spritzen gebe, die du nicht brauchst?«, fragte er.

Das ist ungerecht. Er wusste, dass ich vor Nadeln Angst hatte.

»Einverstanden, ich werde es dir sagen«, erwiderte ich, während ich die imaginären Nadeln zur Seite schob. »Nach der Arbeit essen wir zu Abend. Wir spielen mit den Kindern, bringen sie ins Bett und schauen dann ein paar Stunden fern.«

»Da hast du schon die Antwort. Anstatt fernzusehen, kannst du eine Stunde lang Sport treiben.«

»So spät am Abend?«, fragte ich.

»Es ist nicht ideal, aber es ist besser, als sich in ein Marshmallow zu verwandeln.«

»Ich habe gerade einen Großbildfernseher mit Surroundtonanlage gekauft.«

»Nimm deine Lieblingssendungen auf, während du Sport treibst, und schaue sie dir am Wochenende an«, sagte er.

»Es ist nicht dasselbe, am Wochenende«, beschwerte ich mich.

Dr. Werner betrachtete mich mit stechendem Blick.

»Hör auf, Ausreden zu suchen, und versuche, wenigstens etwas Sport zu treiben, anstatt fernzusehen.«

Er griff zu einem Rezeptblock und begann zu schreiben. »Das ist der Titel eines ausgezeichneten Trainingsbuches. Es gibt drei oder vier einfache Routineübungen, mit welchen du dein Training variieren kannst. Kauf dieses Buch und fang an zu schwitzen.«

»Ich mag es nicht, wenn ich schwitze«, sagte ich zu ihm. »Wenn ich schwitze, fühle ich mich klebrig.«

»Ich will keine Ausreden mehr hören«, sagte er.

»Meine Unterwäsche klebt an meiner Haut«, fuhr ich fort. »Komische Gerüche kommen aus meinen Achselhöhlen.«

Story 8

»Dusche nach dem Training. Ingrid wird das begrüßen«, sagte er.
»Wer will denn schon öfter als einmal pro Woche duschen? Niemand! Das ist Trinkwasserverschwendung.«
»Jetzt hast du mich aber wirklich verärgert«, sagte er. »Dafür mache ich nächste Woche am Samstag einen Hausbesuch um ein Uhr.«
»Wird der von der Versicherung übernommen?«
»Nein, ich bringe den Arztkoffer mit und messe deinen Blutdruck. Da du diesen schönen neuen Fernseher hast, werde ich auch zum Fußballspiel dableiben. Und obendrein werde ich beim Zuschauen in deinem Lieblingsfernsehsessel sitzen.«
»In dem mit dem eingebauten Becherhalter in der Armlehne für die Bierdose?«
»Genau dem. Stell sicher, dass du jede Menge Bier und Knabberzeug da hast«, sagte er.
»Was ist, wenn mein Blutdruck nicht niedriger ist?«
»Dann werde ich jeden Samstag kommen, bis ich eine wesentliche Verbesserung sehe. Vielleicht werde ich meine Familie mitbringen. Das Knabberzeug wird dich ein Vermögen kosten.«

---2---

»Warum sind alle Wohnzimmermöbel außer dem Fernseher und den zwei Lehnstühlen in der Garage?«, fragte mich Ingrid später an jenem Abend.
»Ich brauche Platz zum Trainieren.«
»Kannst du nicht draußen trainieren?«
»Ich werde trainieren, nachdem wir die Kinder ins Bett gebracht haben. Um diese Zeit ist es draußen zu dunkel.«
»Geh ins Fitnessstudio.«
»Ich will zu Hause trainieren, wo ich die Fernsehsendungen anschauen kann, die mir gefallen.«
»Das hört sich nicht gut an«, sagte sie.
»Michael sagte, er würde jeden Samstag kommen und Sportsendungen schauen. Er würde uns alles wegessen, bis ich wieder in Form bin.«
»Lieber er als deine Eltern«, sagte sie.
»Fange nicht an, an meinen Eltern herumzunörgeln«, sagte ich. »Konzentrieren wir uns auf das Trainieren.«
»Du konzentrierst dich auf das Trainieren. Ich mache das nicht«, sagte sie.
»Warum nicht?«, fragte ich.
»Ich trainiere im Fitnessstudio fünfmal pro Woche während meiner Mittagspause.«
»Wir könnten eine Menge Geld sparen, wenn du zu Hause trainieren würdest.«
»Nein, danke. Ich trainiere gerne während der Mittagszeit. Anschließend esse ich etwas Gesundes zu Mittag - Obst und Joghurt. Du solltest versuchen, gesünder zu essen.«
»Ich werde gereizt, wenn ich nicht jeden Tag mindestens zwei Hamburger und Pommes esse«, sagte ich.
Ingrid hob das Buch auf, das am Lehnstuhl lag, und fing an, durch die Seiten zu blättern.
»Michael hat dieses Trainingsbuch empfohlen. Den Aerobic-Teil des Fitnesstrainings werde ich zwischen dem Lehnsessel und dem Fernseher machen, wo genügend Platz ist, während wir abends unsere Sendungen ansehen.«

»Bei der Übung auf Seite zwanzig sollst du schnell gehen und dabei Hanteln schwingen«, sagte sie. »Wie willst du das hier drinnen machen?«

»Da ist genügend Platz, um jeweils ein paar Schritte vor und zurück zu laufen.«

»Was passiert, wenn du eins der Kinder am Kopf triffst, wenn du das machst? Die Hantel würde sie wahrscheinlich umbringen.«

»Die Kinder werden schon im Bett sein.«

Sie warf nochmal einen Blick auf die Übungen.

»Hampelmannsprünge«, sagte sie. »Du sollst zwanzig Minuten lang Hampelmannsprünge machen.«

»Was soll daran falsch sein?«

»Es macht Krach. Das ganze Haus wird wackeln. Ich werde nicht in der Lage sein, den Fernseher zu hören.«

»Das Zimmer ist ja mit Teppich ausgelegt. Das wird den Lärm dämpfen. Und ich werde ganz leicht springen, wie ein Ninja.«

Ingrid schüttelte den Kopf.

»Ich werde in unserem Schlafzimmer fernsehen, während du trainierst«, beschloss sie. »Das ist einfacher für uns beide.«

»Was ist mit unserer wertvollen gemeinsamen Zeit?«

»Wir verbringen gemeinsam Zeit, wenn wir mit den Kindern spielen. Fernsehen ist Entspannungszeit. Ich werde mich im Schlafzimmer besser entspannen können.«

»Dann werde ich einen der Lehnsessel in die Garage bringen. Dadurch werde ich mehr Platz gewinnen«, sagte ich.

---3---

Doktor Michael erschien am folgenden Samstag mit einer Flasche Wein und einer Tüte voller Salzbrezeln. Ingrid führte ihn in unser Wohnzimmer. Alle Möbel waren wieder an ihrem gewohnten Platz. Ernst und Karl, zwei andere Freunde aus meiner Hochschulzeit, saßen schon mit einem Bier auf der Couch. Mit einem großen Verband am Kopf saß ich im Lehnsessel.

»Was ist mit dir passiert?« fragte Michael.

»Das hast du mir angetan«, sagte ich. »Du kannst froh sein, dass ich dich nicht wegen Behandlungsfehler verklage.«

»Was soll ich denn verbrochen haben?«

»Michael, du musst die ganze Geschichte hören«, sagte Ingrid.

»Da werde ich mich lieber vorher mit etwas Wein stärken.«

Er setzte sich und entfernte den Schraubverschluss der Weinflasche.

»Kannst du dir keinen Wein mit Korkverschluss leisten?«, fragte Ernst.

»Das ist ein ausgezeichneter Wein«, antwortete Michael. »Und so es ist wesentlich leichter, die Flasche zu öffnen.«

Michael nahm ein leeres Weinglas vom Couchtisch, schenkte ein und reichte Ingrid das halbvolle Glas.

»Danke Michael, woher hast du gewusst, dass ich das jetzt brauche?«

Story 8

»Wenn ich Klaus' Kopfverband sehe und erfahre, das es eine Geschichte dazu gibt, dann weiß ich, dass du wahrscheinlich eine schwierige Woche hinter dir hast«, sagte er.

Er schenkte ein weiteres Glas für sich selbst ein, setzte sich und schaute mich an.

»Erzähle mir die Geschichte.«

»Noch zehn Minuten, bis das Spiel beginnt«, sagte Karl. »Erzähl es schnell.«

»Moment mal«, sagte Michael. »Was ist mit der Decke passiert?« Er deutete auf ein großes Loch in der Decke über der Couch.

»Das ist Teil der Geschichte«, sagte Karl. »Klaus wollte es uns nicht erzählen, bevor ihr da seid.«

Ich wollte gerade alles erklären, doch Ingrid unterbrach mich. »Ich brauche mehr Wein.«

Sie ergriff die Flasche und füllte ihr Glas nach.

»Das wird mir helfen, die Geschichte nochmals anzuhören, ohne dass ich die Fernbedienung auf Klaus werfe«, sagte sie zu meinen Freunden.

4

Einen kurzen Moment fragte ich mich, warum meine Frau einen kleinen, harten Gegenstand auf mich schleudern wollte. Ich beschloss, ihre Bemerkung zu übersehen, und erzählte meine Geschichte.

»Ich kaufte mir das Buch, das du mir verschrieben hast, dazu ein paar Hanteln und fing an zu trainieren.«

»Prima«, sagte Michael.

»Nicht so prima«, sagte Ingrid. »Er entschied sich, in diesem Zimmer zu trainieren, am Abend während des Fernsehens.«

Michaels Augen weiteten sich. »Oh«, sagte er. »Plötzlich wird mir alles klar.«

»Eine der Übungen verlangte von mir, auf der Stelle zu treten und dabei die Gewichte mit den Armen auf- und abzubewegen. Ich beschloss die Übung mit etwas Step-Aerobic zu kombinieren, und stellte einen kleinen Hocker auf den Boden.«

»Er schaute sich gerade eine von diesen Realityshows an«, unterbrach Ingrid.

»Mir war gar nicht bewusst, dass ich die Gewichte bis zur Decke schwang«, fuhr ich fort.

»Er stieg auf den Hocker und schlug eine Hantel von anderthalb Kilo durch die Decke«, schloss Ingrid.

Michael, Ernst und Karl fingen an, mich auszulachen.

»Wer erzählt hier die Geschichte?«, wollte ich wissen.

»Ich lag auf unserem Bett und schaute mir gerade einen gutes Ärztedrama an«, sagte Ingrid. »Da hörte ich einen Riesenkrach und plötzlich schaute die Hand von Klaus aus dem Boden heraus.«

Die Jungs lachten noch lauter.

»Das ist eine Übertreibung«, schrie ich.

Ingrid ergriff die Fernbedienung und warf mir einen bösen Blick zu. Ich hielt besser meinen Mund.

Michael hob seine Hand hoch. »Ist dir ein Teil der Decke auf den Kopf gefallen?«

»Ingrid wollte nicht, dass ich die Gewichte nochmals verwende, also wählte ich eine andere Trainingsübung aus dem Buch.«

»Eine Aerobic-Übung, bei der man die Knie hochzieht und dann mit den Füßen tritt«, fügte Ingrid hinzu.

»Es war ein sehr gutes Training«, sagte ich.

»Bis er zu nah an den Fernseher gelangte«, sagte Ingrid.

»Hör auf, mich zu unterbrechen«, beschwerte ich mich.

»Er rammte seinen Fuß direkt durch den Fernseher«, sagte Ingrid.

Jetzt johlten meine drei Uni-Freunde. Ernst hielt sich an den Knien und schaukelte nach beiden Seiten. Aus Karls Augen kamen Tränen.

Ich kochte innerlich. Was hätte ich sagen sollen?

»Ich musste am Dienstag in den Laden gehen, um einen neuen Fernseher für das heutige Spiel zu holen. Es war Klaus zu peinlich«, erzählte Ingrid zu Ende.

Es dauerte ein paar Minuten, bis meine Freunde ihre Fassung wieder fanden.

»Du hast mir immer noch nicht erzählt, wie du dir den Kopf verletzt hast«, fragte Michael.

»Ingrid sagte mir, ich müsse an einer Stelle trainieren, die vom neuen Fernseher weit entfernt sei. Deshalb zog ich zu der Seite des Zimmers dort um«, ich zeigte auf eine Stelle neben dem offenen Kamin.

»Außerdem wechselte ich die Trainingsübung.«

»Hampelmannsprünge«, sagte Ingrid.

»Wie hast du dich beim Hampelmannspringen verletzt?«, fragte Michael.

»Wir hatten eine hübsche Glaslampe an der Decke montiert, um diesen Bereich des Zimmers zu beleuchten«, sagte Ingrid.

Sie zeigte auf zwei elektrische Drähte, die jetzt einsam von der Decke neben der Kaminverkleidung baumelten.

»Er hat doch nicht etwa … «, sagte Michael zu ihr.

»Er schaute diese Serie mit den Vampiren«, erwiderte sie.

»Diese Serie, in der die Brüste der Vampirfrauen gezeigt werden«, fügte ich hinzu in der Hoffnung, es würde erklären, warum ich ein drittes Mal versagte.

»Er war so von den Brüsten vereinnahmt, dass er nicht merkte, wie er immer näher zur Lampe hüpfte«, sagte Ingrid.

»Er schlug seine Hände zusammen und zerbrach dabei die Deckenleuchte«, sagte Michael abschließend.

»Große Glasscherben fielen auf seinen Kopf herunter«, sagte Ingrid.

»Das Nächste, woran ich mich erinnere, ist, dass die Wunde mit zehn Stichen im Krankenhaus genäht wurde«, sagte ich.

Sie lachten über mich während der ganzen ersten Spielhälfte. Während einer Pause sagte Michael zu mir: »Ganz im Ernst, du kannst in diesem Zimmer nicht weitertrainieren. Du könntest alles zertrümmern.«

»Ingrid sagte mir, dass ich meine Mittagspause mit ihr im Fitnessstudio verbringen müsse. Auf diese Weise kann sie mich im Auge behalten und sicherstellen, dass ich viel Joghurt esse.«

»Ausgezeichneter Plan«, stimmten alle zu.

STORY 9

In Good Repair

»Wir müssen einen Klempner anrufen«, sagte meine Frau Ingrid zu mir.
 »Warum?«
 »Der Abfallzerkleinerer ist kaputt.«
 »Klempner sind teuer«, erwiderte ich. »Wahrscheinlich kann ich einen neuen Zerkleinerer kaufen und selbst einbauen.«
 »Klaus, ich denke, dass du die Arbeit von einem Fachmann machen lassen solltest.«
 »Hast du denn kein Vertrauen in die handwerklichen Fähigkeiten deines Ehemannes?«, fragte ich.
 »Du bist gut im Heckenschneiden und im Rasenmähen«, sagte sie zu mir.
 »Ich kann auch handwerkliche Arbeit verrichten«, versicherte ich.
 »Wie war das doch mit dem Laternenpfahl, den du vorne im Garten ausgetauscht hast?«, fragte sie.
 »Er funktioniert doch prima.«
 »Er steht schräg und neigt sich ungefähr fünfzehn Zentimeter nach links«, sagte sie.
 »Dadurch fällt mehr Licht auf die Einfahrt.«
 »Und die Sicherung brennt durch, wenn wir das Fernsehgerät einschalten, während das Gartenlicht an ist.«
 »Dafür ist der Elektriker verantwortlich, der die Leitungen gelegt hat«, sagte ich. »Er hat den Stromkreis überlastet.«
 »Ich glaube immer noch, dass wir den Klempner anrufen sollten.«
 Ich debattierte mit Ingrid nicht mehr weiter. Insgeheim plante ich, die Arbeit selbst zu verrichten. Ich würde ihr zeigen, wie einfach es ist, verschiedene Sachen am Haus selbst zu reparieren.

―2―

 Es ist Samstag. Die Kinder verbringen das Wochenende bei meinen Eltern. Ingrid ist gerade los, um ein paar Freunde aus ihrer Studienzeit zu besuchen. Ich werde mindestens sechs Stunden alleine sein. Zeit, mein Vorhaben in die Tat umzusetzen. Ich rief meinen Nachbarn Jürgen an, einen pensionierten Ingenieur, der gleich neben mir wohnt.
 »Kannst du mir heute helfen, einen neuen Abfallzerkleinerer einzubauen?«
 »Sicher.«
 »Komm gleich rüber. Ich habe den neuen Zerkleinerer schon besorgt. Er ist im Keller versteckt.«
 »Ingrid will nicht, dass du diese Arbeit ausführst, nicht wahr?«
 »Warum sagst du das?«
 »Weil du den neuen Zerkleinerer im Keller verstecken musstest. Ich erinnere mich auch daran, dass du einmal dein Badezimmer im Obergeschoss unter Wasser gesetzt hast, als du versucht hast, einen neuen Kaltwasserhahn am Waschbecken anzubringen.«

Story 9

»Das war ein Unfall«, sagte ich.
»Du hast vergessen, den Armaturengriff am Rohr festzuschrauben.«
»Das war nicht mein Fehler. Ich wurde durch die Kinder abgelenkt.«
»Als du den Hauptanschluss im Haus wieder aufgedreht hast, wurde der Handgriff mit solcher Wucht vom Wasserrohr weggesprengt, dass er in der Decke stecken blieb.«
»Erinnere mich bloß nicht daran.«
»Währenddessen warst du im Kellergeschoss und hast nicht gehört, wie das Wasser überall im Badezimmer auf den Boden spritzte.«
»Ich habe diese Geschichte längst vergessen.«
»Der Wasserschaden war so schlimm, dass du die Wohnzimmerdecke erneuern musstest«, sagte Jürgen.
»Willst du mir helfen oder nicht?«
»Ich helfe dir schon. Ich sage ja nur, warum ich weiß, dass Ingrid nicht will, dass du diese Arbeit machst. Ich komme gleich rüber.«

---3---

Zwanzig Minuten später waren wir in meiner Küche und legten unsere Werkzeuge bereit. Jürgen nahm den neuen Abfallzerkleinerer aus seiner Verpackung.
»Zuerst müssen wir den alten Zerkleinerer vom Strom nehmen«, sagte Jürgen.
Er beugte seinen Kopf hinunter und steckte ihn in den Schrank unter dem Spülbecken. Wir hatten schon alle Plastikflaschen, Reinigungsmittel und andere verschiedene Sachen aus dem Schrank herausgenommen, damit sie uns nicht im Weg sein würden. Mit seinem Kopf im Schrank verbrachte Jürgen bereits einige Minuten damit, das ein oder andere zu richten.
Dann sagte er: »Komm hier herunter und schau dir das an.«
Ich steckte meinen Kopf in den Schrank.
»Hier ist das Abflussrohr, das ich gerade vom Zerkleinerer entfernt habe.« Er deutete auf ein weißes Kunststoffrohr, das neben dem Zerkleinerer hing.
»Der Zerkleinerer ist genau hier am Boden des Beckens befestigt.« Er zeigte auf irgendetwas anderes. Eine Art metallischer Vorrichtung. »Setze deinen Schraubenzieher an der Verriegelung an, genau dort, wo sie gebogen ist. Dann klopfe mit dem Hammer leicht darauf, um die Verriegelung zu öffnen und um den Zerkleinerer zu lösen.«
Ich tat was er sagte, aber nichts geschah.
»Die Verriegelung scheint festgerostet zu sein«, sagte ich.
Jürgen erhob sich. Es ist nicht leicht, sich zu bücken und dabei in den Schrank zu schauen.
»Schlage etwas fester drauf«, sagte er.
Ich versetzte dem Schraubenzieher einen mächtigen Schlag. Mit Erfolg! Die Verriegelung löste sich. Der Abfallzerkleinerer fiel vom Haltering.
»Was ist passiert?«, fragte Jürgen.
»Du kannst dir gar nicht vorstellen, wie groß das Loch ist, wenn ein Abfallzerkleinerer auf den Boden eines Küchenschränkchens fällt«, antwortete ich.
»Ich hätte wohl den Zerkleinerer festhalten sollen, als du die Verriegelung gelockert hast.«

In Good Repair

Ich stand auf, damit Jürgen in das Schränkchen schauen konnte.

»Das ist ein ganz schön großes Loch«, stimmte er zu. »Es sieht aus, als ob eine kleine Kanonenkugel den Boden des Küchenschränkchens durchschlagen hätte. Ich habe ein kleines Stück Sperrholz zu Hause. Wir können es zur Reparatur des Loches verwenden. Rühre nichts an, bis ich wieder da bin.«

Während Jürgen weg war, fing ich an, mir Sorgen darüber zu machen, was wohl Ingrid sagen würde, wenn sie nach Hause kommt. Ich brauchte ein Glass Wasser, um einen klaren Kopf zu bekommen. Ich drehte das kalte Wasser auf und ließ es in das Becken laufen. Nach ein paar Sekunden war das Wasser angenehm kalt. Ich füllte ein Glas und setzte mich an den Küchentisch. Jürgen kam ein paar Minuten später zurück.

»Ich konnte das Sperrholz nicht finden. Du musst ein Stück im Geschäft kaufen«, sagte er. »Hey, warum ist da eine große Pfütze auf dem Küchenboden?«

»Welche Pfütze?«

Jürgen sah mein Glas Wasser. »Du hast doch nicht etwa Wasser in den Ausguss laufen lassen, oder?«

Wir starrten beide in den Küchenschrank unter dem Spülbecken.

»Schau dir dieses Schlamassel an«, sagte Jürgen.

»Ich vergaß, dass das Abflussrohr entfernt war.«

»Da müssen ein paar Liter Wasser aus dem Becken raus und in das Loch rein gelaufen sein. Jetzt rinnt es auf den Boden hinaus.«

»Ich werde es aufwischen.«

»Mach das nur. Gehe anschließend in den Laden und besorge ein kleines Stück Sperrholz. Ich gehe nach Hause und werde ein Nickerchen machen. Ruf mich an, wenn du vom Geschäft zurück bist.«

---4---

Ich verbrachte über eine Stunde damit, die Küche zu säubern und ein kleines Stück Holz zu kaufen, um das Loch im Küchenschrank abzudecken. Als ich zu Hause war, rief ich Jürgen an.

»Jürgen musste zu unserem Sohn fahren«, sagte mir seine Frau. »Sie brauchten jemanden, der nach dem Baby schaut, während sie beim Einkaufen sind.«

»Er sollte mir eigentlich bei einer Reparatur helfen«, jammerte ich.

»Enkelkinder gehen vor«, sagte sie zu mir. »Und außerdem, ich dachte, du darfst nichts mehr im Haus reparieren.«

»Darüber rede ich lieber nicht.«

»Ich erinnere mich an deinen Versuch, ein Loch im Dach über deinem Schlafzimmer abzudichten. Du bist das Dach hinunter gerutscht und beinahe in die Büsche gefallen.«

»Das Dach war viel rutschiger, als ich dachte.«

»Wenigstens warst du klug genug, dich an einen Baum im Hinterhof zu binden, bevor du auf das Dach geklettert bist. Musstest du nicht eine Zeitlang am obersten Ast baumeln, bis der Polizist dich rettete?«

»Für ihn war es eine gute Trainingseinheit«, sagte ich. »Ich muss jetzt wirklich gehen.«

Ich legte den Hörer auf. Jetzt hatte ich ein Problem. Jürgen war weg und Ingrid würde in drei Stunden zu Hause sein.

»Es sieht ganz so aus, als ob ich die Arbeit selbst machen müsste«, sagte ich zum Hund, der dasaß und mich mit einem komischen Gesichtsausdruck betrachtete.

Story 9

Ich studierte die Installationsanleitung. Sie war in Japanisch geschrieben. Eine eilige Suche ergab, dass es keine andere Anleitung gab. Ein Gefühl von Panik breitete sich in meinem Magen aus.

―――――――――――――――――――――5―――――――――――――――――――――

Nach fünf Minuten fieberhaften Grübelns kam ich zu dem Schluss, dass mir nur noch eine Vorgehensweise blieb. Zögernd hob ich den Hörer ab und wählte eine weitere Nummer.

Das Telefon läutete einmal. Ich fürchtete mich vor dieser Unterhaltung. Es klingelte ein zweites Mal. Mein Selbstwertgefühl war an seinem tiefsten Punkt seit der siebten Klasse. Ein drittes Klingeln war zu hören. Vielleicht war niemand zu Hause. Leider wurde der Anruf entgegengenommen.

»Hallo«, sagte eine Stimme, die mich jahrelang gequält hatte.

»Hallo Maria. Ich brauche etwas Hilfe.«

»Klaus, das ist aber nett, dass du anrufst«, gurrte meine Schwester Maria ins Telefon. »Worum geht es denn?«

Ich schluckte meinen Stolz hinunter. »Kannst du mir am Telefon erklären, wie man einen Abfallzerkleinerer einbaut?«

»Wann hast du dich entschieden, Klempner zu werden?«

»Seitdem Klempner teurere Autos als meins fahren.«

»Erinnerst du dich noch daran, als du mir helfen wolltest, ein Bücherregal aufzubauen?«, fragte Maria.

Meine Schwester ist ein Jahr älter als ich. Sie war immer schon gut im Aufbauen und Reparieren von Dingen. Als wir Teenager waren, versuchte ich ein paar Mal, ihr zu helfen.

»Erinnere mich nicht daran«, sagte ich.

»Du hast dir dauernd mit dem Hammer auf den Daumen geschlagen. Er schwoll so stark an, dass Mutti die Nägel für dich halten musste.«

»Sie hat nur einen Nagel gehalten«, sagte ich.

»Richtig«, lachte Maria. »Sie gab auf, als du auch auf ihren Daumen geschlagen hast.«

»Ich kann jetzt mit dem Hammer viel besser umgehen«, sagte ich. »Ich könnte die Arbeit wahrscheinlich selbst ausführen aber die Installationsanleitung ist auf Japanisch.«

»Stell das Telefon auf Lautsprecher«, seufzte meine Schwester. »Ich werde dich durch die ganze Angelegenheit leiten.«

―――――――――――――――――――――6―――――――――――――――――――――

Ich verstaute gerade die Werkzeuge, als Ingrid nach Hause kam.

»Wir haben einen neuen Abfallzerkleinerer«, sagte ich zu ihr.

Sie ging in die Küche und schaute unter das Spülbecken.

»Er ist wirklich neu«, sagte sie. »Welchen Klempner hast du angerufen?«

»Ich habe es selbst gemacht.«

»Nein, hast du nicht«, sagte meine reizende Frau. »In der Küche ist nichts kaputtgegangen.«

»Schau nochmals in das Küchenschränkchen«, sagte ich zu ihr. »Unter den Abfalleimer.«

In Good Repair

»Schau nur, wie groß das Loch ist«, rief sie ein paar Sekunden später. »Da passt ja ein Kürbis rein.«
»Ich wollte es mit einem Stück Sperrholz reparieren, aber ich hatte keine Zeit dazu.«
»Wenn das der einzige Schaden ist, den du angerichtet hast, dann bin ich beeindruckt«, sagte Ingrid. »Bist du sicher, dass dir sonst niemand geholfen hat?«
»Am Anfang war Jürgen hier, aber er musste weg.«
»Das muss gefeiert werden. Lasst uns eine Flasche Wein öffnen.«
Sie nahm eine Flasche Chardonnay aus dem Kühlschrank und füllte zwei Gläser.
Wir stießen miteinander an.
»Einen Toast auf meinen Handwerker«, sagte Ingrid, während wir einen kleinen Schluck Chardonnay tranken.
Wir blieben in der Küche, tranken Wein und bereiteten das Abendessen vor. Ingrid widmete sich dem Kochen. Ich deckte den Tisch und machte einen Salat. Ingrid erzählte mir alles Mögliche über ihre Schulfreunde.
»Wir gingen zum Einkaufszentrum und haben dort Sushi zu Mittag gegessen«, sagte sie.
»Wie schön.«
Bis wir uns endlich zum Abendessen setzten, waren Ingrid und ich schon bei unserem dritten Glas Wein angelangt. Ich fühlte mich sehr entspannt.
»So, hast du heute sonst noch mit jemand Interessantem, außer Jürgen gesprochen?«, fragte sie.
»Ich rief meine Schwester Maria an«, erwähnte ich.
»Aha«, sagte Ingrid und zeigte mit dem Finger auf mich. »Maria hat dir geholfen.«
»Unfair«, beschwerte ich mich. »Du hast mir Wein gegeben, um mir die Wahrheit zu entlocken.«
»Ich kann doch nichts dafür, das du keinen Wein verträgst«, kicherte sie.
»Du hast mich schamlos ausgenutzt«, beschwerte ich mich.
»Du brauchst dich nicht zu schämen«, sagte Ingrid. »Es war schlau, jemanden um Hilfe zu bitten.«
»Die Installationsanleitung war auf Japanisch.«
»Nicht jeder ist als Werkzeugfachmann und Mechaniker auf die Welt gekommen«, sagte Ingrid. »Du hast viele andere Talente, die deine Schwester nicht hat.«
»Was zum Beispiel?«
Sie dachte eine Minute nach. »Du kannst wirklich gut meine Füße massieren.«
»Ich will nicht, dass jemand davon erfährt. Man könnte annehmen, ich hätte eine seltsame Neigung.«
»Dein Geheimnis ist bei mir sicher. Ich bin einfach viel glücklicher mit einem Ehemann, der meine Füße massiert, als mit einem Ehemann, der Dinge repariert. Du brauchst dich nicht unsicher deswegen zu fühlen, weil du nicht so geschickt bist, was Reparaturen am Haus angeht. Lass uns lieber Leute beauftragen, die sich damit auskennen.«
»Das klingt nach einer vernünftigen Lösung«, sagte ich. »Du hast keine Ahnung, wie stressig mein Tag gewesen ist.«

STORY 10

All Inclusive

Wir aßen mit Josef und Martina, einem netten Paar aus Bremen, zu Abend. Wir hatten sie zuvor am Nachmittag am Pool an der Insel-Bar getroffen. Sie waren so unterhaltsame Leute, dass wir sie fragten, ob sie uns nicht zum Abendessen Gesellschaft leisten möchten.

»So, was habt ihr zwei heute gemacht?«, fragte Josef.

»Klaus hat zehn Margaritas getrunken und ist am Strand eingeschlafen«, sagte Ingrid. »Jetzt hat er einen schlimmen Sonnenbrand.«

Martina schaute mich an. »Du bist tatsächlich etwas rot«, bemerkte sie.

»Die Sonne hier in Cancun ist wirklich stark. Du musst vorsichtig sein«, sagte Josef. »Trink noch ein paar Margaritas und du wirst dich besser fühlen.«

»Dieser Ort ist so großartig«, sagte Martina. »Wir können essen und trinken, soviel wir wollen, und es ist alles im Preis inbegriffen. Außerdem gibt es ein großartiges Wassersportangebot mit Kajaks, Segelbooten und Schnorcheln direkt hier im Resort.«

»Ich hoffe, meiner Mutter geht es gut bei der Kinderbetreuung«, sagte Ingrid.

»Sie kommt schon klar«, sagte ich.

»Was ist, wenn etwas passiert?«

»Es wird nichts Schlimmes passieren«, sagte ich. »Aber deine Mutter hat die Telefonnummer des Hotels. Sie kann dort jederzeit anrufen und uns suchen lassen.«

»Die Wassergymnastik war ein anstrengendes Fitnesstraining«, erwähnte Ingrid. »Klaus hat es auch ausprobiert, aber er konnte mit dem Tempo nicht mithalten.«

»War das vor oder nach dem Trinkgelage?«, fragte Josef.

»Vorher«, sagte ich. »Otto leitet die Aerobic-Kurse. Er ist wie ein militärischer Ausbilder. Ich verstehe nicht, wie die Frauen alle im Schwimmbad eine ganze Stunde lang ihre Arme schwingen und mit ihren Beinen pumpen konnten.«

»Außerdem gibt Otto täglich um vier Uhr Salsa-Unterricht«, sagte Ingrid. »Als Klaus am Strand schnarchte, hat er mir eine Stunde gegeben.«

»Du hast mir nichts davon gesagt, das Otto dir eine Tanzstunde gegeben hat«, sagte ich. »Ich glaube nicht, das mir das gefällt.«

»Und mir gefällt es nicht, wie du die beiden jungen Mädchen in ihren Tangabikinis angestarrt hast, als sie ihre Wassergymnastik machten«, sagte Ingrid.

Ich schloss meine Augen und erinnerte mich an die zwei wunderschönen jungen Frauen, die Ingrid erwähnte. Sie hatten eine perfekte Bräune, ein paar stilvolle Tätowierungen und glänzend polierte Fingernägel. Allein der Gedanke an sie ließ meine Sonnenbrandschmerzen für ein paar Sekunden lang verschwinden.

»Sie hatten wirklich hübsche Bauchnabelpiercings«, seufzte ich.

Ingrid schlug mich. »Da musst du ja wirklich sehr genau hingeschaut haben, um das zu wissen«, sagte sie.

»Ich kenne die Mädchen, die du meinst«, unterbrach Martina. »Ich habe Schuhe, die älter sind als sie.«

Story 10

»Hast du die zwei Jungs in Cowboyhüten gesehen, die den ganzen Nachmittag im Schwimmbad standen?«, fragte Josef.

»Sie waren beim Wasser-Aerobic«, sagte Ingrid. »Sie tranken mit einer Hand Bier aus großen Thermosbechern und machten Übungen mit der anderen. Es war so lustig.«

»Hört ihr euch die Band an, die heute Abend hier spielt?«, fragte Josef.

»Ich denke, dass wir auf dem Zimmer bleiben und lesen. Mein Sonnenbrand bringt mich um. Viel Spaß euch zweien«, sagte ich.

---—2—---

Zur Cocktailparty des Managers kamen wir um fünf Uhr an. Josef und Martina saßen schon in der Nähe der Bar. Wir leisteten ihnen bei ein paar Drinks Gesellschaft.

»Du siehst nicht sehr gut aus«, sagte ich zu Josef.

»Er hat gestern Abend ein paar Iren in der Karaokebar kennengelernt«, sagte Martina. »Sie haben Bier getrunken und bis Mitternacht gesungen.«

»Und wir mussten heute wirklich früh für einen Tauchgang draußen am Riff aufstehen«, sagte Josef.

»Der Alkohol, das Tauchen, und das Boot, das auf dem Wasser auf- und abschaukelte, machten Josef ganz krank«, sagte Martina.

»Wahrscheinlich sind sie immer noch dabei, das Boot sauber zu machen«, sagte Josef.

»Der Kapitän hat uns aus seinem Boot verbannt, für den Rest der Woche«, beschwerte sich Martina. »Jetzt können wir nicht mehr tauchen gehen.«

»Hättest du deinen Kopf nicht über den Bootsrand hinauslehnen können?«, fragte ich.

»Ich habe es versucht, aber nicht geschafft.«

»Also, was trinkst du jetzt?«, fragte Ingrid.

»Bloß Bier. Ich hoffe, mehr Alkohol wird meinen Magen beruhigen.«

»Was habt ihr heute gemacht?«, fragte Martina.

»Klaus lernte, wie man bei unserem Mietwagen den Rückwärtsgang einlegt«, sagte Ingrid voller Stolz.

Josef und Martina schauten mich leicht befremdet an.

»Wir sind nach Tulum gefahren, um die Ruinen zu sehen«, sagte ich. »Auf dem Weg dorthin hielten wir bei einem Geschäft an und ich parkte das Auto dem Geschäft zugewandt. Als wir wegfahren wollten, konnte ich beim Auto den Rückwärtsgang nicht einlegen.«

»Warum nicht?«

»Ich wusste nicht, wie. Der Schalthebelkopf zeigte die Position des Rückwärtsgangs an, aber ich schaffte es nicht, den Schaltknüppel in diese Position zu bewegen.«

»Wir haben einen netten jungen Mann dafür bezahlt, es uns zu zeigen«, sagte Ingrid.

»Zehn Pesos, um uns zu zeigen, wie die Gänge geschaltet werden, und dreißig Pesos dafür, dass er mich nicht auslacht«, sagte ich.

»Bist du vorher noch nie mit einem Handschaltgetriebe gefahren?«, fragte Martina.

»Doch, aber dieses Auto hatte einen kleinen Ring unterhalb des Ganghebels. Ich musste den Ring hochziehen, um den Rückwärtsgang einzulegen«, sagte ich.

»Das ist ein neuer Trick«, sagte Josef.

»Geht ihr heute zum Abendessen ans Buffet?«, fragte Ingrid Martina.

»Wir haben beschlossen, den Zimmerservice zu nutzen, falls Josef wieder krank wird. Wir werden euch dann wahrscheinlich irgendwann morgen sehen.«

3

»Was hast du dir denn dabei gedacht?«, schrie mich Ingrid an.

»Es war nicht meine Schuld«, sagte ich.

»Du weißt doch nicht einmal, wie man mit einem Spielzeugboot in unserer Badewanne segelt. Wie kommst du darauf, eines der Segelboote des Resorts in einen aufgewühlten Ozean zu steuern?«

»Es hat so leicht ausgeschaut. Die anderen Feriengäste schienen alle mit ihren Segelbooten zurechtzukommen.«

»Aber du hast es geschafft, dein Boot komplett zu zerstören.«

»Die Leute, die an dem Wassersporttresen arbeiten, waren sehr freundlich. Niemand hat mich angeschrien. Weshalb bist du so sauer?«

»Weil wir dem Resort ein neues Segel bezahlen müssen.«

»Können die das Loch nicht einfach wieder zunähen?«

»Dieses Loch war größer als unser Mietwagen.«

Ingrid spazierte ein paar Stunden zuvor an der Küste entlang, als sie auf mein armes Segelboot stieß, welches flach im Wasser lag. Ich stand am Steg und sah den Mitarbeitern der Wassersportabteilung zu, wie sie das Segel vom Mast entfernten. Aufgespießt an einer langen Stange, lag das Segel zwischen den Felsen beim Bootssteg. Die zwei Mädchen mit den lackierten Fingernägeln, Tätowierungen und knappen Badeanzügen standen neben mir. Ingrid erkannte richtigerweise, dass ich die Damen auf eine Vergnügungsfahrt mitgenommen hatte, eine Fahrt, die unglücklich endete. Seitdem ist sie sauer auf mich.

Sie schlug mir auf den Hinterkopf. »Warum hast du den Leuten der Wassersportabteilung gesagt, dass du ein erfahrener Segler seist?«

»Ich wollte die Mädchen beeindrucken«, gab ich zu.

»Und warum bist du mit zwei Mädchen, die noch nicht mal wählen dürfen, Segeln gegangen, anstatt mit deiner Frau?«

»Du wärst nicht gegangen, außer wir hätten jemanden vom Personal gebeten, mir beim Segeln zu helfen«, murmelte ich vor mich hin.

»Na so etwas. Ich glaube, du hattest die Hilfe nötig, oder etwa nicht?«

Glücklicherweise saßen wir an der Theke der zentralen Bar im Resort. In zwei Minuten sollte ein Kurs beginnen. Wir sollten lernen, wie man Martinis macht.

»Lass uns die Vergangenheit vergessen«, sagte ich zu Ingrid. »Ich kann es nicht abwarten zu lernen, wie man Martinis macht.«

Sie schlug mir noch einmal auf den Hinterkopf, um mir sozusagen Glück zu wünschen. Der Klaps war jedoch nicht so heftig wie beim letzten Mal, was ich so auslegte, dass sie nicht mehr so böse auf mich sei. Ich hoffte, nach ein paar Martinis würde sie den ganzen Vorfall vergessen.

Alle Plätze in der Bar waren belegt. Um vier Uhr erschien Otto mit Lukas, unserem Lieblingsbarkeeper.

»Seid ihr alle bereit, etwas über Martinis zu lernen?«, schrie Otto.

Story 10

»Jawohl!«, brüllten wir alle zurück.

Er ging an der ganzen Bar entlang. Als er Ingrid sah, hob er ihre Hand auf und küsste ihren Handrücken.

»Sind alle Aerobic-Lehrer so freundlich?«, fragte ich.

»Das war ein Kuss aus Mitleid. Er hat von dem hoffnungslosen Mann gehört, mit dem ich verheiratet bin.«

»Wir sollten uns auf die Martinis konzentrieren«, sagte ich.

Wir lernten, eine Vielfalt an Martinis zuzubereiten, die ich nicht für möglich hielt. Otto gab Ingrid keinen Handkuss mehr. Ich glaube, er bemerkte meinen finsteren Blick.

4

»Komm, wir paddeln mit dem Kajak hinunter zum nächsten Resort«, sagte Josef zu mir.

»Ich sitze ganz gerne hier am Ozean und schlürfe diese Piña Colada«, sagte ich. »Wieso sollte ich mich zu so etwas Schweißtreibendem hinreißen lassen?«

»Ich habe gehört, dass man in diesem Resort nackt sein darf. Dann können wir all die nackten Leute abchecken.«

»Wer hat dir das gesagt?«

»Die Jungs mit den Cowboyhüten«, sagte Josef.

»Die sind doch seit vier Tagen nicht aus dem Pool herausgekommen. Woher sollten die das wissen?«

»Ihre Frauen arbeiten beim Reisebüro. Sie wissen alles über diese Gegend.«

»Können wir nicht einfach die Küste hintergehen?«

»Es gibt da einen großen Zaun, der den Weg versperrt«, sagte Josef.

Ich stellte meinen Drink hin. »Ein wenig Bewegung würde mir nicht schaden.«

Zehn Minuten später paddelten Josef und ich unsere Kajaks wie besessen in Richtung des benachbarten Resorts. Als wir dort ankamen, erlebten wir eine große Enttäuschung.

»Die haben einen großen Sichtschutz genau vor dem FKK-Strand aufgebaut«, sagte Josef.

»Das ist ungerecht. Um bis hierher gegen den Wind zu paddeln, habe ich mich totgeschuftet und jetzt sehe ich kein bisschen nackte Haut«, fügte ich hinzu.

Wir saßen im Wasser, dreißig Meter vom Strand entfernt, und schaukelten in unseren Kajaks auf und ab.

»Komm, ziehen wir die Kajaks an Land«, schlug ich vor.

Josef zögerte noch.

»Ich bin nicht sicher, dass ich mich ausziehen will«, sagte er.

»Es sind nicht alle nackt in dem Resort. Die Leute vor dem Sichtschutz tragen Badeanzüge.«

Ich konnte sehen wie Josef überlegte.

»Da drüben am Strand neben den Stühlen liegt schon ein Zweierkajak«, sagte ich. »Wir können unsere gleich daneben hinziehen.«

»Das Kajak ist von unserem Resort«, sagte Josef. »Es hat dieselben Markierungen und dieselbe Farbe.«

»Siehst du, wir sind nicht die einzigen, die diese Idee haben. Es wird schon gut gehen. Komm, los geht's!«

Es dauerte noch weitere fünf Minuten, bis Josef den nötigen Mut fand, sein Kajak an Land zu bringen.

»Ich wünschte, ich hätte etwas mehr getrunken«, sagte er, als wir unsere Kajaks aus dem Wasser zogen.

»Also, sollen wir unsere Badehosen ausziehen oder anlassen?«, fragte ich.

All Inclusive

Nach einigem Hin und Her entschieden wir uns, die Badehosen anzulassen. Wir schlenderten hinter dem Sichtschutz herum, der am Strand aufgebaut war. Da lagen zehn oder fünfzehn alte Männer und Damen auf ihren Liegestühlen. Einige hatten Badeanzüge an, aber die meisten waren vollkommen nackt.

»Schau dir bloß all die Falten dieser Leute an«, flüsterte Josef.

Ältere Menschen wirken nicht sehr sexy, wenn sie nackt sind. Ich machte mir im Geiste eine Notiz davon, möglichst viel anzuziehen, wenn ich einmal siebzig bin.

»Komm, wir probieren den Whirlpool aus«, sagte ich.

Wir gingen zu einem großen Whirlpool, der gleich am Strand lag, hinüber. Darin waren mindestens schon zwanzig Leute, die sich unterhielten und entspannten. Alle waren noch ziemlich faltenfrei. Die meisten von ihnen waren nackt. Mir fielen ein paar außerordentlich gutaussehende Leute auf.

»Das wird der Hammer!«, sagte ich, als wir leger ins Wasser stiegen und uns hinsetzten.

Als ich anfing, die anderen Badegäste zu mustern, begann Josef plötzlich, an meine Schulter zu klopfen.

»Was ist los?«, sagte ich, indem ich mich ihm zuwandte.

Er starrte auf zwei Frauen, die mit entblößten Brüsten ungefähr drei Meter vom Whirlpool entfernt in der Sonne saßen. Ich folgte seinem Blick und musste tief Luft holen. Ingrid und Martina hielten Drinks in den Händen und starrten uns entgegen.

―――――――――――――5―――――――――――――

»Du bist so ein Perversling«, sagte Ingrid zu mir, als unser Flugzeug vom Flughafen in Cancun abhob.

»Moment mal. Du warst schließlich auch dort. Oben ohne, wenn ich hinzufügen darf.«

»Ich ging nur zum Bräunen dorthin. Du wolltest nur nackte Mädchen sehen.«

»Gestern warst du noch der Meinung, dass es ganz lustig wäre.«

Sie kicherte und küsste mich auf die Wange. »Ich ärgere dich nur.«

»Hat es dir nichts ausgemacht, dass Josef deine Brust gesehen hat?«, fragte ich.

»Eigentlich nicht. Ich habe meine Scheu verloren, als ich meine Kinder gestillt habe.«

»Martina sah sehr hübsch aus ohne ihr Bikinioberteil«, sagte ich.

Ingrid lachte und schlug mich auf den Arm. Meine Frau schlug mich diese Woche öfter als die ganze übrige Zeit unserer Ehe.

Ich lehnte mich in meinem Sitz zurück und blickte aus dem Fenster. Die Halbinsel Yucatan verschwand aus meinem Blickfeld, als sich das Flugzeug in Richtung Golf von Mexiko entfernte.

»Trotz all der verrückten Sachen, die so passierten, war es ein ganz netter Urlaub«, sagte ich.

STORY 11

Murder Mystery in L.A.

»Das ist eine schlechte Idee«, schreie ich in Karls Ohr.

»In einer Bar etwas trinken?«, fragt er.

»In einer Bar etwas trinken macht mir nichts aus«, sage ich ihm. »Nur nicht in dieser Bar.«

Ernst kommt mit zwei Bier und einem Glas Wein für mich zurück.

»Da sind jede Menge Leute mit großen Plastik-Käsedreiecken auf ihren Köpfen«, brüllt er.

Eine Band bestehend aus Jugendlichen ist auf der Bühne und macht mehr Lärm, als mein Trommelfell ertragen kann. Mir ist leicht schwindelig bei dem Sound. Es fällt schwer, den Worten der anderen zu folgen.

»Gerade deshalb will ich in dieser Bar nichts trinken«, schreie ich zurück. »Lasst uns einen neutraleren Ort aufsuchen.«

Zwanzig Minuten später spazieren wir durch die warme Abendluft von Kalifornien. Wir versuchen, eine Bar zu finden, die nicht mit Leuten aus Wisconsin überfüllt ist.

»Warum müssen die immer vor einem großen Footballspiel diese künstlichen Plastik-Käsedreiecke auf dem Kopf tragen?«, frage ich.

»Was?«, sagen Karl und Ernst. Wir haben immer noch Ohrensausen von dem Krach, den die Band gemacht hat.

»Ich sagte, ich bin zu alt dafür, um mir schlechten Rock 'n' Roll anzuhören«, rufe ich ihnen zu.

Wir drei machen alle mit unseren Frauen eine Woche Ferien in Los Angeles. Die Kinder sind zu Hause bei ihren Großeltern. Heute Abend waren die Damen zu müde, nach dem Abendessen auszugehen. Karl, Ernst und ich entschieden uns, ein paar Bars zu besuchen und uns zu vergnügen. Wir wussten nicht, dass morgen das Footballteam der Uni Wisconsin gegen die Universität von Kalifornien spielt. Halb Wisconsin hat Los Angeles überfallen, um bei dem Spiel dabei zu sein. Wohin man auch blickt, sieht man Leute mit milchig weißer Haut und Plastik-Käsedreiecken auf dem Kopf.

»Die bekommen nicht viel Sonne oben in Wisconsin, oder?«, fragt Ernst.

»Ich glaube, ihre Haut ist so blass, weil die ersten Siedler Wikinger waren«, sagt Karl. »Schaut nur, wie groß diese Leute sind.«

Tatsächlich, es scheint, als wären die Durchschnittsgröße und das Gewicht eines Menschen aus Wisconsin im Vergleich zu einer typischen Person aus Los Angeles doppelt so groß.

»Die letzte Bar war verrückt«, sagt Ernst. »Ich war auf der Herrentoilette und zwei Wisconsin-Fans hielten einen Burschen fest mit einem T-Shirt der Universität von Kalifornien. Sie tauchten seinen Kopf in die Toilette und sangen dazu.«

»Sportfans spinnen einfach«, sage ich zu ihnen. »Da ist eine Bar, die ziemlich ruhig aussieht.«

Wir gehen in ein spärlich beleuchtetes Lokal hinein. Fünf Leute sitzen an der Theke und unterhalten sich mit gedämpfter Stimme. Die übrigen Plätze sind leer.

Wir sitzen an der Bar und bestellen eine Runde Getränke. »Dieses Lokal ist viel weniger stressig«, sage ich.

Story 11

Wir unterhalten uns über unsere Pläne für den nächsten Tag. Die Frauen wollen ins Kunstmuseum ›Los Angeles Museum of Art‹ gehen. Wir wollen die La Brea Tar Pits besuchen.

Mir fällt eine Pfütze am Boden auf, gleich neben der Stelle, wo wir sitzen.

»Da ist etwas am Boden«, sage ich zum Barkeeper.

»Keine Sorge, es ist schon trocken«, sagt er.

»Was ist das?«, frage ich.

»Blut. Irgendein Kerl wurde hier vor einer Stunde erschossen. Er saß auf Ihrem Barhocker.«

»Das erklärt, warum das Lokal so ruhig ist«, sagt Karl.

»Wie stehen die Chancen, dass hier heute Abend noch eine Schießerei stattfindet?«, fragt Ernst.

»Wahrscheinlich bei Null. Wir sollten hierbleiben«, sage ich.

Ein paar Minuten später spüre ich jemanden auf meine Schulter klopfen. Ich drehe mich um und sehe eine umwerfend schöne Frau. Sie reicht mir ein kleines Päckchen.

»Hier ist dein Geld und die Informationen zu deinem Ziel«, sagt sie und geht davon.

Ich bin zu überrascht vom Anblick dieser wunderschönen Frau, um zu reagieren, bis sie fast schon aus der Tür ist.

»Hallo!«, rufe ich. »Wovon reden Sie überhaupt?«

Ich öffne den Umschlag. Er ist mit Einhundert-Dollar-Noten vollgestopft.

»Schaut mal her, Leute. Wir können die ganze Nacht umsonst trinken.«

Wir nehmen das Geld heraus. Außerdem gibt es Bilder eines wirklich fies aussehenden Typen mit einer Narbe an der Wange und einem Ausdruck mit den persönlichen Daten dieses Kerls.

»Was ist das?«, fragt Karl.

Und dann stürmt die Polizei durch die Tür.

---2---

»Ich war mir ziemlich sicher, dass Sie keine professionellen Auftragsmörder sind, als Sie zu heulen angefangen haben«, sagt der Kriminalbeamte zu uns.

»Und warum hat es dann vier Stunden lang gedauert und fünftausend Dollar Anwaltsgebühren gekostet, bis wir gehen durften?«, fragt Karl.

Wir holen unsere persönlichen Habseligkeiten, Gürtel und Schuhbänder am Empfang irgendeines Hochsicherheitstraktes der Polizei in der Nähe von Hollywood ab.

»Der Bezirksanwalt war auf einer Party. Er hat keine Entlassungspapiere unterschrieben, bevor die vorbei war.«

»Wie lautet seine Adresse?«, frage ich. »Ich möchte ihm ein Weihnachtsgeschenk schicken.«

»Werden Sie nicht frech«, sagt der Polizist am Empfang. »Wir hätten Sie die ganze Nacht hierbehalten können.«

»Wir konnten Ihr Gekreische, dass die anderen Insassen Ihnen Angst machen, einfach nicht mehr hören«, sagt der Polizeibeamte.

»Sie haben uns in eine Zelle mit zwei Drogenhändlern, einem verrückten Motorradfahrer und einem Burschen gesteckt, der gerade jemandem das Ohr vom Kopf abgebissen hat«, sagt Ernst.

»Wir haben keine Sonderunterkünfte für Langweiler aus Deutschland«, sagt der Polizist vom Empfang. »Wenigstens sind Sie nicht in die Zelle mit den Verrückten mit Käse auf dem Kopf, geworfen worden.«

»Von dieser Seite betrachtet haben wir Glück gehabt«, sage ich zu den Polizisten.

»Wie steht es mit dem Geld?«, frage ich.

»Das gehört nicht Ihnen. Das sollte der echte Auftragsmörder bekommen.«

»Das muss der Kerl gewesen sein, der erschossen wurde, bevor wir in der Bar eintrafen«, sagt Ernst.

»Wenn Ihre Geheimagenten die Bar beobachtet haben, warum haben Sie dann von der vorangegangenen Schießerei nichts gewusst?«, fragt Karl.

»Wir haben die Bar nicht beobachtet. Wir sind der Frau gefolgt. Die vorausgegangene Schießerei hat niemand gemeldet. Wir verhörten den Barmann zwei Stunden lang, bis er endlich zugab, den Typen einfach in den Müllcontainer geworfen zu haben.«

»Was sind das bloß für Leute, die in dieser Stadt wohnen?«, frage ich. »Jemand wird vor ihren Augen erschossen und sie trinken einfach weiter, während der Barmann die Leiche in einem Müllkontainer entsorgt und dann den Boden putzt.«

»Das waren wahrscheinlich arbeitslose Schauspieler«, sagt der Kriminalbeamte.

»Und was ist mit der Frau, die Sie verfolgt haben?«

»Wir haben sie verloren, als die Polizei in die Bar eindrang.«

»Großartig«, sage ich.

Wir verlassen die Polizeistation und versuchen, ein Taxi zu finden. Es ist halb fünf Uhr morgens und wir haben kein großes Glück. Als wir auf der Straße warten, spüre ich nochmals ein Klopfen auf meiner Schulter. Es ist wieder diese umwerfende Frau.

Dieses Mal habe ich die Geistesgegenwart und halte sie fest. Sie richtet eine kleine Pistole auf mein Gesicht und ich lasse sie los.

»Big Sam sagt, dass ihr das Geld bis Mittag zurückgeben müsst, oder ihr seid geliefert«, sagt sie.

Alle drei starren wir sie an. Sie geht rückwärts in ein wartendes Auto und fährt davon.

»Jetzt sind wir echt in Schwierigkeiten«, sagt Ernst.

Zwei Stunden später verlassen wir die Polizeistation zum zweiten Mal.

»Ich kann es nicht fassen, dass sie uns nicht glauben«, sage ich.

»Ich kann es kaum glauben, dass uns eine Frau mit einer Pistole direkt vor der Polizeistation bedroht hat und niemand hat es gesehen«, sagt Ernst.

»Das erinnert mich an einen wirklich schlechten Film«, sagt Karl.

»Glaubst du, dass dieser Typ, Big Sam, uns Schwierigkeiten bereiten wird?«, fragt Ernst.

»Wir sagen einfach, dass die Frau den falschen Leuten das Geld gegeben hat. Sie ist schuld«, sage ich.

Unser einziges Glück ist, dass die Taxis um halb sieben wieder auf den Straßen sind. Ein schläfriger Fahrer bringt uns in unser Hotel zurück und wir schließen einen Pakt, unseren Frauen überhaupt nichts davon zu erzählen. Gerade als Ingrid aus einem erholsamen Schlaf erwacht, schleiche ich mich ins Hotelzimmer.

»Hast du es dir gut gehen lassen, Klaus?«, fragt Ingrid.

»Das kannst du dir gar nicht vorstellen.«

Story 11

Ich bin zu müde, um mit Ingrid darüber zu diskutieren, welche Sehenswürdigkeiten wir anschauen sollen. Aus diesem Grund stehe ich ein paar Stunden später neben ihr und betrachte dreihundert Jahre alte Gemälde. Ernst, Karl und deren Frauen sind ebenfalls bei uns.

»Ist dieses Kunstmuseum nicht viel schöner als diese Teergruben?«, fragt mich Ingrid.

Ich schaffe es gerade noch, eine Antwort zu murmeln. Es fällt mir schwer genug, die Augen offen zu halten, geschweige denn zu reden. Ich bemerke, das Ernst und Karl ähnliche Probleme haben.

Die Damen beschließen, dass wir im Museum zu Mittag essen.

»Schau mal, die Kantine hat eine vegetarische Speisekarte«, sagt Karls Frau.

»Ihr Männer seid heute so ruhig«, sagt Ernsts Frau, während wir unsere Tofuburger essen. »Was habt ihr eigentlich so spät noch gemacht?«

»Wir hatten einfach Spaß«, murmle ich.

»Das ist schon deine dritte Tasse Kaffee«, sagt Karls Frau zu ihm. »Du wirst heute Nacht nicht schlafen können.«

»Ich versuche doch bloß, den Tag zu bewältigen«, sagt er.

Nach dem Mittagessen sagen wir unseren Frauen, dass wir auf die Toilette müssen.

»Dann treffen wir uns in der Ausstellung nahöstlicher Keramik«, sagt Ingrid.

Um uns wach zu halten, bespritzen wir unsere Gesichter mit Wasser.

Bevor wir hinausgehen können, kommen zwei widerlich aussehende Männer in den Raum und blockieren den Ausgang.

»Wo ist das Geld?«, sagt der Größere von ihnen.

»Die Polizei hat es als Beweismittel beschlagnahmt«, jammere ich. »Sie wollten es uns nicht wiedergeben.«

»Big Sam wird das nicht gefallen«, sagt er.

»Der Kerl, der das Geld erhalten sollte, wurde eine Stunde, bevor wir in die Bar kamen, erschossen«, sagt Karl. »Diese Frau machte einen Fehler und gab Big Sams Geld den falschen Leuten.«

»Warum sollte sich ein professioneller Killer niederschießen lassen, während er auf sein Geld wartet?«, spottete der kleinere Mann.

»Offenbar passieren solche Sachen in Los Angeles andauernd«, antwortet Ernst.

»Ihr könnt froh sein, dass sie das Geld dem Falschen gegeben hat«, sage ich zu ihm. »Die Polizei hatte sie beschattet. Wenn sie den richtigen Killer erwischt hätten, hätte er ihnen wahrscheinlich alles über Big Sam erzählt. Wir hingegen wissen nichts über Big Sam. So gesehen ist es für ihn gut gelaufen.«

»Ich rufe besser Big Sam an«, sagt der größere Bursche. »Ihr bleibt genau, wo ihr seid.«

Er geht hinaus, um seinen Anruf zu tätigen, während sein Partner bei uns in der Toilette bleibt. Wir nutzen die Gelegenheit und setzen uns in drei verschiedene Toilettenkabinen um uns etwas auszuruhen.

Nach fünf Minuten kommt der Große zurück.

»Ihr kommt mit uns. Big Sam möchte euch sehen.«

Wir zögern, aber die beiden zeigen uns ihre Pistolen in den Schulterhalftern, also verlassen wir die Toilette mit ihnen.

Vier Senioren stehen Schlange, um auf die Toilette zu gehen.

»Es wurde ja langsam Zeit, dass Sie mit dem Saubermachen fertig sind«, sagt einer von ihnen. »Unser Reisebus fährt gleich ab und wir müssen hier zehn Minuten auf die Benutzung der Toilette warten. Das ist nicht richtig.«

»Wer hat gesagt, wir hätten sauber gemacht«, frage ich.

»Der Große da«, antwortet einer der Senioren.

»Er hat Sie angelogen«, schreit Karl.

Urplötzlich greifen die vier Senioren mit vollen Harnblasen Big Sams Leute an.

»Ich weiß zwar nicht, was diese Typen für eine Reise machen, aber sie beherrschen alle Judo«, sagt Karl.

»Erinnere mich bitte von nun an daran etwas netter zu alten Leuten zu sein«, sagt Ernst, während wir einen Herrn mit Gehgestell beobachten, wie er Big Sams kleineren Gangster im Würgegriff festhält.

Innerhalb von zwei Minuten sind die Bösewichte bewusstlos und in Handschellen gelegt.

4

Heute besuchen unsere Frauen Pasadena. Ernst, Karl und ich schlafen bis etwa elf Uhr und anschließend essen wir mit unserem Bekannten von der Kripo zu Mittag.

»Wir wussten nicht, das Sie uns gestern gefolgt sind«, sagt Karl.

»Big Sams Leute wussten es ebenso wenig. Daher war es so einfach, sie vor der Toilette zu verhaften.«

»Ihre Leute haben sich gut verkleidet«, sage ich.

»Um ehrlich zu sein, wir haben ein paar Leute eingesetzt, die kurz vor der Pensionierung stehen«, sagt er.

»Und was ist nun mit Big Sam?«, will Ernst wissen.

»Der Staatsanwalt hat mit einem von Sams Männern eine Vereinbarung getroffen. Dieser sagte uns, wo sich Big Sam versteckt hielt und gab zu, dass Sam den Auftrag erteilt hatte, einen seiner Mitbewerber zu töten. Wir haben heute Morgen Sam mitsamt der Frau, die Ihnen das Geld gegeben hat, verhaftet.«

»Das ist aber eine Erleichterung«, sage ich. »Jetzt können wir unsere Ferien zu Ende genießen und unsere Frauen müssen nicht dabei zusehen, wie wir erwürgt oder von einer Planierraupe überrollt werden.«

»Versprechen Sie mir nur, dass Sie Ihre nächsten Ferien an einem anderen Ort verbringen werden«, sagt der Kriminalbeamte.

»Vielleicht probieren wir es in Wisconsin«, sagt Karl. »Die Leute dort scheinen zumindest halbwegs normal zu sein.«

STORY 12

Mommy and Me

»Sie müssen ihr Einhalt gebieten, Herr Dietrich.«

»Was genau macht meine Mutter?«

»Helga erzählt allen in ihrem Altersheim, dass sie zwei Stunden lang an einen Tisch gefesselt gewesen sei und es ihr nicht gestattet gewesen sei, zur Toilette zu gehen.«

Es klang, als ob Dr. Christa Weber, meine Zahnärztin, am Hörer herumnagte, als sie mit mir sprach. Vielleicht knirschte sie mit den Zähnen. Ich wollte ihr schon sagen, das diese Angewohnheit für ihre Zähne schlecht ist, aber das wusste sie wahrscheinlich schon.

Stattdessen sagte ich: »Sie war an keinem Tisch gefesselt. Sie saß in ihrem Behandlungsstuhl. Sie ließen sie nach einer Stunde aufstehen, damit sie auf die Toilette gehen konnte.«

»Ich weiß. Aber Helga erzählt ihren Nachbarn, dass ich sie gefoltert hätte. Vier Leute aus dem Altersheim riefen bereits an, um ihre Termine abzusagen. Eine Dame sagte, sie habe gehört, dass ich keine Zulassung hätte.«

Dr. Weber hörte sich verzweifelt an. Die Hälfte ihrer Patienten wohnte im selben Heim wie meine Mutter. Wenn die glaubten, was meine Mutter erzählte, hätte Dr. Weber sehr viele Einbußen zu befürchten.

Helga Dietrich, meine Mutter, ist achtundachtzig Jahre alt. Sie hat keine Krankheiten. Sie kann ohne Stock gehen. Ihr geistiger Zustand ist sehr gut. Sie hat ein paar kleinere gesundheitliche Probleme, doch sie ist in großartiger körperlicher Verfassung für ihr Alter.

Unglücklicherweise ist meine Mutter mit ihrem Leben nicht zufrieden. Sie bildet sich ein, dass wenn sie nicht glücklich sein könne, auch alle anderen nicht zufrieden sein sollten. Deshalb macht sie alles, um allen anderen das Leben schwer zu machen. Im Moment lässt sie Dr. Weber ihren Unmut spüren.

»Ich werde Mama sofort anrufen«, sagte ich.

»Ich habe es schon versucht. Ihr Telefon ist besetzt. Könnten Sie zu ihr fahren und mit ihr reden? Bitte.«

Ich legte auf und sprang in mein Auto. Während der drei Kilometer langen Fahrt zur Wohnung meiner Mutter fühlte ich, wie mich Schuldgefühle überkamen. Es war meine Schuld, dass Dr. Weber dieses Problem hatte.

Vor ein paar Wochen hatte meine Mutter starke Zahnschmerzen. Sie hatte schon seit Jahren keinen Zahnarzt mehr besucht.

»Wieso soll ich für meine Zähne Geld ausgeben? In ein paar Jahren bin ich sowieso tot«, sagte sie dauernd.

Ich bestand darauf, dass sie meine Zahnärztin Dr. Weber sehen solle.

»Ich werde hingehen, aber ich will keine Röntgenaufnahmen«, sagte sie zu mir.

»Dr. Weber muss Aufnahmen machen, damit sie sehen kann, ob es irgendwelche versteckten Probleme gibt«, sagte ich zu ihr.

»Wie viel werden die Röntgenaufnahmen kosten?«, fragte sie.

»Das spielt keine Rolle. Du brauchst sie.«

»Ich kann mir keine Röntgenaufnahmen leisten.«

»Du hast genügend Geld.«

Story 12

»Du weißt nicht, wie viel Geld ich habe«, sagte Mama.
»Ich kenne deine finanzielle Situation. Ich zahle deine Rechnungen.«
Mama erhob einen neuen Einwand.
»Ich brauche das Geld für den Fall, dass ich in ein Pflegeheim muss.«
»Aber du sollst auch dein Essen ohne Schmerzen kauen können«, sagte ich zu ihr.
Schließlich schaffte ich es, meine Mutter zu Dr. Weber zu bringen. Mama benötigte eine Wurzelbehandlung und eine Krone auf einem ihrer Schneidezähne. Drei andere Zähne hatten Löcher, die behandelt werden mussten.
Vor zwei Tagen arbeitete Dr. Weber an der Wurzelbehandlung und versah Mamas Schneidezahn mit einer vorläufigen Krone. Die ganze Behandlung dauerte zwei Stunden. Mama musste noch zweimal kommen, bis die endgültige Krone eingepasst werden konnte.
Jetzt erzählte Mama den Leuten, dass Dr. Weber ihre Patienten foltere. Wenn ich Mama nicht zu meiner Zahnärztin gebracht hätte, wäre dieses Problem nie entstanden. Jawohl, ich fühlte mich sehr schuldig.

---2---

Als ich Mamas Wohnung betrat, war sie gerade am Telefon.
»Und ich sage dir, sie band mich zwei Stunden lang an einen Tisch. Stell dir vor, was das meinem Rücken antat. Ich kann immer noch nicht meine Beine richtig bewegen«, erzählte Mama irgendjemandem.
»Leg den Hörer auf, Mama!«, rief ich.
Sie hüpfte beinahe hoch beim Klang meiner Stimme.
»Mein Sohn ist gerade zu Besuch gekommen«, sagte sie in den Hörer. »Danke für deinen Anruf.«
»Das war eine meiner Nachbarinnen«, sagte sie, während sie das Telefon in seine Halterung zurückstellte. »Sie wollte alles über meine Krone wissen.«
»Wieso erzählst du den Leuten, dass du dich beim Zahnarzt auf einen Tisch hättest legen müssen?«
»Weil ich genau das tun musste. Mein Rücken bringt mich um.«
»Du hast in einem Behandlungsstuhl gesessen. Sie hat ihn nur nach hinten gekippt.«
»Woher willst du das wissen?«, fragte Mama mit einer gewissen Verärgerung.
»Ich war dabei. Erinnerst du dich nicht daran, dass ich dich zur Zahnarztpraxis gefahren habe und dort die ganze Zeit blieb?«
Sie zog ihr Gesicht in Falten und versuchte, sich zu erinnern. Mama ist klein. Wenn sie ihr Gesicht so verzieht, sieht sie aus wie Yodas ältere Schwester. Ihre lockigen, weißen Haare sind kurz geschnitten. Jede achtzigjährige Frau, die ich je gesehen habe, hat kurzes, lockiges Haar. Vielleicht ist das so etwas wie eine Vorschrift.
Mama trägt auch eine große Brille, deren Farbe im Sonnenlicht zu lila wechselt. Sie versteckt nahezu alle ihre Gesichtszüge. Wenn sie draußen ist, kann man nur die weißen, lockigen Haare und ein lilafarbenes Gesicht sehen. Das ist recht interessant.
Ich beobachtete sie beim Überlegen. Schließlich sagte sie: »Du warst nicht dabei.«
»Doch, war ich. Es gab keinen Foltertisch und Dr. Weber ließ dich nach einer Stunde auf die Toilette gehen.«
»Nein, ließ sie mich nicht. Sie hatte mich zwei Stunden lang an dieses Ding angebunden.«

Mommy and Me

»Ich habe dir geholfen, zur Toilette zu gehen.«

»Sie legte mir ein großes Stück Beton auf die Brust.«

»Das war eine Bleiweste, um dich vor den Röntgenstrahlen zu schützen.«

Mama machte ein zorniges Gesicht. Sie kann es nicht leiden, wenn man ihr widerspricht.

»Du musst aufhören, den Leuten zu erzählen, dass Dr. Weber dich gefoltert habe«, fuhr ich fort. »Die haben bereits ihre Termine abgesagt.«

»Ich habe es nur drei oder vier Leuten erzählt.«

»Schlechte Nachrichten verbreiten sich schnell in deinem Altersheim. Morgen wird sogar der Bürgermeister deine Geschichte kennen, wenn du nicht alle wieder anrufst und ihnen sagst, dass du übertrieben hast.«

Mama wechselte das Thema. »Die Zahnärztin soll mir ja keine große Rechnung schicken.«

»Sie hat dir bereits einen Ausdruck davon gegeben, wie viel alles kosten wird.«

»Warum will sie, dass ich nächste Woche wiederkomme? Ich habe doch bereits meinen neuen Zahn.«

»Das ist nur ein provisorischer Zahn. Du musst noch ein paar Mal hingehen, bis die endgültige Krone gemacht wird. Sie hat dir das bereits gesagt.«

»Hat sie nicht. Sie will bloß mehr Geld haben!«

»Ich war dabei, als sie es dir sagte.«

»Nächstes Mal möchte ich, dass Ursula mich hinbringt.«

»Nein, ich habe dich davon überzeugt, zum Zahnarzt zu gehen. Ich werde dich zu deinen Terminen begleiten.«

»Du warst immer schon ein schlimmer Sohn«, sagte sie zu mir. Das war ihr Lieblingsausspruch.

Ich blieb ungefähr eine Stunde in der Wohnung meiner Mutter, während sie alle ihre Bekannten anrief und ihnen sagte, dass sie mit ihrer Geschichte über die Zahnärztin übertrieben hätte.

3

Sie fragen sich wahrscheinlich, wer Ursula ist. Ist sie eine Verwandte? Eine Sozialarbeiterin? Nein. Ursula ist ein fünfundsiebzig Jahre altes Energiebündel.

Sie verbringt die meiste Zeit damit, in der Stadt Besorgungen für die älteren Leute, die in der Seniorenwohnanlage meiner Mutter wohnen, zu machen. Was es auch sei, sie besorgt es. Sie fährt die Senioren zu Geschäften, Arztpraxen und Krankenhäusern. Sie kauft Lebensmittel für Leute ein, die selbst nicht mehr einkaufen können. Dann hört sie ihnen zu, wenn sie sich beschweren, dass sie die falsche Dosengröße der Bohnen gekauft habe oder, dass die Bananen zu teuer seien.

Manchmal nimmt Ursula sogar die Wäsche eines Kranken mit nach Hause und wäscht sie dort.

Ursula erhält nicht viel Dank für ihre guten Taten. Besonders nicht von Leuten wie meiner Mutter, die glauben, diese guten Taten stünden ihnen ohnehin zu. Erst letzte Woche hatte ich folgende Unterhaltung mit Mama.

»Ursula besuchte mich heute Morgen. Sie hat mir den ganzen Tag durcheinander gebracht.«

»Wie denn das?«

»Sie saß hier und redete eine Stunde mit mir«, sagte Mama.

»Es ist gut, dass du Besuch hattest. Es kommt ja kaum jemand zu dir in die Wohnung.«

»Sie hört mir nie zu.«

Story 12

»Wieso sagt du das?«
»Ich erwähnte meinen Herzinfarkt, den ich vergangenen Sonntag hatte, und sie meinte es wäre nichts gewesen. Woher will sie das wissen?«
»Sie ist eine Krankenschwester, Mama.«
»Na und? Sie ist kein Arzt.«
»Sogar ich wusste, dass du keinen Herzinfarkt hattest. Weißt du noch, als du mich Sonntagnachmittag angerufen und mir deine Symptome beschrieben hast?«
»Ja.«
»Verstopfung und Magenschmerzen sind keine Symptome eines Herzinfarktes.«
»Es war mehr als das. Ich hatte auch Brustschmerzen.«
»Das hast du dazuerfunden. Ich fragte dich nach Brustschmerzen, als du mich angerufen hast, und du hast gesagt, dass deine Brust in Ordnung wäre.«
»Nun, sie sollte mir trotzdem nicht sagen, ich wäre bei guter Gesundheit. Sie kennt schließlich nicht alle meine Beschwerden und Schmerzen.«
»Kennt sie schon«, sagte ich. »Sie bringt dich zum Arzt und sitzt mit dir im Untersuchungszimmer.«
»Sie redet so viel mit dem Arzt, dass er mir für den Besuch mehr berechnet. Ich sage ihr immer schon, nichts mehr zu ihm zu sagen, aber sie hört nicht auf mich.«
»Sie macht das, weil du beim Arzt vergisst, ihm von all deinen Gesundheitsbeschwerden zu erzählen. Deshalb muss Ursula ihm davon erzählen.«
»Na dann soll auch sie für den zusätzlichen Zeitaufwand bezahlen, den er mir in Rechnung stellt.«
»Mama, Ursula ist der netteste Mensch auf dieser Welt. Verlange nicht von ihr, für einen Teil deiner Arztbesuche aufzukommen. Sie könnte es als Beleidigung auffassen.«
»Vielleicht sollte ich sie fragen, ob sie meine Wäsche machen kann«, fuhr sie fort.
Mama nahm es ihr wirklich übel, dass Ursula nie angeboten hat, ihre Wäsche zu machen. Sie fühlte sich übergangen.
»Sie wäscht nur für Leute, die wirklich krank sind. Du bist nicht wirklich krank. Du kannst deinen Wagen zum Waschraum rollen und deine Wäsche selbst machen«, sagte ich.
»Ich bin praktisch körperbehindert. Du hast keine Ahnung, was für Schmerzen ich in meinen Knien habe.«
»Deine Knie sind vollkommen in Ordnung«, sagte ich zu ihr.
»Du warst immer schon ein schlimmer Sohn!«, sagte sie.
Und da war er wieder, ihr Lieblingsausspruch.

―――――――――――――― 4 ――――――――――――――

Sechs Wochen später ...
Freitagabend ist reine Männersache. Und genau das habe ich gemacht. Poker spielen mit meinen Nachbarn Thomas, Ben und Günter. Wir hingen ab, entspannten uns, tranken Bier und unterhielten uns.
Das Leben ist ganz schön anstrengend für mich und meine Mutter gewesen. Vier weitere Zahnarztbesuche über einen Zeitraum von vier Wochen waren nötig, bevor meine Mutter ihre endgültige Zahnkrone auf ihrem schlechten Zahn, sowie neue Füllungen in den anderen drei Zähnen hatte. Ich musste mir achtundzwanzig Tage lang ihre Beschwerden anhören, was für schlechte Arbeit ihre Zahnärztin geleistet habe und wie viel die

ganze Angelegenheit kosten werde. Wenigstens rief sie keine anderen Leute in der Stadt an und beschuldigte Dr. Weber, dass sie Voodoo praktiziere.

»Wie geht es deiner Mutter?«, fragte mein Kumpel Günter.

»Sie erzählt mir dauernd, dass sie in meinem Haus wohnen möchte«, sagte ich.

»Kann jemand bitte die Karten geben«, sagte Ben. »Ich will mein Glück versuchen.«

»Ziehst du wirklich in Betracht, deine Mutter bei dir wohnen zu lassen?«, fragte Günter.

Ich schüttelte meinen Kopf. »Auf keinen Fall. Meine Ehe könnte dieser Belastung nicht standhalten. Außerdem würde sie mich verrückt machen. Ich sage ihr das jedes Mal, wenn sie das Thema anschneidet.«

»Ich wusste nicht, dass deine Mutter so schwierig ist«, sagte Günter.

»Das liegt daran, dass du noch neu hier bist«, sagte Thomas.

»Es gibt viele Leute, die Helga-Geschichten zu erzählen haben«, sagte Günter. »Sie ist eine echte Last.«

»Erinnerst du dich noch an die Party bei Jörg vergangenen Sommer?«, lachte Ben. »Helga schrie uns an, weil wir so viel gegessen hatten.«

»Sie wollte die Reste mit nach Hause nehmen«, fügte Thomas hinzu. »Sie forderte meine Frau auf, den Kartoffelsalat in die Schüssel zurückzutun.«

»Du musst dich so schuldig fühlen, wenn du ihr sagst, dass sie nicht bei dir wohnen kann«, sagte Günter als er die Gewinneinsätze einstrich.

»Ich hatte jahrelang Schuldgefühle. Alles, was ich mache, ist nicht gut genug für sie. Wenn ich fünf Mal in der Woche anrufe, beschwert sie sich, dass meine Frau Ingrid nie anruft. Wenn ich sie zwei Mal die Woche besuche, sagt sie mir, dass die Kinder ihres Nachbarn sie jeden Tag sehen.«

»Woher will sie wissen, was anderer Leute Kinder machen?« fragte Ben.

»Jeder in ihrem Altersheim belügt den anderen damit, wie sehr seine Kinder sich um ihn kümmern. Außerdem geben alle mit ihren Genie-Enkeln an«, sagte ich. »Es ist ein Wettbewerb darüber, wer die besten Verwandten hat.«

»Genug geredet«, unterbrach Günter. »Teil die Karten aus.«

Ich teilte eine neue Runde aus. Ich schaute auf meine Karten. Zwei Könige. Vielleicht gewinne ich endlich einmal den Pott.

Ich habe diese Runde tatsächlich gewonnen, indem ich noch den dritten König zog. Trotzdem kam ich am Ende des Abends mit weniger Geld in meiner Brieftasche nach Hause. Ich gewinne einfach nie beim Poker.

---—5—---

Zwei Wochen später ...

»Wissen Sie, dass Helga die Blumen auf dem Parkplatzgelände abgeschnitten hat?«

Ich hörte Monika zu, der Leiterin der Seniorenwohnanlage, wie sie sich über meine Mutter beschwerte.

»Wie hat sie das geschafft?«, fragte ich. »Mutter kann sich nicht bücken, ohne dass sie auf ihr Gesicht fällt. Wie dem auch sei, sie behauptet, dass sie nicht dort gewesen sei.«

»Irgendwie muss sie es doch geschafft haben. Es gibt acht Augenzeugen. Die kamen gerade von ihrem wöchentlichen Bingospiel, als sie gerade die Blumen in eine Pappschachtel packte. Wenigstens hat sie nur die Blumen direkt neben dem Randstein abgeschnitten.«

Story 12

»Können wir nicht einfach so tun, als ob sie dem Gartenverein geholfen hätte, indem sie einige Pflanzen zurechtstutzte?«, fragte ich.

»Ich glaube nicht, dass der Gartenverein diese Ausrede unterstützen wird. Die Vorsitzende fiel in Ohnmacht, als sie den Schaden heute Morgen sah. Wir mussten den Notarzt rufen.«

»Immerhin ist Mamas Wohnung hübsch dekoriert. Sie sollten die Blumengestecke sehen, die sie gemacht hat«, sagte ich.

»Helga hatte letzte Woche außerdem ein Missgeschick in der Küche«, fuhr Monika fort.

»Sie vergaß schlichtweg, den Herd auszuschalten. Ich bedaure sehr, dass die Feuerwehr kommen musste.«

»Sie wird zur Gefahr für die Allgemeinheit«, sagte Monika.

»Niemand kam zu Schaden. Bitte geben Sie Mama noch eine Chance.«

Sie seufzte und rieb sich die Stirn. Es muss schwierig sein, ein Heim voll alter Leute zu leiten.

»Einverstanden, Herr Dietrich. Aber ich bestehe darauf, dass Ihre Mutter nicht mehr kocht. Sie kann jeden Abend in unserem Hauptspeisesaal zu Abend essen. Es kostet nur sieben Euro und das Essen ist sehr gut.«

»Kein Kochen oder Blumenabschneiden mehr«, versprach ich.

—6—

Ich ging zu Mutters Wohnung und erzählte ihr von meinem Treffen mit Monika.

»Sie kann mich nicht leiden«, sagte Mutter. »Seitdem ich ihr Hündchen mit Ilses Gehstock schlug.«

»Sag mir bitte nicht, dass du ihrem niedlichen, kleinen Hund wehgetan hast«, sagte ich.

»Ich wollte, dass er zu kläffen aufhört. Es war ein kleiner Schubser.«

»Hat sie gesehen, dass du es warst?«

»Nein, ich habe Ilse beschuldigt. Es ist ja ihr Stock.«

»Demnach hast du Ilse in Schwierigkeiten gebracht.«

»Monika hat mir nicht geglaubt. Sie meinte Ilse sei zu schwach, ihren Stock zu schwingen. Wir hatten eine große Auseinandersetzung.«

»Vergessen wir Ilse und den Hund. Ich habe Monika versprochen, dass du jeden Abend im Hauptgebäude essen wirst. Das bedeutet, es wird nicht mehr gekocht. Du wirst auch keine Blumen oder Büsche mehr abschneiden. Und keine Bäume fällen.«

»Sei nicht albern, ich habe doch gar keine Axt. Hallo, ich kann mir doch nicht jedes Mal sieben Euro für ein Abendessen leisten. Ich bin arm.«

Die nächsten fünf Minuten hatten wir eine hitzige Diskussion. Mutter stimmte schließlich den Bedingungen von Monika zu, aber ich musste versprechen, für sie das Abendessen im Hauptgebäude zu bezahlen. Es war mir sieben Euro pro Abend wert, denn so musste ich mich nicht darüber sorgen, dass Mama ihr Wohngebäude niederbrennt.

Mama schaute auf eine Liste, die auf ihrem Küchentisch lag. Sie machte öfters eine Auflistung von Beschwerdepunkten.

»Du fährst nie mit mir irgendwohin.«

Ich dachte ein wenig nach.

»Warum gehen wir nicht ins Kino?«

»Der letzte Film, den wir angesehen haben, war widerlich. Du solltest dich schämen.«

»Es ist doch nicht meine Schuld, dass man in Filmen schlimme Wörter benutzt«, antwortete ich.

»Komm, wir gehen in den Park. Wir können auf einer Bank sitzen und Vögel beobachten.«

»Prima, das hört sich gut an.«

Sie brauchte zehn Minuten, um sich fertig zu machen, noch ein paar Schluck Wasser zu trinken und für alle Fälle auf die Toilette zu gehen. Wir fuhren zu einem Park in der Nähe. Es war kein allzu langer Spaziergang vom Parkplatz zu einer Bank im Schatten der Bäume. Mama musste sich die ganze Zeit bei mir festhalten.

Von der Bank aus konnten wir einen kleinen Teich sehen. Neben dem Teich war ein Spielplatz. Ein kleines Kind verfolgte die Enten nahe dem Wasser.

»Hier ist es schön«, sagte ich.

»Wen interessieren schon Enten?«, sagte Mutter. »Meine Krankenversicherung hat den letzten Arztbesuch nicht bezahlt.«

Ich seufzte. »Wir haben uns darüber schon einige Male unterhalten«, erinnerte ich sie. »Deine Versicherung hat dir eine Abrechnung geschickt, die besagt, dass die Kosten des Besuches mit der Selbstbeteiligung verrechnet wurden.«

»Was ist eine Selbstbeteiligung?«

»Ich habe dir schon drei Mal erklärt, was eine Selbstbeteiligung ist. Warum schreibst du es dir nicht auf?«

»Du hast mir nichts von einer Selbstbeteiligung gesagt. Und was ist mit meinem Augenarzt los? Er hat mir gerade eine Rechnung über fünfundneunzig Euro geschickt. Er ist ein Dieb.«

»Er machte eine komplette ärztliche Untersuchung«, sagte ich zu ihr.

»Irgendein junges Mädchen hat das alles gemacht. Sie ist wahrscheinlich nur eine Krankenschwester. Ich bezahle das nicht.«

»Ursula sagte mir, dass er die meiste Arbeit machte und das Mädchen die Schreibarbeiten«, sagte ich.

»Der Arzt hat ein Sandwich gegessen. Er hat nur zugeschaut. Ich werde ihn verklagen.«

Mein Auge fing an zu zucken. Die Hitze stieg mir ins Gesicht. Ich holte ein paar Mal tief Luft. Es war ein Wunder, dass ich die Ruhe bewahren konnte, obwohl sie sich weiterhin über ihre Ärzte beschwerte. Nach zehn Minuten wusste sie nichts mehr, worüber sie sich beschweren könnte.

Wir saßen noch eine weitere Stunde auf der Bank, genossen die Sonne und unterhielten uns über das Leben.

---—7—---

»Ich war ein guter Junge, warum also tut meine Mutter alles, nur damit ich mich elend fühle?«

»Sie erinnert sich nicht mehr daran, was für ein wunderbares Kind Sie waren«, sagte Dr. Rosenberg.

Dr. Rosenberg ist mein Psychiater. Ich treffe mich jede Woche mit ihm. Er hilft mir dabei, mit den Problemen umzugehen, die ich mit meiner Mutter habe.

»Auf jeden Fall habe ich sie nicht in den Teich geworfen«, sagte ich.

»Das beweist, Sie sind ein großartiges Kind«, sagte er.

»Sie ist einfach nur eine gemeine Frau, nicht wahr?«, fragte ich.

»Wir sind das bereits durchgegangen. Sie ist mit ihrem Leben unglücklich und sie lässt es an jedem aus, der ihr nahekommt.«

»Sie wird sich nie ändern«, sagte ich.

Story 12

»Deshalb lernen Sie hier, wie Sie mit ihr zurechtkommen.«

»Sie macht mich immer noch verrückt.«

»Ja, aber Sie gehen damit besser um. Noch vor einem Jahr konnten Sie nach einem Besuch bei ihr nachts nicht schlafen. Den ganzen Kummer, den sie Ihnen gestern bereitete, haben Sie überstanden, ohne sich die Haare auszureißen. Anschließend haben Sie noch eine schöne Zeit mit ihr verbracht. Das zeugt schon von einem gewaltigen Fortschritt.«

»Ja, wir hatten eine ganz nette Zeit miteinander, nachdem sie aufgehört hatte, über die Ärzte zu meckern.«

»Worüber haben Sie sich unterhalten?«

»Angenehme Sachen. Die Größe und Form ihres Stuhlgangs am Morgen. Den überschüssigen Schleim, der sich in ihrer Nase bildet. Die Nachbarin, die zum kostenlosen, wöchentlichen Mittagessen in der Seniorenwohnanlage geht und dabei möglichst viel Essen für später in ihre Handtasche schaufelt.«

»Hat das nicht Spaß gemacht?«, fragte Dr. Rosenberg.

---8---

»Du machst Fortschritte, weil du deine Mutter im Park nicht erwürgt hast und weil du dich nicht betrunken hast, als du nach Hause gekommen bist?«, fragte Ingrid.

»Das hat Dr. Rosenberg gesagt.«

»Das ist ein Grund zum Feiern. Wir sollten deine Mutter zum Abendessen einladen.«

»Nicht heute Abend.«

»Weiß sie, dass du zu einem Psychiater gehst, weil sie dir gegenüber so bösartig ist?«

»Was brächte es, wenn man es ihr sagen würde? Sie glaubt, sie wäre zu allen nett.«

»Also, was wirst du tun?«

»Was ich bisher getan habe. Ich verbringe Zeit mit ihr, höre mir ihre Beschwerden an, versuche, ihr unglückliches Leben etwas besser zu machen, und widersetze mich dem Drang, sie lebendig zu begraben.«

»Musst du immer noch zum Psychiater?«

»Ich werde wahrscheinlich jede Woche zu ihm müssen, bis sie tot ist.«

»Sie wird noch weitere zwanzig Jahre leben!«

»Das hoffe ich. Kannst du mich bis dahin ertragen?«, fragte ich.

Ingrid schauderte.

»Ich denke, du bist es wert«, sagte sie.

STORY 13

Evolution

»Ich glaube an Gott, aber ich denke nicht, dass er zu sehr in unseren Alltag eingebunden ist. Er hat das Universum erschaffen und die Dinge vor ein paar Milliarden Jahren in Bewegung gebracht. Dann hat er sich zurückgelehnt, um zu beobachten.«

Ich denke einen Moment nach und dann fahre ich fort.

»Die Evolution ist Gottes Weg, die Ordnung in der Welt aufrechtzuerhalten. Wenn etwas anfängt, schief zu laufen, findet die Evolution einen Weg. Manchmal dauert es ein oder zwei Jahrhunderte, aber letztendlich hilft die Evolution der Welt ihre Probleme zu lösen.«

Ich schaue den Mann an, mit dem ich rede. Er scheint nicht interessiert zu sein.

»Vor Jahrhunderten«, fahre ich fort, »machten sich die Menschen Sorgen, an der Pest zu sterben. Sogar noch länger ist es her, dass Menschen keine Milch von Tieren verdauen konnten. Dann trat die Evolution ins Geschehen ein. Unsere Erbanlagen veränderten sich Stück für Stück. Zusätzlich haben neue Technologien unsere evolutionäre Reaktion verstärkt. Letztendlich werden wir resistenter gegen Krankheiten sein, die heute tödlich für uns sind. Das sind großartige Beispiele dafür, wie die Evolution Problemlösungen findet.«

Der Mann reagiert immer noch nicht.

»Ich weiß, was Sie denken«, sage ich zu ihm. »Tödliche Krankheiten sind kein gutes Beispiel, da ja heutzutage viele Menschen an AIDS, Malaria oder Cholera sterben. Aber ich bin sicher, dass die Evolution einen Weg finden wird, wie man auch diese Krankheiten bekämpfen kann.«

Ich ziehe eine Wasserflasche aus meiner Jackentasche und nehme ein paar Schlucke.

»Hier ist ein weiteres Beispiel dafür, wie die Evolution ein Problem löst«, sage ich zu dem Mann. »Sie sind ein Parasit, der anderen Menschen Elend und Leiden verursacht. Die Evolution hat dafür ein Heilmittel gefunden. Nämlich mich!«

Ich begreife, dass ich meine Zeit vergeude. Am Ende kümmert sich dieser Mann doch nicht um meine Weltanschauung. Er hat immerhin drei Schüsse ins Herz abbekommen!

―2―

Ein paar Tage zuvor ...

Ich lehne mich in meinem Drehstuhl zurück und schaue aus dem Bürofenster. Es ist ein schöner Herbstmorgen. Alles ist friedlich und ruhig.

Da höre ich schwere Schritte im Gang. Die Tür öffnet sich und ein großer, vierschrötiger Mann kommt herein. Er blickt mich an, als ob ich eine untergeordnete Lebensform wäre, die er nun sezieren wollte.

»Möchten Sie eine Lebensversicherung beantragen?«, frage ich ihn. »Wenn Sie gesund sind und nicht rauchen, wären Sie für eine Deckungssumme von mindestens einer Million Euro qualifiziert. Ich kann Ihnen sehr günstige Beiträge anbieten.«

Story 13

Sein Blick wandert nun von meinen teuren Möbeln zu den extravaganten Bildern an der Wand.

»Schönes Büro«, sagt er.

»Ja, das stimmt. Ich habe eine neue Kaffeemaschine. Möchten Sie einen koffeinfreien Kaffee haben? Woher haben Sie all diese Narben und diese schiefe Nase? Wenn Sie einen risikoreichen Beruf ausüben, müssen Sie dies in Ihrem Antrag angeben.«

»Hören Sie auf, von der Lebensversicherung zu reden«, sagt er zu mir.

»Ich kann ihren Akzent nicht zuordnen«, erwähne ich. »Russland? Der Balkan vielleicht?«

»Ich komme aus Leipzig.«

Er steckt die Hand in seine Tasche und zieht ein kleines Bild heraus. Er legt es auf meinen Tisch. Ich schaue es mir an und sehe eine junge Frau, etwa vierundzwanzig oder fünfundzwanzig Jahre alt.

»Sie ist sehr hübsch, Ihre Tochter, nicht wahr?«, fragt er.

Mir wird klar, dass es sich hier um einen ernstzunehmenden Besuch handelt. Wir starren uns gegenseitig ein paar Sekunden lang an.

»Auf einmal sind Sie ja ganz still?«, fragt er. »Weil Sie nämlich Ihre Tochter lieben und nicht möchten, dass ihr etwas zustößt.«

»Soll das eine Drohung sein?«, frage ich.

»Nein, ich sage nur, dass Sie alles tun würden, um Ihre Tochter zu beschützen.«

Er gibt mir ein Stück Papier. Darauf steht geschrieben: »Seien Sie bereit. In zwei Tagen. Kleine, unmarkierte Geldscheine.«

Zudem ist noch ein großer Geldbetrag auf das Papier geschrieben. Dann steht er auf und geht hinaus.

---3---

Bei der örtlichen Polizei will niemand etwas von meinen Problemen hören. Sie hat keine Möglichkeiten, sich mit derartigen Straftaten zu befassen. Wenigstens sind sie so nett, mir die Telefonnummer der Landespolizei zu geben.

Ich wähle die Nummer auf meinem Handy und brauche zehn Minuten, um die Antworten aus den verschiedenen Menüs des Antwortsystems der Landespolizei auszuwählen.

Dann spreche ich mit jemandem, der mich mit jemand anderem verbindet, welcher mich wiederum mit dem Kriminalbeamten Frank Müller verbindet. Er arbeitet in der Abteilung, die sich mit Erpressungsfällen befasst. Ich erzähle ihm meine Geschichte. Als ich fertig bin, stelle ich ihm einige Fragen.

»Haben Sie jemanden, der ermitteln wird?«, frage ich.

»Auf jeden Fall.«

»Ich habe gehört, es gibt da mindestens drei weitere Versicherungsleute wie mich, die in den letzten sechs Monaten Opfer einer Erpressung wurden. Ermittelt Ihre Abteilung in diesen Fällen?«

»Ja.«

»Weshalb haben Sie noch niemanden verhaftet?«

»Wir verfolgen einige wertvolle Hinweise.«

»Wurden nicht zwei der Opfer erschossen?«, frage ich.

»Ja«, sagt er.

»Und wurde nicht die Ehefrau des dritten Opfers mit derselben Waffe getötet?«

»Ja, das wurde alles in den Medien berichtet.«
»Warum haben Sie denn überhaupt keine Verdächtigen?«
»Über eine laufende Ermittlung kann ich nicht sprechen.«
»Herr Müller, ich befürchte, dass diese Verbrecher schlauer sind als die Landespolizei.«
»Ich kann dazu nichts sagen.«
»Vielleicht sollte ich ihnen zahlen, was sie verlangen. Ich kann es mir leisten.«
»Zwei Leute haben das gemacht. Sie wurden von der Bande trotzdem umgebracht.«
»Vielleicht wurden sie getötet, weil sie beschlossen, mit der Polizei zusammenzuarbeiten, und die Verbrecher haben das herausgefunden.«
»Dazu kann ich nichts sagen.«
»Das hilft mir nicht weiter. Jedes Mal wenn ich etwas Wesentliches erwähne, antworten Sie mir, dass Sie dazu nichts sagen können.«
»Meine Abteilung arbeitet rund um die Uhr, um diese Bande zu finden. Sie können uns helfen, indem Sie mit mir zusammenarbeiten. Kann ich in Ihr Büro kommen und nach Fingerabdrücken suchen?«
»Er hatte Handschuhe an«, sage ich.
»Na gut, dann treffen Sie sich wenigstens mit mir und machen eine formale Beschwerde.«
»Ich bin mir nicht sicher, ob ich das will. Drei Leute sind tot und es hat nicht den Anschein, dass Sie irgendwelche Fortschritte machen.«
»Warum haben Sie dann angerufen?«
»Das ist eine gute Frage. Lassen Sie mich meine Situation überdenken und dann werde ich mich wieder an Sie wenden.«
Fünf Minuten nach meiner Unterhaltung mit dem Kriminalbeamten Müller rufe ich Joseph Graf an. Er ist der Versicherungsagent, dessen Frau vor fünf Monaten ermordet wurde. Ich bitte ihn, sich mit mir am nächsten Tag zum Mittagessen zu treffen.

4

Joseph Graf sieht furchtbar aus. Sein Gesicht ist ausgemergelt. Sein Bart ist struppig. Er hat Probleme, sich auf die Speisekarte zu konzentrieren.
»Die Medikamente machen es mir schwer, aktiv am Leben teilzunehmen«, sagt er. »Ich bin immer müde.«
Wir unterhalten uns darüber, wie traurig er ist, seitdem seine Frau ermordet wurde. Ich wechsle das Thema nach ein paar Minuten und erkläre, dass dieselbe Verbrecherbande nun meine Tochter bedroht.
»Soll ich die Polizei einschalten?«, frage ich.
»Nein, zahlen Sie ihnen das Geld.«
»Wie lange soll das gehen?«
»Sie haben mir gesagt, sie würden mich nach einem Jahr in Ruhe lassen«, sagt er.
»Haben Sie ihnen geglaubt?«
»Nein, deshalb ging ich zur Polizei.«
»Warum wurde Ihre Frau ermordet?«, frage ich.
»Irgendwoher wussten die Gauner, dass ich mit der Polizei kooperierte.«
»Wie haben die das erfahren?«

Story 13

»Meine nächste Zahlung sollte an einer Tankstelle in der Nähe der Autobahn gemacht werden. Ein paar Kriminalbeamte folgten mir. Sie trugen normale Kleidung, damit sie unter den Leuten an der Tankstelle nicht auffielen. Die Verbrecher müssen sie gesehen haben, da niemand kam, um das Geld abzuholen.«

Er wartet eine Minute and nimmt ein paar Schlückchen Kaffee.

»Ein paar Tage später wurde meine Frau aus unmittelbarer Nähe erschossen. Es war ein Auftragsmord.«

Er fängt an zu weinen.

»Sie wäre noch am Leben, wenn ich nicht zur Polizei gegangen wäre.«

Nach unserem deprimierenden Mittagessen fahre ich ihn zurück zu seinem Haus.

»Ich gehe nicht mehr ins Büro«, sagt er mir. »Ich bin zu deprimiert zum Arbeiten.«

»Sie sollten einen Job bei einer großen Agentur annehmen«, sage ich zu ihm. »Die meisten wären froh, wenn ein so erfolgreicher Verkäufer bei ihnen arbeiten würde. Außerdem wäre es gut für Sie, unter Leuten zu sein.«

Er antwortet nur mit einem niedergeschlagenen Achselzucken.

»Sprechen Sie wenigstens mit einem professionellen Trauerbegleiter«, sage ich.

Ich steuere das Auto in seine Einfahrt.

Er steigt aus dem Auto aus, winkt mir zaghaft zu und schlurft in sein Haus. Ich kehre zurück in mein Büro und mache ein Nickerchen. Für die Pokerrunde muss ich frisch sein.

―――――――――――――――――5―――――――――――――――――

Mein Blick wandert durch die Runde am Tisch von Mitspieler zu Mitspieler. Max, der Drogenhändler, sitzt zu meiner Rechten. Er riecht nach Haargel und Rasierwasser. Seine Freundin steht hinter ihm, beugt sich nieder und küsst sein Ohr. Ich habe Schwierigkeiten, auf meine Karten zu schauen.

Johann, ein Buchhalter, sitzt mir gegenüber. Sein Anzug ist zerknittert, seine Krawatte sitzt schief und die obersten zwei Knöpfe an seinem Hemd sind offen. Seine Whiskyflasche ist bereits halbleer und wir haben noch nicht einmal länger als eine Stunde gespielt.

»Schwerer Tag im Büro, Johann?«, frage ich ihn.

»Einige Regierungsanwälte machen mir das Leben sehr schwer«, antwortet er.

Reinhold, das vierte Mitglied unserer Gruppe, sitzt zu meiner Linken. Reinhold verleiht Geld an Leute, die keine Darlehen von Banken bekommen können. Er verlangt sehr hohe Zinsen. Wenn seine Klienten die Darlehen nicht rechtzeitig zurückzahlen, bricht ihnen sein Assistent die Beine.

Reinholds Assistent sitzt in der Ecke und schaut fern auf einem Großbildschirm. Irgendeine Show über Hausverschönerungen.

Wieso gefallen einem Typen, der als Lebensunterhalt Leute verprügelt, diese dummen Realityshows? Über Geschmack lässt sich nicht streiten.

Wir spielen Poker in einem Raum des Feuerwehrhauses der freiwilligen Feuerwehr Wedding. Der Feuerwehrhauptmann teilt die Karten aus und kassiert fünf Prozent Provision von jedem Pott. Nach den schönen Möbeln im Feuerwehrhaus zu urteilen, hat diese Provision über die Jahre ganz schön viel Geld für das Feuerwehrhaus eingebracht. Ich frage mich, wie viel der Feuerwehrhauptmann davon für sich behält.

Meine Kollegin Lina sitzt auf einem Sofa in der Nähe des Fernsehers. Sie liest ein Buch von Stephen Hawking. Irgendetwas über Sterne und Planeten.

Johann schaut immer wieder kurz auf Lina. Max würde auch schauen, wenn ihm seine Freundin nicht den Blick versperren würde. Reinhold schaut nicht. Er scheint auf sein Blatt konzentriert zu sein. Der Feuerwehrhauptmann behält die Karten und das Geld im Auge.

Lina ist vielleicht fünf Zentimeter kleiner als ich und damit etwa einen Meter achtzig groß. Sie hat mittellange, braune Haare. Auf ihrer Stirn bilden sich leichte Falten, während sie sich auf das Buch, das sie liest, konzentriert. Sie trägt einen bequemen Trainingsanzug, jedoch weder Schmuck noch Schminke.

»Sie ist doch nicht deine Freundin«, sagt Reinhold. »Warum hast du sie mitgebracht?«

»Als Glücksbringer«, sage ich zu ihm. »Ich brauche heute Abend viel Glück. Hoffentlich gewinne ich viel Geld.«

»Hoffentlich gewinnst du nicht«, sagt Reinhold.

»Wie geht es deiner Frau, Johann?«, frage ich.

»Gut.«

Johanns Frau ist die Tochter eines bekannten Berliner Gangsters. Sein Schwiegervater wird ›Alex die Axt‹ genannt. Johann erledigt die finanziellen Angelegenheiten für Alex' Geschäfte.

»Hat irgendjemand das Spiel am letzten Samstag angeschaut?«, frage ich.

Als Antwort erhalte ich ein paar Grummellaute und Flüche. Das ist keine freundliche Gruppe.

Max schiebt seine Freundin sanft von sich. »Sandra, ich kann nicht nachdenken, wenn du dauernd an mir klebst. Geh und schau fern.«

Sie gleitet davon und setzt sich neben Lina.

»Hat jemand von euch schon mal mit der Polizei zu tun gehabt?«, frage ich.

»Wer denn nicht?«, fragt Reinhold.

»Ich habe da gerade eine Sache laufen«, sage ich zu ihnen. »Wisst ihr, ob jemand aus den oberen Rängen Leuten wie uns einen Gefallen tun würde?«

Wir spielen noch ein paar Minuten Karten.

»Wenn der Preis stimmt, überzeugst du die Leute davon, etwas für dich zu tun«, sagt Reinhold.

»Wen?«

»Das kommt darauf an, was du willst.«

»Ich möchte eine Ermittlung stoppen«, sage ich.

»Vielleicht hätte ich da jemanden. Gib mir deine Handynummer.«

Ich schreibe meine Telefonnummer auf ein Stück Papier und schiebe es zu ihm hinüber.

»Lass mir ein paar Tage Zeit«, sagt er.

»Du hast was gut bei mir«, sage ich zu ihm.

Johann wirft seine Karten auf den Tisch und steigt aus, ich ebenso. Reinhold und Max ziehen ein paar Karten.

»Möchte jemand ein Bier?«, frage ich.

Max nickt mir zu. Ich gehe zum Kühlschrank und hole zwei Flaschen Bier. Als ich zum Tisch zurückkomme, schaufelt Max sich die Chips ein.

»Wir haben ein mäßiges Spiel heute Abend«, sagt Reinhold.

Der Feuerwehrhauptmann teilt neue Karten aus. Wir fangen an, uns über Basketball zu unterhalten. Vier Stunden später beschließe ich, nach Hause zu gehen.

»Du hast einen Haufen Geld gewonnen«, sagt Johann, als Lina und ich aufbrechen. »Bleib noch hier, damit wir etwas davon zurückgewinnen können.«

Story 13

»Danke, Johann, aber ich brauche das Geld gerade für etwas anderes.«

»Ach ja, die Sache mit der laufenden Polizeiermittlung«, sagt er.

Wir verlassen das Feuerwehrhaus und gehen die Straße hinunter zu unserem Auto. Auf unserem Weg kommen wir an einer langen, hohen Hecke vorbei. Ich suche in meiner Tasche nach der Fernbedienung fürs Auto.

Plötzlich wirbelt Lina auf ihrem linken Fuß herum. Sie tritt mit ihrem Fuß in das Gesicht eines großen Burschen, der plötzlich hinter der Hecke hervorgekommen ist. Der Schlagstock, den er hält, fällt ihm aus der Hand und er fällt rückwärts auf seinen Hintern.

Ich lehne mich am Auto an, als zwei weitere Männer aus der Dunkelheit herausspringen. Der eine hält einen kleinen Schlagstock in der Hand. Der andere hat ein Messer. Sie sind jung, etwa neunzehn oder zwanzig Jahre alt. Sie sind etwas kleiner als ich, aber wahrscheinlich wiegen sie fünfzehn Kilogramm mehr als ich.

Lina steht ihnen gegenüber. Ihre Knie sind leicht gebeugt. Die Unterarme sind nach oben gerichtet und die Ellbogen am Körper angelegt. Ihre Fäuste sind leicht geballt. Der linke Fuß steht vorne und die rechten Zehen zeigen nach außen. Beide Fersen sind vom Boden gelöst. Das ist die traditionelle Muay-Thai-Kampfhaltung.

Die zwei harten Kerle schauen zu ihrem Freund, der am Boden sitzt. Er hält seine Hände vor das Gesicht. Blut quillt zwischen seinen Fingern hervor.

Sie zögern und Lina greift an. Der Typ mit dem Schlagstock versucht auszuholen. Zu spät.

Linas Ellbogen zertrümmert seine Nase und ihr linkes Bein zieht ihm die Füße unter sich weg, bevor sich sein Schläger auch nur fünf Zentimeter bewegt.

Als er hinfällt, weicht sie tänzerisch einem Messerstich des zweiten Mannes aus. Er sticht zu fest zu und verliert dabei das Gleichgewicht. Lina geht schon zum Angriff über, bevor er sich fangen konnte.

Sie stößt ihm ihr Knie in die Niere und schlägt ihm seitlich auf den Kiefer mit einer harten, kurzen Geraden. Sein Körper sackt durch die Wucht des Schlages zu Boden.

Als er hinfällt, tänzelt sie zum Kerl mit dem Schlagstock und stampft ihm in den Schritt. Er wimmert und wird ohnmächtig.

Dann schlurft sie zurück zu dem Mann mit dem Messer, der nun am Boden liegt. Sie tritt ihm gegen den Kopf. Er lässt das Messer fallen und bleibt reglos liegen.

Inzwischen hat sich unser erster Angreifer wieder auf die Beine gestellt. Er fummelt an einer Pistole herum, die in seiner Hosentasche steckt. Seine Hände sind glitschig von dem Blut aus seiner Nase und seinem Mund. Das macht es schwierig für ihn, die Pistole zu fassen.

Ich schlage ihm lässig mit einem kleinen Knüppel aus meiner Tasche auf die Kopfseite. Er sackt auf dem Pflaster in sich zusammen.

»Du brauchst ein Schulterhalfter«, sage ich zu dem bewusstlosen Mann. »Das erleichtert das Ziehen der Pistole.«

»Er kann dich nicht hören«, sagt Lina.

Sie ist nicht einmal außer Atem. Wir setzen uns beide in mein Auto und fahren davon.

»Woher wussten sie von dem Pokerspiel?«, fragt sie.

»Vielleicht sind sie Mitglieder der freiwilligen Feuerwehr«, sage ich.

Evolution

Der Mann aus Leipzig mit dem komischen Akzent ruft mich am nächsten Morgen an. Auf meinem Handy! Wie hat er diese Nummer bekommen?

»Sie werden mein Geschenk um zwei Uhr zum Parkplatz am Treptower Park bringen«, sagt er.

»Nein«, antworte ich.

Schweigen in der Leitung.

»Sie haben das Geschenk nicht?«, fragt er.

»Ich habe es, aber ich fahre nicht den ganzen Weg dort hinunter, um Sie zu treffen.«

»Ich mache keine Witze. Sie müssen tun, was ich sage.«

»Wenn Sie Ihr Geld haben wollen, dann werde ich es Ihnen an einem Ort geben, den ich vorschlage.«

Er denkt ein paar Sekunden nach.

»Wenn die Polizei dort ist, werde ich es wissen. Ich bin sehr vorsichtig.«

»Keine Sorge«, sage ich zu ihm, »die Polizei wird nicht dort sein.«

Nach zwanzig Sekunden Stillschweigen sagt er: »In Ordnung, wohin wollen Sie das Geschenk bringen?«

»Ich werde Sie am U-Bahnhof Kottbusser Tor in Neukölln treffen. Das ist ein schöner, offener Platz.«

»Haben Sie Angst, dass ich Ihnen etwas antun könnte?«

»Ich will Zeugen haben.«

»Denken Sie daran«, sagt er zu mir, »wenn die Polizei kommt, werde ich es wissen.«

»Verstanden«, sage ich.

»Wo wir gerade dabei sind, nehmen Sie auch Schecks?«

Nicht einmal ein Kichern ist zu hören.

Ein paar Stunden später stehe ich am Bahnhof Kottbusser Tor und lese eine Zeitung. Ein Zug hält und zehn Leute steigen aus. Dann rumpelt der Zug weiter. Niemand beachtet mich. Mein neuer Freund geht die Plattform hinunter und steht vor mir.

»Wo ist mein Geschenk?«, fragt er.

Das ist eine gute Frage, da ich ja keinen Koffer oder Rucksack dabei habe.

»Es ist in der Nähe«, sage ich. »Bevor ich es hole, können wir eine Art Vereinbarung treffen?«

Er wirkt amüsiert.

»Ziehen Sie Ihre Jacke aus«, sagt er.

Nachdem ich das getan habe, klopft er mir mit seinen Händen die Brust, den Bauch, Rücken und die Oberschenkel ab. Nach ein paar Minuten hört er auf.

»Sie tragen keine Abhörgeräte. Jetzt können wir uns unterhalten. Die Vereinbarung lautet, dass Sie mir jeden Monat etwas bezahlen müssen.«

»Das ist eine Menge Geld«, sage ich. »Können wir Ihren Boss anrufen und etwas anderes vereinbaren?«

»Mein Boss verhandelt nicht.«

»Besteht die Möglichkeit, dass ich einen Prozentsatz meines Einkommens zahlen könnte? Ich verdiene nicht jeden Monat gleich viel.«

»Schluss mit dem Gerede. Bringen Sie mich zum Geld«, antwortet er.

Der Kerl scheint entschlossen zu sein. Also führe ich ihn hinter den Bahnsteig und die Stufen hinunter. Auf halbem Weg liegt ein Rucksack auf den Stufen. Ein elektrischer Verteilerkasten ist an der Wand ungefähr zwei Meter über den Stufen angebracht. Als er auf den Rucksack blickt, greife ich nach der Pistole, die oben auf dem Verteilerkasten liegt, und schieße ihm dreimal ins Herz.

»Sie hätten die Lebensversicherung abschließen sollen«, sage ich zu seiner Leiche.

Story 13

---------- 7 ----------

Die Pistole hat einen Schalldämpfer, damit niemand die Treppen hinunter eilt, um zu sehen, was passiert ist. Ich rufe Lucia kurz an.

»Es ist erledigt«, sage ich zu ihr.

Zwanzig Sekunden später höre ich rasselnde Geräusche. Die Mitglieder meines Teams verschließen die Türen oberhalb und unterhalb der Treppe mit einer Kette. Das gibt mir Zeit zum Nachforschen. Ich sehe in seinen Taschen nach. Nichts. Ich ziehe seine Kleider aus und suche nach Tätowierungen oder Narben. Nichts. Währenddessen erkläre ich ihm meine Evolutionstheorie. Sie erinnern sich doch noch an den Monolog zu Beginn dieser Geschichte, oder?

Ich hacke seine Finger ab und stecke sie in eine Plastiktüte. Es ist viel einfacher, Fingerabdrücke von den abgehackten Fingern zu machen und DNA daraus zu gewinnen, als die ganze Leiche zu transportieren.

Ich gehe die Treppen hinunter und klopfe unten an die verschlossene Tür. Anja öffnet eine Kette und macht die Tür auf. Sie versperrt die Tür wieder mit der Kette und wir gehen zu ihrem Auto. Mit etwas Glück wird die Leiche ein paar Wochen lang nicht entdeckt werden. Schließlich sind wir hier in Neukölln.

---------- 8 ----------

Anja fährt uns vom Bahnhof weg. Sie trägt einen Businessanzug. Ihr Pferdeschwanz ist durch eine etwas reifer wirkende Frisur ersetzt worden.

»Wieso trägst du diesen Anzug«, frage ich sie.

»Ich gleiche mich den Pendlern an«, sagt sie.

»Lass mich beim Versicherungsbüro raus. Ich habe um halb fünf einen Termin. Du kannst die Finger zum Hauptquartier mitnehmen. Nimm auch die Pistole. Sag Lucia, sie soll sie beseitigen.«

»Hast du bei dem Kerl im Treppenhaus eine Bewusstseinsbeeinflussung durchgeführt?«

»Ich tat es, als wir am Bahnsteig waren. Was glaubst du, wieso er mir freiwillig folgte?«

»Und das machte es leichter für dich, ihn zu erschießen.«

»Sicher. Ich gab ihm den Denkanstoß, auf den Rucksack zu schauen. Er hat mich nicht einmal bemerkt, als ich nach der Pistole griff. Aber ich hätte es wahrscheinlich auch machen können, ohne sein Bewusstsein zu trüben.«

»Ich weiß, wie schnell du bist«, sagt sie.

»Ich bin mit dem Alter nicht langsamer geworden«, erinnere ich sie.

»Da hat aber jemand schlechte Laune.«

»Ich hasse es einfach, Leute zu erschießen.«

»Aber du machst es trotzdem.«

»Vergiss nicht, ich bin doch der Agent im Außeneinsatz. Jemand muss die Drecksarbeit machen.«

»Sag mir nochmal warum alle glauben, dass du ein Versicherungsagent wärst«, sagt sie.

»Meine besondere Fähigkeit offenbart sich auf verschiedene Weise. Ich kann die Psyche einer Person so beeinflussen, dass sie nicht weiß, was vor sich geht. Ich kann ihr Kurzzeitgedächtnis ändern. Ich kann sie zu einfachen Handlungen veranlassen, wie zum Beispiel auf einen Rucksack zu schauen oder eine Pistole fallen zu lassen. Und ich kann sie in den Glauben versetzen, das ich jemand anders wäre.«

Evolution

»Kannst du einen ganzen Raum voller Menschen hypnotisieren?«, fragt sie.

»Es ist keine Hypnose. Ich weiß nicht einmal, wie ich meine Fähigkeit beschreiben soll, aber sie funktioniert nur bei einzelnen Personen und bei kleinen Gruppen.«

»Wo ist die Person, als die du dich ausgibst?«, fragt Anja.

»Ich habe ihn und seine Tochter für ein paar Wochen auf eine nette Reise nach Spanien geschickt. Sie sind gerne gegangen, nachdem ich ihm erklärt hatte, dass unser Top-Analytiker meinte, er wäre das nächste Anschlagsziel.«

»Wer ist dein Top-Analytiker?«

»Roland.«

»Nicht ich?«

»Du bist die ranghöchste Analytikerin.«

»Gut«, sagt sie.

Ein Augenblick der Stille stellt sich ein, als ich das schöne Stadtzentrum Neuköllns bewundere.

»Ich hoffe, dass du nicht wirklich Versicherungen verkaufst«, sagt Anja.

»Ich habe noch nicht eine verkauft. Die Leute glauben mir nicht, wenn ich ihnen die Vorteile einer Lebensversicherung erkläre. Anscheinend habe ich kein ehrliches Gesicht.«

Wir schweigen noch eine Minute, als wir auf die Autobahn auffahren.

»Du stellst heute eine Menge Fragen«, sage ich zu Anja.

»Ich übe meine Kommunikationsfähigkeiten.«

»Denkst du daran, Rechtsanwältin zu werden?«

»Nein, ich versuche nur, ein besseres Mitglied unserer Einheit zu sein.«

»Hat Lucia irgendetwas zu dir gesagt?«

»Sie erwähnte, dass ich an meiner Sozialkompetenz arbeiten müsse.«

»Weil du den Bildschirm auf Roland geworfen hast?«

»Er kann manchmal so nerven.«

Ich muss kichern.

»Was glaubst du, für wen der Tote gearbeitet hat?«, fragt sie.

»Roland ist ziemlich sicher, dass es ein hohes Tier von der Landespolizei ist.«

»Und du glaubst ihm?«

»Er lag niemals daneben mit all seinen anderen Prognosen. Einer der Typen, mit denen ich Poker spiele, wird mir ein paar Namen senden, die ich mir ansehen werde.«

»Wieso lassen dich diese Gangster beim Poker mitspielen?«

»Ich habe einmal eine Menge Arbeit als Freiberufler gemacht. Manchmal erledigte ich Jobs für Kriminelle. Die kennen meinen Ruf.«

»Da du doch die Psyche von Leuten beeinflussen kannst, wieso gewinnst du dann nicht jedes Mal einen Haufen Geld, wenn du Poker spielst?«

»Weil ich nicht will.«

»Wieso nicht?«

»Ich spiele mit diesen Typen, um Informationen zu sammeln, nicht, um Geld zu gewinnen. Deshalb spiele ich an verschiedenen Orten mit verschiedenen Gruppen. Ich versuche normalerweise, ein bisschen zu gewinnen und ein bisschen zu verlieren. Was ich auf keinen Fall will, ist, die ganze Aufmerksamkeit auf mich zu ziehen, indem ich dauernd gewinne.«

Story 13

»Gestern Abend hast du eine Menge Geld gewonnen.«
»Ich habe mich hinreißen lassen. Ich versuchte, auf das Mädchen, das dort war, Eindruck zu machen.«
»Auf Lina?«
»Auf jemand anderen. Die war vielleicht heiß.«
»So genau wollte ich das gar nicht wissen!«, schreit mich Anja an.
Es wird wieder ruhig im Auto. Anja übt ihre Fertigkeiten im dichten Auffahren und Fahrspurwechseln. Einige Autos hupen uns an.
»Winke ihnen doch mit der Pistole zu«, sagt sie zu mir.
»Das ist Neukölln. Die haben vermutlich größere Waffen.«
»Hast du dem Toten deine Evolutionstheorie erzählt?«, fragt sie.
»Ich erklärte ihm meine Theorie, als ich seine Kleider durchsuchte.«
»Glaubst du nicht, dass es etwas komisch ist, Toten etwas zu erzählen?«, fragt sie.
»Jeder, der einen Friedhof besucht, spricht zu den Toten«, sage ich.
»Das ist etwas anderes. Die erklären nicht ihre Weltanschauung. Wie auch immer, wir haben unsere besonderen Kräfte nicht durch die Evolution erhalten.«
»Wie haben wir diese sonderbaren Gaben dann erhalten?«
»Außerirdische aus dem Weltall haben ihre DNA bereits in der Steinzeit den menschlichen Chromosomen hinzugefügt. In der Folge kommt alle paar Generationen dabei etwas Ungewöhnliches heraus - wie wir.«
»Das ist albern«, sage ich.
»Nicht so albern wie dein Glaube an einen Gott, der nicht existiert.«
»Ich kann es kaum glauben, ich arbeite mit einer Atheistin«, rufe ich aus. »Der Rest des Kommandos wird davon hören.«
»Niemand hat gesagt, dass wir unser Team ›Das Kommando‹ nennen«, sagt sie.
»Aber es hatte auch niemand etwas dagegen.«
»Wir wollten dich nicht kränken. Es ist ein bescheuerter Name.«
»Mir gefällt er. Vielleicht können wir Jacken bestellen, wo am Rücken ›Das Kommando‹ draufsteht.«
»Ich finde, wir sollten über den Namen abstimmen«, sagt sie.
»Wir werden sehen.«

—————————9—————————

Am selben Abend läutet das Telefon. Ich hebe ab und höre wieder eine Stimme mit einem fremden Akzent.
»Wo ist er?«
»Wer ist da?«
»Stellen Sie sich nicht so bescheuert an. Ich frage nochmal - wo ist er?«
»Reden Sie von einem Typen, den ich heute treffen sollte?«, frage ich.
»Hören Sie auf mit der Zeitverschwendung. Beantworten Sie die Frage.«
»Ich weiß nicht«, sage ich. »Ich war eine halbe Stunde lang am Bahnhof in Neukölln, betete, dass ich nicht von irgendeinem Pendler ausgeraubt werde, und Ihr Mann ist nie aufgetaucht.«
»Er war dort. Was ist mit ihm passiert?«
»Ich weiß nicht?«

Evolution

So ging es einige Minuten weiter. Er behauptete dauernd, ich hätte etwas getan, und ich sagte ihm dauernd, dass ich nichts getan habe. Ich habe gelogen, aber der Typ am Telefon wusste das nicht. Schließlich entschied er, dass ich die Wahrheit sagte. Wer würde denn schließlich annehmen, dass jemand mit meinem sonnigen Gemüt jemandem ins Herz schießen und seine Finger abhacken könnte.

»Ich komme auf dich zurück«, sagt er.

»Das bekomme ich oft von Mädchen zu hören«, sage ich, als er den Anruf beendet.

Am nächsten Tag lese ich in der Zeitung, dass der Mann, den ich erschossen hatte, bereits gefunden wurde. Irgendein emsiger Hausmeister sägte die Kette durch, welche die Tür verschloss, und entdeckte die Leiche.

Im Bericht wird vermutet, dass es sich um eine Hinrichtung der Mafia handele. Ich möchte am liebsten die Reporterin anrufen, um die Geschichte richtigzustellen, aber dann entscheide ich mich dagegen. Sie würde mir nicht glauben.

Später schlendere ich zum Mittagessen in ein örtliches Restaurant.

Eine neunzig Jahre alte Kellnerin kommt herüber, um meine Bestellung aufzunehmen.

»Was gibt es heute als Tagesgericht?«, frage ich.

»Zwiebelsuppe und Wurst vom Lamm.«

»Schmeckt es gut?«

»Woher soll ich das wissen? Ich esse hier nicht.«

»Wieso nicht?«

»Ich muss auf mein Cholesterin achten.«

»Servieren Sie noch Frühstück?«

»Kein Frühstück mehr nach elf Uhr. So steht es auch auf der Speisekarte.«

»Ich denke gerade an den Thunfischsalat. Ist er frisch?«

»Werden Sie heute noch etwas bestellen, oder sind Sie hier, um eine Meinungsumfrage zu machen?«

»Ich dachte, Sie würden sich über etwas Unterhaltung freuen«, sage ich zu ihr. »Schließlich ist hier nicht gerade sehr viel los.«

»Nun, meine Füße tun mir weh«, sagt sie zu mir, »also beeilen Sie sich und bestellen Sie etwas.«

»Ich nehme einen Hamburger und eine Cola.«

Die Kellnerin schreibt meine Bestellung auf ihren Notizblock und geht weg. Zehn Minuten später setzt sich ein hässlicher Typ genau neben mich an die Theke. Das ist ungewöhnlich, da es noch jede Menge freier Hocker gibt. Die Leute in Berlin wollen normalerweise nicht unmittelbar neben jemandem sitzen, wenn es sich vermeiden lässt.

»Nächste Woche zahlst du das Zweifache«, sagt er zu mir. »Ich werde am Dienstag in deinem Büro sein. Keine Treffpunktänderungen.«

Dann geht er. Ich spreche in ein Ansteckmikrofon an meiner Jacke.

»Er ist auf dem Weg nach draußen. Braune Haare, einen Meter fünfundachtzig, wiegt ungefähr fünfundneunzig Kilo. Er trägt eine dunkle Jacke und Jeans. Sieht aus, als ob er eine Rauferei mit einem Zug verloren hätte.«

Ich habe einen kleinen Empfänger in meinem Ohr, damit ich die Person am anderen Ende hören kann. Ein Privatdetektiv, der mich seit gestern unauffällig begleitet.

»Ich habe ihn«, berichtet der Privatdetektiv. »Ich rufe dich später an und sage dir, wo er hingefahren ist.«

Gerade jetzt bringt die Kellnerin meinen Hamburger. Er schmeckt köstlich. Ich hinterlasse ein ordentliches Trinkgeld, bevor ich gehe.

Story 13

Der Rest des Tages verläuft ohne besondere Ereignisse. Ich lese ein paar Handbücher darüber, wie man Zahnversicherungen an Leute verkauft, die sie nicht wollen. Ich spiele ein paar Spiele am Bürocomputer. Dann mache ich ein Kreuzworträtsel. Als nächstes mache ich ein Nickerchen. Schließlich gehe ich online und lese Klatschgeschichten über Hollywoods Berühmtheiten. Tausende Webseiten sind dem gewidmet.

Um halb sieben ruft meine Privatdetektivin zurück.

»Der Typ ging zu einem alten Wohnblock in Kreuzberg, holte seine Wäsche ab und hat sie in einem Waschsalon in der Nähe gewaschen.«

»Ist dir aufgefallen, ob auf irgendeinem der Schlafanzüge, die er gewaschen hat, Kaninchen waren?«

»Kaninchen?«

»Ja, junge Kaninchen. Ich liebe Schlafanzüge mit Kaninchen.«

»So nahe bin ich nicht herangekommen.«

»Solche Sachen sollten dir auffallen. Ich habe vor, deinem Vorgesetzten einen Beschwerdebrief zu senden.«

»Paul, ich habe keinen Vorgesetzten.«

»Das habe ich vergessen. Wo ist dieser Typ jetzt?«

»Er trinkt gerade etwas in einem Restaurant in Friedrichshain.«

»Gib mir die Adresse. Ich werde in einer halben Stunde dort sein.«

»Brauchst du eine Wegbeschreibung?«

»Natürlich nicht, ich habe ein Navi.«

Als ich zum Restaurant komme, sehe ich meinen Mann, wie er am Ende der Bar sitzt. Ich setze mich auf den Platz neben ihm. Er sieht mich an. Ich lächle. Er erkennt mich nicht. Wie ich zuvor schon erwähnte, gibt mir meine besondere Fähigkeit die Kontrolle darüber, was Leute sehen und hören.

»Sind diese Navigationssysteme nicht erstaunlich?«, frage ich den Typen.

»Lassen Sie mich in Ruhe«, brummelt er.

»Mein Navi hat einen österreichischen Akzent. Ich tue gerne so, als ob ich mit Arnold Schwarzenegger fahren würde.«

»Wenn Sie mich nochmal anreden werde ich Ihnen eine reinhauen.«

In diesem Moment richte ich meine ganze Kraft auf ihn, um sein Bewusstsein zu trüben.

»Warum trinken Sie Ihr Glas nicht aus und dann machen wir eine kleine Fahrt«, sage ich zu ihm.

Er schüttet das restliche Bier hinunter und folgt mir hinaus zu meinem Auto.

»Setzen Sie sich rein und entspannen Sie sich«, sage ich zu ihm. »Ich werde fahren.«

Ich fessele den Herrn mit Handschellen an die Beifahrertür und rufe Lucia an. Wir vereinbaren, uns an einer verlassenen Baustelle in der Nähe des Flughafens zu treffen. Zwanzig Minuten später ist der Kopf des Typen wieder klar, aber seine Hände und Füße sind gefesselt.

Lucia spricht mit ihm. Lucia hat diese interessante Fähigkeit. Sie unterhält sich mit Leuten und die erzählen ihr alles, was sie wissen will. Sie kann nicht erklären, wie sie es macht, genau wie ich nicht weiß, wie meine Bewusstseinsverwirrung funktioniert. Aber es ist eine großartige Gabe.

Unglücklicherweise weiß dieser Typ nicht viel. Lucia findet seinen Namen heraus, dass er aus der Ukraine kommt und dass er vor zehn Monaten in Deutschland mit einem Aeroflot-Flugzeug angekommen ist. Er erzählt ihr, dass da noch ein paar weitere Ukrainer mit ihm arbeiten, aber er kennt ihre Namen nicht. Er gibt ihr drei Adressen von Wohnungen, wo seine Kollegen möglicherweise sind, aber er weiß nicht, wer die Operation leitet.

»Er erhält alle seine Anweisungen über ein Handy«, sagt mir Lucia, nachdem sie ihr Verhör beendet hat.

»Was sollen wir mit ihm machen?«, frage ich.

»Lass wieder die Bewusstseinseintrübung über ihn kommen. Mach, dass er die letzten paar Stunden vergisst.«

Lucia gibt mir eine Pistole mit einem Schalldämpfer.

»Das ist die Waffe, mit der du den ersten Ukrainer erschossen hast«, sagt Lucia zu mir. »Gib sie diesem Typen und setz ihn in der Nähe einer Polizeistation ab.«

»Großartige Idee. Es wäre am besten, wenn er nackt wäre, damit die Polizei ihn sofort bemerkt.«

»Das hört sich gut an«, sagt Lucia.

Lucia fährt zu unserer Zentrale zurück. Ich lasse den Mann auf dem Rücksitz meines Wagens in einen Schlaf versinken und schreibe ein Geständnis für ihn. Dann entferne ich seine Kleidung, klebe ihm das Geständnis auf die Brust und fahre ihn zu einer Polizeistation im nächsten Ort.

Ich halte vor dem Gebäude und sage ihm, dass er aus dem Auto aussteigen soll. Er ist angeschlagen, aber schafft es, die Pistole zu halten, als er nackt in die Station hineingeht, um mit den freundlichen Polizisten zu reden. Manchmal liebe ich einfach meine Arbeit.

---10---

»Ich dachte, das wäre alles geregelt«, sage ich zu Roland am Telefon. »Ich will uns ›Das Kommando‹ nennen.«

»Anja überzeugte Lucia, dass wir über einen Namen abstimmen sollten«, sagt er zu mir.

»Wie wäre es mit ›Männer in Schwarz‹.«

»Sehen Lucia, Anja und Lina aus wie Männer?«

»Eher nicht.«

Roland entschließt sich, das Thema zu wechseln.

»Wo ist das Geld, das du beim Pokerspiel gewonnen hast?«

»Es liegt auf meinem Bürotisch. Ich hatte noch keine Zeit, es zur Bank zu bringen.«

»Lucia sorgt sich darüber, dass du es dazu verwenden könntest, um Ferien zu machen.«

Lucia ist die Chefin, aber manchmal glaube ich, dass sie sich zu viel Sorgen ums Geld macht.

»Sag ihr, sie soll sich entspannen«, sage ich.

»Du weißt, dass ich Buchhaltung online lerne«, sagt Roland.

»Ich bin sicher, du lernst sehr viel.«

»Lucia lässt mich bei den finanziellen Angelegenheiten der Firma mithelfen«, sagt er.

»Warum sollte ich davon wissen?«, frage ich ihn.

»Sie hat mir die Verantwortung für die Kostenabrechnung übertragen. Ich muss deine Pokergewinne nachverfolgen können.«

»Ich habe ein besonderes System«, sage ich zu ihm. »Wenn ich beim Poker gewinne, behalte ich das Geld und benutze es für meine geschäftlichen Ausgaben. Auf diese Art brauche ich keine weitere Kostenabrechnung auszufüllen bis das Geld alle ist.«

»So sollst du es nicht machen«, sagt Roland.

»Warum nicht? Es ist einfach und es spart Zeit.«

»Aber wir sehen dann nicht deine tatsächlichen Ausgaben. Alles, was wir wissen, ist, dass du Geld in einem Pokerspiel gewinnst und es dann während der nächsten paar Wochen für geschäftliche Zwecke ausgibst. Wir wissen nicht, wie viel du gewinnst oder wohin das Geld tatsächlich geht.«

»Glaube mir, du willst das nicht wissen.«

»Lucia will es aber.«

»Sag Lucia, dass ich Außenagent bin und kein Buchhalter.«

»Ich sage ihr überhaupt nichts. Du redest mit ihr«, sagt Roland.

»Hat Lucia die Adressen geprüft, die wir von dem Ukrainer erhalten haben?«

»Ja, aber die Wohnungen waren leer.«

Ich lege auf, als Roland versucht, mich daran zu erinnern, wann die nächste Kostenabrechnung fällig ist. Warum muss es so kompliziert sein, ein kleines Unternehmen wie das unsere zu führen. Eine Minute später rufe ich Lucia an.

»Roland belästigt mich wegen der Kostenabrechnungen.«

»Gib ihm, was er haben will.«

»Ich mag diese Arbeit«, sage ich zu ihr. »Die Arbeit ist aufregend. Sie ist sicherer als die freiberufliche Arbeit, die ich gemacht habe. Die Bezahlung ist nicht schlecht und wir bekommen ausgezeichnete Krankenversicherungsleistungen. Die sind immer von Vorteil für den Fall, dass eine Kugel meine inneren Organe durchdringt.«

»Außerdem darfst du mit einem Team ausgezeichneter Leute zusammenarbeiten«, erinnert sie mich.

»Ich wollte das gerade sagen«, antworte ich. »Ich wollte auch gerade sagen, dass meine Stellenbeschreibung nichts von Kostenabrechnungen erwähnt.«

»Wir haben keine Stellenbeschreibung für das, was du machst«, erinnert mich Lucia.

»Wenn du eine schreibst, dann stelle sicher, dass ich keine Kostenabrechnungen abgeben muss.«

Ich höre sie seufzen.

»Können wir später darüber sprechen?«, fragt sie mich.

»Okay, denk einfach daran, dass ich meine Meinung nicht ändern werde.«

---11---

Am nächsten Tag sitze ich im Versicherungsbüro. Nachdem ich zehn Minuten lang einen Artikel über Invaliditätsversicherungen gelesen habe, bin ich so müde, dass ich fast von meinem Stuhl falle. Ich drücke die Kurzwahl auf meinem Handy, um mit Lucia zu sprechen.

»Was ist los?«

»Ist unsere Privatdetektivin in der Nähe?«

»Ja.«

»Sag mir nochmals, warum ich einen Babysitter brauche.«

»Du brauchst Rückendeckung für den Fall, dass die Bösen eine kleine Armee zu dir schicken.«

»Hast du heute meine E-Mail erhalten? Reinhold hatte mit ein paar Namen Erfolg.«

»Anja und Roland überprüfen diese Namen gerade.«

»Warum schnappen wir uns nicht diese Leute, die mir Reinhold genannt hat, werfen sie in eine der Arrestzellen im Bürokeller und du holst die Wahrheit aus ihnen heraus. Das ist leichter als eine Computerrecherche durch Anja und Roland.«

»Du willst ranghohe Beamte der Polizei entführen?«

»Sicher, ich kann sie mit einem Bewusstseinszauber beeinflussen, damit sie sich nicht daran erinnern, wie wir aussehen.«

»Ich ziehe eine unauffälligere Arbeitsweise vor«, sagt Lucia.

»Brauchen die Kinder Unterstützung bei ihren Nachforschungen?«

»Nein, bleib dort und tu so, als ob du ein Versicherungsvertreter wärst. Rufe potentielle Kunden an.«

»Ich hasse diese Tätigkeit. Alle schreien mich an und legen auf.«

»Du musst an deinen Verkaufsfähigkeiten arbeiten.«

»Ich habe nicht einmal eine Zulassung, Versicherungen zu verkaufen. Was passiert, wenn jemand eine Police von mir kaufen will?«

»Ich glaube nicht, dass du dich darum sorgen musst.«

Ich verbringe den Rest des Tages damit, auf ein Dutzend bewaffneter Männer zu warten, die durch meine Tür hereinstürmen, aber nichts passiert. Verdeckte Aufklärungsarbeit ist nicht immer spannend.

Schließlich geht es auf fünf Uhr zu. Ich brauche einen Kaffee und gehe daher zu einem nahegelegenen Café. Meine Privatdetektivin ist wahrscheinlich gleich hinter mir. Ich bestelle einen Latte mit extra Schaum, zahle der Dame drei Euro und setze mich hin.

Ich denke gerade über die hohen Kosten von Kaffee in Berlin nach, als sich jemand mit einer Zeitung in der Hand in den Sessel neben mir hinsetzt. Er lehnt sich vor und sieht mich mit grimmiger Miene an.

Ich lasse meine Tasse etwas zittern und verschütte etwas von dem Getränk auf den Tisch. Das jedoch nur, um ihn wissen zu lassen, dass sein finsterer Blick eine Wirkung hat.

»Ich sagte dem anderen Typ, dass ich das Geld am Dienstag bringen würde«, flüstere ich.

Der Kerl schaut mich mit einem verwirrten Ausdruck an und zeigt mir eine Pistole, die er unter der Zeitung versteckt hält.

»Der andere Mann wurde nackt vor einer Polizeistation gefunden. Er wurde festgenommen und ich glaube, Sie hatten etwas damit zu tun.«

Ich blicke ihn nichtssagend an.

»Ich habe ihn nicht ausgezogen, falls Sie das meinen«, sage ich zu ihm.

»Lassen Sie uns irgendwo hingehen, wo wir ungestört reden können«, sagt er. »Sie werden mir alles erzählen.«

Ich werfe ihm einen besorgten Blick zu und sage: »Bitte tun Sie mir nicht weh.«

»Wir werden einen Spaziergang machen«, sagt er. »Lassen Sie das Getränk stehen.«

Ich schaffe es, ein oder zwei Zitterbewegungen vorzutäuschen, als wir das Café verlassen. Wir gehen zum Parkplatz. Sarah, die Privatdetektivin, lehnt an einem Auto und liest ein Magazin.

Ich überwältige den Typ mit einer vollen Bewusstseinstrübung, gerade als wir Sarah erreichen. Er bleibt stehen und senkt seine Hände. Ich nehme die Pistole und helfe ihm in den Vordersitz des Wagens.

Sarah nimmt auf dem Fahrersitz Platz, während ich ihn an der Beifahrertür mit Handschellen anhänge. Ich springe auf den Rücksitz und wir fahren weg.

»Du siehst sehr hübsch in deinem Trenchcoat aus«, sage ich zu Sarah.

»Ich bin froh, dass er dir gefällt«, sagt sie. »Wieso lässt sich der Mann von uns kampflos mitnehmen?«

»Ich habe etwas in sein Getränk getan, als wir in dem Café waren.«

Es ist besser, wenn Sarah nicht weiß, dass ich besondere Fähigkeiten besitze. Wir fahren ein paar Minuten lang stillschweigend.

Story 13

»Musst du Kostenabrechnungen ausfüllen?«, frage ich sie.

»Wenn ich für Lucia einen Job erledige, muss ich immer eine Kostenabrechnung und ein Zeitprotokoll einreichen. Lucia besteht darauf.«

»Wie steht es mit den Leuten von der Sicherheit?«, frage ich.

»Ich zahle ihnen einen festen Preis für jeden Einsatz. Sie geben mir die Quittungen für irgendwelche speziellen Dinge, die sie kaufen müssen.«

Meiner Gruppe gehört die Sicherheitsfirma einer Briefkastengesellschaft. Sarah leitet die Firma und ist die einzige Vollzeitangestellte. Die Sicherheitsfirma stellt Arbeitskräfte und Ausrüstung, um spezielle Aufgaben für unsere Kunden zu erledigen. Sarah hat eine lange Liste von Söldnern und ehemaligen Mitgliedern der Streitkräfte, die sie für jegliche Einsätze anheuern kann, je nach den benötigten Kenntnissen.

»Roland fängt an, Lucia bei der Bürobuchhaltung zu helfen«, sage ich zu ihr. »Er geht mir jetzt schon auf die Nerven, damit ich meinen Papierkram rechtzeitig abgebe.«

»So etwas machen Erwachsene nun einmal«, sagt Sarah. »Sie erledigen ihren Schreibkram.«

»Fang bloß du nicht an, mir von der Verantwortung Erwachsener zu erzählen«, sage ich zu ihr. »Ich bin mir nicht einmal ganz sicher, ob du alt genug bist, Alkohol trinken zu dürfen.«

Sarah ist im gleichen Alter wie Roland. Sie sind seit ihrer Kindheit befreundet. Ihre Eltern waren beide Privatdetektive und als sie aufwuchs, half sie ihnen bei den Ermittlungen. Sie übernahm das Familienunternehmen, als sie in Rente gingen.

Roland stellte sie kurz danach Lucia vor. Über die nächsten paar Jahre beauftragte Lucia Sarah mit einer Reihe besonderer Aufgaben. Sarah erwies sich als großartige Detektivin. Innerhalb weniger Jahre wurde unser Team zum wichtigsten Kunden von Sarah.

Schließlich bat Lucia sie, die Sicherheitsabteilung zu leiten. Sarah arbeitet immer noch für andere Kunden, aber widmet den größten Teil ihrer Zeit der Hilfe unseres Teams.

»Warum hast du mich heute gebraucht?«, fragt Sarah. »Alles, was wir gemacht haben, war, einen harmlosen Kerl ins Auto zu setzen.«

»Wir waren nicht sicher, was geschehen würde«, sage ich ihr. »Es hätten fünf Männer mit Kampfhunden und Panzerfäusten sein können. Es hat sich herausgestellt, dass du entbehrlich warst, aber es ist immer gut, auf Nummer sicher zu gehen.«

»Nettes Wort«, sagt sie zu mir. »Entbehrlich. Wo hast du das gelernt?«

»Ich überrasche Leute immer gerne mit meinem breiten Wortschatz.«

Während Sarah fährt, reden wir ein bisschen über die örtlichen Fußballmannschaften.

Sarah steuert den Wagen auf einen kleinen Parkplatz neben einem Lagerhaus im Ortsteil Marzahn. Lucia wartet neben einer offenen Metalltür. Ein hoher Zaun macht es für jeden unmöglich, das Parkplatzgelände von der Straße aus zu sehen.

Ich schließe die Handschellen unseres Gefangenen auf. Lucia führt ihn in das Gebäude. Bis die Bewusstseinstrübung abklingt, wird er in einer Sicherungszelle im Keller des Lagerhauses sein.

Nun, warum ist das Hauptquartier in Marzahn? Wahrscheinlich hat Lucia einen Vorzugspreis für das Gebäude bekommen.

»Du musst mir einen Gefallen tun«, sagt Sarah zu mir, als wir wegfahren.

»Willst du, dass ich dir einen guten Tätowierer empfehle?«

»Nein, danke.«

»Was kann ich sonst noch für dich tun?«

»Ich habe einen neuen Kunden. Die Leute, gegen die ich für ihn ermitteln soll, sind sehr gefährlich. Kannst du mir helfen?«

»Wieso ich?«

»Weil du wirklich gut bist, wenn es um Gewalttätigkeit geht.«

»Lina ist eine bessere Kämpferin«, sage ich zu ihr. »Verstehe mich nicht falsch, ich kann ganz gut Leute verprügeln, aber sie ist besser.«

»In diesem Fall könnte es sein, dass geschossen werden muss.«

»Erzähle mir die Einzelheiten«, sage ich.

12

Zwei Tage später ...

»Ich zähle eine Stimme dafür, uns ›Das Kommando‹ zu nennen, und vier Stimmen dagegen«, sagt Lucia.

»Ich will die Stimmen nochmals zählen«, sage ich zu ihr.

»Paul, es gibt nur fünf Stimmen. Ich werde sie nicht noch einmal zählen.«

»Aber jede gute Mannschaft braucht einen Namen.«

»Es sieht so aus, als würdest du wieder verlieren«, sagt Anja. »Genau wie du damals wolltest, dass wir eine Katze als Maskottchen kaufen. Diese Abstimmung war auch vier zu eins. Ich glaube, ich sehe da ein Muster.«

Anja ist unsere Informationsexpertin. Sie verbringt ihre Zeit damit, eine Menge von Daten zu analysieren, um nach Verhaltensmustern zu suchen. Wenn sie etwas Ungewöhnliches findet, bittet sie Roland um Hilfe. Er sieht sich die Daten an und macht Voraussagen.

Anja hat sich alle Daten rund um die Verbrechen gegen bekannte Versicherungsvertreter in Berlin angeschaut und entdeckte ein paar interessante Muster. Roland überprüfte die Muster und sagte uns, der Verantwortliche für die Erpressungsoperation sei vermutlich an der Spitze der Polizeibehörde zu finden gewesen. Er fand ebenso heraus, wer das nächste Opfer sein würde. Diese Informationen werden unsere Arbeit sicherlich beschleunigen.

Anja und Roland verwalten auch die Anlagenportfolios unserer Gruppe und sie verdienen dabei jede Menge Geld. Lucia verwendet dieses zusätzliche Geld, um neue technische Spielereien und Waffen zu kaufen.

Roland hat noch ein Talent. Er ist ein sagenhafter Hacker. Kein Computer oder Netzwerk ist sicher, wenn Roland sich entschließt, eine bestimmte Information zu suchen.

Sie wissen ja bereits, dass Lina eine großartige Kämpferin ist. Ihre Reflexe sind schneller als die einer Kobra und sie kann jede Kung-Fu- oder Karatebewegung innerhalb von Sekunden erlernen. Zusätzlich nimmt sie auch an Tortendekorationswettbewerben teil.

Lucia arbeitete fünfundzwanzig Jahre lang für verschiedene Vollzugsbehörden. Wie ich schon erwähnte, hat sie die besondere Gabe, Leute dazu zu bringen, dass sie die Wahrheit sagen. Während ihrer Karriere benutzte sie diese Gabe, um einige bedeutende Fälle zu lösen. Es war schwierig, aber sie schaffte es, ohne dass jemand ihre besondere Gabe bemerkte.

Lucia ging vor fünf Jahren, als sie fünfzig Jahre alt wurde, in Rente. Anstatt das Gärtnern zu erlernen, begann sie, unser Team zu formieren.

Während ihrer Karriere hielt Lucia Augen und Ohren offen, um andere mit besonderen Talenten zu finden. Zum Zeitpunkt ihres Renteneintritts hatte sie eine Liste von zehn möglichen Kandidaten für das Team. Sechs

Story 13

dieser Kandidaten stellten sich als Leute mit normalen Fähigkeiten heraus. Vier von uns waren etwas Besonderes. Ich war der Erste auf ihrer Liste.

Als sie mit mir sprach, sagte ich zu ihr, dass sie zu viele Comicbücher gelesen habe. Aber sie überzeugte mich, wir würden Spaß haben, gute Taten vollbringen, ein paar Leute erschießen und viel Geld verdienen. Somit unterschrieb ich. Das war vor vier Jahren.

Als Nächstes rekrutierte sie Anja von einer Expertenkommission der Regierung. Roland kam zu uns als Computerspezialist vom BND. Lina war die letzte Rekrutin. Sie trainierte LKA-Agenten in Selbstverteidigungstechniken.

Aber ich schweife ab. Zurück zur eigentlichen Geschichte.

Wir treffen uns in unserer großartigen Basis. Sie war früher ein Vorratslager für Klempnerbedarf. Es liegen immer noch verrostete Rohr- und Eckstücke in einigen der ungenutzten Räume verstreut.

»Wie geht es unserem Gefangenen?«, frage ich.

»Er ist bei den Sicherheitsbehörden.«

»Warum?«

»Es hat sich herausgestellt, dass er ein Russe ist, der seit ein paar Jahren illegal hier ist«, sagt Lucia.

»Er weiß nichts über die Ukrainer. Jemand rief ihn vor ein paar Tagen an und heuerte ihn an, dich zu foltern, bis du ihm sagst, was mit den ersten zwei Männern passiert ist.«

»Können wir das Gespräch nachverfolgen?«

»Der Anruf wurde von einem Einwegtelefon gemacht. Derjenige, der den Einsatz leitet, ist ganz schön schlau.«

Während Lucia und ich miteinander sprechen, beginnen Anja und Roland eine Diskussion darüber, ob Mendelejew besondere evolutionäre Kräfte hatte oder nicht. Ich frage Lina, ob Mendelejew der Premierminister von Russland ist.

»Nein, er erfand das Periodensystem, damals im 19. Jahrhundert«, sagt sie zu mir. »Er sagte auch die Eigenschaften von Elementen voraus, die noch nicht entdeckt waren.«

Roland und Anja debattieren ein paar Minuten. Dann fangen sie an, sich anzuschreien. Dann fangen sie an, miteinander zu kämpfen.

»Kämpft, kämpft, kämpft«, feuere ich sie an.

Lina steht auf und schlägt Anja und Roland ein paar Mal mit einem Holzstab, den sie gerne mit sich herumträgt, auf die Beine.

»Au, hör auf. Das tut weh«, sagt Roland.

»Lasst uns die Besprechung beenden«, sagt Lina.

Anja und Roland stehen vom Boden auf und reiben sich die Schienbeine. Sie setzen sich auf ihre Plätze. Jetzt, nachdem sie wieder unsere Aufmerksamkeit hat, spricht Lucia weiter.

»Arno überprüft immer noch die DNA und die Fingerabdrücke, um die Herkunft der Ukrainer festzustellen. Vielleicht ergibt sich daraus ein Anhaltspunkt.«

Arno ist ein Freund von Anja. Ich glaube, sie mag ihn. Sie haben sich kennengelernt, als sie an ihrer Promotion arbeitete. Zu dieser Zeit hatte Arno bereits einen Doktortitel in Chemie und war ein Experte für Proteine und Ähnliches. Vor ein paar Jahren haben wir Arno in seinem eigenen Forschungslabor ausgerüstet und förderten einige seiner Projekte. Als Gegenleistung agiert er als unser eigenes, privates, kriminaltechnisches Labor.

»Irgendwelche Fortschritte mit den Namen, die ich von Reinhold bekommen habe?«, frage ich.

Evolution

»Noch nicht«, antwortet Roland. »Ich schreibe gerade ein paar Spezialprogramme, um Informationen über Ukrainer, die nach Deutschland gekommen sind, ans Licht zu bringen. Ich schaue mir auch alle von den Landespolizisten bearbeiteten Transaktionen an, von denen Pauls Freund sagt, dass sie gewillt seien, Schmiergelder anzunehmen. Ich werde so viele Jahre zurückgehen wie ich kann, um zu sehen, ob es dort irgendwelche Zusammenhänge gibt.«

»Reinhold ist nicht gerade mein Freund«, sage ich.

»Haben wir einen Kunden, der für diesen Fall zahlt?«, fragt Lina.

»Nein«, sagt Lucia. »Wir zahlen dafür aus eigener Tasche.«

»Wie rechtfertigen wir die Kosten?«, fragt Roland.

»Manchmal tun wir etwas, weil es getan werden muss«, antwortet Lucia. »Und das ist jetzt der Fall.«

»Ich habe doch nur gefragt«, sagt Roland.

»Nun, jetzt weißt du es.«

Wir unterhalten uns ein paar Minuten lang über etwas anderes. Roland wird es langweilig und er fängt mit einem Computerspiel an. Zehn Minuten später ruft Anja zu ihm hinüber.

»Roland, hast du verstanden, was Lucia zuletzt gesagt hat?«

»Ich bin gerade bei Level zehn«, murmelt er.

Anja versucht, den Aus-Knopf auf Rolands Laptop zu drücken. Er schubst sie mit einer Hand weg und tippt mit der anderen Hand weiter. Sie zieht ihn von seinem Platz.

»Ich möchte nur einmal eine Besprechung erleben, wo sich niemand streitet«, sagt Lucia zu mir.

»Sie streiten sich nicht wirklich«, sage ich zu ihr.

»Es ist deine Schuld«, sagt sie.

»Wieso beschuldigst du mich?«

»Du reichst deine Berichte nicht ordnungsgemäß ein, du feuerst diese Kinder an, wenn sie verrückt spielen und du beschwerst dich, weil du in Marzahn arbeiten musst. Ich kann zehn andere Fälle benennen, wo du ein schlechtes Beispiel darstellst.«

Plötzlich bemerken wir, dass uns die anderen drei beobachten.

»Okay, Papa und Mama haben eine kleine Auseinandersetzung. Aber macht euch keine Sorgen, wir haben euch noch lieb«, sage ich zu ihnen.

Sie rollen die Augen.

»Nur noch eine geschäftliche Angelegenheit«, sage ich, »und dann könnt ihr weiterstreiten.«

»Worum geht es?«, fragt Anja.

»Sarah hat einen Fall, den sie alleine nicht bearbeiten kann.«

»Erzähle uns davon«, sagt Lucia.

---13---

»Sarah muss gegen einen Motorradclub ermitteln.«

»Geil«, sagt Lina.

»Wer hat sie angeheuert?«, fragt Lucia.

»Der Vorsitzende des Clubs. Einer in seiner Gang bestiehlt sie. Er möchte, dass Sarah seine Leute beobachtet und herausfindet, wer das Geld nimmt.«

Story 13

»Woher weiß er, dass Geld fehlt?«, fragt Lucia.

»Der Clubpräsident führt monatliche Aufzeichnungen über ihre Einkommen. Die Einnahmen in diesem Jahr waren niedriger als im letzten Jahr, obwohl die Preise höher sind.«

»Klingt nach einer ganzen Menge Spaß«, sagt Anja. »Ich wollte schon immer einmal auf einer großen Harley Davidson herumfahren.«

»Da ist ein großes Motorradtreffen nächste Woche oben an der Ostsee«, erzähle ich ihnen. »Die Gang wird dort sein und eine Menge illegaler Sachen machen. Sarah denkt, das sei der beste Ort, den Dieb zu finden.«

»Gehen wir alle hin?«, fragt Anja.

»Ja, ich habe Sarah klargemacht, dass sie nicht alle Gangmitglieder beaufsichtigen kann. Daher werden wir alle hingehen und helfen. Ich wusste, dass euch ein Ausflug gefallen wird.«

»Juhu, ein Wochenende an der Ostsee«, sagt Lina.

--------14--------

Ein paar Tage später ...

»Es ist Donnerstag«, erinnert uns Lina. »Zeit, an die Ostsee zu fahren.«

»Ist es nicht ein bisschen zu früh?«, frage ich. »Wir haben gerade zu Mittag gegessen.«

»Wir wollen auf dem Ausstellungsgelände herumgehen und die Sachen ansehen, die von den Händlern angeboten werden«, sagt Lina.

Anja hält eine glänzende, schwarze Lederjacke hoch. Sie hat Fransen an den Ärmeln.

»Die sind ausgezeichnet«, sagt sie zu Lucia.

»Die wären noch viel besser, wenn wir einen Teamnamen am Rücken hätten«, sage ich.

»Es wird Zeit, dass du diese Idee aufgibst«, sagt Roland.

»Haben wir noch irgendwelche Hinweise gefunden, die uns bei der Verfolgung der Erpresser helfen könnten?«, fragt Lina.

»Nein«, sagt Anja, »Rolands Programme haben uns noch keine Resultate geliefert.«

»Während der nächsten paar Tage sollten wir uns über die Ukrainer keine Gedanken machen und uns auf die Motorradgang konzentrieren«, sagt Sarah zu uns.

Sie kam vor ein paar Minuten an und trug einen kleinen Koffer mit Kleidung für das Wochenende.

»Wo werden wir unterkommen?«, fragt Anja.

»Ich habe das Hotelbuchungssystem gehackt«, sagt Roland. »Die haben ein Hotel ungefähr acht Kilometer von dem Ort entfernt, wo das Treffen abgehalten wird. Ich habe die Namen von sechs bestehenden Reservierungen gelöscht und mit unseren Namen ersetzt. Wir haben schöne Zimmer, aber so manches Gangmitglied wird bitterböse sein, wenn er versucht, einzuchecken.«

»Ist die Ausrüstung fertig?«, fragt mich Lucia.

»Die Waffen sind sauber, die Kommunikationsausrüstung ist einsatzbereit, die Computer funktionieren und der Lieferwagen ist beladen. Alles, was wir noch tun müssen, ist unsere Koffer einzuladen.«

»Anja und Roland haben bereits die vier Mitglieder des Motorradclubs identifiziert, die höchstwahrscheinlich klauen«, sagt Lucia. »Einer leitet den Drogenverkauf. Ein anderer ist für die Waffenschmuggel-Transaktionen der Gang verantwortlich. Der Dritte leitet die Gangaktivitäten in Sachen LKW-Entführungen und der Vierte organisiert das Prostitutionsgeschäft. Das sind die Männer, denen wir folgen werden.«

»Wir sind das gestern durchgegangen, als du uns die Aufträge ausgehändigt hast und uns die Bilder von jeder Zielperson gegeben hast«, erinnert sie Roland.

»Es kann nicht schaden, das Ganze nochmal fünf Minuten durchzugehen«, sagt sie zu ihm.

Alle stöhnen, als sie weitermacht und alles wiederholt, was sie uns am Tag vorher bereits gesagt hat. Lucia erwischt mich dabei, wie ich Grimassen hinter ihrem Rücken schneide.

»Au«, sage ich, als sie mir auf die Schläfe schlägt.

»Habt ihr alle die Wegbeschreibung zum Hotel und zum Ausstellungsgelände?«, fragt Lucia.

»Ich habe sie ausgedruckt, nur für den Fall, dass unsere Handys keinen Empfang haben«, sagt Roland.

Er gibt jedem von uns eine Kopie. Wir schnappen unser Gepäck und gehen durch die Hintertür des Lagerhauses. Drei glänzende Motorräder und ein großer Lieferwagen stehen auf dem Parkplatzgelände.

Der Lieferwagen sieht eher wie ein Lastwagen aus. In den Seitenwänden des Lasters befinden sich Stauräume, wo alle unsere Geräte gelagert sind. Im mittleren Bereich sind drei Stühle und eine kleiner Tisch am Boden festgeschraubt. Wir können ihn als Büro benutzen, sobald wir geparkt sind. Das Führerhaus hat Platz für vier Personen.

Ich habe alle Fahrzeuge ein paar Tage vorher gemietet. Lucia sperrt das Gebäude ab, während die Kinder unser Gepäck in den Lieferwagen bringen. Anja, Roland und Lina ziehen ihre Lederjacken an, schwingen sich auf ihre Motorräder und donnern davon. Sarah, Lucia und ich folgen ihnen im Lieferwagen. Wir sind alle begeistert über den Ausflug.

Später am Nachmittag fahren wir auf das Ausstellungsgelände, wo das Treffen stattfindet. Die nächsten paar Stunden verbringen wir damit, die Imbissbuden zu überprüfen, die rings um vier große Zelte aufgebaut sind. Zum Abendessen kaufen wir eine Auswahl an Bratwürsten, Popcorn und Erfrischungsgetränken.

Motorradfahrer von überallher beginnen bereits einzutreffen. Sie sehen gemein aus. Ich bin froh, dass meine Knarre voll geladen ist.

Um neun Uhr donnern unser Kunde und seine Gruppe von Schurken in das Ausstellungsgelände. Ekelhafte, hässlich aussehende Leute.

---15---

Wir teilen uns auf, um unsere vier Zielpersonen zu verfolgen. Mein Typ ist ganz schön langweilig. Ich beobachte ihn dabei, wie er eine Menge Bier trinkt und mit seiner Freundin streitet, während sie auf dem Ausstellungsgelände herumgehen. Ungefähr um elf Uhr höre ich eine bekannte Stimme hinter mir. Ich drehe mich um und sehe Anja und Roland, wie sie an einer Imbissbude lehnen.

»Roland, iss nicht so viel Zuckerwatte«, sagt Anja.

»Du bist nicht meine Mutter«, sagt Roland zu ihr.

Ich gleite zu ihnen hinüber.

»Ich glaube nicht, dass ihr Sonnenbrillen braucht, da es schon dunkel ist«, sage ich.

»Ja schon, aber damit sehen wir so cool aus!«, antwortet Anja.

»Hat dein Typ irgendetwas Verdächtiges gemacht?«, fragt Roland.

»Nichts Ungewöhnliches soweit. Er ist gerade seine Freundin losgeworden und ging hinüber zu dem Mann, dem du folgst.«

»He, da geht ein Mitglied einer anderen Gang hinüber, um mit ihnen zu reden«, sagt Roland.

Story 13

»Ich gehe ein bisschen näher ran«, sagt Anja.

»Nicht notwendig«, sage ich. »Wir können ihnen von hier aus zuhören.«

Ich ziehe ein kleines Gerät aus meiner Tasche und richte es auf die drei Motorradfahrer.

»Das ist das Neueste in der Mikrofontechnik«, sage ich zu ihnen, als ich mir einen kleinen Ohrhörer ins linke Ohr stecke.

»Was sagen sie?«, fragt Anja mich.

»Es scheint nicht zu funktionieren.«

»Ich dachte, du hast alle Geräte geprüft?«

»Na gut, ich habe die meisten geprüft.«

»So viel zur modernsten Technik«, sagt Anja. »Ich gehe näher ran. Schaut mal, wie ich mit der Umgebung verschmelze.«

»Ich glaube nicht, dass sie gut dazupasst«, sage ich zu Roland, als sich Anja von uns wegbewegt. »Sie hat noch alle ihre Zähne, riecht gut und ihre Fingernägel sind sauber. Sie sieht aus wie eine Fußballmutti in Lederjacke.«

Die Motorradfahrer stehen vor einem Verkaufsstand, wo Armbänder und Ohrringe verkauft werden. Anja geht lässig bis auf einen Meter Entfernung zu den Motorradfahrern und tut so, als ob sie einige Artikel betrachten würde. Binnen einiger Minuten starren die drei Männer sie an. Einer der Biker sagt irgendetwas. Die anderen lachen. Ein zweiter Biker packt sie am Arm und sagt etwas anderes. Sie klatscht ihm eine.

»Bleib hier«, sagt Roland.

Er geht hinüber zu den drei Bikern und versucht, Anja wegzuziehen. Zwei von ihnen halten ihn fest. Die drei Biker schubsen und ziehen meine zwei Partner in ein nahegelegenes Zelt. Der Verkäufer sieht, was passiert, aber tut nichts.

Zehn Sekunden später gehe ich in das Zelt.

Außer ein paar Musikern, die sich für ihre nächste Vorstellung aufwärmen, ist das Zelt leer. Einer von ihnen sieht, wie sich Anja und Roland abplagen, und schreit die Biker an. Der Biker, der Anja festhält, lässt sie mit einer Hand los. Er dreht sich von ihr weg und zeigt dem Musiker den Mittelfinger. Das ist ein Fehler.

Sie holt einen kleinen Schlagstock aus ihrer Tasche hervor und schwingt ihn auf das Bein des Mannes. Der Schlagstock trifft sein Schienbein. Der Kerl brüllt und fällt auf den Boden.

Anja schwingt den Schlagstock zurück und lässt ihn auf einen der Männer sausen, der Roland festhält. Er versucht, sich zu ducken, aber Roland wehrt sich so sehr, dass er Mühe hat, auszuweichen. Der Schlagstock trifft ihn direkt an der Stirn. Er zerbröselt wie ein alter Keks.

Anja dreht sich zum ersten Mann um. Er liegt am Boden und hält sein Bein. Sie stampft ihm mit ihrem Biker Stiefel auf das andere Knie und er schreit.

Der dritte Mann greift Anja und versucht, sie wegzuziehen, bevor sie noch mehr Schaden anrichtet. Plötzlich fällt er hin. Er liegt zuckend am Boden. Ich bemerke, dass Roland eine Elektroschockpistole in der Hand hält. Roland gibt zwei Bikern einen Fußtritt, als er und Anja sich von ihnen entfernen.

»Nun, ich denke, ihr seid aufgeflogen«, sage ich zu ihnen. »Warum geht ihr nicht in den Essbereich und mischt euch dort unter.«

»Das war großartig«, sagt Roland.

»Danke für deine Hilfe«, sagt Anja zu ihm, »aber ich hatte es unter Kontrolle.«

Als sie weggehen, fangen sie an darüber zu streiten, ob Anja alle drei Biker alleine geschafft hätte. Ich schlendere hinüber zu den Musikern und stelle mich vor.

»Ihr hättet beinahe ein bisschen Ärger bekommen«, sage ich.

»Ich hasse diese Auftritte«, sagt der Gitarrenspieler. »Die Biker fangen immer an, Ärger zu machen.«

»Aber die Bezahlung ist gut und an der Ostsee ist es schön um diese Jahreszeit«, sagt der Schlagzeuger.

»Was passiert mit den drei Kerlen, die da drüben am Boden liegen?«, frage ich.

»Die werden irgendwann aufstehen und dann in den Wald gehen, um high zu werden.«

»Einer von ihnen ist total weg«, erwähne ich.

»Es fährt so jede halbe Stunde ein Wagen vom Sicherheitsdienst vorbei. Wenn er dann noch immer dort ist, werden sie ihn zur Erste-Hilfe-Station mitnehmen.«

»Ich glaube, ich werde über das Mädchen mit dem Schlagstock ein Lied schreiben«, sagt der Schlagzeuger. »Sie war erstaunlich.«

---16---

Am nächsten Morgen vergleichen wir unsere Notizen.

»Der Kerl, der für den Drogenverkauf verantwortlich ist, klaut nicht«, sagt Sarah.

»Woher weißt du das?«, fragt Lucia.

»Lina und ich überprüften gestern Abend den Arbeitsablauf. Er ist ein guter Manager. Zwei Männer führen Buch darüber, wie viel sie jedem Drogenkurier geben und wie viel Bargeld der Drogenkurier zurückbringt. Es wäre für jeden, der in der Sache involviert ist, unmöglich, auch nur irgendetwas zu stehlen.«

»Anja und Roland schickten ihren Mann mit einer gebrochenen Kniescheibe ins Krankenhaus. Dazu verpassten sie meinem Mann eine Gehirnerschütterung. Diese Männer haben gestern Abend nichts gestohlen«, sage ich.

Lucia hat Anja und Roland bereits für ihren Kampf mit den Bikern verziehen. Sie gibt mir die Schuld an allem. Bloß weil das Mikrofon nicht funktionierte.

»Der Mann, den ich verfolgte, ist der Dieb«, sagt Lucia. »Er ist für das Prostitutionsgeschäft zuständig.«

»Ich habe keine Prostituierten gesehen«, sagt Roland.

»Sie kamen in einem separaten Kleinbus. Die Gang hat fünfzehn Zelte hinten im Wald aufgestellt. Die Mädchen haben von den Zelten aus gearbeitet. Sie machten ein florierendes Geschäft.«

»Wieso hat mir niemand etwas von diesen Zelten gesagt?«, will ich wissen.

»Woher willst du wissen, dass der Zuständige gestohlen hat?«, fragt Sarah.

»Ich habe die Anzahl der Männer und Frauen gezählt, die in die jeweiligen Zelte gingen«, sagt Lucia. »Ich schätzte den Gesamtbetrag, den die Prostituierten verdienten, indem ich die Zahl der Kunden mit den Kosten jeder Transaktion multiplizierte. Der Mann, der die Operation leitet, hat weniger als fünfzig Prozent meiner Schätzung abgeliefert.«

»Wieso konnte der Geschäftsführer des Clubs das nicht herausfinden?«, frage ich.

»Er war eine Stunde, nachdem die Gang angekommen war, total blau. Er hätte niemals wissen können, wie viele Kunden bedient wurden.«

Ein paar Stunden später verpasse ich dem Mann, der für die Prostituierten verantwortlich ist, eine Bewusstseinstrübung und ziehe ihn in unseren Lieferwagen. Lucia spricht mit ihm zehn Minuten lang und zeichnet seine Antworten auf.

Story 13

Erinnern Sie sich noch daran, dass sie die Wahrheit aus jedem herausbekommen kann? Der Mann sagt ihr, wie lange er schon stiehlt, wie viel er gestohlen hat und wo sich das Tresorfach befindet, in dem er das Geld aufbewahrt.

Nach dem Verhör entferne ich Lucias Stimme von der Aufzeichnung. Dann mache ich zwei Kopien, damit Sarah eine davon ihrem Kunden geben kann. Schließlich bringe ich das Gedächtnis des Bikers durcheinander und dann lasse ich ihn einschlafen.

Wenn er aufwacht, wird er denken, ein furchterregender Kerl mittleren Alters hätte ihn in einen Lieferwagen gezerrt, gefesselt und gedroht, ihm ein Messer in den Augapfel zu stoßen, wenn er kein volles Geständnis ablegen würde.

Lucia entfernt sich und ich rufe Sarah am Handy an. Ein paar Minuten später bringt sie den Vorsitzenden des Motorradclubs in den Lieferwagen.

»Wer ist dieser Typ?«, fragt er, als er mich sieht.

»Ich bin ihr angeheuerter Schläger«, sage ich zu ihm.

»Du siehst nicht so hart aus.«

»Aber immerhin hart genug, um ein volles Geständnis von deinem Mann zu erhalten. Hier ist die Aufnahme.«

Er schaut auf seinen Mitarbeiter, der gefesselt ist, und in der Ecke des Wagens schläft.

»Was habt ihr mit ihm gemacht?«

»Glaub mir, das willst du nicht wissen.«

Der Kopf der Bande ist sehr glücklich, nachdem er die Aufnahme abgespielt hat. Er zieht ein Bündel Hundert-Euro-Scheine aus seiner Tasche und bezahlt Sarah. Dann schleppt er seinen Mann aus dem Lieferwagen und übergibt ihn ein paar Mitarbeitern. Ich bemerke, wie Sarah ein wenig weint, als die Biker uns verlassen.

»Was ist los?«

»Sie werden diesen Mann umbringen. Ich hätte ihn der Polizei übergeben sollen.«

»Wenn du ihn nicht der Gang überlassen hättest, hätten sie versucht, uns zu töten«, sage ich zu ihr. »Außerdem hat mir der Kerl während des Verhörs erzählt, dass er an einigen Morden schuld ist, wovon niemand etwas weiß.«

»Ich fühle mich immer noch nicht wohl dabei.«

Gerade in diesem Moment kommen Lucia und der Rest unserer Gruppe. Roland trägt eine große Packung Popcorn und eine große Flasche Coca-Cola.

»Können wir hier bleiben, bis das Bikertreffen vorbei ist?«, fragt Lina.

»Klar, gebt die Motorräder am Sonntag beim Verleih ab und wir holen euch dort ab«, sagt Lucia.

Sarah unterhält sich mit Lucia ein paar Minuten lang und entschließt sich, ein Auto zu mieten und alleine wieder zurück nach Berlin zu fahren.

»Sie braucht etwas Zeit für sich selbst«, sagt mir Lucia ein paar Minuten später.

»Es ist ja nicht so, als hätte sie dem Typen in den Kopf geschossen«, sage ich. »Sie musste ihn der Gang überlassen.«

»Aber sie ist immer noch sehr beunruhigt.«

Lucia und ich fahren mit dem Lieferwagen davon. Wir beschließen, die Nacht in einer kleinen, niedlichen Frühstückspension in Neuruppin zu verbringen.

»Weißt du«, sage ich zu Lucia, »es wäre leichter gewesen, wenn du einfach jeden der vier Gangmitglieder unter vier Augen befragt hättest. Du hättest alle Antworten erhalten, ohne dass wir das Wochenende auf dem Bikertreffen verbringen müssen.«

»Wenn ich das so gemacht hätte, hätten Sarah und der Gangleiter alle beide bemerkt, dass ich besondere Fähigkeiten besitze.«

»Stimmt«, sage ich.

»Außerdem war es ein amüsantes Wochenende. Den Kindern hat es viel Spaß gemacht, Lederjacken zu tragen und auf riesigen Motorrädern umherzufahren«, sagt Lucia.

»Sarah behielt eine Kopie des Geständnisses für sich«, sagt mir Lucia ein paar Minuten später. »Sie hat vor, es der Polizei zu geben, mitsamt anderen Beweisen über illegale Tätigkeiten der Gang, die sie dieses Wochenende gesammelt hat.«

»Achte darauf, dass sie ein paar Monate wartet und dass sie es so macht, dass die Gang es nicht zu ihr zurückverfolgen kann«, sage ich.

»Werde ich tun.«

---17---

Der Mittwoch bringt gute Nachrichten.

»Roland fand die Namen und die Bilder von drei weiteren Ukrainern, die möglicherweise in der Erpressungsgang involviert sind«, sagt Anja.

»Wie hat er das gemacht?«, fragt Lina.

»Er hat ein Programm geschrieben, welches die Daten von Aeroflot-Passagieren mit der Datenbank der ukrainischen Polizei abglich. Das Programm identifizierte vier vorbestrafte Männer, die mit Aeroflot letztes Jahr in dieses Land eingeflogen sind. Der Mann, den Lucia in der Nähe des Flughafens verhörte, war einer von ihnen. Die anderen drei kommen aus der gleichen Stadt.«

»Wissen wir, wie die anderen drei Männer aussehen?«, fragt Lina.

»Ja«, sagt Anja. »Glücklicherweise dokumentiert Aeroflot den Lichtbildausweis jedes Passagiers.«

»Ich freue mich nicht darauf, wochenlang die Bilder dieser Typen Leuten in ganz Berlin zu zeigen«, sage ich.

»Die ukrainischen Einwanderer in Berlin sind in zwei sehr kleinen Gebieten konzentriert«, sagt Lucia zu mir. »Es wird nicht lange dauern, sie zu finden.«

An diesem Abend fahren Lina, Sarah und ich in den ukrainischen Stadtteil. Wir fahren in separaten Autos. Lina treibt sich in Billardkneipen herum. Sarah überprüft die Lebensmittelgeschäfte und Waschsalons. Ich nehme mich der Bars und der Stripclubs an. In der ersten Nacht hatten wir kein Glück.

»Ich traf in der Billardkneipe zwei Automechaniker, die mich heiraten wollen«, sagt mir Lina am Handy, als ich nach Hause fahre.

In der zweiten Nacht probieren wir dieselbe Gegend. Sarah ruft mich um zwei Uhr morgens an.

»Hast du irgendwas gefunden?«, fragt sie.

»Niemand erkennt sie auf den Bildern«, sage ich zu ihr.

»Hast du einen Lapdance bekommen?«, fragt sie.

Story 13

»Die Damen, die in diesen Klubs tanzen, sind nicht mein Typ«, sage ich zu ihr. »Und einige Barkeeper drohten, sie würden mir die Nase umgestalten, wenn ich nicht aufhören würde, ihre Kunden zu belästigen.«

»Wie aufregend«, sagt Sarah.

»Wo bist du gerade?«, frage ich.

»Ich helfe Lina, die Bilder in den Billardkneipen herumzuzeigen.«

»Amüsiert ihr euch?«

»Ein Kerl mit dem Namen Georgi zeigte mir, wie man den Billardstock hält.«

»Schön, in ein paar Jahren kannst du auf Tour gehen.«

»Georgi sagt, dass ich mich nicht genügend konzentriere.«

»Fühlst du dich besser wegen des Mannes, der die Bikergang bestohlen hat und den du ausgeliefert hast?«, frage ich.

»Ich denke, ich kann damit leben.«

»Gut.«

In der nächsten Nacht haben wir Glück. In einem Rattenloch, einer Bar neben einer zugenagelten Tankstelle, treffe ich einen Kerl, der die Männer auf den Bildern erkennt, die ich ihm zeige.

»Die leben alle in einer Wohnung in meinem Gebäude«, sagt er. »Sehr schlimme Männer.«

---18---

Fünfunddreißig Minuten später treffen mich Lina und Sarah vor dem Gebäude, wo sich die Ukrainer befinden. Wir setzen uns in mein Auto, um eine Telefonkonferenz mit Lucia zu machen.

»Wir brauchen Gefangene«, sagt mir Lucia am Telefon. »Erschießt sie nicht alle.«

»Ich bleibe draußen für den Fall, dass jemand versucht, über die Feuerleiter herunterzukommen«, sagt Sarah. »Außerdem kann ich mich so um die Polizei kümmern, sollte sie unerwartet auftauchen.«

Ich benutze eine dünne Stahlstange, um die Eingangstür des Gebäudes aufzubrechen. Ich mache nicht zu viel Lärm. Glücklicherweise ist es spät in der Nacht. Alles ist ruhig, als Lina und ich die Stufen hinaufschleichen. Meine Pistole hat einen Schalldämpfer. Es hat keinen Sinn, die Leute aufzuwecken.

Unsere Strategie ist einfach. Lina wird auf die Bösewichte einprügeln, bis sie aufgeben. Wenn sie nicht aufgeben, werde ich auf sie schießen. Hoffentlich wird einer von ihnen noch so lange leben, dass Lucia sich mit ihm unterhalten kann.

Wir schleichen im ersten Stock den Flur entlang und lauschen an der Tür der Wohnung mit der Türnummer 2. Durch die Tür hören wir laute Schnarchgeräusche. Schnarchen ist gut. Unsere Widersacher schlafen.

Ich bemerke, wie Lina einen Schlagring auf ihre rechte Hand streift.

»Wozu brauchst du denn den?«, frage ich.

»Ich will mir nicht die Fingernägel abbrechen. Ich habe sie gerade erst gemacht.«

»Ich glaube nicht, dass das funktioniert.«

Ich benutze meinen bewährten Dietrich, um die Tür zur Wohnung leise zu öffnen. Wir treten ein und sehen zwei schlafende Männer auf einem Sofa vor einem kleinen Fernseher. Ich schlage ihnen mit meinem Schlagstock auf den Kopf. Während ich ihnen Handschellen anlege, gleitet Lina den Flur entlang, um deren Kumpel zu finden.

Unglücklicherweise haben sie eine Katze. Wer denkt schon daran, dass ukrainische Gauner Katzen mögen? Das Mistvieh lässt ein Jaulen los, als Lina den Flur entlangläuft.

Als sie die Schlafzimmertür erreicht, wird diese aufgestoßen. Der dritte Mann, durch die Katze gewarnt, springt Lina an. Der Kerl ist schnell.

Er packt Lina an der Kehle, bevor sie sich bewegen kann. Er ist fünf Zentimeter größer und zwanzig Kilogramm schwerer als Lina. Er stößt sie gegen die Wand und fängt an, sie zu würgen. Ich sitze auf dem Sofa und beobachte den Kampf.

Lina schmettert ihr Knie in seine Leiste. Er lässt ihren Hals los und sie versucht, ihm die Nase mit der Handfläche zu brechen. Er blockiert den Schlag mit seinem Unterarm und schwingt den Ellbogen auf ihre Wange zu. Sie dreht den Kopf zur Seite und der Ellbogen hämmert hinter ihr ein Loch in die Wand.

Lina geht zurück ins Wohnzimmer, um mehr Platz zu haben. Ihr Gegner folgt ihr auf dem Fuße. Der Kniestoß in seine Leiste hat ihn nicht langsamer gemacht. Das ist ein harter Kerl.

Sie schwingt einen Aufwärtshaken mit der Schlagringfaust auf sein Kinn zu. Er blockiert den Schlag und rammt sie mit seinem Oberkörper. Lina hat die Balance einer Balletttänzerin. Sie hüpft einen halben Meter zurück und landet in perfekter Kampfhaltung.

Er schwingt seine muskulöse Faust nach ihr. Sie wehrt sie mit dem Unterarm ab. Ich höre einen Knochen brechen. Er versucht, sie mit einem Roundhouse-Kick in die Seite zu treffen. Sie hebt ihr Bein und fängt den Stoß mit der Außenseite ihres Unterschenkels ab.

Sie zuckt zusammen und springt einen weiteren Schritt zurück. Er schiebt sich nach vorne, täuscht an und schlägt zu. Dann tritt er schnell zurück und schwingt ein Bein auf ihren Kopf zu. Der Tritt ist schnell und heftig. Sein Bein wird ganz unscharf, als es auf sie zurast.

Aber Lina ist eine erstaunliche Kämpferin. Sie duckt sich unter das Bein und hämmert mit dem Schlagring auf sein anderes Knie. Ich höre ein Geräusch, wie wenn Eis zerbricht, und der Typ ächzt. Erstaunlicherweise geht er nicht zu Boden. Er stellt seinen anderen Fuß zurück auf den Boden und weicht zurück.

Ich weiß nicht, ob er über einen Teppich stolpert oder ob sein gebrochenes Knie nachgab. Aber er stolpert nur ein wenig, gerade genug, um Lina die Gelegenheit zu geben, einen neuen Angriff zu starten. Sie nähert sich sehr schnell und stößt ihm wieder mit dem Knie in die Leiste. Dann knickt sie seinen Kopf mit einem Ellbogenschlag gegen das Kinn zurück. Das lässt seinen Hals ungeschützt. Sie schlägt ihm mit dem Schlagring auf die Luftröhre.

Der Kerl sackt zusammen. Ich gehe hinüber und sehe ihn an. Seine Kehle ist zerschlagen. Er ringt nach Atem, der niemals kommen wird. Langsam verschwindet der Glanz aus seinen Augen.

Ich schicke Sarah eine Nachricht mit meinem Handy und sie kommt sofort mit Klebeband und Säcken herauf. Sarah und ich verbinden die zwei bewusstlosen Männer und stecken sie in zwei große Säcke. Dann schleppen wir sie hinunter zu meinem Auto.

Während wir uns bemühen, die Kerle loszuwerden, durchsucht Lina die Wohnung. Sarah und ich laden die Männer in mein Auto und ich laufe zurück, um Lina zu helfen. Sarah hilft ihr die Treppen hinunter, während ich eine Tasche voller Sachen trage, auf die wir Lina zufolge einen Blick werfen sollten. Linas Arm hängt an ihrer Seite herab.

Auf unserem Weg hinunter begegnen wir einer anderen Bewohnerin des Gebäudes, die durch den Lärm aufwachte. Beim Vorbeigehen setze ich eine Bewusstseinstrübung bei ihr ein. Wir lassen den toten Mann in der Wohnung. Als wir beim Auto ankommen, werfe ich einen Blick auf die Sachen, die Lina in die Tasche geworfen hat.

Story 13

»Einen Laptop, einige Handys, Rechnungen und ein Scheckheft. Vielleicht haben wir ein paar Beweise.«

»Ich muss meinen Arm röntgen lassen«, sagt Lina.

»Kannst du mit einem Arm fahren?«, frage ich.

»Sicher«, antwortet sie.

Ich brauche Lina nicht daran zu erinnern, zu der Privatklinik zu gehen, die unser Team für medizinische Notfälle benutzt. Sie wird von einem Arzt geleitet, der Leute versorgt, die bar zahlen und nicht ihre richtigen Namen verwenden. Bevor wir wegfahren, zieht mich Lina zur Seite.

»Du hast diese Bewusstseinsbeeinflussung nicht bei dem Ukrainer benutzt, oder?«

»Auf keinen Fall«, sage ich. »Ich habe zur Abwechslung gerne einmal bei einem fairen Kampf zugeschaut. Du hast ihn ohne meine Hilfe besiegt.«

Sie nickt selbstgefällig. Lina ist sehr wetteifernd.

---19---

Am nächsten Tag haben wir eine weitere Besprechung.

»Was hast du von unseren ukrainischen Gefangenen erfahren?«, frage ich Lucia.

»Sie haben mir von fünf weiteren Opfern erzählt, die ihnen eine Menge Geld bezahlten«, sagt sie.

»Sie machen das schon länger, als wir dachten«, sage ich. »Waren die anderen Opfer Versicherungsagenten?«

»Nein, sie waren unabhängige Finanzberater.«

»Das ist beinahe das Gleiche«, sage ich. »Weißt du, wer der Boss ist?«

»Noch nicht. Roland zieht noch immer Informationen aus dem Computer, den du in ihrer Wohnung gefunden hast. Diese Männer waren blöd genug, eine Liste ihrer Aktivitäten aufzubewahren. Wir wissen, wo sie wohnten, mit wem sie gesprochen haben, wann sie Anrufe von ihrem Boss erhielten, solche Dinge halt. Ich hoffe, all das wird uns irgendwie helfen.«

»Und wann glaubst du, werden wir etwas Konkretes wissen?«, fragt Lina.

Sie hat einen Gips am Arm und humpelt etwas beim Gehen.

»In ein paar Tagen, so hoffe ich.«

Anja ruft mich zwei Tage später an.

»Wir haben ihn«, sagt sie.

»Nun, wer ist das große Verbrechergenie?«

»Ein Hauptmann bei der Landespolizei mit dem Namen Philip Jung.«

»Wie habt ihr ihn gefunden?«

»Reinhold gab uns seinen Namen neben ein paar anderen. Wir prüften alle seine Kreditkartenquittungen und weißt du was?«

»Was?«

»Er bezahlte einen Zahnarzt dafür, einem der Ukrainer einen Zahn zu ziehen. Kannst du das glauben?«

»Ich bin überrascht, dass er nicht bar zahlte«, sage ich.

»Das war sein einziger Fehler.«

»Da habe ich also drei Nächte lang umsonst in Berlin Frauen mit Schnurrbärten beim Ausziehen beobachtet.«

»Es war die Mühe wert, da wir den Rest der Gang gefunden haben.«

»Was hat Lucia mit den beiden Gefangenen gemacht?«

»Mit einer Schleife verpackt und zu einem Typen namens Müller bei der Landespolizei geschickt. Wir gaben ihm auch die Namen der anderen Opfer, die Auflistung der Aktivitäten, die die Ukrainer führten, und informierten ihn darüber, dass Hauptmann Jung die Zahnbehandlung für den einen bezahlte.«

»Das sollte ihn glücklich machen«, sage ich.

In der folgenden Woche steht ein großer Bericht in der Zeitung. Hauptmann Philip Jung von der Landespolizei wurde festgenommen und angeklagt, eine große Erpressungsoperation in Berlin geleitet zu haben. Die Zeitung berichtet detailliert über die Opfer und listet die Namen der ukrainischen Gauner auf, die für die Drecksarbeit angeheuert wurden.

Zwei Tage später steht noch ein Artikel in der Zeitung. Die Ermittler fanden ein Bankschließfach und zwei Offshore-Bankkonten, die dem Hauptmann Jung gehören. Die Konten enthalten einige hunderttausend Euro. Das Schließfach ist voller ungeschliffener Diamanten.

»Die hätten nie etwas über das Geld und das Schließfach herausgefunden, wenn ich nicht dem Kriminalbeamten Müller eine anonyme E-Mail geschickt hätte«, sagt Roland.

»Ist nur schade, dass die Welt nie etwas von deinem Talent erfahren wird, Straftaten dank deiner Hackerfähigkeiten aufzudecken«, sage ich ihm.

Die Kautionsanhörung von Hauptmann Jung wird von einem Richter geleitet, der ihm ein paar Gefälligkeiten schuldet. Er wird aus der Haft entlassen, nachdem er eine Kaution von einer halben Million Euro hinterlegt hat. So laufen die Dinge in Berlin, wenn man Freunde hat.

Die Angelegenheit beruhigt sich etwas, während Roland und Anja den Computer der Ukrainer nach weiteren Beweisen durchforsten, um sie an den Kriminalbeamten Müller zu senden. Und dann schluckt Hauptmann Jung eine halbe Flasche Gift und stirbt zu Hause. Wir haben am nächsten Tag eine Teambesprechung.

»Glaubst du, die Polizei hatte genügend Beweise, um Hauptmann Jung auf lange Zeit ins Gefängnis zu schicken?«, frage ich Lucia.

»Ich glaube nicht. Wenn er einen guten Anwalt beauftragt hätte, hätte er bestenfalls ein paar Jahre absitzen müssen.«

»Weshalb hätte er sich dann umbringen sollen? Roland, hast du das vorausgesehen?«

»Wenn ich gedacht hätte, dass er Gift nehmen würde, hätte ich vor ein paar Tagen bereits aufgehört, nach Beweisen zu suchen.«

»Vielleicht müssen wir die Dinge aus einem anderen Blickwinkel betrachten«, schlug Lucia vor.

---20---

Zwei Wochen später ...

»Sie sehen heute etwas besser aus«, sage ich zu Joseph Graf.

Wir essen belegte Brote, die ich ihm mit nach Hause gebracht habe.

»Haben Sie aufgehört, die Medikamente zu nehmen?«

»Ja«, sagt er zu mir. »Ich habe mit einer Trauerbegleiterin gesprochen, wie Sie bei unserem letzten Mittagessen vorgeschlagen haben. Sie hat mir geholfen, mich mit dem Verlust meiner Frau auseinanderzusetzen. Ich bekomme mein Leben endlich wieder in den Griff.«

Story 13

»Das ist großartig.«

Wir unterhalten uns etwas mehr über seine Therapiesitzungen. Aufgrund meiner Bewusstseinszauberei glaubt er immer noch, dass ich ein Freund von der Versicherung wäre. Schließlich komme ich zur Sache.

»Sie haben es fast geschafft«, sage ich zu ihm.

»Wie bitte?«, fragt er.

»Sie wissen ja, die Erpressungen, den Mord an ihrer Frau und sogar die Ermordung von Hauptmann Jung.«

»Ich weiß nicht, wovon Sie sprechen«, sagt er.

»Doch, das wissen Sie. Wir wissen, dass Sie die ganze Erpressungsoperation leiteten.«

»Sind Sie von der Polizei?«

»Ich gehöre einer Gruppe an, die die letzten vierzehn Tage damit verbracht hat, jeden Aspekt ihres Lebens zu untersuchen«, sage ich. »Sie haben Hauptmann Jung angeworben, um die Ukrainer herüberzubringen. Sie wählten die Erpressungsopfer aus. Sie erschossen drei Leute, eine davon war ihre eigene Frau. Und Sie haben Hauptmann Jung vergiftet, als die Dinge langsam aus dem Ruder gerieten.«

»Sie sind verrückt«, sagt er zu mir. »Wo ist ihr Beweis?«

»Wir haben den Ort gefunden, wo Sie das Gift kauften. Die haben immer noch die Überwachungsvideos von allen Transaktionen, die an jenem Tag gemacht wurden. Ihr Gesicht ist in dem Video sehr klar zu erkennen. Außerdem erinnert sich der Kassierer an Sie.«

Herr Graf zieht eine Pistole aus der Tasche und richtet sie auf mich. Ich sitze ruhig da, als er um den Esstisch herum kommt und mich abtastet, um zu sehen, ob ich eine Waffe oder ein Abhörgerät bei mir trage. Dann setzt er sich hin und beißt ein weiteres Stück von seinem Truthahnbrot ab. Die Pistole ist immer noch auf mich gerichtet.

»Es ist sehr dumm von Ihnen, hierherzukommen und diese Sachen zu sagen«, sagt er zu mir. »Haben Sie geglaubt, ich würde Sie bezahlen, damit Sie schweigen?«

»Ich wollte nur die Genugtuung haben, Ihnen von Angesicht zu Angesicht zu sagen, dass Sie mit ihren Verbrechen nicht davongekommen sind.«

Er lacht mich aus.

»Sie haben einen schweren Fehler gemacht«, sagt er.

»Eigentlich machte Hauptmann Jung den Fehler. Wenn er nicht für die Zahnarztbehandlung des Ukrainers mit seiner Kreditkarte bezahlt hätte, wären Sie alle beide außer Verdacht. Wir hatten nicht genügend Beweise dafür, irgendjemanden wegen irgendetwas anzuklagen, bis wir die Kreditkartenzahlung fanden.«

»Wenn Sie ›wir‹ sagen, von wem reden Sie dann eigentlich?«, fragt er.

»Meine Gruppe. Ich wollte uns ›Das Kommando‹ nennen, aber wir hatten eine Abstimmung und ich verlor. Deshalb nennen wir uns einfach das Team. Ich darf nicht einmal Teamjacken kaufen.«

»Sind Sie high?«, fragt er mich. »Das ergibt doch keinen Sinn. Was für eine Abstimmung?«

»Das spielt keine Rolle.«

Joseph Graf seufzt.

»Sie werden mir von Ihrem Team erzählen.«

»Nein, werde ich nicht.«

»Wenn Sie es nicht tun, werde ich Ihnen ins Knie schießen und dann ins andere Knie und dann in den Ellbogen, bis Sie es mir schließlich sagen.«

Ich wende eine Bewusstseinstrübung auf ihn an. Er senkt seine Arme und lässt sie an der Seite herunterhängen. Ich nehme die Pistole und lege ihm Handschellen an. Dann rufe ich Sarah auf dem Handy an. Sie kreuzt einige Minuten später auf.

»Hast du ihm Tabletten ins Getränk getan?«, fragt sie.

»Wie bitte?«, frage ich.

»Er schläft beinahe. Wie hast du das geschafft?«

»Ich habe es beinahe vergessen. Ich habe ihm etwas ins Getränk getan.«

»Was machen wir nun?«, fragt Sarah.

»Du fesselst ihn. Ich platziere genügend Beweise, um ihn mit jedem Verbrechen der letzten zehn Jahre in Verbindung zu bringen. Dann rufe ich die Polizei von Grafs Handy aus an.«

---21---

»Hier ist Kriminalbeamter Frank Müller, unser Gespräch wird aufgezeichnet. Darf ich bitte Ihren Namen haben?«

»Der ist unwichtig.«

Ich spreche mit einer komischen Stimme, nur um ihn zu ärgern.

»Sie sagten unserer Empfangsdame, dass Sie mir mit einigen meiner Fälle helfen wollen.«

»Ja, ich habe sie für Sie gelöst.«

»Ich werde mit Ihnen nicht sprechen, es sei denn, Sie nennen mir Ihren Namen.«

»Dann werden Sie aber wirklich dumm aussehen, wenn ich den Zeitungen meine Information übermittle und erwähne, dass Sie nicht daran interessiert waren, mir zuzuhören.«

Ich höre ihn unter seinen Atemgeräuschen murmeln.

»Okay, reden Sie.«

»Ein Mann mit dem Namen Joseph Graf ermordete seine Frau vor etwa sechs Monaten. Sie dachten, sie sei wegen einer verpfuschten Erpresserzahlung umgebracht worden, jedoch hat er den Abzug betätigt.«

»Und woher wissen Sie das?«

»Er hat die Pistole nie weggeworfen. Schicken Sie jemanden zu seinem Haus. Sie wissen doch, wo er wohnt. Er ist gefesselt und die Waffe liegt gleich neben ihm am Boden. Seine Fingerabdrücke sind überall darauf.«

Müller braucht ein paar Sekunden, um das sacken zu lassen.

»Können Sie einen Moment warten?«, fragt er.

»Wenn Sie das machen, werde ich auflegen und Sie werden nicht die ganze Geschichte kennen. Im Übrigen, ich benutze gerade Grafs Handy.«

»Okay, reden Sie weiter.«

»Die zwei Versicherungsagenten wurden mit derselben Pistole getötet, aber das wissen Sie schon.«

»Ja.«

»Herr Graf war der Drahtzieher hinter dem Erpressungsvorhaben. Er hat Hauptmann Philip Jung angeworben und ermordete ihn, als Hauptmann Jung auf Kaution frei war.«

»Woher wissen Sie das?«

»Ich habe neben der Waffe einen Zettel hingelegt. Darin steht, wo das Gift gekauft wurde. Das Geschäft hat eine Überwachungskamera, deren Aufnahmen zeigen, wie Graf das Gift kauft. Der Geschäftsführer wartet darauf, dass Sie das Band abholen. Der Kassierer erinnert sich außerdem daran, wie Graf das Gift kaufte.«

Story 13

»Was sonst noch?«, fragt er.

»Vergleichen Sie die Bankauszüge von Graf mit denen von Hauptmann Jung. Sie werden sehen, dass es da einander entsprechende Abbuchungen und Einzahlungen gibt.«

»Jung hatte Offshore-Konten. Wir konnten die Zahlungen nicht verfolgen. Das Geld schien vom Himmel gefallen zu sein«, sagt er.

»Sie brauchen einen besseren Hacker. Mein Mann wird Ihnen eine detaillierte Erklärung per E-Mail darüber senden, wie das Geld von einem Konto zum anderen bewegt wurde. Sobald Sie alle Unterlagen vorliegen haben, werden Sie sehen, dass Jung und Graf wie siamesische Zwillinge miteinander verbunden waren.«

»Wer sind Sie?«

Ich lege auf.

—22—

Fünf Tage später bringen die Zeitungen einen großen Bericht über Joseph Graf und Hauptmann Philip Jung. Lina liest ihn uns allen vor.

»Du hast die Finger des ersten Ukrainers in Grafs Haus platziert«, sagt Anja. »Das ist widerlich!«

»Ich fand es eine nette Geste«, sage ich.

»Die Polizei wird feststellen, dass Graf nicht die Finger seines eigenen Angestellten abschneiden würde«, sagt Roland.

»Wahrscheinlich, aber es gibt den Reportern und Bloggern etwas, worüber sie sich auslassen können.«

»Warum hat Graf seine Frau und die zwei Versicherungsleute getötet?«, fragt Lina.

»Sie hat ihn dauernd angeschrien, den Toilettensitz unten zu lassen«, scherzt Roland.

Ich schmunzle etwas.

»Das ist ein guter Witz.«

»Könnten wir uns über Mordopfer bitte nicht lustig machen?«, bittet Lucia.

»Vor ein paar Jahren hat er eine Lebensversicherung über zehn Millionen Euro auf seine Frau zu seinen Gunsten abgeschlossen«, erklärt Anja. »Damals fing er an, darüber nachzudenken, wie er sie loswerden könnte, ohne dabei erwischt zu werden. Was schließlich zu diesem ganzen Erpressungsplan führte.«

»Kein schlechter Plan«, sagt Roland. »Er wird seine Frau los und schließt sich selbst gleichzeitig als Verdächtigen aus.«

»Ich weiß nicht, warum er die beiden Versicherungsleute tötete«, sage ich zu ihnen. »Ich dachte nicht daran, ihn danach zu fragen.«

»Graf war ein schlauer Bursche«, sagt Anja. »Wir hatten Glück, dass Hauptmann Jung den einen Fehler machte.«

»Meint ihr, die Polizei versteht meine E-Mail über den Geldverkehr zwischen Graf und Jung?«, fragt Roland.

»Wahrscheinlich. Ich werde den Kriminalbeamten Müller in ein paar Tagen anrufen, um dem nachzugehen. Er wird wahrscheinlich wieder mit mir reden wollen.«

»Warum?«, fragt Anja.

»Sarah ist hier nicht irgendwo im Büro, oder?«, frage ich.

»Nein, sie arbeitet heute an einem anderen Fall«, sagt mir Lucia.

»Gut. Um Anjas Frage zu beantworten, Sarah und ich haben Grafs Haus gesäubert, damit die Polizei unsere Fingerabdrücke nicht finden würde. Dann habe ich ein wenig Bewusstseinszauber bei Graf eingesetzt, um sicherzustellen, dass er sich nicht daran erinnern würde, uns jemals gesehen zu haben. Daher ist Müller wahrscheinlich sehr interessiert daran herauszufinden, wer ich bin und wie es mir möglich war, den Fall zu lösen.«

»Von dem Geld und den Diamanten, die sie von Hauptmann Jung erhielten, und was auch immer sie in den Konten von Graf finden, werden die Opfer den Großteil ihres Geldes zurückbekommen«, sagt Lucia.

»Glaubst du, dass die Beweise, die du im Haus hinterlassen hast, genug sind, um ihn zu überführen?«, fragt Anja.

»Ich denke schon. Roland hat auch ein paar finanzielle Transaktionen erfunden, die Graf mit den Ukrainern in Verbindung bringen. Wenn die Polizei die Bankunterlagen von Graf untersucht, werden ihnen diese Transaktionen wie Warnsignale ins Auge springen«, sage ich ihr.

»Ihr seid so unehrlich«, sagt Lina.

Am selben Abend liegen Lucia und ich zusammen im Bett. Ich reibe ihr die Füße. Sie mag das. Lucia sagt mir, dass sie morgen einen neuen Standort für das Büro suchen wolle.

»Warum?«, frage ich.

»Wir können viel Geld verdienen, wenn wir die Marzahn-Immobilie in Wohnungen umwandeln und sie dann verkaufen. Der Immobilienmarkt erholt sich langsam«, sagt sie.

»Wo sollen wir uns umschauen?«, frage ich.

»Ich dachte an Mariendorf. Das ist eine schöne kleine Gegend und liegt direkt an der Bahnstrecke nach Berlin. Außerdem gibt es dort großartige Restaurants. Du hattest nie eine Beziehung mit einer Maria, oder?«

»Nicht, dass ich wüsste.«

Ich reibe ihr die Füße noch etwas länger.

»Ich brauche eine neue Pistole«, sage ich.

»Reibst du mir deshalb die Füße?«

»Vielleicht.«

»Wie wäre es, wenn du mir eine Weile den Rücken massierst. Danach können wir über Pistolen reden.«

www.ingramcontent.com/pod-product-compliance
Lightning Source LLC
Chambersburg PA
CBHW081414230426
43668CB00016B/2232